VISUAL QUICKPRO GUIDE

UNIX

FOR MAC OS X 10.4 TIGER

Matisse Enzer

Peachpit Press

Visual QuickPro Guide
Unix for Mac OS X 10.4
Matisse Enzer

Peachpit Press
1249 Eighth Street
Berkeley, CA 94710
510/524-2178
800/283-9444
510/524-2221 (fax)
Find us on the World Wide Web at: http://www.peachpit.com
To report errors, please send a note to errata@peachpit.com
Peachpit Press is a division of Pearson Education

Editor: Whitney Walker
Production Coordinator: Myrna Vladic
Copy Editor: Elissa Rabellino
Tech Editor: Scott M. Neal
Compositor: Jerry Ballew
Indexer: Rebecca Plunkett

Notice of rights

Notice of liability

Trademarks

ISBN 0-321-24668-3

9 8 7 6 5 4 3 2 1

Printed and bound in the United States of America

Dedications

The first edition of this book was dedicated to David Hawkins,

```
{apple|decwrl|hplabs}!→ well!dhawk
```

It was David who taught me my first serious addition to a Unix command line:

```
command | awk '{print $3}' | sort |
→ uniq -c | sort -nr
```

and this quote from Horace—

To know all things is not permitted.

—to which David's response was

But you can still go deeper . . .

David died on July 24, 2000. There is an online memorial at www.river.org/~dhawk/memorial.html.

This second edition is dedicated to someone I haven't met yet—someone who picks up this book, uses it, and years later realizes the quixotic turns that his or her life has taken as a result of delving into the strange land that we call Unix.

Acknowledgments for the first edition

Creating a book is like creating software—if it is any good, it is almost certainly a team effort. Here's a list of the people who made this book happen, and if we've left anyone out, it is entirely the author's fault.

Marjorie Baer brought the author in on this project and instigated the whole effort. Without her, it wouldn't even have started.

Cliff Colby and Victor Gavenda helped with the basic outline of the book.

Howard Rheingold, Freddy "Are We Really?" Hahne, Pilar "Power P" Johnson, and Eugene Alexander provided the sort of encouragement that makes life worth living.

Ron Liskey made the priceless suggestion that we set a schedule for how much to write each week and *stick to it.* Tim Pozar provided help with the history of BSD and open-source Unix. The crew that hangs out in the Macintosh and Unix conferences on the WELL provided numerous valuable contributions, especially Chris Carroll, Paul Bissex, and Sean Harding, along with Barrett Brassfield, Joel Westerberg, John F. Whitehead, Mark Binder, Matthew Hawn, Michael C. Berch, Tara L. Andrews, Thomas Armagost, and James Waldrop. Waldrop and Ken Hipschman tackled the technical editing and attempted to correct the author's more flagrant mistakes. Elissa Rabellino provided kind, careful, and thorough copyediting. Myrna Vladic, Phyllis Beaty, David Van Ness, and Lisa Brazieal handled the production challenges with aplomb.

Many thanks to Ernest Prabhakar and Grace Kvamme at Apple Computer: Ernest for answering a slew of questions about obscure issues such as whether or not NetInfo might be used to override `/etc/mail/sendmail.cf`, and Grace for being the patient intermediary between a pesky author and an overloaded Ernest.

And finally, Howard Baldwin, the editor, provided priceless encouragement and patient support to a first-time author who probably caused more trouble than he knows. Thanks, Howard.

Acknowledgments for the second edition

As always, many, many people's efforts went into bringing this edition to print. The credits for a book should be like movie credits, rolling on for several minutes.

Whitney Walker stepped in as editor and carefully handled all the behind-the-scenes coordination the author is grateful to have never seen. Scott M. Neal did an excellent job of checking the technical accuracy of the author's wild and unsubstantiated claims—any remaining technical errors are all the author's fault. Elissa Rabellino once again managed to save the English language from complete geekification, and Ernie Prabhakar once again put up with and actually answered piles of questions, only rarely saying, "That's a feature, not a bug."

Cliff Colby at Peachpit gets the credit and blame for talking the author into doing this again. Thanks to Myrna Vladic and Jerry Ballew for making the finished product look so good, and to Rebecca Plunkett for compiling a thorough index.

Loren Rosen, Paul Bissex, Pete Hanson, John Brewer, John F. Whitehead, and the rest of the gang at the WELL once again provided comments, ideas, questions, and inspiration: aurum, barrett, bbear, betsys, biscuit, bslesins, bubbles, cactus, cascio, chet, combs, davgam, dblan, dmd, gail, howard, hrh, jacob, jal, jax, jbrewer, jef, jeffreyp, jfw, karish, loren-rosen, agnus, marvy, mattrose, mcb, mnemonic, mpk, mtrbike, mz, nickw, pac, realfun, rtswimm, satyr, siino, spackard, sungja, tenney, thevoidmstr, tux, wolfy, and ymike.

TABLE OF CONTENTS

Introduction **xi**
Who Is This Book For? xiii
What's in This Book? xiv
How to Use This Book xvi
Requirements xix

Chapter 1: What Is Unix, and Why Is It Good? **1**
The Advantages of a Unix-Based Mac OS 2
But First, a Little History 5
How Mac OS X's Unix Differs from Mac OS 9 . . . 9
What You Can Do with Mac OS X and Unix . . . 10
How You Will Be Working with Unix 14
Where to Find More 22

Chapter 2: Using the Command Line **23**
Getting to the Command Line 24
Understanding the Shell Prompt 26
Using a Command 27
Using Common Commands 35
About Commands, Processes, and Jobs 40
About Spaces in the Command Line 45
Wildcards 47
About Standard Input and Output 49
Creating Pipelines of Commands 51
Running a Command in the Background 53
Opening Files from the Command Line 57
Creating a Simple Unix Shell Script 58

Chapter 3: Getting Help and Using the Unix Manual **63**
Using the Unix Manual 64
Printing man Pages 69
Using Commands' Built-in Help 71
Using the Web to Get Help 73
Getting Help from Other People 74

Chapter 4: Useful Unix Utilities 75
Mac OS X–Specific Utilities 76
File Compression and Archiving 79
File and Text Processing 83
Searching for Text Inside Files 95
Searching for Files 104
Viewing and Editing Files 112
Sending E-mail 113
Network Analysis 115
Using the Internet 118

Chapter 5: Using Files and Directories 119
Seeing the Whole File System 120
Seeing Where You Are in the File System 123
Understanding and Using Unix Filenames 124
Moving Around in the File System 128
Seeing the Contents of Directories 130
Viewing the Contents of Text Files 134
Creating Files and Directories 138
Copying Files and Directories 139
Renaming or Moving Files 141
Deleting Files and Directories 142
Getting Information About Files and Directories 143
About Links (the Unix Version of Aliases) 151

Chapter 6: Editing and Printing Files 155
Editing Files with vi 156
About vi's Two Modes 161
Navigating Using vi 164
Saving a File in vi 167
Quitting vi 168
Changing and Deleting Text 169
emacs—an Editor Without Modes 177
Printing Files 179

Chapter 7: Configuring Your Environment with Unix 187
Finding Configuration Files 189
Configuring Your Shell 190
Environment Variables 192
Shell Aliases 198
Shell Settings 202
Configuring vi 207
Configuring Mac OS X Defaults from the Command Line 208

Chapter 8: Working with Permissions and Ownership **211**
About Users and Groups 212
The Root User—Permission to Do Anything .. 217
Understanding Permissions and Ownership ... 218
Setting and Changing Permissions 225
Changing Ownership 231
Default Permissions for File Creation 234
Recognizing Permission Problems 235

Chapter 9: Creating and Using Scripts **241**
Common Uses of Shell Scripts 242
Creating a Shell Script 243
Using Variables 246
Using Arguments 251
Using Commands Within Commands 255
Doing Arithmetic and Using Expressions 257
Using Control Structures 259
Getting User Input 272
Creating and Using Functions 274

Chapter 10: Connecting over the Internet **277**
About Hostnames 278
Logging In to Another Unix Machine 279
Copying Files Across the Internet 288
Advanced Interactions 307

Chapter 11: Introduction to System Administration **309**
About root 310
Becoming Another User 316
Keeping Backups 318
Managing User Accounts and Groups 322
Monitoring System Usage 340
Running Regularly Scheduled Commands 345
System Log Files 357
The Boot Sequence 359
Creating New LaunchDaemons and StartupItems 362
Troubleshooting Tips 371

Chapter 12: **Security** **377**
Security Checklist 378
Physical Security 379
Choosing Good Passwords 380
Protecting Yourself from Internet Attacks 383
Searching for Files That Make You root 397
Keeping Up-to-Date 398
Monitoring Files for Changes 401

Chapter 13: **Installing Software from Source Code** **405**
Installing from Source Code—the Basics 406
Using Fink to Install Software 408
Manually Installing from Source Code 422
Installing Perl Modules 431

Chapter 14: **Installing and Configuring Servers** **451**
Setting Your Machine's Hostname 452
Controlling the AppleShare Server 457
Activating the SSH Server 459
Configuring an Internet E-mail Server 460
Activating the FTP Server 465
Apache: A Web Server 475
The MySQL Database Server 483
Even More Servers 504

Appendix: **Darwin-only Unix Commands** **505**

Index **510**

INTRODUCTION

This book is the most comprehensive beginner's guide to Unix on the market. If you have never used Unix before, jump right in—this book was written first and foremost for you. If you are an experienced Unix user wondering about Mac OS X, take it from us, Mac OS X really is Unix—not almost, not sort of, but actual, real Unix with the Lovely Mac Interface.

This book deals almost exclusively with the command-line interface to Darwin—which is the version of Unix that Mac OS X is built upon. Unix is an operating system, and obviously you have used other operating systems in the past—at the very least, you have used the Macintosh operating system, and perhaps Windows, or even DOS. Unix is different. The other operating systems have a sharp distinction between the operating system itself and the applications you use with it. In Unix, the distinction is much less clear.

In learning Unix, you will use a collection of separate applications to do things like copy files, create new folders, view such information as file size and date modified, and perform all the tasks that in other operating systems are part of the one big application that is the "operating system."

It has been said that if Unix were an airplane, it would have been built by all the frequent fliers who over the years showed up at the airport with new and/or improved pieces for the airplane. Each time someone had a better, faster (and sometimes even easier) way of doing something, all the other frequent fliers—along with the engineers working for the airplane manufacturer—would crowd around and argue over the benefits of the new tool.

In many cases a new tool (or toy) became a standard part of the airplane. Unix was invented in 1969, but it wasn't until the early 1980s that engineers at the

University of California, Berkeley, added the code for communicating on the Internet directly into the core (or *kernel*) of Unix. The tools for viewing files and monitoring the operating system have evolved constantly over the years.

New tools are added frequently. Each of them is a separate piece of software, with its own collection of features, options, and tricks for using it; and all of them (or almost all) are designed to be combined with each other in the way that words are combined to make a sentence.

All this means that Unix has evolved organically over the past 30-plus years, and continues to evolve, very much as a language evolves. In this book, we teach you how to think and act in Unix step-by-step, providing you with both a sequential learning process and a reference you can return to in the days to come as you become more and more adept.

Learning Unix is like learning a language—it all comes together to make some kind of sense, but there are idiosyncrasies and bits of historical stuff that pop up. It is not smoothly monolithic, but rather it is gloriously rich and complex. Instead of words, though, Unix has tools.

In Unix we call these tools *commands*, and you will start thinking about "which command to use" just as if you were some kind of authority figure, or wizard, which indeed you are on your way to becoming. Unix experts sometimes speak of "invoking" commands, as if they were magic spells. Perhaps that is not far from the truth.

You will see more similarity between Unix and language as you recognize that Unix commands achieve much of their value from the ways in which they can be combined with each other and even modified as the need arises.

This book teaches you how to perform the tasks necessary to accomplish traditional actions with your computer. Performing a task in Unix is frequently a matter of using two or more commands in a particular sequence. For example, you will use one command to create a new folder, another command to move within that folder, then another command to create a file, and still another command to set the permissions on the file so that you can control who is allowed to use it.

Unix is a world where a string of commands displays a specificity so unique, it results in an exact execution of your intention. Although such an incantation may seem obscure to a novice, the experienced user will see only directness, simplicity, and precision. We'll help you move from the former to the latter.

Who Is This Book For?

This book was written primarily with two audiences in mind:

- Beginners who have never or barely used Unix before.

  You are the folks who we expect will actually read and use this book. We don't expect you to know anything at all about Unix before you read the book (but you will know a great deal about it when you are done). We'll teach you all the basic Unix skills and provide you with a solid reference book to turn to in the future. If you start at the beginning (often a good idea!) and work your way through, this book will give you an excellent foundation in Unix.

  We assume that you are adventurous, creative, and curious (hey, you *are* a Mac user, after all). We also assume that you have experience with the Macintosh and have become comfortable with the Aqua interface introduced in Mac OS X. If you are new to Mac OS X, we suggest that you also read Peachpit Press's *Mac OS X Tiger: Visual QuickStart Guide*, by Maria Langer (Peachpit Press; www.peachpit.com).

- Expert Unix users.

  You have installed and configured Unix systems in your sleep. You know the differences between the System V and BSD versions of the `ps` command. You have a favorite in the `vi` versus `emacs` debate. Your Unix-novice Mac-using friends keep calling you for help with `cd` and `ls`.

  If you already know your way around Unix, the simple fact is that you already know your way around 90 percent of Unix on Mac OS X. As we describe in Chapter 1, Mac OS X includes a complete Unix system, Darwin, that is based mostly on FreeBSD 4.4 and that you can use just like any other Unix system. Yes, there are a few differences (marked in this book with the Darwin mascot, Hexley), but mostly it's the same as other Unix systems you have used.

  We hope you'll buy this book by the caseload and give copies to friends who are new to Unix, so that they'll stop pestering you with basic questions.

What's in This Book?

Simply put, an introduction to Unix. An introduction that is both broad and deep, and yet assumes no prior Unix experience.

We give you instructions on how to perform dozens of tasks using standard Unix tools. Probably 90 percent of what you will learn from this book applies to other Unix systems, such as GNU/Linux, FreeBSD, and Sun Microsystems' Solaris.

The book consists of 14 chapters, containing several hundred specific tasks that cover everything from the basics of using the Unix command line to Unix system administration and the installation and configuration of Unix software.

An introduction to Unix

We start off by introducing you to Unix itself in Chapter 1, "What Is Unix, and Why Is It Good?" in which we explain what Unix is and describe the relationships between Mac OS X, Unix, Darwin, and Aqua.

The basics of the Unix command-line interface

In Chapter 2, "Using the Command Line," we teach you the basics of the command-line interface. This is the primary interface to Unix, and almost every task in the book is performed using only the keyboard; the mouse is hardly used at all.

In Chapter 3, "Getting Help and Using the Unix Manual," we teach you how to find and read the Unix documentation and how to get more help.

In Chapter 4, "Useful Unix Utilities," we give you instructions for the most common and useful Unix utility programs, including file compression and searching for text, as well as for a few utilities that are unique to Mac OS X. (In the appendix, we provide a list of more than 100 Unix commands that are unique to Darwin/Mac OS X.)

Chapter 5, "Using Files and Directories," provides more detailed instruction in the fundamental Unix skills of moving around your disk, and of viewing, creating, copying, and renaming directories and files (*directory* is what Unix calls a folder).

Beyond the basics: Editing, permissions, and programming

Chapter 6, "Editing and Printing Files," is devoted to the use of Unix tools to perform these functions. We teach you how to use the standard Unix editor (called `vi`), which is a keyboard-only editor (no mouse!) that is available on virtually every Unix system in the world.

In Chapter 7, "Configuring Your Environment with Unix," we teach you how to create shortcuts (*aliases* in Mac-speak) for commands and change settings (called *environment variables*) that many Unix programs use.

Chapter 8, "Working with Permissions and Ownership," teaches you how to work with one of Unix's more complex facets. We show you how to view the permission settings on files, how to change them, and what each of the dozens of possible settings means.

Chapter 9, "Creating and Using Scripts," is an introduction to simple Unix programming. We teach you about the fundamental building blocks of all programming and how to use each of them: variables, arguments, expressions, control structures, user input, and functions.

Using the Internet

Chapter 10, "Connecting over the Internet," covers several different methods for interacting with other machines over the Internet. These include logging in to other machines using a command-line interface, and transferring files between machines.

Intermediate skills: System administration and security

Chapter 11, "Introduction to System Administration," is a hefty introduction to managing Unix systems. We show you how to use the all-powerful *root* account, add and remove users, back up essential files, run commands automatically, monitor system use, and perform some basic repairs using Unix tools.

In Chapter 12, "Security," you'll learn about the security of your machine and how to improve it, and we pay particular attention to measures that can protect your machine from attacks that come across the Internet.

Installing and configuring software

The last two chapters take you deeper into Unix by teaching you about the installation and configuration of Unix software.

Chapter 13, "Installing Software from Source Code," gives instructions on how to download and install the vast collection of Unix software that is available in *source code* form. This is software for which the underlying programming code is available for download, and that you then turn into usable software though a process called *compiling*.

Chapter 14, "Installing and Configuring Servers," continues the theme of software installation by concentrating on *server* software. This is software that runs on your Mac to provide services to other machines over a network (typically over the Internet). Chapter 14 teaches you how to do several useful jobs, all from the command line, of course: set your machine's *hostname*; activate and deactivate various built-in servers (including setting up an *anonymous FTP server*); configure your Mac to receive incoming e-mail; create and install a CGI script in the Web server; and install, configure, and use the MySQL database server.

Learning Darwin/Mac OS X Commands

Finally, we provide an appendix listing of Unix commands that are found only in Darwin/Mac OS X. For example, the `open` command lets you "double-click" a file from the command line. (Out of the more than 1100 Unix commands found in Mac OS X, about 100 of them are unique to Darwin.)

How to Use This Book

Unix for Mac OS X 10.4: Visual QuickPro Guide is designed so that each chapter builds upon the skills and understanding taught in the preceding chapters. So before we teach you how to edit files using Unix tools (in Chapter 6, "Editing and Printing Files"), for example, we show you how to work with files in general (in Chapter 5, "Using Files and Directories").

- If you are completely new to Unix, we recommend that you work your way through the book chapter by chapter, at least through Chapter 12, "Security."
- If you already know a bit of Unix, take a few minutes to skim through the first six chapters, and if you already know the information we cover, see if you want to work through it in detail. Then decide if you want to work through the book chapter by chapter or use it as a reference as you poke around Mac OS X on your own. You'll find instructions on getting to the command line in Chapter 2, "Using the Command Line."
- If you are a hotshot Unix expert, gift-wrap the book and give it to your favorite Mac user. (But photocopy the appendix first.)

Most of this book consists of specific tasks laid out in a step-by-step fashion, with accompanying illustrations and examples of your input and the computer's output. The chapters and tasks are intended to be used as a tutorial, to teach you how to perform and understand the particular tasks and larger concepts. The book is also meant to be a reference work you will come back to as you continue to learn Unix, and as you find and create more uses for Unix.

Graphic conventions

We use the following graphic conventions throughout this book:

Keyboard symbols

Where we want to indicate that you must press a particular key, we use special symbols such as [Return] and [Control].

Whenever we show you a command or line of text to type into the computer, we assume that you will press [Return] at the end of the line unless we tell you not to. To avoid visual clutter and repetition, we do not put the [Return] symbol at the end of every line.

Bold

Used for figure and table references. For example: "**Figure 0.1** shows the 'layers' of Mac OS X, with the Aqua user interface on 'top' and the Darwin Unix layer at the foundation. **Table 0.1** is an example of a table."

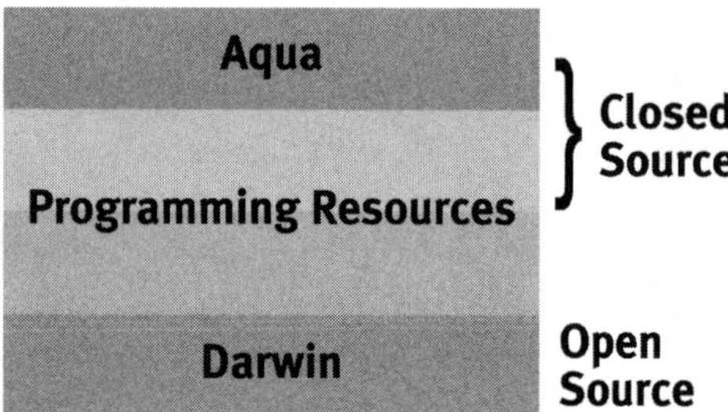

Figure 0.1 Diagram showing a very simplified view of the software layers in Mac OS X, with the Aqua user interface on top and the open-source Unix layer called Darwin at the foundation.

```
g4-cube:~ matisse$ cal 05 2023
      May 2023
 S  M Tu  W Th  F  S
    1  2  3  4  5  6
 7  8  9 10 11 12 13
14 15 16 17 18 19 20
21 22 23 24 25 26 27
28 29 30 31

g4-cube:~ matisse$
```

Figure 0.2 Example of using the Unix command line. The **`code text in bold`** is typed by you, the user; all the `other text` comes from the computer.

Table 0.1

Example of a Table

TABLE ENTRY	MEANING/DESCRIPTION
Unix	A multiuser, multitasking operating system available in more than 100 different versions.
POSIX	A standard for Portable Operating System Interface for Unix.

About "vanilla"

Throughout this book we use the made-up user name "vanilla" (and sometimes another one called "puffball").

Whenever you see vanilla, you should substitute your own short user name. Your home directory has the same name as your short user name.

`code text`

Used for Unix command-line text, including Unix commands and filenames. Basically, if you see something in code text, that means it is literally what would be typed into or come out of the computer. If a line of text is too long for this book's text margins, one or more gray arrows indicate the continuation of a single line of code. For example, the following should be typed as one long line:

```
find . -type f -print0 | xargs -0 grep
→ -l Darwin | mail -s "Files containing
→ 'Darwin' somebody@example.com
```

`code text in bold`

Used in figures to distinguish text you type in from text that comes from the computer. **Figure 0.2** has an example of how `code text` and **`code text in bold`** appear in a figure: The command line that the user typed is `cal 05 2023`, and everything else came from the computer.

`code italics`

These indicate text that you type into the computer but where you must substitute the appropriate value for the italicized text. For example, if you see

`ls -l` *`filename`*

then you would type the `ls -l` part literally, and then the name of a file instead of *`filename`*.

body-text italics

Used for emphasis and also to introduce words and phrases that are likely to be unfamiliar to Unix novices. For example, "The Unix concept of the *working directory* is similar to the GUI concept of the active window."

Case sensitivity

In Unix, filenames and command names are case sensitive. The standard Mac OS X file system (HFS Plus) is a *case-preserving, case-insensitive* file system. This means that it preserves the case when it stores filenames, but ignores case when looking for filenames, so you cannot have two files in the same folder if the only difference in their names is case: file1 and FILE1. This means that there are some situations in which "COMMAND" and "command" are the same, but because those are exceptions and because case sensitivity is the Unix standard, we assume that all commands and filenames are case sensitive unless otherwise noted.

Darwin-specific features

The image in **Figure 0.3** is Hexley, the mascot/logo for Darwin, which is the name of the Unix part of Mac OS X (see www.hexley.com). We use Hexley to indicate features of Mac OS X's Unix environment that differ from those of most other Unix versions. These features are available only in the open-source version of Unix (called Darwin) used in Mac OS X. Most of the Unix features of Mac OS X do *not* differ from those of other Unix systems.

Figure 0.3 This is Hexley; the mascot/logo for Darwin. *Darwin* is the name of the version of Unix used as the foundation of Mac OS X.

Figure 0.4 A Finder window showing the top level of the system disk. The folder containing the Developer Tools is highlighted.

Requirements

There are a few requirements for effectively using this book. Odds are, you already have all of them covered.

Adventurous and enthusiastic attitude

This is the most important requirement. If you meet this one, you will be able to master the others or do without them. Learning Unix is about learning a richly diverse collection of tools that are part of a lively ecosystem of software development. Unix is an environment for collaborative computing, and by stepping into it, you become part of an ongoing human phenomenon.

OK, enough philosophy. Here are the technical requirements:

Mac OS X 10.4 Tiger

This book is based on Mac OS X version 10.4 Tiger. All the examples in this book should work with Mac OS X 10.4.2. If you have an earlier version of Mac OS X, then a few things will be different from their descriptions in this book.

Be an administrator

You must be logged in as an administrative user for many of the tasks covered in this book, particularly for installing software and conducting system-admin tasks. If you aren't sure what an administrative user is, go to the Help menu in the Finder and search on *administrative user*.

Have the Developer Tools installed

Many important parts of this book require that you have the Mac OS X Developer Tools installed. This is a collection of software included with Mac OS X but not always installed by default.

Depending on which version of Mac OS X you have, the Developer Tools may already be installed. If you have a folder called Developer at the top level of your hard drive, then the Developer Tools are installed. **Figure 0.4** shows a Finder window with the Developer folder highlighted.

The Developer Tools may be on a separate DVD or CD that you must install. If you don't have the DVD or CD, there may be an installer application in your Applications folder (in the Installers folder). Also, you can find links to download the Developer Tools from Apple's "Tools" page (http://developer.apple.com/tools) or Developer Connection site: http://connect.apple.com. You will need a (free) Developer Connection account to use the site.

Connection to the Internet

Many of the tasks in the book assume that your machine is connected to the Internet, particularly those tasks involving interacting with other machines over networks.

What Is Unix, and Why Is It Good?

1

Mac OS X is the most significant advance in desktop computing since the introduction of the original Mac interface.

This book is a small part of a big revolution: the introduction of the Unix operating system to regular computer users. Never before have so many people had access to a common platform that is powerful, stable, and open to being reshaped through the collaborative efforts of all who contribute. Mac OS X provides a real "Mac interface" to a real Unix operating system, so if you are using Mac OS X, you're using Unix. Unix is an industrial-strength operating system specifically designed for always-on, network-connected computers that run multiple applications and are shared by many users. There are many different "flavors" of Unix and Unix-like operating systems; GNU/Linux and Mac OS X are by far the most common on desktop and laptop computers. If you have heard of Linux, it would be roughly correct to say that Mac OS X gives you everything Linux gives you, but with a Mac interface.

Since its creation in 1969, Unix has evolved into one of the world's most popular operating systems for servers and increasingly for desktop use. Moreover, Unix is an excellent environment for creating new software. Apple built Mac OS X on top of a version of Unix called Darwin. If you're a Mac user who wants to push the boundaries of what you can do with your computer, here's what Unix can do for you.

The Advantages of a Unix-Based Mac OS

While Unix is best known as a server operating system—most of the servers on the Internet run Unix—it's also been the desktop operating system for engineers, software developers, and system administrators. But Mac OS X is placing a Unix-based system on millions of desktops. With Unix under the hood of Mac OS X, Macintosh users are now able to take advantage of software developments beyond the boundaries of Apple Computer, while still enjoying the elegance and ease of use for which the Mac OS is famous.

Basing Mac OS X on the Darwin operating system gave it three important features that, for all its advantages, the Mac OS had not previously had: stability, flexibility, and openness.

Stability

Even the most devoted Macintosh user will admit that system crashes have been an unfortunate but predictable part of everyday life. Unix systems, however, are extremely difficult to crash. Thanks to *protected memory*—the memory each application uses that is unavailable to any other application—with Mac OS X your Macintosh will continue running even when one or more applications crash. You can simply restart the crashed application without having to restart your Mac.

If your system doesn't have protected memory, a badly behaving application can disturb the memory space of another application, or even of the operating system itself—often with nasty results. Macintosh operating systems before Mac OS X didn't include protected memory—which explains all those system crashes!

A feature called *preemptive multitasking* allows the operating system to limit the amount of computational resources devoted to each application by prioritizing between tasks. Before Mac OS X, the Mac OS employed *cooperative* multitasking—in which each application is *supposed* to behave and play well with the other applications on a machine. You can guess what happens when cooperatively multitasked applications don't cooperate.

Flexibility

Unix was designed to allow different programs to be connected in an almost infinite variety of ways. Because thousands of utilities are available for Unix (and because they work together so well), Unix users can customize their work environments relatively easily, building their own tools when the need arises. Mac OS X itself comes with around 500 utilities, most of which can be easily combined with other programs (see Chapter 4, "Useful Unix Utilities," for a roundup of the ones you're most likely to use). Because of this (and its portability), Unix is the ideal environment for developing new software.

Openness

Like other open-source versions of Unix, such as Linux, Darwin is open—that is, the inner workings are open to examination and change. You can download, study, and alter its programming source code at will. (In fact, versions of Darwin other than Apple's already exist.) Say you want to create a server that

What's in a Name?

Strictly speaking, *Unix* is a trademarked term that's been variously owned by AT&T, Novell, and now the Open Group (www.opengroup.org). Only Unix versions with the correct legal pedigree can use that name. In reality, though, most people casually refer to all the various "flavors" as Unix.

enables you to synchronize an iPod with any computer over the Internet, or one that sends faxes on demand from a catalog of files—whatever software you create is likely to use an existing piece of Unix software as its starting point.

By allowing people to examine and change their operating systems, open-source software is central to the ongoing evolution and spread of Unix, resulting in a software-development environment that will continue to increase in stability, flexibility, and power.

Unix's ability to connect different programs together provides almost infinite flexibility. Combine this with Unix's built-in support for TCP/IP (the networking protocol that defines the Internet) and other networking tools, and you have an operating system—Mac OS X—that's ready to take you into a future where you can build your applications, and every computer has the ability to be a server.

Whatever capability you want to add to an application, you can probably do it in Darwin. As a Mac enthusiast, you may have had limited exposure to any kind of programming, but you'll be able to expand your horizons by accessing the Unix underlying Mac OS X. Even if you're brand-new to programming, delving into Unix is the best way to start.

Other Versions of Unix

Over the years, many versions of Unix have been developed—some by large corporations (for example, Sun Microsystems' Solaris and Hewlett-Packard's HP/UX), and some by small companies and individuals working for their own pleasure. The most famous of the latter is the open-source GNU/Linux operating system, which combines the work of hundreds of programmers from around the world and has been adopted by thousands of companies. (For example, IBM announced in January 2002 a mainframe computer designed specifically for Linux, and in 2005 Brazil's National Institute of Information Technology is planning to make computers running Linux available to citizens at subsidized prices of $500 or less.)

A good list of dozens of versions of Unix is available at www.ugu.com/sui/ugu/show?ugu.flavors.

Becoming a sophisticated user

Thus, you should read this book because you want a deeper understanding of your computer, and to get your fingers and hands and mind inside of it. Using Unix is about moving from being a consumer of software and systems to being a creator of software and systems. This means pushing the envelope of how you interact with the operating system, delving into areas where most users don't go, in order to develop capabilities that most users don't have. Mac OS X makes this possible because Unix is an operating system for developing and building, for getting into the nitty-gritty.

Since much Unix software is created by volunteers, you're benefiting from the hard work of thousands of users. But using Unix means you will always tweak, modify, and configure to get the software to do what you want. By bringing an industrial-strength server to your desktop, Apple has taken desktop computing to another level—in much the same way that Macintosh-plus-PostScript laser printers brought high-quality print publishing and graphics tools to the desktop. None of this is automatic, though, and using Unix places a greater burden on you. If you're coming to Unix expecting the shrink-wrapped experience of the Mac OS or Windows, you're bound to be disappointed.

You will work with Unix primarily from the command line in the Terminal application (more about that in the next chapter). You will put together lots of odd-sounding commands, creating tiny and not-so-tiny scripts and programs to give the machine capabilities it never had before. Not only will you be customizing your machine and creating software, but also you will be customizing your world, and indirectly the world that the rest of us live in.

Most people won't really notice that Mac OS X is Unix based. In fact, most people will use their Mac OS X Macintoshes just as they always have—writing in their word processors, creating images in graphics software, and editing sound and video.

Some of the Unix tools in Mac OS X were available in some form for Mac OS 9, but the Unix versions are included with Mac OS X (for example, a Web server and an e-mail server). With Mac OS X, you are more likely to work with these applications for a couple of reasons. Mac OS X is so stable that you won't be afraid of messing up your computer. More important, if you use a "pure" Unix tool, like the Apache Web server, then the skills you learn, and the system you build, will be transferable to almost any other Unix environment with little effort.

Unix is more hands-on than the graphical user interfaces you're accustomed to. However, if you're ready to experience new heights of computing creativity, you'll find that you have a more personalized and robust system on your hands by the time you finish this book.

From Multics to Unix

Unix wasn't actually named until about a year into its development—at which point the wordplay on the preceding Multics project was intentional (*uni*, meaning *one*, as opposed to *multi*, meaning *many*). The tradition of puns and word games in Unix software continues to this day, as you'll see in later chapters when we introduce programs such as `less`, which is an improvement on an earlier program called `more`. More became less, you see.

But First, a Little History

"What we wanted to preserve was not just a good environment in which to do programming, but a system around which a fellowship could form. We knew from experience that the essence of communal computing, as supplied by remote-access, time-shared machines, is not just to type programs into a terminal instead of a keypunch, but to encourage close communication.

—Dennis M. Ritchie, coinventor of Unix, from "The Evolution of the Unix Time-Sharing System," **AT&T Bell Laboratories Technical Journal** ***63, No. 6, Part 2, October 1984 (http://cm.bell-labs.com/cm/cs/who/dmr/hist.html)***

How did Unix end up as the underpinning of the Mac OS? In 1997, after a series of unsuccessful attempts to update the Macintosh operating system—remember Pink and Copland?—Apple bought NeXT, the computer company that Apple cofounder Steve Jobs had started 12 years earlier after he was forced out of Apple. NeXT had developed a powerful operating system with an elegant user interface, but it had failed to become commercially successful. (Of course, commercial success is not the only way to gauge the quality of a product. None other than Tim Berners-Lee, inventor of the World Wide Web, used a NeXT machine for his development work on hypertext.)

When Apple bought NeXT, it got the code for NeXT's operating system, development tools, and user interface. But, more important, it got Steve Jobs and a culture of Unix-based development. The NeXT operating system (called NextStep), while largely written from scratch, was a version of Unix, and the NeXT engineers were used to a Unix culture—that is, employing powerful, flexible tools and systems in an environment of creative engineering. Given the effect on Apple's operating-system development, some people say that, culturally, NeXT bought Apple.

Mac OS X is based on a new version of Unix called Darwin. Darwin is a direct descendant of the Unix technology underlying NextStep, yet virtually every component has been significantly upgraded by a massive infusion of new open-source software, as well as some significant Apple-specific innovations. The cultural influence of NeXT and the software itself played a huge part in moving Apple toward the values of openness, flexibility, and stability.

Where did those values come from? They were part of Unix from its beginnings. Unix

continues on next page

Unix Pioneer: Bill Joy

Perhaps most recognizable to the general population as the chief scientist and cofounder of Sun Microsystems, Bill Joy is known in the Unix community as the primary designer of the Berkeley Software Distribution (BSD) version of Unix.

Among Joy's many contributions are the NFS (Network File System) protocol, the open-source version of TCP/IP, and the `vi` text editor.

After BSD Unix's introduction in 1983, it became the first widely distributed open-source version of Unix and has been the basis for numerous later versions of Unix, including Darwin, the core of Mac OS X.

More information about Bill Joy is available at www.answers.com/topic/bill-joy.

was born in 1969 from the efforts of a small group of scientists working at AT&T's Bell Labs to create an operating system that would allow the group to continue the kind of collaborative programming it had been doing on an earlier project called Multics. Thus, from the very beginning, Unix was conceived as both a multiuser and multitasking system—that is, one that many people and many programs could use simultaneously and harmoniously.

In the late 1970s, the University of California, Berkeley, used Unix extensively in its computer science department, several of whose members contributed features to the operating system. A key contribution: building in support for TCP/IP (the networking protocol suite that defines the Internet), added in the early 1980s. Virtually all current versions of Unix use the Berkeley networking code or its derivatives. Eventually, the version of Unix that came out of the university was dubbed the Berkeley Software Distribution (BSD). The Darwin layer of Mac OS X is directly based on BSD along with NextStep (mentioned above). As with Linux, you can run Darwin by itself on many hardware platforms (including the Intel architecture); however, it won't look like Mac OS X without the proprietary components Apple provides in Mac OS X.

Think of Mac OS X as having several layers: The bottom, or foundation, layer is Darwin (**Figure 1.1**). On top of Darwin are a number of proprietary software components that Apple has added. Above it all is the layer that users see—the graphical interface called Aqua. You can use Mac OS X for traditional Macintosh tasks without ever being aware of the layers underneath Aqua, including Darwin.

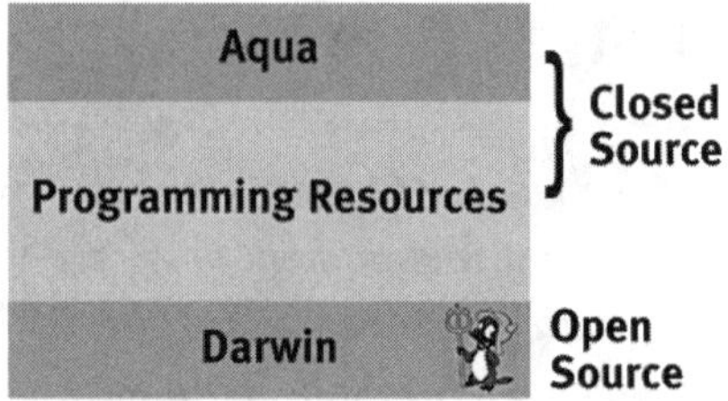

Figure 1.1 Apple built the latest version of its operating system, Mac OS X, on top of a version of Unix called Darwin. Between the Aqua interface and the underlying operating system are Apple-specific layers.

Unix Pioneer: Linus Torvalds

Linus Torvalds is widely known as the inventor of Linux, a completely open-source Unix-like operating system. Torvalds wrote the core of Linux, called the *kernel*, and released the first version in 1991.

Besides the Linux kernel, Torvalds's most significant contribution to Unix has been his ability to gently and productively facilitate and coordinate the efforts of literally hundreds of programmers whose work makes up the current version of the Linux kernel.

Torvalds made a key decision when he released the code for the Linux kernel under a software license called the GNU General Public License (GNU GPL), which requires anyone making changes to the source code to make those changes freely available to the world. Most installed versions of Linux come with hundreds of other pieces of software also licensed under the GNU GPL, and so the name GNU/Linux is usually more accurate when speaking of Linux.

More information about Linus Torvalds is available at www.answers.com/topic/linus-torvalds.

Torvalds's own homepage is at www.cs.helsinki.fi/u/torvalds.

Beyond Unix: Other Open Systems

Mac OS X includes many open-source technologies that are also helping to revolutionize the information infrastructure of society.

- **HTML**—The ease of creating documents using Hypertext Markup Language drove the growth of the Web. Anyone viewing a Web page can see, copy, and modify the underlying HTML. The HTML standard is coordinated by the World Wide Web Consortium (www.w3c.org/MarkUp/).
- **Apache Web server (http://httpd.apache.org)**—By far the most popular Web server in the world, Apache provides a huge variety of configuration options and can be altered easily to add new ones. Mac OS X comes with Apache (see Chapter 14, "Installing and Configuring Servers").
- **Perl** (www.perl.org)—This powerful scripting and programming language (which comes with Mac OS X) is used in scripts as short as 20 lines and in large object-oriented applications with thousands of lines of code.
- **C**—The programs listed here and those included in every version of Unix are written—with few exceptions—entirely in the C programming language. To learn more, check out *The C Programming Language,* Second Edition, by Brian W. Kernighan and Dennis M. Ritchie (Prentice Hall, 1998; http://cm.bell-labs.com/cm/cs/cbook)—the fundamental book on the topic—or "The Development of the C Language" (http://cm.bell-labs.com/cm/cs/who/dmr/chist.html).
- **SSH**—The Secure Shell tool facilitates secure connections between computers. The open-source version is maintained by the OpenBSD project (www.openssh.org).
- **GCC**—The GNU Compiler Collection translates programming source code into machine-executable applications. It's maintained by the Free Software Foundation (www.gnu.org/software/gcc/gcc.html).
- **Postfix** and **Sendmail** (www.postfix.org and www.sendmail.org)—Mac OS X comes with both of these common mail-server software applications, which you can use to set up your Mac OS X computer to be your own mail server.

Apple not only utilizes these open technologies, but also submits improvements to these and other open-source technologies so that other open-source users benefit, even if they are not using Mac OS X—open source is not only taking, but also giving back to the community.

Unix Pioneer: Dennis M. Ritchie

Dennis M. Ritchie has been a computer scientist with Bell Labs for 35 years. He is most famous for having assisted Ken Thompson in inventing Unix and for being the primary creator of the C programming language (with Brian Kernighan in 1972). Ritchie is also a parent of another operating system, called Plan 9, that is well-known to the community of people who develop operating systems. He is currently head of the System Software Research Department at Bell Labs, where he helped develop a new operating system called Inferno and currently manages a group of researchers.

Dennis M. Ritchie's homepage: www.cs.bell-labs.com/who/dmr.

Unix History Timeline

Some key dates in the development of different Unix versions:

- **1970**—Ken Thompson suggests the name *Unix* for the fledging operating system born in 1969 at AT&T Bell Labs.
- **1973**—The kernel (core) of Unix is rewritten in the C language, making it the world's first operating system that's "portable"—that is, able to run on multiple kinds of hardware.
- **1977**—First BSD (Berkeley Software Distribution) version is released. Licensees must also get a license from AT&T.
- **1983**—Version 4.2 BSD is released. By the end of 1994, more than 1000 licenses are issued. AT&T releases its commercial version, System V.
- **1983**—AT&T releases System V release 3. IBM, Hewlett-Packard, and others base their own Unix-like systems on this version.
- **1989**— NeXT releases NextStep which includes an operating system based on 4.3 BSD as well as a sophisticated graphical user interface and well-regarded set of tools for developers. Ten years later Apple will release revised versions of much of NextStep as Mac OS X.
- **1991**—Linus Torvalds releases version 0.02 of Linux, an open-source, Unix-like operating system.
- **1992**—Bill Jolitz releases 386/BSD, a full version of Unix with no AT&T code.
- **1992**—Sun Microsystems releases Solaris, a version of Unix based on System V release 4, incorporating many BSD features.
- **1994**—BSD4.4-Lite is released by the University of California, Berkeley. It is entirely free of legal encumbrances from the old AT&T code. Version 1.0 of Linux is also released this year; Linux incorporates features from both AT&T's System V and BSD versions of Unix.
- **1999**—Apple Computer releases Darwin—a version of BSD Unix and the core of the Mac OS X.

For More on Unix History

- **CrackMonkey** (http://crackmonkey.org/unix.html)—A history of Unix, including a discussion of its important flavors.
- **The Evolution of the Unix Time-Sharing System** (http://cm.bell-labs.com/cm/cs/who/dmr/hist.html)—Coinventor Dennis M. Ritchie offers a technical and social history of Unix.
- **"Overview of the GNU Project"** (www.gnu.org/gnu/gnu-history.html)—A history of the Free Software Foundation's efforts to create an open and free version of Unix.
- **Open Source: Darwin** (http://developer.apple.com/darwin)—Apple's official Darwin Project site, where you can download source code and find links to other related projects.
- **OpenDarwin.org** (http://opendarwin.org)—General-purpose site about Darwin, including links to mailing lists.
- **The GNU-Darwin Distribution** (http://gnu-darwin.sourceforge.net)—Web site that "aims to be the most free Darwin-based Unix distribution."

How Mac OS X's Unix Differs from Mac OS 9

The immediate, obvious difference between Unix and Mac OS 9 is the user interface. Until Mac OS X, the various graphical interfaces available to Unix users all fell short of the elegance and polish to which Macintosh users are accustomed.

It is a tribute to the architecture of Mac OS X that you can use it as a Macintosh operating system and never have to see any significant Unix underpinnings. Never, that is, unless you want to learn Unix.

From a more technical point of view, when Mac OS X is compared with Mac OS 9 (and earlier Macintosh operating systems), several important differences stand out. As we noted earlier, Unix uses protected memory and preemptive multitasking, and has other capabilities that let applications share memory, processors, and applications in a stable and reliable way.

As a result, it is hard for one misbehaving application to affect any other application or the operating system itself. Yes, applications can still crash in Mac OS X, but rarely do they take the whole OS down with them. Not only will you suffer fewer crashes, but they'll impact your other work less.

Unix, and thus Mac OS X, is also a multiuser operating system. It's designed from the ground up with the assumption that many people will be using the computer, often simultaneously. Just as the applications' activities are kept separate, so too are the actions of each user. Even if 50 people are using the Macintosh, it is hard for any one of them to mess up the work of the other ones.

Another way Mac OS 9 differs from Mac OS X is in the arrangement of files and folders (called *directories* in Unix) and the way information about each file is stored.

You will also see an icon that looks like a house show up as a shortcut in the Finder navigation dialog, the Save dialog, and so on. This icon will be labeled with your short user name and represents your *home directory*. This concept of each user's home directory as the only place where you normally create files is a thoroughly Unix idea arising directly from Unix's nature as a multiuser system, and is a major change from Mac OS 9.

Apple has strived to mask these differences in Mac OS X, but they are still there, and you must be aware of them if you want to do serious Unix work (or even just be a Mac OS X "power user").

In your day-to-day use of Mac OS X, you'll find that many of the ways it differs from Mac OS 9 have more to do with Aqua, than with Unix. For example, the Dock was new to Mac OS X, but it wasn't a "Unix change." In this book, we'll focus specifically on the Unix characteristics of Mac OS X, not the differences that came from Aqua.

What You Can Do with Mac OS X and Unix

What do you want to do? Do you want to create movies with iMovie and make them available over the Internet? With the Unix-based Mac OS X, that task is easy: You simply drag the movies into the Sites folder in your home directory, then enable Web sharing. Are you a programmer who works on Unix systems? With Mac OS X you can install the same software on your desktop (or laptop) Mac that you use on your Unix servers you develop for, enabling you to have a complete development and test environment on your own machine. Would you like to run your own radio station? You can easily use your Mac OS X machine to run the Darwin Streaming Server, which provides powerful streaming-audio capabilities. Do you want your schedule to be constantly available to friends and family, your résumé always accessible to potential employers? You can provide all those things with greater reliability on a Unix platform.

Beyond the foundation of increased stability, flexibility, and openness, Unix brings a number of more specific features to Mac OS X that are fundamental to the way you will use it. Key among these is the way it supports multiple users and multiple processes.

Accommodating multiple users

As we've said earlier, Unix is a multiuser environment and intentionally keeps each user's actions separate to create a more stable environment.

On a Unix system you are never alone (unless you started the machine in single-user mode, which we'll discuss in Chapter 11, "Introduction to System Administration"; if you already know what that means, keep quiet until the others have a chance to catch up). Unix assumes there are going to be many users running programs on the system.

When you log in to a Unix system, you identify yourself with a user name and password that have already been entered into the system by an administrator (if you are working on your own Mac OS X system, you will have created at least one account for yourself when you installed the operating system). This enables the operating system to keep your files and actions separate from everyone else's and is a major factor in Unix stability and security.

✔ Tip

- You can see a list of who is logged in to your system using the command-line `w` and `who` commands. See Chapter 11 for more information on using the `w` and `who` commands.

All the files you create in the normal course of using the system are "owned" by you. Every file and every running program (known as a *process*) on a Unix system is owned by a user. All the important system files—that is, the ones that make up the actual operating system—are owned by a special super user called *root*. The root account is all-powerful, and you must exercise great care when using it (see Chapter 11 for more on root).

Not every user account on the system is intended for use by a human. Unix systems, including Mac OS X, come with a number of special user accounts with names like "nobody" and "daemon." The system uses these accounts to own processes that should not have the power of the root account.

Each regular user account on a Unix system has its own area in the file system called its *home directory*. This is where all the files a given user creates and owns are normally stored. Unix keeps track of who owns each file and allows (or disallows) various operations based on the ownership of files.

Preemptive multitasking

On Unix systems, you might have not only multiple programs running, but also multiple copies of the same program running. Even with just a single person logged in, running a few applications, several dozen processes will be running at any given moment, each with its own separate memory allocation. In fact, the operating system keeps a number of different processes running even if you are not doing anything.

When the machine starts up, the initial process (called *init*), which is owned by the super-user root, begins. The init process then starts many other processes, which are also owned by root.

✔ Tip

- You can see a list of all the processes on your system using the `ps` and `top` commands. See Chapter 11 for more information on monitoring system usage.

Parents and children

Every process in Unix is the child of some other process, except for that first process, init, which is the mother of all processes. This concept of processes' having parents and children comes up frequently in Unix.

When you log in to a Unix system, you start a process that you alone own. The exact process depends on which Unix system you are using, and how you log in to it. This process will be the parent (or grandparent, or great-grandparent) of every process you start on the system after logging in.

When you log in using the Mac OS X graphical user interface, you start a process called WindowServer, which you own.

Every program you run will have the WindowServer process as an ancestor. In other words, if you start up an application such as BBEdit, a popular text editor, then BBEdit's parent process will be WindowServer. If you start up the command-line interface (the Terminal application), you might then start more programs using the Terminal application. Those programs will have Terminal as their parent, and WindowServer as their grandparent, and so on.

So, even if you are the only person using your Mac, you might have several dozen processes running. In addition to a process for the programs you are running, there will always be dozens of other processes—some owned by the root account and some owned by other system accounts.

Applications vs. Programs vs. Commands

All applications are programs—the terms are synonymous. In this book we use the term *application* to refer to complex programs used for a variety of related tasks—for example, Adobe Photoshop is an application for graphics manipulation. In Unix you often see the term *command*, which can refer either to an application that handles some specific task (such as copying files) or to a built-in feature of a larger program or application. For example, the command for copying files is the `cp` command, which is in fact a small program. The command to move from one folder into another folder (*directory*, in Unix terms) is the `cd` command, which is actually part of a larger program called the *shell*. See Chapter 5, "Using Files and Directories," for more on the `cp` and `cd` commands.

Files and the filesystem

Unix brought a number of changes to the Mac OS with regard to files and the filesystem (see the sidebar "What Is a Filesystem?" for its definition).

From the user's point of view, the most prominent changes (as compared with Mac OS 9) involve the handling of file security, the storage of files, and the use of a different syntax for describing a file's location.

Files and security

On an old Mac OS system, you could alter or delete any file. You could put files from the System Folder in the Trash and cause all kinds of trouble, even accidentally. On a Unix system, every file is owned by some user. The operating system restricts the ability to create, change, or delete files based on ownership of the file/folder and the permissions applied to it. So, one user cannot alter or delete files created by another user, and you are unlikely to cause any serious damage to the operating system (the exception: the root user can do anything).

Folders are called *directories*

What Mac users call a *folder* Unix users call a *directory.* A directory that is inside another is called a *subdirectory.* It is important to know which directory you are "in," because when you're working from a command line, there is no visual cue, such as an active window. Know the concept of the "current directory" in Unix—that's where you're currently working.

File paths use / instead of :

In Mac OS 9 and earlier, file-path designations use colons. (By *file-path designations* we mean how you would spell out—in writing—the location of a file showing all the enclosing folders.) In Mac OS X, Unix uses the / (slash) instead of the : (colon) to separate the parts of a file path. In Mac OS 9, then, the path of the FileMaker Pro application would look like that in **Figure 1.2**.

In Mac OS X, the same path would appear as shown in **Figure 1.3**.

Notice that the name of the hard drive doesn't show up anymore. In Unix, drives don't have names. The Mac OS X Aqua interface does have names for drives, and they do appear in the Finder, thanks to some tricks of the Mac OS X Finder. But at the underlying Unix/Darwin level, even in Mac OS X, drives don't have names. (They do have *device names*, which look like `/dev/disk0s3`. For more on the Unix way of looking at the your disk[s], check out "Seeing the Whole File System" and especially Figure 5.1 in Chapter 5.)

Unix presents all the available hard disks as a single hierarchy of directories and files. There are ways to see which disks contain which files, but usually, when dealing with

```
MyBig Disk:Applications (Mac OS 9):FileMaker Pro 5 Folder:FileMaker Pro
```

Figure 1.2. This is how the path of the FileMaker Pro application would look on the Mac OS 9 file system.

```
/Applications (Mac OS 9)/FileMaker Pro 5 Folder/FileMaker Pro
```

Figure 1.3 This is how the path of the FileMaker Pro application looks on the Mac OS X filesystem.

files in Unix, you pay attention to only the *full pathname* of the file. See Chapter 5 for more about using pathnames.

Even with the differences cited above, the Unix filesystem is organized similarly to what you are used to on a Mac.

If you use / instead of *:* in your pathnames, and think of as your startup disk as being named / in Unix, you're getting closer to understanding the way Unix thinks of files, directories, and subdirectories.

What Is a Filesystem?

In Unix, the terms *filesystems* and *file sysem* are often used interchangeably. Furthermore, the term *filesystem* is used in two different ways. The first way is more informal and refers to the complete hierarchy of directories. The second way refers to a single storage area that has been formatted for use by the operating system. The "single storage area" is often, but not always, a single disk partition. Filesystems contain directories and files but never other filesystems.

Example of the first form: "/ is the root directory of the filesystem."

Example of the second form: "It is common to have two or more filesystems on the same physical disk."

Get used to filename extensions

Another difference between Mac OS 9 and Mac OS X is in Mac OS X's use of filename extensions—you know, those things at the end of all the filenames on the Web and on PCs, such as .html, .txt, and .jpg.

From the very start, the Mac OS has cleverly kept track of a file's characteristics: what type of file it is; what application opens it; if the file is being used by another application; if the file is locked. Unix doesn't store as much information about each file along with each file. In particular, Unix has no fundamental concept of a file's "type" or "creator" (Mac OS X does, but only for files that were created with Mac file information).

Unix's filename extensions indicate a file's type. This is not as powerful as the Macintosh approach, but it is the standard in the Unix world. (This is no surprise, given which operating system the original Web servers used and the one most Web servers still use today.) Mac OS X tries to have it both ways and, in the Mac spirit, uses the old Mac approach in some cases and the standard Unix approach in other cases. But in order to play well with others, Mac OS X incorporates filename extensions. You can decide whether to display them in the graphical interface, but when you use the command line they will always be there.

Files created by Macintosh applications will have the Macintosh creator and type attributes, but files created by non-Mac applications, including all non-Mac Unix applications, will have only the filename extension (if any) to indicate what kind of file they are.

How You Will Be Working with Unix

You are probably already using your Macintosh for a variety of tasks, working in applications that take advantage of the lovely Aqua interface. As you dig below the surface and start using the Darwin layer of Mac OS X, you will be performing operations that are either unique to Unix or better suited to the Unix environment.

Working from the command line

The command line is the primary user interface in Unix. Most Unix software packages are designed to be installed and configured from the command line.

It is from the command line that you will be installing software and manipulating files (copying, moving, renaming, and so on). You might even start editing files using the command-line tools.

One of the most powerful aspects of the command line is in how it allows you to connect a series of commands together to accomplish some task. **Figure 1.4** shows an example of connecting three commands together in order to find all the files in a folder that contain the word *success* and e-mail the resulting list of filenames to yourself.

The command line in Figure 1.4 is composed of three major parts separated by the vertical bar (|) character, which is called a *pipe*. (Note: The first part uses the `find` command to produce a list of the names of all the files (not folders) in the current folder (by using the `-type f` option) and all those inside it. The output of that command is passed (*piped*) via the | character to the next command, `xargs` (*arguments*). This second part applies the `grep` (*search*) command to each filename in turn, searching the file for the string `success` and producing a list of the filenames where the string was found. That second list is piped to the third part, the `Mail` command, which sends the list to the specified e-mail address. The ampersand (&) at the end tells Unix to do all this "in the background," which means that we do not have to wait for the processes to finish before issuing a new command—we can go on with our work at the command line. Don't worry if every little thing doesn't make sense yet—you will learn about each aspect of that command in the following chapters. Understand that part of the power of Unix comes from the fact that many small parts can be combined to do bigger tasks, as seen above. See Chapter 2, "Using the Command Line," for more details.

Under Mac OS X, the most common way to get to the command line is through the Terminal application (found in the Utilities folder under Applications).

```
find . -type f -print0 | xargs -0 grep -l success | Mail address@hostname.com &
```

Figure 1.4 This command line shows how to connect commands together—in this case, finding all the files in a folder that contain the word *success* and then e-mailing the resulting list of filenames to yourself. `/System/Library/StartupItems/Apache/Apache` handles the starting (and stopping) of the Apache Web server.

Editing files from the command line

In order to really harness the power of Unix, you will want to learn how to edit files using a command-line text editor. Unix is file-centric and uses text files to control almost every aspect of software configuration. Although it's difficult for most Mac users to learn at first, editing files from the command line lets you change files without leaving the command-line environment in which most of your Unix work will occur. Furthermore, the ability to edit files from the command line will make it easy for you to work on other Unix systems besides Mac OS X, something you are almost certain to do once you get further into Unix.

Unix Commands Have Strange Names

Unix commands often have very terse obscure and/or arbitrary-sounding names. Examples: `awk`, `grep`, and `chmod`.

This contributes to Unix's (justly earned) reputation as a difficult operating system to use, requiring users to memorize a great deal in order to become proficient.

Because you are probably itching to know how those three commands got their names, here's the story: `awk`, a text-processing system, got its name from the initials of the three people who created it. `grep`, a command for searching inside text, got its name from the commands used in an earlier program to "globally find a regular expression and print." `chmod` is a command to change the permissions associated with a file and means *CHange MODe*.

Programming and scripting

Developed *by* programmers *for* programming, Unix is—not surprisingly—an excellent programming environment, and many of its strengths (and some of its weaknesses) stem from that heritage.

Although you don't need Mac OS X or Unix to create software, if you're using Unix, you'll probably at least poke around with programming—perhaps first modifying existing programs and then moving on to create new ones. In addition to its terrific stability, Unix provides an environment in which it's easy to connect varying tools in an equally various number of ways. And when you need them, you can create new commands, extending your tool kit as you work.

You can also write simple scripts to automate tasks—for example, to perform backups, automate the transfer of files to other systems, calculate the rate of return on an investment, or search text for certain phrases and highlight them. You could write scripts to create a small database-backed Web site, or to convert batches of images for use on the Web, or to analyze voter-registration or campaign-contribution records. Some users never stop creating new applications: We call them *programmers.*

Mac OS X comes with tools to create and run programs in AppleScript, Perl, Bourne shell, and a couple of other Unix scripting languages. The Mac OS X developer tools include software that allows you to create programs in C, C++, Objective-C (the primary language for native Mac OS X software), Java, Ruby, and Python as well. (Throughout this book we assume that you have in fact installed the Developer Tools. If not, refer back to the Introduction.) With the exception of AppleScript, none of these programming

continues on next page

languages were available to Mac users in the past unless they installed third-party software (such as MacPerl or the CodeWarrior compiler). The Mac OS X Developer Tools also include the Xcode and Interface Builder applications, which are graphical interfaces for developing software projects written in C, Objective-C, C++, and Java.

Shell scripts

The vast majority of Unix scripting is done using *shell scripts*. These are written using the language of a Unix *shell*. A Unix shell is the program that provides the command-line interface you will be using. A shell accepts typed commands and provides output in text form; it is a "shell" around the operating system. The Bourne shell is one of the oldest command-line interpreters for Unix (see Chapter 2). Bourne shell scripts are used as part of the system startup and shutdown process in virtually all versions of Unix, and Mac OS X is no exception (although it uses fewer than most versions of Unix; see "The Boot Sequence" in Chapter 11). Also, when you are using Mac OS X from the command line (which is what this book is all about), you will normally be using an advanced version of the Bourne shell, called `bash` (for *Bourne again shell*).

If you are excited or impatient, you probably want to take a look at one of the Mac OS X system-startup scripts right now! Here's how to do it.

To view a system-startup script:

1. Open a Mac OS X (not Classic) text editor—for example, the TextEdit application, which you can access through TextEdit in the Applications folder.
2. Open the file `/System/Library/` ➝ `StartupItems/Apache/Apache`.

   The file will be opened in read-only mode, so you need not worry about damaging it.

You are looking at the script that starts up the Apache Web server when your machine starts up (**Figure 1.5**).

```
#!/bin/sh

##
# Apache HTTP Server
##

. /etc/rc.common

StartService ()
{
        if [ "${WEBSERVER:=-NO-}" = "-YES-" ]; then
             echo "Starting Apache web server"
             if [ ! -e /etc/httpd/httpd.conf ] ; then
                       cp -p /etc/httpd/httpd.conf.default /etc/httpd/httpd.conf
             fi
             apachectl start
             if [ "${WEBPERFCACHESERVER:=-NO-}" = "-YES-" ]; then
                  if [ -x /usr/sbin/webperfcachectl ]; then
                       echo "Starting web performance cache server"
                       /usr/sbin/webperfcachectl start
                  fi
             fi
        fi
}

StopService ()
{
        if [ -x /usr/sbin/webperfcachectl ]; then
             echo "Stopping web performance cache server"
             /usr/sbin/webperfcachectl stop
        fi
        echo "Stopping Apache web server"
        apachectl stop
  }

RestartService ()
{
        if [ "${WEBSERVER:=-NO-}" = "-YES-" ]; then
             echo "Restarting Apache web server"
             apachectl restart
             if [ "${WEBPERFCACHESERVER:=-NO-}" = "-YES-" ]; then
                  if [ -x /usr/sbin/webperfcachectl ]; then
                       echo "Restarting web performance cache server"
                       /usr/sbin/webperfcachectl restart
                  fi
             fi
        else
             StopService
        fi
}

RunService "$1"
```

Figure 1.5 The script `/System/Library/StartupItems/Apache/Apache` is used to start and stop the Apache Web Server.

Figure 1.6 is an example of a script you might use in Mac OS X to make a group of files open in Photoshop when they're double-clicked from the Finder. Using this script and some additional Unix commands, you could instruct your machine to find every file ending in .jpg within a directory (folder) and have those files launch Photoshop when double-clicked from the Finder. And by altering the script, you could do the same thing for just those files that already have the Mac type code for JPEGs, GIFs, and others. (The *type code* is a four-character code that identifies the type of each file. It's a pre–Mac OS X feature that many Mac applications still use.)

This example may look scary now, but don't worry—once you learn some Unix, it will make more sense. For now, just let it wash over you, and understand that when you've read this book (and thus know a bit of Unix), you'll be able to create this sort of script fairly easily. (See Chapter 9, "Creating and Using Scripts," for more on creating shell scripts.)

```
#!/bin/sh
# This a comment. Comments help make the code easier to read.
# This script takes one or more filenames as arguments and
# sets the Creator Code for each one to Photoshop.

GETINFO="/Developer/Tools/GetFileInfo"
SETFILE="/Developer/Tools/SetFile"

#  8BIM is the Creator Code for Photoshop
NEW_CREATOR="8BIM"
changed_files=0
total_files=0
for file in "$@" ;   # All the command-line arguments are in $@
do
       total_files=`expr $total_files + 1`;  # keep track of total
       if [ ! -f "$file" ];  # if it is not a file
       then
            echo "skipping '$file' - it is not a file."
       elif [ -w "$file" ];  # If it is writable...
       then
            creator=`$GETINFO -c "$file"`; # Get the Creator code of this file
            if [ !  "$creator" = \"$NEW_CREATOR\" ] ; # If it is not already set...
            then
                 # Set the file to have the new creator code
                 $SETFILE -c "$NEW_CREATOR" "$file"
                 changed_files=`expr $changed_files + 1`
            fi
       else
            echo "skipping '$file' - not writable"
       fi
done

echo "Checked $total_files files"
echo "Set $changed_files files to have creator $NEW_CREATOR"
skipped=`expr $total_files - $changed_files`
echo "Skipped $skipped files"
```

Figure 1.6 You might use this script in Mac OS X to make a group of files open in Photoshop when they're double-clicked from the Finder.

Perl

Perl is one of the most popular programming languages in the world. Although you can use it to build large, complex programs, it is easy enough to learn that most people begin using it to write small utility programs or CGI programs for Web sites.

Because Perl excels at text processing and can easily interact with SQL databases, it's ideal for building Web pages as well as other data-manipulation projects.

Figure 1.7 is a code listing of a Perl script that outputs plain-text files in reverse—the last line comes out first. This would be difficult, if not impossible, using traditional Macintosh applications.

Java

Although newer than many other programming languages, Java has already spread far and wide—partly because it is powerful and partly because its creator, Sun Microsystems, has promoted it very well.

Programs written in Java can run on only one kind of machine, but that machine is a *virtual machine*—a piece of software. Because a virtual machine is software, it can be written for different hardware platforms. Java virtual machines exist for every major operating system, and an increasing number of small hardware devices (such as cell phones) are able to run Java code. Programs written in Java can often run without changes on many different platforms. The Mac OS X Developer Tools come with a Java compiler and a Java virtual machine. The Java programming language has a large set of tools for creating graphical user interfaces and for communicating across networks.

```
#!/usr/bin/perl
# This a comment. Always use comments.
#
# This script takes one or more file names as arguments and
# outputs the files one line at a time, in reverse order.
# I.e. The last line of the last file comes out first.

while ( $file =  pop(@ARGV) ) {
   open FILE, "$file"; # Open the file for reading
   @lines = <FILE>;    # Read the entire file into @lines
   close FILE;
   while ( $line = pop(@lines) ) {
        print $line;
   }
}
```

Figure 1.7 This Perl script code listing outputs plain-text files in reverse, with the last line first.

C

The C programming language is to programming what Greek is to literature—the language of heroes. C is the language in which Unix as we know it was written, and most of the utility programs used with Unix were written in C. In the Unix world, the people who invented Unix could be thought of as heroes, and they wrote their great works in C.

The core of every Unix operating system (the *kernel*) is written almost entirely in C, as is virtually every common Unix utility program, such as `ls`, `pwd`, and `grep`. Many important Unix applications, such as Sendmail and the Apache Web server, are also written in C. In addition, C++, Objective-C, and a number of other important languages stem from or are related to C.

Because so much Unix software is written in C, you're likely to at least modify existing C code if you spend much time working on the Unix platform.

Interacting with other Unix machines

Much of what people do with their Unix systems involves connecting to other Unix systems—for example, logging in to a machine that hosts a Web site to edit files and install software, or arranging to automatically transfer files between two Unix machines.

To ease this process, Mac OS X comes with a widely used program called `ssh` (*Secure Shell*) that facilitates secure (encrypted) connections to other machines over the Internet. With `ssh` you can connect from the command-line interface to other Unix machines, and the information exchanged is protected from being read if intercepted. Other programs also use `ssh` to work over encrypted connections.

Running servers

One of the biggest differences between Mac OS 9 and Mac OS X is that the latter allows you to *reliably* run servers (such as a Web server or an e-mail server) on your computer. You could run these types of servers on Mac OS 9, but because Mac OS 9 was much more likely to crash, you probably wouldn't consider it for serious use. Also, most of the software available for these kinds of servers on Mac OS 9 was closed-source proprietary software, so if the vendor changed its business plan or went out of business, you were left with unsupported software. With Mac OS X, you can use the widely installed, open-source applications that most servers on the Internet use.

You might run a server to provide a service to the rest of the world. Or you might run one because you're developing a system that uses it—for example, a shared calendar/event-planning system—and you want to test it on your local machine and/or network before deploying it. There are all kinds of servers; the following are just two of those available to you as a Mac OS X user.

APACHE WEB SERVER

Apache is the most popular Web server in the world—that is, more Web sites use Apache servers than any other. Apache is highly configurable, so it can be adapted to many different situations and specific requirements. Apache comes installed in Mac OS X.

DARWIN STREAMING SERVER

The Darwin Streaming Server (http://developer.apple.com/darwin/projects/streaming/) is an open-source version of Apple's QuickTime Streaming Server, allowing you to "broadcast" audio and video content on the Internet.

Using other Unix applications

In addition to the specific applications mentioned above, there are thousands of Unix applications available. Most are free, some are commercial packages, some are open source. With Mac OS X you can use many of these existing applications to monitor network status, analyze data such as Web-server log files, run mailing lists, create Web publishing systems, and more.

Because there are so many, we can't list even a tenth of them. Below are a few that give some sense of the variety available, plus links to places where you can find more.

Ruby on Rails

Ruby is a relatively new programming language, and Ruby on Rails (www.rubyonrails.org) is a framework for building Web applications. While not a server itself, Ruby on Rails provides a comprehensive and tightly integrated collection of tools for use with a Web server and SQL database server. RubyForge offers a software package called RubyGems that simplifies obtaining and installing Ruby software (http://rubyforge.org/projects/rubygems).

Samba Windows file-sharing software

Samba lets you share files from your Macintosh with Windows users over a network. The name Samba comes from SMB (Server Message Block), which is the Windows file-sharing protocol. Mac OS X has included an SMB server (Windows File Sharing) since version 10.2.

SQL database engines

If you are a Mac database user, you have heard of FileMaker Pro, which is a great database with a great user interface. But FileMaker Pro doesn't understand SQL (Structured Query Language), which is what all the big serious databases use. Most database-backed Web sites use SQL databases.

A number of SQL database engines are available for Mac OS X, including MySQL, PostgreSQL, ProSQL, Oracle, Sybase, and others.

Image manipulation with GIMP

GIMP (GNU Image Manipulation Program) (www.gimp.org) is a no-cost Unix version of Photoshop. Even though GIMP is not as powerful as the main commercial alternative, it is free of charge and open source, and it runs on many Unix platforms. Using GIMP requires that you install X Windows.

X Windows

X Windows is the underlying mechanism for providing a graphical user interface on most Unix systems. The graphical interface for Mac OS X uses a different method, Apple's proprietary Aqua interface, but many Unix programs were built to use X Windows. Mac OS X comes with a version of X Windows already installed (as `/Applications/X11`).

A powerful feature of X Windows is that it provides a graphical display on your computer for Unix programs that are running on other machines over the Internet. That is, if you are running X Windows on your Mac, and you have an account on another Unix machine somewhere on the Internet, you may be able to run software on the remote machine and see the graphical display on your Mac. When you run X Windows on

continues on next page

your computer, you are running an X Windows *server* that can provide graphical display services to software running on other machines. For more on Unix programs that use X Windows see www.macgimp.org

Blogs and content-management systems

You can install and run many different software packages for managing online content such as intranets and blogs (as in *weblogs*, easily editable Web-based journals). For example, the Zope-based Plone content-management system (www.zope.org and http://plone.org) will run on Mac OS X, as can the Movable Type blog publishing system (www.sixapart.com/moveabletype) and many others (http://dmoz.org/Computers/Internet/On_the_Web/Weblogs/Tools/Publishers).

E-mail list management with Mailman or Majordomo

Mailman (www.gnu.org/software/mailman/) and Majordomo (www.greatcircle.com/majordomo) are free, open-source application for managing multiple e-mail lists. To use either, you must set up your Macintosh as an e-mail server. The Mac OS X Server has Mailman already installed. Using either Mailman or Majordomo, you can run dozens of mailing lists, with different configurations for each one. For example, one list may require that new subscribers be added by the list owner, while another may allow anyone to self-subscribe via e-mail. Both applications support list archives and digests as well as many other features.

Where to Find More

Thousands of Unix programs are available, with more being created every day. Here are a couple of places to look.

The FreeBSD Ports Collection

This collection (www.freebsd.org/ports) offered more than 12,000 open-source applications as of early 2005. These are all Unix programs that work on a number of different Unix versions. Because the Darwin layer of Mac OS X is based largely on FreeBSD, most of these programs should work on Mac OS X.

The easiest way to install many of the FreeBSD programs (and other Unix programs) on Mac OS X is to use the Fink program (http://fink.sourceforge.net), which is covered in Chapter 13, "Installing Software from Source Code."

Mac OS X Apps

This Web site (www.macosxapps.com) provides a large and growing collection of Mac OS X applications, most of which have graphical interfaces and can be installed in a manner familiar to Mac users. Many of these programs are not "pure" Unix programs, in that they make use of proprietary Mac OS X features such as the Aqua interface. Still, many take advantage of the Unix core of Mac OS X, and so this site is a good place to explore.

2

Using the Command Line

The command line is the primary interface to Unix. While there are many graphical interfaces for Unix systems, the command-line interface gives you the greatest control over the system. Furthermore, the command-line interface is virtually identical on every Unix system you are likely to use, from Mac OS X to Linux, FreeBSD, and Solaris. Of course there are differences, but there are far more similarities. Once you learn how to use the command line on Mac OS X, you will be comfortable using it on any Unix system.

A reminder before we go further: Whenever a task in this book asks you to type something, always press Return at the end of the line unless the task description specifically tells you not to.

Getting to the Command Line

The primary way to get to the command line in Mac OS X is with the Terminal application.

Terminal is an Aqua application that allows you to open multiple windows, each of which provides a place to enter commands and see output from those commands.

Because Terminal utilizes the Aqua User Interface of Mac OS X, you can do anything you'd expect from a Mac graphical application—you can print, copy text and paste into other windows, and adjust preferences such as color and font size.

Practically all of your command-line work in Mac OS X will be done using Terminal.

To open Terminal:

- Locate the Terminal application in the Finder by going to the Applications folder and opening the Utilities folder.
- Double-click the Terminal application icon.

  A Terminal window containing a shell prompt opens (**Figure 2.1**).

The shell prompt you see will probably be different from what is displayed in Figure 2.1 because the default prompt contains the *hostname* (in this case, `user-vc8f9gd`) of your machine and your short user name (`vanilla` in Figure 2.1). See "Customizing your shell prompt" in Chapter 7, "Configuring Your Environment with Unix," for more on this.

✔ Tips

- Put the Terminal icon in the Dock. You will be using it often.
- When adjusting your Terminal preferences (under Window settings in the Terminal menu), always stick with a *monospace* (also called *fixed-width*) font like Monaco (the default) or Courier. Command-line software assumes you are using a monospace font, and proper text layout in Terminal depends on this.
- Experiment with different colors and font sizes for the text and background in Terminal. For example, we prefer 12-point bright green text on a black background because it looks like the screen on an "old-fashioned" computer terminal.
- Open more than one Terminal window (by clicking New Shell in the File menu), and give each one a different color scheme as a way to differentiate them. You can have as many Terminal windows open as you like.

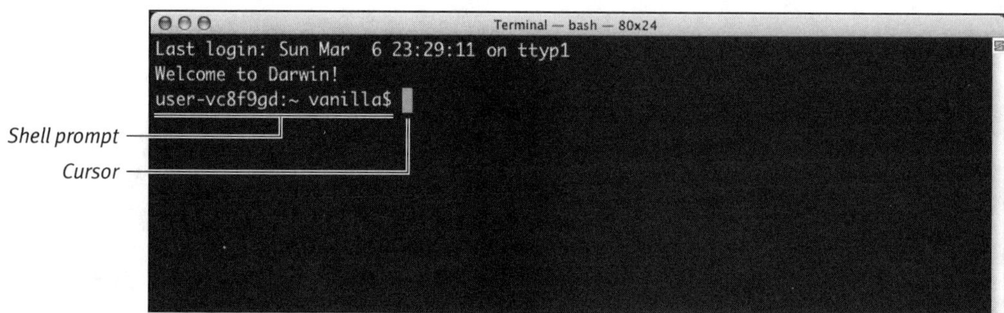

Figure 2.1 A window opened in the Terminal application.

Other ways to get to the command line

Using Terminal is by far the most common way to get to the Mac OS X command line, but there are other ways that are useful after you have become proficient in using Unix. One way is to log in directly to the command line instead of going through the Terminal application in Aqua. You must have set the login window to show "Name and password," not to automatically log in as a user, nor to display a list of users. You do this in the System Preferences Accounts pane, in the Login Options dialog. (Note: The Aqua interface will not be available until you log out of the command line.)

To log in to the command line interface:

1. Enter `>console` as your user name in the login screen. Leave the Password field empty (**Figure 2.2**).
2. Click Login or press Return.

   This switches you directly to the Darwin layer of Mac OS X. A command-line login prompt appears, in white text on a black background (**Figure 2.3**).

   To go back to the Aqua login window, press Control D. Otherwise, proceed to log in to the Darwin layer.
3. Type your short user name, and press Return (remember to press Return after typing each task item). Note: On every other Unix system in the world, this would be called your *user name*, but Mac OS X uses the concept of *short user name* to distinguish it from the regular Mac user name.

   A command-line password prompt appears.
4. Type your password at the Password prompt.

   Nothing appears on the screen as you type. If you get it wrong, you get another Login prompt, and you are back at the beginning of step 4. If you get it right, the shell prompt appears on your screen.
5. Type `logout` to return to the Aqua login screen.

   There is a long pause before Aqua starts up—as much as a minute. Be patient.

At the time that this book was being written, this method of logging in would not work in Mac OS X 10.4.0 through at least 10.4.2. In fact, it would freeze your machine, requiring you to reboot. We expect that Apple will soon solve the problem. This method does work in Mac OS X 10.3.9.

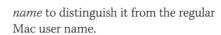

Another way to get to the command line is to start up the machine in *single-user mode*. This boots the machine directly into the Darwin layer so that the command line comes up instead of Aqua. You cannot start Aqua from this mode without rebooting. You should only boot to single-user mode if you are extremely comfortable using Unix. See Chapter 11, "Introduction to System Administration," to learn how to boot into single-user mode.

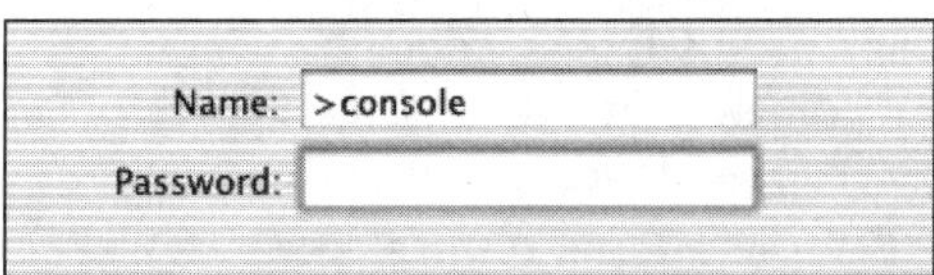

Figure 2.2 You can use the name `>console` to log in to the command line instead of Aqua.

```
Darwin/BSD (yourhostname.domainname.com) (console)
login:
```

Figure 2.3 When you click the Login button, you are switched directly to the Darwin layer of Mac OS X and see the Darwin login prompt.

Understanding the Shell Prompt

The first thing you see in the Terminal window is the shell prompt (as we saw in Figure 2.1). The *shell* is a program that sits between you, the user, and the operating system. You type commands to the shell, and the shell reads the input, interprets its meaning, and executes the appropriate commands. This is similar to the way the Finder accepts your mouse clicks, interprets their meaning (single click? double click? drag?), and then performs an appropriate action (select item, open item, move item). The shell prompt is a string of text telling you that your shell is waiting for a command line.

The Shell window (in the Terminal folder under Preferences) allows you to specify which shell the Terminal application will use—but don't change the default until you have mastered the material at least through the end of Chapter 5, "Using Files and Directories." Throughout this book we assume you are using the default shell (`bash`) unless noted otherwise. Now that you know what the shell is, let's start using it.

A Variety of Shells

There are many different shell programs available. The default shell on Mac OS X is called `bash`. Other shells available on Mac OS X are `sh`, `csh`, `ksh`, `tcsh`, and `zsh`. Mac OS X comes with manuals for all of these shells, which you can read at the command line with `man` *`shell`*—for example, `man bash`. See Chapter 3, "Getting Help and Using the Unix Manual."

The `sh` shell is the oldest commonly used shell—`sh` just means *shell*. It is also called the *Bourne shell* after its principal author, Steve Bourne of Bell Labs. Many important system files are actually small programs (scripts) written using `sh` commands. See Chapter 9, "Creating and Using Scripts."

The default shell for Mac OS X (and for most Linux systems) is `bash` (for *Bourne again shell*—one of those Unix puns we warned you about). An improved version of the old standby `sh`, `bash` adds many useful features to `sh` while preserving the ability to use all `sh` commands (`bash` is backward compatible with `sh`).

The `csh` shell borrows some of its command syntax from the C programming language (hence the `c`) and was designed to be an improvement over the `sh` shell for interactive use. The `tcsh` shell is a more advanced form of the `csh` shell (the `t` comes from two old DEC operating systems). Many Unix experts consider the `csh` shell a poor tool for creating scripts. A classic essay making that case is "Csh Programming Considered Harmful" (www.faqs.org/faqs/unix-faq/shell/csh-whynot). In Mac OS X versions prior to 10.3, the `tcsh` shell was the default shell.

You can learn more about the `tcsh` shell at www.tcsh.org.

The `ksh` (the KornShell) was created by David G. Korn at AT&T Bell Laboratories and is backward compatible with the Bourne shell (`sh`), while adding many features from `csh` and greatly improving performance. The `ksh` shell is widely used by programmers and system administrators. You can find more information about `ksh` at www.kornshell.com.

The `zsh` shell was designed as an improvement on `ksh`. It has a command syntax very different from that of `csh` and `tcsh`. You can learn more about `zsh` at www.zsh.org. If you find out why it is called `zsh`, let me know.

Using a Command

To use commands, you type them into the shell at the prompt. The shell executes the command line and displays output (if any), and then gives you another shell prompt. When the shell prompt comes up again, even if there's no other output, your shell is ready to accept another command.

Many command lines (but not all) produce output before returning a new shell prompt. It is quite common in Unix for a command to produce no visible output if it is successful (if it fails, a command should always produce output). In Unix, silence implies success.

To run a command:

- `ls /Developer/Tools`

  This is the `ls` command, which lists the names of files and directories. The output of the command—a list of the tools installed in the `/Developer/Tools` directory—appears, and then a new shell prompt follows (**Figure 2.4**).

  The command line you just used consists of two parts: the command (`ls`) and an argument (`/Developer/Tools`).

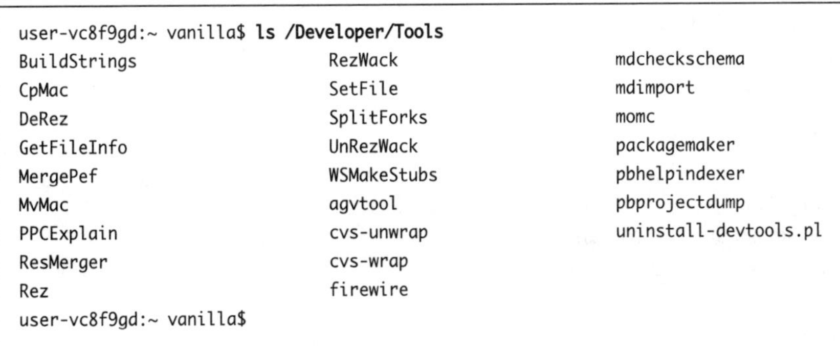

```
user-vc8f9gd:~ vanilla$ ls /Developer/Tools
BuildStrings          RezWack          mdcheckschema
CpMac                 SetFile          mdimport
DeRez                 SplitForks       momc
GetFileInfo           UnRezWack        packagemaker
MergePef              WSMakeStubs      pbhelpindexer
MvMac                 agvtool          pbprojectdump
PPCExplain            cvs-unwrap       uninstall-devtools.pl
ResMerger             cvs-wrap
Rez                   firewire
user-vc8f9gd:~ vanilla$
```

Figure 2.4 When you type the command line `ls /Developer/Tools`, this is what you see.

The parts of a command line

The parts of a command line are separated by spaces. Basic command lines have up to four kinds of components:

- The command (required)
- *Options* (or *switches* or *flags*) (optional)
- *Arguments* (optional)
- *Operators* and special characters (optional)

Figure 2.5 shows the different parts of a typical command line (you'll recognize this as the command from Figure 1.4 in Chapter 1, "What Is Unix, and Why Is It Good?" that searched for all instances of the word *success* in a particular directory).

Each command may have multiple options and multiple arguments.

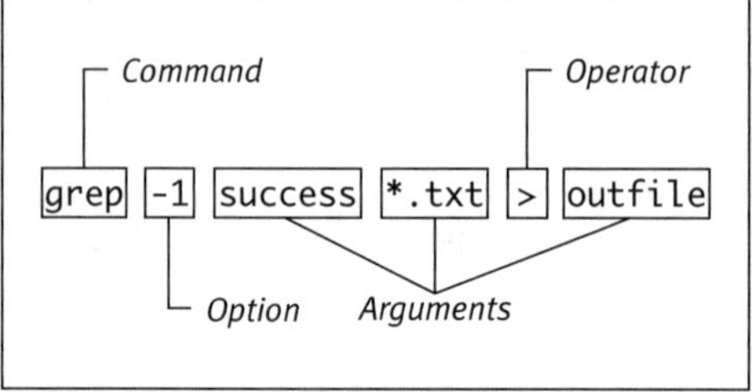

Figure 2.5 The parts of a command line are separated by spaces, and basic command lines have up to four kinds of items in them. This shows the separate parts of the command line.

About the "command" part of the command line

When you enter a command line, the shell assumes that the first item on the line is a command.

There are two types of commands: those that are built into the shell you are using and those that are separate files somewhere on your disk. For example, if you run the `cd` command from the `bash` shell, you will execute the separate program `/usr/bin/cd`; the `tcsh` shell has a built-in `cd` command.

The overwhelming majority of Unix commands are separate programs—that is, Unix commands are usually individual files that are actually small (or not-so-small) programs that perform a specific function, such as listing the contents of a directory (that would be the `/bin/ls` command).

Unix Commands vs. Mac Applications

Traditional Macintosh applications tend to have a great many features that allow you to accomplish complete projects all from within one application. For example, you can create and manipulate complex documents in a page-layout program. Unix takes a different approach.

In Unix, commands are often focused on specific steps you use in a variety of different tasks. For example, where the Mac has a single application (the Finder) for performing many tasks involving files, Unix uses a collection of separate "applications": the `ls` command lists the contents of a directory, the `cd` command switches from one directory to another, the `cp` command copies files, the `mv` command renames files, and so on.

This difference in approach shows a key difference in philosophy between the traditional Mac and Unix ways of thinking. In Unix, you are expected to combine commands in various ways to accomplish your work; in traditional Mac applications, the program's author is expected to have anticipated every kind of task you might want to accomplish and provided a way of doing that.

Unix provides a collection of smaller, "sharper" tools and expects you to decide how to put them together to accomplish your goals.

Your PATH—how the shell finds commands

When the shell sees a command, it evaluates whether it is a built-in command—that is, one that is part of the shell itself. If the command is *not* built in, then the shell assumes the command is an actual file on the disk and looks for it.

If the command does not contain any / (slash) characters, then the shell searches in a list of places known as your `PATH` for a file whose name matches the command name (see the description of the `PATH` environment variable in Chapter 7). If the command contains any / characters, then the shell assumes you are telling it not to search your `PATH` but instead to interpret the command as a *relative or absolute path* to the command file. Relative and absolute paths are two ways of specifying Unix filenames on the command line, and we explain relative and absolute paths in Chapter 5.

About command options

Options (also called *switches* or *flags*) modify the way a command behaves. Most commands have at least a few options available, and many commands have a large number of options. As we noted when we talked about Unix's flexibility in Chapter 1, options frequently can be combined.

See Chapter 3 to learn how to ascertain the available options for each command.

To use one option with a command:

- `ls -s /Developer/Tools`

  The `-s` option modifies the output of the `ls` command, asking for the size of each file. That number (in *blocks*, which correspond to disk space) is now displayed alongside each filename (**Figure 2.6**).


```
user-vc8f9gd:~ vanilla$ ls -s /Developer/Tools
total 2144
 48 BuildStrings                    448 WSMakeStubs
 56 CpMac                            32 agvtool
224 DeRez                             8 cvs-unwrap
 40 GetFileInfo                       8 cvs-wrap
256 MergePef                          0 firewire
 56 MvMac                            64 mdcheckschema
168 PPCExplain                        8 mdimport
 48 ResMerge                         72 momc
264 Rez                               8 packagemaker
 48 RezWack                          40 pbhelpindexer
 48 SetFile                          56 pbprojectdump
 48 SplitForks                       48 uninstall-devtools.pl
 48 UnRezWack
user-vc8f9gd:~ vanilla$
```

Figure 2.6 When you type this command line, `ls -s /Developer/Tools`, which has one option, the output lists the size of each file in blocks.

Here's a case where we want to combine two options in a command. The `-s` option gave us file sizes, using a unit of measurement (blocks) that might not always have the same value (blocks are usually 512 bytes but might vary, depending on a setting called `BLOCKSIZE`). If we add the `-k` option, the sizes are shown in kilobytes, regardless of how `BLOCKSIZE` is set. (`BLOCKSIZE` is an *environment variable*; see Chapter 7.)

To use multiple options with a command:

- `ls -s -k /Developer/Tools`
  Simply supply both of the options you want.
- You can combine two or more options:
  `ls -sk /Developer/Tools`
  This produces the same output as in the first case and saves typing two characters. **Figure 2.7** shows the output of both command lines. (Unix commands are short and cryptic because the programmers who invented them wanted to lessen the amount of typing they needed to do.)

```
user-vc8f9gd:~ vanilla$ ls -s -k /Developer/Tools
total 1072
 24 BuildStrings                              224 WSMakeStubs
 28 CpMac                                      16 agvtool
112 DeRez                                       4 cvs-unwrap
 20 GetFileInfo                                 4 cvs-wrap
128 MergePef                                    0 firewire
 28 MvMac                                      32 mdcheckschema
 84 PPCExplain                                  4 mdimport
 24 ResMerger                                  36 momc
132 Rez                                         4 packagemaker
 24 RezWack                                    20 pbhelpindexer
 24 SetFile                                    28 pbprojectdump
 24 SplitForks                                 24 uninstall-devtools.pl
 24 UnRezWack
user-vc8f9gd:~ vanilla$ ls -sk /Developer/Tools
total 1072
 24 BuildStrings                              224 WSMakeStubs
 28 CpMac                                      16 agvtool
112 DeRez                                       4 cvs-unwrap
 20 GetFileInfo                                 4 cvs-wrap
128 MergePef                                    0 firewire
 28 MvMac                                      32 mdcheckschema
 84 PPCExplain                                  4 mdimport
 24 ResMerger                                  36 momc
132 Rez                                         4 packagemaker
 24 RezWack                                    20 pbhelpindexer
 24 SetFile                                    28 pbprojectdump
 24 SplitForks                                 24 uninstall-devtools.pl
 24 UnRezWack
```

Figure 2.7 This shows that there's no difference between what you get when you use the -s and -k options separately and when you combine them in the -sk option.

About command arguments

Most commands accept one or more *arguments*. An argument is a piece of information the command acts upon, such as the name of a file to display. It's similar to the object of a sentence.

You used a command with a single argument in the tasks above. The single argument was `/Developer/Tools`, the folder whose contents you wanted to list. A command line can contain multiple arguments.

To use multiple arguments with a command:

◆ `ls /Developer /Developer/Tools`

You simply add as many arguments as needed on the command line, separated by spaces. In this example, the `ls` command gets two arguments and lists the contents of both directories (**Figure 2.8**).

✔ Tips

- You can combine multiple options with multiple arguments—for example, `ls -sk /Developer /Developer/Tools`
- Remember that the shell expects the parts of a command line to be separated by spaces. If an argument has spaces in it, then you need to protect the embedded space(s) from being interpreted as separators. See "About Spaces in the Command Line," later in the chapter.

Operators and special characters in the command line

A number of special characters often appear in command lines, most frequently the >, |, and & characters.

These special characters are used for a variety of powerful features that manipulate the

```
user-vc8f9gd:~ vanilla$ ls /Developer /Developer/Tools
/Developer:
ADC Reference Library Extras
Applications                    Headers                 Palettes
Documentation                   Java                    Private
Examples                        Makefiles               Tools

/Developer/Tools:
BuildStrings                    RezWack                 mdcheckschema
CpMac                           SetFile                 mdimport
DeRez                           SplitForks              momc
GetFileInfo                     UnRezWack               packagemaker
MergePef                        WSMakeStubs             pbhelpindexer
MvMac                           agvtool                 pbprojectdump
PPCExplain                      cvs-unwrap              uninstall-devtools.pl
ResMerger                       cvs-wrap
Rez                             firewire
user-vc8f9gd:~ vanilla$
```

Figure 2.8 The `ls` command gets two arguments, `/Developer` and `/Developer/Tools`, and lists the contents of both directories.

output of commands. The most common of these operators make it easy to save the output of a command to a file, feed the output of one command into another command, use the output of one command as an argument to another command, and run a command line "in the background" (that is, letting you get a shell prompt back even if the command takes an hour to run).

The use of these powerful features is covered later in this chapter (see "Creating Pipelines of Commands").

Table 2.1 summarizes the most frequently used command-line operators and special characters, with examples of their use.

Stopping commands

Some commands run for a long time, and sometimes they can get "stuck" (perhaps because a command is waiting for some other process to finish, or because of a network problem, or for any number of other reasons) and neither give output nor return you to a shell prompt. In those cases, you need a way to stop a command once you have started it. Here are two ways to stop a command.

If you are waiting for the shell prompt to appear, then you use Control C to stop the command.

To stop a command with Control-C:

- Press Control (usually at the lower left of your keyboard) and simultaneously press C. This sends what is called an *interrupt* signal to the command, which should stop running and bring up a shell prompt.

✔ Tip

- If using Control C doesn't work, as a last resort you can close the Terminal window, overriding the warning that appears. The stuck command will be stopped. It doesn't hurt Unix for you to close the window; it's just annoying for you.

To stop a command using the kill command:

- `kill` *`pid`*

  You use the `kill` command to stop other commands if you already have a shell prompt. You need to know the *process ID* of the command you want to stop. For details on obtaining process ID numbers, see "About Commands, Processes, and Jobs," later in this chapter.

  The `kill` command doesn't always kill a process. It actually sends a signal asking it to stop. The default signal is hangup.

  Sometimes that isn't strong enough. In those cases you can use signal 9, the kill signal that cannot be ignored:

  `kill -9` *`pid`*

  Using signal 9 terminates the target with extreme prejudice—the stopped command has no chance to clean up before exiting and may leave temporary files around.

Table 2.1

Operators and Special Characters

Symbol	Example and Meaning
>	*command* > *filename*
	Redirect output to `file`.
>>	*command* >> *filename*
	Redirect output, appending to `file`.
<	*command* < *filename*
	command gets input from `file`.
|	*cmdA* | *cmdB* (sometimes called the *pipe* character)
	Pipe output of *cmdA* into *cmdB*.
&	*command* &
	Run *command* in background, returning to shell prompt at once.
` `	*cmdA* `` `cmdB` `` (often called *backtick* characters)
	Execute *cmdB* first, then use output as an argument to *cmdA*.

USING A COMMAND

Getting help for a command

Most commands have associated documentation in the Unix help system. Unfortunately, Unix help is almost always written for the experienced programmer, not for the novice user, so we have devoted all of Chapter 3, "Getting Help and Using the Unix Manual," to clarifying it.

You can skip ahead to Chapter 3 and come back if you like, but here is the bare minimum you need to at least begin to explore the help available for commands.

To read the Unix manual for a command:

1. `man` *command*

   This displays the Unix manual for a command. **Figure 2.9** shows the first screen of the manual for the `ls` command, displayed by typing `man ls`.

   The `man` command displays the Unix manual entry for the named command, one screen at a time.

2. To move forward one screen, press the [Spacebar] once.

3. To move backward one screen, press [B] once.

4. To quit from the `man` command and return to a shell prompt: [Q].

   You should be back at the shell prompt.

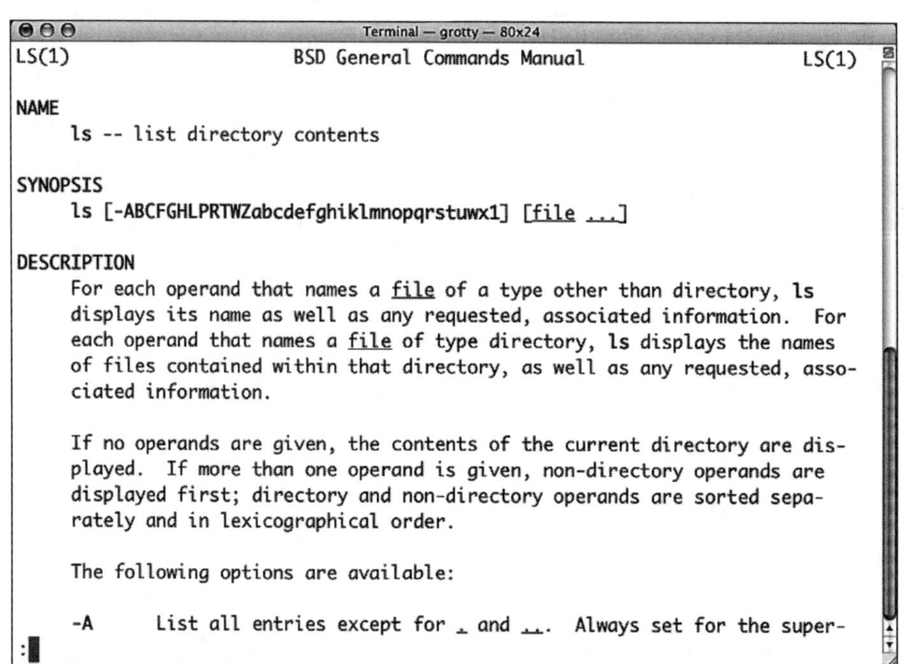

```
LS(1)                    BSD General Commands Manual                   LS(1)

NAME
     ls -- list directory contents

SYNOPSIS
     ls [-ABCFGHLPRTWZabcdefghiklmnopqrstuwx1] [file ...]

DESCRIPTION
     For each operand that names a file of a type other than directory, ls
     displays its name as well as any requested, associated information.  For
     each operand that names a file of type directory, ls displays the names
     of files contained within that directory, as well as any requested, asso-
     ciated information.

     If no operands are given, the contents of the current directory are dis-
     played.  If more than one operand is given, non-directory operands are
     displayed first; directory and non-directory operands are sorted sepa-
     rately and in lexicographical order.

     The following options are available:

     -A      List all entries except for . and ... Always set for the super-
:
```

Figure 2.9 When you request help from the Unix manual by typing in a command like `man ls`, you get a page with an explanation of that entry (this shows only part of an output).

Using Common Commands

You've already learned how to perform some basic Unix commands, but now let's run through a series of commands you'll use on a regular basis (we'll go into detail on several of these in later chapters).

To perform some basic commands:

1. `cd`

   The `cd` command (*change directory*) produces no output. Used with no arguments, it tells your shell to set your "working directory" to your home directory (`/Users/`*`shortusername`*) and "takes you home" from wherever you are.

2. `pwd`

   This command displays your present working directory —where you "are" in the Unix filesystem. **Figure 2.10** shows typical output from the `pwd` command.

3. `ls`

   Figure 2.11 shows typical output from `ls`, which lists the names of files and directories. The actual output depends on what you have in your home directory.

4. `echo "Hello there"`

   The output from the `echo` command consists of its arguments (in this case, the words `Hello there`) (**Figure 2.12**). It also automatically adds a new line (try it with the `-n` option to not add the new line).

pwd—Compare with Aqua

In Aqua, the Finder tells you where you are, using the names and positions of windows. One window is always the active window, and the title bar of that window tells you the name of the folder. If the window is the Finder window, then the directory name in the title bar is the equivalent of what the Unix `pwd` command shows.

```
user-vc8f9gd:~ vanilla$ pwd
/Users/vanilla
user-vc8f9gd:~ vanilla%
```

Figure 2.10 The pwd command shows your present working directory—where you "are" in the Unix filesystem.

```
user-vc8f9gd:~ vanilla$ ls
Desktop      Library     Music       Public
Documents    Movies      Pictures    Sites
user-vc8f9gd:~ vanilla$
```

Figure 2.11 The `ls` command lists the names of files and directories. The actual output will depend on what you have in your home directory.

```
user-vc8f9gd:~ vanilla$ echo "Hello There"
Hello There.
user-vc8f9gd:~ vanilla$
```

Figure 2.12 The output from the echo command consists of two arguments (in this case, `"Hello there"`).

5. `echo "Hello $USER, welcome to Unix."`

   Figure 2.13 shows output from echo, using the $USER environment variable in an argument. $USER is replaced by your short user name (the $ usually indicates that the following term is a variable, and the shell substitutes the value of the variable before executing the command.

6. `echo "$USER created this" > file.txt`

   In this case, the output from the echo command doesn't go to your screen, but rather it is *redirected* into the file named file.txt, either creating the file with this specific content or copying over anything within it. For more on redirection and output, see "About Standard Input and Output," later in this chapter.

7. `ls`

   Figure 2.14 shows the output from the ls command. The files listed now include file.txt, created in the previous step.

8. `cat file.txt`

   The cat command, derived from *concatenate*, displays the contents of the file (**Figure 2.15**), again based on the command in step 6 (*concatenate* actually means *combine*; if you read the Unix manual section on cat with man cat, you will see how it can be used to combine several files).

echo—Compare with Aqua

The Aqua interface doesn't really have any equivalent of the echo command. The echo command exemplifies a tool that is unique to command-line interfaces.


```
user-vc8f9gd:~ vanilla$ echo "Hello $USER, welcome to Unix."
Hello vanilla, welcome to Unix.
user-vc8f9gd:~ vanilla$
```

Figure 2.13 This shows the output from echo, using the $USER environment variable in an argument. $USER will be replaced by your short user name.

```
user-vc8f9gd:~ vanilla$ ls
Desktop         Library        Music         Public        file.txt
Documents       Movies         Pictures      Sites
user-vc8f9gd:~ vanilla$
```

Figure 2.14 This output from the ls command now includes file.txt.

```
user-vc8f9gd:~ vanilla$ cat file.txt
vanilla created this
user-vc8f9gd:~ vanilla$
```

Figure 2.15 The cat command, derived from *concatenate*, displays the contents of a file.

cp—Compare with Aqua

In the Finder, you copy files by Option-dragging them, or by selecting them and choosing File > Duplicate. After copying them, you can rename them in a separate operation.

At the command line, you select files to be copied by naming them and then entering their new names at the same time.

9. `cp file.txt filecopy.txt`

   `cp` stands for *copy*. You have made a copy of file.txt called filecopy.txt. Run the `ls` command again to see it (**Figure 2.16**).

10. `rm filecopy.txt`

    The `rm` command *removes* the file forever. The file is not moved to the Trash, and there is no undo. The `rm` command is serious business. Run the `ls` command again to confirm that it is gone.

11. `mkdir testdir`

    The `mkdir` command creates (or *makes*) a new *directory* (that's what Unix calls folders), in this instance named `testdir`.

12. `open .`

    This opens the current directory in the Finder. You should see the file called file.txt and the directory `testdir` (**Figure 2.17**).

```
user-vc8f9gd:~ vanilla$ ls
Desktop        Library      Music        Public       file.txt
Documents      Movies       Pictures     Sites        filecopy.txt
user-vc8f9gd:~ vanilla$
```

Figure 2.16 Running the `ls` command again shows that you have made a copy of file.txt called filecopy.txt.

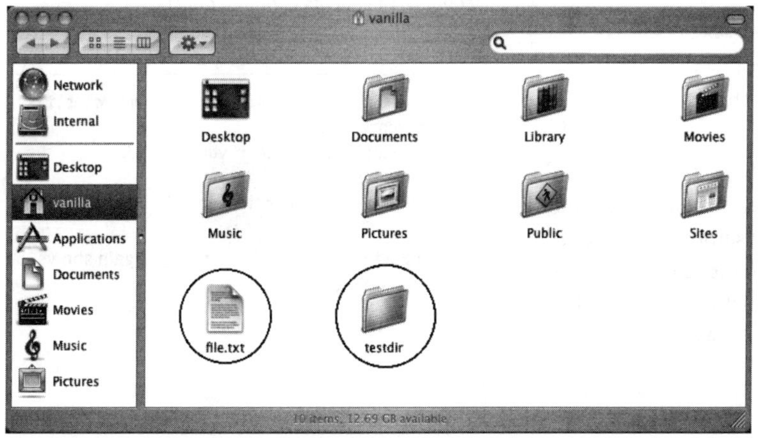

Figure 2.17 The Finder window now shows the new file and directory.

13. `cd testdir`

    You have told your shell to change from the current directory to the directory named `testdir`. Notice that your shell prompt has changed to reflect your new directory (**Figure 2.18**).

14. `pwd`

    This confirms that you are indeed in the new directory (**Figure 2.19**).

15. `date`

    The `date` command displays the current date and time (**Figure 2.20**); unless you've perfected time travel, your output will be different.

16. `date > dates.txt`

    This redirects the output of the `date` command into a file named dates.txt. It is often useful to save the output of a command.

17. `date >> dates.txt`

    This time we redirect the output using the >> operator (this redirects the output and appends it to the file instead of replacing the contents).

18. `cat dates.txt`

    The file contains the results of both redirects from steps 16 and 17 (**Figure 2.21**).

19. `mv dates.txt newname.txt`

    The `mv` command renames (or *moves*) a file. You can think of the command line as being

    `mv` *`oldname newname`*

    In Unix, a file's name is actually the name of its location, so the same command is used to rename and to move files. Run the `ls` command to see that the file dates.txt has been renamed to newname.txt (**Figure 2.22**).

```
user-vc8f9gd:~ vanilla$ cd testdir
user-vc8f9gd:testdir vanilla$
```

Figure 2.18 After you use the cd command, the shell prompt changes.

```
user-vc8f9gd:testdir vanilla$ pwd
/Users/vanilla/testdir
user-vc8f9gd:testdir vanilla$
```

Figure 2.19 Running the pwd command again shows your new working directory.

```
user-vc8f9gd:testdir vanilla$ date
Sun Mar6 17:29:27 PST 2005
user-vc8f9gd:testdir vanilla$
```

Figure 2.20 The date command displays the current date and time.

```
user-vc8f9gd:~/testdir vanilla$ date >
   dates.txt
user-vc8f9gd:~/testdir vanilla$ date >>
   dates.txt
user-vc8f9gd:~/testdir vanilla$ cat
   dates.txt
Sun Mar6 17:30:30 PST 2005
Sun Mar6 17:30:41 PST 2005
user-vc8f9gd:~/testdir vanilla$
```

Figure 2.21 Using redirection, you get a file that contains the results of both redirects.

```
user-vc8f9gd:~/testdir vanilla$ mv dates.txt
   newname.txt
user-vc8f9gd:~/testdir vanilla$ ls
newname.txt
user-vc8f9gd:~/testdir vanilla$
```

Figure 2.22 Running the ls command again shows the renamed file.

```
user-vc8f9gd:~/testdir vanilla$ ls
dates.txt newname.txt
user-vc8f9gd:~/testdir vanilla$
```

Figure 2.23 Running the `ls` command again shows the file created with the >> operator.

```
user-vc8f9gd:~/testdir vanilla$ ls
user-vc8f9gd:~/testdir vanilla$
```

Figure 2.24 Note that when there is nothing to list, the `ls` command gives no output.

```
user-vc8f9gd:~/testdir vanilla$ cd
user-vc8f9gd:~ vanilla$
```

Figure 2.25 Your shell prompt changes when you use the cd command.

cat—Compare with Aqua

Not only does the `cat` command display a single file (as shown in step 8 above), but it can be given multiple filenames as arguments in order to display them all, in one long output (hence the name *concatenate*).

The closest thing Aqua has to the `cat` command is the ability to open multiple files with one application by selecting several files and dragging them all onto an application icon, but there isn't really a direct equivalent.

mv—Compare with Aqua

In the Finder, you move files by dragging them to their new locations. Renaming them is a separate operation.

At the command line, you can move and rename files in the same operation.

20. `date >> dates.txt`

    The >> operator appends to an existing file and will create a file if it doesn't already exist (**Figure 2.23**).

21. `rm *.txt`

    The * operator is used in the command line as a *wildcard* to match all the files ending in .txt. As a result, the `rm` command actually receives two arguments—`dates.txt` and `newname.txt`—and acts on both of them. For more on wildcard operators, see "Wildcards," later in this chapter. Run the `ls` command to confirm that there are now no files in the current directory; you simply get a shell prompt back (**Figure 2.24**).

22. `cd`

    This takes you back to your home directory. Notice that your shell prompt changes (**Figure 2.25**).

< and >—Compare with Aqua

The Aqua interface has no equivalent to the command line's ability to redirect input and output. This is a good example of the difference between the Unix command-line interface and a graphical interface such as Aqua.

The command line is text oriented: Everything is assumed to be text output and can be fed into anything else. (See especially the | operator later in this chapter, in "Creating Pipelines of Commands.")

In Aqua, each application is assumed to produce output of a different kind, and applications cannot normally feed their output directly into each other without saving to a file first.

About Commands, Processes, and Jobs

Commands fall into two categories: Some commands are built into the shell you are using (for example, the cd command), while most are separate programs.

To see a list of basic Unix commands:

◆ `ls /bin`

The /bin directory contains all of the commands we used in the examples earlier in this chapter (except open, which is in /usr/bin). Each command appears as a separate file (**Figure 2.26**). Notice that your shell program (bash) is included. It, too, is essentially a command, albeit a larger, interactive one.

✔ Tip

■ Other places that contain Unix commands are /usr/bin, /sbin, and /usr/sbin. (The *bin* is short for *binary*, as most Unix commands are binary files. Not all commands are binary files; some are executable text files, or *scripts*.)

```
user-vc8f9gd:~ vanilla$ ls /bin
[          df            launchctl     pwd          tcsh
bash       domainname    link          rcp          test
cat        echo          ln            rm           unlink
chmod      ed            ls            rmdir        wait4path
cp         expr          mkdir         sh           zsh
csh        hostname      mv            sleep        zsh-4.2.3
date       kill          pax           stty
dd         ksh           ps            sync
user-vc8f9gd:~ vanilla$
```

Figure 2.26 The /bin directory contains all the commands we used in the examples earlier in this chapter.

Every time you issue a command that is not already built into a shell, you are starting what Unix calls a *process* or a *job*. You will encounter both terms in Unix literature.

Every process is assigned an identification number when it starts up, called the *PID* (for *process ID*), as well as its own slice of memory space (this is one of the reasons why Unix is so stable—each process has its own inviolable memory space). At any given moment, there are dozens of processes running on your computer.

To see all the processes you own:

- `ps -U username`

  Fill in your short user name for *username*. **Figure 2.27** shows typical output with a variety of programs running. Notice how even Aqua programs like iTunes are listed—underneath it all, they are all running on Unix.

  The first column of output lists the PID of each process. (Review "Stopping commands," earlier in this chapter, for an example of using a PID number.)

```
user-vc8f9gd:~ vanilla$ ps -U vanilla
PID     TT     STAT   TIME    COMMAND
 104    ??     Ss     0:04.54 /System/Library/Frameworks/ApplicationServices.framew
 394    ??     Ss     0:04.05 /System/Library/CoreServices/loginwindow.app/Contents
 404    ??     S      0:06.27 /System/Library/CoreServices/RemoteManagement/ARDAgen
 934    ??     Ss     0:00.75 /System/Library/CoreServices/pbs
 939    ??     S      0:01.90 /System/Library/CoreServices/Dock.app/Contents/MacOS/
 941    ??     S      0:10.61 /System/Library/CoreServices/SystemUIServer.app/Conte
 942    ??     S      0:21.78 /System/Library/CoreServices/Finder.app/Contents/MacO
 945    ??     S      1:13.69 /Applications/Utilities/Terminal.app/Contents/MacOS/T
2302    ??     R      0:05.97 /Applications/iTunes.app/Contents/MacOS/iTunes -psn_0
2303    ??     Ss     0:07.00 /Applications/Firefox.app/Contents/MacOS/firefox-bin
2305    ??     SNs    0:00.63 /System/Library/Frameworks/CoreServices.framework/Ver
2307    ??     S      0:00.92 /System/Library/CoreServices/System Events.app/Conten
2309    ??     S      0:00.08 /Applications/iTunes.app/Contents/Resources/iTunesHel
 949    p1     S      0:00.19 -bash
2282    p2     S+     0:00.03 -bash
user-vc8f9gd:~ vanilla$
```

Figure 2.27 When you type ps -U *username*, you see the variety of programs running, even Aqua programs like iTunes.

To see all the processes on the system:

1. `ps -aux`

   Figure 2.28 shows typical output from using the `-aux` options to `ps` (for *processes*).

2. `ps -auxw`

   Figure 2.29 shows output when using the `-auxw` options. The `w` makes the output wider (wide enough that the lines will wrap around in the Terminal window).

Table 2.2 shows the common options for the `ps` command. Use `man ps` for the complete list.

✔ Tips

- You can use two w's to make the output even wider—for example, `ps -auxww`. In fact, using two w's whenever you use the `ps` command can be considered a "best practice."
- Combine the `-U` option with the `-aux` options to show a particular user's processes: `ps -aux -U` *`username`*.

```
user-vc8f9gd:~ vanilla$ ps -aux
USER       PID  %CPU  %MEM  VSZ      RS     STT   STAT  STARTED   TIME     COMMAND
nobody     405  5.0   0.2    61748   1600   ??    R     Thu11AM   3:28.91  /System/Li
vanilla    945  1.3   3.3   123960  21452   ??    S     Sat09AM   1:16.86  /Applicati
windowse   396  1.0   3.2   112992  20716   ??    Ss    Thu11AM   1:50.25  /System/Li
vanilla   2303  0.4   4.7   281760  30512   ??    Ss     5:46PM   0:12.13  /Applicati
vanilla   2302  0.3   5.0   121472  33012   ??    S      5:46PM   0:06.91  /Applicati
root        54  0.0   0.2    27768   1088   ??    Ss    Wed10PM   0:00.94  /usr/sbin/
root        81  0.0   0.0    27212    192   ??    Ss    Wed10PM   0:00.00  /usr/libex
root        96  0.0   0.8    54792   5104   ??    Ss    Wed10PM   0:30.57  /System/Li
vanilla    104  0.0   0.6   179148   3908   ??    Ss    Wed10PM   0:04.56  /System/Li
root       105  0.0   0.2    27360   1604   ??    Ss    Wed10PM   0:00.03  xinetd -do
root       134  0.0   0.0    29268    176   ??    Ss    Wed10PM   0:00.00  nfsiod -n
root       148  0.0   0.7    37864   4912   ??    Ss    Wed10PM   0:22.84  /usr/sbin/
root       154  0.0   0.0    27268    184   ??    Ss    Wed10PM   0:00.00  rpc.lockd
root       158  0.0   0.1    27468    360   ??    Ss    Wed10PM   0:33.01  ntpd -f /v
root       174  0.0   0.2    29368    988   ??    Ss    Wed10PM   0:00.05  /usr/sbin/
root       179  0.0   0.2    28472   1500   ??    Ss    Wed10PM   0:01.55  /usr/sbin/
root       314  0.0   0.2    29216   1216   ??    Ss    Thu11AM   0:15.23  /usr/sbin/
vanilla    394  0.0   0.6    74868   3792   ??    Ss    Thu11AM   0:04.07  /System/Li
vanilla    939  0.0   2.2    98924  14100   ??    S     Sat09AM   0:01.91  /System/Li
root       947  0.0   0.2    27420   1620   p1    Ss    Sat09AM   0:00.04  login -pf
vanilla    949  0.0   0.1    27772    852   p1    S     Sat09AM   0:00.22  -bash
root      2280  0.0   0.3    27420   1668   p2    Ss     5:33PM   0:00.04  login -pf
vanilla   2282  0.0   0.1    27772    832   p2    S+     5:33PM   0:00.03  -bash
vanilla   2307  0.0   1.5    82732   9744   ??    S      5:47PM   0:00.93  /System/Li
vanilla   2309  0.0   0.9    44832   5692   ??    S      5:47PM   0:00.12  /Applicati
root       247  0.0   0.0        0      0   ??    Z     31Dec69   0:00.00  (LAServer)
root      2317  0.0   0.1    27248    388   p1    R+     5:53PM   0:00.01  ps -aux
root         1  0.0   0.1    28300    524   ??    S<s   Wed10PM   0:01.44  /sbin/laun
root        25  0.0   0.0    27224    160   ??    Ss    Wed10PM   0:00.00  /sbin/dyna
root        29  0.0   0.1    28176    936   ??    Ss    Wed10PM   0:03.01  kextd
user-vc8f9gd:~ vanilla$
```

Figure 2.28 Using the -aux options to ps gives you this typical output.

```
user-vc8f9gd:~ vanilla$ ps -auxw
USER      PID   %CPU %MEM  VSZ     RSS    TT   STAT  STARTED  TIME      COMMAND
vanilla   945   8.3  4.1   130136  27092  ??   S     Sat09AM  1:23.99
/Applications/Utilities/Terminal.app/Contents/MacOS/Terminal -
root      2327  1.4  0.1   27248   388    p1   R+    5:59PM   0:00.01   ps -auxw
windowse  396   1.2  3.5   116484  23252  ??   Us    Thu11AM  1:55.65
/System/Library/Frameworks/ApplicationServices.framework/Frame
vanilla   942   0.8  3.4   108676  21964  ??   S     Sat09AM  0:21.99
/System/Library/CoreServices/Finder.app/Contents/MacOS/Finder
vanilla   949   0.5  0.1   27772   860    p1   S     Sat09AM  0:00.26   -bash
vanilla   2303  0.3  4.7   282832  30792  ??   Ss    5:46PM   0:28.74
/Applications/Firefox.app/Contents/MacOS/firefox-bin -psn_0_19
vanilla   2302  0.1  5.0   121472  32876  ??   S     5:46PM   0:08.04
/Applications/iTunes.app/Contents/MacOS/iTunes -psn_0_2228225
root      56    0.0  0.2   28772   1460   ??   Ss    Wed10PM  0:01.69   /usr/sbin/securityd
root      57    0.0  0.1   27824   436    ??   Ss    Wed10PM  0:03.79   /usr/sbin/notifyd
root      58    0.0  0.3   31008   2036   ??   Ss    Wed10PM  0:03.07   /usr/sbin/DirectoryService
root      60    0.0  0.2   28020   1064   ??   Ss    Wed10PM  0:11.63   /usr/sbin/mDNSResponder -
launchdaemon
root      62    0.0  0.1   28200   712    ??   Ss    Wed10PM  0:00.03   /usr/sbin/KernelEventAgent
root      63    0.0  0.2   28760   1148   ??   SNs   Wed10PM  4:33.89   /usr/sbin/launchd_helperd
root      64    0.0  0.2   27552   1208   ??   Ss    Wed10PM  0:01.46   /usr/sbin/netinfod -s local
root      65    0.0  0.1   27244   684    ??   Ss    Wed10PM  0:03.36   /usr/sbin/syslogd
root      67    0.0  0.1   27632   748    ??   Ss    Wed10PM  0:00.31   /usr/sbin/distnoted
user-vc8f9gd:~ vanilla$
```

Figure 2.29 Using the -auxw options to ps gives you this partial output; adding the w gives you a wider output.

Table 2.2

Common Options for ps

Option	Meaning
-a	Display processes owned by all users.
-u	Display more information, including CPU usage, process ownership, and memory usage.
-x	Include any process not started from a Terminal window.
-w	Wide listing—display the full command name of each process up to 132 characters per line. If more than w is used, adding ps will ignore the width of your Terminal window.
-U *username*	Show process for specified user.

To see a constantly updated list of the top processes:

1. `top`

   The `top` command displays a frequently updated list of processes, sorted by how much processing power each one is using—that is, which one is at the *top* of the list of resource usage (**Figure 2.30**). (The reason they're at 0% is that most processes, at any given time, aren't using that much processor time.)

   `top` runs until you stop it by typing the following command:

2. `q`

   This stops the `top` command and returns you to a shell prompt.

✔ Tip

- If you want to save the output of `top` to a file (such as using the > redirect operator), then use the `-l` switch and specify how many samples you want. For example, to get three samples, use

  `top -l3 > toplog`

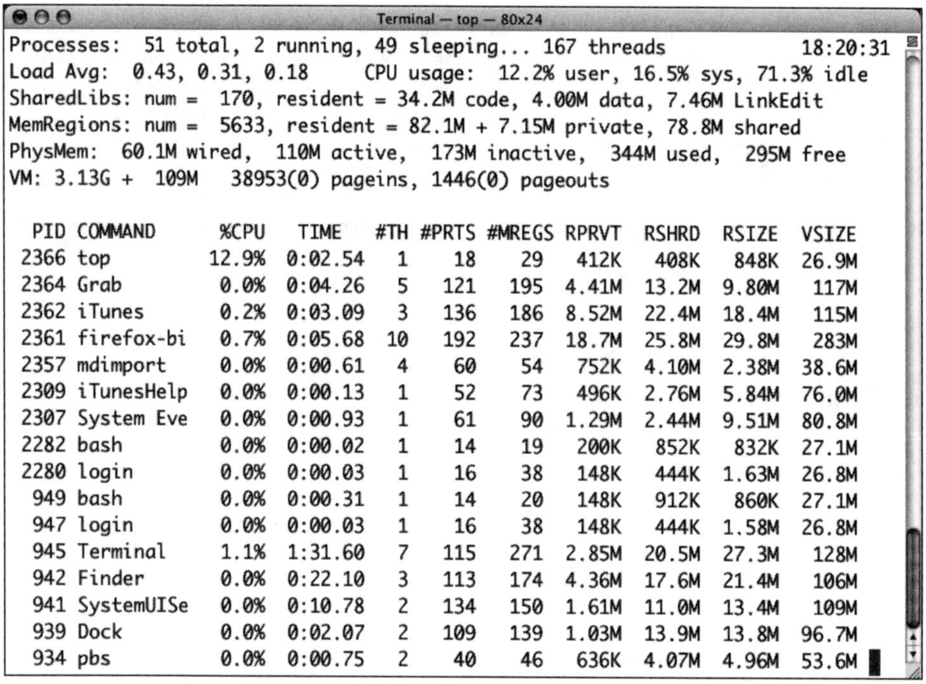

```
Terminal — top — 80x24
Processes:  51 total, 2 running, 49 sleeping... 167 threads            18:20:31
Load Avg:  0.43, 0.31, 0.18     CPU usage:  12.2% user, 16.5% sys, 71.3% idle
SharedLibs: num =  170, resident = 34.2M code, 4.00M data, 7.46M LinkEdit
MemRegions: num =  5633, resident = 82.1M + 7.15M private, 78.8M shared
PhysMem:  60.1M wired,  110M active,  173M inactive,  344M used,  295M free
VM: 3.13G +  109M   38953(0) pageins, 1446(0) pageouts

  PID COMMAND      %CPU   TIME   #TH #PRTS #MREGS RPRVT  RSHRD  RSIZE  VSIZE
 2366 top         12.9% 0:02.54   1    18     29   412K   408K   848K  26.9M
 2364 Grab         0.0% 0:04.26   5   121    195  4.41M  13.2M  9.80M   117M
 2362 iTunes       0.2% 0:03.09   3   136    186  8.52M  22.4M  18.4M   115M
 2361 firefox-bi   0.7% 0:05.68  10   192    237  18.7M  25.8M  29.8M   283M
 2357 mdimport     0.0% 0:00.61   4    60     54   752K  4.10M  2.38M  38.6M
 2309 iTunesHelp   0.0% 0:00.13   1    52     73   496K  2.76M  5.84M  76.0M
 2307 System Eve   0.0% 0:00.93   1    61     90  1.29M  2.44M  9.51M  80.8M
 2282 bash         0.0% 0:00.02   1    14     19   200K   852K   832K  27.1M
 2280 login        0.0% 0:00.03   1    16     38   148K   444K  1.63M  26.8M
  949 bash         0.0% 0:00.31   1    14     20   148K   912K   860K  27.1M
  947 login        0.0% 0:00.03   1    16     38   148K   444K  1.58M  26.8M
  945 Terminal     1.1% 1:31.60   7   115    271  2.85M  20.5M  27.3M   128M
  942 Finder       0.0% 0:22.10   3   113    174  4.36M  17.6M  21.4M   106M
  941 SystemUISe   0.0% 0:10.78   2   134    150  1.61M  11.0M  13.4M   109M
  939 Dock         0.0% 0:02.07   2   109    139  1.03M  13.9M  13.8M  96.7M
  934 pbs          0.0% 0:00.75   2    40     46   636K  4.07M  4.96M  53.6M
```

Figure 2.30 The top command displays a frequently updated list of processes, sorted by how much processing power each one is using.

The Danger of a Space Misplaced

A bug in the installation software for an early version of iTunes could cause the erasure of an entire hard drive if the first character in the drive's name was a space.

The installation script did not allow for that possibility and neglected to use quotes where it should have. Even professional programmers occasionally have trouble dealing with spaces in filenames on Unix systems.

About Spaces in the Command Line

As we have seen, the shell uses spaces to separate the parts of the command line. Having two or more spaces separate a command from its options or its arguments doesn't change anything. When your shell acts on your command line, it breaks it into pieces by looking at where the spaces are. The following command lines both do the same thing:

```
ls -l
ls        -l
```

But this one is very different:

```
ls - l
```

In the first two cases the shell sees two items: `ls` and `-l`. In the third case the shell sees three items: `ls`, `-`, and `l`.

But there are times when you have to include a space inside an argument—such as in a filename that itself contains spaces. Consider what would happen if you tried the command line

```
ls -l /Desktop DB
```

If you don't do something special to handle spaces in command-line arguments, you will have problems. The shell treats the spaces as separators, and you will get unexpected and probably undesired results (**Figure 2.31**).

Here are two ways to handle spaces safely in command-line arguments.

```
user-vc8f9gd:~ vanilla$ ls -l /Desktop DB
ls: /Desktop: No such file or directory
ls: DB: No such file or directory
user-vc8f9gd:~ vanilla$
```

Figure 2.31 When you use unprotected spaces in a command-line argument, the shell treats each word as a separate argument.

To protect spaces using quotes:

1. `ls -l "/Desktop DB"`

   When you enclose the argument in quotes, the shell treats everything within the quotes as a single entity.

2. You may also use single quotes:

   `ls -l '/Desktop DB'`

✔ Tip

- Using single quotes around a string of characters eliminates the effect of any special character, including the $ we saw earlier for environment variables. Compare

  `echo 'hello $USER'`

  with

  `echo "hello $USER"`

  The first one echoes the exact characters, while the second identifies the user.

To protect spaces using the backslash:

- `ls /Desktop\ DB`

  The backslash character (\) is often used in Unix to *escape* a character. This means "make the next character not special." In this case it removes the special meaning of "separator" from the space character. This is called *escaping a character*.

✔ Tip

- Many Unix shells (including the default shell on Mac OS X) provide a feature called *filename completion*. When typing a part of a command line that is an existing filename, you can type just part of it and then press Tab; the shell tries to fill in the rest of the filename for you. The filename completion feature will also automatically escape spaces (and other special characters) in filenames.

Wildcards

Arguments to commands are frequently filenames. These might be the names of files the command should read, copy, or move. If you want to act on a number of files, you don't want to have to type every filename, especially when all the filenames have some pattern in common. For example, you might want to do something with a group of files whose names all start with Hello.

That's where *wildcards* come in. Wildcards (often called *glob-patterns*) are special characters you can type in a command line to make a command apply to a group of files whose names match some pattern—for example, all files ending in .jpg.

When the shell reads a command line, it expands any glob-patterns by replacing them with all the filenames that match. The shell then executes the command line, using the new list of arguments with the command.

To use a glob-pattern to match all filenames starting with Hello:

◆ `ls Hello*`

The asterisk (*) is the glob character that matches any number (zero or more) of characters.

The shell finds all the filenames that begin with Hello and substitutes that list for the `Hello*` on the command line.

So if the directory contains files with the names Hello, HelloTest, and HelloGoodbye, then the shell changes the command line with the wildcard into

```
ls -l Hello HelloTest HelloGoodbye
```

✔ Tip

■ You can use more than one glob-pattern in a command line, such as

```
rm *.jpg *.gif
```

This removes all the .jpg and .gif files from the current directory.

To use a glob-pattern to match only one single character:

◆ `ls File?`

The ? character matches any single character. So the example above would match files with names such as FileA, File3, Files, and so on. It would not match File23 because the pattern matches only one character.

✔ Tip

■ You can combine the ? and * glob characters together. For example,

```
ls ??.*
```

This would list files whose names begin with exactly two characters, followed by a period, followed by anything. (The period is matched literally.)

More-specialized glob-patterns

Sometimes you want to use a list of files that match a more specific pattern. For this you might use a more complex kind of pattern.

To match a range of characters:

1. `ls /var/log/system.log.[0-3].gz`
   would result in output similar to that shown in **Figure 2.32**.
   The [and] characters are used to create a glob-pattern called a *character class*. The resulting pattern matches any single character in the class. A range of characters can be indicated by using the hyphen, so that [0-3] is the same as [0123].
2. Ranges may be alphabetical as well as numeric:
   `ls Alpha-[A-D]`
3. Unix filenames are case sensitive. You can match either case by including both in the character class:
   `ls Alpha-[A-Da-d]`

✔ Tip

- You can create a character class that is quite arbitrary—for example, the glob-pattern
  Photo-[AD]
  matches only Photo-A and Photo-D.

To negate a character class:

- Use the ^ character as the first character in the character class.
  When you do this, the glob-pattern *[^3-8] matches anything that does not end in 3, 4, 5, 6, 7, or 8 (the * matches anything; the [^3-8] means "do not match 3-8").

Patterns and rules similar to those described here are used in many different Unix tools, especially in a set of tools called *regular expressions*. See Chapter 4, "Useful Unix Utilities," for more on regular expressions.

```
user-vc8f9gd:~ vanilla$ ls /var/log/system.log.[0-3].gz
/var/log/system.log.0.gz       /var/log/system.log.2.gz
/var/log/system.log.1.gz       /var/log/system.log.3.gz
user-vc8f9gd:~ vanilla$
```

Figure 2.32 This shows the output when you use a glob-pattern—in this case [0-3]—for a range of characters.

About Standard Input and Output

Normally, the output from command lines shows up on your screen. You type in a command and press Return, and the resulting output appears. This is actually a special case of the more general-purpose way that Unix handles both input and output.

All Unix commands come with two input/output devices, called `stdin` (for *standard input*) and `stdout` (for *standard output*). You can't see the `stdin` and `stdout` devices the same way you see a printer, but they are always there. You might like to think of `stdin` and `stdout` as valves or hose connectors stuck on the outside of every command. Think of the `stdout` connector as being fed to your screen, and your keyboard feeding data to the `stdin` connector.

You have seen redirection of `stdout` with the > and >> operators earlier in this chapter. In this section, you will learn more about redirecting `stdout`, and also how to redirect `stdin`—that is, to have a command get input from someplace other than the keyboard—and how to connect the `stdout` of one command to the `stdin` of another, creating what is called a *pipeline*. This ability to connect several commands together is one of the most important features of Unix's flexibility.

Besides `stdin` and `stdout`, there is one more virtual connection on each command, `stderr` (for *standard error*), which is the output connection for warning and error messages. If a command issues an error message, it comes out of the `stderr` connector, which is normally connected to your screen (same as `stdout`). If you redirect `stdout` to a file (with >), `stderr` still goes to your screen. You can redirect `stderr` as well, though.

`stdin`, `stdout`, and `stderr` are often capitalized in Unix manuals and literature. Both upper- and lowercase usage is correct.

Figure 2.33 illustrates the concept of the `stdin`, `stdout`, and `stderr` connectors.

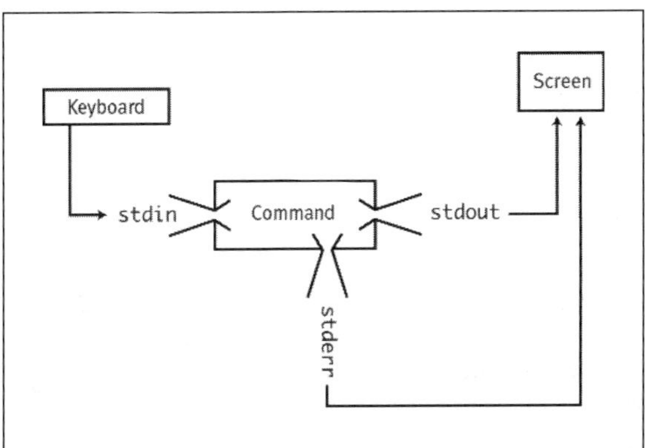

Figure 2.33 Here's how the normal connections of `stdin`, `stdout`, and `stderr` work.

Redirecting stdout

The most common form of redirection is to redirect the output of a command into a file using the > operator, which you saw in examples earlier in this chapter. You will redirect `stdout` to a file when you want to save the output for later use, such as editing or viewing.

To save output in a file:

- Add > *`filename`* to the command line.

  For example,

  `ls /Users > users`

  redirects the output into the file named users. If the file does not already exist, it is created. If the file does exist, the contents are *irrevocably overwritten.*

✔ Tip

- Sometimes you'll want to simply throw away the output of a command without ever seeing it. To do this, redirect the output into the special file called `/dev/null`. For example,

  `noisy_command > /dev/null`

  Anything written to `/dev/null` is simply discarded. It's a good place to send insults and complaints.

Sometimes you will want to *add* the redirected output to a file instead of overwriting the contents.

To append output to a file:

- Use >> *`filename`* at the end of the command—for example,

  `ls /Users >> users`

  redirects the output to the end of the file called users, or creates the file if it did not already exist.

Redirecting stderr

`stderr` can be redirected as well. One reason to do this is to save errors into a log file. Another reason is to not have warning and error messages cluttering up your screen.

To redirect stderr to a file:

- 2> *`filename`*

  puts the `stderr` output into the named file. You can use 2>> to append rather than overwrite an existing file.

  You can send both `stdout` and `stderr` to the same file with

  `command` `2>&1` *`filename`*

(If you are using the `tcsh` shell, you cannot redirect `stdout` and `stderr` separately, but you can make them both go into the same file using >&.) For example:

`command` `>&` *`filename`*

Redirecting stdin

Sometimes you'll want a command to get its input from a file you have prepared. For example, you might have prepared the text of an e-mail message and want to feed it into the mail command, or you might have a list of filenames you want to feed into a program.

Most Unix commands allow you to redirect standard input and have it come from a file instead of the keyboard.

To take standard input from a file:

- Add < *`filename`* to the end of the command.

  For example, if you have a file that contains a list of 30 filenames, you might type

  `ls -l < list_of_files`

  instead of

  `ls -l` *`file1 file2 file3`*

  . . . and so on.

Creating Pipelines of Commands

Another way to manipulate `stdin` and `stdout` is to have one command take its input directly from the output of another command. To do this, Unix uses the |, or *pipe*, character to connect commands together to form *pipelines*, with the `stdout` of each command being piped into the `stdin` of the next one. The `stderr` is not affected by the pipeline. The use of pipes enables you to create an almost infinite variety of command lines processing input and output to what are nothing more than miniature custom applications.

To pipe the output of one command into another:

1. Type the first command that produces output, but don't press Return until the last step below.

   This can be any command (along with options and arguments) that produces output on `stdout`. For example,

   `ls -l /bin`

   lists the contents of `/bin`, where the executable files for many commands are stored (**Figure 2.34**). But let's say we want to see only the modification date and the filename. Noticing that this information starts 38 characters into each line, we might pipe the output of the `ls` command into the `cut` command, telling `cut` to show us only from character 38 to the end of each line.

```
user-vc8f9gd:~ vanilla$ ls -l /bin
total 8816
-r-xr-xr-x   2  root  wheel      18104 Jan 31 01:13 [
-rwxr-xr-x   1  root  wheel     581680 Jan 31 00:23 bash
-r-xr-xr-x   1  root  wheel      14380 Jan 31 01:04 cat
-r-xr-xr-x   1  root  wheel      23792 Jan 31 00:50 chmod
-r-xr-xr-x   1  root  wheel      19108 Jan 31 00:51 cp
-r-xr-xr-x   2  root  wheel     347060 Jan 31 00:52 csh
-r-xr-xr-x   1  root  wheel      19016 Jan 31 01:12 date
-r-xr-xr-x   1  root  wheel      27012 Jan 31 00:51 dd
-r-xr-sr-x   1  root  operator   22984 Jan 31 00:51 df
-r-xr-xr-x   1  root  wheel      14440 Jan 31 05:03 domainname
-r-xr-xr-x   1  root  wheel      13712 Jan 31 01:13 echo
-r-xr-xr-x   1  root  wheel      56480 Jan 31 01:05 ed

(...output truncated for brevity...)
```

Figure 2.34 Running `ls -l /bin` lists the contents of `/bin`, where the executable files for many commands are stored.

2. Add the | character at the end of the command.

   The | character catches the output from what is on its left and passes it to the `stdin` of what is on its right.

3. Add the command that will receive its input from the pipe. Continuing our example, the command line would now look like this:

   `ls -l /bin | cut -c38-`

   and the result would look like that shown in **Figure 2.35**.

   Now you can press Return. Or if you wanted to redirect the output of the pipeline to a file, the final command line would be

   `ls -l /bin | cut -c38- > outfile`

Assuming your computer is connected to the Internet, you can pipe the output of any command into an e-mail message for another user on the Internet.

```
user-vc8f9gd:~ vanilla$ ls -l /bin | cut -c38-
 Jan 31 01:13 [
 Jan 31 00:23 bash
 Jan 31 01:04 cat
 Jan 31 00:50 chmod
 Jan 31 00:51 cp
 Jan 31 00:52 csh
 Jan 31 01:12 date
 Jan 31 00:51 dd
 Jan 31 00:51 df
 Jan 31 05:03 domainname
 Jan 31 01:13 echo
 Jan 31 01:05 ed
(...output truncated for brevity...)
```

Figure 2.35 Running `ls -l /bin | cut -c38-` gives this partial output.

To pipe the output of a command into e-mail:

- *command* `| mail -s "`*subject*`"` *address*

  command can be any command line that produces output on `stdout`. *subject* is the subject of the e-mail message, and *address* is a valid e-mail address. For example:

  ```
  ls -l /usr/bin | mail -s
  → myself@xyz.com
  ```

Running a Command in the Background

Some commands take a while to run. For example, a command that searches through a large number of files or a command that must read a large amount of input may take more time than you're willing to spend twiddling your thumbs.

It is a simple matter to have a command run in the background and get a shell prompt right away so that you can keep working. The command keeps running—you can stop it or bring it to the foreground if you like—but you can let the operating system worry about the command while you do other things.

To run a command line in the background:

- Add the & character at the end of the command line.

  At the end of any command line, you can add the & character so that the entire command line runs in the background.

The shell shows you the background job number and the process ID number for each command on the command line, and gives you a shell prompt right away. **Figure 2.36** shows an example of getting three samples from the top command and sending them in e-mail.

Once the job is finished running, the shell displays a notice the next time it gives you a new shell prompt. That is, the shell does not spontaneously notify you, but it waits and displays the notice along with the next shell prompt (**Figure 2.37**).

✔ Tip

- If a background job needs input from you, it simply sits and waits patiently—possibly forever. Before putting a job in the background, you should have a good idea of how it behaves normally.

The [1] is the Job ID number

2653 is the process ID of the mail command

```
user-vc8f9gd:~ vanilla$ top -l3 | mail -s "3 samples from top" matisse@matisse.net &
[1] 2653
user-vc8f9gd:~ vanilla$
```

Figure 2.36 Running a command in the background, here you've gotten three samples from the top command and sent them in e-mail. (Hey, please send them to yourself, not the author!)

```
user-vc8f9gd:~ vanilla$
[1]+Done                    top -l3 | mail -s "3 samples from top" matisse@matisse.net
user-vc8f9gd:~ vanilla$
```

Figure 2.37 The shell notifies you when the job is completed.

You can have several jobs running in the background, and you can bring any of them back to the foreground, or stop any of them by using the `kill` command, discussed earlier in this chapter.

To see a list of jobs running in the background:

- `jobs`

  The `jobs` command displays a list of background jobs started from the current shell (**Figure 2.38**). (Insert gratuitous Steve Jobs joke here.) If you have multiple Terminal windows open, each has its own list of background jobs. Even if a job consists of multiple commands (processes), it has a single job number.

To bring a job to the foreground:

1. `jobs`

   Run the `jobs` command to get a list of job numbers. Pick the one you want to bring back to the foreground.

2. `fg %`*n*

   Use the `fg` command (meaning *foreground*) to bring the job from the background. You identify the job with `%` and its job number: `%1` for job 1, `%2` for job 2, and so on.

   The job is now running in the foreground.

   If you omit the job number, then the job you most recently put in the background will be brought to the foreground.

✔ Tip

- Once a job is in the foreground, you can stop it with Control C, or with the following method.

To stop a background job:

1. `jobs`

   This shows you the list of all jobs running.

2. `kill %`*n*

   where *n* represents any number, such as

   `kill %2`

   This is the same `kill` command we saw earlier in the chapter, only this time instead of the process ID we are using the job ID. The same options apply here. The `kill` command by itself sends a hang-up signal to each process in the job, requesting that it quit; `kill -9` sends kill signals that can't be ignored, stopping the job in its tracks.

Sometimes you might not realize that a command is going to take a while to finish until after you start it. You might have pressed Return and find yourself waiting for the job to finish. Or maybe you want to temporarily stop a job, get a shell prompt, do something else, and then return to the job that was stopped. You can *suspend* the job and get a shell prompt back right away.

A suspended job will be in the background, but it won't keep running; that is, its memory remains active, but it consumes no processor time. You can bring it back to the foreground, or tell it to run in the background, just as if you had started it initially with an `&` at the end of the command line.

```
user-vc8f9gd:~ vanilla$ jobs
[1]+Stopped                  vm_stat 5
[2]-Running                  top -l3 | mail -s "3 samples from top" matisse@matisse.net &
user-vc8f9gd:~ vanilla$
```

Figure 2.38 Running the jobs command gives you a list of jobs running in the background.

Compare with Aqua

The Unix concept of putting a command in the background is very much like the traditional Mac or Aqua situation where you have an application running in one window and you open a window for a different application. The first application continues to run, and you can get on with other things.

To suspend a job:

◆ Control Z

Figure 2.39 shows what happens when you use Control Z to suspend the `top` command while it is running. The shell shows you the job ID and process ID of the suspended job, and returns you to a shell prompt. The `^Z` you see in Figure 2.39 is what is displayed when you press Control Z.

✔ Tip

■ You can bring the job back to the foreground as described above using the `fg` command. If the job you want to bring back to the foreground is the one you just suspended, use `fg` by itself with no arguments.

```
SharedLibs: num = 93, resident = 22.5M code, 1.57M data, 5.52M LinkEdit
MemRegions: num = 3234, resident =142M + 7.07M private, 84.3M shared
PhysMem:60.1M wired, 71.8M active,245M inactive,377M used,263M free
VM: 2.34G + 45.8M 9564(0) pageins, 0(0) pageouts

PID   COMMAND     %CPU   TIME      #TH   #PRTS  #MREGS  RPRVT   RSHRD   RSIZE   VSIZE
439   Mozilla     1.7%   36:35.72   6     87     437    26.6M   25.4M   43.2M    109M
396   AOL Instan  1.7%   31:01.89  10    121     170    10.7M   11.0M   16.2M   79.3M
379   Eudora 5.1  0.0%    7:26.90   7    112     162    6.49M   12.5M   11.2M    100M
356   httpd       0.0%    0:00.13   1      9      65     140K   1.25M    612K   2.38M
329   tcsh        0.0%    0:00.61   1     24      17     508K    676K    996K   5.99M
328   ssh-agent   0.0%    0:01.23   1      9      14      80K    352K    172K   1.29M
327   Terminal    1.7%    0:51.57   5    114     103    2.89M   7.12M   6.08M   68.5M
325   sh          0.0%    0:00.01   1     16      13     164K    640K    556K   1.69M
^Z
[1]+ 736 Suspended                    top
user-vc8f9gd:~ vanilla$
```

Figure 2.39 Using Control Z suspends the top command.

If you have suspended a job and decide you want the job to keep running, but in the background, you can do that, too.

To have a suspended job continue running in the background:

- `bg %n`

  For example,

  `bg %2`

  tells job number 2 to start running again, but to do so in the *background*. **Figure 2.40** shows an example of starting a job, suspending it, running another command, and then starting up the suspended job again in the background.

✔ Tip

- If the suspended job is the one you most recently suspended, you can use `bg` with no arguments.

```
user-vc8f9gd:~ vanilla$ find /Developer -name "*.htm" > found_files
^Z
[1]    +    Stopped         find /Developer -name "*.htm" >found_files
user-vc8f9gd:~ vanilla$ uptime
22:04 up 4 days, 3 mins, 3 users, load averages: 0.25 0.09 0.03
user-vc8f9gd:~ vanilla$ bg %1
[1]    +    find /Developer -name "*.htm" >found_files &
user-vc8f9gd:~ vanilla$
```

Figure 2.40 When you suspend a job, you can restart it in the background using `bg %n`.

Opening Files from the Command Line

One of the great things about using the Unix command line in Mac OS X is that you are also using a Macintosh. So how do you access graphical Mac applications or AppleScripts from the command line? Apple provides a set of command-line tools to do exactly that.

To "double-click" a file from the command line:

◆ `open filename`

The `open` command performs the equivalent of double-clicking each of its arguments. For example,

```
open *.doc FunReport
```

is the same as double-clicking all the .doc files in the current directory, along with the file FunReport. The default application for each file is used just as if you had double-clicked the icons in the Finder.

✔ Tips

- You can specify which application to use with the `-a` switch (or option)—for example,

  ```
  open -a "BBEdit 6.5" found_files
  ```

  would open the file called found_files using the BBEdit 6.5 application.

- The `open` command is often used to open the current directory in the Finder:

  ```
  open .
  ```

To run an AppleScript from the command line:

◆ `osascript scriptname`

The `osascript` command executes the script named by its argument.

✔ Tip

- If you are an experienced AppleScript programmer, read the Unix manual page for `osascript` by typing

  ```
  man osascript
  ```

  You will also be interested in learning about the `osacompile` and `osalang` commands.

The Importance of Editing Text in Unix

Editing text from the command line is a crucial part of using Unix.

Unix system-configuration files, system-startup files, source code for software, and much documentation are all contained in text files, which you will have occasion to edit when using the command line.

While you can certainly use your favorite Aqua text editor or word processor to edit text in Mac OS X, you will need to be able to edit files directly from the command line if you do any serious command-line work. Also, if you want to be able to use other Unix systems besides Mac OS X, you will need to learn how to edit files using one of the command-line tools.

Chapter 6, "Editing and Printing Files," teaches you the basics of using the most common command-line text editor, the `vi` editor. In this chapter, you will use the simpler `pico`/`nano` editor, which is adequate for the example of creating a shell script but is not appropriate for more complex Unix work, such as editing system-startup files. (The `nano` editor is a compatible replacement for the more well-known `pico` editor, but `nano` has a less restrictive license and more features. On Mac OS X 10.4 the `pico` command actually runs `nano`.)

Creating a Simple Unix Shell Script

A *shell script* is a text file that contains a series of shell commands. Shell scripts are used for a wide range of tasks in Unix; Chapter 9 covers complex shell scripts that contain loops, functions, and other features associated with computer programming. But here we'll talk about simpler shell scripts, which are often just a series of command lines intended to be executed one after the other.

When you create a script you'll be using frequently, you should save it in a place where your shell normally looks for commands. This way, you can run the script by simply typing its name, as you would for any other command. The list of places where your shell looks for commands is called your PATH, and we teach you how to change your PATH in Chapter 7.

The standard place to store scripts for your personal use (as opposed to scripts intended for use by all users) is the `bin` directory inside your home directory. Mac OS X (as of version 10.4) ships without this directory's having been created for each user and without its being on the list of places where your shell looks for commands (your PATH), so before we have you create a script, we show you how to create this directory and add it to your PATH. (See Chapter 7 for more on your PATH.)

To create your personal bin directory:

1. `cd`

   This ensures that you are in your home directory.

2. `mkdir bin`

   This creates a new directory called `bin` (a standard Unix name for directories that contain commands, scripts, or applications).

✔ Tip

- See Chapter 5 for more on the `mkdir` command.

To add your bin directory to your PATH:

1. `cd`

   This ensures that you are in your home directory. (You can skip this step if you have just done the task above, but it doesn't hurt to do it again.)

2. `export PATH=$PATH:~/bin`

   This adds the `bin` directory inside your home directory to the list of places your shell searches for commands. The next step takes care of doing this for all future Terminal windows you open.

3. `echo 'export PATH=$PATH:~/bin' >> .bash_profile`

   This command line adds a line of code to a configuration file used by your shell. Every new Terminal window you open will have the new configuration.

   Be careful to type it exactly as shown—the placement of spaces and the use of single quotes must be replicated exactly. Be sure to type both greater-than signs (that way, if you happen to already have a .bash_profile, you will be appending to it, not replacing it).

   The text contained inside the single quotes is added as a new line to the end of the file .bash_profile that is inside your home directory. You may check that this was successful by displaying that file with

   `cat bash_profile`

   The last line of the output should be

   `export PATH=$PATH:~/bin`

Unix shell scripts can be written for any of the available shells, but the standard practice is to write shell scripts for the `sh` shell. The `sh` shell can be expected to behave in the same way on any Unix system.

Here is an example of creating a simple shell script that shows you a variety of status information about your computer.

To create a shell script to show system status:

1. `cd`

   This makes sure you are in your home directory.

2. `cd bin`

   This changes your current directory to the `bin` directory.

3. `nano status.sh`

   This starts up the nano editor, telling it to edit (and create) the file status.sh (**Figure 2.41**).

   We name the new script with a .sh extension as a reminder that it is written using the `sh` scripting language.

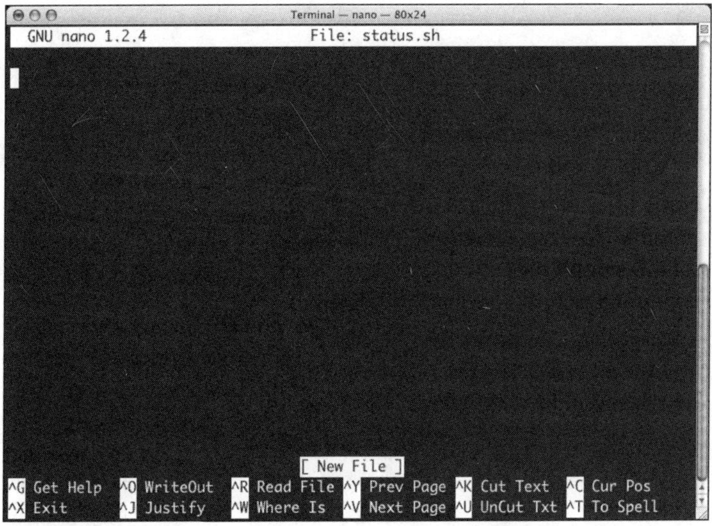

Figure 2.41 This is what you see when you start the nano editor.

4. Type in the script from **Figure 2.42**. Note that the highlighted lines use the *backquote*, or *backtick*, character—this is the [`] character, which is usually in the upper left of your keyboard (to the left of [1]).

5. [Control][X]

   Pressing [Control][X] causes the nano editor to quit. nano asks if you want to save the changes you have made (**Figure 2.43**).

```
#!/bin/sh
# This is a comment. Comments are good.
# This is my first shell script.
echo "System Status Report"
date
echo -n "System uptime and load:" ;uptime
echo -n "Operating System: " ; sysctl -n kern.ostype
echo -n "OS Version: " ; sysctl -n kern.osrelease
echo -n "OS Revision number: " ; sysctl -n kern.osrevision
echo -n "Hostname: " ; sysctl -n kern.hostname
bytes=`sysctl -n hw.physmem`
megabytes=`expr $bytes / 1024 / 1024`
echo "Physical memory installed (megabytes): $megabytes"
```

Figure 2.42 This is the code listing of a system-status script. Pay special attention to the backtick ([`]) characters.

```
Save modified buffer (ANSWERING "No" WILL DESTROY CHANGES) ?
 Y Yes
 N No              ^C Cancel
```

Figure 2.43 The nano editor asks if you want to save changes.

6. y

   Type a y to tell nano that yes, you want to save the changes you have made.

   nano then asks you to confirm the filename to save to (**Figure 2.44**).

7. Press Return.

   nano exits, and you are back at a shell prompt.

8. chmod 755 status.sh

   The chmod command (*change mode*) sets the file status.sh to be an executable file. See Chapter 8, "Working with Permissions and Ownership," for more on the chmod command.

   Next you will actually run the script you have created.

9. ./status.sh

   Figure 2.45 shows typical output from the command. You have just created your first new command.

Welcome to Unix!

Figure 2.44 The nano editor asks you to confirm the filename you're using.

```
user-vc8f9gd:~/bin vanilla$ status.sh
System Status Report
Sun Mar6 23:03:28 PST 2005
System uptime and load:23:03up 4 days,1:01, 4 users, load averages: 0.45 0.19 0.09
Operating System: Darwin
OS Version: 8.0.0
OS Revision number: 199506
Hostname: user-vc8f9gd.biz.mindspring.com
Physical memory installed (megabytes): 640
user-vc8f9gd:~/bin vanilla$ status.sh
System Status Report
Sun Mar6 23:11:59 PST 2005
System uptime and load:23:11up 4 days,1:10, 4 users, load averages: 0.09 0.09 0.07
Operating System: Darwin
OS Version: 8.0.0
OS Revision number: 199506
Hostname: user-vc8f9gd.biz.mindspring.com
Physical memory installed (megabytes): 640
user-vc8f9gd:~/bin vanilla$
```

Figure 2.45 Typing ./status.sh shows you output from the command you have just created.

3 Getting Help and Using the Unix Manual

There are four ways to get help when using Unix: from external documentation such as this book, Web sites, and other similar materials; from the extensive Unix reference manuals that come with every version of Unix, including Mac OS X; from the built-in help that comes with most commands; and from other people via online discussion systems, e-mail, user groups, and, yes, calling your friends on the telephone. You are already taking the first approach, so this chapter concentrates on the other three.

The Unix reference manual is a collection of files called `man` *pages*, which are specially formatted files intended to be viewed with the `man` command. Unix `man` pages are written for an audience of experienced programmers, not for novice users, so to understand Unix `man` pages, you need to understand the conventions used in them.

Mac OS X comes with almost 3000 Unix `man` pages. Most of these are copied from the FreeBSD version of Unix, the one used to create Mac OS X's Darwin layer. Some of these pages come from Apple itself, and some come from the software that Apple acquired when it bought NeXT. As of this writing (summer 2005), Apple has made progress updating the `man` pages to be Darwin specific, but the job is not yet done. Fortunately, most of the `man` pages do not require updating; unfortunately, there is no easy way to know which ones do require it.

Command-line programs almost always provide a minimal level of built-in help—usually just enough to show you the options and arguments the command expects. Still, that is often enough to remind you of the proper way to use the command.

Help from other people is the most valuable kind, and it's available from a variety of sources. At the end of this chapter is a list of the best places to look.

Using the Unix Manual

Every Unix command is supposed to have an associated man page that describes the command and the options available for using it. You read man pages using the man command.

Unix man pages are arranged into eight or nine sections, depending on which flavor of Unix you are using. Mac OS X uses the nine sections shown in **Table 3.1**. (These are the nine standard sections from BSD Unix, plus a section for the Tcl/Tk programming language.) Look in the various subdirectories of /usr/share/man to see all the man pages that come with Mac OS X.

Wherever you see a Unix command name followed by a number in parentheses—for example, date(1)—the number refers to the section of the manual with which the command is associated. Thus, chown(2) refers to the chown documented in section 2 of the manual, while chown(8) refers to the chown documented in section 8 of the manual.

Throughout this book we use the Unix convention of referring to a manual entry by saying "see man *entry*." *entry* is usually a command name—for example, we might say "see man ls" to look at the manual entry of the ls command. *entry* can also represent anything else the manual covers; some system-configuration files have manual entries.

To display a man page:

1. The short answer is: man *command*

   For example,

   man man

   shows you the man page for the man command. **Figure 3.1** is a code listing showing the beginning of the Unix man page for the man command. It is probably rather confusing at this point, which is why we have this chapter to explain Unix man pages.

Table 3.1

Sections of the Mac OS X/BSD Unix Manual

Section	Contents	
1	*General Commands*	Commands you use most frequently, such as man and grep.
2	*System Calls*	Commands (actually *functions*) provided by the operating system for use in programming, mostly in the C language, such as getlogin and setuid.
3	*Library Functions*	Tools for programmers that are available in a variety of languages (C, Perl, Tcl, and others), such as opendir and Text::Soundex.
4	*Kernel Interfaces Manual*	More-advanced tools for programmers, mostly in the C language, such as stdout and urandom.
5	*System File Formats*	Man pages for the most important system-configuration files, describing their use for system administration, such as appletalk.cfg and launchd.conf.
6	*Games*	This covers games, but Mac OS X comes with only one command-line game, banner. If you have a printer connected, try banner -w 80 "Unix" | lp.
7	*Miscellaneous Information*	Character-set definitions; file types; filesystem information, such as hier, which shows the filesystem hierarchy; and ascii, which describes the ASCII character set.
8	*System Manager's Manual*	Servers and system-administration commands, such as halt (to shut down the system) and httpd (the Apache Web server).
9	*Kernel Developer's Manual* *Tcl and Tk Built-in Command*	The Tcl/Tk programming language gets its own section of the Unix manual, describing all of the Tcl functions and libraries available, such as lindex and tk_messageBox. See man tclsh for an interactive Tcl shell.

Look in the various subdirectories of /usr/share/man to see all man pages that come with Mac OS X.

```
[localhost:~] vanilla% man man

man(1)                                                          man(1)



NAME
       man - format and display the on-line manual pages

SYNOPSIS
       man [-acdfFhkKtwW] [--path] [-m system] [-p string] [-C config_file]
       [-M pathlist] [-P pager] [-S section_list] [section] name ...


DESCRIPTION
       man formats and displays the on-line manual pages. If you specify sec-
       tion, man only looks in that section of the manual. name is normally
       the name of the manual page, which is typically the name of a command,
       function, or file. However, if name contains a slash (/) then man
       interprets it as a file specification, so that you can do man ./foo.5
       or even man /cd/foo/bar.1.gz.

       See below for a description of where man looks for the manual page
       files.


OPTIONS
       -C config_file
            Specify the configuration file to use; the default is
            /usr/share/misc/man.conf. (See man.conf(5).)

       -M path
            Specify the list of directories to search for man pages. Sepa-
            rate the directories with colons. An empty list is the same as
            not specifying -M at all. See SEARCH PATH FOR MANUAL PAGES.

       -P pager
            Specify which pager to use. This option overrides the MANPAGER
            environment variable, which in turn overrides the PAGER vari-
            able. By default, man uses /usr/bin/less -is.
```

Figure 3.1 Typing man man lets you see the man page for the man command itself (this is partial output).

2. Here is a longer, more useful answer. The generalized syntax of how to display a Unix `man` page is this:

```
man [-acdfFhkKtwW] [-path] [-m
→ system] [-p string] [-C config_file]
→ [-M pathlist] [-P pager] [-S
→ section_list] [section] name ...
```

What does that mean? It is the technical way in which Unix command syntax is described. This format, though daunting at first, is a concise and accurate way of showing how a command should be used, and you will see this format constantly in Unix documentation.

The `man` pages for commands all begin with a synopsis of the command using the format shown above. It is well worth your time to learn this syntax.

Figure 3.2 shows an element-by-element translation of the specification for the `man` command itself.

According to the specification, the only required argument to the `man` command is the name of the manual entry you want (it is the only argument *not* inside square brackets), but there are many available options. You must read the `man` page itself to learn what the options mean.

Here are the meanings for the options you are most likely to use:

`-a` Displays all the `man` pages that match the command name you supply (the final argument to the `man` command). Normally the `man` command shows only the first match (searching the manual starting from section 1).

`-d` Displays debugging information instead of the actual manual page(s).

`-k` Finds a list of the manual pages that contain the entry in their one-line description. (The entry is the final, and required, argument to the `man` command.) `man -k` *`string`* is the same as `apropros` *`string`*. See "To search for a `man` page," below.

`-K` Similar to the `-k` (lowercase) option, but searches the full text of all `man` pages for the string. Can be slow but is very useful.

`-h` Displays a help message for the `man` command.

`-t` Produces PostScript output by passing the output of the `man` command through another program (called `troff`). If you use this option, you will almost certainly want to save the output in a file or pipe it to a program that understands PostScript. (See "Printing `man` Pages," later in this chapter, and "Redirecting `stdout`" and "Creating Pipelines of Commands," in Chapter 2, "Using the Command Line.")

-w Shows the locations of the actual man page files instead of showing the pages themselves. Try combining this with -a.

-M You must supply a list of one or more directories (separated by colons) right after this option. The directories are searched for man pages instead of the default locations (which are all in /usr/share/man).

✔ Tips

- Print a pretty version of a man page with

  `man -t name | lp`

- Use the man command to read about each new command in this book. Many commands have options that go beyond what we're covering.
- In some cases, man pages in two sections of the manual have the same name. Using the -a switch displays all the entries for a given name.
- Look at the ends of most man pages for a "SEE ALSO" section that lists related commands. A related command might be more useful than the one you first thought to use.

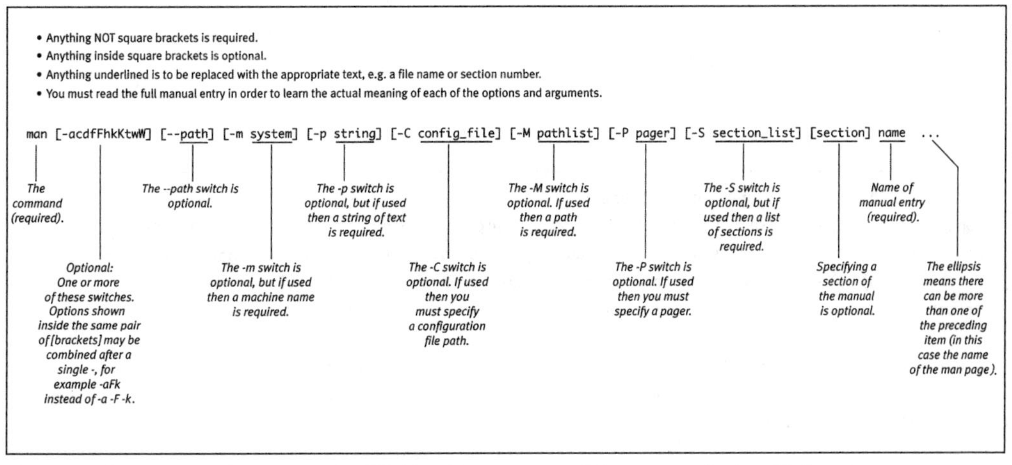

Figure 3.2 The man pages for commands all begin with a synopsis of the command using this format.

Sometimes you may not be sure which command you want. The apropos command can be used to search the title lines of all the manual pages.

To search for a man page:

- apropos *keyword*

  For example, if you were looking for commands related to appletalk, you would try

  apropos appletalk

  Figure 3.3 shows the result (reformatted slightly for print). Each entry lists the name of a man page, the section it belongs to, and usually a one-line description of the man entry.

✔ Tips

- Of course, you can try man apropos to learn more about the apropos command.
- On many Unix systems (including Mac OS X), man -k is the same as apropos.
- You can also search for man pages by looking in the directories inside /usr/share/man and /usr/local/man.
- The apropos command searches the "whatis" database, which is updated every Sunday morning starting at 3:15 a.m. as long as your Mac is on at that time. You can manually update the database with the following command:

  sudo /usr/libexec/makewhatis.local

  You will be prompted for your password, and the command will take a while to run. (See "Running Regularly Scheduled Commands" in Chapter 11, "Introduction to System Administration.")

```
user-vc8f9gd:~ vanilla$ apropos appletalk
appleping(1)      -    exercises the AppleTalk network by sending packets to a named host
appletalk(8)      -    enables you to configure and display AppleTalk network interfaces
at_cho_prn(8)     -    allows you to choose a default printer on the AppleTalk internet
atlookup(1)       -    looks up network-visible entities (NVEs) registered on the
                       AppleTalk network system
atprint(1)        -    transfer data to a printer using AppleTalk protocols
atstatus(1)       -    displays status information from an AppleTalk device
user-vc8f9gd:~ vanilla$
```

Figure 3.3 The apropos command can be used to search the title lines of all the manual pages.

Printing man Pages

Unix `man` pages are plain-text files written using a special formatting syntax (see `man mdoc` for a tutorial). The raw files are not suitable for printing because they contain text that the `man` command uses to produce boldface, underlining, and other text formatting, but in many cases you can translate the `man` page into HTML or PostScript.

Note that the printing techniques described here work for many, but not all, `man` pages, simply because some converters may not be able to handle certain formatting commands (the `man` pages may have been written at different times). However, you'll always be able to see the text on the screen—on the printed page you may get truncated text or missing paragraph breaks.

See Chapter 6, "Editing and Printing Files," for more on printing from the command line.

To print a man page to a PostScript printer:

◆ `man -t` *`command`* `| lp`

For example, if you want a printed `man` page for the `date` command:

```
man -t date | lp
```

You are using the `-t` option of the `man` command to produce PostScript output and piping that into the `lp` command. If you're not using a PostScript printer, you will probably get a nicely formatted result because Mac OS X includes open-source Unix software that helps non-PostScript printers print PostScript. (If you are curious, see the Gimp-Print Web site, http://gimp-print.sourceforge.net, for more about this software.)

✔ Tip

■ If you wanted to save the PostScript version of a `man` page, perhaps for use in some future project, then you would simply redirect the output of the `man` command to a file:

```
man -t date > date.ps
```

Besides converting `man` pages to PostScript, you can also convert many of them to PDF or HTML (or TIFF, or JPEG, or many other formats). This will allow you to view pages in the Preview application or a Web browser and print them to any printer.

To convert a man page to PDF:

1. `man -t` *`command`* `>` *`command`*`.ps`

   This creates a PostScript file from the `man` page. It is important that you include the .ps at the end of the output filename.

2. `open command.ps`

   This opens the PostScript file. By default, the file opens in the Preview application, which automagically converts it to PDF for display.

3. Choose File > Save in the Preview application.

   You get the standard Mac save-file dialog, where you choose the name and location for saving the file.

4. Choose PDF from the Format menu in the dialog.

   Notice that you have the choice of several formats.

5. Click Save.

   You're done.

To convert a man page to HTML:

1. Find the raw `man` page.

   Use the `-w` option to the `man` command—for example:

   ```
   man -w bash
   ```

   `bash` is just the name of the command for which we want the `man` page. Even though `bash` is your shell, it is still just another command.

   ```
   groff -man -Thtml
   → /usr/share/man/man1/bash.1 >
   → bash.html
   ```

   (You might see some debugging output on your screen from the `groff` command, but you can ignore it. The new file, bash.html, will not contain the debugging text. The `groff` command is the GNU version of the `roff` (*runoff*) typesetting system and provides a variety of formatting features.

2. You can now try viewing the HTML page with your default browser, even from the command line:

   ```
   open bash.html
   ```

✓ Tip

- Some `man` pages convert better than others. If you know HTML, you may be able to edit poorly formatted HTML versions to fix conversion problems.

Using Commands' Built-in Help

The most common way to learn about a command is to read its built-in help. Many commands support an option that displays information about the command, and almost all commands display a *usage* message (saying how they are best used) if they are invoked with improper arguments or options.

Built-in help is terse, often consisting only of a usage message using the format shown in Figure 3.2. Still, it is easily available and often reminds you of the available options and required arguments.

There isn't a consistent way to get built-in help from commands, but there are several ways that work.

To see the built-in help from a command:

- Try invoking the command with the `--help` option (that's two hyphens).

  For example, try

  `softwareupdate --help`

  Some commands (like `softwareupdate`) provide an extensive listing of available options (see **Figure 3.4** for a partial listing from the `ssh` command).

  For some commands, the `--help` option is not valid, and for others it looks like a valid option but doesn't provide any help.

```
user-vc8f9gd:~ vanilla$ softwareupdate --help
usage: softwareupdate <mode> [<args> ...]
       -l | --list              List all appropriate updates
       -d | --download          Download Only
       -i | --install           Install
                <label> ...     specific updates
                -a | --all              all appropriate updates
                -r | --recommended      only recommended updates
                -u | --url <url> ...    from signed package URLs
       Per-user preferences:
       --ignore <label> ...         Ignore specific updates
       --reset-ignored              Clear all ignored updates
       --schedule (on | off)        Set automatic checking

       -h | --help          Print this help
user-vc8f9gd:~ vanilla$
```

Figure 3.4 Some commands (like softwareupdate) give an extensive listing of available options; this is the result when you type softwareupdate --help.

◆ In some cases, using a single hyphen gives something useful:

  `ssh -help`

  Even though `-help` is not a valid option to the `ssh` command, it still gives you some insight. Most commands give a "usage" message when invoked with an invalid option or without a required argument. **Figure 3.5** shows the output from `ssh` when invoked with the `-help` option.

◆ In some cases the `-h` option will produce a help message.

  The `man` command is an example of a command that will give you a help message if you invoke it with the `-h` option:

  `man -h`

✔ Tips

- Try deliberately using an invalid option, such as `-XXX`, and see what happens.
- If the built-in help is not helpful or is missing, just refer to the `man` page.

```
user-vc8f9gd:~ vanilla$ ssh -help
ssh: illegal option - h
usage: ssh  [-1246AaCfghkNnqsTtVvXxY] [-b bind_address] [-c cipher_spec]
            [-D port] [-e escape_char] [-F configfile] [-i identity_file]
            [-L port:host:hostport] [-l login_name] [-m mac_spec] [-o option]
            [-p port] [-R port:host:hostport] [user@]hostname [command]
user-vc8f9gd:~ vanilla$
```

Figure 3.5 What you get when you type `ssh -help`.

Using the Web to Get Help

One of the best ways to find help for a Unix problem is to do a Google search (www.google.com). Besides maintaining an extremely large database of Web pages, Google also provides search results from Usenet discussion groups, which can include a wealth of technical information and often provide better answers to Unix problems than other Web searches do.

✔ Tips

- Click the "Groups" link at the top of the page for results limited to online discussion groups such as Usenet. **Figure 3.6** shows an example of search results using this approach.
- If you are looking for help with an error message, enter the exact text of the error, in quotes.
- Try using quotes to enclose any two or more words when you want to find them as a single unit.
- Put a - (hyphen) in front of words you want to exclude from search results—for example, *-windows* to exclude results that mention the Windows operating system.

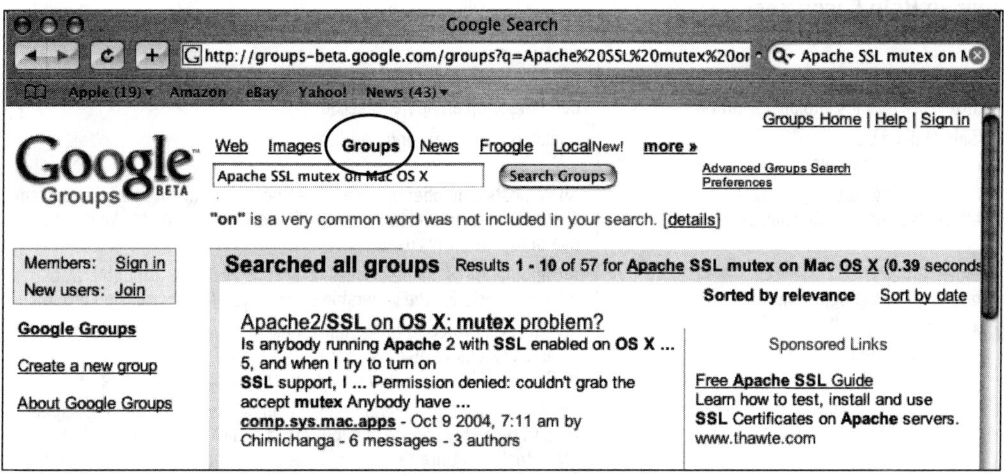

Figure 3.6 Search results from Google, limited to online discussion groups. Shown in the Safari browser.

Getting Help from Other People

Unix evolved organically, with features and commands being added piecemeal over the years. Even with all of the books written about Unix, person-to-person interaction remains the best way to become comfortable with using Unix, and it's often the only way to learn about new features or the more sophisticated uses of features you already know about.

Becoming connected to other Unix users is your best route to Unix mastery. **Table 3.2** shows several good places to start.

Table 3.2

Human Help Resources

Resource	What and Where
Apple Discussions (http://discussions.info.apple.com)	Apple's official Mac OS X discussion forums. No charge, but you need to set up an Apple ID account.
Apple Mailing Lists (http://lists.apple.com)	E-mail lists for users and developers.
Darwin mailing lists (http://developer.apple.com/darwin/mail.html)	Apple hosts a number of e-mail lists about the Darwin operating system. The Darwin-UserLevel and DarwinOS Users lists are most likely to be useful to a new Unix user.
Google Groups (http://groups.google.com)	A combination of online discussion groups available through a Web interface. Includes the venerable Usenet system of discussion groups.
Mac OS X Hints (www.macosxhints.com)	A Web site devoted to tricks, hints, help, and arcana about Mac OS X. Includes extensive discussion forums. Created and run as a labor of love by Rob Griffiths. If you find the site useful, consider donating $10.
The WELL (www.well.com, or from the command line `telnet well.com`)	The WELL has been a vibrant online community since 1985. Participants tend to be highly literate and interested in a wide range of subjects. The Macintosh and Unix discussion areas are extremely high quality and worth the $10/month fee all by themselves. Several of the people who helped with this book are WELL users.

4

Useful Unix Utilities

Unix's flexibility arises from its large collection of tools and the ease of combining different tools to accomplish tasks. This is a key part of the Unix culture of computing.

When we say "utility" here, we mean a command or other software that is commonly used in a variety of situations and is frequently combined with other commands to perform a useful task. For example, the `sort` command is usually used to sort the output of other commands. Unix utilities have been designed to be combined easily.

You've seen in Chapter 2, "Using the Command Line," how the output of a command can be piped into the input of another command. This allows you to create an almost infinite variety of command lines using different commands, options, and arguments.

Because there are so many commands, just knowing what is available is a big part of being able to use Unix effectively. This chapter is intended to introduce you to the more common and useful Unix utilities. Almost all the commands described in this book are found on every Unix system you are likely to use.

An important exception is the `mdfind` command, which enables you to do Spotlight searches from the command line. (In the appendix, "Darwin-only Unix Commands," you will find a list of Unix commands that are more or less unique to Mac OS X/Darwin.) One of the best features of Unix is that even though different versions exist and are constantly being updated, the skills you learn on one Unix system will help you on all Unix systems.

Mac OS X–Specific Utilities

Some utilities on your system are specific to Mac OS X/Darwin; the appendix describes almost all these commands. Here we will describe a few of them, the ones a beginner is most likely to use, and those that do not fit easily into one of the other categories in this chapter (see also the `textutil` and `mdfind` commands later in this chapter).

Throughout this book we mark commands that are specific to Darwin with the Darwin logo:

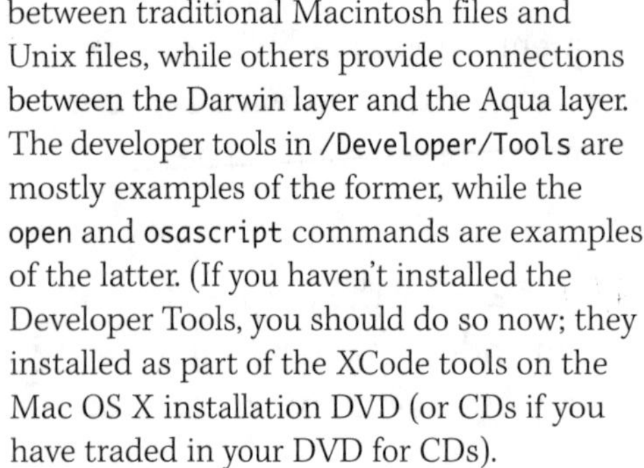

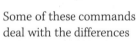

Some of these commands deal with the differences between traditional Macintosh files and Unix files, while others provide connections between the Darwin layer and the Aqua layer. The developer tools in `/Developer/Tools` are mostly examples of the former, while the `open` and `osascript` commands are examples of the latter. (If you haven't installed the Developer Tools, you should do so now; they installed as part of the XCode tools on the Mac OS X installation DVD (or CDs if you have traded in your DVD for CDs).

The following are the most important of the Mac OS X–specific commands you are likely to use in day-to-day work.

open—"Double-click" files and directories from the command line

The `open` command in Unix works the same way as a double-click on the Mac: It lets you open one or more files from the command line. And with the `-a` option you can achieve an effect similar to drag and drop by specifying an application to use when opening a file. See `man open` for the Unix manual entry and Chapter 2 of this book for an example of using `open`.

osascript—Run AppleScript from the command line

AppleScript is the Mac-specific scripting language that allows you to control Mac applications from scripts (see the "Learning AppleScript" sidebar). In Mac OS X you can run AppleScripts from the command line using the `osascript` command.

To get a list of the Open Scripting Architecture (OSA) languages installed on your system, use `osalang`. For documentation on AppleScript itself, see www.apple.com/applescript.

Need Help?

In Chapter 3, "Getting Help and Using the Unix Manual," we showed you how to use the `man` command to search for commands by keyword. Some of the commands in this chapter are covered in detail elsewhere in this book. In each case, we'll refer you to the appropriate chapter rather than repeat the information. In any event, it is a good idea to read the Unix manual entry for each of the commands described here. Even if you don't understand all of what you read, you will get a good sense of what is possible and will see references to other related commands (in the "See also" section of each `man` page). For more on using the Unix manual, refer back to Chapter 3.

To run an AppleScript from the command line:

◆ `osascript filename`

This executes the AppleScript contained in the file represented by *filename*.

For example, if you have a script called `playsong` that contains

```
tell application "iTunes"
open file
→ "MyDisk:Users:vanilla:Desktop:
→ slow_ride.mp3"
end tell
```

then the command line

```
osascript playsong
```

would run the AppleScript, launching iTunes and opening the slow_ride.mp3 file (**Figure 4.1**).

✔ Tip

- Notice that AppleScript expects files to be described using colons to separate the names of folders. This is quite different from Unix commands, which expect you to use the slash character (/), prevalent throughout this book.

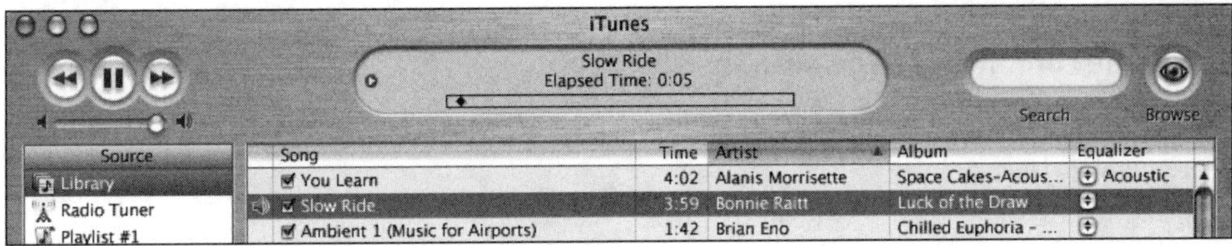

Figure 4.1 iTunes running a file opened from the command line.

Learning AppleScript

AppleScript is a complete language for controlling your Macintosh using scripts. Here are some resources for learning more about AppleScript:

◆ The main Apple Computer Web site for AppleScript is www.apple.com/applescript.

◆ Go to the AppleScript Documentation page (http://developer.apple.com/documentation/AppleScript/index.html).

pbcopy and pbpaste—Command-line interface to the pasteboard ("clipboard")

The `pbcopy` and `pbpaste` commands copy and paste data between `STDIN/STDOUT` and the Mac OS X clipboard. (See "About Standard Input and Output" in Chapter 2.)

This means you can copy something onto the clipboard from the command line and then paste it in an Aqua application, and you can copy something in an Aqua application and paste it into a command line. Currently `pbcopy` and `pbpaste` handle only plain text, Encapsulated PostScript (EPS), and rich text format (RTF).

To copy the contents of a file onto the clipboard:

- `pbcopy < filename`

  The contents of the file are now on the clipboard. If the file contents are not plain text, EPS, or RTF, then nothing is placed on the clipboard. If you now choose "paste" in an Aqua application, the contents of the file will appear.

To paste from the clipboard into a command line:

1. Copy something into the clipboard in an Aqua application.

   `pbpaste > filename`

2. The file now contains whatever you copied in step 1. (Only plain-text, RTF, and EPS content will be pasted.)

File Compression and Archiving

If you've been using a Mac, you have most likely seen files compressed using StuffIt, Aladdin Systems' popular file-compression utility.

In the Unix world there are a handful of commands, already part of the operating system, that are used for archiving and compressing files. It's likely that command-line software you download from the Internet will be compressed using these tools.

gzip

`gzip` is a program for compressing files. The `g` in `gzip` is from *GNU* (see the sidebar "What Is a GNU?"), and the `zip` is a reference to an earlier program called `zip`. `gzip` is not the same as `zip`, though. The older `zip` program not only compresses files, but it also combines multiple files and/or directories into a single file. The `gzip` program is more widely used than `zip` in the Unix world because `gzip` provides better compression (smaller files), and the Unix `tar` command is the commonly used program to combine multiple files into a single file. (The version of `tar` on Mac OS X can also compress its output with `gzip`. See `tar` below.)

To compress a file using gzip:

◆ `gzip` *`filename`*

`gzip` attempts to replace the files named in its arguments with compressed files, adding the .gz extension to the filename (`gzip` may not be able to replace a file if the file with the new name already exists and cannot be changed, in which case you get an error message). So if the original filename is Picture 1.tiff, the compressed filename will be Picture 1.tiff.gz.

Figure 4.2 shows an example of compressing all the .tiff files in the current directory. Notice how `gzip` did not change the modification times of the files, but it changed the group ownership (see "About Users and Groups" in Chapter 8, "Working with Permissions and Ownership," for more on group ownership of files).

```
localhost:~/Desktop vanilla$ ls -l *.tiff
-rw-r--r--    1 vanilla      wheel        186590 Apr 14 20:49 Picture 1.tiff
-rw-r--r--    1 vanilla      wheel        569553 Apr 15 10:41 Picture 2.tiff
-rw-r--r--    1 vanilla      vanilla      517795 Apr 15 10:51 Picture 3.tiff
localhost:~/Desktop vanilla$ gzip *.tiff
localhost:~/Desktop vanilla$ ls -l *.tiff.gz
-rw-r--r--    1 vanilla      vanilla      93648 Apr 14 20:49 Picture 1.tiff.gz
-rw-r--r--    1 vanilla      vanilla      170010 Apr 15 10:41 Picture 2.tiff.gz
-rw-r--r--    1 vanilla      vanilla      119743 Apr 15 10:51 Picture 3.tiff.gz
localhost:~/Desktop vanilla$
```

Figure 4.2 Compressing a set of files using gzip.

✔ Tips

- You can use gzip to compress the output of other commands. Just pipe the output of the other commands into gzip and redirect the output to a file. (See Chapter 2 to review pipelines.) For example:

  ```
  grep root /var/log/mail.log | gzip >
  → output.gz
  ```

  That command line runs the grep command to search for the string root in the file /var/log/mail.log. The output of grep (the lines containing root) is piped into the gzip program, and the output of gzip is redirected into the file output.gz.

- If you use gzip to compress a Mac file that has a resource fork, the file loses both its icon and its association with the application that created it, and thus it may become useless. To safely compress traditional Mac files, use StuffIt.

gunzip

Of course, once you have a compressed file, you'll want to know how to uncompress it.

To uncompress a gzipped file:

- `gunzip filename.gz`

  gunzip replaces the compressed file with the uncompressed version, removing the .gz filename extension. For example:

  ```
  gunzip "Picture 1.tiff.gz"
  ```

  replaces Picture 1.tiff.gz with Picture 1.tiff.

✔ Tips

- You can use gunzip in a pipeline. If you want the output of gunzip to go into a pipe, use the -c option:

  ```
  gunzip -c filename.gz | command
  ```

  When gunzip is used this way, it does not replace the compressed file.

- You can use the -t option to prevent removal of the compressed file.

What Is a GNU?

GNU is a recursive acronym (an acronym that refers to itself) that stands for *Gnu's Not Unix*. The GNU project is the domain of the Free Software Foundation, which coordinates a huge volunteer effort to create a complete Unix-like operating system that has the following four freedoms:

- Freedom to run the program, for any reason
- Freedom to study the internal workings of the program, and to alter them to suit you
- Freedom to redistribute copies so that you can help other people
- Freedom to make the program better, and make your changes available to the public, so that the others benefit from your efforts

There are hundreds of GNU software packages. There is even a GNU-Darwin project: the GNU-Darwin Distribution (http://gnu-darwin.sourceforge.net).

There's more information on the GNU project and the Free Software Foundation at GNU's Not Unix! (www.gnu.org).

tar

In many cases you will want to compress an entire directory (folder). Unlike the StuffIt program, `gzip` does not compress directories. To deal with this, you use another program from the command line, called `tar`, which creates a single file from a directory and all its contents (a *tar file*). `tar` was originally used only for making backups to tape systems (hence its name, for *tape archive*), but is now used far more frequently to combine entire folders into a single `tar` file prior to compression.

The version of `tar` included with Mac OS X can simultaneously combine a directory full of files into one file and compress the result with `gzip`.

To archive a directory using tar:

- `tar -cvzf` *`newfile`*`.tar` *`directoryname`*

  The `tar` command needs the `-c` option to tell it to create a new archive.

  The `v` option tells `tar` to "be verbose" and show you the names of all the files it is processing. You can leave it out if you like.

  The `z` option tells `tar` to compress the result using `gzip`. Leave it out if you don't want compressed output.

  The `f` option tells `tar` that you are specifying a filename for the new archive. Without the `f` option, `tar` assumes that you are trying to write to an attached tape drive. The `f` option must come last right before the new filename, *not* before the source filename.

  Figure 4.3 shows a listing of the contents of the `code` directory and then output from `tar` when you create a `tar` file with

  `tar -cvzf code.tar.gz code`

  `tar` does not replace the original directory.

  Notice that the output from `tar` in Figure 4.3 lists all the files and subdirectories that are included in the archive (a result of the `-v` for "verbose" option).

```
localhost:~/Desktop vanilla$ ls -l code
total 16
-rw-r--r--  1 matisse     staff      156 Nov  4 09:57 Changes
-rw-r--r--  1 matisse     staff      1444 Nov  4 09:57 README
drwxr-xr-x  4 matisse     staff      92 Apr 16 12:44 src
[localhost:~/Desktop] vanilla% tar -cvzf code.tar.gz code
code
code/Changes
code/README
code/src
code/src/syntax.c
code/src/syntax.h
localhost:~/Desktop vanilla$ ls -l code.tar.gz
-rw-r--r--  1 matisse     staff      3203 Apr 16 12:56 code.tar.gz
localhost:~/Desktop vanilla$
```

Figure 4.3 Listing the contents of a directory and then archiving it with `tar`.

✔ Tips

- tar has a plethora of options. See man tar for the complete list.
- If you want to use the tar command in a pipeline, use the special filename - (a hyphen). This is especially useful if you are working on a Unix system where the version of tar cannot compress its output. On those systems you might use

  `tar -cvf - code | gzip > code.tar.gz`

Of course, once you have a tar file, you want to be able to reverse the process and turn it back into a directory (this is called *untarring* or *unpacking*).

To unpack a tar archive:

- `tar -xvzf code.tar`

  This produces output as shown in **Figure 4.4**. The -x option tells tar that you want to extract files from a tar file. The v and f options have the same meanings as before: v means "be verbose," and f means "extract from a file, not a tape drive."

  Omit the z option if the archive is not compressed.

  Unlike gunzip, tar does not replace the archive when you extract files from it.

  If there is already a directory called "code" in the directory where you do this, then the extracted files will be placed inside it, possibly overwriting existing files.

```
localhost:~/Desktop vanilla$ tar -xvzf code.tar.gz
code
code/Changes
code/README
code/src
code/src/syntax.c
code/src/syntax.h
localhost:~/Desktop vanilla$
```

Figure 4.4 Extracting the contents of a compressed tar file. If the directory "code" already exists, the extracted files will be placed inside it, possibly overwriting existing files.

File and Text Processing

As you have probably noticed, the Unix command line is very file oriented. Almost everything you do involves at least one file, and often several. Here are a few of the most commonly used command-line tools for processing files. They function equally well in pipelines for processing text that comes directly from other commands without being saved to a file first.

wc—Counting lines, words, and bytes

The wc command displays a count of lines, words, and bytes contained in its input. Input to wc can be one or more files specified as arguments; wc also takes input from stdin (see Chapter 2 to review stdin).

To count the number of lines, words, and bytes in a file:

◆ wc *filename*

For example,

wc /etc/hostconfig

counts the contents of the file

/etc/hostconfig

showing 32 lines, 45 words, and 540 bytes (**Figure 4.5**). (The file /etc/hostconfig is one of the many system-configuration files in the /etc directory.)

```
localhost:~ vanilla$ wc /etc/hostconfig
         32    45    540 /etc/hostconfig
localhost:~ vanilla$
```

Figure 4.5 Counting the number of lines, words, and bytes in a file with wc. Your output may have different numbers.

✔ Tips

- The -l option displays only the number of lines, -w the number of words, and -c the number of bytes. The default behavior is the same as when using the -lwc options together. **Figure 4.6** shows a comparison of output from each option.
- If you give wc more than one file as an argument, it gives you a line for each and a summary line adding up the contents of all of them (**Figure 4.7**).

```
localhost:~ vanilla$ wc /etc/hostconfig
         32    45    540 /etc/hostconfig
localhost:~ vanilla$ wc -lwc /etc/hostconfig
         32    45    540 /etc/hostconfig
localhost:~ vanilla$ wc -l /etc/hostconfig
         32    /etc/hostconfig
localhost:~ vanilla$ wc -w /etc/hostconfig
         45    /etc/hostconfig
localhost:~ vanilla$ wc -c /etc/hostconfig
        540    /etc/hostconfig
localhost:~ vanilla$
```

Figure 4.6 Comparing the results of using different options with wc.

```
localhost:~ vanilla$ wc /etc/*.conf
      20    90    753  /etc/6to4.conf
      22    47    576  /etc/gdb.conf
      57   361   2544  /etc/inetd.conf
       0     0      0  /etc/kern_loader.conf
      46   199   1160  /etc/named.conf
       1     6     44  /etc/ntp.conf
       2     4     44  /etc/resolv.conf
      21   144    983  /etc/rtadvd.conf
       0    12     52  /etc/slpsa.conf
      50   273   1602  /etc/smb.conf
      18    66    724  /etc/syslog.conf
      12    29    238  /etc/xinetd.conf
     249  1231   8720  total
 localhost:~ vanilla$
```

Figure 4.7 Counting lines, words, and bytes in several files at once.

sort—Alphabetical or numerical sorting

The sort command takes its input either from files named in its arguments or from stdin and produces sorted output on stdout. The default sorting is in alphabetical order. You can also sort numerically.

For the following tasks, create two plain-text files (you may use the nano editor as described in Chapter 2). The first file should be called "data" and should contain three lines:

```
100 pears
2 apples
1 orange
```

The second file should be called "data2" and contain three lines:

```
1 dog
1 cat
10 fish
```

To sort alphabetically:

- `sort data data2`

  This produces the output shown in **Figure 4.8**. The results are correct, but something looks wrong. The problem is that 100 is alphabetically lower than 2. The next task shows you how to sort numerically.

To sort numerically:

- `sort -n data data2`

  This produces the output shown in **Figure 4.9** (n stands for *numeric*).

✔ Tips

- Add the -r option to *reverse* the sort order:
  `sort -nr data data2`
- You can, of course, use sort in a pipeline:
  `ls -s /usr/bin | sort -n`
- To save the output, use output redirection:
  `sort -n data > sorted`

```
localhost:~ vanilla$ sort data data2
    1 cat
    1 dog
    1 orange
    10 fish
    100 pears
    2 apples
localhost:~ vanilla$
```

Figure 4.8 Sorting alphabetically. Note how the line starting with 100 appears before the line starting with 2.

```
localhost:~ vanilla$ sort -n data data2
    1 cat
    1 dog
    1 orange
    2 apples
    10 fish
    100 pears
localhost:~ vanilla$
```

Figure 4.9 Sorting numerically with sort.

```
localhost:~ vanilla$ sort data | uniq
     bird
     cat
     dog
     mongoose
     snake
localhost:~ vanilla$
```

Figure 4.10 uniq deletes duplicates so that there is only one of each line.

```
localhost:~ vanilla$ sort data | uniq -c
     2 bird
     3 cat
     2 dog
     1 mongoose
     1 snake
localhost:~ vanilla$
```

Figure 4.11 Getting a count of each entry, using uniq.

```
localhost:~ vanilla$ sort data | uniq -c |
sort -rn
     3 cat
     2 dog
     2 bird
     1 snake
     1 mongoose
localhost:~ vanilla$
```

Figure 4.12 Sorting the counted entries using sort -rn.

- If you give the uniq command one argument, it will use that as a filename to take its input. If you give it two arguments, uniq assumes that the second one is the name of an output file, and it will copy the results of its output to the second file, *overwriting its contents*:

  `uniq infile outfile`

uniq—Only one of each line

The uniq command takes sorted text as input and produces output with duplicate lines removed.

To display only the unique lines:

1. Create a file called data containing the following lines:

   ```
   dog
   cat
   mongoose
   cat
   bird
   dog
   snake
   cat
   bird
   ```

2. `sort data | uniq`

   This produces the output shown in **Figure 4.10**.

3. But what if you want to know how many of each line there was? Adding the -c (*count*) option to uniq:

   `sort data | uniq -c`

   produces the output shown in **Figure 4.11**.

4. But now the output is no longer sorted numerically. So:

   `sort data | uniq -c | sort -rn`

   Pipe the output through sort again, with the rn option for *reverse numerical* sorting, and you get output as shown in **Figure 4.12**.

✔ Tips

- If you want to have uniq act on more than one file, use sort to act on them simultaneously:

  `sort file1 file2 file3 | uniq`

File and Text Processing

cut

The `cut` command is used to extract parts from each line of a file or pipeline of data and send the result to `stdout`. (see Chapter 2 for more about *standard output*, or `stdout`.) For example, the log files created by Web servers record several fields of data, including date/time of request, what the user requested, and how many bytes were sent to the browser. **Figure 4.13** shows a sample from `/var/log/ httpd/access_log` (this is your Web-server access log if you have enabled Personal Web Sharing by going to the Apple menu and choosing System Preferences and then Sharing).

Let's say you want to extract only the URLs that were requested in order to determine the most popular pages. `cut` allows you to specify what separates (or *delimits*) the fields in each line. The default separator is a tab character (commonly used in *tab-delimited* files). In our example below, you will instead use the space character. If you look at each line of the data in Figure 4.13, you'll see that the field you want is field number 7; that is, if you break a line into pieces, wherever a space occurs, the seventh piece has the URL in it (for example, in the first line, the seventh field contains `/~matisse/images/macosxlogo.gif`).

To print only one field from a file using spaces as a separator:

- `cut -d " " -f 7`
  `→ /var/log/httpd/access_log`

  This produces output like that shown in **Figure 4.14**.

  Notice how we used quotes around a space character; otherwise, the shell would not pass the space character to `cut` as our choice for the `-d` option. (See "About Spaces in the Command Line" in Chapter 2.)

```
66.47.69.205 - - [14/Mar/2002:14:53:48 -0800] "GET /~matisse/images/macosxlogo.gif HTTP/1.1" 200 2829
66.47.69.205 - - [14/Mar/2002:14:53:48 -0800] "GET /~matisse/images/apache_pb.gif HTTP/1.1" 200 2326
66.47.69.205 - - [14/Mar/2002:14:53:48 -0800] "GET /~matisse/images/web_share.gif HTTP/1.1" 200 13370
66.47.69.205 - - [14/Mar/2002:14:54:00 -0800] "GET /~matisse/cgi-bin/test HTTP/1.1" 200 25
66.47.69.205 - - [14/Mar/2002:14:54:29 -0800] "GET /~matisse/cgi-bin/test HTTP/1.1" 200 25
66.47.69.205 - - [14/Mar/2002:15:08:27 -0800] "GET /~matisse/upload.html HTTP/1.1" 200 397
66.47.69.205 - - [14/Mar/2002:15:33:48 -0800] "GET /~matisse/images/web_share.gif HTTP/1.1" 200 13370
66.47.69.205 - - [14/Mar/2002:15:33:50 -0800] "GET /~matisse/images/web_share.gif HTTP/1.1" 200 13370
```

Figure 4.13 Example of contents of a Web-server log from `/var/log/httpd/access_log`.

```
localhost:~ vanilla$ cut -d " " -f 7 /var/log/httpd/access_log
/~matisse/images/macosxlogo.gif
/~matisse/images/apache_pb.gif
/~matisse/images/web_share.gif
/~matisse/cgi-bin/test
/~matisse/cgi-bin/test
/~matisse/upload.html
/~matisse/images/web_share.gif
/~matisse/images/web_share.gif
localhost:~ vanilla$
```

Figure 4.14 Using cut to print one field from a file, using the space character as the field separator.

Each line in the original file represents one request made to your Web server, so each URL is from one request. You might already have realized that we could get a quick count of the requests by using the `sort` and `uniq` commands covered earlier in this chapter:

```
cut -d " " -f 7
→ /var/log/httpd/access_log | sort |
→ uniq -c | sort -nr
```

gives us output like that in **Figure 4.15**.

✔ Tips

- You can print more than one field:

  ```
  cut -d " " -f 1,7 /var/log/httpd/
  → access_log
  ```

  Figure 4.16 shows the result.

continues on next page

```
localhost:~ vanilla$ cut -d " " -f 7 /var/log/httpd/access_log | uniq -c | sort -nr
         3 /~matisse/images/web_share.gif
         2 /~matisse/cgi-bin/test
         1 /~matisse/upload.html
         1 /~matisse/images/macosxlogo.gif
         1 /~matisse/images/apache_pb.gif
localhost:~ vanilla$
```

Figure 4.15 Using cut to feed a pipeline.

```
localhost:~ vanilla$ cut -d " " -f 1,7 /var/log/httpd/access_log
66.47.69.205 /~matisse/images/macosxlogo.gif
66.47.69.205 /~matisse/images/apache_pb.gif
66.47.69.205 /~matisse/images/web_share.gif
66.47.69.205 /~matisse/cgi-bin/test
66.47.69.205 /~matisse/cgi-bin/test
66.47.69.205 /~matisse/upload.html
66.47.69.205 /~matisse/images/web_share.gif
66.47.69.205 /~matisse/images/web_share.gif
localhost:~ vanilla$
```

Figure 4.16 Printing two fields with cut.

- You specify the field separator in `cut` with the `-d` option (for *delimiter*). This allows you to specify a different field separator than the default (a tab character). If you use a separator of ", then `cut` will break the line into fields wherever a " appears. For example, in

  ```
  cut -d\" -f 2 /var/log/httpd/
  → access_log
  ```

  the \ is required before the " to remove its special meaning to the shell.

  Figure 4.17 shows the result. See how field 2 contains a chunk of information that is enclosed in quotes. Field 1 is everything before the first " in the line, field 2 is the text between the first and second ", and field 3 is everything after that second ". Try using different delimiters on different files and see what you get.

- The `cut` command has several useful options, including the ability to extract only specific character positions—for example, only characters 42–54. This is very useful when dealing with *fixed-length records*, like those produced by older databases, and the output of many Unix commands—for example, piping the output of `ls -l` through `cut -c42-54` will display only the date/time portion of each line. See `man cut` for more information.

```
localhost:~ vanilla$ cut -d\" -f 2 /var/log/httpd/access_log
GET /~matisse/images/macosxlogo.gif HTTP/1.1
GET /~matisse/images/apache_pb.gif HTTP/1.1
GET /~matisse/images/web_share.gif HTTP/1.1
GET /~matisse/cgi-bin/test HTTP/1.1
GET /~matisse/cgi-bin/test HTTP/1.1
GET /~matisse/upload.html HTTP/1.1
GET /~matisse/images/web_share.gif HTTP/1.1
GET /~matisse/images/web_share.gif HTTP/1.1
localhost:~ vanilla$
```

Figure 4.17 Using a different field separator with cut.

awk

The awk program, a multifeatured text-processing tool, gets its name from the initials of its three inventors (Aho, Kernighan, and Weinberger; Kernighan is Brian Kernighan, coinventor of the C programming language).

The basic idea behind awk is that it looks at each line of an input file and performs some action on each line. awk has its own language for defining the actions, and the resulting scripts can be quite complex. See man awk.

A common use of awk is to send to stdout only certain fields from a file or pipeline of data, just like with the simpler cut command described above. In the case of awk the default separator is *whitespace*. Whitespace is any blank space in a line, including any run of the space character and/or tabs. This is different from what we saw above with cut, where we set the delimiter to a single space character—by default, awk treats any number of spaces or tabs as a delimiter, instead of treating each single space as a delimiter. Also awk ignores whitespace at the very beginning of a line, and this fact can make awk a better choice than cut in some cases.

In the next task, we first show how awk does the same job as cut in extracting one field from a file. In the following task we show you a comparison between how awk and cut handle whitespace.

More About sed and awk

The standard reference for these two venerable Unix utilities is *sed & awk*, by Dale Dougherty and Arnold Robbins (O'Reilly; www.oreilly.com/catalog/sed2).

To use cut to print only one field from a file:

- ```
  awk '{print $7}'
  ➝ /var/log/httpd/access_log
  ```

  This produces the same output that cut produced in Figure 4.14. The output should look the same as the example using cut from the previous section in this chapter; likewise,

  ```
  awk '{print $7}' /var/log/httpd/
  ➝ access_log | sort | uniq -c |
  ➝ sort -nr
  ```

  gives us the same output as shown for cut in Figure 4.15.

✔ Tips

- You can print more than one field:

  ```
  awk '{print $1,$7}'
  ➝ /var/log/httpd/access_log
  ```

  The output should be the same as in Figure 4.16.

- You can vary the field separator in awk with the -F option (for *field*). This allows you to specify a different field separator than the default (whitespace). If you use a separator of ", then awk will break the line into fields wherever a " appears. For example, in

  ```
  awk -F\" '{print $2}'
  ➝ /var/log/httpd/access_log
  ```

  the \ is required before the " to remove its special meaning to the shell.
  ```

To compare how cut and awk process whitespace:

1. `ls -sk /usr/bin | less`

   This shows the sizes (in kilobytes) of all the files in /usr/bin—refer to **Figure 4.18**. Notice how the lines actually begin with two or more space characters.

   The output of ls is piped through the less command. See "Viewing the Contents of Text Files" in Chapter 5, "Using Files and Directories." You can proceed to the next screenful of output by pressing Spacebar, or return to the shell prompt by pressing Spacebar.

2. `ls -sk /usr/bin | awk '{print $1}'`

   This pipes the output of the ls command through awk, printing only the first field, which in this case consists of the sizes (in kilobytes) of the files in /usr/bin.

3. `ls -sk /usr/bin | cut -d " " -f 1`

   This pipes the output from ls through cut, with the delimiter set to a single space character. The result is that we get no numbers at all in the output, because all the lines from ls begin with a space, and so cut considers the first field to be empty—there is nothing before the first occurrence of the delimiter on each line. Figure 4.18 shows the results of all three command lines above.

```
localhost:~ vanilla$ ls -sk /usr/bin | less

          104 a2p
          156 acid
           16 aclocal
           16 aclocal-1.6
           60 addftinfo
          164 afmtodit
. . . (output abbreviated for space) . . .
localhost:~ vanilla$ ls -sk /usr/bin | awk '{print $1}'
104
156
 16
 16
 60
164
. . . (output abbreviated)
localhost:~ vanilla$ ls -sk /usr/bin | cut -d " " -f 1


(many blank lines)

localhost:~ vanilla$
```

Figure 4.18 Comparing how awk and cut deal with whitespace.

sed

sed is a *stream editor*—that is, a tool for editing streams of data, whether in a file or the output of some other command.

Create a file called `sedtest`, using the text in **Figure 4.19**. You can use `sed` to make it rhyme by changing all the occurrences of *love* to *amore*.

To convert all occurrences of *love* to *amore*:

- `sed "/love/s//amore//" sedtest`

  produces output as shown in **Figure 4.20**.

✔ Tip

- If you are using `sed` to change a file and then redirect its output to a new file, check the new file to make sure it's correct, and then replace the old file with the new file.

textutil

The `textutil` command appears only in Mac OS X/Darwin and allows you to easily convert files from one format to another. Introduced in Mac OS X 10.4, `textutil` can convert to and from plain text, RTF, RTFD, HTML, Microsoft Word, Microsoft Word XML (wordml), and webarchive.

One especially cool `textutil` feature is that it creates HTML files converted from Word documents that are remarkably "clean" and meet strict HTML 4.01 specifications, way better than HTML created by Word's Save As feature. Another great thing about `textutil` is that you can create Microsoft Word documents from other formats without having Word installed on your machine. (Note that the Mac OS X application TextEdit can read Word files.) However, `textutil` is not perfect. If you convert from format X to Y to Z and back to X, the final result will be pretty close to the original, but not exactly the same.

```
There's just no better foray then the one they call love.
When the moon hits your eye, like a big pizza pie, that's love.
When an eel grabs your hand, and won't let go, that's love.
```

Figure 4.19 A sample data file. But it doesn't rhyme very well.

```
localhost:~ vanilla$ sed "/love/s//amore/" sedtest
There's just no better foray then the one they call amore.
When the moon hits your eye, like a big pizza pie, that's amore.
When an eel grabs your hand, and won't let go, that's amore.
localhost:~ vanilla$
```

Figure 4.20 Using sed to make the data rhyme. (Given the prevalence of puns in Unix, it seems only natural that we should add a few.)

To convert a file format using textutil:

- `textutil -convert format oldfile`

  Where *format* is one of `txt`, `html`, `rtf`, `rtfd`, `doc`, `wordml`, or `webarchive`. The command produces a new file whose name is based on the new format—for example, file.html—if converted to HTML. The new file is placed in the same directory as the old file (which may be overridden with the `-output` option). The old file must be in one of the above formats. Here's an example of converting a file to Microsoft Word format:

  ```
  textutil -convert doc  resume.html
  ```

  That creates a file called resume.doc in your current directory (notice how the .doc extension was added).

✔ Tips

- As always, read the `man` page for the full list of available options, such as combining multiple files into a single converted file using the `-cat` (*concatenate*) option in place of the `-convert` option. You can also specify the output filename or extension with other options. For example,

  ```
  textutil -cat html -output all.html
  → *.doc
  ```

  would create a file called `all.html` containing the content from the .doc files in the current directory.

- Some options only work if the command is run from a shell that has access to the Aqua user interface (technically to a program called Window Server). Basically, that means the command is run from a shell inside the Terminal application, rather than a shell that you logged in to using `ssh` or `telnet` (as described in Chapter 10, "Connecting over the Internet").

- The Mac OS X Spotlight system and the `mdfind` command (described later in this chapter) search metadata that can be set or viewed with `textutil`.

- This section deals with `textutil(1)`, the `textutil` command covered in section 1 of the Unix manual, not `textutil(n)`, the one covered in section n. See Chapter 3 for more on `textutil (n)`.

Perl

Perl is a programming language equally suited to small tasks and large, complex programs. (See www.perl.org.)

In this chapter, we are showing Perl in its role as a text-processing utility—a general-purpose tool in the same category as `awk`, `cut`, and `sed`.

Following is an example of creating a very small utility program written in the Perl language that provides a feature not available from any existing command.

Earlier in this chapter, you learned how to sort data alphabetically or numerically, but what if you simply want to look at a file backward—seeing the last lines in the file first? This might come up if you are looking at a file consisting of date/time entries and you want to see the latest ones first.

Although Unix provides numerous tools for situations like this, there are still times when you want to do something beyond what the current tools provide. Users of other operating systems look to a catalog of software to see if they can buy a tool that will serve the purpose, or, failing that, wait for someone else to create a new tool. Unix users build their own. And often Unix users choose Perl as the programming language in which to build their new tools.

Perl excels at text processing and allows you to do some things very easily that would be difficult or impossible using other tools.

Perl is a complete programming language used for everything from simple utility scripts to very large and complex programs containing tens of thousands of lines of code. Teaching Perl is beyond the scope of this book, but we do want to give you some sense of how useful it is and pique your interest in learning more (see the sidebar "Resources for Learning Perl"). And we cover the basics of Unix shell scripts in Chapter 9, "Creating and Using Scripts."

Our example here is a short script that reverses the order of its input—the last line of input comes out first, and the first line comes out last, regardless of alphabetical or numerical sort order.

The steps are similar to the ones in Chapter 2, in the section "Creating a Simple Unix Shell Script":

```
#!/usr/bin/perl
# script to reverse input
@input = <>;
while ( @input) {
    print pop(@input);
}
```

To create a script that will reverse its input:

1. `nano ~/bin/reverse`

   This opens the `nano` editor and creates the script (called `reverse`) in the `bin` directory of your home directory, as we did in Chapter 2 with the system-status script. (Make sure you have added `~/bin` to your `PATH` as described in Chapter 2 in "Creating a Simple Unix Shell Script.")

   The following lines are entered into the `nano` editor:

2. `#!/usr/bin/perl`

   This must be the first line. It tells Unix to use Perl when running this script.

3. `# script to reverse input, by JME → 2005-04-21`

   This line is just a comment, to remind us what the script does. Include your initial or e-mail address and the date. Comments are good. We love comments.

continues on next page

Resources for Learning Perl

- If you have never heard of Perl, a good place to start is the Perl Directory About Perl (www.perl.org/press/fast_facts.html).
- If you are looking for online documentation, mailing lists, and other support resources, then go to the Perl Directory Online Documentation (www.perl.org/support/online_support.html).
- You can start right on your Mac with `man perl`.
- A primary resource for beginning Perl programmers is *Learning Perl, 3rd Edition*, by Randal L. Schwartz and Tom Phoenix (O'Reilly; www.oreilly.com/catalog/lperl3).
- The definitive programmer's guide is *Programming Perl, 3rd Edition*, by Larry Wall, Tom Christiansen, and Jon Orwant (O'Reilly; www.oreilly.com/catalog/pperl3).
- If you are looking to start learning how to use Perl for CGI programming, then check out *Perl and CGI for the World Wide Web: Visual QuickStart Guide, 2nd Edition*, by Elizabeth Castro (Peachpit Press; www.peachpit.com/title/0201735687).

4. `@input = <>;`

   This line causes all input to go into a variable called `@input`. Each line of input is stored as a separate item in the variable. (Think of this variable as a stack of plates—each time we add an item, we are adding a plate to the stack. In Perl, the @ indicates a list of things, or "stack of plates," which is also called an *array*.)

5. `while ( @input ) {`

   This is the start of a loop that will continue as long as there is anything left in the `@input` variable.

6. `print pop( @input );`

   This line removes the most recently added item (`pop`) from the `@input` array and sends it to `stdout` (the `print` function). (The `pop` function "pops" the last "plate" off the "stack.")

7. `}`

   This ends the loop. While the script is running, Perl checks here to see if there is anything still in `@input`, and if there is, it executes the `print pop(@input);` line again; otherwise, Perl proceeds to the next line.

   There isn't a next line in this case, so the script stops running when `@input` is empty.

8. You can stop entering text, and exit from the `nano` editor, by pressing Control X.

9. `nano` will ask you if you want to save the changes; you say yes by pressing y.

10. `nano` asks you to confirm the name you are using to save the file. You confirm by pressing Return.

    You'll be back at the shell prompt.

11. `chmod 755 ~/bin/reverse`

    That makes the script executable so that you can run it later (remember that `chmod` means *change mode*; the `755` refers to the mode that sets permissions; see Chapter 8 for more details).

    You're done.

Congratulations—you've created a new Unix command by writing a Perl script.

To display input backward using reverse:

◆ `reverse` *`filename`*

  This sends the contents of the file *filename* to `stdout`, last line first. **Figure 4.21** shows a comparison between using `cat` and `reverse` on the same file.

  You can use multiple files—for example,

  `reverse file1 file2 file3`

  You can use `reverse` in a pipeline:

  `ls -l | reverse`

```
localhost:~ vanilla$ cat poetry.txt
And the coming wind did roar more loud,
And the sails did sigh like sedge;
And the rain poured down from one black cloud;
The Moon was at its edge.
localhost:~ vanilla$ reverse poetry.txt
The Moon was at its edge.
And the rain poured down from one black cloud;
And the sails did sigh like sedge;
And the coming wind did roar more loud,
localhost:~ vanilla$
```

Figure 4.21 Comparing the output of cat and reverse.

Searching for Text Inside Files

It is extremely common when using Unix to want to search for specific words or strings of characters inside text files or to search the long output of some command. The main Unix command for this is `grep`.

Using grep

To search for a string in a text file:

- `grep string file`

  For example,

  `grep memory /etc/rc`

  finds all the lines in the file `/etc/rc` that contain the string `memory` (in this case there was only one line, so only one line was returned) (**Figure 4.22**).

```
localhost:~ vanilla$ grep memory /etc/rc
echo "Starting virtual memory"
localhost:~ vanilla$
```

Figure 4.22 Using grep to find the string memory in a file.

To make the search case insensitive:

- Use the `-i` option. For example,

  `grep -i apple /etc/services`

  Figure 4.23 shows part of the result. Note how both `apple` and `Apple` are found.

✔ Tips

- To see the output one screenful at a time, pipe the output of `grep` through the `less` pager:

  `grep -i apple /etc/services | less`

- You can use Control C to interrupt the command and get back to the prompt.

Not All greps Are the Same

We cover the version of `grep` that comes with Darwin/Mac OS X. Different flavors of Unix come with different versions of the `grep` family (`grep`, `egrep`, `fgrep`, `agrep`), so the exact behavior of each command will vary slightly depending on the version installed on your system. The best way to see the differences is to read the Unix `man` pages for each command.

```
localhost:~ vanilla$ grep -i apple /etc/services
. . .
asip-webadmin   311/udp     # AppleShare IP WebAdmin
asip-webadmin   311/tcp     # AppleShare IP WebAdmin
#                           Ann Huang <annhuang@apple.com>
aurp            387/udp     # Appletalk Update-Based Routing Pro.
Aurp            387/tcp     # Appletalk Update-Based Routing Pro.
Appleqtc        458/udp     # apple quick time
Appleqtc        458/tcp     # apple quick time
#                           <murali_ranganathan@quickmail.apple.com>
appleqtcsrvr    545/udp     # appleqtcsrvr
appleqtcsrvr    545/tcp     # appleqtcsrvr
. . .
localhost:~ vanilla$
```

Figure 4.23 Performing a case-insensitive search with grep. Your output depends on your machine's configuration. (Partial output shown.)

To search for a string in multiple files:

- Simply add more files to the argument list, perhaps by using wildcards. For example,

  `grep -i network *`

  As we discussed in Chapter 2, the `*` (asterisk) is a special character expanded by the shell to be a list of many files.

  This is probably the most common use of `grep`—to find all the occurrences of a string throughout multiple files. When searching multiple files, `grep` adds the filename at the beginning of each line of output so that you know which file each line came from:

  `grep " boot" /etc/rc*`

  gives output as shown in **Figure 4.24**. Notice the use of quotes to make the search string include a space character (searches for `" boot"` instead of just `boot`); try removing the quotes to see the difference.

✔ Tip

- If you give an argument to `grep` that is a directory (instead of a regular file), `grep` gives you an error message saying that the file "is a directory." You can tell `grep` to skip directories by adding the `-d skip` option—for example,

  `grep -d skip NETWORK */*`

```
localhost:~ vanilla$ grep " boot" /etc/rc*
/etc/rc:     echo "CD-ROM boot procedure complete"
/etc/rc:     echo "Configuring kernel extensions for safe boot"
/etc/rc.netboot:# Prevent inadvertent problems caused by interrupting the shell during boot.
localhost:~ vanilla$
```

Figure 4.24 Using grep to search multiple files for a string that includes a space.

Where grep Gets Its Name

`grep` gets its name from *g/RE/p*, which is a representation of the commands in the old Unix editor `ed` to "globally search for a *reg*ular *e*xpression and *p*rint."

Regular expressions make up a complex and powerful system for matching patterns and are available in many Unix programs. We'll cover a small part of regular expressions in this chapter.

The `grep` program is the main Unix command for searching text files or a stream of text (such as the output of another program). The output of `grep` is every line that contains the search string. The default is for searches to be case sensitive.

To recursively search all the files in a directory:

◆ Use the -r option. For example,

```
grep -ri network
→ /System/Library/StartupItems
```

performs a case-insensitive search (note the -i option) of all the files inside /System/Library/StartupItems and all its subdirectories.

✔ Tip

■ Using the -r option to grep can cause the command to take a long time to complete, so you might want to redirect the output to a file and put the job in the background (review "Redirecting stdout" and "Running a Command in the Background" in Chapter 2):

```
grep -ri network
→ /System/Library/StartupItems >
→ found.txt &
```

To find the lines that do not match:

◆ Use the -v option.

```
grep -v tcp /etc/services
```

finds all the lines in the directory /etc/services that do not contain the string tcp.

To search the output of another command:

◆ Pipe the output of the other command through grep.

```
last | grep reboot
```

shows all the reboots this month.

(The last command shows a history of logins to your machine, as well as crashes and reboots. Type man last.)

✔ Tip

■ Use multiple greps in the pipeline to narrow your request.

```
last | grep reboot | grep "Feb 16"
```

finds all the reboots on February 16. See how the first grep filters the output of the last command, and the second grep filters the output further, narrowing down the result.

The grep and egrep (e for *extended*) programs have a huge number of options. **Table 4.1** lists some of the more common ones. See the Unix manual for more (type man grep).

Table 4.1

Options for grep and egrep

Option	Meaning
-i	Ignore case.
-v	Show only lines that do not match.
-n	Add line numbers.
-l	Show only the names of files in which matches were found.
-L	Show only the names of files without a match.*
-r	Recursively search directories.*
-d skip	Skip arguments that are directories.*

* These options are not as common as the others, but Mac OS X does have them.

Using patterns in your search

You will often want to search for something more complicated than a literal string of characters. You might want to search only for lines that begin with a certain string, or for lines that contain a range of dates, such as `Feb 15` or `Feb 16`.

The `egrep` command supports an extremely powerful (and complex) pattern-matching system called *regular expressions*. The `re` in `egrep` stands for *regular expression*. (The `grep` command also supports a small number of regular expressions. To avoid switching back and forth, we will stick with `egrep` here.)

Regular expressions are used in a large number of situations in Unix, not only with the `grep` and `egrep` commands. For example, the Unix programs `sed`, `awk`, and `vi` all use regular expressions, as do the C, Perl, Tcl, Python, and Java programming languages. The basic syntax of regular expressions is the same or very similar in a variety of situations, so once you learn how to use them in one area, you have a head start on using them in another.

Regular expressions are built up like mathematical formulas (see the sidebar "Learning More About Regular Expressions"). You can do a lot with the few rules we'll show you here.

An important concept to grasp in using regular expressions is that when you search for "hello," you are really searching for a pattern consisting of six *atoms* (*h, e, l, l,* and *o*). In regular expressions, an atom is a part of the overall expression that matches one character. The most common kind of atom is simply a literal character, so the atom *h* matches the letter *h*. But atoms don't stop there. For example, the atom *[a-d]* matches one letter from the range *a, b, c,* or *d*. (The *[and]* are used to define a set of characters.) So when you see the word *atom* used in the examples below, keep in mind that an atom can be as simple as one character, or it can be a more complex notation that matches one character from a list of possibilities.

Regular expressions have a few major rules, which are demonstrated in the examples below.

Also, note that you always enclose the pattern inside single quotes; this is to prevent the shell from misinterpreting any of the characters used in *regexes* (as they're traditionally called) that have special meaning to the shell: [] {} . * .

Compare with Aqua

Mac OS X provides a nice graphical interface for finding strings of text in files on your Mac, and in some ways it can do a better job than `grep`. Spotlight (introduced in Mac OS X 10.4) is a powerful and elegantly designed graphical interface for searching your hard disk. Spotlight searches the names and contents of files and presents the results grouped by types of files. It also builds indexes of files, which speeds up searching. And, of course, it is mostly a point-and-click interface.

In practice, `grep` is often easier to use than Spotlight (once you get used to the command line); for example, it is rather hard in Spotlight to focus your search on a few specific files, whereas with `grep` you can supply any arbitrary list of files as arguments on the command line.

To find lines starting with a specific string of characters:

- Put a ^ at the beginning of the string;

  `grep ^# ~/bin/reverse`

  finds only lines beginning with #, and `grep -v ^# script.pl` would find all lines *not* beginning with #. **Figure 4.25** shows the output from both command lines.

  The ^ character in a regex is called an *anchor* because it anchors the search string to the start of the line.

To find lines ending with a string:

- Putting a $ at the end of the string

  `grep today$ filename`

  finds only lines ending with `today`.

  The $ anchors the search string to the end of the line.

✔ Tip

- If you anchor a pattern to both the start and the end of line—for example, `^word$`—then only lines that exactly match will be found. That is, only lines that consist solely of the pattern, with nothing before or after.

```
localhost:~ vanilla$ cat ~/bin/reverse
#!/usr/bin/perl
# reverse cat script
#
@file = <>;
while ( @file ) {
   print pop(@file);
}

localhost:~ vanilla$ grep ^# ~/bin/reverse
#!/usr/bin/perl
# reverse cat script
#
localhost:~ vanilla$ grep -v ^# ~/bin/reverse
@file = <>;
while ( @file ) {
   print pop(@file);
}

localhost:~ vanilla$
```

Figure 4.25 Using a pattern that matches the character at the start of a line.

Testing regular expressions

Regular expressions can get quite complex, and learning how to use them takes practice. Luckily there is an easy way to test them to see if they match what you think they will match.

If you use one of the `grep` commands (`grep` or `egrep`) with a pattern but without giving it a filename or input from a pipe, then it waits for you to type input and repeats back to you any lines that match.

In most of our examples we use the `egrep` command because it supports *extended* regular expression. In cases where we don't need extended regexes, we will use plain old `grep`.

To test a regular expression:

1. `egrep 'regular expression'`

   For example:

   `egrep '^[hH]ello'`

   (Using both upper- and lowercase letters means you're looking for both instances.)

   Notice you are not giving `egrep` a file to search. When you press Return, you get a blank line. `egrep` is waiting for you to type in a line of text, which it will check against the pattern. **Figure 4.26** shows the next few steps in this task with the text you type highlighted (in **bold**) and the Mac's response in `plain` text.
2. Type in a line of text that you think should (or should not) match the pattern, and press Return. For example:

   `Hello, nice to meet you.`

   If the shell displays (repeats back to you) the line you typed, then the expression matched (the example above should match). Otherwise, it did not match.
3. Type in another line of text to check:

   `Say, Hello world`

   This does not match the pattern in step 1 because the line does not match the ^ anchor ("look at the beginning of the line").
4. To exit from the test, press Control C.

Learning More About Regular Expressions

Regular expressions are used not only with the `grep` program but also with multiple Unix programs and programming languages.

Here are a few places to learn more about *regexes* (as they are known to Unix experts):

- Learning to Use Regular Expressions (http://gnosis.cx/publish/programming/regular_expressions.html).

  A nice online tutorial, though it assumes you are working with regular expressions in one of the many programming languages that use them.
- Electronic Text Center: Using Regular Expressions (http://etext.lib.virginia.edu/helpsheets/regex.html).

  An introduction to regular expressions that describes the history and main concepts, and gives examples of their use.
- *Mastering Regular Expressions: Powerful Techniques for Perl and Other Tools*, by Jeffrey E. F. Friedl (O'Reilly, 1997; www.oreilly.com/catalog/regex).

  Considered by many to be the standard in-depth work on regular expressions.

```
localhost:~ vanilla$ egrep '^[hH]ello'
Hello, nice to meet you.
Hello, nice to meet you.
Say, Hello world
^C
localhost:~ vanilla$
```

Figure 4.26 Testing a regular expression.

```
localhost:~ vanilla$ egrep '[FNW]orm A-100'
Worm A-100 is a very virulent worm.
Worm A-100 is a very virulent worm.
Norm A-100 isn't really normal.
Norm A-100 isn't really normal.
Form A-100 must be filled out in pink ink.
Form A-100 must be filled out in pink ink.
^C
localhost:~ vanilla$
```

Figure 4.27 Using an atom that matches any character in a list.

```
localhost:~ vanilla$ egrep '[^FNW]orm A-100'
Worm A-100 no longer matches.
Either does Norm A-100.
Nor even Form A-100.
But form A-100 does because of the lowercase f.
But form A-100 does because of the lowercase f.
See you in Dorm A-100
See you in Dorm A-100
how about this?
^C
localhost:~ vanilla$ /Applications (Mac OS
9)/FileMaker Pro 5 Folder/FileMaker Pro
```

Figure 4.28 Using an atom that matches any character not in the list.

✔ Tips

- In each of the tasks below, try testing the regular expression with several different lines of input to see how each one behaves. Try to predict what will and will not match.
- If you make a mistake while typing a test expression, you may notice that the D key doesn't work the way you expect. Instead, press Control U, which will erase the whole line. This is a very useful trick that works in many command-line situations.

To find lines containing a string in which one character can vary:

◆ Use square brackets to create an atom from a list of characters. For example:

`egrep '[FNW]orm A-100'`

The atom `[FNW]` means "one character that matches any of the three atoms `F`, `N`, or `W`." **Figure 4.27** shows examples of testing this pattern with three different matching lines.

To create an atom that is anything *not* in a list:

◆ Use the `^` character as the first character in the list. For example:

`egrep '[^FNW]orm A-100'`

Figure 4.28 shows examples of testing this pattern (again, you type the text that's in bold). Matching lines will *not* contain any of the following:

`Form A-100`

`Norm A-100`

`Worm A-100`

This line will match:

`Dorm A-100`

✔ Tips

- Notice how the last example is different from the -v option (described earlier). The -v option finds all lines that do not match the whole pattern. The example here finds lines that contain `'orm A-100'` but only if the first letter before `'orm'` is *not* F, N or W.
- Notice that the use of ^ here is different from using ^ as the start-of-line anchor. The ^ behaves differently when it is the first character in a square-bracket list.

To create an atom from a range of numbers:

- Use `egrep` and put square brackets around the range:

```
egrep 'Feb 1[5-9]' mail.log
```

The `[5-9]` means "5, 6, 7, 8, or 9" in regular-expression language.

✔ Tip

- You can use multiple lists, such as `[2-3][0-5]` (that means "20-35").

To create an atom from a range of letters:

- Use `egrep` and the square brackets, and `a-z` for lowercase, `A-Z` for uppercase. For example:

```
egrep 'Appendix [B-D]' book.txt
```

✔ Tip

- You can make the range case insensitive by using lowercase and uppercase ranges in the atom:

```
egrep 'Appendix [B-Db-d]' book.txt
```

To use a wildcard character:

- Use the `.` character to mean "any single character." For example:

```
egrep '.oy'
```

behaves as shown in **Figure 4.29**. Notice that the line that begins with `oy` doesn't match, because there is no character before the `oy`.

To find lines in which an atom is repeated zero or more times:

- Use the `*` quantifier. (That's an asterisk on your keyboard, but it's generally referred to as a *star* in Unix speak.) For example,

```
grep 'Form A-10*'
```

behaves as shown in **Figure 4.30**.

In this case the atom is the `0.` The `*` quantifier means "zero or more of the preceding atom." Notice how it found the line in which `0` did not appear at all.

✔ Tip

- Be careful when using the `*` character. If an argument contains a `*` and you don't want the shell to expand it to a list of filenames (see "Wildcards" in Chapter 2), then you must make sure that any use of `*` on the command line is enclosed in quotes or that you escape the `*` by preceding it with a backslash; for example:

```
grep fo\*bar *.txt
```

In that case the shell would expand the second `*` to match all the filenames that end in .txt, but the shell would pass the string `fo*bar` to `grep` as an argument without expanding the `*`.

```
localhost:~ vanilla$ egrep '.oy'
toy should match
toy should match
so should boy
so should boy
even coy
even coy
but not this line
oy this one doesn't match either!
but oy, this one does.
but oy, this one does.
^C
localhost:~ vanilla$
```

Figure 4.29 Using a . (period) to match any single character.

```
localhost:~ vanilla$ grep 'Form A-10*'
Form A-100
Form A-100
Form A-10
Form A-10
Form A-1
Form A-1
^C
localhost:~ vanilla$
```

Figure 4.30 Using * to match zero or more of an atom.

More rules and tools for building regex atoms

The regex examples shown above allow you to perform some fairly sophisticated matching, but there are a lot more ways to create atoms and patterns. **Table 4.2** describes several additional tools you will find useful in constructing more complex patterns. All the tools and rules in Table 4.2 require egrep. The real key is to experiment using the testing approach described above.

Table 4.2

Rules and Tools for Regex Atoms

Rule	Tool/Meaning
Match 1 or more	Use the + quantifier, "one or more of the preceding atom."
Match 0 or 1	Use the ? quantifier, "zero or one of the preceding atom."
Exact number	Put the number in braces; [a-c]{3} means "any character from the list a-c repeated exactly three times."
Alternatives	Put each alternative in parentheses, and separate them with the pipe character; '(Fox)|(Hound)' means "match lines containing either Fox or Hound."
Match special characters	If you want to match characters that have special meanings in a regex such as [or ^, then escape (that is, remove any special meaning from) them with a \; for example, \[will match a literal [. Inside a square-bracket list, you do not need to escape anything.
Match ^ inside a list	To include the ^ character in a square-bracket list, put it anywhere except first in the list; for example, [a-c^] matches a, b, c, or ^.

Searching for Files

While grep and egrep are great for searching inside files, they don't look at the names of files or other information about the files, such as size or modification date. For that, Mac OS X provides other tools.

Spotlight and mdfind

In version 10.4 of Mac OS X, a powerful new search feature called Spotlight was added.

Spotlight searches two areas of the operating system that are always up-to-date. Every time a file is saved, Mac OS X now updates the *metadata store* and the *content index*. The metadata store and content index are only updated if the file being saved is recognized by one of the metadata importers installed on your machine. Mac OS X comes with numerous metadata importers that recognize files created with all the common Apple applications, such as iTunes, iChat, iCal, Pages, and Keynote, as well as most of the common file formats used by Microsoft Office documents, image formats, PDF files, and so on. Apple strongly encourages developers of applications that use new file formats to create metadata importers. (For more on Spotlight, check out the Apple Web site at http://developer.apple.com/macosx/spotlight.html).

The mdfind command allows you to search the same data sources that Spotlight uses, but from the command line. However, mdfind will only return the names of files that the user has permission to see. (See Chapter 8 for more on Unix permissions.)

The metadata stored by Mac OS X includes obvious things like the filename, date and time it was last changed, and so forth, but it can also include a large number of other metadata *attributes*, such as keywords,copyright information, and number of pages. **Table 4.3** is a partial list of metadata attributes. Apple's list of metadata attributes is available at http://developer.apple.com/documentation/Carbon/Reference/MetadataAttributesRef/. The mdls command can be used to display the metadata attributes for a file.

The mdfind and mdls commands are available only in Mac OS X/Darwin.

Table 4.3

Some Metadata Attributes

Attributes in *italics* may be set from the command line on files converted to another format using the `textutil` command. For a longer list of attributes, see http://developer.apple.com/documentation/Carbon/Reference/MetadataAttributesRef/.

File-System Metadata Attribute Keys

Metadata attribute keys describe the file-system attributes for a file. These attributes are available for files on any mounted volume.

Attributes Common to Many File Types	
ATTRIBUTE	DESCRIPTION
kMDItemFSCreationDate	The date when the contents of the file were created. This is different from the file-creation date. It can be used to store information on when the file contents were first created or first modified.
kMDItemAuthors	The author, or authors, of the contents of the file. Can be set with `textutil` using the `-author` option.
kMDItemContentModificationDate	Date and time when the content of this item was modified.
kMDItemCreator	Application used to create the document content (for example, *Pages* or *Keynote*).
kMDItemKeywords	Keywords associated with this file. For example, *Birthday* or *Important*. Can be set with `textutil` using the `-keywords` option.
kMDItemOrganizations	Companies or organizations that created the document. Can be set with `textutil` using the `-company` option.
kMDItemPageHeight	Height of the document page, in points (72 points per inch). For PDF files this indicates the height of the first page only.
kMDItemPageWidth	Width of the document page, in points (72 points per inch). For PDF files this indicates the width of the first page only.
kMDItemSubject	Subject of the item. Can be set with `textutil` using the `-subject` option.
kMDItemTextContent	Contains a text representation of the content of the document. Applications can search for values in this attribute but are not able to read the content of this attribute directly.
kMDItemTitle	The title of the item. For example, this could be the title of a document, the name of a song, or the subject of an e-mail message. Can be set with `textutil` using the `-title` option.
Image Metadata Attribute Keys	
ATTRIBUTE	DESCRIPTION
kMDItemAlbum	Title for a collection of media. This is analogous to a record label or photo album.
kMDItemBitsPerSample	The number of bits per sample. For example, the bit depth of an image (*8-bit*, *16-bit*, and so on).
kMDItemColorSpace	The colorspace model used by the document contents. For example, *RGB*, *CMYK*, *YUV*, or *YCbCr*.
kMDItemOrientation	The orientation of the document contents. Expected values: *0* (landscape) *1* (portrait).
Video Metadata Attribute Keys	
ATTRIBUTE	DESCRIPTION
kMDItemCodecs	The codecs used to encode/decode the media.
kMDItemMediaTypes	The media types present in the content.
kMDItemTotalBitRate	The total bit rate, audio and video combined, of the media.
Audio Metadata Attribute Keys	
ATTRIBUTE	DESCRIPTION
kMDItemAudioSampleRate	Sample rate of the audio data contained in the file. The sample rate is a float value representing hz (audio_frames/second). For example: *44100.0*, *22254.54*.
kMDItemKeySignature	Musical key of the song in the audio file. For example: *C*, *Dm*, *F#m*, *Bb*.

To search for files using mdfind:

- `mdfind query`

  `mdfind` produces a list of files that match the query. The query is a string that is matched (without regard to upper/lowercase) against the central metadata store. In the simplest case, the query can be just a single word. For example,

  `mdfind susie`

  would produce a list of files where any of their metadata included the string `susie`—it could be in the files' name, in the content, in the `kMDItemKeywords` attribute, in the `kMDItemOrganizations` attribute, and so on.

✔ Tips

- Documentation for the query language used by `mdfind` is available at http://developer.apple.com/documentation/Carbon/Conceptual/SpotlightQuery/. **Table 4.4** shows some examples of queries.
- You can list the metadata attributes on a file with the `mdls` command:

  `mdls file`

- To have `mdfind` ignore permissions on files it finds, do the search using the `sudo` command (covered in Chapter 11, "Introduction to System Administration"):

  `sudo mdfind query`

- You can use the `-live` option to `mdfind` to have it continuously and instantly update its output to show the number of files that match the query. As files are added or removed, the count will change.
- Consider using the `-0` option to pipe the output of `mdfind` through the `xargs` command. For example, to back up every file that mentions peaches, you would use the following:

  ```
  mdfind -0 peaches | xargs -0 -J % cp
  → % /Volumes/Backups/
  ```

  See `man xargs` for more—it is a very powerful command.
- You may use the `-onlyin` option to limit `mdfind` results to files in a particular directory.
- As of Mac OS X 10.4, there is only one command-line tool for setting or changing metadata attribute values. The `textutil` command is primarily designed for converting files from one format to another (for example, from Microsoft Word to HTML) but also allows setting a few metadata attributes (like `kMDItemAuthor`) on the converted files. See `man textutil` for more information.

Table 4.4

Complex Queries Using mdfind

Find files that mention *jack*, but only in your Documents folder:	`mdfind -onlyin ~/Documents jack`
Find all HTML docs that mention *refactoring* in their content:	`mdfind "(kMDItemKind == 'HTML Document'c) && (kMDItemTextContent == 'refactoring'wc)"`
All PDF's that mention *dashboard*:	`mdfind "(kMDItemKind == 'PDF document'c) && (kMDItemTextContent == 'dashboard'wc)"`
Find PDF documents where the height (of the first page) is less than or equal to 842 pixels:	`mdfind "(kMDItemKind == 'PDF document'c) && (kMDItemPageHeight <= 842)"`
Find files that use the Palatino and/or Arial fonts:	`mdfind "(kMDItemFonts == Palatino) || (kMDItemFonts == Arial)"`

locate

The `locate` command searches a database of files for filenames that match its argument. The `locate` database contains the names of almost all the files on the system (it omits some files for security reasons). The `locate` command is available on most versions of Unix, unlike `mdfind`, which is (currently) available only in Mac OS X/Darwin. Also, since `locate` searches *only* filenames, it will sometimes be easier to use than trying to restrict a different search tool to search only filenames.

This means that `locate` can perform a very fast search of practically the whole system, but it only finds files that existed as of the last database update. The database is rebuilt weekly (Sundays at 4:30 a.m. on Mac OS X). See the "Running Regularly Scheduled Commands" section in Chapter 11 to learn how to change that.

If you are looking for a file you believe has been around since before the last Sunday update, `locate` is a good way to look for it.

To use locate to search for a file:

◆ `locate` *`string`*

`locate` produces a list of file paths that include the string. Note that it is case sensitive:

`locate security`

and

`locate Security`

produce different results, as shown in **Figure 4.31** (partial results shown).

✔ Tips

- `locate` tends to produce voluminous output, so consider piping its output through `grep` to filter it or through `less` to see it one screen at a time. For example:

  `locate security | grep Library`

  or

  `locate security | less`

- Want to count how many files `locate` located? Pipe it through `wc -l`:

  `locate security | wc -l`

```
localhost:~ vanilla$ locate security
...
/Library/Documentation/Services/apache/misc/security_tips.html
/System/Library/Frameworks/JavaVM.framework/Versions/1.3.1/Home/lib/security
/System/Library/Frameworks/JavaVM.framework/Versions/1.3.1/Home/lib/security/cacerts
/System/Library/Frameworks/JavaVM.framework/Versions/1.3.1/Home/lib/security/java.policy
/System/Library/Frameworks/JavaVM.framework/Versions/1.3.1/Home/lib/security/java.security
...
localhost:~ vanilla$ locate Security
...
/Library/Receipts/SecurityUpdate10-19-01.pkg
/Library/Receipts/SecurityUpdate10-19-01.pkg/Contents
/Library/Receipts/SecurityUpdate10-19-01.pkg/Contents/Resources
/Library/Receipts/SecurityUpdate10-19-01.pkg/Contents/Resources/BundleVersions.plist
/Library/Receipts/SecurityUpdate10-19-01.pkg/Contents/Resources/da.lproj
...
localhost:~ vanilla$
```

Figure 4.31 Comparing results for `Security` and `security` when using `locate`. (Your output will differ, but you get the idea.)

find

While `locate` is fast and simple, `find` is more flexible, allowing you not only to search for patterns in filenames, but also to specify multiple criteria. You can search by type of file (directory versus plain file), modification date, size, and many more. See the Unix `man` page (`man find`) for a complete list and several good examples.

The first argument to `find` is always a directory name, which tells `find` where to start looking (it can be `.` for the current directory, `/` for the root directory, or any other path). You then specify options to tell `find` which files will match, and finally what to do with each matching filename. The default is to send each matching filename to `stdout`, but you can do other things, such as execute a command using each found filename as an argument.

To search for files based on name:

- `find` *`dirname`* `-name "`*`pattern`*`"`

  For example,

  `find ~ -name "Picture*"`

  would show all the files in your home directory whose names begin with `Picture` (**Figure 4.32**). (Your shell interprets the `~` (tilde) character as "my home directory." See Chapter 5.) The quotes around `Picture*` are important. Without them the shell would interpret the `*` instead of passing it to `find`. We want the `find` command to get `Picture*` as the value for the `-name` option.

To search for files based on type:

- Use the `-type` option to select the file type you want, such as directories.

  `find ~/Documents -type d`

  finds all the directories inside your Documents directory (**Figure 4.33**).

  To find only regular files, use `-type f`. See `man find` for a complete list of available types.

✔ Tip

- Combine the `-type` option with the `-name` option to find only files that match both name and type.

  `find ~ -type d -name "Picture*"`

  looks in your home directory (~) and finds only directories whose names begin with the string `Picture`.

A very cool feature of `find` is its ability to find every file that has been modified after some specific reference file, such as one with a particular date. One use of this feature would be in scripts that perform backups.

```
localhost:~ vanilla$ find ~ -name "Picture*"
/Users/vanilla/Documents/Picture of Susan
/Users/vanilla/Pictures
/Users/vanilla/Pictures/Picture 1.jpg
/Users/vanilla/Pictures/Picture 2.jpg
/Users/vanilla/Pictures/Picture 3.jpg
/Users/vanilla/Pictures/Picture 4.jpg
localhost:~ vanilla$
```

Figure 4.32 Finding all the files in your home directory whose names start with `Picture`.

```
localhost:~ vanilla$ find ~/Documents -type d
/Users/vanilla/Documents
/Users/vanilla/Documents/Contracts
/Users/vanilla/Documents/Misc.
/Users/vanilla/Documents/PartyPlans
localhost:~ vanilla$
```

Figure 4.33 Using the `-type d` option to find only directories.

To find every file modified after a reference file:

- `find dirname -newer filename`

  For example,

  `find . -newer "Figure 4.27.doc"`

  searches the current directory and all the subdirectories contained inside it for files that have been modified more recently than the file Figure 4.27.doc.

  Figure 4.34 shows what the output might look like. Notice how the current directory (.) showed up in the list. This is because a directory is considered "modified" whenever a file is added to or removed from it.

✔ Tip

- `Find` can also find files that have (or have not) been modified, accessed, or created in the past *n* 24-hour periods, where *n* is any whole number. For example, this will find files that have been modified less than one day ago:

  `find . -mtime -1`

  and this will find files modified more than two days ago:

  `find . -mtime +2`

One last thing we will show you about `find` is how to apply a command line to every file that `find` discovers. That is, the `find` command produces a list of files, and you may want to use each of those filenames as an argument to a command, over and over. One reason to do this would be to use `grep` to search each of the found files. Another reason would be to move the found files to a new location, and a third reason would be to remove each of the found files. The possibilities are endless.

`find` provides a built-in option for executing a command on each file, the `-exec` option. However, this option does not handle files with spaces in their names very well. Also, if a large number of files are involved, the `-exec` option is noticeably slower than using a command called `xargs`.

The alternative is to pass the output of `find`, via a pipe, to another command, called `xargs`. The `xargs` command takes a list of files on `stdin` and executes its arguments as a command line once for every filename it is passed. Normally `xargs` will put the filename at the end of the command, but see the `-J` option, described in a tip below.

```
localhost:~ vanilla$ find . -newer "Figure 4.27.doc"
.
./Chapter 4.doc
./Figure 4.28.doc
./Figure 4.29.doc
./Figure 4.30.doc
./Figure 4.31.doc
./Figure 4.32.doc
./Word Work File D 3702
./Word Work File D 4
localhost:~ vanilla$
```

Figure 4.34 Searching the current directory for files modified after a reference file.

To apply a command to each file found:

- ◆ `find . -name "*.doc" -print0 | xargs → -0 ls -sk`

  The first part of the `find` command should be familiar by now—you are finding all the files in the current directory whose names end in .doc. The `-print0` option tells `find` not to put a *newline* character at the end of each line of output, but instead to use a special character (called the *null* character), which never appears in filenames.

  You then pipe the output of `find` into `xargs`. The `-0` option to `xargs` tells it to use the null character (instead of spaces) as the separator between filenames. `xargs` then executes the command line `ls -sk` *`filename`* on each filename that it gets from the pipe.

  The result will look like **Figure 4.35**, giving us the size (in kilobytes) of every .doc file in the current directory and all its subdirectories.

✔ Tips

- The `xargs` command normally puts each incoming argument at the end of the command line, but you can use the `-J` option to put the argument in the middle of a command line:

  ```
  mdfind -0 Apples | xargs -0 -J % cp
  → % /Volumes/Backups/
  ```

  copies all the files found by `mdfind` into the directory `/Volumes/Backups`. The `-J %` option tells `xargs` to replace the `%` in the following command line with the argument it is processing.

```
localhost:~/Documents/OS X vanilla% find . -name "*.doc" -print0 | xargs -0 ls -sk
  204 ./Chapter 0 - Introduction/Introduction.doc
  136 ./Chapter 0 -TOC/Outline.doc
   32 ./Chapter 0 -TOC/Outline_Comments_me.doc
  180 ./Chapter 0 -TOC/Outline_v2.doc
  260 ./Chapter 0 -TOC/Outline_v2.hb.doc
  184 ./Chapter 0 -TOC/Outline_v3.doc
  448 ./Chapter 0 -TOC/Outline_v4.doc
   64 ./Chapter 0 -TOC/TOC.doc
   64 ./Chapter 0 -TOC/TOC2.doc
  188 ./Chapter 1/Chapter 1 v2.doc
  160 ./Chapter 1/Chapter 1 v2beta.doc
  204 ./Chapter 1/Chapter 1 v5a/Chapter_1_v5a.doc
   24 ./Chapter 1/Chapter 1 v5a/Figure 1.2.doc
  localhost:~/Documents/OS X vanilla$
```

Figure 4.35 Finding the sizes of all the .doc files in the current directory.

- You could get just the numbers with

  ```
  find . -name "*.doc" -print0 | xargs
  -0 ls -sk | awk '{print $1}'
  ```

  And if you wanted to add them up, you would create a Perl script called add containing

  ```
  #!/usr/bin/perl
  while (<>) {
       $sum += $_;
  }
  print "$sum\n";
  ```

  and then use the command line

  ```
  find . -name "*.doc" -print0 | xargs
  ➝ -0 ls -sk | awk '{print $1}' | add
  ```

  (If you are an experienced Unix user, we acknowledge that, yes, you could use an awk script instead of the Perl script.)

The fact that a complicated command line like the one we've been using is just a grouping of simpler commands into a problem-solving entity shows the power, and also the simplicity, of the Unix command line. Compare the command line above with creating a Workflow in the Mac OS X Automator application (http://developer.apple.com/macosx/automator.html).

which

The `which` command is used specifically to find out which version of a command should be executed. When you enter a command line, Unix looks for the command in a series of directories named in a list called your `PATH`, and executes the first matching command it finds. (See Chapter 7, "Configuring Your Unix Environment," to learn how to alter your `PATH`.)

Sometimes there will be more than one command with the same name among the various directories in your `PATH`. The `which` command tells you which one will actually be executed.

To search your path for a command:

◆ `which` *command*

  For example,

  ```
  which ls
  ```

  shows you that the `ls` command is `/bin/ls`, and `which cd` shows you that the `cd` command is `/usr/bin/cd`.

Viewing and Editing Files

All the commands mentioned here are covered in more detail in Chapter 5 and Chapter 6, "Editing and Printing Files"; we covered nano in Chapter 2.

Viewing files

The less, cat, head, and tail commands (described below) are all used for viewing files. For more detailed information on these four commands, see Chapter 5.

less—The less command is a *pager*—a utility for viewing a long stream of text one screen (or *page*) at a time. When you are viewing a Unix man page, you are seeing it *paged* through less.

cat—The cat command is used to combine (*concatenate*) files together. It is frequently used to simply display an entire file without pausing.

You can think of cat as a way of displaying short files, and less for displaying long files.

head—The head command is used to show just the beginning of a file or other output.

tail—If head shows the beginning, can you guess what tail does?

Editing files

The three most common Unix tools for editing text files are vi, emacs, and nano. We'll cover these in more detail in Chapter 6.

vi—vi is a full-featured command-line text editor. It is found on virtually every Unix system and is the primary editing tool we cover in this book.

emacs—emacs is another full-featured text editor and has far more features than vi (including a built-in adventure game). Many programmers prefer emacs to vi, and the debate over which editor is best sometimes seems religious rather than rational.

nano—This is a fairly simple text editor. It is intended to work like another simple editor called pico (the Pine Composer), and in versions of Mac OS X prior to 10.4 pico was supplied instead of nano. nano has a less restrictive license than pico.

Sending E-mail

If your Mac OS X system is connected to the Internet, you can easily send e-mail from the command line using the `mail` command.

mail

The `mail` command lets you compose and send e-mail from the command line (`sendmail`, on the other hand, is server software for transporting messages). It can also be used for reading e-mail if your Mac is set up to receive mail, but we don't cover that here. Instead, we cover the `pine` program, a better tool for reading e-mail from the command line, in Chapter 15, "More Open-Source Software."

To send e-mail from the command line:

1. `mail` *`username@host.domain`*

   You give the `mail` command one argument: the address you want to send to.

   The `mail` command responds by prompting you for a subject. **Figure 4.36** shows the complete process of sending e-mail from the command line.

2. Enter a subject line and press Return.

   `mail` responds by waiting for you to enter your message.

3. Enter the body of your message.

   Note that `mail` lacks any kind of fancy editing capability. You must press Return at the end of each line (there is no automatic word wrap).

4. When you're done, type a period on a line by itself and press Return.

   That is how `mail` knows you are done with your message. `mail` responds as shown in Figure 4.36 with `EOT` (*End of Transmission*).

   Your e-mail is on its way, and you get a shell prompt back.

Any command that produces text on `stdout` can be piped into `mail`. You can specify a subject on the command line with the `-s` option (`s` for *subject*).

A common reason for piping command output into the `mail` command is to run a command that takes a while to finish, pipe it into `mail`, and run the whole command line in the background (see Chapter 2). This allows you to get back to a shell prompt and get on with your work, and eventually receive e-mail when the process is done. You might do this if you want to find all the MP3 files in your home directory and e-mail yourself a list.

```
localhost:~ vanilla$ mail susan@cool.domain.net
Subject: Is it soup yet?
This is the message body. You must press enter at the end of
each line.

When you want a blank line press return twice.
.
EOT
localhost:~ vanilla$
```

Figure 4.36 Sending e-mail from the command line.

To pipe output from any command into mail:

- ```
  find ~ -name "*.mp3" | mail -s "My
  → MP3 files" myaddress@host.domain &
  ```
  This pipes the output of the `find` command into `mail`. The `&` at the end of the command line runs the whole thing in the background (as we noted in Chapter 2).

Another useful trick with `mail` is to take the message body from a file by redirecting `stdin`.

To take the message body from a file:

- ```
  mail -s "here is the file"
  → address@host.domain < memofile
  ```
  This passes the contents of the file to `mail` as the message body. (See "Redirecting `stdin`" in Chapter 2 for more on how the < operator works.)

  Unless the message is made up only of plain text (that is, no images or other non-text material), it will not show up properly. The `mail` command is very old and predates the common use of e-mail attachments. If you want to send anything besides plain-text e-mail from the command line, you should use `pine`.

Pine

`Pine` is a command-line e-mail program that takes over your whole Terminal window (though it is a "full-screen" program, it won't take over your whole Mac screen, just the Terminal window you run it from). It can handle e-mail attachments.

`Pine` was developed as an easier-to-use alternative to another full-screen command-line e-mail program, called `elm`. The name `Pine` stands for *Pine is not elm.* (The `Pine` program is capitalized, the `pine` command is not.)

We cover the installation and use of `Pine` in Chapter 15.

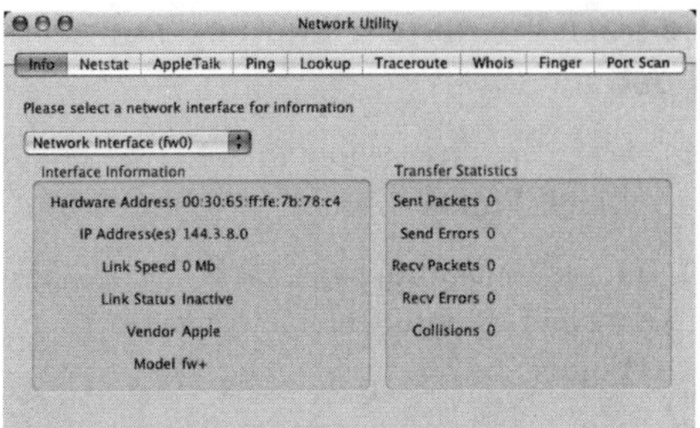

Figure 4.37 The Info pane of Network Utility.

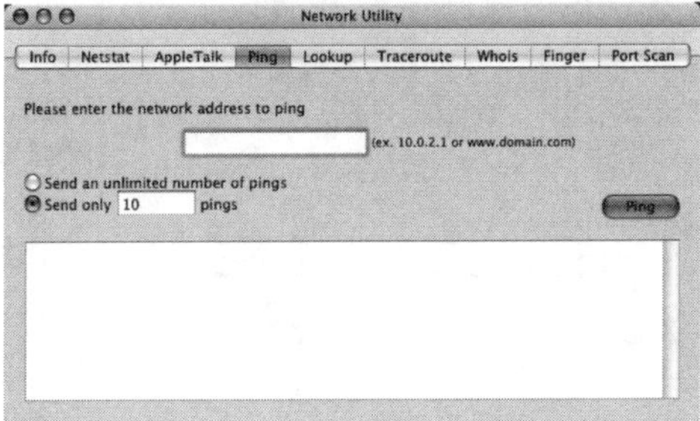

Figure 4.38 The Ping pane of Network Utility.

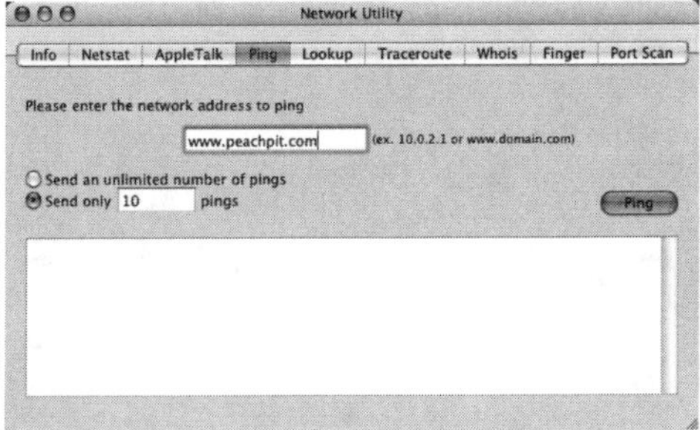

Figure 4.39 Entering a domain name for `Ping` testing.

Network Analysis

Being a multiuser operating system from its start, Unix has always been intended for use on a network. If your Mac OS X machine isn't already connected to a network, it is likely to be at some point. In this section we describe some of the tools for analyzing network activity that come with Mac OS X.

Network Utility

Network Utility (/Applications/Utilities/Network Utility) is an Aqua program that provides a graphical interface for several common network-analysis tasks.

To launch Network Utility:

- Double-click the Network Utility icon, or at the command line enter

  ```
  open "/Applications/Utilities/Network
  → Utility.app"
  ```

  The Network Utility application opens to its Info pane (**Figure 4.37**).

To see if another Internet host is active:

1. Select the Ping tab of Network Utility.

   The Ping pane opens (**Figure 4.38**).

2. Enter a domain name or an IP address to test.

   Figure 4.39 shows a domain name entered for testing. A domain name is the part of a Web address (URL) after the two slashes. It consists of two or more words separated by dots—for example, *www.peachpit.com*. An IP (Internet Protocol) address is a set of four numbers separated by dots. Each number in an IP address is between 2 and 254.

   You can adjust the number of pings (essentially, a request for a response) that you want to send.

continues on next page

3. Click the Ping button.

   Network Utility sends a series of short messages (called *Internet Control Message Protocol* [*ICMP*] *packets*) to the remote machine and expects responses. The results are shown in the lower portion of the window (**Figure 4.40**).

   If the packets do not make it to the remote machine and back again, you will see gaps in the `icmp_seq` numbers. These indicate a packet loss of greater than 1 percent, especially high time values (that is, the time it took to conduct the ping), or no response at all. (To properly test for packet loss, send at least 100 pings.) Normal time values depend on the nature of your Internet connection. Frequent testing of a handful of remote machines over a period of a few weeks will give you an idea of what is normal for your connection. Some networks are configured to block the kind of packets used in these tests, so in a few cases a machine or network appears unreachable even though it is functioning normally.

✔ Tip

- You can run the same test from the command line with

  ```
  ping -c 10 www.peachpit.com
  ```

See `man ping` for many more options.

When your computer connects to another on the Internet, the data being exchanged passes through a series of intermediate special-purpose computers called *routers*. Routers connect networks together (the Internet is an internetwork system, like *inter*state or *inter*national, hence the name).

It is possible to see a list of the routers between your computer and any particular destination you connect to through the Internet. The list can and does vary as networks are added, dropped, and reconfigured.

To trace the route to another Internet host:

1. Select the Traceroute tab in Network Utility (**Figure 4.41**).

2. In the Traceroute pane, fill in the domain name or IP number of a host to test (**Figure 4.42**).

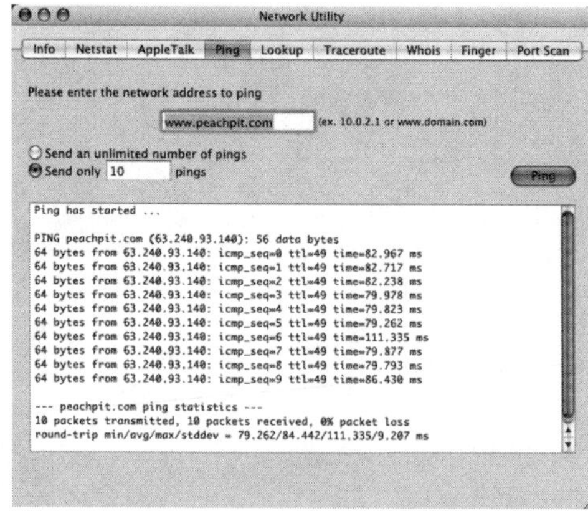

Figure 4.40 What happens when you send ten pings to www.peachpit.com.

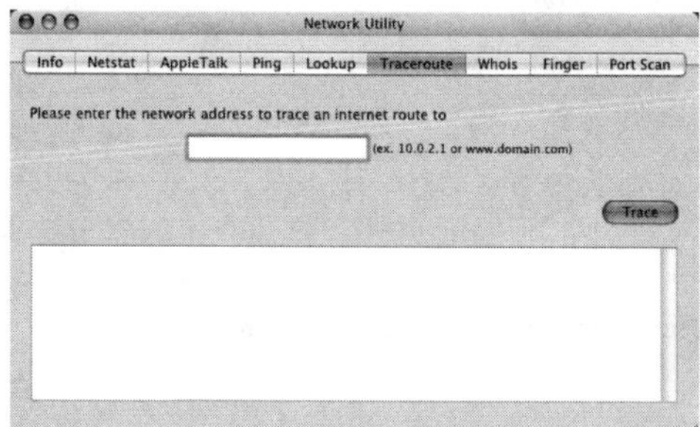

Figure 4.41 The Traceroute pane of Network Utility.

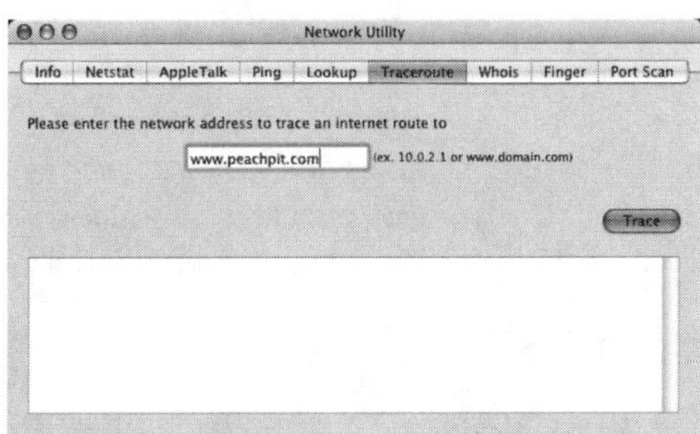

Figure 4.42 Entering a domain name for Traceroute testing.

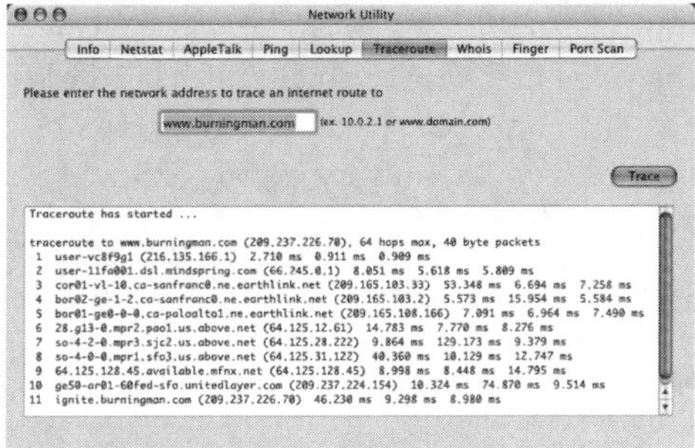

Figure 4.43 The results of using Traceroute on www.peachpit.com.

3. Click the Trace button.

The trace results appear in the lower part of the Traceroute pane (**Figure 4.43**).

Each line shows one router with the three round-trip times (in milliseconds) for data sent between your computer and the router. If the connection along the way is bad, the round-trip time is replaced with an asterisk (*).

✔ Tip

- You can run the same test from the command line with

  `traceroute www.burningman.com`

  See `man traceroute` for more options.

Network Utility has half a dozen more features, some of which have a dozen or more options. While they are beyond the scope of this book, you can't hurt your Mac by trying them. **Table 4.5** contains a brief description of the panels other than Info, along with their command-line equivalents.

Table 4.5

Network Utility Features

Feature	Description
Netstat	Gives information about raw data that has been sent and received through your network (Ethernet) connection. See `man netstat` for the command-line version.
AppleTalk	Configure and display information about your AppleTalk network. See `man -k appletalk` for a list of AppleTalk-related command-line utilities, such as the `appletalk` command.
Ping	Tests to see if another machine is reachable through the Internet. See `man ping` for the command-line version.
Lookup	Used to find information about Internet addresses (both domain names and IP numbers). See `man dig` for the command-line version.
Traceroute	Shows the routers in between your machine and another machine on the Internet. See `man traceroute` for the command-line version.
Whois	Used to find information about domain names (as opposed to specific machine addresses—use Lookup for that). Finds who owns the domain name and who is responsible for translating addresses in that domain into IP addresses (the "DNS" servers for the domain). See `man whois` for the command-line version.
Finger	Used to find information about users logged in to other machines on the Internet. Few Internet hosts allow incoming finger requests. See `man finger` for the command-line version.
Port Scan	Used to see what services a particular Internet host is providing, such as Web server or e-mail server. There is no direct command-line equivalent.

Using the Internet

The tools described here are the main programs you will use to interact with other machines over the Internet. Although, technically speaking, anything you do over the Internet involves interacting with another machine, these tools are the ones you will use more intensively for command-line work.

telnet

`telnet` is a command for connecting to another machine. Use it to log in to the other machine and get a shell prompt from it, just as the Terminal application gives you a shell prompt on your machine.

`telnet` is mostly deprecated these days because it sends data and passwords without encryption, and does not provide the kind of secure connections that `ssh` provides. See Chapter 12, "Security," and `man telnet` for more details.

ssh

`ssh` (*Secure Shell*) is a tool for creating encrypted connections to other machines over the Internet. Like `telnet`, `ssh` can be used to log in to another machine. It can also be used to create secure connections between machines for file transfer (see the "`scp`" section below), or to relay incoming data to a different machine for handling, among other capabilities.

`ssh` is the preferred tool for connecting to other machines through the Internet. The basic command line to log in to another machine is

```
ssh yourname@host.domain
```

See Chapter 12 and `man ssh` for details.

scp

`scp` (*Secure Copy*) is a tool for transferring files between machines on a network. `scp` uses `ssh` to provide an encrypted connection. See Chapter 12 and `man scp` for details.

ftp and sftp

`ftp` (*File Transfer Protocol*) is an old tool for transferring files between machines on the Internet. It provides a way of logging in to an FTP server and interactively exchanging files. Because the FTP protocol sends passwords and data without encryption, it shares the vulnerabilities of `telnet` and is less desirable than `scp` or a new alternative, `sftp` (*Secure* `ftp`). See Chapter 12, `man ftp`, and `man sftp` for details.

Lynx

`Lynx` is a command-line, text-only Web browser.

Mac OS X doesn't come with `Lynx`; see Chapter 15 to learn how to install it. (See also the `curl` and `wget` commands, covered in Chapter 10.)

5 Using Files and Directories

This chapter is all about showing you how to use files and directories "the Unix way." You have done most of the things in this chapter before, using the Finder. This includes seeing what files and directories are available, copying files, renaming files, and getting information about files. In Aqua you use one application (the Finder) for many different file-related tasks. In Unix you use many different applications (that is, commands) to navigate among directories and to create, change, delete, and examine files and directories.

Almost every command you use in Unix involves one or more files or directories. In most cases, when we say "file" when referring to Unix, we mean "file or directory."

All the tasks in this chapter assume that you have a Terminal window open and that you have read Chapter 2, "Using the Command Line."

Seeing the Whole File System

An important difference between the Unix and Aqua (and Mac OS 9) approaches to files and directories is the way the user sees disks and the locations of files.

Aqua displays files in folders, which are in turn located on *volumes*. (There is one or more volume per disk. Volumes show up in the Finder looking like disks.) Each volume has its own hierarchy of files and folders.

In Unix there is only one hierarchy of directories and files. If you have more than one volume on your system, then each volume is a part of one centralized hierarchy, rather than appearing as separate volumes on the desktop, as in Mac OS 9. The beginning of the hierarchy is the *root directory. The root directory is always on the volume that you booted from*—it contains the kernel of the operating system. **Figure 5.1** shows the hierarchy of your entire file system contained on three disks. (See the sidebar "Disks, Partitions, Volumes, and Removable Devices" for even more details.)

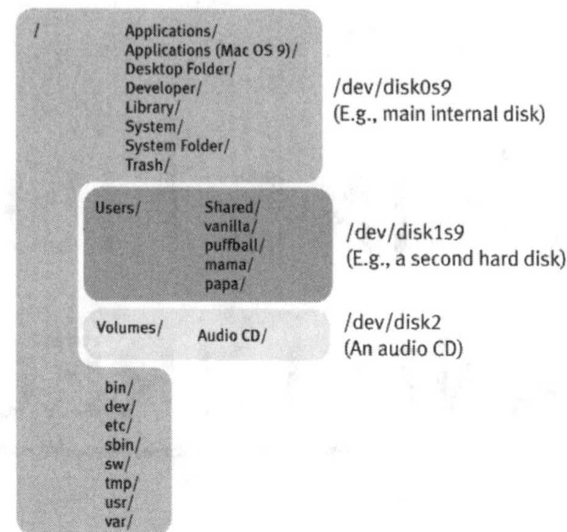

Figure 5.1 There is only one hierarchy of files on your system no matter how many disks and volumes you have. Unix uses a file in the /dev directory to represent each volume, so `/dev/disk0s9` represents "disk zero, slice 9."

To see the contents of the root directory:

◆ `ls /`

  As discussed in Chapter 2, the `ls` command (for *list*) shows the names of files and directories. It can be used with any number of arguments. If an argument is the name of a directory, then the contents of that directory are shown; **Figure 5.2** shows the contents of the root directory.

Your first thought may be, "Where did my disk(s) go?" You may have noticed that the disks you see in the Finder didn't show up in that listing. The answer is that disks and/or volumes are displayed in a normal Unix listing of the root directory. (In Unix, virtually everything is a file of some kind.) Unix uses a special file in the /dev directory to represent each disk and volume on the system. The /dev (for *devices*) directory contains files that represent various physical and virtual devices, so /dev/stdin represents the STDIN we talked about in Chapter 2 and /dev/disk0 represents the first physical disk. Then /dev/disk1 would be a second disk, and /dev/disk0s2 would be "disk 0, slice 2" (a *slice* is also known as a *partition*, or *volume*).

```
localhost:~ vanilla$ ls /
Applications      Library       automount      mach           tmp
Desktop DB        Network       bin            mach.sym       usr
Desktop DF        System        cores          mach_kernel    var
Developer         Users         dev            private
Installers        Volumes       etc            sbin
localhost:~ vanilla$
```

Figure 5.2 Typing `ls /` shows the contents of the root directory. Your output depends on your machine's configuration.

Disks, Partitions, Volumes, and Removable Devices

On Unix systems, there is always a single hierarchy containing all files and folders available to the operating system, regardless of how many physical disks or other devices are attached.

Each storage device (disk, CD, and so on) shows up in the master hierarchy (the file system) as a directory.

Physical disks may be divided (*partitioned*) into two or more *volumes* (also called *partitions* and *filesystems*).

On a Unix system the boot volume is always the root of the whole file system. (Note that the file system may have multiple filesystems—that is, volumes.)

In the Finder and other Aqua applications, each volume will appear as if it were a separate disk.

In Darwin—that is, at the command line—each volume is said to be *mounted on* a directory. (So the boot volume is mounted on the / directory.) In Figure 5.1, the second internal disk is mounted on the /Users directory, and we say that /Users is the *mount point* for the second disk (which is also represented by a special file, /dev/disk1s9; all "devices" are represented by special files in the /dev directory).

In Darwin/Mac OS X, removable devices are mounted on directories automatically created inside the /Volumes directory, so in Figure 5.1, the Audio CD is mounted on the /Volumes/Audio CD directory.

The df command will show a list of filesystems and mount points. (Remember that *filesystem* and *volume* and *partition* all mean the same thing.) See man df for more. Figure 11.40 in Chapter 11 shows an example of using the df command.

Compare with Aqua

Normally the Aqua interface hides much of the contents of the root directory when it is viewed in the Finder. This is probably because Apple doesn't consider the items it has hidden to be useful to an Aqua-only user. You can change this on a per-user basis by using the command-line utility `defaults` to turn on an option called `AppleShowAllFiles`. Here is the command line to do this:

```
defaults write com.apple.finder Apple
→ ShowAllFiles ON
```

See `man defaults` and also "Configuring Mac OS X Defaults from the Command Line" in Chapter 7, "Configuring Your Environment with Unix."

The Aqua interface tries to keep you away from the more hard-core Unix files and folders.

If you choose Go to Folder from the Go menu in the Finder and then type in a / (slash), you are shown a list of the disks and partitions on your system, along with the Network icon.

You *can* use the Go to Folder dialog to navigate into some of the hidden directories; for example, if you type in */usr*, you are shown the contents of the `/usr` directory as shown in **Figure 5.3**. You just can't see the root directory itself.

Some Aqua applications let you navigate to the root directory by typing in the "Go to" field of the Open dialog. Even then, however, the view you get does not show every file and directory in the root directory. If you know the full path of a hidden file or directory, you may navigate to it by entering the full path. (Some Aqua applications, notably the BBEdit text editor, have an Open Hidden choice under the File menu.)

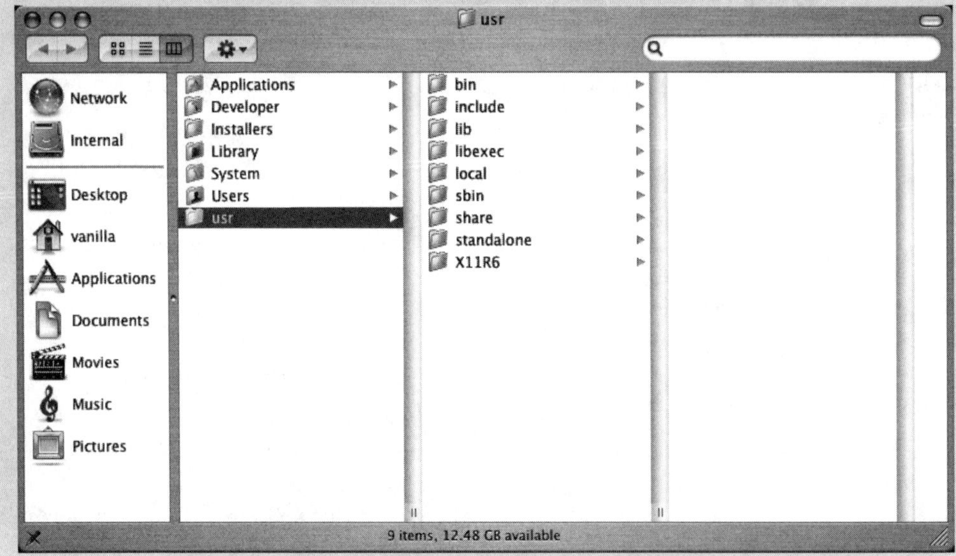

Figure 5.3 Result of entering */usr* in the Go to Folder dialog from the Finder's Go menu.

Seeing Where You Are in the File System

At the Unix command line, you are always "in" some directory in the file system. The directory you are in right now is called your *current working directory* (often shortened to either *working directory* or *current directory*).

The current directory is the default directory for commands that read or create files. For example, if you give a command a filename to read, and you do not specify where to look for that file, the command will look for it in the current directory.

When you first open a Terminal window, your working directory is your home directory. Your home directory has the same name as your short user name. As you perform various tasks, you will frequently change your working directory. You can think of your working directory as being similar to the active Finder window—that is, the currently active Finder window, the one "in front."

To display the current working directory:

- pwd

  The pwd command "prints" the location of the working directory (**Figure 5.4**). The command doesn't actually print anything—it just outputs the path, and your screen is the normal place for output from commands.

  The working directory is the default directory for a large number of actions. For instance, the `ls` command lists the contents of the working directory by default. (Throughout this book we use *vanilla* as an example of a short user name; of course, you will see and use your own short user name instead.)

```
localhost:~ vanilla$ pwd
/Users/vanilla
localhost:~ vanilla$
```

Figure 5.4 Typing pwd shows your current working directory. Yours will be different, of course.

Compare with Aqua

The Unix concept of the *working directory* is similar to the graphical user interface (GUI) concept of the active window—the window that currently is the subject of actions like File > Close.

Here's another way to compare the Unix working directory with Aqua. Think of what happens when you save or open a file from within an Aqua application. The dialog that appears starts you off in whatever folder the application most recently used. That folder is similar to the current working directory.

Understanding and Using Unix Filenames

You use filenames constantly in Unix. Almost every command covered in this chapter, and most commands in Unix, accept one or more filenames as arguments. Those filenames can be entered in two different forms: as *relative paths* or as *full paths* (also called *absolute paths*).

The difference between relative and full paths is simple but critical. A path tells you not only the name of a file, but also its location in the file system. A path is like a set of directions telling you how to get somewhere.

Full paths *always* begin with a / (slash) and give the absolute location of the file in the file system; that is, they give you "directions" to the file starting from the root directory. Every full path is completely unique.

Relative paths *never* begin with a /, and they give you directions to the file starting from your working directory—that is, from where you are right now. The same relative path can refer to different files, depending on where it is used.

To use a full path as an argument:

- `ls /Developer/Tools`

  Use a full path as a filename when you want it to refer to the same location, no matter what your working directory is when you type the command (**Figure 5.5**).

  The path `/Developer/Tools` means, "Starting from the root directory, look for a directory called `Developer`, and then inside there look for an entry called Tools."

✔ Tip

- Use full paths when you are not sure where you are, or when you want to make certain you are referring to a specific version of a file.

To use a relative path as an argument:

- `ls Sites/images`

  Use a relative path as a filename when you want the path to refer to a location in your current working directory (**Figure 5.6**).

```
localhost:~ vanilla$ ls  /Developer/Tools
BuildStrings          RezWack          mdcheckschema
CpMac                 SetFile          mdimport
DeRez                 SplitForks       momc
GetFileInfo           UnRezWack        packagemaker
MergePef              WSMakeStubs      pbhelpindexer
MvMac                 agvtool          pbprojectdump
PPCExplain            cvs-unwrap       uninstall-devtools.pl
ResMerger             cvs-wrap
Rez                   firewire
localhost:~ vanilla$
```

Figure 5.5 Using a full path for a filename means you get the same result regardless of your current directory.

```
localhost:~ vanilla$ ls  Sites/images
apache_pb.gif         macosxlogo.gif        web_share.gif
localhost:~ vanilla$
```

Figure 5.6 Using a relative path as a filename.

The path `Sites/images` means, "Starting from the current directory, look for a directory called `Sites`, and then inside there look for an entry called images." If you started from your home directory, then the path would resolve to

`/Users/vanilla/Sites/images`

If you used that relative path from a working directory of

`/Volumes/ExtraSpace`

then the path would resolve to

`/Volumes/ExtraSpace/Sites/images`

To use a more complex relative path:

- `ls ../../Developer/Tools`

  Each `..` is a special directory name that means "one step closer to the root directory" (see the sidebar "Two Special Directory Names" for more details). Each `..` takes you one step closer to `/`, so starting from a working directory of `/Users/vanilla`, the first `..` refers to `/Users`, and the second `..` refers to `/` itself. (The `..` path is often said to refer to the *parent directory*.)

  So the path `../../Developer/Tools` means, "Starting from the working directory, take two steps toward the root directory and then look for a directory called `Developer`, and then inside that for Tools."

Having the shell type the filename for you

Now that you have been typing some longer paths, you will be happy to learn about the *filename completion* feature of some Unix shells (see Chapter 2 to review shells).

Filename completion is a way of having the shell type most of the filename for you. You can use it whenever you are typing a filename or path that already exists.

To use filename completion:

1. Type any command that will use a filename as an argument.

   For example, to see the long-form listing of contents of the `/etc/httpd/users` directory, type `ls -l` (make sure to type a space after the `-l`).

2. Type the beginning of the filename. For example, in this case the beginning would be `/e`.

   Figure 5.7 shows the command line up to this point.

3. Press Tab .

   The shell tries to fill in the rest of the path, or at least as much of the path as is unique. In this case, there is only one entry in `/` that begins with `e`, so the shell fills in `/etc/` and then waits for you to continue (**Figure 5.8**).

4. Type a little more of the filename.

   In this case, just type an `h`, so that your command line now looks like this:

   `ls -l /etc/h`

continues on next page

```
localhost:~ vanilla$ ls -l /e
```

Figure 5.7 To use filename completion, you start by typing the beginning of the filename.

```
localhost:~ vanilla$ ls -l /etc/
```

Figure 5.8 When you press Tab, the shell will try to fill in the rest of the filename.

Two Special Directory Names

There are two very special directory names: `.` and `..` (that's a single dot and a double dot).

The `.` directory name always translates to the full path of the working directory. So if your working directory is `/Users/puffball/bin`, then the relative path `./script.sh` translates to `/Users/puffball/bin/script.sh`.

Anytime you are using a path, you can use the directory name `..` to mean "one step closer to the root directory." So if your working directory is `/usr/local/bin`, then the path `../../sbin` translates to `/sbin` (each `..` goes one step closer to `/`).

The `..` directory name refers to the *parent directory*, and you will often see that term in Unix documentation.

The `.` in `script.sh` does *not* have any special meaning. The `.` and `..` have their special meanings only when they are used *as* a directory name, not as *part of* a directory or filename.

5. Press Tab .

   In this case, there are many entries in `/etc/` that begin with `h`, so the shell beeps. If you then press Tab again, the shell displays all the entries that match (**Figure 5.9**). You should see the one you want among the entries listed.

   Notice how the shell repeats the partial command line after showing you the possible matches.

6. Type just enough of the filename to make it unique. In this case, that would be a `t`, so your command line now looks like this:

   `ls -l /etc/ht`

7. Press Tab .

   The shell fills in some more, so now your command line looks like this:

   `ls -l /etc/httpd/`

8. Press Tab again, twice.

   The shell shows you everything in `/etc/httpd/` (**Figure 5.10**) and repeats the partial command line.


```
localhost:~ vanilla$ ls -l /etc/h
hostconfig              hostconfig~   hosts.lpd
hostconfig.applesaved   hosts    httpd
hostconfig.applesaved2     hosts.equiv localhost:~ vanilla$ ls -l /etc/h
```

Figure 5.9 If there is more than one possible match when you press Tab, the shell beeps. If you then press Control D, all the available matches are displayed. The list in this figure may be a little different from what you'll get on your system.

```
localhost:~ vanilla$ ls -l /etc/httpd/
httpd.conf                  httpd.conf.default          mime.types.default
httpd.conf.applesaved       magic                       users
httpd.conf.applesaved2          magic.default
httpd.conf.bak              mime.types
localhost:~ vanilla$ ls -l /etc/httpd/
```

Figure 5.10 Another example of the shell's displaying possible matches after you press Tab and Control D.

A Special Name for Home

The ~ (tilde) character has a special meaning when used on the command line in a path. It translates to "the home directory of the user" whose username follows the ~. So ~puffball translates to /Users/puffball.

If the ~ is used without a user name, for example, in ~/Documents, then it translates to the home directory of whichever user is running the command.

The actual locations of users' home directories are different on different Unix systems, and in some cases different users on the same system may have their home directories in different places. For example, in Mac OS X, regular users have their home directories in /Users, but the root user's home directory is /var/root.

Using the ~ character lets the shell do the work of figuring out where a user's home directory is, so you can use ~puffball without having to know exactly where puffball's home directory is, and you can use ~/ to refer to your own home directory regardless of your working directory.

9. Repeat the process of typing a little more of the filename and pressing Tab until the filename you want is filled in.

   In this case, it should be sufficient to type a u and then press Tab. That should fill in the whole filename you want:

   ```
   ls -l /etc/httpd/users/
   ```

10. If there are more arguments, type them in.

    In this example, there would not be any more arguments. In other cases you might have more filenames or other arguments to add to the command line.

11. Press Return when the command line is complete. **Figure 5.11** shows the final result. (You should see a line for each user on your system.)

✔ Tips

- Use filename completion as much as you can, because it will help you avoid misspellings.
- The instructions above cover the default shell, bash; if you are using the tcsh shell, then in step 5, instead of the second Tab you would press Control D.


```
localhost:~ vanilla$ ls -l /etc/httpd/users/
total 32
-rw-r--r--   1 root   wheel   142 Mar 14 14:50 howard.conf
-rw-r--r--   1 root   wheel   207 Mar 14 14:52 matisse.conf
-rw-r--r--   1 root   wheel   141 Jan 28 13:16 noway.conf
-rw-r--r--   1 root   wheel   143 Dec 26 12:48 vanilla.conf
localhost:~ vanilla$
```

Figure 5.11 The result of the completed command line. Your output depends on the user accounts you've created on your system.

Moving Around in the File System

When using Unix, you will frequently want to change your working directory because the current directory is the default location for many commands (the terms *current directory* and *working directory* are used interchangeably in Unix documentation, as discussed above in "Seeing Where You Are in the File System"). For example, the `ls` command lists the contents of the current directory if given no arguments. If you never changed your working directory, you would often need to type very long paths and would be more likely to make mistakes.

To change your working directory:

- `cd Public`

  The `cd` command takes either no arguments or one argument and produces no output (unless it fails to work; remember that in Unix, "Silence means success"). The argument to `cd` is the path of a directory that will become your new working directory (in this case, `Public`). If you do not supply an argument, `cd` takes you to your home directory. You can see where you are with `pwd`.

  Notice how your shell prompt changes to reflect your new working directory. **Figure 5.12** shows the shell prompt before and after the `cd` command. See the sidebar "A Special Name for Home" for an explanation of the ~ (tilde) character.

  In this example, `Public` is a *relative path*, but quite often you will use a *full path*:

- `cd /etc/httpd`

  takes you to `/etc/httpd` regardless of where you were.

```
localhost:~ vanilla$ cd Public
localhost:~/Public vanilla$
```

Figure 5.12 Using cd to change your current directory. Your prompt also changes.

✔ Tip

- You can use the special directory name `..` with the `cd` command:

  `cd ../..`

To move back to your home directory:

- `cd`

  If you use the `cd` command with no arguments, it will take you back to your home directory.

Filenames Are Case Sensitive

Unix systems, including Darwin, use case-sensitive filenames. So at the command line, a file or directory named `Public` is not the same as one named `public`.

Your Mac uses a format for its disks called the Mac OS Extended (or HFS Plus) file system. The Mac OS Extended format is a "case-preserving, case-insensitive" file system. Apple has done a very nice job of dealing with this in Mac OS X.

If you are working at the command line on a Mac OS Extended partition (Mac OS Extended format is the normal way a Mac OS X partition will be formatted), then file and directory names are case insensitive.

It is possible to format a disk using a case-sensitive version of the Mac OS Extended format, but this is not recommended; see "Mac OS X 10.3: The Dangers of Case-Sensitive HFS+" (www.macfixit.com/staticpages/index.php?page=2003111009264885) for a discussion of the issues.

If you are working in a UFS partition (a common way of formatting in the Unix world), then file and directory names are case sensitive, and if you look at a UFS folder from the Finder, you will see that you can have two files whose names differ only in case—for example, FOO and foo.

Seeing the Contents of Directories

We normally think of a directory as "containing" files, but in reality a directory is just a special kind of file. A directory contains a list of entries. Each entry is the name of a file or another directory—this is an important concept. In Unix, the only place where a file's name is stored is in the directory. Filenames are not stored inside the files themselves. When you rename a file, you are changing the entry in a directory, but not changing the file. And when you remove a file, you are removing the file's name from a directory.

The operating system removes the file if there are no other directory entries for that file. This becomes very important when trying to understand *hard links*, which are described below in the section "About Links (the Unix Version of Aliases)." (Hard links are a way of having more than one directory entry that refers to the same actual file.)

To list the contents of the current directory:

- `ls`

  You see all of the nonhidden entries in the current directory (see below for an explanation of hidden files and how to view them).

```
localhost:~ vanilla$ ls /bin /sbin
/bin:
[               df              launchctl       pwd             tcsh
bash            domainname      link            rcp             test
cat             echo            ln              rm              unlink
chmod           ed              ls              rmdir           wait4path
cp              expr            mkdir           sh              zsh
csh             hostname        mv              sleep           zsh-4.2.3
date            kill            pax             stty
dd              ksh             ps              sync

/sbin:
SystemStarter           md5                     newfs_msdos
Autodiskmount           mknod                   nfsd
Clri                    mount                   nfsiod
Disklabel               mount_afp               nologin
Dmesg                   mount_autofs            ping
Dump                    mount_cd9660            ping6
Dumpfs                  mount_cddafs            quotacheck
dynamic_pager           mount_devfs             rdump
fibreconfig             mount_fdesc             reboot
fsck                    mount_ftp               restore
fsck_hfs                mount_hfs               route
fsck_msdos              mount_msdos             routed
halt                    mount_nfs               rrestore
ifconfig                mount_ntfs              rtsol
ip6fw                   mount_smbfs             service
ipfw                    mount_synthfs           shutdown
kerberosautoconfig      mount_udf               slattach
kextload                mount_volfs             tunefs
kextunload              mount_webdav            umount
launchd                 newfs
launchd_debugd          newfs_hfs
localhost:~ vanilla$
```

Figure 5.13 Supplying multiple arguments to `ls` to see the contents of more than one directory.

To list the contents of any directory:

- `ls path`

  If *path* is a directory, then the contents of the directory are shown. The *path* is always optional with the `ls` command. If it is omitted, the default *path* is `.` (the current directory).

  You can list the contents of several directories by specifying multiple paths on the command line. **Figure 5.13** shows the output from the command line

  `ls /bin /sbin`

  (Each of the files listed is actually a command. Use the `man` command described in Chapter 4, "Useful Unix Utilities," to learn about each of them.)

Hidden files

Unix normally does not show you files whose names begin with a `.` (a period, or *dot* in Unix-speak). These *dot files* are typically configuration files that are used by programs such as your shell when they start up, and thus they are something like the preferences files that littered your System Folder in pre–OS X versions of the Mac OS. See the sidebar "More About Hidden Files" for details.

To see hidden files:

- Use the `-a` or `-A` option to `ls`.

  Unix (and the Mac OS X Finder) hides files whose names begin with a `.` (dot).

  Adding the `-a` option shows all dot files (`-a` for *all files*).

  The `-A` option is the same as `-a` except that the two special directory names `.` and `..` are not shown. In this case, it's `-A` for *almost all.*

  Figure 5.14 compares the output of

  `ls`

  `ls -a`

  `ls -A`

```
localhost:~ vanilla$ ls
Current Projects        Library           Pictures       bin
Desktop                 Movies            Public         system-status
Documents               Music             Sites
localhost:~ vanilla$ ls -a
.                       .lpoptions        Music
..                      .ssh              Pictures
.CFUserTextEncoding     .viminfo          Public
.DS_Store               Desktop           Sites
.Trash                  Documents         Stuff
.bash_history           Library           bin
.bash_profile           Movies
localhost:~ vanilla$ ls -A
.CFUserTextEncoding     .ssh              Music
.DS_Store               .viminfo          Pictures
.Trash                  Desktop           Public
.bash_history           Documents         Sites
.bash_profile           Library           Stuff
.lpoptions              Movies            bin
localhost:~ vanilla$
```

Figure 5.14 Using the `-a` and `-A` options to `ls` reveals dot files. Your output may be different.

Getting more information from ls

The -l option to ls gives the "long" form of its output, listing one line for each entry and giving information about the file's size, date of last change, and other information.

See the section "Getting Information About Files and Directories," later in this chapter, for more on the -l option.

Sorting the output of ls

The default for ls is to sort its output alphabetically. By using the -t option you can cause the output to be sorted according to the *time* the file was last changed.

To sort the list by time instead of name:

- Use the -t option to ls.

  This is most useful when it's combined with the -l option (for example, ls -lt *.jpg), because the -l option causes the modification date and time to be displayed.

  Figure 5.15 compares the output of ls -l with ls -lt.

To reverse the sort order:

- Use the -r option (r for *reverse*).

  Figure 5.16 compares the output of ls with ls -r.

✔ Tip

- If you want to find out which files in a directory were most recently modified, use ls with the l, t, and r options:

  ls -ltr

  That puts the most recently modified files at the bottom of the list, so even if the list of files is very long, the last thing on your screen is the most recently modified file.

```
localhost:~/Documents vanilla$ ls -l
total 48
-rw-r--r--    2 vanilla    staff    55 Jan     2 17:37 foo
-rw-r--r--    1 vanilla    staff    331 May    8 19:04 novel.txt
-rw-r--r--    1 vanilla    staff    134 May    8 19:06 report.txt
-rw-r--r--    2 vanilla    staff    55 Jan     2 17:37 test1.txt
-rw-r--r--    1 vanilla    staff    87 Jan     2 17:38 test2.txt
-rw-r--r--    1 vanilla    staff    62 Jan     2 17:38 test3.txt
drwxr-xr-x    3 vanilla    staff    264 May    5 13:39 vi-practice
localhost:~/Documents vanilla$ ls -lt
total 48
-rw-r--r--    1 vanilla    staff    134 May    8 19:06 report.txt
-rw-r--r--    1 vanilla    staff    331 May    8 19:04 novel.txt
drwxr-xr-x    3 vanilla    staff    264 May    5 13:39 vi-practice
-rw-r--r--    1 vanilla    staff    62 Jan     2 17:38 test3.txt
-rw-r--r--    1 vanilla    staff    87 Jan     2 17:38 test2.txt
-rw-r--r--    2 vanilla    staff    55 Jan     2 17:37 foo
-rw-r--r--    2 vanilla    staff    55 Jan     2 17:37 test1.txt
localhost:~/Documents vanilla$
```

Figure 5.15 Adding the -t option causes ls to sort by the time of last modification.

To list only files matching a pattern:

See the entry on command-line wildcards in Chapter 2 or pipe the output of `ls` through `grep` (review Chapter 4 or `man grep`).

Sometimes you will want to list everything in a directory, including what's in any subdirectories, and any subdirectories of those directories, and so on. This is known as a *recursive* listing. There is an easy way to do this:

To recursively list the contents of a directory:

- `ls -R` *path*

  If *path* is a directory, then `ls` recursively lists the contents of *path* and its subdirectories (in this case, `R` is for *recursive*). **Figure 5.17** compares the output from

  `ls ~/Sites`

  and

  `ls -R ~/Sites`

  Notice how with the `-R` option, the listing shows the contents of the two subdirectories.


```
localhost:~/Public vanilla$ ls
cgi-bin            dancer       images       index.html    upload.html
localhost:~/Public vanilla$ ls -r
upload.html        index.html   images       dancer        cgi-bin
localhost:~/Public vanilla$
```

Figure 5.16 Using the `-r` option causes `ls` to reverse the sorted order of its output.

```
localhost:~/Public vanilla$ ls ~/Sites
images             index.html       test
localhost:~/Public vanilla$ ls -R   ~/Sites
images             index.html       test

/Users/vanilla/Sites/images:
apache_pb.gif      macosxlogo.gif   web_share.gif

localhost:~/Public vanilla$
```

Figure 5.17 Using the `-R` option tells `ls` that you want a recursive directory listing.

Viewing the Contents of Text Files

Because Unix uses text files for so many things (including system configuration, source code, log files, and documentation), you will frequently want to view the contents of text files. Unix provides many tools to do this, and we've described the more common ones here. To learn how to edit text files, see Chapter 6, "Editing and Printing Files."

All the tools shown here apply not only to viewing text files but also to seeing the output of other commands; that is, you can pipe the output of commands into the tools shown here. (Review the Chapter 2 section "Creating Pipelines of Commands.")

The two most common ways to view text files are with the commands `cat` and `less`. We have seen these commands in earlier chapters, but we will go into more detail about them here.

The `cat` command (short for *concatenate*) combines all of its input and sends it without any pauses to `stdout` (review the Chapter 2 section "About Standard Input and Output" for more on `stdout`).

Remember that the `less` command is a *pager*, a program that displays one page or screen of a file at a time, waiting for your command to show the next page.

Using a pager

The two most common pager programs are called `more` and `less`. The `less` program is an advanced version of the `more` program, so that is the one we describe here. (The `more` program was invented first, and it gets its name from the fact that you have to keep asking it to show you *more* of a file. The `less` command's name is the sort of recursive word game that Unix programmers love: `less` is an improved version of `more`; thus `less` is more.)

To view a file one screen at a time:

1. `less` *`path`*

   If your Terminal window is 24 lines high, then each "page" is 23 lines long—that is, one line less than your Terminal height. `less` uses the bottom line of the window to display status information and to accept some commands from you.

2. If you want to go forward one page, press the Spacebar.

3. If you want to go back one page, press B (for *back*).

4. If you want to skip forward to the next occurrence of `string`, type

   `/string`

   and then press Return.

5. If you want skip back to the prior occurrence of `string`, type

   `?string`

   and then press Return.

6. If you want to go directly to line 23, type `23G` (that's an uppercase `G`).

7. If you want to go directly to the end of the file, type `G` (that's an uppercase `G`, for *go*).

8. If you want to exit from `less`, type `q` (for *quit*).

✔ Tip

- Pipe the output of other commands into `less` so that you can see their output one page at a time. For example,

  ```
  grep Copyright *.c
  ```

  searches all the `.c` files in the current directory for the string `Copyright` (see Chapter 4 or `man grep` for details on `grep`).

  The resulting output could be very long, so you pipe it through `less`:

  ```
  grep Copyright *.c | less
  ```

Sometimes you want to see an entire file without pausing. Perhaps you know the file is very short, or you want to use the Terminal window's scroll bars to move up and down. You might want to select the text with the mouse to copy or print it.

Another reason to see an entire file is to join two or more files together. Unix provides the `cat` tool for this purpose.

To see an entire file without pausing:

- `cat` *`path`*

  The `cat` command gets its name from *concatenate,* and in fact that is what it does—it concatenates (or combines) all the files in its argument list and sends them to its output. For example,

  `cat file1 file2 file3`

  results in the contents of all three files appearing on your screen without a break.

✔ Tips

- Use `cat` to concatenate several files into one new file:

  `cat` *`file1 file2 file3`* `>` *`newfile`*

- Use the `-n` option to number lines. For example:

  `cat -n script.pl`

  Figure 5.18 shows an example of using `cat -n` to see a file with line numbers. (The example uses the script you created in Chapter 2.)

- Use the `-s` option to "squeeze out" extra blank lines, resulting in single-spaced output. For example:

  `cat -s` *`file1 file2`* `>` *`newfile`*

- As always, see the `man` page for more options: `man cat`.

```
localhost:~ vanilla$ cat -n ~/bin/status.sh
     1	#!/bin/sh
     2	# This is a comment. Comments are good.
     3	# This is my first shell script.
     4	echo "System Status Report"
     5	date
     6	echo -n "System uptime and load:" ;  uptime
     7	echo -n "Operating System: " ; sysctl -n kern.ostype
     8	echo -n "OS Version: " ; sysctl -n kern.osrelease
     9	echo -n "OS Revision number: " ; sysctl -n kern.osrevision
    10	echo -n "Hostname: " ; sysctl -n kern.hostname
    11	
    12	bytes=`sysctl -n hw.physmem`
    13	megabytes=`expr $bytes / 1024 / 1024`
    14	echo "Physical memory installed (megabytes): $megabytes"
localhost:~ vanilla$
```

Figure 5.18 Using `cat -n` adds line numbers to the output of `cat`.

Seeing just the beginning or end of a file

Sometimes you want to see just the first (or last) few lines of a file. You might want to confirm that the file contains what you expect, or to see the last lines added to a log file.

The Unix commands head and tail show you the beginning or end (respectively) of their input.

To view just the beginning of a file:

- head *path*

  For example:

  `head /conf/config.txt`

  The head command shows you the first 10 lines of a file.

You can control the number of lines to display by giving the number as an option. For example,

`head -15 /etc/rc`

displays the first 15 lines of the system-configuration file /etc/rc (**Figure 5.19**).

To view just the end of a file:

- tail *path*

  For example:

  `tail /var/log/mail.log`

  The tail command works just like the head command, but it shows you the end of a file. For example,

  `tail -100 /var/log/mail.log`

  displays the last 100 lines of the system mail log.

```
localhost:~ vanilla$ head -15 /etc/rc
 #!/bin/sh
# Copyright 1997-2004 Apple Computer, Inc.

. /etc/rc.common

export -n SafeBoot
export -n VerboseFlag
export -n FsckSlash
export -n NetBoot

if [ -d /System/Installation -a -f /etc/rc.cdrom ]; then
        /etc/rc.cdrom multiuser
        # We shouldn't get here; CDIS should reboot the machine when done
        echo "CD-ROM boot procedure complete"
        halt
localhost:~ vanilla$
```

Figure 5.19 The head command shows the specified number of lines from the start of its input.

✔ Tip

- The `head` and `tail` commands can both be used on multiple files; add as many filenames as you need on the command line. For example:

  `tail file1 file2` or `head *.html`

  The output will have each file's name. Remember that you can use full or relative paths wherever you are using filenames.

We've mentioned system log files several times because Unix systems keep a variety of log files to record system events (startup and shutdown, e-mail being sent or received, and Web pages served by a Web server, to name a few).

Checking the addition of new lines to a log file is very useful. You might be debugging a piece of software or watching to see the effect of some change to your network. You could continuously run the `tail` command, but it is far more useful to tell the `tail` command to simply keep showing you any new lines as they are added.

To view the end of a file while it is growing:

1. Use the `-f` option to `tail`.

   `tail -f /var/log/system.log`

   shows all lines being added to the main system log file as they are added.

   The `-f` (for *follow*) option shows you the end of the file and keeps displaying new lines as they are added. Unix experts call this "tailing a file."

2. When you want to stop `tail -f`, press Control C.

✔ Tips

- Keep an extra Terminal window open when you need to run `tail -f`. That way, you can see the file you are tailing in one window and do your work in the other one.
- Pipe the output of other commands through `head` or `tail` to see just the start or end of the output. For example,

  `last | tail`

  shows just the last ten lines of output from the `last` command (which shows all log-ins, crashes, and reboots in the current month; see `man last`).

More About less

The `less` program has a large number of options and an even larger number of commands for moving around inside a file. Type `man less` at a shell prompt to read the Unix manual entry on `less` for a complete (if rather technical) description of its capabilities and features.

More About Hidden Files

Mac OS X uses a variety of files and directories that are hidden from casual view. In most cases you will have no reason to mess with these files, but as you get further in Unix, you will want to know what they are and why they are there.

A good summary of the hidden files and folders used by Mac OS X is at "Mac OS X Hidden Files & Directories" (Westwind Computing; www.westwind.com/reference/OS-X/invisibles.html).

Also, see Chapter 7 for a discussion of how to make some hidden files appear in the Finder.

Creating Files and Directories

There are many ways to create files and directories from the command line. The method you choose depends on your purpose. Two common purposes are to capture the output of a command into a file, and to create a new, empty directory. Chapter 6 covers the more complex tasks of editing files from the command line, but we'll go over the basics here.

To create a new directory:

◆ `mkdir` *path*

The `mkdir` command (for *make directory*) takes one or more arguments, each of which is a *path* of a new directory. The path (as with all path arguments) may be relative or absolute. The `mkdir` command produces no output unless an error is encountered.

✔ Tip

■ Use `ls` to check that your new directory was created (**Figure 5.20**).

To create a series of nested directories:

◆ Use the `-p` option to `mkdir`.

For example,

`mkdir -p test/`*`dir1/dir2`*

makes all the directories in the path if they do not already exist (`p` for *path*). So if `test` already exists, only *dir1* and *dir2* will be created; if `test` and *dir1* already exist, then only *dir2* will be created.

To create an empty file:

◆ `touch` *path*

The `touch` command takes one or more paths as arguments. If any of the files do not exist, they are created. The `touch` command updates the file's access time on each file. You could create several empty files at once. The following would create three files (assuming none already existed—if one of them did, its timestamp would be updated, but the contents of the file would be unaffected):

`touch file1 ../test/file2 /tmp/file3`

Creating a file from command output

The output of most commands can be sent into a file instead of your screen by adding `>` *`path/to/file`* at the end of the command line. If the file already exists, the old contents are replaced. Use `>>` to append or create instead of replacing the old contents. (Review the section "To save output in a file" in Chapter 2.)

```
localhost:~ vanilla$ ls
Current Projects Library       Pictures          bin
Desktop          Movies        Public            system-status
Documents        Music         Sites
localhost:~ vanilla$ mkdir "My Projects"
localhost:~ vanilla$ ls
Current Projects Library       My Projects       Sites
Desktop          Movies        Pictures          bin
Documents        Music         Public            system-status
localhost:~ vanilla$
```

Figure 5.20 Use the `ls` command to check that `mkdir` really created a directory. (What you see will be different.)

Copying Files and Directories

In the Finder, you select files to copy by clicking and Option-dragging them or by choosing File > Duplicate.

In Unix, you select files to copy by typing their names and/or paths as arguments to the `cp` command (`cp` for *copy*). You can use wildcards (see Chapter 2), and the files need not all start in the same directory.

The behavior of the `cp` command depends on its arguments. It will behave one way if its last argument is a directory and another way if its last argument is a file. The `cp` command produces no output unless it encounters an error.

To copy a file in the same directory:

- `cp` *`oldfilename newfilename`*

  If *`newfilename`* is an existing nondirectory file, then `cp` will attempt to overwrite the file, replacing its contents.

To copy a file into a directory:

- `cp` *`oldfilename directorypath`*

  If the last argument to `cp` is a directory, then the file is copied *into* the directory and the copy has the same name as the original.

  ```
  cp /etc/appletalk.cfg .
  ```

  creates a copy of `/etc/appletalk.cfg` in the current directory (represented by `.`), and the copy is also named appeltalk.cfg.

To copy a file from one directory into another and change its name:

- `cp oldfilename` *`directory/newname`*

  Simply make sure that the last argument to `cp` is a path to a file, not to a directory. For example:

  ```
  cp /etc/appletak.cfg /tmp/atalk.copy
  ```

To copy more than one file at a time:

- `cp` *`file1 file2 directorypath`*

  For example:

  ```
  cp script.pl config.pl bin/
  ```

  When `cp` is used with more than two arguments, it assumes that the last argument is a directory (you get an error message if it is not). All the files are then copied into the directory.

  The source files need not all be in the same directory. The following example would copy all the .mp3 files from the `/tmp` and `Public/` directories into the `Music/` directory:

  ```
  cp /tmp/*.mp3 Public/*.mp3 Music/
  ```

To copy an entire directory:

- `cp -R` *`directory destination`*

  For example:

  ```
  cp -R /etc/httpd .
  ```

  copies the entire `/etc/httpd` directory into the current directory.

  With the `-R` option, `cp` recursively copies directories named in its arguments. The *`destination`* (last argument) must be a directory—often it will be simply `.` for *current directory*.

  ```
  cp -R file1 dir1 dir2 dir3
  ```

  copies *`file1`* and all of *`dir1`* and *`dir2`* into *`dir3`*.

✔ Tip

- Add the `-p` option to tell `cp` to attempt to preserve the file-modification times and permissions from the source file(s). For example,

  ```
  cp -Rp /etc/httpd .
  ```

  We say "attempt" because some information about the files may not be preserved unless you execute the command as root, using the `sudo` command described in Chapter 11. Without the `-p` option, when `cp` overwrites an existing file, it will still preserve some information about the overwritten file, such as its modification time.

To copy (only) the contents of an entire directory:

- `cp -R` *`directory/ destination`*

  If you append a / to the path of a directory you are copying, then the *contents* of that directory are copied. This is tricky. These two command lines are *not* the same:

  ```
  cp -R /etc/httpd .
  cp -R /etc/httpd/ .
  ```

  The extra / in the second command line changes its behavior. With the trailing / on the source directory, cp copies only *the contents* of the directory and not the directory itself.

  Table 5.1 shows more options for the cp command.

Table 5.1

More Options for cp

Option	Meaning
-i	*Inquire* before overwriting existing files.
-f	Attempt to remove files that cannot be overwritten. Ignores -i.
-p	Attempt to *preserve* file permissions and modification dates.
-H	Used with -R, causes symbolic links on the command line to be followed (overrides some of the behavior of -R). The symbolic links in the copied directory are still copied, not followed.
-L	Used with -R, this causes all symbolic links to be followed, not copied. The difference here from the -H option is that with the -H option symlinks that are inside a copied directory will be copied, but with the -L option those symlinks will be followed.

Old Mac Files in the Unix World

In Mac OS 9 and earlier, files saved on a Mac actually consisted of either one or two parts, or *forks*. The *data* fork was always present; this was where the file data was stored. The *resource* fork contained icons and other resources associated with the file, such as which application to use when opening it. When these two-part files were copied to non-Macintosh systems, the resource fork was lost unless special steps were taken, such as encoding them into a single binhex file.

On all non-Darwin versions of Unix, and on Mac OS X before version 10.4, the standard Unix tools for manipulating files do *not* preserve the resource fork on an old-style Mac file. So if you copy a file using cp on one of these systems, the resource fork will be missing from the copy.

Starting with Mac OS X 10.4, the cp and mv commands will recognize and preserve resource forks. In versions of Mac OS X before 10.4, you can use the two commands /Developer/Tools/CpMac and /Developer/Tools/MvMac instead. These commands do not have all the options of the standard cp and mv commands. See man CpMac and man MvMac for details.

Renaming or Moving Files

As we mentioned previously, a file's path is both its name and its location, so renaming a file is really the same as moving a file. In Unix, to move is to rename, and to rename is to move. When you move a file from one directory to another, you are removing the file's name from the first directory and adding it to the list of files in the second directory. You are actually modifying the directory, not the file.

To move or rename a single file or directory:

- `mv` *`oldpath newpath`*

  If the final element of *newpath* does not exist, then the old file is moved/renamed to the new path. For example, if *newpath* is `food/pizza/toppings` and toppings. does not exist, then the old file is renamed toppings. If `food` or `food/pizza` did not exist, you would get an error.

  If *newpath* is an existing directory, then the old file is moved into the destination directory.

  If you add a trailing / to the destination directory name, `mv` makes sure that it is in fact a directory (you get an error if it is not).

  If *newpath* is an existing file, then `mv` silently attempts to overwrite the old file (you can make it ask you first, with the `-i` option). You cannot overwrite directories. If there is an existing directory where you want to move something, you must rename or delete the existing directory first.

To move several files at once:

- `mv` *`path1 path2 path3 destinationpath`*

  The `mv` command handles arguments in a manner very similar to that of the `cp` command described above.

  If the `mv` command is used with more than two arguments, it assumes that the final argument is a directory name and moves all the earlier files into that directory. **Table 5.2** shows the options for the `mv` command.

Table 5.2

Options for mv

Option	Meaning
`-i`	*Inquire* before overwriting existing files.
`-f`	*Force* no warnings when overwriting files (that is, you don't want to be notified about files' being changed).

Deleting Files and Directories

In Unix, when you remove a file or directory, it is gone forever.

In Unix, when you remove a file or directory, it is gone forever.

In Unix, when you remove a file or directory, it is gone forever.

Are we clear on this? The file is not moved to the Trash, where you can go back and retrieve it later. Yes, it is theoretically possible to recover a deleted file, but unless you're with the CIA and have a government agency behind you, don't count on it. (See the sidebar "To Use the Trash from the Command Line.")

To remove a file:

- `rm path`

  You can *remove* multiple files by supplying multiple paths as arguments; for example, the following would remove the two named files and all files in the current directory whose names end in .jpg:

  `rm file1 file2 *.jpg`

To remove an empty directory:

- `rmdir path`

  If the directory named by *path* is not empty, you get an error message. As with many commands, you can supply multiple file paths.

To remove a directory and everything inside it:

- Use the `-r` option with `rm`. For example:

  `rm -r file1 directory1/ file2`

  Table 5.3 shows the options for the `rm` command.

✔ Tips

- Be extremely careful with `rm`. Consider moving the file(s) to `~/.Trash` instead.
- Be especially careful when using wildcards in arguments; for example, `rm *` would remove every file (except dot files) from the current directory. Think twice before doing that.
- Some people like to configure their shells so that `rm` is always used with the `-i` option. See Chapter 7 to find out how to create an alias of `rm` in your shell so that it becomes `rm -i`.

Table 5.3

Options for rm

Option	Meaning
-d	Remove empty *directories* as well as files.
-r	*Recursively* remove directories and their contents; implies -d.
-f	*Force*—attempts to override permission restrictions and does not report errors.
-i	*Inquire* before removing each file; type a y to confirm.

To Use the Trash from the Command Line

When you use the Finder, the files you put in the Trash are actually moved into a "hidden" directory in your home directory, called `.Trash` (in Unix, files whose name starts with a `.` are not normally displayed).

Instead of deleting files, you can move them to the Trash with

`mv -i filename ~/.Trash`

The `-i` (for *inquire*) option prompts you before overwriting a file with the same name in the `.Trash` directory. This is different from the Finder behavior in which the filename of the newly trashed file gets changed, instead of the older trashed file of the same name being deleted. (See Chapter 9, "Creating and Using Scripts," for a script that emulates the Finder behavior.)

Getting Information About Files and Directories

Besides a file's name and contents, you probably want to know many other pieces of information about it. All Unix systems provide a way to get the following information about files:

- File sizes
- File types
- Time and date last modified
- Who owns the file
- The *permissions* on files

(See Chapter 7 for more on permissions and ownership.)

Darwin (and thus Mac OS X) provides a way to get a great deal more information about files. In version 10.4 of Mac OS X, Apple introduced a brand new method for keeping track of additional data about files (*metadata*) and also a radical new method for updating indexes of file information (the *metadata store* and *content index*). The metadata store and content index are the basis for the Spotlight feature of Mac OS X, and these indexes are instantly updated every time a file is created or changed. We covered searching the metadata store and content index with the `mdfind` command in Chapter 4, and also mentioned examining the metadata for a file with the `mdls` command. In this chapter we will go into a bit of detail about the `mdls` command.

But first we will describe the way to get file information that works on all Unix systems.

Using the ls command to get file information

The `ls` command is the standard Unix command for "listing" information about files and directories. In this book we have already shown how to use `ls` to list the contents of directories. The command is also used to obtain many kinds of information besides filenames.

Options for the ls Command

The `ls` command has more than two dozen available options and can show many kinds of information about files. The Unix manual page on `ls` (`man ls`) is where you can see all of them. The most commonly used option is `-l`, for *long listing*. Other commonly used options are `-t`, to sort the output by the last-modified time, and `-a`, to show files whose names begin with a . (*dot files*). Another interesting option is the `-e` option, to display the Access Control List (ACL) associated with a file (see Chapter 8, "Working with Permissions and Ownership," for more on ACLs).

To see file type, size in bytes, date modified, owners, and permissions:

- `ls -l` *path*

  Use the `-l` option to the `ls` command (`-l` for *long form*).

  `ls -l /`

  shows you a long-form listing of your root directory (**Figure 5.21**).

  Figure 5.22 shows what the different parts of the output mean.

To show file sizes in kilobytes:

- Use the `-s` and `-k` options together:

  `ls -sk` *path*

  The `-s` option means "List sizes," and the `-k` option means "List sizes in kilobytes." If you omit the `k` option, the size is listed in *blocks,* which vary in size depending on the version of Unix and how the disk was formatted. On our disk in Mac OS X, each block is .5 Kbyte.


```
localhost:~ vanilla$ ls -l /
total 9642
drwxrwxr-x      30 root     admin     1020 Mar 26 09:29 Applications
-rw-r--r--       1 root     admin     3584 Mar 26 09:58 Desktop DB
-rw-r--r--       1 root     admin     2 Jan 14 18:48 Desktop DF
drwxrwxr-x      13 root     admin     442 Jan 17 14:38 Developer
drwxrwxr-t      43 root     admin     1462 Mar 26 09:29 Library
drwxr-xr-x       1 root     wheel     512 Mar 26 10:10 Network
drwxr-xr-x       4 root     wheel     136 Mar 26 09:26 System
drwxrwxr-t       8 root     admin     272 Mar 26 09:26 Users
drwxrwxrwt       4 root     admin     136 Mar 26 10:10 Volumes
drwxr-xr-x       4 root     admin     136 Jan 14 18:20 automount
drwxr-xr-x      40 root     wheel     1360 Mar 26 09:20 bin
drwxrwxr-t       2 root     admin     68 Nov 14 02:31 cores
dr-xr-xr-x       2 root     wheel     512 Mar 26 10:09 dev
lrwxr-xr-x       1 root     admin     11 Mar 26 09:20 etc -> private/etc
lrwxr-xr-x       1 root     admin     9 Mar 26 10:09 mach -> /mach.sym
-r--r--r--       1 root     admin     597876 Mar 26 10:09 mach.sym
-rw--r--r--      1 root     wheel     4312948 Mar 19 19:56 mach_kernel
drwxr-xr-x       6 root     wheel     204 Mar 26 10:09 private
drwxr-xr-x      63 root     wheel     2142 Mar 26 09:26 sbin
lrwxr-xr-x       1 root     admin     11 Mar 26 09:22 tmp -> private/tmp
drwxr-xr-x      11 root     wheel     374 Jan 17 14:29 usr
lrwxr-xr-x       1 root     admin     11 Mar 26 09:23 var -> private/var
localhost:~ vanilla$
```

Figure 5.21 Using `ls -l` to get information about files. (Your output may differ.)

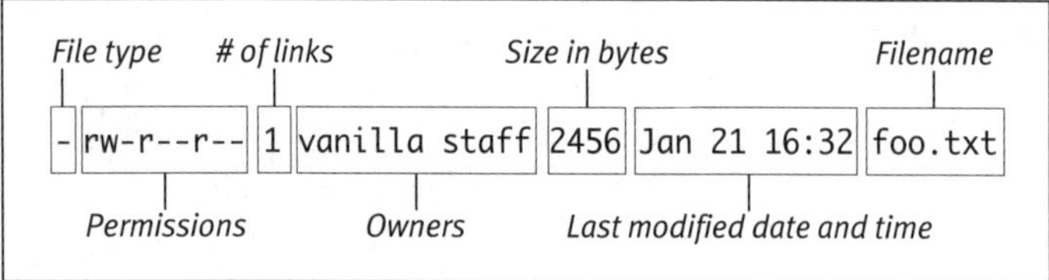

Figure 5.22 This diagram shows what the output of `ls -l` means.

Displaying file metadata

The `mdls` command lists the metadata associated with a file but is only available in the Darwin/Mac OS X version of Unix. It was introduced in Mac OS X 10.4 (along with the `mdfind` command, covered in Chapter 4). See the "Searching for Files" section of Chapter 4 for more details about metadata; briefly, the metadata displayed by `mdls` is the same metadata that the Spotlight feature of Mac OS X searches. For more on Spotlight see "Working with Spotlight" (http://developer.apple.com/macosx/spotlight.html).

To list the metadata attributes of a file:

◆ `mdls` *`path`*

  This displays the metadata associated with the file or directory whose path you supplied. For example:

  ```
  mdls /Developer/Examples/Dashboard/
  ➝ Documentation/DashboardTutorial.pdf
  ```

  Figure 5.23 shows this.

continues on next page

✔ Tips

- You can restrict the output of `mdls` to a single metadata attribute using the `-name` option—for example:

  `mdls -name kMDItemTitle`
  `→ Documents/Unix-VQP-05.doc`

- We provide a partial list of metadata attributes in Table 4.3 in Chapter 4, and a longer list is available in "Introduction to Spotlight Metadata Attributes Reference" (http://developer.apple.com/documentation/Carbon/Reference/MetadataAttributesRef).


```
localhost:~ vanilla$ mdls /Developer/Examples/Dashboard/Documentation/DashboardTutorial.pdf
/Developer/Examples/Dashboard/Documentation/DashboardTutorial.pdf -------
kMDItemAttributeChangeDate              = 2005-04-14 13:19:33 -0700
kMDItemAuthors                          = ("Apple Computer, Inc.")
kMDItemContentCreationDate              = 2004-06-16 23:38:06 -0700
kMDItemContentModificationDate          = 2004-06-16 23:38:06 -0700
kMDItemContentType                      = "com.adobe.pdf"
kMDItemContentTypeTree                           = (
          "com.adobe.pdf",
          "public.data",
          "public.item",
          "public.composite-content",
          "public.content"
)
kMDItemCreator                          = "XEP 3.7.8 Client"
kMDItemDisplayName                      = "DashboardTutorial.pdf"
kMDItemEncodingApplications             = ("XEP PDF Generator \U2013 RenderX, Inc.")
kMDItemFSContentChangeDate              = 2004-06-16 23:38:06 -0700
kMDItemFSCreationDate                   = 2004-06-16 23:38:06 -0700
kMDItemFSCreatorCode                    = 0
kMDItemFSFinderFlags                    = 0
kMDItemFSInvisible                      = 0
kMDItemFSLabel                          = 0
kMDItemFSName                           = "DashboardTutorial.pdf"
kMDItemFSNodeCount                      = 0
kMDItemFSOwnerGroupID                   = 80
kMDItemFSOwnerUserID                    = 0
kMDItemFSSize                           = 346134
kMDItemFSTypeCode                       = 0
kMDItemID                               = 661176
kMDItemKind                             = "PDF Document"
kMDItemLastUsedDate                     = 2004-06-16 23:38:06 -0700
kMDItemNumberOfPages                    = 40
kMDItemPageHeight                       = 792
kMDItemPageWidth                        = 612
kMDItemSecurityMethod                   = "None"
kMDItemTitle                            = "Dashboard Tutorial"
kMDItemUsedDates                        = (2004-06-16 23:38:06 -0700)
kMDItemVersion                          = "1.3"
localhost:~ vanilla$
```

Figure 5.23 Displaying a file's metadata using the `mdls` command.

Table 5.4

File Types from ls -l

First Character	Meaning
-	Regular file.
d	Directory.
l	Symbolic link. A special kind of file that contains the path of another file, similar to a Mac alias.
b	*Block special files* represent physical devices that deal with blocks of data, such as disks (or drives).
c	*Character special files* represent devices that deal with streams of characters, such as modems.
s	*Socket links* (also called *named pipes*) are special files that connect to programs. Writing data to the file actually "pipes" the data to the program.

Discerning different types of files

Not all files are the same. For example, some files are directories, while others are special files the operating system uses to interact with disks and other devices.

Even among regular files there are differences. For example, some files are images, others consist of programming source code in various languages, and some are compiled applications. Among files created with Mac Classic applications, there are attributes such as *stationery* (if a Mac file is marked as stationery, then it is a sort of template—a read-only document you use as a starting place for creating new documents) and *creator*.

There are several ways to find out a file's type, each showing different kinds of information.

To see file types using ls -l:

- Examine the output from `ls -l`.

  The first character of each line tells you what kind of file it is. **Table 5.4** summarizes the meaning of the first character in the output.

- If you want information about a directory, then add the `-d` option:

  `ls -ld` *`directorypath`*

  The `ls` command reports information about the directory file itself, not its contents.

To see basic Unix file-type information:

- Use the -F option to ls:

  ls -F *path*

  The -F (for *file type*) option distinguishes directories, executable files (Unix commands), and symbolic links by adding / after directories, @ after symbolic links, and * after executables. **Figure 5.24** compares ls / with ls -F /.

To guess file types from hundreds of possibilities:

- file *path*

  The file command attempts to figure out what kind of file each argument is. It uses a set of tests defined in the /usr/share/file/magic file. The file command can recognize more than 100 file types, but it is not 100 percent accurate. Some of the file types that file will try to recognize are image formats (such as JPEG, GIF, and PNG), programming languages (C, Perl, and Java), and compressed file formats (StuffIt archives, ZIP files, and Unix compress format).

  As with most commands that deal with filenames, you can supply as many paths as you like.

  file /etc/*

  applies the file command to everything in the /etc directory.

  Most of the files in the /etc directory are text files, but the file command is able to look inside them and make an educated guess about what *kind* of text file each one is (**Figure 5.25**).

```
localhost:~ vanilla$ ls /
Applications        Network        bin         mach.sym       usr
Desktop DB          System         cores       mach_kernel    var
Desktop DF          Users          dev         private
Developer           Volumes        etc         sbin
Library             automount      mach        tmp
g4-cube:~ vanilla$ ls -F /
Applications/       Network/       bin/        mach.sym       usr/
Desktop DB          System/        cores/      mach_kernel    var@
Desktop DF          Users/         dev/        private/
Developer/          Volumes/       etc@        sbin/
Library/            automount/     mach@       tmp@
localhost:~ vanilla$
```

Figure 5.24 The -F option to ls adds characters to some filenames showing file type. (Your output may differ.)

Working with Classic Mac metadata

In Mac OS X 10.4 a new system of storing file metadata was introduced (see "Displaying file metadata" earlier in this chapter, and "`mdfind`" in Chapter 4); because of this we will refer to the kind of metadata used in the Mac OS prior to Mac OS X as *Classic Mac metadata*.

The challenges of integrating pre–Mac OS X files with a Unix system are numerous and difficult. Apple has done quite an amazing job of providing backward compatibility for files created with older applications, while allowing thousands of Unix tools to operate. Still, there are some issues a command-line user should be aware of. (An excellent paper on some of the technical problems Apple has had to deal with is available online at USENIX 2000; www.wsanchez.net/papers/USENIX_2000/.)

Traditional Mac applications, and some Mac OS X applications, use an older system of storing information about each file that standard Unix commands do not understand. For example, the Finder can mark a file as "locked," and Unix command-line programs will not be able to alter the file, but neither will they tell you why you can't change them—you'll just get an error when trying to delete or rename a locked file.

(You can use the Darwin/Mac OS X version of the `ls` command with the `-lo` options:

```
ls -lo filename
```

to show if a file is "locked": the notation `uchg` [*unchangeable*] is added to the output for locked files.)

The `GetFileInfo` command (provided as part of the Mac OS X Developer Tools collection) will show you this Mac-specific information.


```
localhost:~ vanilla$ file /etc/*
/etc/6to4.conf:                    ASCII text
/etc/6to4.conf.applesaved:         ASCII text
/etc/6to4.conf.applesaved2:        ASCII text
/etc/6to4.conf.applesaved3:        ASCII text
/etc/X11:                          directory
/etc/afpovertcp.cfg:               ASCII English text
/etc/aliases:                      symbolic link to `postfix/aliases'
/etc/aliases.db:                   Berkeley DB 1.85 (Hash, version 2, native byte-order)
/etc/appletalk.cfg:                ASCII text
/etc/appletalk.nvram.en0:          data
/etc/authorization:                XML document text
/etc/authorization.cac:            XML document text
/etc/bashrc:                       ASCII text
/etc/crontab:                      ASCII English text

(Partial output)
```

Figure 5.25 The `file` command attempts to figure out what kinds of files are in the directory. (Again, your output may differ.)

To see the Mac metadata for a file:

- `/Developer/Tools/GetFileInfo` *path*

  For example,

  `/Developer/Tools/GetFileInfo`
  `→ /usr/share/doc/bash/bash.pdf`

  is shown in **Figure 5.26**.

  The attributes line lists a series of file attributes. Each letter represents one attribute that is either On (uppercase) or off (lowercase). See **Table 5.5** for the meaning of each attribute.

  Unlike many other Unix commands, `GetFileInfo` does not handle multiple filenames as arguments.

  `GetFileInfo` is installed in a directory where your shell will not normally find it, so when you use the command, you must use its full path:

  `/Developer/Tools/GetFileInfo`

  For instructions on how to configure your shell to look in more places for commands, see Chapter 7.

✔ Tip

- If a file is locked, you can unlock it from the command line using the `SetFile` command, described below. See also the `chflags` command (`man chflags`).

To set the Mac metadata for a file:

- `/Developer/Tools/SetFile -a` *letter path*

  For example,

  `/Developer/Tools/SetFile -a l "My File"`

  unlocks the file `My File`.

  `/Developer/Tools/SetFile -a T ~/`
  `→ Documents/Letter`

  turns the file Letter into stationery.

  See Table 5.5 and `man SetFile` for the meaning of each option/attribute.

✔ Tip

- Check that the attribute was set with the `GetFileInfo` command described above.

Table 5.5

File Attributes from GetFileInfo

Option/Attribute	Meaning
a or A	Alias file
v or V	Invisible*
b or B	Bundle
s or S	System (name locked)
t or T	Stationery
c or C	Custom icon*
l or L	Locked
i or I	Inited*
n or N	No INIT resources
m or M	Shared (can run multiple times)
e or E	Hidden extension*
d or D	Desktop*

*Note: Uppercase means on, lowercase means off. Options and attributes with * are allowed with folders.

```
localhost:~ vanilla$ /Developer/Tools/GetFileInfo /usr/share/doc/bash/bash.pdf
file: "/usr/share/doc/bash/bash.pdf"
type: ""
creator: ""
attributes: avbstclinmedz
created: 03/13/2005 14:31:45
modified: 03/13/2005 14:31:45
localhost:~ vanilla$
```

Figure 5.26 The `GetFileInfo` command reveals Mac-specific metadata.

About Links (the Unix Version of Aliases)

A Mac alias is a special file that "points to" another file. Unix has its own way of doing this, using *links*. Actually, Unix has two kinds of links: *symbolic links* (or *symlinks* in the Unix vernacular) and *hard links*. Hard links are sometimes simply called *links*, and symlinks are sometimes called *soft links*.

Both symlinks and hard links are created with the `ln` command (**Table 5.6**).

A hard link is virtually indistinguishable from the original file. It is simply a second name for the exact same chunk of data on your disk.

Symlinks are more similar to Mac aliases than hard links are, so we will address them in detail first.

Table 5.6

Options for ln

Option	Meaning
-f	Force the link to remove any existing file at the target location, if possible.
-h	If the target path is a symbolic link, do not follow it. Use with the -f option to replace a symbolic link with a hard link.
-s	Create a symbolic link instead of a hard link.

Using symbolic links

Symlinks are special files that contain the path (relative or absolute) to another file.

When seen from the Finder, symlinks look and behave (mostly) like Mac aliases. (When Mac aliases are examined from the command line, they look like empty files unless you examine them with the `GetFileInfo` command described above, in which case the `A` attribute will be present.)

Mac aliases still point to the original file even if the alias and/or the original file is moved. Unix symlinks are less intelligent.

For instance, symlinks that use full paths can be moved around and still work (because a full path always points to the same place), but symlinks that use relative paths will stop working if they're moved (unless the link and original file move together and maintain the relative relationship). This is because symlinks point at a path, not at the actual file's data the way that Mac aliases do. If the symlink points to an original file that is moved, the symlink will stop working because the path no longer has the original file.

If you look at a symbolic link with `ls -l`, you see the path that the link points to. **Figure 5.27** shows that the `/etc` directory is actually a symlink to `/private/etc`, and `/mach` is actually a symlink to `/mach.sym`.

The first example shows a symlink that points to a relative path, and the second example shows a symlink pointing to a full path.

continues on next page

```
localhost:~ vanilla$ ls -ld /etc
lrwxrwxr-t  1 root          admin          11 Feb 25 17:40 /etc -> private/etc
localhost:~ vanilla$ ls -l /mach
lrwxrwxr-t  1 root          admin           9 Feb 25 17:40 /mach -> /mach.sym
localhost:~ vanilla$
```

Figure 5.27 You can make symlinks by using either full or relative paths.

You use the Unix `ln` command to create hard links and the `-s` option to create symbolic links. (Notice that the syntax of the `ln` command is similar to that of the `cp` command, covered earlier in this chapter.)

To create a symbolic link:

1. Type `ln -s` but don't press Return yet.
2. Type the path to the existing file or directory.

   Think about whether you want to use a relative path or a full path for the existing file.

   These are different commands:

   ```
   ln -s /Users/vanilla/Documents/
   → letter.doc .
   ```

   ```
   ln -s ../Documents/letter.doc .
   ```

   They both create a symlink called `letter.doc` in the current directory, but the first one points to an absolute path, while the second one points to "one step toward the root directory, then down into Documents, then letter.doc."

   Remember, a full path continues to work even if the symlink is moved, and a relative path continues to work if the original *and* the symlink are moved together—say if you copy a collection of directories and files to another computer.
3. Type the path or name of the symlink, and press Return.

   If the path you type is an existing directory (for example, the current directory), then the symlink will have the same name as the original file and will be created in that directory.

   ```
   ln -s ../file.txt .
   ```

   creates a symlink called `file.txt` in the current directory. That symlink will point to `../file.txt` (remember, `.` is just another name for the current directory; it is a perfectly valid path).

   If you want to give the symlink a different name than the original, just type a pathname that ends in the new name (or, more simply, a new filename). The symlink will be created with that name:

   ```
   ln -s ../file.txt newname
   ```

✔ Tips

- Use symlinks when you want it to be obvious where the links point. Anyone can use `ls -l` to see where a symlink points.
- Use symlinks whenever you want to make a link to a directory.
- Use symlinks when you want to link to a file on a different disk or partition.
- Do not use symlinks when you want the link to keep working when the original file moves.
- Unix tools deal with symbolic links in different ways, sometimes acting upon the symlink file itself, sometimes acting upon the original. For example, the `-H`, `-L`, `-P`, and `-R` options to `cp` all affect how `cp` handles symlinks. For this reason, it is important to be aware of the presence of symlinks even if you did not create them. For instance, the `rm` program never follows symlinks; it will remove them but not follow the link to remove the original file.
- If you remove the original file, a symlink stops working—you get a "File not found" error if you try to use it. But if you put a new file at the location that the symlink points to, then the symlink works, regardless of what file is there (even if it's not the original) This is different from the way Finder aliases work, even though from the Finder it is hard to distinguish an alias from a symlink (they appear as the same icon).

Using hard links

At the beginning of this chapter, we described how Unix directories are special files that contain a list of file and directory names. Filenames are stored as entries in directories. These entries are *links* between the filename and the actual physical location on the disk partition where the file is stored (called an *inode*). Every file has at least one hard link. A hard link is essentially a name for a file, an entry in a directory. So a file's actual data occurs only once on the disk (at the location specified by its inode), but it can appear in more than one directory, or even twice in the same directory but with different names, which are called *hard links*.

Hard links are used partly for the same reasons as symbolic links (for example, as a space-saving mechanism), but, more important, they are used so that any of the links can be deleted and all the other links will still work (contrast this with symbolic links, where if the original file is deleted, the symbolic links will no longer point to anything).

Hard links differ from symbolic links in some important ways:

- You cannot make a hard link to a directory.
- You cannot make a hard link to a file on a volume that is different from the one containing the link.
- Hard links continue to work even if the original file and/or the link is moved around on the disk.
- If you move a hard link to a different disk or partition, it becomes a new file, no longer connected in any way to the original. That is, if you edit the link after moving it, the original file is not affected at all, and vice versa.
- Perhaps most interestingly, hard links continue to work even if the original file is deleted. Now how can that be?

While symbolic links are actually tiny files that contain the path of the original, hard links are extra names for the original file. Every time a hard link is created or deleted, the operating system makes a note about it in the data stored on disk about the file.

Keeping in mind that filenames are actually hard links, when you use `rm` to remove a file, you are really removing a link, not a file. The "link count" is reduced by one. The file itself is not removed until the last hard link is removed. As long as at least one hard link for a file remains, the file will still exist.

You can see the number of hard links to a file with `ls -l`. Figure 5.22 shows where to find the number of links in the output from `ls -l`.

Because a hard link points to the actual location of a file on the disk (to the inode for the file), you cannot create a hard link on one disk that points to a file on another disk (or volume). For that, you need to use symlinks.

To create a hard link:

- `ln existingpath newpath`

  With hard links, it makes no difference if the paths you use are relative or full. In either case, a new directory entry is created.

  If the new path you enter is an existing directory path, then the link is created inside that directory and has the same name as the original.

✔ Tips

- Use a hard link when you want the link to keep working even if the original file is moved or removed.
- Just as with `cp`, if you supply `ln` with more than two arguments, it assumes the last argument is a directory and creates links inside that directory for each of the earlier arguments.

6

Editing and Printing Files

Learning how to edit text files from the command line is the second most important Unix skill, right after learning how to use the command line itself. That's because text files form the basis of many activities we'll cover later in this book. Unix uses text files to store the vast majority of system configurations. Most system-administration tasks involve editing text files. Installing Unix software often requires you to edit a text file or two, and the scripts you create are also text files.

Text files in Unix are all stored as plain-text files. That is, there is no font, color, sizing, style, or other formatting information stored in the file. Unix text files are intended to be displayed using a `monospaced` font, so that every character takes up the same amount of space on the line. Unix uses a different end-of-line character than Macintosh programs use, so a text file created in a Macintosh word processor will look strange when viewed in a Unix text editor. (Some Macintosh programs, such as BBEdit, offer the option to save files with Unix-style line endings.)

In Chapter 2, "Using the Command Line," you used a simple Unix text editor called `nano` to edit a file from the command line. `nano` is a fine editor for casual editing of text files, but for a variety of reasons (such as difficulty in handling very long lines), it is not the best choice for performing serious Unix administration work, such as editing system-configuration files. In order to properly perform Unix system-administration tasks, you need to use a more powerful text editor.

There are two standard powerful Unix text editors, `vi` and `emacs`. Mac OS X comes with both of them. In this book we are going to show you some basic `vi` skills because `vi` is more widely available on different Unix systems. (See the sidebar "BBEdit—an Excellent Text Editor," for a useful Mac-centric solution.)

Once you know how to create and edit files from the command line, you will of course be curious about how to print them. At the end of this chapter we'll show you a couple of ways to do this.

Editing Files with vi

The vi editor is the *visual interface* to an older and even more basic editor called ex. ex displays only a single line at a time, because it was created for use on typewriter-like terminals. vi added *full-screen* capabilities for use on video display systems. Full screen means that vi takes up the entire Terminal window. vi uses the last line of the Terminal window, called the *status line*, to display information.

In order to keep your files neatly organized, start by creating a new directory in which to practice editing files (you might want to review Chapter 5, "Using Files and Directories").

To create a directory for use in practicing with vi:

1. `cd ~/Documents`

   This takes you to the Documents directory in your home directory.

2. `mkdir vi-practice`

   This creates the new directory, called vi-practice.

3. `cd vi-practice`

   This sets your current directory as ~/Documents/vi-practice

Super-quick start

vi is a complete application, with dozens of options, features, and commands. In order to work with vi, though, you have to have a file, so here is a quick task to start vi, enter some text, save it, and quit from vi. Later in the chapter, we will go into the details of each step. (See also the sidebar "vi Improved—the vim Editor.")

Learning vi with the vimtutor Program

Another resource for learning vi is the vimtutor program. This is a command-line program that gives you a short tutorial in using the vim editor. (See the sidebar below.)

The tutorial should take about 30 minutes to complete and is available in several languages. The default language is whatever your system default is, which is what you get if you just run vimtutor. You can specify the language with a two-letter code (en for English, es for Espanol, fr for French, and so on). So for Spanish, you'd use vimtutor es.

vi Improved—the vim Editor

The version of vi that comes with Mac OS X is actually an improved version called vim (short for vi *improved*); since not all Unix systems have vim (but virtually all have vi), we are sticking with the basic vi information in this book. Most distributions of Linux also provide vim.

vim includes multiple levels of undo, the ability to move the cursor with the arrow keys even in edit mode, and other features.

The vi command /usr/bin/vi is actually a symlink to /usr/bin/vim (see "About Links [the Unix Version of Aliases]" in Chapter 5), and when you run vi, the program is able to tell that it was invoked as vi instead of vim. But anywhere we tell you to use vi, you can type vim instead.

More information about vim is available at www.vim.org.

To create a file using vi:

1. `vi` *path*

   path is the path to the file you want to edit and will typically be the name of a file in the current directory. For example:

   `vi shopping-list`

   This brings up the `vi` editor and fills your Terminal window (note that the name of the file appears in the status line at the bottom of the window) (**Figure 6.1**).

   If the file does not already exist, it will be created when you first save from within `vi`. This is very similar to the procedure with word processors familiar to you, except that you are specifying the new filename when you start `vi`.

   The highlighted rectangle at the top left of the window is the *cursor*, which is similar to the insertion bar you see in a regular Macintosh word processor, except that this type of cursor always sits *on* a character, not between two characters. (Your cursor might look different. You can select a different cursor in the Terminal application preferences; in this book we assume you are using the default *block cursor*.)

   You also see a series of tilde (~) characters running down the left side. They are `vi`'s way of telling you that those lines are empty lines at the bottom of the window. In this case they almost fill the window because you haven't entered anything yet.

2. The next step is to switch to *edit mode* (also called *insert mode* because it lets you insert text) and enter some text:

   `i`

   Do *not* press Return.

   That is just the lowercase letter *i*. (There are many ways to enter edit mode in `vi`—we'll go into detail on them in the section "About `vi`'s Two Modes.")

   The text `-- INSERT --` appears in the status line. Not all versions of `vi` behave this way, so you cannot always rely on this indication.

continues on next page

Figure 6.1 This is what you see when you start up `vi`.

Now that you are in edit mode, you can do the following:

3. Type in at least five lines of text just so you have enough to work with in the rest of the task. You must press Return at the end of each line (see the sidebar "Word Wrap in vi").

   Figure 6.2 shows a sample view after you have entered several lines of text.

4. Save the file. To do that, you must switch back to *command mode*, so press Esc.

   The text `-- INSERT --` disappears from the status line.

   There is no need to press Return after pressing Esc.

   If you are unsure whether you switched back to command mode, press Esc again. Terminal will beep if you are already in command mode. There is no harm in pressing Q several times (that is, if you don't mind the beep).

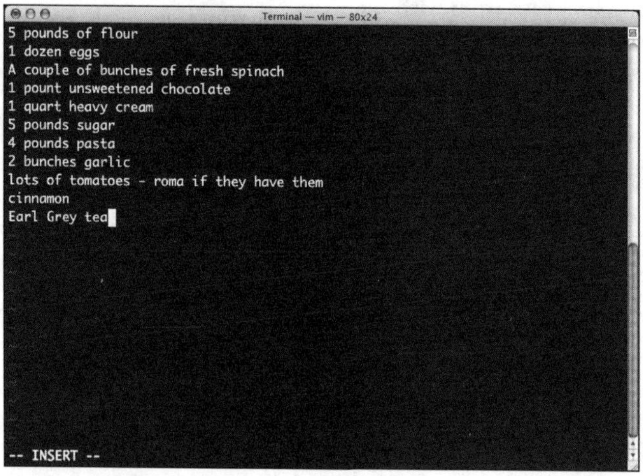

```
Terminal — vim — 80x24
5 pounds of flour
1 dozen eggs
A couple of bunches of fresh spinach
1 pount unsweetened chocolate
1 quart heavy cream
5 pounds sugar
4 pounds pasta
2 bunches garlic
lots of tomatoes - roma if they have them
cinnamon
Earl Grey tea

-- INSERT --
```

Figure 6.2 Our shopping list entered into the file using vi.

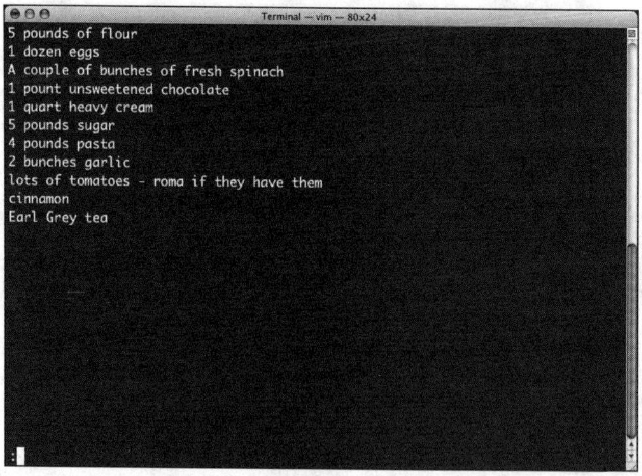

```
Terminal — vim — 80x24
5 pounds of flour
1 dozen eggs
A couple of bunches of fresh spinach
1 pount unsweetened chocolate
1 quart heavy cream
5 pounds sugar
4 pounds pasta
2 bunches garlic
lots of tomatoes - roma if they have them
cinnamon
Earl Grey tea

:
```

Figure 6.3 When you type a colon in command mode, the cursor drops to the vi status line.

5. Now you can save the file:

   `:w`

   Notice how the cursor drops to the status line as soon as you type the colon character (**Figure 6.3**).

   Also, the status line shows that you saved the file after you pressed [Return]. (Remember to press [Return] at the end of a line unless we tell you not to.)

6. `:q`

   You are back at the shell prompt, and you've created a file using `vi`.

7. `cat shopping-list`

   Run the `cat` command to verify that the new file exists and contains what you typed into it (**Figure 6.4**).

Obviously, there is a lot more to `vi` than this example. Now that you have created a file, we will explore `vi`'s different modes, as well as how to move around inside a file, change and delete text, copy and paste, and search and replace.

✔ Tip

- If you are using a version of `vi` where

  `-- INSERT --`

  doesn't appear in the status line when you are in insert mode, then you might be able to turn it on by typing

  `:set showmode`

  from the command mode. An example would be in Mac OS X prior to 10.4.


```
localhost:~/Documents/vi-practice vanilla$ cat shopping-list
5 pounds of flour
1 dozen eggs
A couple of bunches of fresh spinach
1 pound unsweetened chocolate
5 pounds sugar
4 pounds pasta
2 bunches garlic
lots of tomatoes - roma if they have them
cinnamon
Earl Grey tea
localhost:~/Documents/vi-practice vanilla$
```

Figure 6.4 Using the `cat` command to verify that the new file exists and contains what you typed into it.

Starting vi

The vi command can be started with or without specifying filenames on the command line.

The most common way to start vi is to give it one pathname as an argument. If the file already exists, it will be loaded into vi when you launch the editor. If the file does not exist, it will be created the first time you save from within vi. You can also start vi with no arguments, in which case you must supply a filename when you first save the file.

vi also allows you to enter multiple arguments and provides a way to edit each file in turn.

To start vi and edit or create a single file:

◆ `vi` *`pathname`*

pathname can be a full or relative path (review relative paths in Chapter 5). Most commonly, you simply supply the name of a file in the current directory:

`vi` *`myfile`*`.txt`

If the file does not exist, it is not created until you save your work.

To start vi without specifying a filename:

◆ `vi`

This starts up the vi program, using a temporary file. (The path of the temporary file appears on the status line.) To save text entered into this temporary file, you must supply a name for the file when you save it.

To start vi with multiple filenames:

◆ `vi` *`file1 file2 file3`* `...`

You can supply as many files as arguments as you like. vi starts up and displays the first file in the list.

You can move to the next file with the `:n` command (from command mode only), but only after you have saved any changes to the file.

You can move to the next file and discard changes with the `:n!` command.

✔ Tip

■ You can use command-line wildcards to open several files. For example,

`vi *.txt`

opens all the files in the current directory whose names end in .txt.

About vi's Two Modes

The most important thing to learn about vi is that it has two modes: *command mode* and *edit mode*.

A good way to start thinking about vi's two modes is to compare vi with any graphical user interface (GUI) word processor you have used, but imagine that the only way to move the pointer or select text is by typing commands. That presents a problem: How does the software know when you are typing a command, and when you are typing text to go into the file?

vi handles the problem of distinguishing commands from text by its two modes. In edit mode (also sometimes called *insert mode*), anything you type is inserted into the file. In fact, the only thing you can do in edit mode is enter text and move around inside the file using the arrow keys. In some older versions of vi, you can't even move around in edit mode, but happily Mac OS X comes with a version that does allow you to use the arrow keys while in edit mode.

In command mode, anything you type is interpreted as a command. Saving and quitting involve using commands, and so does moving to the beginning or end of the file, or selecting a range of text to replace, or searching for text, and so on. Anything you would use the mouse for in a GUI word processor is accomplished from command mode in vi.

You must be in command mode in order to save a file, quit, undo, search and replace, copy and paste, and perform all similar functions.

Typing the same thing in the two different modes will have very different results. This is probably the most difficult thing to get used to in vi, along with the fact that you cannot use the mouse (all moving of the cursor in both modes is done from the keyboard.)

Switching to command mode

Switching to command mode from edit mode is the simplest task in vi—there is only one way to do it.

To switch back to command mode:

- Press Esc.

  The Esc key is located at the upper-left corner on most Macintosh keyboards. This is the only way to switch back to command mode from edit mode. If you are already in command mode, you will get a beep.

✔ Tip

- If you aren't sure whether you are in command mode, go ahead and press Esc. Once you hear the beep, you'll know you are in command mode.

Switching to edit mode

When you first start vi, you are always in command mode. In order to enter text, you must switch to edit mode.

Before switching to edit mode, you should see where exactly the cursor is in the file and think about where you want the next text to be inserted (just as with the insertion bar in GUI word processors).

There are several ways to switch to edit mode, and the method you choose determines where the new text will go. For instance, if you want the new text to be inserted *after* (to the right of) the current cursor position, then you will choose one particular method of switching to edit mode. If you want the new text to be inserted *before* (to the left of) the cursor, then you will choose a different method.

All of the one-letter commands shown here for switching to edit mode take effect immediately—that is, you do not press Return after any of them.

To enter edit mode and add text before the cursor:

- `i`

  Do not press Return. The `i` command (for *insert*) lets you edit to the left of wherever the cursor was when you typed `i`.

✔ Tip

- This is usually the way you want to switch to edit mode, but be careful—when you want to add text to the end of a line, use the method shown next.

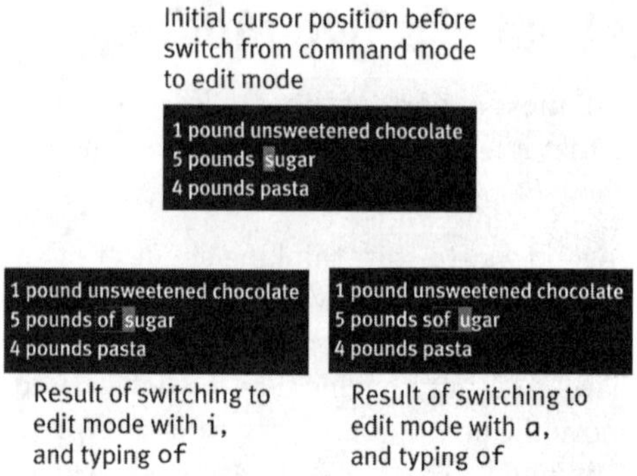

To enter edit mode and add text after the cursor:

- `a`

  The `a` command (for *append*) switches you to edit mode and lets you add text *after* (to the right of) the cursor position. (Compare with the `i` command, which lets you *insert* text before the cursor position.)

Figure 6.5 compares the results of these first two methods.

✔ Tip

- The `a` command is the one to use when you want to add text to the end of a line.

To enter edit mode and add text below the current line:

- `o`

  The `o` command (lowercase letter *o*) *opens* a new line below the one you were on. New text is entered on that line (**Figure 6.6**).

Initial cursor position before switch from command mode to edit mode

```
1 pound unsweetened chocolate
5 pounds sugar
4 pounds pasta
```

```
1 pound unsweetened chocolate
5 pounds of sugar
4 pounds pasta
```

Result of switching to edit mode with `i`, and typing `of`

```
1 pound unsweetened chocolate
5 pounds sof ugar
4 pounds pasta
```

Result of switching to edit mode with `a`, and typing `of`

Figure 6.5 Text is inserted either before or after the initial cursor position, depending on how you switch to edit mode.

Initial cursor position before switch from command mode to edit mode.

```
1 pound unsweetened chocolate
5 pounds sugar
4 pounds pasta
```

```
1 pound unsweetened chocolate
5 pounds sugar

4 pounds pasta
```

Result of switching to edit mode with the `o` command.

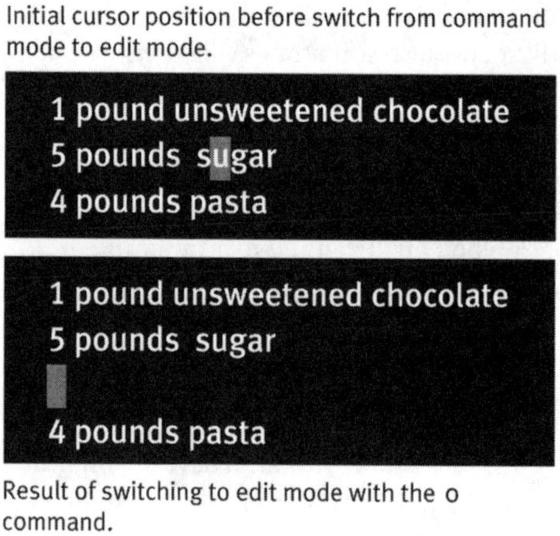

Figure 6.6 Using the `o` command to switch to edit mode opens a new line below the one you were on.

Initial cursor position before switch from command mode to edit mode

```
1 pound unsweetened chocolate
5 pounds sugar
4 pounds pasta
```

```
1 pound unsweetened chocolate

5 pounds sugar
4 pounds pasta
```

Result of switching to edit mode with the uppercase O command

Figure 6.7 Using the uppercase O command to switch to edit mode opens a new line above the one you were on.

To enter edit mode and add text above the cursor:

- O

  The uppercase O command does the same thing as the lowercase o, except it opens a line above the one you were on (**Figure 6.7**).

Table 6.1 summarizes the most common ways to switch from command mode to edit mode in vi.

Table 6.1

Switching to Edit Mode in vi

Where to Add New Text	Command
Before the cursor	i
After the cursor	a
Below the current line	o
Above the current line	O

Word Wrap in vi

An excellent feature of vi is its ability to deal with very long lines of text, far wider than the 80 columns that are the default display in a Terminal window.

You have to press Return at the end of each line in vi, unlike what you do with paragraph-based word processors you are probably used to.

You can tell vi to automatically insert a return character when you get within *x* columns of the right edge of the Terminal window. To do this, make sure you are in command mode (press Esc) and then type

```
:set wm=5
```

for auto returns within five columns of the edge. You can change that number to anything convenient. If you want that option to always be on, put the following line in a file in your home directory called .exrc:

```
set wm=5
```

Navigating Using vi

In vi you do all of your navigation within the Terminal window with the keyboard, and almost all of it from command mode.

Think of your file as having a grid of lines and columns, each one a character wide and high. Your basic cursor movements are up, down, left, and right.

Figure 6.8 shows the vi cursor on line 5, column 13.

To see which line you are on:

- Control G
  The status line displays the line number where the cursor is and also indicates whether the file has unsaved changes ("modified") or not ("unmodified") (**Figure 6.9**).

Basic cursor movement

Newer versions of vi (including the version included with Mac OS X) allow you to move the cursor by using the arrow keys while in either command or edit mode. But not every version of vi allows this. Some versions support the arrow keys only in command mode, and some do not support the arrow keys at all, regardless of which mode you are in.

```
/usr/bin/login (ttyp2) 80x24
5 pounds of flour
1 dozen eggs
A couple of bunches of fresh spinach
1 pound unsweetened chocolate
1 quart heavy cream
5 pounds sugar
4 pounds pasta
2 bunches garlic
lots of tomatoes - roma if they have them
cinnamon
Earl Grey tea
(remember to exercise heavily after eating all of this)
~
```

Figure 6.8 The vi cursor is on line 5, column 13.

```
shopping-list: unmodified: line 5 of 12 [41%]
→ col 13
```

Figure 6.9 Pressing Control G displays the cursor position on the vi status line.

vi Cheat Sheets

There are hundreds of vi cheat sheets on the Web. Here are a few in different styles.

vi Editor Cheat Sheet (K Computing; www.kcomputing.com/vi.html). Has a link to an excellent PDF cheat sheet that is very graphically oriented. Highly recommended.

vi Editor Cheat Sheet (University of the Virgin Islands, Center for Administrative Computing; http://cac.uvi.edu/miscfaq/vi-cheat.html). A text-based cheat sheet that covers many commands.

VI Cheat Sheet (Tufts University, Computational Mechanics Studio; http://ase.tufts.edu/mechanical/compstudio/help/vihelp.html). A short, text-based cheat sheet.

Table 6.2 shows commands for moving the cursor that will work in command mode with every version of `vi`. Also see the sidebar "`vi` Cheat Sheets."

You do *not* press [Return] after any of the commands shown in Table 6.2. In fact, pressing [Return] by itself in command mode is another way to move down one line.

Table 6.2

Basic vi Moves

Move the Cursor	Command
Left one column	h or [←]
Right one column	l or [→]
Up one line	k or [↑]
Down one line	j or [↓]
To the end of this line	$
To the start of this line	^
Down one screen	[Control][F] (similar to "page down")
Up one screen	[Control][B] (similar to "page up")
Go to line 23 of file	23G
Go to last line of file	G

Navigating by searching for text

Another very common way to navigate within a file when using `vi` is to search for a string of characters, which moves the cursor to the next occurrence of the string. You may search forward (toward the end of the file) or backward (toward the top of the file). In either case, the search will "wrap" around the top or end of the file.

Remember that these commands must be executed from command mode, and that you can make sure you are in command mode by pressing [Esc].

To move forward to the next occurrence of a string:

1. /

   The cursor drops to the status line in your Terminal window (**Figure 6.10**).

continues on next page

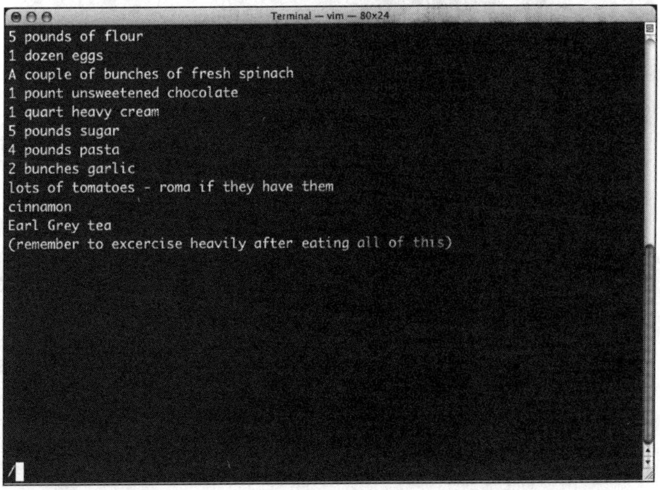

```
Terminal — vim — 80x24
5 pounds of flour
1 dozen eggs
A couple of bunches of fresh spinach
1 pount unsweetened chocolate
1 quart heavy cream
5 pounds sugar
4 pounds pasta
2 bunches garlic
lots of tomatoes - roma if they have them
cinnamon
Earl Grey tea
(remember to excercise heavily after eating all of this)

/
```

Figure 6.10 The cursor drops to the bottom line as soon as you type a slash to search from command mode.

2. Type the string you want to search for.

   The search string is case sensitive (**Figure 6.11**). (The search string in Figure 6.11 is `Ea`.)

3. Press Return to execute the search.

   The cursor moves to the next occurrence of the string, which was actually above where we started searching (note the "wrapped" comment in the status line) (**Figure 6.12**).

✔ Tips

- To repeat the last search and move to the next occurrence of the string, use the `n` command. (You do *not* press Return after typing the `n`.)
- To repeat the search in the opposite direction, use `N` (uppercase *N*). (Again, do not press Return.)

To move backward to the previous occurrence of a string:

- This is exactly the same as searching forward, except you use ? instead of `/`.

  Once again, the cursor drops to the status line as soon as you press ?.


```
5 pounds of flour
1 dozen eggs
A couple of bunches of fresh spinach
1 pount unsweetened chocolate
1 quart heavy cream
5 pounds sugar
4 pounds pasta
2 bunches garlic
lots of tomatoes - roma if they have them
cinnamon
Earl Grey tea
(remember to excercise heavily after eating all of this)




/Ea
```

Figure 6.11 Enter a case-sensitive search string, and press Return.

```
5 pounds of flour
1 dozen eggs
A couple of bunches of fresh spinach
1 pount unsweetened chocolate
1 quart heavy cream
5 pounds sugar
4 pounds pasta
2 bunches garlic
lots of tomatoes - roma if they have them
cinnamon
Earl Grey tea
(remember to excercise heavily after eating all of this)
~
~
~
~
~
search hit BOTTOM, continuing at TOP
```

Figure 6.12 Note the comment in the status line "search hit BOTTOM, continuing at TOP."

Saving a File in vi

vi offers features similar to the familiar Save and Save As features found in most Macintosh applications.

To begin, you must be in command mode. All save commands in vi begin with a colon. This drops the cursor to the last line of your Terminal window and tells vi you are about to enter a command that affects the entire file.

You will see that many vi commands begin by the user's typing a colon (:). If the cursor doesn't drop to the status line when you type a colon, then you have forgotten to switch to command mode. In those cases, delete (press Delete) the colon you inserted and press Esc.

You always press Return at the end of vi commands that start with a colon.

To save the current file:

- `:w`

  The `:w` command (for *write to disk*) saves the current file. If you do not supply a filename, your changes will be saved to disk in the temporary file that, unbeknownst to you, vi was already using.

To save the file with a new filename:

- `:w` *pathname*

  The current version of the file is saved at *pathname*.

  You are still "in" the file you started on after the save; that is, using `:w` *pathname* doesn't change which file you are editing.

  Usually the *pathname* is simply a filename to save the file in the current directory, but there is no reason why you cannot save to a file somewhere else; you just have to supply a proper (relative or full) pathname. For example,

  `:w ~/Documents/newfile.txt`

  saves a copy of the file you are editing as newfile.txt in the `Documents` directory of your home directory, regardless of where you were when you started vi.

✔ Tip

- The `:w` *pathname* feature is useful if you started vi without specifying a filename.

To save and attempt to override warnings:

- `:w!`

  Sometimes you get warnings that vi is unable to save a file when you use the `:w` command. Often the problem is related to the file's *permissions*—that is, who has permission to read, write, and copy it (we'll cover permissions in detail in Chapter 8, "Working with Permissions and Ownership"). As long as you either own the file or have write permission in the directory containing the file, using `:w!` will override permission warnings.

Quitting vi

As much as you probably love using vi, sooner or later you will want to do something else, maybe anything else. Knowing when and how to quit is one of life's great lessons. Quitting from vi is pretty easy, as long as you have saved all your changes. You can combine saving and quitting if you like. If you try to quit from vi with unsaved changes, vi will give you a warning on the status line (**Figure 6.13**). You can override the warning if you want to quit without saving.

To quit vi if you have saved all changes:

- :q

  vi quits and returns to the shell prompt.

  If you forgot to save any changes, then vi displays a warning message in the status line and does not quit.

To combine saving and quitting:

- :wq

  The file is saved, and vi quits.

To quit without saving:

- :q!

  vi quits even if there are unsaved changes to the file.

BBEdit—an Excellent Text Editor

The BBEdit program is a GUI text editor. Available in both "lite" freeware and full-featured commercial versions, BBEdit is a powerful tool for editing plain-text files such as HTML, programming source code, and Unix text files.

The commercial version will allow you to perform all your Mac OS X system-administration tasks. Because it is a commercial version, we did not use it as the primary editor discussed in this book—we don't want you to have to buy something else in order to use this book. Still, we heartily recommend BBEdit lite to anyone who works with plain-text files on a Mac.

BBEdit is available from Bare Bones Software (www.barebones.com).

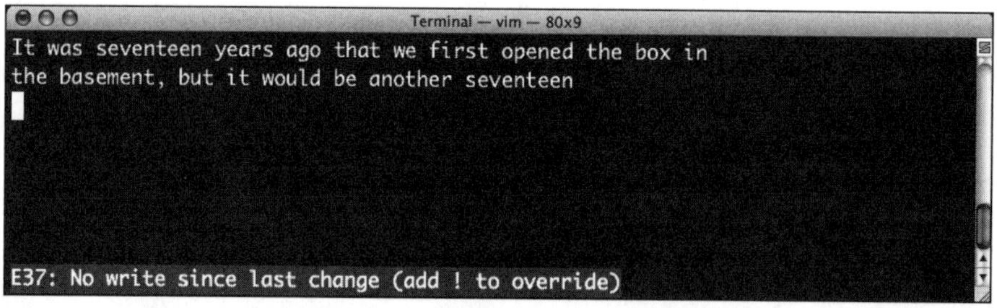

```
Terminal — vim — 80x9
It was seventeen years ago that we first opened the box in
the basement, but it would be another seventeen

E37: No write since last change (add ! to override)
```

Figure 6.13 vi gives you a warning on the status line if you try to quit while leaving unsaved changes.

Changing and Deleting Text

Besides the basics of entering text, saving, and quitting, you often use vi to change text that has already been saved. Sometimes you will simply want to delete text; other times you will want to alter existing text.

Deleting text is simpler, so we'll look at that first.

Deleting text

You can delete text from either edit mode or command mode.

The basic rule for deleting text in edit mode is: You can delete text by pressing Delete.

The version of vi in Mac OS X 10.3 and later allows you to use edit mode to delete any text in the file, and it will "word-wrap" backward past the start of the line to the previous line.

From command mode, you may delete any text in the file. Any text deleted while in command mode is saved temporarily in memory (similarly to the way the traditional Mac concept of the Clipboard works) and is available for pasting. See the section "Copy and paste," later in this chapter.

To delete text from edit mode:

- Press Delete

  It's that simple. No need to press Return.

To delete one character from command mode:

- x

  The x command (for *excise*) deletes the character under the cursor. You do not press Return, just type the x.

  There are many ways to delete text from command mode. **Table 6.3** summarizes the most important methods.

To delete one line of text from command mode:

- dd

  The dd command deletes the current line (the line the cursor is on). Do not press Return.

Notice how most of the methods shown in Table 6.3 follow a pattern consisting of the d command followed by something that indicates how much text to delete. You do not press Return for any of these commands except one (because that command ends with a number of lines, and vi doesn't know if you are entering a single-digit number or more digits until you press Return).

Table 6.3

Deleting Text from Command Mode in vi

To Delete This	Type This
Character under the cursor	x
Two characters	2x
From here to end of line	d$
This whole line	dd
Five lines (including this one)	d5 Return
From this line to end of file	dG
From this line to line 27	d27G
From here forward to *string*	d/string
From here back to *string*	d?string
From cursor to end of word	dw

Changing text

You can change text in either command or edit mode.

To change text in edit mode, press Delete over it and retype.

Changing text from command mode is usually a matter of selecting a range of text with a command that switches you into edit mode; then what you type after switching replaces the selected text. This is very much like selecting text with the mouse in a GUI word processor: As soon as you type something after making the selection, the selected text disappears.

It is important to note that many of the text-changing examples below combine the change-text command (`c`) with one of the navigation techniques we talked about earlier in this chapter. For example, `c24G` actually does the following:

1. Deletes all the text from the current cursor position through line 24 (inclusive).
2. Switches you into edit mode.

So whatever you type next will replace the deleted text (which is available for pasting with the `p` command; see the section "Copy and paste").

To change from the cursor position to the end of the word:

1. `cw`

Do *not* press Return.

The word will disappear, and whatever you type next will be inserted where the word was.

Figure 6.14 shows the text before using the `cw` command, and **Figure 6.15** shows what happens when you type `cw`. Basically, the word disappears and you are placed into insert mode. (In some versions of `vi`, the word does not disappear until you begin typing the replacement. Instead, the last character of the word changes to a `$` when you type `cw`, to indicate that it is about to be replaced.)

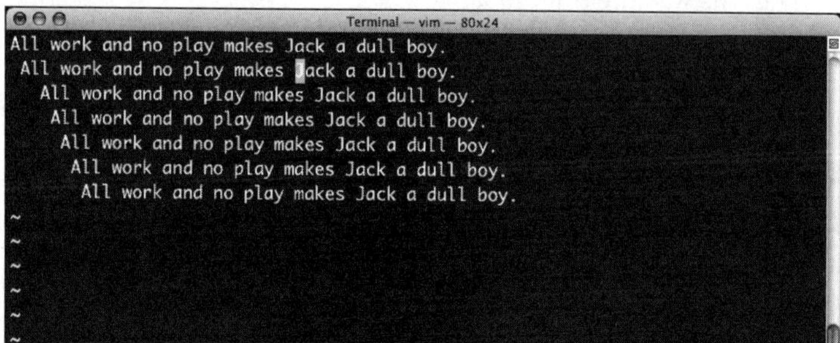

Figure 6.14 Example of text before typing the cw command to change one word in command mode.

2. Enter the new text.

   In **Figure 6.16** we show what you would see if you typed `George`.

3. Press [Esc] to exit insert mode.

To change text from the cursor to the end of the line:

◆ `c$`

  The `c$` command means "change to end-of-line." This command removes the text from the current position to the end of the current line and puts you into edit mode. (Again, in some versions of `vi`, the text will not disappear until you start typing the replacement text.)

✔ Tip

■ There is a shortcut for this command—`C` (an uppercase *C*).

To change text from the cursor to the next occurrence of a given string:

1. `c/`*`string`*

   You must press [Return] at the end of the search string. This is a good example of combining the `c` command with a movement command we showed you earlier (`/`*`string`*). Using this command to change text will delete all the text from the current cursor position to the next occurrence of *`string`*, and switch you to edit mode. (As with the tasks above, in some versions of `vi`, the text will not be deleted until you begin to type the replacement.)

2. Type the replacement text.

✔ Tip

■ You can also search backward, so that `c?`*`string`* selects text from the current cursor position to the previous occurrence of *`string`* (toward the top of the file).

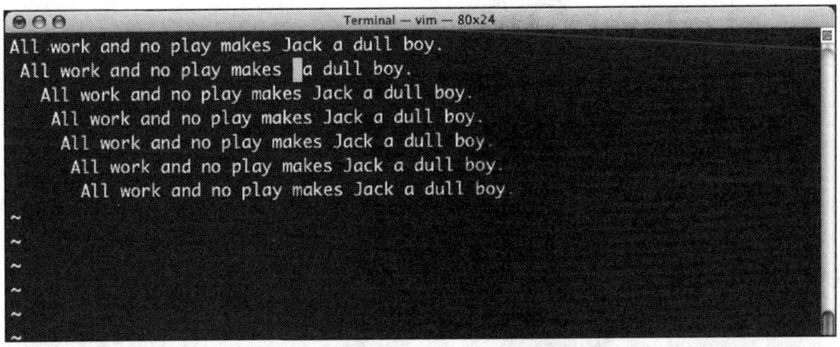

Figure 6.15 After the cw command is typed, the word disappears.

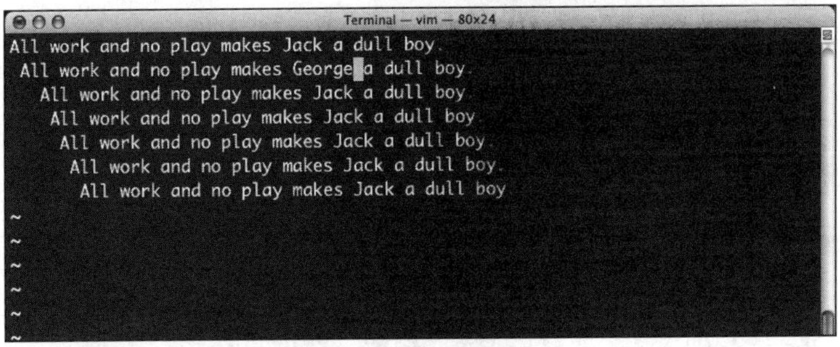

Figure 6.16 Whatever you type next replaces the selected text.

To change text from the current line to a specific line number:

1. c5G

   Of course, you replace 5 with whatever line number you want. This selects the text from the current line to the specified line number—all the lines are included. The screen updates as soon as you type the G, showing the selected lines deleted and leaving you in edit mode. **Figures 6.17** and **6.18** show text before and after the c5G command.

2. Type the replacement text.

   Remember that you are still in edit mode when you are done.

Sometimes you want to change just one character. Here is an easy way to change one character without having to go into edit mode and back.

To change just the character under the cursor:

1. r

   The r command selects just the character under the cursor. Do not press Return.

2. Type the replacement character.

   Unlike most other editing commands, r lets you stay in command mode as you do this—you are not left in insert mode when done.

To flip the case of the character that is under the cursor:

- ~

  Typing ~ (the tilde) switches the character under the cursor from upper- to lowercase, or vice versa. This command does not switch you into edit mode. Again, do not press Return.

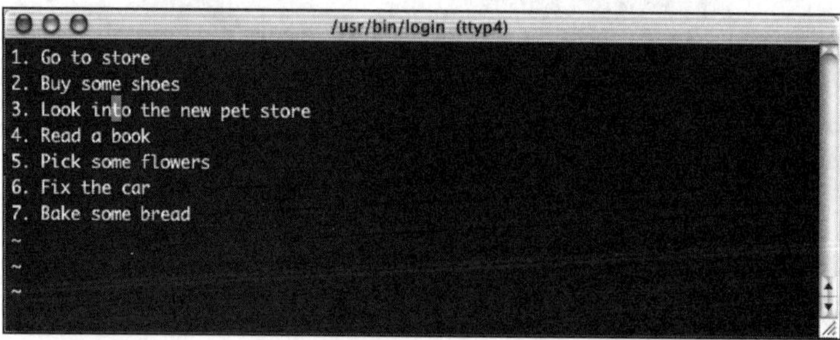

Figure 6.17 Example of text before using the c5G command.

Figure 6.18 After you type c5G, the selected lines are removed.

The version of vi in Mac OS X has multiple levels of undo—that is, you can undo not only the last change you made, but each change going back to when you opened the file for editing.

To undo the last change:

- u

  Do not press Return. The u command undoes the last edit you made anywhere in the file, even if the cursor has moved since the change was made, and even if you have saved the change. You can use this command several times in a row to take advantage of multiple levels of undo.

To revert to the last saved version:

- :e!

  Then press Return. vi reloads the last saved version of the file.

Copy and paste

vi supports fairly easy copy-and-paste functions. Like the commands for changing text, the copy command (y for *yank*) may be combined with many of the movement commands to select ranges of text and copy them.

To copy the current line:

- y

  Then press Return. This yanks the current line into the vi equivalent of the Clipboard; it's called the *buffer* and is totally separate from the regular Mac Clipboard.

Once you have yanked text, you can paste it.

To paste the contents of the buffer:

- p

  Do not press Return. The p (for *paste*) command inserts the contents of the buffer at the cursor.

  If the buffer's content is one or more lines, the text is inserted below the current line.

  If the buffer's content is less than a full line, it is inserted into the current line to the right of the cursor.

✔ Tip

- The uppercase P command also pastes, but it pastes either *above* the current line or to the *left* of the cursor.

To paste multiple copies simultaneously:

- Precede the p command with a number.

  For example, 10p pastes ten copies of the buffer's content.

To copy several lines into the buffer:

- Precede the y command with a number.

  For example, to copy the current line plus four more lines (five lines total), type 4y.

To paste deleted text:

- Any deleted text may be pasted using the p and P commands.

There is no separate "cut" command in vi. All deleted text is "cut" and available for "pasting"—this includes text deleted using d$, dw (delete to the end of the word), 10d Return (delete this and the next ten lines), x, 5x, and so on—and it goes into the same buffer as yanked (copied) text.

Search and replace

Search and replace in vi is done in command mode using commands on the status line. Like the commands to save and quit, the search and replace commands all begin with a colon, which drops the cursor to the command line, and all end with pressing Return.

(To simply search for a string of text without replacing it, see "Navigating by searching for text," earlier in this section.)

The general format of the search-and-replace command is
`:[optional range of lines]s/Old/New/`
`→ [optional modifiers]`

You will always type the colon, the s, and the three slashes. *Old* and *New* may be patterns using a simple subset of the regular expressions you learned in Chapter 4, "Useful Unix Utilities."

To create a general search-and-replace command:

1. Type a colon to drop to the vi command line.
2. As an option, you can enter a *range* of lines to be affected. This is a pair of specifiers separated by a comma. For example, 23,57 indicates lines 23 through 57 (inclusive). Use the specifier . for "the current line" and $ for "the end of the file." For example, use .,23 to indicate the current line through line 23 (either up or down from the current line without wrapping around the top or bottom of the file). Using .,$ would mean "from the current line through the end of the file." If you do not specify a range, only the current line is affected (the same as a range of .,.).
3. Type s (for *substitute*).
4. Type a slash: /
5. Enter the target (search) pattern.
6. Type another slash.
7. Enter the replacement pattern.
8. Type a third slash.
9. Enter any optional modifiers, such as g, for "global on each line."
10. Press Return to execute the command.

Here is a series of increasingly complex search-and-replace commands.

To replace the first Foo with Bar on the current line:

◆ `:s/Foo/Bar/`

This is the simplest form of a search and replace in `vi`. Only the first occurrence of `Foo` on the current line will be replaced with `Bar`.

To replace every Foo with Bar on the current line:

◆ `:s/Foo/Bar/g`

In this case you are adding the `g` modifier so that the change affects the line "globally"; that is, every occurrence of the first string is replaced.

To replace every occurrence in the file:

◆ `:1,$s/Foo/Bar/g`

When you add a range of lines, the change affects more than the current line. In this case the range `1,$` means from the first line in the file through the end of the file. If you leave off the `g` modifier, only the first occurrence of `Foo` on each line will be changed.

✔ Tip

■ The range need not start at line 1. A range of `55,$` would affect lines 55 through the end of the file.

To replace from one line to another line:

◆ `:15,23s/Foo/Bar/g`

Here the range is from line 15 through line 23.

To replace from the current line to the end of the file:

◆ `:.,$s/Foo/Bar/g`

Here the range begins with the `.` character, which means "the current line"—that is, the line the cursor was on before you typed the colon.

To replace from the current line and five more lines below it:

◆ `:.,+5s/Foo/Bar/g`

The `+5` in this range means "the current line plus five more below it."

To replace from the current line and seven more lines above it:

◆ `:.,-7s/Foo/Bar/g`

The `-7` here means "the current line plus seven lines above."

To replace text only when it occurs at the start of a line:

◆ Put the `^` character at the beginning of the target string.

This command replaces `Foo` only when it occurs as the very first thing on a line:

`:1,$s/^Foo/Bar/`

(No need for the `g`, since you are only looking for `Foo` at the start of each line.)

To replace text only when it occurs at the end of a line:

◆ Append `$` to the target string.

This command replaces `Foo` only when it occurs as the very last thing on a line:

`:1,$s/Foo$/Bar/`

To include a / in either the target or replacement string:

- You use the backslash (\) to *escape* the / character. By escape we mean that you remove the special meaning of the following character. This is similar to how you learned to use backslashes in Chapter 2 to escape spaces in command-line arguments. (The term *escape* in this context has nothing to do with the Esc key.)

  If you wanted to replace every occurrence of `/usr` with `/usr/local`, you would use the following:

  `:1,$s/\/usr/\/usr\/local/g`

  There are three un-escaped slashes in that command: The first, third, and sixth (last) / characters are not escaped in this example.

`vi` has a great many more commands available. **Table 6.4** shows a few of the most useful ones, and the sidebar "`vi` Cheat Sheets" tells you where to find some handy guides to keep near your keyboard.

✔ Tip

- All of the above `:set` commands may be placed (without the `:`) in your `~/.exrc` file to be executed every time you start `vi`. For example, you might have the following in your `~/.exrc` file:

```
set ai
set ruler
set wm=7
```

To repeat the last editing command:

- `.`

  The `.` command (that's just a period without pressing Return) repeats the last direct command that changed text. A *direct command* is one that did not use the `:` to drop to the status line.

Table 6.4

More vi Commands

Command	What It Does
`J`	Joins the next line to this one.
`%`	Finds the matching closing parenthesis or brace. Position cursor on a (){}[] first.
`:set ruler`	Displays row#,column#.
`:set all`	Shows current settings.
`:set ai`	Turns on auto-indentation.
`:set noai`	Turns off auto-indentation.
`:set number`	Shows line numbers on left.
`:set nonumber`	Turns off line numbers.
`:set wm=5`	Sets wrap margin to five characters from right edge.

emacs—an Editor Without Modes

The emacs editor was invented by Richard M. Stallman, who is better known today as the founder of the Free Software Foundation and the GNU project.

emacs is what's known as a *modeless* editor—you don't have to switch back and forth between command mode and edit mode. emacs is not quite as widely used as vi, but it is very popular, and even though it's a large application with many features, its basics are actually easier than vi's.

To start emacs:

- emacs *filename*

  emacs starts up. Like vi, emacs is a full-screen editor that fills your Terminal window. **Figure 6.19** shows a Terminal window after starting emacs.

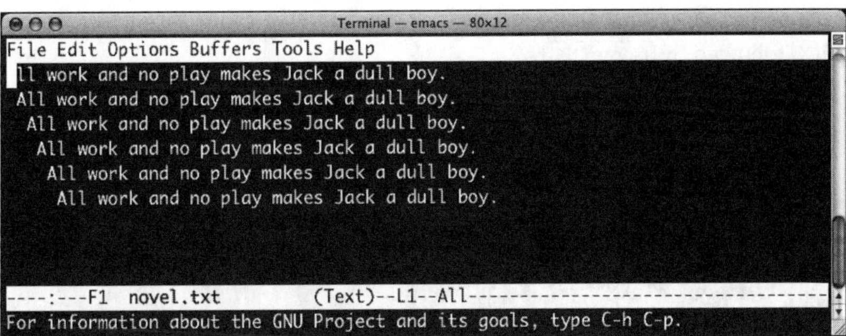

Figure 6.19 emacs is another full-screen editor.

To move around in the file:

- Use the arrow keys.

To change text:

- Type to insert text; to remove text, press [Delete]. emacs automatically wraps lines for you.

To save changes:

1. [Control][X]

   emacs commands use the [Control] key. Most commands consist of two (or more) control characters. The save command is [Control][X], followed immediately by [Control][S]. (That means do not press [Return] or any other key between this step and the next one.)

2. [Control][S]

   The file is saved.

To quit:

1. [Control][X]

   Like the save command, the quit command is a pair of [Control] combinations: [Control][X] followed by [Control][C].

2. [Control][C]

   If there are unsaved changes, emacs asks if you want to save (**Figure 6.20**).

   To save changes, type y; to abandon changes, type n.

You can find more information about emacs on the man page (man emacs), which includes instruction on running an interactive tutorial feature from within the emacs program.

✔Tip

- If you want to see an example of why emacs is way different from other commands we have shown you, try this: Start emacs, press [Esc][X], and then type hanoi-unix and press [Return]. You will see a text-based display of solving of the classic Towers of Hanoi problem. The emacs program is really a complete environment for interacting with your machine, far more than simply a text editor. Remember that to quit, you press [Control][X] and then [Control][C].

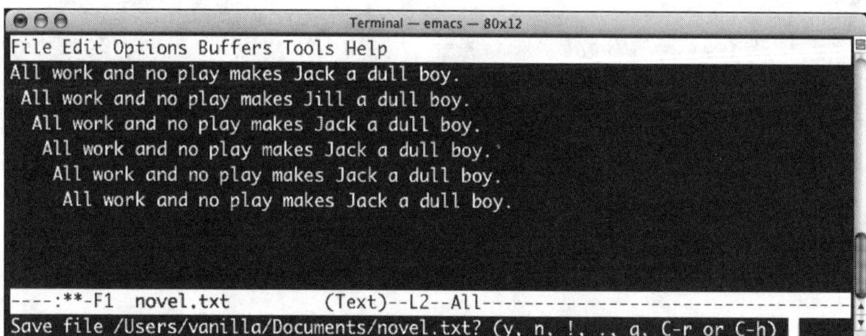

Figure 6.20 If you attempt to quit from emacs with unsaved changes, you will be asked if you want to save.

Printing Files

Now that you are creating files from the command line, you will undoubtedly want to print them. Of course, you can open the files in a GUI text editor or word processor and print using the standard Mac print dialog, or simply select text in your Terminal window and choose Print from the Shell menu. But once you start using the command line, you will often want to stay there and not switch to a GUI application unless you absolutely have to. That means you'll want to print from the command line.

Also, you may want to create a script that sends information to a printer, so you will need a command line you can put in the script.

Here's the very short version (see the rest of this section for more gory details):

```
lp filename
```

You can print only certain types of files from the command line. Generally, you can print files in standard file formats such as plain text, PostScript, GIF, PDF, JPEG, and TIFF, but you cannot print proprietary file formats from the command line—for example, files in the native format of the applications that created them. That means no AppleWorks or Microsoft PowerPoint files. Those need to be printed from within the applications that created them; the applications actually convert the file to another format for printing.

Unix Pioneer: Richard M. Stallman

Richard M. Stallman (known in the Unix community by his lowercase initials, rms) is a programmer with a major vision of programming as an art form that should share its fruits with all of society.

The reputation of rms in the Unix world is that of a passionate, dedicated, visionary, and dogmatic advocate for free software (*free* as in *freedom*, not as in *free beer*).

His contributions to the Unix world have been crucial in making Unix as open and flexible as it is today. He is the principal author of some vital pieces of Unix software and is the founder of the Free Software movement. This is a worldwide effort to create and maintain software with which users have the freedom to examine and change its inner workings and to share their changes with anyone they wish.

One key piece of software that rms is responsible for is the GNU C compiler (gcc), the most widely available compiler in the world.

Besides creating a number of important pieces of software, rms also created the basic license agreement under which most open-source Unix software is distributed. The GNU GPL (General Public License) gives permission to use a piece of software, to examine and alter its source code, and to redistribute the altered version of the software, but only if the altered source code is also distributed under the same GNU GPL license. The Linux operating system is the most well-known collection of GNU GPL software.

Richard M. Stallman's personal Web site is www.stallman.org; to learn more about the Free Software Foundation, visit www.fsf.org and www.gnu.org.

How printing works on a Macintosh

Starting in Mac OS X 10.2, all printing is handled using the Common Unix Printing System, or CUPS (see the sidebar). **Table 6.5** lists some command-line utilities for use with CUPS.

It is important to understand that printers generally can only print documents that are sent to them already converted into a format the printer can understand. For example, printers are not able to understand a Microsoft Excel spreadsheet or a JPEG image.

When you print from within a conventional Macintosh application such as Adobe Photoshop, AppleWorks, or Excel, the application converts the document from the application's native format to a format that the Macintosh printing system can handle (typically PDF for Mac OS X applications and PICT format for Classic applications). The Mac printing system then does another conversion and hands the result to the actual printer.

Some printers expect documents to be sent to them as PostScript files, and other printers expect documents to be formatted using a proprietary page-description language like Hewlett-Packard's PCL (Printer Control Language), and still others desire what is called Raster input (each dot's position is explicitly specified). This is why each printer needs software specifically designed for that printer. In Mac OS X Classic mode (and Mac OS 9 and earlier), the printer-specific software shows up in the Chooser. In Mac OS X, Apple has preinstalled the software that converts files to the format used by each supported printer (called a *filter*). You can also install new filters, which is what often happens when you install the software for a new printer.

CUPS—the Common Unix Printing System

CUPS is an open-source printing system for Unix. It uses its own Web server (listening on port 631) to receive printing requests. In Mac OS X, this is limited to your own machine unless you allow outside access.

The CUPS software attempts to determine what kind of file you are printing and passes it to the appropriate CUPS *filter* for conversion into the format used by your printer. You can add filters as they become available.

CUPS comes with extensive documentation and a very nice Web interface for managing print jobs. The CUPS homepage is www.cups.org. You can see a basic overview of the CUPS system at http://localhost:631/overview.html. The CUPS documentation is at http://localhost:631/documentation.html. The user's manual is http://localhost:631/documentation.html. And the actual management system is at http://localhost:631/, but please be careful not to simply start adding and deleting printers without any knowledge of how that can mess up your Mac OS X printing!

Table 6.5

CUPS Printing Utilities

Goal	Command and Help
Get status	`lpstat` information
Export printer	`cupsaddsmb` for Windows
Manage printers	`lpadmin` or http://localhost:631/printers/

Two Ways to Print: lp vs. lpr

The `lp` (*line printer*) and `lpr` (*line printer request*) commands are the two most common Unix commands for printing. In Mac OS X, both commands have been configured to use CUPS.

The `lp` command was originally developed as part of BSD Unix, and the `lpr` command comes from the AT&T System V version of Unix.

In Mac OS X you will see no practical difference between the commands.

The two commands do have different options, as comparing the `man` pages will show.

Printing PostScript

If you have Mac OS X 10.3 or later, you do not need a PostScript printer to print PostScript—CUPS will convert the PostScript file for you.

The version of CUPS installed with Mac OS X before version 10.3 will *not* convert PostScript files for printing on a non-PostScript printer. However, you can install additional software that supports this, enabling you to print PostScript files to non-PostScript printers. See Gimp-Print (http://gimp-print.sourceforge.net/MacOSX.php3).

Printing from the command line

You print documents from the Mac OS X command line using the `lp` or `lpr` command (see the sidebar "Two Ways to Print: `lp` vs. `lpr`"). Wherever we refer to the `lp` command in a task, you can substitute the `lpr` command if you like. In either case, the file(s) you print will be passed through CUPS, and CUPS will use a filter to convert the file(s) into a format that your printer can understand.

Both `lp` and `lpr` take filenames as arguments, passing the files to CUPS for processing. You can also pipe the output of any command line into `lp` or `lpr`. As long as the command output is a format that CUPS supports, it prints properly.

The CUPS software recognizes most standard file types, such as plain text and GIF, JPEG, PNG, and TIFF images, as well as PDF and PostScript files.

CUPS converts the file to the format your printer uses, assuming that your printer is one of the many supported by CUPS.

Note that HTML files print as plain text, not as you see them in a Web browser. That is because HTML files are actually plain-text files containing the source code that tells a Web browser what to display.

Support for additional printers is added either through software updates from Apple (see the Software Update tool in System Preferences) or by downloading new printer drivers and installing them (see the sidebar "Support for More Printers and File Formats").

To print a single file from the command line:

◆ `lp filename`

Here the `lp` command sends the file named *filename* to your default printer. For example, you can print the 44-page-long Software Users Manual for CUPS with

```
lp /usr/share/doc/cups/sum.pdf
```

Here's a file with only one page:

```
lp "/Library/Desktop Pictures/Black &
→ White/Mojave.jpg"
```

To print multiple files:

◆ `lp file1 ...`

Just supply all the filenames as arguments on the command line. For example,

```
lp hello.pdf flower.jpg smiles.tiff
```

prints all three files.

To print the output from a command:

◆ `command line | lp`

For example,

```
find /Users/vanilla -name "*.png" | lp
```

prints a list of all the .png files in vanilla's home directory. The output of the command line is sent to `lp`.

As long as the output is a format recognized by CUPS, it prints properly, so commands that produce output in the form of image files, PDF, and PostScript can all be sent directly to the `lp` command. For example,

```
man -t ssh | lp
```

pipes the PostScript output of the `man` command (because of the `-t` option) to the `lp` command, which pushes it through CUPS, where it eventually gets to the printer.

To see information about printers:

◆ `lpstat -p`

The `lpstat` command is used to obtain information about CUPS. The `-p` option displays the list of available printers (**Figure 6.21**).

There are several more useful options to `lpstat`; for example, the `-d` option shows the current default printer (**Figure 6.22**), the `-R` option shows all jobs waiting to print, and the `-t` option shows all available information. See `man lpstat` for a list of all options.

```
localhost:~ vanilla$ lpstat -p
printer HP_Color_LaserJet_4500 is idle.  enabled since Jan 01 00:00
printer SC_860hUSBi is idle.             enabled since Jan 01 00:00
localhost:~ vanilla$
```

Figure 6.21 Using `lpstat -p` to see a list of available printers.

```
localhost:~ vanilla$ lpstat -d
system default destination: SC_860hUSBi
localhost:~ vanilla$
```

Figure 6.22 Using `lpstat -d` to see the system default printer.

Support for More Printers and File Formats

Apple adds support for additional printers every so often, and these are available to you via the online Software Update system (see Software Update in System Preferences).

Support for additional printers and file formats (as when printing PostScript files to non-PostScript printers) is also available through the hard work of many open-source programmers. An excellent resource for upgrading your CUPS system is the Gimp-Print project (http://gimp-print.sourceforge.net). Look for the Mac OS X link.

Gimp-Print is a source of high-quality open-source print drivers, and you will almost certainly see improved print quality using its software.

Gimp-Print, in combination with the ESP-Ghostscript software (both available at the Gimp-Print Web site), enables you to print PostScript files to non-PostScript printers such as the USB inkjet printers that are common for home and small-office use.

To set the default printer:

- `sudo lpadmin -d` *`destination`*

  The `sudo` command attempts to run the rest of the command line as root—that is, with the maximum privileges possible on a Unix system. The `sudo` command is covered in detail in Chapter 11, "Introduction to System Administration," but for now you can just enter the command line as shown above. Trust me.

  If you haven't used the `sudo` command within the previous few minutes, you will be asked for your password; enter it.

  You are using the `lpadmin` command to set the default printer.

  The *`destination`* is a printer name from the list supplied by the `lpstat -p` command (described above). For example,

  ```
  sudo lpadmin -d sudo lpadmin -d
  → SC_860hUSBi
  ```

To print to a non-default printer:

- `lp -d` *`destination filename`*

  Use the `-d` option to specify a printer name (as reported by `lpstat -p`)—for example,

  ```
  lp -d HP_Color_LaserJet_4500
  → bigfile.ps
  ```

  It is critical that the printer name be entered exactly as reported by `lpstat`. So if the printer name has spaces in it, you must either enclose it in quotes or escape the spaces with \.

  Note: If you are using the `lpr` command, use the `-P` option instead of `-d`.

Printing to AppleTalk printers

This is actually pretty easy. You can print files on AppleTalk printers using the atprint command. First you have to select the printer from the command line, but only once—after that your selection is remembered.

As a disclaimer, since we no longer have access to AppleTalk printers, we were unable to test this section on Tiger for this edition of the book. However, the information from the last edition is still helpful for those of you using AppleTalk printers.

To select an AppleTalk printer with at_cho_prn:

1. sudo at_cho_prn

   at_cho_prn means "AppleTalk choose printer." The sudo command attempts to run the rest of the command line as root—that is, with the maximum privileges possible on a Unix system. Remember that the sudo command is covered in detail


```
/usr/bin/login (ttyp1)
[matisse@knowledge matisse]$ sudo at_cho_prn
1    Zone1                              2    Zone2
3    Zone3


ZONE number (0 for current zone)?
```

Figure 6.23 The at_cho_prn command shows you a list of available AppleTalk zones.

```
/usr/bin/login (ttyp1)
[matisse@knowledge matisse]$ sudo at_cho_prn
1    Zone1                              2    Zone2
3    Zone3


ZONE number (0 for current zone)? 1
Zone:Zone1
Looking up printers...
```

Figure 6.24 Once you select a zone, at_cho_prn searches for printers in that zone.

in Chapter 11, but for now you can just enter the command line as shown above.

If you haven't used the sudo command within the previous few minutes, you will be asked for your password; enter it.

When the at_cho_prn command runs, it shows you a list of the AppleTalk zones your machine can see (**Figure 6.23**).

2. Enter the zone number to search, and then press Return.

   Once you enter a zone number, at_cho_prn searches the zone for printers (**Figure 6.24**) and displays a numbered list of all the printers found.

3. Enter the printer number from the list.

   You select a printer by typing its number and pressing Return (**Figure 6.25**).

4. You're done.

   The selected printer will now be used for command-line printing with the atprint command.

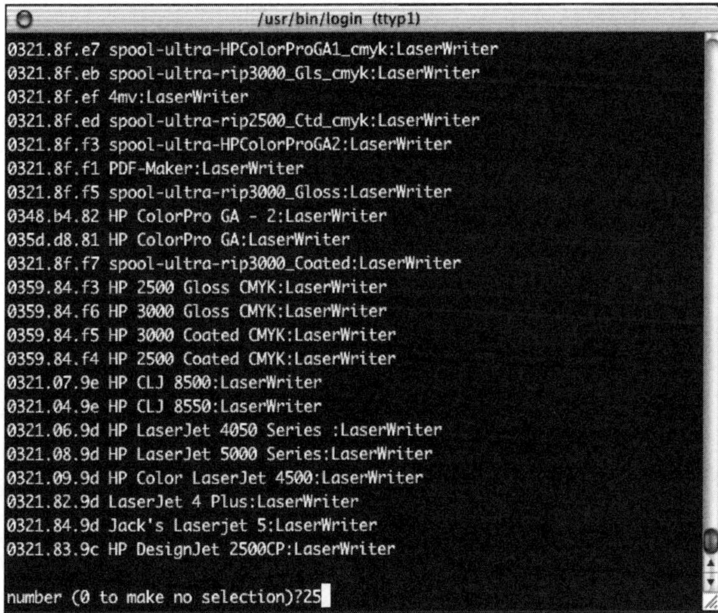

Figure 6.25 You select a printer in at_cho_prn.

To print to an AppleTalk printer:

- `atprint < filename`

  For example,

  ```
  atprint < myfile.ps
  ```

  The `atprint` command sends its input to an AppleTalk printer (the last printer selected using `at_cho_prn`, described above).

  You do not supply the filename to print as an argument to `atprint`. Rather, you must supply the file contents as input to the command, using the < input redirection operator (see Chapter 2) or piping the output of a command to `atprint`. For example,

  ```
  last -25 vanilla | atprint
  ```

  sends the output of the last command to the default AppleTalk printer.

✔ Tip

- You can override the default printer and specify the printer you want to use as an argument to `atprint`—for example,

  ```
  atprint "HP Color LaserJet
  → 4500: LaserWriter@Zone1"
  → < myfile.pdf
  ```

  See the `man` page for a more detailed description of available options.

7 Configuring Your Unix Environment

As a Mac user you are accustomed to configuring your Mac with various graphical user interface (GUI) tools. For example, you configure the Finder using the Finder > Preferences window, and you configure the default audio output device using the Sound pane in System Preferences. But how do you configure Unix programs such as your shell? This chapter shows you the basics of using the command line to configure Unix command-line programs (like your shell and the `vi` editor), and also shows you how you can use the command line to configure virtually any Mac OS X application, including the Finder.

Unix programs that can be configured by a user get their configuration from configuration files and/or from variables such as environment variables. Configuration files are usually read by Unix programs only when they start up. These configuration files contain settings and commands that determine how the programs will behave—for instance, the files can modify the list of places your shell looks for the commands you enter (that list is called your `PATH`).

In addition to traditional Unix configuration files, Mac OS X also uses a system of storing default settings (called the *defaults system*) that is inherited from NextStep. The Mac OS X defaults system allows using the Unix command line to control the defaults for Aqua applications, such as the Finder, Microsoft Word, and Safari, as well as the deep internals of the Mac OS X operating system itself.

Examples of configuring your Unix environment include

- Customizing your shell prompt so that it displays information you want to see
- Creating shortcuts for commonly used command/option combinations
- Changing the defaults for the Finder so that it displays all files, including ones normally hidden (such as the `/usr` directory)
- Making it easier to use additional software you install; for example, if you add `/Developer/Tools` to your `PATH`, then you can use the commands in the `/Developer/Tools` directory without typing their full pathnames
- Configuring specific programs such as `vi` to turn on various options whenever you use them, much the same way that traditional Mac programs often have a preferences window

Examples of using the Unix command line to configure an Aqua application include

- Configuring the Finder to show hidden files, such as `/usr`
- Configuring the Terminal application so that focus automatically switches to whichever window your mouse is in ("focus follows mouse")

The first program to configure is your shell, since your shell is the primary program you use to interact with Unix. We will also show you how to configure the `vi` editor by editing a configuration file it uses (see Chapter 6, "Editing and Printing Files," to learn how to use `vi`).

It should come as no surprise by now that you configure your shell by editing text files.

Am I Configuring the Terminal Application or My Shell?

There's an important distinction to understand here.

The Terminal application you are using to access the command line in Mac OS X is not the same as your shell.

Terminal is a regular Mac OS X graphical application, like your Web browser or word processor. When you open a new window in Terminal, the application runs the appropriate Unix shell (determined by the Terminal application's preferences). Terminal is the program that is handling the screen display and keyboard input for the shell. When you type something in Terminal, the Terminal application passes that to the shell, and when the shell produces output, Terminal draws it on your screen.

The subtle point here is that there are actually other ways besides Terminal in which you can use your shell. One example: You can connect to your Mac using the command line over a network from another machine, which we'll cover in Chapter 10, "Connecting over the Internet." So when we tell you in this chapter that a change you make will take effect "in the next Terminal window you open," that is really a shorthand way of saying that the change will take effect in the next instance of your shell that you run, and that the easiest way to see it is to open a new Terminal window.

Finding Configuration Files

User-configurable Unix programs (including your shell, the vi editor, and others) look for configuration files in your home directory when they start up. Most of the commands you have learned so far are not user configurable; neither the ls nor the cd command uses configuration files, for example. They do accept options on the command line but do not read any configuration files when you run them.

Many configuration filenames begin with a dot (.), so they are called *dot files* (use ls -a to see them). Often the filenames end in "rc" (for *resource*). For example, the main configuration file for the bash shell is ~/.bash_profile, a configuration file for the tcsh shell is ~/.tcshrc, and the configuration file for the vi editor is called ~/.exrc (ex is an older editor, and vi provides a "visual interface" for it). There are actually several configuration files available for each shell, and **Table 7.1** lists the more common ones. In this chapter, we will concentrate on the ones you would change in the course of normal use. These files each have settings and commands for the particular program being configured. (Remember that ~ [the tilde] is a synonym for your home directory.)

Configuration files for shells are actually scripts. This means they are a series of commands written in the scripting language for the corresponding shell. They make use of variables, if-then conditions, and other scripting elements, such as loops. (See Chapter 9, "Creating and Using Scripts," for more on scripts.)

Table 7.1

A Summary of Common Shells

Shell	Name and Description
sh	**Bourne shell.** The oldest and most standardized shell. Widely used for system-startup files (scripts run during system startup). Installed in Mac OS X.
bash	**bash** (Bourne Again Shell). An improved version of sh. Combines features from csh, sh, and ksh. Very widely used, especially on Linux systems. See the Bash Reference Manual online (www.gnu.org/manual/bash/bash.html). The default shell in Mac OS X 10.3 and later.
csh	**C shell.** Provides scripting features that have a syntax similar to that of the C programming language (originally written by Bill Joy). Installed in Mac OS X.
ksh	**Korn shell.** Developed at AT&T by David Korn in the early 1980s. ksh is widely used for programming. It is now open-source software, although you must agree to AT&T's license to install it. See the KornShell Web site (www.kornshell.com).
tcsh	An improved version of csh. The t in tcsh comes from the TENEX and TOPS-20 operating systems, which provided a command-completion feature that the creator (Ken Greer) of tcsh included in his new shell. Wilfredo Sanchez, formerly lead engineer on Mac OS X for Apple, worked on tcsh in the early 1990s at the Massachusetts Institute of Technology. The default shell in Mac OS X 10.2 and earlier.
zsh	**Z shell.** Created in 1990, zsh combines features from tcsh, bash, and ksh, and adds many of its own. Installed in Mac OS X. The Web site for Z shell is http://zsh.sourceforge.net.

Configuring Your Shell

The first thing you need to know is which shell you are using. The default shell on Mac OS X is `bash`.

It's very easy to find out which shell you are using. One simple command line will show you.

To determine which shell you are using:

◆ `echo $SHELL`

`$SHELL` is an *environment variable* (more about these in the "Environment Variables" section below) that contains the full path of the shell you are using. Unless you have changed from the Mac OS X default, you will see `/bin/bash` (**Figure 7.1**).

✔ Tips

- You can change the shell that the Terminal program uses by selecting Preferences from the Terminal menu. If you want to change your default login shell (so that the new shell is used no matter how you get to the command line), see "Changing a user's login shell" in Chapter 11, "Introduction to System Administration."
- See Chapter 11 for instructions on changing your login shell, not only within the Terminal application, but also for when you connect to your Mac from another machine over a network using a command-line interface.

To configure your shell, edit the appropriate configuration file(s). **Table 7.2** lists the configuration files for the most common shells.

Unless you have changed the default Mac OS X setup, you configure your shell by editing your `~/.bash_profile` file.

Note that some of the files are the system-wide defaults (those located in the `/etc` directory), and some are user files (located in each user's home directory). Also, some configuration files are executed only for *interactive* shells—these are shells that give you a command-line prompt (as opposed to a shell program started by a script or other process).

Table 7.2

Common Configuration Files

Shells and Configuration Files in Order of Execution (remember that the ~ character is shorthand for *your home directory*)	
BASH	
/etc/profile	Systemwide configuration file for the bash and sh shells (**Figure 7.2**).
/etc/bashrc	Systemwide configuration file for bash interactive shells (**Figure 7.3**).
~/.bash_profile	The first personal configuration file that bash looks for.
~/.bashrc	This file is executed for interactive shells unless the shell is your login shell (the shell that starts up when you open each Terminal window).
~/.bash_logout	Executed when you log out from a bash login shell.
TCSH	
/etc/csh.cshrc	Systemwide configuration file for the tcsh and csh shells. This is the first file that tcsh executes when it starts up.
/etc/csh.login	Systemwide configuration for tcsh and csh, executed only for interactive shells.
~/.tcshrc	The main personal configuration file for your tcsh shell. If tcsh doesn't find this, it looks for a .cshrc file.
~/.login	This file is executed after the .tcshrc file, but only if the shell is an interactive login shell. It won't be used if some other process is starting the shell.
~/.logout	tcsh executes this file when you log out of an interactive shell.

```
localhost:~ vanilla$ echo $SHELL
/bin/bash
localhost:~ vanilla$
```

Figure 7.1 Displaying the contents of the SHELL environment variable.

```
# System-wide .profile for sh(1)
PATH="/bin:/sbin:/usr/bin:/usr/sbin"
export PATH

if [ "${BASH-no}" != "no" ]; then
        [ -r /etc/bashrc ] && . /etc/bashrc
fi
```

Figure 7.2 /etc/profile is the main sh and bash configuration file. This is a shell script written in sh.

```
# System-wide .bashrc file for interactive bash(1) shells.
if [ -n "$PS1" ]; then PS1='\h:\w \u\$ '; fi
# Make bash check it's window size after a process completes
shopt -s checkwinsize
```

Figure 7.3 /etc/bashrc is the systemwide configuration file for bash interactive shells.

Environment Variables

In the configuration files for your shell, you will most commonly change the contents of various environment variables.

A *variable* is simply a piece of memory with a name. When the variable is used, the contents stored in memory are substituted for the name.

Usually, when a program stores something in a variable, the stored information is intended only for that program and is not available to any other program. (You can think of variables as private to the program that created them.) Environment variables are an exception to this.

Environment variables in Unix not only are available to the process that set them, but also are passed to any child processes at the moment the child process is created. (Review Chapter 2, "Using the Command Line," for an explanation of processes.) So if you set an environment variable in your shell, then any command you run from that shell will be able to read the contents of that variable. And any processes created by the child will also "inherit" all the environment variables that were set when it was created (**Figure 7.4**). Note that shell variables, such as the prompt (which determines your shell prompt), are not passed to children.

Many programs use this ability to read information provided by their parents and to configure their behavior—think of it as programs' adapting to their environment.

When your shell starts up, it automatically sets a number of environment variables. You can create more and alter the ones that have already been set. By convention, the names of environment variables are capitalized, as in `PATH`. When you want to obtain the value that is stored in a variable, you add a `$` to it. Adding the `$` to the variable name tells the shell that the value stored in the `PATH` variable should be substituted at that point, as in `$PATH`. So the *name* of the variable is `PATH`, and to get its contents we use `$PATH`. If you have used the VisualBasic (or just BASIC) programming language, this will be familiar.

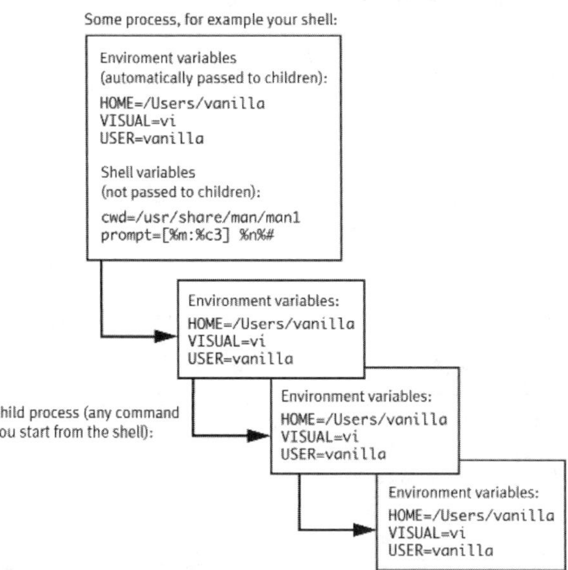

Figure 7.4 Illustration of how environment variables set by parent processes are passed to child processes.

Table 7.3

Common Environment Variables	
VARIABLE	MEANING
HOME	Full path of home directory
SHELL	Full path of login shell
USER	User name (a.k.a. *short name* in Mac OS X)
PATH	List of directories containing commands
LOGNAME	Same as USER
PWD	Full path of present working directory
MANPATH	List of directories containing man pages
TERM	Used to control how text is displayed in command-line applications
VISUAL	Name of the "visual" editor (such as vi, emacs, nano) to be used when another program wants you to edit a file. The visual editor is expected to be one where you can see multiple lines of a file at the same time.
EDITOR	Name of an editor to be used when editing files. Some programs will use the value of this variable if the VISUAL variable is not set.

To see all your environment variables:

- env

  The env command shows you all of the environment variables that are currently set (**Figure 7.5**). For an explanation of common variables, see **Table 7.3**.

  The env command is actually a good example of a child's inheriting its environment from its parent. When you run the env command, your shell is the parent process that "spawns" a child process to run env. When env runs, it inherits its parent's environment and then reads and displays its own environment.

✔ Tip

- The tcsh shell has the setenv command, which is normally used to set an environment variable. If used with no arguments, setenv produces a neatly formatted list of all your environment variables.

```
localhost:~ vanilla$ env
TERM=xterm-color
SHELL=/bin/bash
SSH_CLIENT=192.168.0.23 51989 22
SSH_TTY=/dev/ttyp1
USER=vanilla
MAIL=/var/mail/vanilla
PATH=/bin:/sbin:/usr/bin:/usr/sbin:/Users/vanilla/bin
PWD=/Users/vanilla
SHLVL=1
HOME=/Users/vanilla
LOGNAME=vanilla
SSH_CONNECTION=192.168.0.23 51989 175.122.221.13 22
_=/usr/bin/env
OLDPWD=/Users/vanilla
localhost:~ vanilla$
```

Figure 7.5 The command env shows all of the current environment variables.

You should leave most environment variables alone—they are set automatically to their correct values. For example, the USER variable has your user name, and changing it will simply confuse any program that tries to use it to determine which user you are.

Sometimes you will want to change environment variables, though; for example, the crontab program (used to schedule automatic execution of commands, discussed in Chapter 11, "Introduction to System Administration") reads the VISUAL environment variable to decide which editor to launch.

Setting environment variables is simple.

To change or create an environment variable in bash (or sh):

1. `VISUAL=vi`

   Make sure there are no spaces on either side of the equals sign.

2. `export VISUAL`

   The export command sends variables into the environment.

   Without the export step, the VISUAL variable would be set, but only as a *shell variable*, which is a variable that the shell can read but that will not be passed on to any child processes it creates.

3. Test the setting with `echo $VISUAL` (**Figure 7.6**).

✔ Tips

- The bash shell (but not the older sh shell) allows setting an environment variable in a single step using the export command:

  `export VISUAL=vi`

- If you want the setting to be made each time you start a shell, put the two command lines' export command line in your ~/.profile file.

- If the value contains spaces, make sure to enclose it in quotes:

  ```
  ORGANIZATION="Tony's Pizza"
  export ORGANIZATION
  ```

```
localhost:~ vanilla$ VISUAL=vi
localhost:~ vanilla$ export VISUAL
localhost:~ vanilla$ echo $VISUAL
vi
localhost:~ vanilla$
```

Figure 7.6 Setting an environment variable in the bash or sh shell.

```
[localhost:~] vanilla% setenv VISUAL vi
[localhost:~] vanilla% echo $VISUAL
vi
[localhost:~] vanilla%
```

Figure 7.7 Setting an environment variable in the tcsh or csh shell.

To change or create an environment variable in tcsh (or csh):

1. `setenv VISUAL vi`

   This sets the environment variable named `VISUAL` to have the value `vi`.

2. Test that it worked:

   `echo $VISUAL`

   Figure 7.7 shows the result.

✔ Tips

- As with the `bash` shell, if the value contains spaces, make sure to enclose it in quotes:

  `setenv ORGANIZATION "Tony's Pizza"`

- If you want the setting to be made each time you start a `tcsh` or `csh` shell, put the two command lines' `export` command line in your `~/.cshrc` file.

- To reset (or *unset*, in Unix terminology) an environment variable, simply leave off the value:

  `setenv VISUAL`

Environment variables that are set at a shell prompt will last only for as long as you use the current shell in each session. That is, the setting disappears when you log out.

To make a durable change to an environment variable:

1. Edit the shell configuration file in your home directory.

   For `bash`, this would be

   `~/.bash_profile`

   For `tcsh` or `csh`, use

   `~/.cshrc`

2. Add the commands to the end of the file.

   Use the commands described in the tasks above—for example, to set the `VISUAL` variable to `vi` for the `bash` shell:

   `export VISUAL=vi`

3. Save the file.

4. Quit the editor.

   The change will take effect with the next shell you start.

5. Open a new Terminal window.

6. Test that the variable is set:

   `echo $VISUAL`

✔ Tips

- A faster way to add a single line to a file is to use the output redirection you learned in Chapter 2. Replace steps 1–4 above with

  ```
  echo export ORGANIZATION=\"Tony\'s
  → Pizza\" >> ~/.bash_profile
  ```

- Make sure to use >> and not a single > character. If you use only >, you will wipe out the current contents of your `.bash_profile` file.

- Notice how you have to escape the quotes by preceding them with backslashes so that the shell itself doesn't try to interpret them. You want the quotes to be part of the arguments to the `echo` command so that they end up in the `~/.bash_profile` file.

Changing your PATH

Every time you execute a command by using only the command's name (for example, `ls` or `pwd` as opposed to the full path of the command, like `/usr/bin/ls`), your shell looks for the command in a list of directories. That list is stored in the `PATH` environment variable. The `PATH` list provides a shortcut for finding commands.

If it weren't for the `PATH` list, you would have to type `/bin/ls` instead of `ls`, and `/usr/bin/vi` instead of `vi`. The command-line utilities supplied with the Mac OS X Developer Tools are located in `/Developer/Tools` (some of those utilities, such as `GetFileInfo` and `SetFile`, are described in Chapter 5, "Using Files and Directories"). The `/Developer/Tools` directory is not normally in your `PATH`, so if you use any of the commands in `/Developer/Tools`, you need to type their full pathnames, unless you add the directory `/Developer/Tools` to your `PATH`. Here's how to do that.

If you are using the `bash` shell, you can add a directory to your `PATH` by directly setting the `PATH` environment variable. Putting this setting in your `~/.bash_profile` ensures that it takes effect each time you start a new shell.

Adding a directory to your PATH in bash:

1. Edit your `~/.bash_profile` file.

   (Review Chapter 5 about editing files from the command line.)

   If you are using the `vi` editor, the command is

   ```
   vi ~/.bash_profile
   ```

2. Add a line to the file that says

   ```
   export PATH="$PATH:/Developer/Tools"
   ```

   Notice how the new value includes the current value of `$PATH`, then a colon (no spaces!), and then the new directory. Without `$PATH` in the new value, the result would be to replace the old `PATH` with just the single new directory—not at all what you want.

3. Save the file.

4. Quit the editor.

   The change takes effect the next time you start a shell.

5. Open a new Terminal window to test the change.

6. `env`

   You'll see the new directory at the end of the list in the `PATH` variable.

✔ Tip

- To make the change for your current shell, execute the same command that you added to the `.bash_profile` file:

  ```
  export PATH="$PATH:/Developer/Tools"
  ```

If you are using the `tcsh` shell, you'll make the change in your `~/.tcshrc` file.

Adding a directory to your PATH in tcsh:

1. Start by editing your `~/.tcshrc` file.

   If you are using `vi`, the command is

   ```
   vi ~/.tcshrc
   ```

2. Add a line that says

   ```
   set path = ( $path /Developer/Tools )
   ```

   This may seem a little odd. After all, you are trying to set the `PATH` environment variable, not `path`. What's going on? Well, `tcsh` uses an unusual method to set the `PATH` variable.

   `tcsh` requires that you set the shell variable `path`, and then `tcsh` sets the actual `PATH` environment variable. As discussed earlier, shell variables are created in your shell and are only available in the shell you are currently using. They are not passed on to child processes the way that environment variables are.

3. Save your file (the command will depend on which editor you're using).

4. Quit the editor (this command will also depend on which editor you're using).

   The change will take effect in the next shell you start.

5. Open a new Terminal window to test the change.

6. `env`

   You'll see the new directory at the end of the list in the `PATH` variable.

Shell Aliases

Shell aliases are shortcut names for commands and have nothing to do with Finder aliases (see "About Links [the Unix Version of Aliases]" in Chapter 5). Each alias consists of one word (or even one letter) that you can use instead of a longer command line. For example, you may find yourself using the command `ls -F` a lot. You can easily make a shortcut for that command: `lf`, for example. So when you use `lf` where the shell expects a command, then the shell will substitute `ls -F`.

You can create aliases at the command line or by adding them to a configuration file.

Aliases created at the command line are only in effect for as long as you use that shell—that is, they disappear when you close that Terminal window. If you want an alias to always be available, you must put it in a configuration file.

To create a temporary alias in bash:

1. `alias shortcut='replacement'`

   For example:

   `alias lf='ls -F'`

   Note that there are no spaces before or after the equals sign.

2. `alias`

   Used without any arguments, the alias command shows all your current aliases, including the one you just created. **Figure 7.8** shows both of the above commands in action.

   Aliases created at the command line will disappear when you exit the shell. The next task shows how to create a `bash` alias that is always available.

```
localhost:~ vanilla$ alias lf='ls -F'
localhost:~ vanilla$ alias
alias lf='ls -F'
localhost:~ vanilla$
```

Figure 7.8 Using the `alias` command to set a temporary alias and then again (with no arguments) to display current aliases.

To create a permanent alias in bash:

1. Edit your `~/.bash_profile` file.

   For example, using vi:

   `vi ~/.bash_profile`

2. Add a line with the alias—for example,

   `alias lf='ls -F'`

3. Save the file.

4. Quit the editor.

   The new alias is set for the next shell you start.

5. Open a new Terminal window to check that the alias is set:

   `alias`

   You should see your new alias in the list:

   `alias lf='ls -F'`

To see all your current aliases:

- `alias`

  The `alias` command with no arguments displays all your current aliases. The first item on each line is the alias (which must always be a single string, with no spaces), and the rest of the line is the full command for which the alias is a shortcut.

Aliases in the `tcsh` and `csh` shells are set using almost the same syntax as in `bash`—basically, you use a space instead of the = sign.

To create a temporary alias in tcsh or csh:

1. `alias lf 'ls -F'`

   This creates an alias called `lf`, which the shell translates into `ls -F` whenever you use `lf` as a command. Make sure to enclose the last argument in quotes, either single or double, so that everything after the alias name is treated as a single entity.

2. Check to see that the alias is set:

   `alias`

   The line

   `lf ls -F`

   should be included in your aliases now.

✔ Tips

- If you want to have a `tcsh` shell alias use arguments from the command line inside the alias definition, you can use `!:1` for the first argument, `!:2` for the second, and so on. You may use `!*` to include all the arguments. You must escape the `!` in the alias definition. So to define an alias called `myword` that takes its first argument and searches for it inside the file `~/mydictionary`, you would use

  ```
  alias myword 'grep \!:1
  → ~/mydictionary'
  ```

- For example, you could use that alias in this way:

  `myword banana`

  as a shortcut for

  `grep banana ~/mydictionary`

To create a permanent alias in tcsh (or csh):

1. Edit your `~/.tcshrc` file (for the `csh` shell use `~/.cshrc`).
2. Add a line with the alias

   `alias lf 'ls -F'`
3. Save the file.
4. Quit the editor.

   The new alias is set for the next shell you start.
5. Open a new Terminal window to check that the alias is set:

   `alias`

   You should see your new alias in the resulting list.

✔ Tip

- A set of example aliases for the `tcsh` shell is contained in the file `/usr/share/tcsh/examples/aliases`.

Shell functions

Unlike aliases in the `tcsh` shell, aliases in `bash` cannot have command-line arguments included in them. However, `bash` allows you to create *shell functions*, which can make use of their arguments.

The term *shell function* applies to a series of shell command lines. This is similar to an alias, except that a shell function can be many lines long, and you may use the special variables `$1` for the first argument, `$2` for the second, and so on.

Shell functions should be defined in your `~/.bash_profile`.

To create a shell function in bash:

1. Open your `~/.bash_profile`.

   The entire function you will be entering is shown in **Figure 7.9**. This sample function looks up a word in two different files that make up a dictionary.
2. Enter a comment and the first line of the new function.

   You may put the function anywhere in your `.bash_profile`. Usually, adding new functions at the end of the file is easiest.

   Lines that begin with # in your `.bash_profile` are comments and are ignored by the shell:

   ```
   # shell function to search for a
   → word in Webster's dictionary
   ```

   In this example you are creating a function called `word`; the actual function definition begins with the function name:

   `word () {`

   The parentheses tell `bash` that this is a function definition. The brace ({) marks the beginning of the commands in the function.
3. Enter the body of the function:

   ```
   grep $1 /usr/share/dict/web2
   grep $1 /usr/share/dict/web2a
   ```

   Notice that the function can have more than one line of commands.

   The `$1` is a variable that will be replaced with the first argument when you use the function in a command line. (Read the file `/usr/share/dict/README` for a description of the web2 and web2a files.)

4. Finish the function definition with a closing brace: }.

   Double-check that what you entered looks like Figure 7.9.

5. Save the file.

6. Quit the editor.

   The new function will be in effect with the next Terminal window you open.

7. Open a new Terminal window.

8. Test the function by trying it on the command line. If you are using the example function from Figure 7.9, then the first argument you supply is used in the function. The function searches two different files for its first argument.

9. `word auspic`

   You should get the output shown in **Figure 7.10**. Your new shell function, `word`, takes its first argument (the `$1` in the function) and searches for it in the two files. The function is really a short shell script (see Chapter 9) but is part of your personal shell configuration.

```
# shell function to search for a word in Webster's dictionary
word () {
    grep $1 /usr/share/dict/web2
    grep $1 /usr/share/dict/web2a
}
```

Figure 7.9 Code listing of a bash shell function. The files web2 and web2a refer not to the World Wide Web but to Webster's Second International Dictionary, whose 1934 copyright has expired.

```
localhost:~ vanilla$ word auspic
auspicate
auspice
auspices
auspicial
auspicious
auspiciously
auspiciousness
auspicy
inauspicious
inauspiciously
inauspiciousness
unauspicious
unauspiciously
unauspiciousness
ultra-auspicious
localhost:~ vanilla$
```

Figure 7.10 Using the new shell function to look up *auspic* in the dictionary.

Shell Settings

Your shell uses a variety of settings that you will want to change from time to time. You should read the man page for your shell to learn about dozens of possible settings—for example, man bash.

You may want your shell prompt to be shorter, or to display the date, time, or some other specific piece of information. This is easy to do by adding a line to your shell configuration file.

Another setting you may want to change is umask, which controls the permissions given to any new file you create. (Chapter 8, "Working with Permissions and Ownership," goes into detail on permissions.)

Customizing your shell prompt

Both tcsh and bash provide ways to customize your shell prompt. The simplest customization would be to simply have your prompt be a word or phrase, such as Type something:, but far more interesting is the ability to have the prompt include information about what is going on in your shell.

The bash shell uses a set of special formatting codes to allow the inclusion of things like the current directory and date in the prompt. You put these codes into a shell variable (called PS1) that bash reads to determine your prompt.

In Unix we call these *escape sequences* because they all start with the backslash character, which is frequently used in Unix to alter the meaning of the following character, usually by removing some special meaning (*escaping* the character). But in this case, the use of the backslash creates a special meaning for the following character, so \d becomes the date, and \u becomes your user name.

Table 7.4 shows some common escape sequences for the bash shell prompt.

Table 7.4

Some bash Prompt Escape Sequences

Escape Sequence	Meaning
\d	The date in "weekday month date" format (for example, "Tue May 26")
\h	Your computer's Internet hostname up to the first "."
\H	Your computer's Internet hostname
\j	The number of jobs currently managed by the shell
\s	The name of the shell program (for example, bash)
\t	Current time in 24-hour HH:MM:SS format
\T	Current time in 12-hour HH:MM:SS format
\@	Current time in 12-hour a.m./p.m. format
\u	Your user name.
\v	The version of bash you are using—for example, 2.05
\w	Your current directory
\W	Base name (last part) of your current directory
\\	A backslash

See man bash for the complete list.

```
bash-2.05$ PS1='\t:\w > '
10:17:03:~ >
```

Figure 7.11 Changing your bash shell prompt on the command line.

In Mac OS X 10.4 the default bash shell prompt is set in /etc/bashrc and uses the format

'\h:\w \u\$ '

It produces a prompt that looks like

hostname:~ vanilla$

The \h becomes whatever your machine's name (called the *hostname*) is; the \w becomes your current working directory; and the \u becomes your user name. The $ is reproduced literally. Notice the space included in the format, after the $. The space ensures that whatever you type next to the prompt isn't smooshed up against the $, which would be hard to read.

In the tasks below, you will set your prompt to show the current time in 12-hour a.m./p.m. format followed by a colon, and the current directory, followed by the > character and a space.

Don't worry about making a mistake—the changes you make will be in effect only for the single Terminal window in which you perform this task. Once you are satisfied that you have it right, you can add the setting to your ~/.bash_profile file to have it take effect for all future shells you start up (that is, all future Terminal windows).

To temporarily customize your bash shell prompt:

- PS1='\t:\w > '

  Make sure there are no spaces on either side of the equals sign. Your shell prompt will immediately change, as in **Figure 7.11**.

  Note that even though this looks as if you are setting an environment variable (because PS1 is capitalized), you aren't. You are setting a variable (the PS1 variable), but you are setting it for this shell only. Unlike environment variables, this variable will not be passed on to child processes of this shell.

To make a durable customization of your bash shell prompt:

1. Open your `~/.bash_profile` file.
2. Add a line with the new setting.
   Using the example from the previous task, you would add
   `PS1='\t:\w > '`
3. Save the file.
4. Quit the editor.
   The change will take effect with the next Terminal window you open.
5. Open a new Terminal window.
   You will see your new prompt.

The procedure for customizing a `tcsh` shell prompt is similar to that for the `bash` shell. The `tcsh` shell also uses a set of special formatting codes to allow the inclusion of things like the current directory and date in the prompt. The `tcsh` shell calls these formatting codes *prompt macros*.

Table 7.5 lists the common prompt macros available for the `tcsh` shell prompt.

For example, the default prompt for `tcsh` uses the formatting pattern

`[%m:%c3] %n%#`

If your computer's hostname is violet, your user name is vanilla, and your current directory is `/usr/share/man/man1`, then the prompt would be

`[violet:share/man/man1] vanilla%`

See how the `%m` gets replaced with `violet`, the `%c3` gets replaced with `share/man/man1`, the `%n` gets replaced with `vanilla`, and the `%#` gets replaced with `%`.

The following tasks show you how to customize your shell prompt so that it shows the current time (in 12-hour a.m./p.m. format), followed by your current directory, followed by your user name.

Table 7.5

Some tcsh Prompt Macros

Formatting Sequence	Turns into This
`%/`	Your current directory.
`%~`	Your current directory, but with your home directory shown as ~ and other home directories shown as `~user`.
`%c`	The last part of the current directory. If followed by a number *n* (for example, `%c3`), then only the last *n* components (directories) are shown. Your home directory and other users' home directories are shown, as with `%~` above.
`%C`	Same as `%c` but does not show home directories with a ~.
`%M`	Your computer's Internet hostname.
`%m`	The hostname up to the first ".".
`%B (%b)`	Start (stop) bold mode.
`%U (%u)`	Start (stop) underline mode.
`%t`	The time of day in 12-hour a.m./p.m. format.
`%T`	Like `%t` but in 24-hour format.
`%%`	A single `%`.
`%n`	Your user name.
`%d`	The weekday in day format.
`%D`	The day in dd format.
`%w`	The month in mon format.
`%W`	The month in mm format.
`%y`	The year in yy format.
`%Y`	The year in yyyy format.
`%#`	A % for normal users and a # for the root user (helps you know if you are logged in as root).

See `man tcsh` for the complete list.

Shell Settings

Once you are satisfied that you have it right, you can add the setting to your ~/.tcshrc file to have it take effect for all future shells you start up (that is, all future Terminal windows).

To temporarily customize your prompt in tcsh:

- `set prompt='%t:%c3 %# '`

  Your prompt immediately changes, as shown in **Figure 7.12**. Note the space at the end of the prompt—right after the # and before the last '. That space is actually part of the prompt, so when you type a command, it is visually separated from the prompt.

To make a durable customization of your tcsh shell prompt:

1. Open your ~/.tcshrc file.
2. Add a line with the new setting.
3. Using the example from the previous task, add

   `set prompt='%t:%c3 %# '`
4. Save the file.
5. Quit the editor.

   The change will take effect with the next Terminal window you open.
6. Open a new Terminal window to see your new prompt.

```
localhost:~ vanilla$ set prompt='%t:%c3 %# '
11:32am:~ %
```

Figure 7.12 Changing your tcsh shell prompt on the command line.

Changing your umask

When you create a new file or directory, the initial permissions are determined by the umask (*user mask*) setting of the shell that created the file. So the umask is a shell configuration that affects the permissions of any file you create. (See Chapter 8 for more on permissions.)

Your umask setting can be either temporary or durable, like your shell prompt, which you customized in the tasks above.

You use the umask command to set (and view) your umask. Used with no arguments, umask simply displays your current umask setting. To set your umask, you supply one argument, which is an octal (base eight) number of one to four digits. If you use fewer than four digits, zeros are added to the left to bring up the total to four digits—so 2 becomes 0002, and 22 becomes 0022, for example. See Chapter 8 for an explanation of how the umask is applied to determine file permissions, and of what those permissions mean. In most Unix documentation, umasks are shown as three-digit numbers, because the four-digit form is rarely needed. So in most cases, we will show umasks as three-digit values.

In Mac OS X your default umask is 0022, which means that any new files you create will be readable by every user of your Mac but only writable by you. A common change is to set one's umask so that newly created files are writable not only by oneself but also by other users in the same *group* (see Chapter 8 for more on groups). The umask setting for this is 002 (which can be abbreviated simply as 2).

To temporarily change your umask:

1. umask 002

   The change takes effect at once and lasts until you log out of the shell or change it again.

2. Verify that the change took effect:

   umask

   Figure 7.13 shows an example.

✔ Tip

- In some shells—for example, the tcsh shell—the leading zeros in your umask are not displayed, so a umask of 0022 appears as 22.

Changing your umask for all future shells is simply a matter of putting the same command in your shell configuration file.

To make a durable change to your umask:

1. Open the startup file for your shell.

   For bash, edit ~/.bash_profile.

   For tcsh, edit ~/.tcshrc.

2. Add a line with the umask command and the new umask.

   For example, to have your umask set to 002, add a line that says

   umask 002

3. Save the file.

4. Quit the editor.

   The change will take effect on the next shell you start.

5. Open a new Terminal window.

6. umask

   to confirm it's correct.

```
localhost:~ vanilla$ umask
0022
localhost:~ vanilla$ umask 002
localhost:~ vanilla$ umask
0002
localhost:~ vanilla$
```

Figure 7.13 Changing your umask on the command line.

Configuring vi

In addition to reading configurations from your shell, the vi editor will also read configurations from a text file, and since we've already shown you how to use it (in Chapter 6), we'll show you some common configuration settings you may want to use.

To configure vi:

1. Open your ~/.exrc file (using vi or any other text editor).
2. Add the setting(s) you wish to use.

   For example, to have word wrap (indicated by wm) always be on, and to set it to kick in within five characters of the right edge of the window, add a line that says

   `set wm=5`
3. To set a tab stop every four spaces (instead of the default eight), add a line that says

   `set tabstop=4`

   Table 7.6 lists some common setting possibilities, and of course you should read the vi man page to see the full list.
4. Save the file.
5. Quit.

   That is:

   `:wq`

   The new settings will be in effect the next time you use vi.

✔ Tip

- You can turn off a setting with

  `:set no` *`settingname`*

  For example, to turn off auto-indent, you would use

  `:set no ai`

Table 7.6

Common vi Configuration Settings

Setting	Meaning
`set autoindent`	vi will insert tabs and spaces at the start of each line to make the first character you type line up with the first character of the line above.
`set extended`	Allows extended regular expressions to be used in searches. In Chapter 4, "Useful Unix Utilities," see the section "Searching for Text" for a discussion of regular expressions.
`set ruler`	Causes vi to display the position of the cursor at the bottom of the window (as two numbers: line, column).
`set showmode`	Displays the current mode (command or insert) on the status line.
`set tabstop=n`	Tells vi how many spaces between each tab stop. If you set it to 4, then pressing [t] will advance the cursor only four spaces.
`set wm=n`	Turns on automatic word wrap. vi will automatically insert a new-line character when you get within *n* columns of the right edge of the window.

CONFIGURING VI

Configuring Mac OS X Defaults from the Command Line

Mac OS X uses a system for storing settings called the *defaults system*. The defaults system stores settings such as those you make in the preferences of Mac OS X applications and the various *panes* (formerly called *control panels*) in System Preferences.

The defaults system is one of the things that Mac OS X (or, more properly, Darwin) inherits from its NeXT ancestor. In most cases you should continue to use the GUI tools for seeing and changing these settings, but in some cases you may want (or need) to view or make changes from the command line. **Figure 7.14** is an excerpt from the man page for the `defaults` command.

Mac OS X defaults are stored in files using a format called *plist* format (see `man plist`). Each user's preferences are stored in `~/Library/Preferences` inside his or her home directory. For example, your Safari Preferences are stored in `~/Library/Preferences/com.apple.Safari.plist`. Systemwide defaults are stored in `/Library/Preferences`, so the Software Update program's settings (which are not user-specific) are stored in `/Library/Preferences/com.apple.SoftwareUpdate.plist`.

Mac OS X comes with a GUI application for viewing and editing .plist files, the Property List Editor (located in `/Developer/Applications/Utilities`), but here we will show you how to manipulate these files the preferred way using the `defaults` command.

```
Defaults allows users to read, write, and delete Mac OS X user defaults
from a command-line shell. Mac OS X applications and other programs use
the defaults system to record user preferences and other information that
must be maintained when the applications aren't running (such as default
font for new documents, or the position of an Info panel). Much of this
information is accessible through an application's Preferences panel, but
some of it isn't, such as the position of the Info panel. You can access
this information with defaults

Note: Since applications do access the defaults system while they're run-
ning, you shouldn't modify the defaults of a running application. If you
change a default in a domain that belongs to a running application, the
application won't see the change and might even overwrite the default.
```

Figure 7.14 Excerpt from the man page for the `defaults` command.

To read preferences for an application:

- `defaults read` *`domain`*

  The `domain` value is in the format *`domain.company.Application`*.

  The domain for the Finder is `com.apple.Finder`, and for the Firefox Web browser it's `org.mozilla.firefox`.

  For example, to read your settings for the Finder, you would run

  `defaults read com.apple.Finder`

  which produces output like that shown in **Figure 7.15**.

✔ Tips

- There can be a great deal of output, so you might want to pipe the output through `less`:

  `defaults read com.apple.Finder | less`

- You can get a list of all the available domain values with

  `defaults domains`

  The output will be a (long) comma-separated list of domains for which you have defaults.

```
{
    ComputerOptions = {
        ComputerBackgroundType = DefB;
        ComputerIconViewArrangeBy = dnam;
        ComputerIconViewIconSize = 64;
        ComputerIconViewScrollPosition = {h = 0; v = 0; };
        ComputerListViewColumnFlags = 1;
        ComputerScrollPosition = {h = 0, v = 0; };
        ComputerToolbarVisible = 1;
        ComputerUseCustomIconViewOptions = 1;
        ComputerUseCustomListViewOptions = 1;
        ComputerViewStyle = icnv;
    };
    CopyProgressWindowLocation = "397, 51";
    EmptyTrashProgressWindowLocation = "457, 51";
.
.
.
(output truncated for space)
```

Figure 7.15 Using the `defaults` command to show your Finder settings. (Output is abbreviated.)

To configure the Finder to display hidden files:

1. `defaults write com.apple.Finder`
   `→ AppleShowAllFiles -string ON`

   The general form of the command is

   `defaults write` *`domain key value`*

   See `man defaults` for more details.

   You need to restart the application (the Finder in this case) for the change to take effect.
2. Log out of Mac OS X.
3. Log in again.

   You will see files and folders that were previously hidden, as shown in **Figure 7.16**.

   You can remove the configuration change with

   ```
   defaults write com.apple.Finder
   → AppleShowAllFiles -string OFF
   ```

   and then restart the Finder.

✔ Tip

- Some longtime Unix users prefer to have "focus follows mouse" on their Terminal windows. As soon as the cursor moves over the window, whatever you type goes to that window, without your having to click it or bring it to the front. This behavior is the default in some graphical interfaces for Unix. You can use the `defaults` command to make the Terminal application behave this way:

  ```
  defaults write com.apple.Terminal
  → FocusFollowsMouse -string YES
  ```

  and turn it off with

  ```
  defaults write com.apple.Terminal
  → FocusFollowsMouse -string NO
  ```

  You need to restart Terminal for the change to take effect.

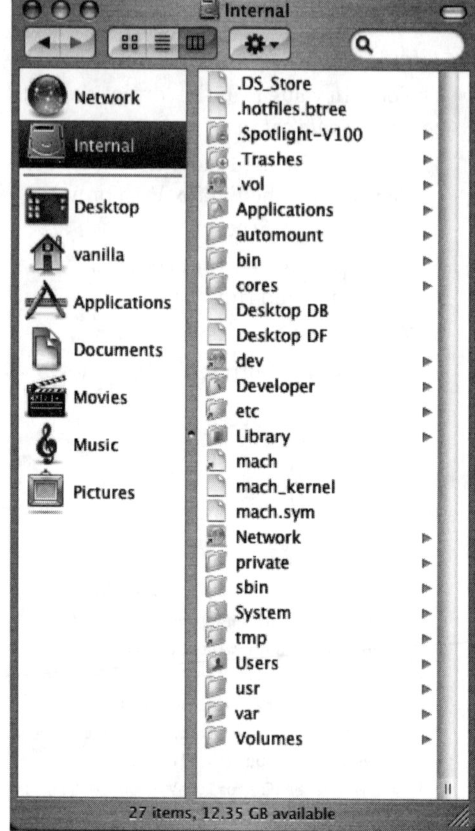

Figure 7.16 A Finder view of the root level of the system disk after using the `defaults` command to turn on `AppleShowAllFiles`.

Working with Permissions and Ownership

8

The dual concepts of *permissions* and *ownership* in Unix are not only an important part of Unix's high level of stability—they are also the foundation for its system of security.

This chapter covers these two critical concepts, and from the very first we want to impress upon you the difference between them. Even Unix veterans are sometimes tripped up when they haven't sufficiently separated the two concepts in their minds.

It's really quite simple. Think "Who owns it?" and "What permission do they have?" *Ownership* in Unix deals with *who* controls something. *Permissions* deals with *what* the owners (and others) can do with something. Every file is "owned" by one user and one group. Every file has a set of "permissions" that define what the owning user, group, and all others may do with it.

This chapter describes the ownership and permissions features available on every Unix and Unix-like system you are likely to encounter. We'll show you what users and groups are, how to see who owns each file, and how to understand and set the permissions on a file. Because the setting of permissions in Unix involves so many possible combinations, we use several tables and examples to allow you to compare different permission settings and to read an explanation for each. Starting in version 10.4, Mac OS X also supports an extremely powerful (and equally complex) ownership and permissions feature called Access Control Lists (ACLs) At the end of this chapter we describe ACLs and give some examples of their use.

About Users and Groups

Because Unix is a multiuser system, it is quite normal to have many users (also called *user accounts*) on your computer. You could even have hundreds if your computer is being used as a server that many people can access, perhaps to retrieve their e-mail.

To help manage system security, Unix uses *groups* to organize several users together so that you can grant file access to all of them. A user is always a member of at least one group and may be a member of many groups. Think of how employees in a company might be organized—everyone has access to the e-mail system, but only certain people in the accounting department have access to financial information. Thus, the people in accounting are members of two different groups for security purposes: They are members of group "staff" and also group "finance."

Every single file and directory on a Unix machine is owned by one user and one group. When a file is created, its ownership and permissions are based on the user who created it.

A file starts its existence under the ownership of the user who created it and within one of the groups that user belongs to (usually the user's *primary group*—for more on groups, see the following section, and the entries for 2775 and 2000 in Tables 8.3 and 8.4, respectively). The file also has a set of permissions assigned to it, based on the `umask` of the user; the `umask` defines which permissions are *not* granted (or are "masked out") for files you create (review "Changing your `umask`" in Chapter 7, "Configuring Your Environment with Unix").

Every user account on a Unix system has a name and a number. The name is what Mac OS X calls your *short name*. In the Unix world, this short name is variously referred to as your *login name*, your *user name*, and frequently simply *user*. The number is referred to as the *user ID*, or *uid*.

Every user account on a Unix system belongs to at least one *group*. Like users, groups have both names and ID numbers. A Unix group contains a list of users. As we mentioned, users are frequently members of more than one group. The group's ID number is often referred to as the *gid*. See Chapter 11, "Introduction to System Administration," to learn how to add users to a group.

In some Unix systems (including Mac OS X 10.4 Tiger) a new group is normally created when you create a new user account. The new group has the same name as the user's user name, and the gid number is the same as the new uid number. The new user will be the only member of this *user private group*. The group ownership on users' home directories will be their user private group. On other Unix systems (and Mac OS X before 10.3), new user accounts typically all belong to a single group and their home directories have that group ownership. On Mac OS X before 10.4 this would be the staff group.

Seeing all the users and groups on your system

Even if you created only one account when you installed Mac OS X, you still have more than a dozen "users" on your system. This is because Unix has a number of special user accounts that are never intended to be directly used by any human. These other "users" exist so that system files and processes may be owned and operated with differing sets of privileges. There are also a number of groups that exist for the same purpose.

To see a list of all the users on your system:

◆ `nidump passwd .`

The `nidump` command (*NetInfo dump*) is a Darwin-specific command (derived from the NeXT operating system) that displays information from a database called NetInfo (**Figure 8.1**).

Each line of output from `nidump` is a colon-separated series of entries for one user.

continues on next page

```
localhost:~ vanilla$ nidump passwd .
nobody:*:-2:-2::0:0:Unprivileged User:/var/empty:/usr/bin/false
root:*:0:0::0:0:System Administrator:/var/root:/bin/sh
daemon:*:1:1::0:0:System Services:/var/root:/usr/bin/false
unknown:*:99:99::0:0:Unknown User:/var/empty:/usr/bin/false
lp:*:26:26::0:0:Printing Services:/var/spool/cups:/usr/bin/false
postfix:*:27:27::0:0:Postfix User:/var/spool/postfix:/usr/bin/false
www:*:70:70::0:0:World Wide Web Server:/Library/WebServer:/usr/bin/false
eppc:*:71:71::0:0:Apple Events User:/var/empty:/usr/bin/false
mysql:*:74:74::0:0:MySQL Server:/var/empty:/usr/bin/false
sshd:*:75:75::0:0:sshd Privilege separation:/var/empty:/usr/bin/false
qtss:*:76:76::0:0:QuickTime Streaming Server:/var/empty:/usr/bin/false
cyrusimap:*:77:6::0:0:Cyrus IMAP User:/var/imap:/usr/bin/false
mailman:*:78:78::0:0:Mailman user:/var/empty:/usr/bin/false
appserverusr:*:79:79::0:0:Application Server:/var/empty:/usr/bin/false
clamav:*:82:82::0:0:Clamav User:/var/virusmails:/bin/tcsh
amavisd:*:83:83::0:0:Amavisd User:/var/virusmails:/bin/tcsh
jabber:*:84:84::0:0:Jabber User:/var/empty:/usr/bin/false
xgridcontroller:*:85:85::0:0:Xgrid Controller:/var/xgrid/controller:/usr/bin/false
xgridagent:*:86:86::0:0:Xgrid Agent:/var/xgrid/agent:/usr/bin/false
appowner:*:87:87::0:0:Application Owner:/var/empty:/usr/bin/false
windowserver:*:88:88::0:0:WindowServer:/var/empty:/usr/bin/false
matisse:********:501:20::0:0:Matisse Enzer:/Users/matisse:/bin/bash
vanilla:********:502:502::0:0:Sample User:/Users/vanilla:/bin/bash
howard:********:503:503::0:0:Howard Baldwin:/Users/howard:/bin/bash
jose:********:504:20::0:0:Jose Marquez:/Users/jose:/bin/bash
whitney:********:505:20::0:0:Whitney Walker:/Users/whitney:/bin/bash
securityagent:*:92:92::0:0:SecurityAgent:/var/empty:/usr/bin/false
tokend:*:91:91::0:0:Token Daemon:/var/empty:/usr/bin/false
remote:eq2myO/rZb/v2:503:503::0:0:Remote Desktop User:/Users/remote:/bin/bash
appserver:*:79:79::0:0:Application Server:/var/empty:/usr/bin/false
localhost:~ vanilla$
```

Figure 8.1 Using `nidump` to see a list of all the user accounts on the system. Your list will differ.

Figure 8.2 shows the meanings of the most important entries. Notice the primary group ID entry. Every user is a member of at least one group, called his or her *primary group*.

✔ Tip

- `nidump` reads from a database that contains a variety of system information. The database is a series of files in `/var/db/netinfo`. If you are experienced with other Unix systems, then `nidump` is one big difference with Mac OS X/Darwin. The output from `nidump` looks like the `/etc/passwd` file that other Unix systems use. See also the sidebar "Creating Users and Groups."

To see a list of all the groups on your system:

- `nidump group .`

  Figure 8.3 shows the output of this command, and **Figure 8.4** is a diagram showing what the parts of each line mean. Note that several users shown in Figure 8.1 have group 20 as their primary group. In Figure 8.3 we see that group 20 is called "staff."

✔ Tip

- Even though only the root user is listed in the entry for group staff, there are still users who are members of it—they are those users who have group 20 listed as their primary group in Figure 8.1. So to see all the users who are a member of a group, you have to look in two places: the output of both

  `nidump passwd .`

  and

  `nidump group .`

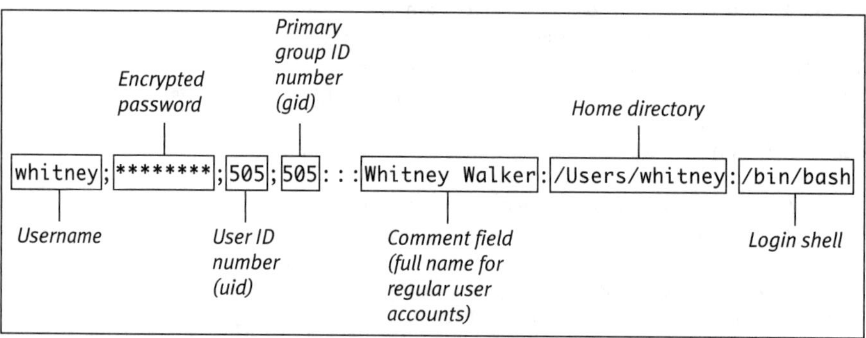

Figure 8.2 Diagram showing the important parts of each line in the output from `nidump passwd`.

```
localhost:~ vanilla$ nidump group .
nobody:*:-2:
nogroup:*:-1:
wheel:*:0:root
daemon:*:1:root
kmem:*:2:root
sys:*:3:root
tty:*:4:root
operator:*:5:root
mail:*:6:
bin:*:7:
staff:*:20:root
lp:*:26:
postfix:*:27:
postdrop:*:28:
utmp:*:45:
uucp:*:66:
dialer:*:68:
network:*:69:
www:*:70:
mysql:*:74:
sshd:*:75:
qtss:*:76:
mailman:*:78:
appserverusr:*:79:matisse,vanilla,remote
admin:*:80:root,matisse,vanilla,remote
appserveradm:*:81:matisse,vanilla,remote
clamav:*:82:
amavisd:*:83:
jabber:*:84:
xgridcontroller:*:85:
xgridagent:*:86:
appowner:*:87:
windowserver:*:88:
accessibility:*:90:
unknown:*:99:
everyone::12:
authedusers::50:
interactusers::51:
netusers::52:
consoleusers::53:
owner::10:
group::11:
smmsp::25:
matisse:*:501:
vanilla:*:502:
howard:*:503
jose:*:504
whitney:*:505
securityagent:*:92:
tokend:*:91:
remote:*:503:
peachpit:*:1000:matisse,whitney
localhost:~ vanilla$
```

Figure 8.3 Using nidump to get a list of all the groups on the system. Your results will differ.

It is very easy to see which groups a particular user belongs to.

To see which groups you belong to:

- groups

  The groups command displays a list of all the groups you are a member of (**Figure 8.5**).

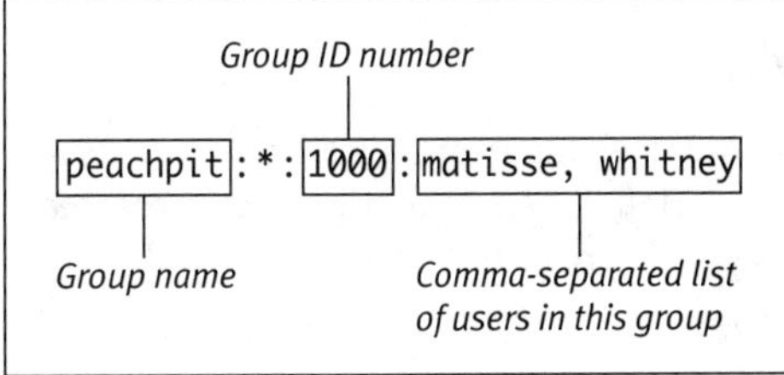

Figure 8.4 Diagram showing the important parts of each entry in the list of groups.

```
localhost:~ vanilla$ groups
vanilla appserveradm appserverusr admin
localhost:~ vanilla$
```

Figure 8.5 Using the groups command to see which groups you belong to. Your results will differ.

About Users and Groups

To see which groups another user belongs to:

- `groups username`

  You use the same `groups` command to see which groups a user other than yourself belongs to. For example, to see which groups the user vanilla belongs to, type

  `groups vanilla`

  Figure 8.6 shows sample results using users and groups from Figures 8.1 and 8.3.

✔ Tip

- Membership in groups is not secret information. Any user on the system can see which groups other users are members of.

```
localhost:~ vanilla$ groups matisse
matisse appserveradm appserverusr admin peachpit
localhost:~ vanilla$
```

Figure 8.6 Using the groups command to see the groups another user belongs to. Again, your results will differ.

Creating Users and Groups

The Darwin methods for adding, modifying, and deleting users and groups are different from those used by all other Unix systems. The current (Mac OS X 10.4) approach uses something called Directory Service and is an evolved version of software developed by NeXT.

Using the Mac OS X graphical interface, users may be added or deleted, and their passwords may be changed, from the Accounts pane in System Preferences. See Chapter 11 for more and the `man` pages for `DirectoryService`, `dscl`, and `dseditgroup`.

Why Mac OS X Uses sudo Instead of a Root Login

By emphasizing the use of the sudo command, Apple made it slightly less convenient for users to perform commands as root. Its goal: discouraging average Mac OS X users from working as root because of the danger that they could irreparably damage their systems, requiring a reinstall of the operating system. Apple probably thought it was making this more inconvenient than it actually did. Its intent, though—that naive users be protected from accidentally messing up their systems—was a good idea.

The Root User—Permission to Do Anything

There is one very special user account on every Unix system: the one with the user name *root*. This account is also called the *superuser*, because it has the power to override every safeguard on the system.

The root account on a Unix system has full control over every file on the system.

The root account is what is sometimes called a *role account*, meaning it exists to fill a role rather than being intended for a specific person to use. On some systems more than one person will be able to use the account.

On most Unix systems, you use the root account to perform system-administration tasks. In practice, this means that on those Unix systems you either log in as the root user or use the su (*switch user*) command to assume the role of the root user after having logged in with your regular account.

Mac OS X uses a slightly different approach, in which you never actually log in as root but instead use a command called sudo (*superuser do*) to perform specific commands with the power of root (see the sidebar "Why Mac OS X Uses sudo Instead of a Root Login" for a discussion of why Mac OS X does this differently). Using the sudo command is covered in Chapter 11, but you need to be aware at this point that there is a way to override any of the permission restrictions described in this chapter.

Understanding Permissions and Ownership

As we noted in the introduction, permissions and ownership in Unix are two tightly related but different concepts. While each file (and each process) is owned by one user and one group, each file also has a set of permissions that define what can be done with that file by the three different categories: 1) the user who owns it, 2) the group that owns it, and 3) everyone else (all users who are neither the owning user nor members of the owning group).

The first step to understanding permissions and ownership is to learn how to determine the permissions and ownership of a file. If you have worked through Chapter 5, "Using Files and Directories," you have already learned to use the `ls` command with the `-l` option to get the long-format listing of files in a directory. Now you will learn exactly what the permission and ownership portions of those listings mean. (Review Chapter 2, "Using the Command Line," and Chapter 5 if the commands below are unfamiliar to you.)

To create a file and a directory to use as examples:

1. `cd`

   This ensures that you are in your home directory.

2. `mkdir examples`

   This creates a new directory called `examples`.

3. `cd examples`

   This changes your working directory so that your current directory is now `~/examples`.

   Create a directory and file inside the `examples` directory.

4. `mkdir testdir`

   This creates a new directory called `testdir`.

5. `date > testfile`

   Creates a new file called testfile, containing the current date and time.

The following task assumes that you have created the directories and files in the task above, and that your current directory is `~/examples`.

To view the permissions and ownership of all files in the current directory:

- `ls -l`

  This shows the long-form listing of all the files in the current directory (**Figure 8.7**).

Figure 8.8 shows what the different parts of the listing mean. Notice that there is a part of the listing that shows the permissions and a part that shows the ownership, and that ownership has two parts: user and group. We'll go into more detail about the permissions part a little later on (just a preview: `r` stands for *read*, `w` stands for *write*, `x` stands for *execute*, and `-` means *no permission*, in sets of three characters for each of these—user, group, and all others). For more about ACLs (Access Control Lists) see "Using ACLs" later in this chapter.

```
localhost:~ vanilla$ ls -l
drwxr-xr-x      2 vanilla     staff     24 Jan 24 11:30 testdir
-rw-r--r--      1 vanilla     staff     29 Jan 24 11:30 testfile
localhost:~ vanilla$
```

Figure 8.7 Using `ls -l` to view the permissions and ownership of all the files in the current directory.

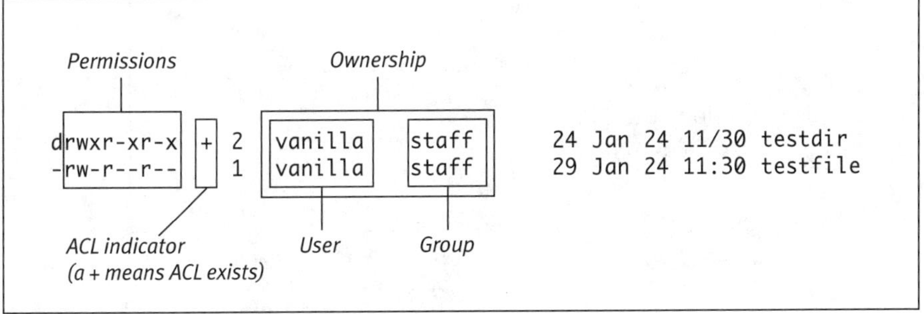

Figure 8.8 Diagram showing which parts of the listing are the permissions and which parts are the ownership information.

To list permissions for specific files:

- Supply the filenames as arguments to `ls -l`.

  For example,

  `ls -l testfile`

  shows the permissions and ownership for only the file testfile. You may supply multiple file and directory names as arguments.

  If any of the arguments are directory names, then the *contents* of the directory are listed.

To see the permissions for a directory:

- Add the `-d` option to `ls -l`:

  `ls -ld testdir`

  Figure 8.9 compares the output of

  `ls -l ~/examples`

  with

  `ls -ld ~/examples`

  In the first case the directory's contents are listed. The addition of the `-d` option shows the permissions for the directory itself instead of its contents.

```
localhost:~ vanilla$ ls -l ~/examples
total 8
drwxr-xr-x     2 vanilla    staff    24 Jan 24 11:30 testdir
-rw-r-r-      1 vanilla    staff    29 Jan 24 11:30 testfile
localhost:~ vanilla$ ls -ld ~/examples
drwxr-xr-x     2 vanilla    staff    92 Jan 24 11:29 /Users/vanilla/examples
localhost:~ vanilla$
```

Figure 8.9 Comparing the output of `ls -l` and `ls -ld` when a directory is an argument.

Compare with Aqua

In Aqua you can view (and set) some of the permissions for files by selecting a file (or directory) in the Finder and choosing Get Info from the File menu. Then click the Ownership & Permissions triangle, and then the Details triangle. In **Figure 8.10**, you see the Get Info window displaying the permissions of the `~/examples` directory used in Figure 8.8.

The Aqua interface does not provide a way to list the permissions for several files together in one window, nor does it display the execute permission (described in the next section) or allow you to set all the possible permutations of permissions.

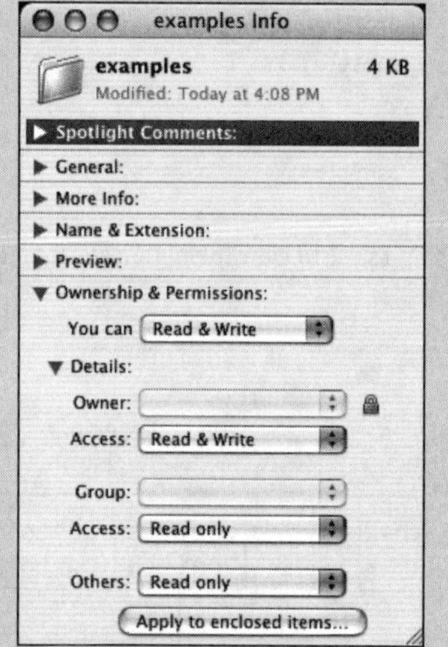

Figure 8.10 The Show Info window displaying the permissions of the `~/examples` directory used in Figure 8.8.

The types of permission

The permissions settings for a file in Unix pack a lot of information into only nine characters. **Figure 8.11** shows how the permissions listing of nine characters is divided into three groups of three characters each for the owning user, group, and all others.

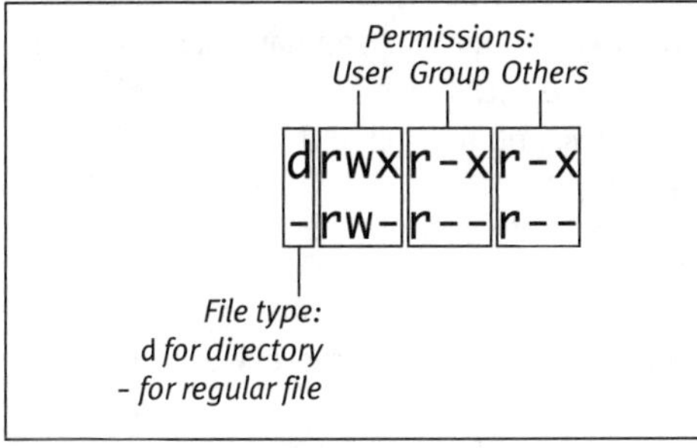

Figure 8.11 Diagram showing which parts of the permission listing are for read, write, and execute permission.

There are three kinds of file permission in Unix, and each kind may be different for each of the three categories of owners (owning user, owning group, and all others).

The three main kinds of permission, for both files and directories, are

- Read permission
- Write permission
- Execute permission

In the nine characters of a permission listing, each set of three shows the read, write, and execute permission for the user, group, and others, respectively. **Figure 8.12** shows how letters indicate that permission is granted and a hyphen (-) signifies that permission is not granted.

Each type of permission (read, write, execute) has a different meaning for files than for directories.

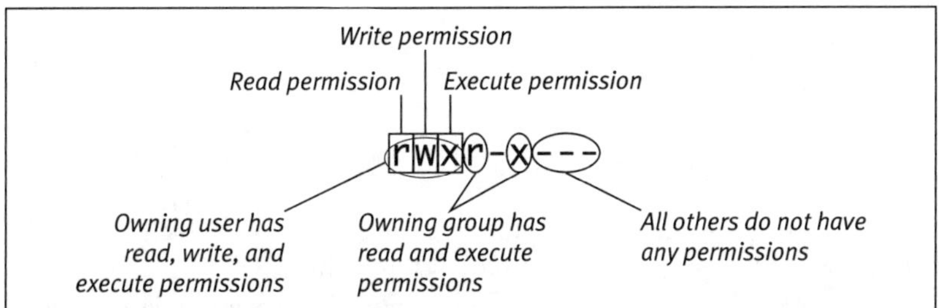

Figure 8.12 Annotated example of permission information showing the three groups of three characters indicating permissions for the user, group, and others. Permission settings: - means "no permission;" and a letter means "this permission is granted."

What permissions mean for files

Read permission means that you can read the file. If you have read permission on a file, then you can see its contents with commands like `cat` and `less`, copy it with `cp`, and so on. You can view the file with an editor like `vi`, but you can't alter the file unless you also have write permission.

Write permission means that you can change the file. You need write permission to edit the file or rename it. Note that if you have read permission but not write permission, you can make a copy of the file, and because you own the copy, you can alter it.

Execute permission means that if a file is a script, or program, you need to have execute permission to actually run, or *execute*, the program. Type `ls -l /bin` and see how the user, group, and others all have execute permission on all of the programs in that directory (you'll see the `ls` program itself in there, too).

What Permissions Mean for Directories

Read permission means that you can list the directory contents. Remember that a directory is actually a special kind of file whose content is a list of file and directory names.

Write permission means that you can change the directory name, and create and delete files inside the directory, and you can also change the permissions of files that you own inside the directory. Since a directory is really a special kind of file that contains a list of names, having permission to write to the directory means that you have permission to change the list, which includes changing filenames, and adding and removing files. See the sidebar "Deleting Files."

Execute permission means that you may `cd` into or through the directory. If you have read permission on a directory but not execute permission, then you can use `ls` to see the contents of the directory but cannot use `cd` to go into the directory.

Deleting Files

You do not actually need write permission on a file to delete the file.

To create or delete a file, you need only have write permission for the directory containing the file. This is because when you delete a file, you are really deleting its name from the list of items in a directory, and that means you are altering (writing) the *directory*. Review the section "Using hard links" at the end of Chapter 5 for more on how filenames are actually entries in directories.

If you try to delete a file for which you do not have write permission but that is in a directory where you have write permission, you get a warning, but you are allowed to delete the file.

Looked at another way, if a user has write permission on a directory, he or she can delete every file inside that directory. There is a way to prevent that by setting the "sticky bit" in a directory. See `man sticky`.

Examples of permissions

Using a set of examples is a good way to increase your understanding of ownership and permissions.

Figure 8.13 shows a sample listing of eight files (three of which are directories). The explanations below all refer to Figure 8.13.

In each of the examples, we tell you what the permission *mode* is on the file. The permission mode is a numerical representation of the permission settings on the file—for example, 644 or 755. We explain these numerical modes in great detail later in the section "Changing permissions with absolute modes."

file1 is the most common case. The user who owns the file (vanilla) has permission to read the file and write (or modify) it. Everyone else has permission to read it. The permission mode on this file is 644.

file2 is readable and writable by the owner, and readable by anyone in group "staff." No one else can read or write to the file. The mode on this one is 640.

file3 has the standard permissions for an executable program or script. The owner has read, write, and execute permissions; everyone else has read and execute permissions. Only the execute permission is needed to actually run the program/script; the read permission allows making copies of the file. The mode is 755.

file4 is an interesting case. The owner, vanilla, has read and write permission. Members of group "losers" have no permissions, and everyone else has read permission. What's going on here? When you try to use a file, the operating system checks permissions in this order: user, group, other. So if you are the user who owns the file, the user permissions are used. If not, the system checks to see if you are in the group that owns the file. If so, the group permissions are used, and if you are not the owner or in the group, the "other" permissions apply. Only one set of permissions is applied. So in the case of *file4*, everybody has read permission *except* people in group losers. The mode is 604.

continues on next page

```
-rw-r--r--   1 vanilla   admin    21 Jan 24 15:21 file1
-rw-r-----   1 vanilla   admin    21 Jan 24 15:22 file2
-rwxr-xr-x   1 vanilla   admin    21 Jan 24 15:22 file3
-rw-r-----   1 vanilla   losers   21 Jan 24 15:22 file4
-rw-rw-r--   1 vanilla   team1    21 Jan 24 15:22 file5
drwxr-xr-x   1 vanilla   admin    21 Jan 24 15:22 directory1
drwxrwxr-x   1 vanilla   admin    21 Jan 24 15:22 directory2
drwx------   1 vanilla   admin    21 Jan 24 15:22 directory3
```

Figure 8.13 Sample listing of eight files showing different permission modes.

file5 has the most common permissions for a file that is part of a group project. The owner and any user in group "team1" have read and write permission; everyone else has read-only permission. The mode is 664.

directory1 has the standard permissions for nonprivate directories. The owner has read, write, and execute permissions; everybody else has read and execute permissions. Everyone can list the contents of the directory and can `cd` into it, but only the owner can create files inside it. The mode is 755.

directory2 has the most common permissions for a directory used in a group project. Permissions are the same as with *directory1* except that any member of group staff also has write permission on the directory. The mode is 775.

directory3 has the standard permissions for a private directory. The owner has read, write, and execute permissions; everybody else (including people in group staff) has no permissions—they cannot see anything in the directory or even `cd` into or through it. The mode is 700.

Be Careful with the Execute Bit

Be sure not to turn on execute permission for files that are not actually intended to be run as commands. Executing a file that was not created as a command file could cause undesirable results as the operating system attempts to read the file's contents as executable. Usually you simply get an error message, but if the file's contents happen to contain something that the system thinks is actually executable, you could lock up your Terminal window or lose data.

Setting and Changing Permissions

Although "permissions" means different things for files than for directories, you use the same command to set permissions for both files and directories.

Only the user who owns a file may change its permissions (but see the "sudo—the Mac OS X way of using root" section in Chapter 11, on how to use the sudo command to override this limitation).

You use the chmod (*change mode*) command to set the permissions of files.

The general form of a command line for chmod is

chmod *mode file*

where *mode* is the permission setting, and *file* is a filename or even multiple filenames.

The *mode* argument is in one of two forms: *symbolic* or *absolute*.

Table 8.1

Symbolic Mode Changes

(This is a partial list.)

Symbol	Meaning
Symbols for the "Who" Part	
u	Applies change to the owning user.
g	Applies change to the owning group.
o	Applies change to all others.
a	Applies change to all (user, group, and others).
Symbols for the "Operator" Part	
+	Adds the following permissions.
-	Removes the following permissions.
Symbols for the "Who" Part	
r	Read permission.
w	Write permission.
x	Execute permission.

Symbolic modes are best used to make changes to permissions on a file when you want to alter some of its permissions but leave others unchanged.

Absolute modes are used to set all of the permissions for a file at once.

So if you want to add read permission to a file without disturbing any of the other permissions on the file, you use a symbolic mode. An example of this would be adding read permission to a file for the owning group without changing the permissions for the user or others.

On the other hand, if you want a file to have a specific set of permissions for the user, the group, and others all at once, then you should use an absolute mode. An example of this would be if you wanted to set a file to be readable and writable by the owning user, and only readable by the owning group and others.

Changing permissions with symbolic modes

The basic syntax of a symbolic mode is *who operator what.*

For example,

ug+w

would appear in a command line as

chmod ug+w *file*

The ug are the "who" (user and group), the + is the "operator" (add), and the w is the "what" (write permission). Many combinations are possible. **Table 8.1** shows the meanings of each of the characters.

Here are a few tasks that use symbolic modes to change permissions.

To add read permission to a file for the owning group:

◆ `chmod g+r` *`file`*

  For example,

  `chmod g+r myfile.txt`

  Figure 8.14 shows the permissions before and after using this command line.

To remove read permission on a file for the owning group:

◆ `chmod g-r` *`file`*

  For example,

  `chmod g-r myfile.txt`

  Figure 8.15 shows the before and after for this command line.


```
localhost:~ vanilla$ ls -l myfile.txt
-rw-------    1 vanilla    staff    29 Jan 24 11:30 myfile.txt
localhost:~ vanilla$ chmod g+r myfile.txt
localhost:~ vanilla$ ls -l myfile.txt
-rw-r-----    1 vanilla    staff    29 Jan 24 11:30 myfile.txt
localhost:~ vanilla$
```

Figure 8.14 Comparing permissions before and after adding read permission for the group with `chmod g+r`.

```
localhost:~ vanilla$ ls -l myfile.txt
-rw-r-----    1 vanilla    staff    29 Jan 24 11:30 myfile.txt
localhost:~ vanilla$ chmod g-r myfile.txt
localhost:~ vanilla$ ls -l myfile.txt
-rw-------    1 vanilla    staff    29 Jan 24 11:30 myfile.txt
localhost:~ vanilla$
```

Figure 8.15 Comparing permissions before and after removing read permission for the group with `chmod g-r`.

To add read permission for the group and others:

- chmod go+r *file*

  For example:

  chmod go+r myfile.txt

  Figure 8.16 shows the before and after for this command line.

To add write permission for the group and others:

- chmod go+w *file*

  For example,

  chmod go+w myfile.txt

  Figure 8.17 shows the before and after for this command line.

To remove write permission for the group and others:

- chmod go-w *file*

  For example,

  chmod go-w myfile.txt

  Figure 8.18 shows the before and after for this command line.

  Notice how changing the permissions does not change the file's modification time.

```
localhost:~ vanilla$ ls -l myfile.txt
-rw-------    1 vanilla    staff    29 Jan 24 11:30 myfile.txt
localhost:~ vanilla$ chmod go+r myfile.txt
localhost:~ vanilla$ ls -l myfile.txt
-rw-r--r--    1 vanilla    staff    29 Jan 24 11:30 myfile.txt
localhost:~ vanilla$
```

Figure 8.16 Comparing permissions before and after adding read permission for the group and others with chmod go+r.

```
localhost:~ vanilla$ ls -l myfile.txt
-rwxr--r--    1 vanilla    staff    29 Jan 24 11:30 myfile.txt
localhost:~ vanilla$ chmod go+w myfile.txt
localhost:~ vanilla$ ls -l myfile.txt
-rw-rw-rw-    1 vanilla    staff    29 Jan 24 11:30 myfile.txt
localhost:~ vanilla$
```

Figure 8.17 Comparing permissions before and after adding write permission for the group and others with chmod go+w.

```
localhost:~ vanilla$ ls -l myfile.txt
-rw-rw-rw-    1 vanilla    staff    29 Jan 24 11:30 myfile.txt
localhost:~ vanilla$ chmod go-w myfile.txt
localhost:~ vanilla$ ls -l myfile.txt
-rw-r--r--    1 vanilla    staff    29 Jan 24 11:30 myfile.txt
localhost:~ vanilla$
```

Figure 8.18 Comparing permissions before and after removing write permission for the group and others with chmod go-w.

Changing permissions with absolute modes

An absolute mode consists of a three- or four-digit number, such as 644 or 2775.

In practice you use these modes in this fashion:

```
chmod 644 file
```

That would set the permissions on *file* to be read and write (6) for the user, and read-only (4) for the group and others.

Most of the time you use three-digit numbers for absolute modes, so we address those first.

Each digit in a three-digit absolute mode represents the permissions for the user, the group, and others, in that order. The value of each digit is based on adding up the values of the kinds of permissions being assigned.

- Read permission has a value of 4.
- Write permission has a value of 2.
- Execute permission has a value of 1.

Figure 8.19 shows the values for the absolute modes for each type of permission. Add up the columns to get the mode—for instance, for the user to have all permissions, add 4+2+1 to get 7 for the first column; for the group to have read and execute permissions, the value is 4+1, and so on.

Table 8.2 shows the meanings of each of the eight possible mode values (0–7) for each digit in an absolute mode. Some of you might be thinking this looks like a base-8 (octal) numbering system. You would be correct.

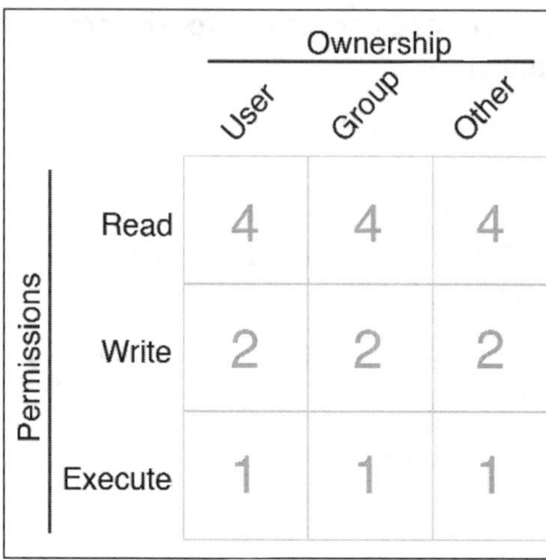

Figure 8.19 Diagram showing the values for the absolute modes for each type of permission.

Table 8.2

Value of Each Digit in a Three-Digit Absolute Mode

Value	Meaning
0	No permission granted to this owner.
1	Execute permission only.
2	Write permission only.
3	Execute permission and write permission (1 + 2 = 3).
4	Read permission only.
5	Execute and read permission (1 + 4 = 5).
6	Write permission and read permission (2 + 4 = 6).
7	Execute, read, and write permission (1 + 2 + 4 = 7).

To set a file's permissions using absolute mode:

- `chmod mode file`

  For example,

  `chmod 644 myfile.txt`

  sets myfile.txt to be readable and writable by the owning user (4 + 2 = 6), and readable by the group and others.

  `chmod 755 myscript.sh`

  makes myscript.sh readable, writable, and executable (4 + 2 + 1 = 7) by the user, and readable and executable (4 + 1 = 5) by the group and others. These same permissions (755) are the standard permissions for nonprivate scripts and programs, as well as nonprivate directories (**Table 8.3**).

  Table 8.3 shows the most common permission settings using absolute mode. This table includes some four-digit modes. When a four-digit mode is used, the first digit has a different set of meanings from the other three. **Table 8.4** and **Table 8.5** (next page) show the meanings of the values for each of the positions in three- or four-digit mode for files (Table 8.4) and for directories (Table 8.5). **Table 8.6** shows the options for the chmod command.

Table 8.3

Common Permission Modes

Mode	Common Use
644	For files. Readable and writable by owning user, readable by everyone else.
755	For directories and programs (commands, scripts, and so on). For directories, this mode allows owning user to create and delete files in the directory, allows everyone to list directory contents and cd into or through the directory. For files, allows owning user to alter the file, allows everyone to read and to execute the program.
664	Same as 644 but also allows owning group to alter the file. Used for files that are part of a group project.
775	For program files (scripts, commands, and so on). Same as 755 but also gives write permission to the owning group so that anyone in the group may alter the file.
2775	Like 775 but adding the 2 at the beginning "sets the group id bit" and means that for directories any file or directory created inside this directory is owned by the same group that owns the parent directory, and for executable files the script or program will run with the group permissions of this file.
600	For private files. The owning user has read and write permission. No one else has any permissions.
700	For private directories or private executable files. The owning user has read, write, and execute permission. No one else has any permissions.

✔ Tip

- The most useful option for the chmod command is -R (*recursively*), which allows you to change the permissions on a directory and everything inside it all at once. For example,

  `chmod -R go-rwx private_dir`

  removes read, write, and execute permissions for group and others from the directory *private_dir* and everything inside it. But be careful. It would probably be a mistake to do something like

  `chmod -R g+x mydirectory`

  because that adds group execute permission to the directory and everything inside it. If the directory contained any files that were not actually scripts or programs, they would end up appearing as executable, and if someone tried to run one of them as a command, it could cause unpredictable results.

Table 8.4

Mode Values for File Permissions

Permission	Mode	Why and When
User read	0400	So that the owning user may read it.
User write	0200	So that the owning user may change it.
User execute	0100	So that the owning user may execute it.
Group read	0040	So that the owning group may read it.
Group write	0020	So that the owning group may change it.
Group execute	0010	So that the owning group may execute it.
Others read	0004	So that all others may read it.
Others write	0002	So that all others may change it.
Others execute	0001	So that all others may execute it.
Setuid	4000	Execute file as owning user ("Set user id on execution"). This property is removed and must be reset each time the file is changed (edited).
Setgid	2000	Execute file as owning group ("Set group id on execution"). This property is removed and must be reset each time the file is changed (edited).
Sticky bit	1000	A directory whose *sticky bit* is set has special restrictions on file deletion. In order to delete or rename a file inside a sticky directory, a user must have write permission on the directory or own the directory, and must also own the file. The root user is not restricted by sticky directories. The `/private/tmp` directory in Mac OS X is a sticky directory (and `/tmp` is a symbolic link to it). See `man sticky` for more on the sticky bit.

Table 8.5

Mode Values for Directory Permissions

Permission	Mode	Why and When
User read	0400	So that the owning user may list contents.
User write	0200	So that the owning user may create and delete files inside it.
User execute	0100	So that the owning user may `cd` into or through it.
Group read	0040	So that the owning group may list contents.
Group write	0020	So that the owning group may create and delete files inside it.
Group execute	0010	So that the owning user may `cd` into or through it.
Others read	0004	So that all others may list contents.
Others write	0002	So that all others may create and delete files inside it.
Others execute	0001	So that all others may `cd` into or through it.
Setuid	4000	No effect.
Setgid	2000	Any files or directories created inside this directory are owned by the same group that owns this directory.

Table 8.6

Options for the chmod Command

Option	Meaning
-R	Makes changes recursively. Used when changing permissions on a directory and everything it contains.
	The next three options only work in combination with the -R option. Only one of the following may be used. If more than one is used, the last one on the command line takes precedence.
-H	If the -R option is specified, symbolic links on the command line are followed. (Symbolic links encountered in the directory traversal are not followed.) See Chapter 5 for more on symbolic links.
-L	If the -R option is specified, all symbolic links are followed.
-P	If the -R option is specified, no symbolic links are followed.

Table 8.7

Options for the chgrp and chown Commands

OPTION	MEANING
-R	Makes changes recursively. Used when changing permissions on a directory and everything it contains.
	The next three options only work in combination with the -R option. Only one of the following may be used. If more than one is used, the last one on the command line takes precedence.
-H	If the -R option is specified, symbolic links on the command line are followed. (Symbolic links encountered in the directory traversal are not followed.) See Chapter 5 for more on symbolic links.
-L	If the -R option is specified, all symbolic links are followed.
-P	If the -R option is specified, no symbolic links are followed.
-f	Ignore errors (force silence). This option squelches error messages resulting from inadequate permissions—for example, if you try to change the group ownership to a group to which you do not belong.

Changing Ownership

Files have two kinds of owners—the user owner and the group owner. Only root can change a file's user ownership. You cannot "give away" a file.

In order to change a file's group ownership, you must be both the file's user owner and a member of the new group, or you must perform the change as root. Furthermore, when a file's group ownership is changed, the `setuid` and `setgid` properties are removed unless the change was made by root. This avoids some potential security problems (see the sidebar "What the `setuid` and `setgid` Properties Do" for more on this).

Group ownership can be changed using either the chgrp (*change group*) or chown (*change owner*) command.

To change the group ownership using chgrp:

- chgrp *newgroup file*

  For example,

  chgrp www index.html

  changes the group ownership of file index.html to www. You must be the file's owner and a member of the new group to perform this. **Figure 8.20** shows an example of changing the group ownership of a file using chgrp. **Table 8.7** shows the options for the chgrp and chown commands.

```
localhost:~/Sites vanilla$ groups
vanilla appserveradm appserverusr admin www
localhost:~/Sites vanilla$ ls -l index.html
-rw-r--r--    1 vanilla   vanilla   5754 Jan 17 14:18 index.html
localhost:~/Sites vanilla$ chgrp www index.html
localhost:~/Sites vanilla$ ls -l index.html
-rw-r--r--    1 vanilla   www       6186 Apr 30  2001 index.html
 localhost:~/Sites vanilla$
```

Figure 8.20 Using chgrp to change the group ownership of a file.

Changing Ownership

✔ Tip

- It is often useful to use the `-R` option to change the group ownership of an entire directory. For example,

  `chgrp -R www webteam`

  changes the directory `webteam` and all it contains so that it is owned by group www.

To change the group ownership using chown:

- `chgrp :`*`newgroup file`*

  For example,

  `chown :web index.html`

  The only difference between using this and using `chgrp` is the addition of the colon before the group name. The reason for this funny syntax is that the `chown` command is designed to change the user ownership and/or the group ownership of a file, and the first argument to `chown` is in the form

  `user:group`

  However, you can leave out the user or group portion to change only one or the other. If you leave out the user portion, you must still use the colon. See the next task for how to use `chown` to change the user ownership (which may be done only by root).

As we've mentioned above, a file's user ownership can be changed only by the root user. On Mac OS X the standard way to perform a command as root is to use the `sudo` command. The following task shows how to change a file's user ownership using `sudo` and `chown`. (See Chapter 11 for more on `sudo`.)

To change the user ownership using chown:

1. `sudo chown `*`newuser file`*

   For example,

   `sudo chown whitney index.html`

   changes the user ownership of the file index.html to whitney.

   The `sudo` command requires that you enter your password if you haven't used it within the last five minutes.

What the setuid and setgid Properties Do

If an executable file such as a script has the `setuid` property turned on, and if the file is executable by users other than the owning user (group or other executable), then when the program is run by someone other than the owning user, the process has the same permission as the owning user. This means you can create a script that alters files on which only you normally have write permission, and you can allow other people to run that script. Obviously this can be both useful and dangerous, like giving out the keys to your house. A similar situation occurs with `setgid` permission: The process runs with the permission of the owning group.

When a user (other than root) changes the group that a file belongs to and `setuid` and `setgid` properties are removed, the properties must be reset as a security precaution. This helps avoid accidentally giving too much power to other users. If you truly want the file to have `setuid` or `setgid` permission, after changing its group you must reset the `setuid` and/or `setgid` permission.

2. Enter your password if asked.

   The command is executed after you enter your password and press [Return].

   Figure 8.21 shows before and after views of using this command line.

To change the user and group ownership simultaneously:

1. `sudo chown newuser:newgroup file`

   For example,

   `sudo chown vanilla:www index.html`

2. Enter your password if asked.

   The command is executed when you enter your password and press [Return].

   Figure 8.22 shows the before and after of this command line.

✔ Tip

- The chown command uses the same options as the `chgrp` command. It is often useful to change an entire directory full of files at once:

  `sudo chown -R howard:www web_images`

  changes the directory `web_images` and all it contains to be owned by the user howard and the group www.

```
localhost:~/Sites ls -l index.html
-rw r--r--    1 vanilla      vanilla      5754 Jan 17 14:18 index.html
localhost:~/Sites sudo chown whitney index.html
Password:
localhost:~/Sites ls -l index.html
-rw-r--r--    1 whitney      vanilla      5754 Jan 17 14:18 index.html
localhost:~/Sites
```

Figure 8.21 Using chown to change a file's user ownership.

```
localhost:~/Sites ls -l index.html
-rw-r--r--    1 whitney      vanilla      5754 Jan 17 14:18 index.html
localhost:~/Sites sudo chown vanilla:www index.html
Password:
localhost:~/Sites ls -l index.html
-rw-r--r--    1 vanilla      www          5754 Jan 17 14:18 index.html
localhost:~/Sites
```

Figure 8.22 Using chown to simultaneously change the user and group ownership.

Default Permissions for File Creation

When a file or directory is created, its initial permissions are determined by a setting called umask. A umask is a value similar to an absolute mode that is subtracted from full permissions to determine the permissions. A typical umask would be 022 or 002. Chapter 7, "Configuring Your Environment with Unix," explains how to see, and change, your umask. You may see umasks displayed as one- or two-digit numbers; in those cases, assume that zeros are added to the left, so a umask of 2 is really 002.

"Full permissions" for files are considered to be 666 (readable and writable by everyone) and for directories to be 777 (readable, writable, and executable by everyone). You always have to explicitly change a file's permission to make a non-directory file (such as a script) executable.

The net result is that if you have a umask of 022, for example, and create a new directory, the permission on the directory is 755 (777 – 022), and if you create a new file, the permission is 644 (666 – 022).

Table 8.8 shows the effect of various umasks on the creation of new files and directories.

Table 8.8

Effect of umask on New File Permissions

UMASK	FOR FILE	FOR DIRECTORY
022	644 (rw-r--r--)	755 (rwxr-xr-x)
002	664 (rw--rwr--)	775 (rwxrwxr-x)
077	600 (rw-------)	700 (rwx------)
066	622 (rw-------)	733 (rwx--x--x)

Recognizing Permission Problems

Ninety percent of day-to-day problems in running Unix systems are permissions-related. Most often, some process tries to write to a file or directory that it doesn't have permission to write to. Maybe it did yesterday, but someone accidentally or carelessly changed it, and then something stopped working.

Permission problems show up in so many ways that it is not reasonable to try to list them here, but there are a few rules you can follow to spot permission problems.

Often the first sign is an error message containing the words "Permission denied." Sometimes it is accompanied by more information—for example,

```
/usr/local/bin/script.sh: permission
→ denied: /etc/foo [3]
```

This is telling you that line 3 of the script `/usr/local/bin/script.sh` failed because it did not have enough permission to do something with `/etc/foo`. You have to look inside the script to see what exactly was going on, but you have a good place to start.

Some things to keep in mind:

1. To create a new file, rename a file, delete a file, or change a file's permissions, the process must have write permission in the directory where the file is being created.
2. To change an existing file, you must have write permission on the file.
3. To `cd` into a directory, the process must have execute permission on the *full path* of the directory. So to `cd` into `/Users/vanilla/Sites/images/big_images`, the processes doing the `cd` must have execute permission on the following:

   ```
   /
   /Users
   /Users/vanilla
   /Users/vanilla/Sites
   /Users/vanilla/Sites
   /images
   /Users/vanilla/Sites
   /images/big_images
   ```
4. To list the contents of a subdirectory, you must have read permission for it, as well as permission to `cd` into the directory where it's stored. So to list the contents of `/Users/vanilla/Sites/images/big_images`, you must be able to `cd` into `/Users/vanilla/Sites/images` and have read permission on big_images. You do not need to be able to `cd` into a directory to list its contents.

To correct a permission problem:

1. Write down the permissions of the files or directories you think should change.

   You might try redirecting the output of `ls -l` into a file, for example:

   `ls -l bad_file > permission_save`
2. Change the permissions to what you think will fix the problem.
3. Test the fix.

   If the fix doesn't work, change the permissions back to what they started as, and think through the problem again. Go back to step 2. Lather, rinse, repeat.

Using ACLs

Starting with version 10.4 Mac OS X supports a form of permissions called an Access Control List (ACL). ACLs are special files, normally hidden from view, that allow you to specify in excruciating detail the kinds of access that users have to a file or directory. For example, using an ACL, you can give permission to append to a file but not to delete it, or to delete or create a file, but not to alter an existing file. And you can give these permissions separately to each user or group in the ACL.

ACLs are not enabled by default in the regular version of Mac OS X, but they are enabled in Mac OS X Server (see www.apple.com/server/documentation). There is also an article on understanding ACLs at www.afp548.com/article.php?story=20050506085817850. Or, check out Apple Training Series: Mac OS X Server Essentials, soon to be published by Peachpit Press, for much more about ACLs than we are able to cover here.

To enable ACLs:

◆ `sudo fsaclctl -a -e`

Enter your password if asked for it.

You will see a line of output for each filesystem (volume, partition) you have mounted, with at least the root filesystem being listed:

```
ProcessVolume: processing /
```

✔ Tips

- You can learn more about ACLs from the `man` page for the `chmod` and `ls` commands. These describe how to set and read ACLs. For example, to set an ACL you might do

```
chmod +a "admin allow write"
→ filename
```

- The folks at Ars Technica wrote an article that provides an excellent overview of the changes to Mac OS X that were introduced in version 10.4. The section on ACLs is http://arstechnica.com/reviews/os/macosx-10.4.ars/8.

To add an ACL entry:

◆ Use the `+a` option to the `chmod` command.

For example, the following would add an entry to the ACL for the file *filename*, allowing anyone in group dancers to append to the file (write data to the file but not overwrite any existing data in the file):

```
chmod +a "dancers allow append"
→ filename
```

Table 8.9 lists ACL permission keywords, **Table 8.10** lists the most common ACL-related options for the `chmod` command,

continues on page 238

Table 8.9

ACL Permissions

Keyword	Description
Permissions available for both files and directories:	
delete	Deletes the object. You can delete an object if you have this permission or the delete_child permission on the immediate parent directory.
readattr	Reads the object's basic attributes (filename, size, and so on)
writeattr	Changes the normal Unix attributes of the object.
readextattr	Reads the object's extended attributes—these are the attributes used in Spotlight searches.
writeextattr	Alters the object's extended attributes.
readsecurity	Reads the object's ACL.
writesecurity	Writes an object's ACL.
chown	Changes the object's ownership.
Permissions available only for directories:	
list	Lists the contents of the directory.
search	Looks up files by name.
add_file	Adds a file.
add_subdirectory	Adds a subdirectory.
delete_child	Deletes any object in the directory. (See also the delete permission, above.)
file_inherit	Causes files (not directories) to inherit ACL settings.
directory_inherit	Causes subdirectories (not files) to inherit ACL settings.
limit_inherit	Causes an inherited ACL entry to not be inherited any further down the hierarchy—it stops here, so this one only applies to inherited entries.
only_inherit	The entry is inherited but has no effect.
Permissions available only for non-directories:	
read	Like the standard Unix read permission—allows reading the file contents.
write	Allows writing to the file.
append	Like write, but only allows writes into areas in the file that have not already been written.
execute	Like the standard Unix execute permission for a file.

Table 8.10

ACL Options for the chmod Command

Option	Description
+a	Set (add) an ACL entry.
+a# *n*	Add an entry at position *n* (lowest number is 0)
-a	Remove an entry.
-a# *n*	Remove entry at position *n* (lowest position is 0)
=a# *n*	Rewrite an existing entry at position *n*.
-E	Read the ACL entries (separated by newlines) from STDIN, so you can redirect input from a file with chmod -E < *acl_entries_file*
-i	Removes the "inherited" setting from all entries in the named file(s)' ACLs. See the man page for chmod for more on complex inheritance possibilities of ACL entries.
-I	Removes all inherited entries from the named file(s)' ACLs.

and **Figure 8.23** shows several examples of setting ACLs.

You can view the ACL for a file using the `ls` command:

```
ls -le filename
```

The `e` option (*extended*), when combined with the `l` option, will show the ACL for the specified file. See **Figure 8.23** for some examples.

✔ Tips

- ACL entries normally get added to the "top" of the ACL list (in position 1 as shown by the `ls -le` command), but you can specify a position for a new ACL entry by using the `+a#` option—for example:

  ```
  chmod +a# 3 "probies deny write"
  → inbox
  ```

  would put the new ACL entry at position 3. If there was already an entry at position 3, it would now be at position 4.

- ACLs support specifying (for directories only) how ACL settings are passed down to files and directories contained inside the directory. This is called *inheritance*. See the `man` page for `chmod` for details.

To remove an ACL entry:

- Use the `-a` or `-a#` option to the `chmod` command.

  For example,

  ```
  chmod -a "probies deny write"
  → filename
  ```

  will remove the (exactly matching) ACL entry. You can use the `-a#` option to remove an entry by its index number:

  ```
  chmod -a# 3 filename
  ```

  will remove the third ACL entry.

To alter an existing ACL entry:

- Use the `=a#` option to the `chmod` command.

  For example, to replace the ACL entry in position 2:

  ```
  chmod =a# 2 "dancers allow read"
  → filename
  ```

Adding an ACL entry to allow group "dancers" to write to a file:

```
root# ls -le
total 8
-rw-r--r--  1 vanilla wheel     13 Jul 11 20:18 file1
root# chmod +a "dancers allow write" file1
root# ls -le
total 8
-rw-r--r-- + 1 vanilla         wheel     13 Jul 11 20:18 file1
 0: group:dancers allow write
```

Adding an ACL entry on a directory to allow group dancers to add files to the directory:

```
root# ls -le
total 0
drwxr-xr-x  2 root   wheel     68 Jul 11 20:23 dropbox
root# chmod +a "dancers allow add_file" dropbox
root# ls -le
total 0
drwxr-xr-x + 2 root   wheel     68 Jul 11 20:23 dropbox
 0: group:dancers allow add_file
```

(Notice how the second use of `ls -le`, after adding an ACL entry, added a + to the output of `ls`.)

Adding an ACL entry giving user "vanilla" three permissions (add_file, list, and search) on the directory:

```
root# chmod +a "vanilla allow add_file,list,search" dropbox
root# ls -le
total 0
drwxr-xr-x + 2 root   wheel     68 Jul 11 20:29 dropbox
 0: user:vanilla allow list,add_file,search
 1: group:dancers allow add_file
```

Removing an ACL entry by position number:

```
root# ls -le
total 0
drwxr-xr-x + 2 root   wheel     68 Jul 11 20:29 dropbox
 0: user:vanilla allow list,add_file,search
 1: group:dancers allow add_file
root# chmod -a# 1 dropbox
root# ls -le
total 0
drwxr-xr-x + 2 root   wheel     68 Jul 11 20:29 dropbox
 0: user:vanilla allow list,add_file,search
```

Figure 8.23 Examples of setting and changing ACLs.

Creating and Using Scripts

A script is simply a text file that contains a series of commands. By definition, a script must be read and executed by a program called an *interpreter*, a separate program that understands the commands in the script.

You may already be familiar with scripts written in AppleScript or JavaScript. In the Unix world, we often speak of *shell scripts*—scripts that are written to be interpreted by one of the Unix shells, such as `sh`, `bash`, and `tcsh`. These scripts use exactly the same commands that you would type at the command line using the corresponding shell. Indeed, one of the reasons for using a script is to reduce the chance of mistyping a complicated command line. So when you see the term *Bourne shell script*, you know it's referring to a script that is written to be interpreted by the Bourne shell (`/bin/sh`). See `man sh` for the online manual for the Bourne shell.

Think of a shell script as a small computer program. The languages available for writing shell scripts are numerous, but by far the most commonly used is the Bourne shell. This is because the Bourne shell has been around so long, it has become the de facto standard for programming system-configuration files and for system administration. A script written for the Bourne shell is likely to run properly on the widest variety of Unix systems. So in this chapter we will show you the basics of Bourne shell scripts.

In Chapter 2, "Using the Command Line," you created a simple shell script. Now you will delve more deeply into scripting, learning the basic tools through which all shell scripts are made: commands, operators, variables, conditionals, loops, and functions. Sound like computer programming? It is, but don't worry—you don't have to become a programmer to benefit from understanding and using scripts, and if you do want to get further into programming, then shell scripts are a good place to start.

Common Uses of Shell Scripts

Although there are virtually unlimited uses for shell scripts (for example, we know of at least one that generates Web pages that are thumbnail indexes of images: www.acme.com/software/thumbnail_index), there are some uses that are more common than others. Here are the most common uses of shell scripts.

System-startup configuration files

Mac OS X/Darwin keeps its system-startup files in /System/Library/StartupIt (virtually every other version of Unix keeps similar scripts in /etc/rc.d or /etc/init.d).

Automating common tasks

One example is the Bourne shell script /etc/weekly, which is run once each week by a scheduling program called launchd. (See Chapter 11, "Introduction to System Administration," to learn about the launchd command.) The /etc/weekly script rebuilds a couple of databases and compresses a few system log files. You can open it using vi or nano if you like—you won't hurt anything by reading the file.

Creating new utilities for your personal use

In Chapter 2 you created a simple script to show a system status report. As you become more comfortable with Unix, you will undoubtedly create several small scripts to automate tasks, provide new commands, and in general handle problems that the existing set of commands doesn't quite cover. One example might be a shell script that allows you to use the Macintosh Trash from the command line.

Creating a Shell Script

Shell scripts are text files, so you create them the same way as any other text file. At the command line, that typically means using an editor like `vi`, `nano`, or `emacs`, but you can also use a GUI text editor or even a word processor. Just be sure to save the files as plain-text files (often called "Text Only" in save-file dialogs), which means no font information, no boldface or underlining, just plain text. (Review Chapter 5, "Using Files and Directories," for details on editing files from the command line.)

The first task simply takes you through the steps of creating an extremely minimal script. Subsequent tasks add features to the script covering the basic elements of scripting:

- Using variables
- Using arguments
- Using expressions
- Using control structures
- Getting user input
- Creating and using functions

To create a simple shell script:

1. Create a new file called myscript.sh in your text editor.

   The filename can actually be anything you like. The .sh extension indicates that the file is a Bourne shell script; however, this is simply a file-naming convention and is not required. It is the first line of the file itself that determines the kind of script.

2. Enter the first line of the script:

   `#!/bin/sh`

   Make sure there are no spaces before the #. This first line is very special. See the sidebar "The All-Important Shebang Line of a Script."

   This script is a Bourne shell script. The commands in it are read and executed by the program `/bin/sh`.

3. Enter a comment to describe what the script does.

   Lines that begin with just a # are comments and are ignored when the script is executed, as are blank lines. (Exception: the very first line, as described in the sidebar "The All-Important Shebang Line of a Script.")

   `# This script just says hello.`

4. Enter the first actual command line in the script:

   `echo "Hello, I am a script."`

   Notice that this line would work perfectly well if you entered it at the command line, even if you are using a shell other than the Bourne shell, such as the `tcsh` shell. That's because the lines in shell scripts are simply Unix command lines. Even though this script uses the Bourne shell, many command lines are identical in both the Bourne and `tcsh` shells. The `echo` command in this example is a separate program (`/bin/echo`), executed by the Bourne shell when it gets to this line in the script.

5. Save the file.

   Use the appropriate command for your editor to save the file.

6. Quit the editor.

   You should be back at a shell prompt.

   Now you must make the script executable.

7. `chmod 755 myscript.sh`

   Changing the mode to 755 (review modes in Chapter 8, "Working with Permissions and Ownership") gives anyone the ability to read and execute the script file, while giving you (the owner) the additional permission to edit it.

continues on next page

8. You can now execute the script with the command line

   ```
   ./myscript.sh
   ```

   Figure 9.1 shows a code listing of the script, and **Figure 9.2** shows the result of running it from the command line.

   You need to use the ./ to specify a path to the script because the script is not in your PATH (which is the list of places where your shell looks for commands; see "Environment Variables" in Chapter 7, "Configuring Your Environment with Unix"). But see the next task to learn how to have the script be available just like any other command—that is, without having to type the path to it but simply by typing the script name.

Running a script without using a path

You can run a shell script by typing its name on the command line, just as if it were any other Unix command. In order for this to work, you must do a few things with the script, described in the following task.

To create a shell script that can be used like a command:

1. Make sure the script is executable.
2. Make sure the script is in a directory listed in your PATH environment variable.

   For most scripts you create for your own personal use, the best place to put them is in your ~/bin directory—that is, the bin directory inside your home directory. This directory is not installed with Mac OS X—you need to create it. (Remember: The ~ character is a shortcut for specifying your home directory.)

   If you have not already done so, you should add your ~/bin directory to your PATH environment variable (instructions for doing this are in the "Changing your PATH" section of Chapter 7). Scripts intended for systemwide use should go in /usr/local/bin. (/usr/local should already exist on your system, but you may need to create /usr/local/bin).

   You can either create the script in the appropriate place to begin with, or use the cp or mv command to copy or move the script into place—for example,

   If ~/bin does not exist, then create it with

   ```
   mkdir ~/bin
   ```

   Move the script into ~/bin:

   ```
   mv myscript.sh ~/bin/
   ```

3. You can now run the script by simply typing its name.

   If you are using the tcsh shell, you'll need to run the rehash command for any shell that is already running. When it starts up, the tcsh shell scans the directories listed in your PATH.

✔ Tip

- Be careful about creating scripts that have the same names as existing commands.

  The standard date command is /bin/date. If you use date on a command line without specifying a path, then a date script in either ~/bin or /usr/local/bin is executed instead of the standard /bin/date command. This is because the shell looks in the directories in your PATH in order, and your ~/bin directory and /usr/local/bin are listed earlier than /bin in your PATH.

```
#!/bin/sh
# This script just says hello.
echo "Hello, I am a script."
```

Figure 9.1 Code listing of a simple script. It has only one line of executable code.

```
localhost:~ vanilla$ ./myscript.sh
Hello, I am a script.
localhost:~ vanilla
```

Figure 9.2 Running the new script from the command line.

The All-Important Shebang Line of a Script

In a shell script, the # character at the start of a line marks that line as a comment—to be ignored when the script is executed. But when the first two characters in a file are `#!`, then the rest of the first line is assumed to be a path to a program that knows how to execute the rest of the file (an *interpreter*). The operating system executes the interpreter and hands it the script file as input. If the first two characters are not `#!`, then the operating system assumes that the file consists of compiled machine-readable binary code and will try to execute it directly.

The # character is often called a *sharp* (as it is in musical notation), and the `!` character in Unix is pronounced "bang" (the literal sense of an exclamation point), hence *shebang*.

This trick of looking at the first two bytes of a file has been part of Unix for more than 20 years, starting in an early version of BSD Unix version 4, around early 1980. The shebang line is one of the mechanisms that make shell scripts so common in Unix.

You can still run a shell script without the shebang line by supplying the script filename as an argument to the shell program itself—for example,

```
sh myscript
```

passes `myscript` as an argument to the `sh` command, which will then read the file as series of commands, ignoring any shebang line (because the shebang line looks like a comment).

So if the first line of the file contains

```
#!/bin/sh
```

the operating system will execute the program located at `/bin/sh` and feed it the whole file as input.

If the first line of a script is

```
#!bin/sh
```

when you run it, you will probably get the error message "Command not found." Why? Because when you run the script, the operating system looks for `bin/sh` and doesn't find it. The line is missing the / before `bin`. A simple typographical error like that can lead to a lot of frustration. (Extra credit: Can you think of a situation in which that typo would not cause an error message? Hint: What if your working directory is /?)

Using Variables

Can you think back on all that stuff you learned in high school algebra? Things like

$a^2 - b^2 = (a - b)*(a + b)$

or

$E = MC^2$

Those letters are variables, essentially storage containers with names. Any time you see a variable, you are supposed to replace it with whatever is in the container. That's really all a "variable" is.

For example, if we take the first formula above, and store 5 in the variable *a* and 3 in the variable *b*, then when we *access a* we get 5 and when we access *b* we get 3; so we would read the formula as

$5^2 - 3^2 = (5 - 3)*(5 + 3)$

(which, if you are curious, works out to 25 – 9 = (2)*(8), which is 16 = 16).

It is common in programming to want to use the contents of a variable inside a string of text; for example, if you have

```
"Hello $name"
```

you probably want to replace the variable `$name` with its contents to create a new string of text. In computer programming, the act of replacing a variable with its contents to create a new string of text is called *interpolating* (which is not at all the same as turning someone over to the international police organization Interpol).

All computer programming makes heavy use of variables. There are two major things you do with variables: *assign* something to them (store information in the container) and interpolate them—that is, replace the variable(s) with the contents of the container(s).

In a shell script, you assign a value to a variable using the = operator. It copies the value on the right side into the variable on the left side. For example:

```
greeting="Top of the morning to you."
```

or

```
maximum_length=25
```

or

```
# Speed of light in furlongs/fortnight
C=1802617500000
```

Variables are replaced with their contents (that is, interpolated) any time they appear in a command line with a **$** in front of their name:

```
echo "Then he said: $greeting"
```

The following task creates a script that assigns a value to a variable and then interpolates it in a command line. This is commonly done to store an error or warning message in a variable so that it may be used in several places in the script. That way, if you want to change the message, you only have to change it in one place.

To assign a value to a variable and then interpolate it:

1. Edit a new script file. For example,
   ```
   vi newscript.sh
   ```
2. The first line is the same as before:
   ```
   #!/bin/sh
   ```
3. Enter some comments to explain what the script does:
   ```
   # This script assigns values to
   → variables
   # and then interpolates them.
   ```
4. `line1="The queen, my lord, is dead."`

```
#!/bin/sh
# This script assigns values to variables
# and then interpolates them.

line1="The queen, my lord, is dead."
line2="She should have died hereafter."

# Now interpolate the variables.
echo "SEYTON: $seyton"
echo "MACBETH: $macbeth"
```

Figure 9.3 Code listing of a script that assigns values to two variables and then interpolates them.

```
localhost:~ vanilla$ ./myscript.sh
SEYTON: The queen, my lord, is dead.
MACBETH: She should have died hereafter.
localhost:~ vanilla
```

Figure 9.4 Running the script that uses variables.

About Those Algebraic Equations

The first one we listed shows how to calculate the difference between two squared numbers. So the difference between 9^2 and 4^2 is (9 – 4) times (9 + 4). That is, 81 – 16 equals 5 times 13. Check it out. Works every time. Pretty cool, huh? For more, see "The Difference of 2 Squares" (www.mste.uiuc.edu/users/dildine/sketches/Diff2sq.htm).

The second equation is Einstein's famous formula expression of his special theory of relativity, that energy (*E*) is equal to mass (*M*) multiplied by the square of the velocity of light (*C*). That formula plus a lot of technology can get you global thermonuclear war if you are not careful. For more, see "Einstein Explains the Equivalence of Energy and Matter" (www.aip.org/history/einstein/voice1.htm).

5. `line2="She should have died`
   `→ hereafter."`

   Assigning a value to a variable in a Bourne shell script is very simple. You start the line with the variable name. This can be any combination of letters, numbers, and the underscore character, _ (for example, a variable named `item_23_01` is fine). However, variable names may not begin with a number.

   Right after the variable name you put an equals sign (=). Do *not* put any spaces before or after the = sign.

   After the = sign comes the value that is stored in the variable. The value can be a number or text. If the value has spaces inside it, enclose the value in quotes.

6. Add another comment:

   `# Now interpolate the variables.`

7. `echo "SEYTON: $line1"`

8. `echo "MACBETH: $line2"`

   Interpolating a variable is simply a matter of using the variable name in a command line with `$` added to the beginning of the variable name.

   When the shell reads any command line, either one entered at a shell prompt or one found in a script, the first thing the shell does is interpolate variables that start with `$`.

   Figure 9.3 is a code listing of a script that assigns a value to a variable and then interpolates it, and **Figure 9.4** shows the result of running the script.

✔ Tip

- If you want to include quotes in the value, then you escape the quotes with backslashes:

  `response="MACBETH: \"Liar and slave!\""`

Using Variables

It is quite common to use the value of a variable inside the assignment of another variable. This is easy to do because the shell performs *variable interpolation* on all the variables in a line before executing the command at the start of a line.

To use a variable inside another variable:

- Simply use a variable with the **$** inside the value of a new variable.

  For example,

  ```
  first_name="Alexis"
  last_name="Pushkin"
  full_name="$first_name $last_name"
  ```

  Figure 9.5 is a code listing of a complete script that uses a variable inside the value assigned to another. **Figure 9.6** shows the output of the script.

The first line of output comes from line 8 of the script. Notice how the contents of `$message` are what were assigned to it on line 6. The assignment of a new value to `$directory` on line 7 does not change what was already assigned to `$message`. On line 9, there is a new assignment using `$directory`, which has a new value. The second line of output (which comes from line 10 of the script) shows this.

Using a command inside a variable

It is very common in shell scripts to store the name of a command in a variable and then use the variable in a command line later in the script. This is commonly done to allow the same command to be used in many places in the script, but to have only one place where it needs to be changed if you decide to use a different command later.

```
#!/bin/sh
# Example of using a variable inside the value
# assigned to another variable.

directory="/Applications (Mac OS 9)"
message="OS 9 applications are in \"$directory\""
directory="/Applications"
echo "$message"
message="OS X applications are in \"$directory\""
echo "$message"
```

Figure 9.5 Code listing of a script that uses variables inside the values assigned to other variables.

```
localhost:~ vanilla$ ./newscript.sh
OS 9 applications are in "/Applications (Mac OS 9)"
OS X applications are in "/Applications"
localhost:~ vanilla
```

Figure 9.6 Output of the script in Figure 9.5.

To use a command inside a variable:

1. Assign the command name to a variable. For example,
   `command="ls"`
2. Use the variable (with $) anywhere you want to use the command.
   For example,
   `$command /usr`
   Figure 9.7 is a code listing of a script that uses a command in a variable, and **Figure 9.8** shows the output of the script.

✔ Tips

- Use variables in scripts whenever you want the same thing to appear in more than one place. This minimizes the number of places where you need to make changes.
- Try creating the script in Figure 9.7 and changing the command to `ls` and `options` to different options for the `ls` command—for example, `-ld` and/or `-F`.

```
#!/bin/sh
# This script uses a command name in a variable

# The du command shows disk usage
command="du"
# The -s option means "summary". The -k means "in kilobytes"
options="-sk"

directory="/Developer/ADC Reference Library"

# Note the use of quotes around $directory in the command line
echo "Trying $command with options $options on '$directory/*'"
$command $options "$directory"/*
```

Figure 9.7 Code listing of a script that uses a command name in a variable.

```
localhost:~ vanilla$ ./diskuse.sh
Trying du with options -sk on '/Developer/ADC Reference Library/*'
672     /Developer/ADC Reference Library/docSet.xml
552852 /Developer/ADC Reference Library/documentation
4  /Developer/ADC Reference Library/index.html
67944   /Developer/ADC Reference Library/indexes
107800 /Developer/ADC Reference Library/referencelibrary
10780   /Developer/ADC Reference Library/releasenotes
23936   /Developer/ADC Reference Library/samplecode
11452   /Developer/ADC Reference Library/technicalnotes
28832   /Developer/ADC Reference Library/technicalqas
localhost:~ vanilla
```

Figure 9.8 Output from the script in Figure 9.7.

Using environment variables in a script

In previous chapters (especially Chapter 7), you learned about a special kind of variable called an *environment variable*. When you execute a script, you are creating a child process of your shell, and so the script's processes inherit your shell's environment. As a result, you can use all of your shell's environment variables in your scripts. Note that assigning anything into an environment variable in a script does not change the contents of that variable for the parent process (your shell), but sets it for any child processes the script creates.

To use an environment variable in a script:

◆ Use the environment variable as you would any other variable.

For example,

`echo "Hello $USER"`

`echo "Your home directory is $HOME"`

Figure 9.9 is a code listing of a script that uses environment variables, and **Figure 9.10** shows the output from the script. Note that the script uses the sudo command (which we introduced in Chapter 8) to gain extra privileges. These privileges are needed because Mac OS X (starting in version 10.4) puts some files in each user's home directory that are not owned by the user. Without them, the du command in the script would fail when it tried to read those files. (The sudo command will be covered in more detail in Chapter 11).

```
#!/bin/sh
# This script uses environment variables

command="du"
options="-sk"
command_line="$command $options $HOME"

echo "User is:                  $USER"
echo "Home directory is:        $HOME"
echo "Command line will be:     $command_line"
echo "Disk space usage in kilobytes:"
sudo $command_line
```

Figure 9.9 Code listing of a script that uses environment variables.

```
localhost:~ vanilla$ ./envscript.sh
User is:                vanilla
Home directory is:      /Users/vanilla
Command line will be:   du -sk /Users/vanilla
Disk space usage in kilobytes:
Password:
2160    /Users/vanilla
localhost:~ vanilla
```

Figure 9.10 Output from the script in Figure 9.9.

Table 9.1

Special Variables

VARIABLE	USE / MEANING
$0	The name with which the script was called on the command line.
$1	The first command-line argument.
$2	The second command-line argument, and so on, up to $9.
$@	A list of all the command-line arguments.
$#	The number of command-line arguments.
$?	The exit status of the most recent command. (0 means success; other numbers mean some kind of error.)

Using Arguments

You can pass arguments to scripts just as with any other command. The arguments to a script are accessed inside the script using a series of special variables (**Table 9.1**).

The variable `$0` contains the name of the script itself; the first argument to a script can be obtained from `$1`, the second argument from `$2`, and so on. Arguments with more than one digit must be written with braces around the number—for example, `${10}`, `${25}`.

When you supply options to a script, such as `-A` or `-r`, the script thinks of them as simply arguments. So in the command line

```
myscript.sh -A foo
```

`$0` contains `myscript.sh`, `$1` contains `-A`, and `$2` contains `foo`. `$3` contains nothing (because there were only two arguments).

To use command-line arguments in your script:

- You simply use the special variables as you would any other variable. For example,

  `echo "The first argument was $1"`

  Figure 9.11 is a code listing that shows the use of the special variables for command-line arguments, and **Figure 9.12** shows the output of the script. Notice how the second and third arguments in Figure 9.12 are enclosed in quotes. Without the quotes, only the first three words would have been printed out (`What`, `a`, and `long`).

There are a couple of ways to handle large numbers of arguments. The first is to use the `shift` command. The `shift` command (which typically appears on a line all by itself) moves all of the arguments "down" one step. That is, after you use `shift`, `$1` contains what used to be in `$2`, `$2` contains what used to be in `$3`, and so on.

One good reason to use `shift` is if you do not know how many arguments will be passed to your `script`. First check to see if `$1` contains anything each time you call `shift`. As long as it does, you know you have (at least) one more argument to process. Alternatively, you can use the special variable `$@`, which contains a list of all the arguments. By using

```
#!/bin/sh
# This script uses the special variables for
# command line arguments.

echo "Hey $USER called me:  $0"
echo "First argument: $1"
echo "Second argument: $2"
echo "Third argument: $3"
```

Figure 9.11 Code listing of a script that uses special variables to access command-line arguments.

```
localhost:~ vanilla$  ./args.sh What "a long strange trip" "it's been"
Hey vanilla called me: ./args.sh
First argument: What
Second argument: a long strange trip
Third argument: it's been
localhost:~ vanilla
```

Figure 9.12 Output from the script shown in Figure 9.11.

$@ in combination with a *loop* (see "Using loops," later in the chapter), it is possible to *iterate over* (a programming term for *running through*) all of the script's arguments, regardless of how many there are.

To use shift to access arguments:

1. Put the `shift` command on a line by itself.

   For example,

   ```
   echo "First argument was: $1"
   echo "Ninth argument was: $9"
   shift
   ```

2. Use any of the special variables, such as $1 or $2. For example,

   ```
   echo "Here's one: $1"
   echo "And here's nine: $9"
   ```

   After `shift` is used, all the arguments are "shifted" over, so if you think of the list of arguments as something like $1, $2, $3, $4, $5, $6, $7, $8, $9, you can picture using `shift` to move all the arguments one place to the left.

   The contents of $1 disappear (they do not go into $0), and whatever was in ${10} goes into $9. For example, if before `shift` is used, $0 contained `myscript.sh`, $1 contained `-A`, $2 contained `100`, and $3 was empty, then after the `shift` statement $0 would still contain `myscript.sh`, $1 would now contain `100`, and $2 would be empty.

   You can use `shift` as many times as you like in your script.

To refer to the entire list of arguments:

◆ Use the special variable $@.

  The special variable $@ contains all of the command-line arguments (only the arguments—it does not contain $0). You can use it to pass all the arguments your script received to a command inside your script. For example,

  ```
  ls "$@"
  ```

  Figure 9.13 is a code listing of a script that is a simple replacement for the `rm` command. Instead of deleting the files named in its arguments, this script uses `mv` to move them all into the user's Trash (the `.Trash` directory in the user's home directory). See the sidebar "Compare with Aqua: Using the Trash from the Command Line," on the next page, for some important differences between moving files with this

continues on next page


```
#!/bin/sh
# trash - script for moving files to the Trash
# from the command line.

# Each user's Trash is a directory called .Trash in their
# home directory
trash_directory="$HOME/.Trash/"

# We use $@ to pass all the arguments
mv "$@" "$trash_directory"
```

Figure 9.13 Code listing of a script that moves files to the Trash from the command line, using $@ to pass all the command-line arguments.

script and actually dragging a file to the Trash in the Finder. **Figure 9.14** shows an example of using this script, including how to see the contents of the Trash from the command line. Notice how you can use command-line wildcards with the script. The argument `badfile*` in Figure 9.14 ended up matching two files: `badfile1` and `badfile2`, and all four arguments were captured in `$@` and passed to the `mv` command in the script.

Figure 9.15 shows the Finder view of the Trash folder after using the script.

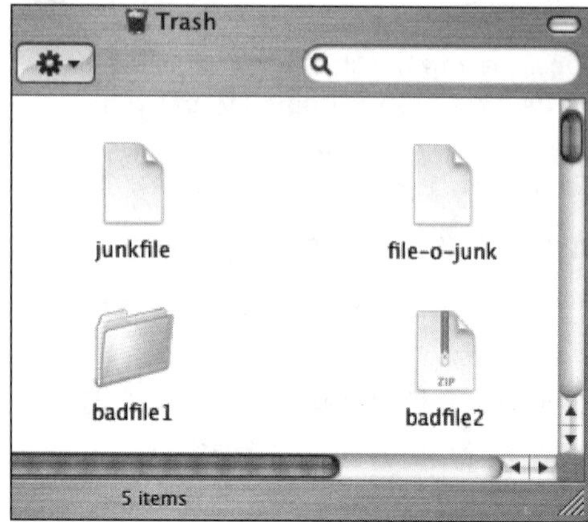

Figure 9.15 The Finder view of the Trash folder after using the script for moving files to the Trash.

✔ Tip

- Create this script with the name "trash," and follow the instruction in "Running a script without using a path" at the beginning of this chapter. This script is one you could use every day.

```
localhost:~ vanilla$ ./trash junkfile file-o-junk badfile*
localhost:~ vanilla$ ls .Trash
badfile1    badfile2     file-o-junk    junkfile
[localhost:~]
```

Figure 9.14 Example of using the script in Figure 9.13.

Compare with Aqua: Using the Trash from the Command Line

The script in Figure 9.13 allows you to move files to the Trash instead of using the Unix `rm` command, but there are some important differences between the behavior of this script and the way the Finder uses the Trash.

When you drag a file to the Trash, a check is performed in the Finder to see if a file with the same name already exists in the Trash. If so, the new file is renamed by adding a 1 at the end of its name, or a 2 if this is the second duplicate, and so on. There can be only one file with any particular name inside a folder (or directory).

The Finder won't simply replace the older file, since the whole point of the Trash is that using it is not the same as actually deleting a file.

The script shown in Figure 9.13 is not as sophisticated as the Finder. If a file with the same name as an argument has already been moved to the Trash, this script will overwrite the older file.

Later in this chapter we will show you how to improve the script to make its behavior more like the Finder's use of the Trash.

Using Commands Within Commands

Now that you have used variables and arguments, you are probably wondering how to have your scripts do something simple like adding two numbers together and storing the results in a variable. The answer to this lies in using a powerful feature of Unix shells called *backquoted commands*. Backquoted commands enable you to incorporate one command line within another command line. The backquote (also called a *backtick*) is the ` character, usually found in the upper left corner of your keyboard, just above [Tab]. The backquote ` is *not* the same as the apostrophe, ', so be careful not to confuse the two.

You use backquoted commands in scripts any time you want to store the output of a command line in a variable. You also use them when you want to create a command line in which part of the command line comes from the output of some other command.

We mentioned the use of backquotes briefly in Chapter 2, and now we will go into more detail about them.

To use backquotes in a command line:

- Enclose part of a command line in backquotes. The part of the command line you enclose in backquotes must itself be a valid command line:

  ```
  file `which ls`
  ```

  Any time the shell sees a part of a command line that is enclosed in backquotes (`which ls` in the example above), it executes the enclosed commands first, just as if they were a complete command line of their own. In this case, it will return the full path of the `ls` command.

  The shell takes the output (`/bin/ls`, in the case of the example) and replaces the backquoted portion of the original command line with the output from the backquoted command. So the command line would then read

  ```
  file /bin/ls
  ```

  The shell executes this final command line, which in this case gives the output

  ```
  /bin/ls: Mach-O executable ppc
  ```

  This tells you that the actual executable file for the `ls` command is a "Mach-O executable ppc," which means that it is a binary file, not a text file, compiled for the PowerPC chip.

To save the output of a command in a variable:

- Start a command line as you would for a normal variable assignment. For example,

  `today=`

- Put the backquoted command right after the = sign. For example,

  ``today=`date` ``

  When the line is executed, the shell first executes the backquoted portion, and then stores the output of that portion in the variable. **Figure 9.16** is a code listing of a script that stores the output of a backquoted command in a variable. The `+%A, %B %d` is a formatting argument for the `date` command. `%A` is the full weekday name, `%B` is the full month name, and `%d` is the two-digit day of the month. See `man date` and `man strftime` for details on the available formatting options. Notice that the backquoted command may include arguments (in this case a formatting string for the `date` command). **Figure 9.17** shows the output from the script in Figure 9.16.

✔ Tip

- You can (and should) test whatever you put in backquotes by typing it at a shell prompt first.

```
#!/bin/sh
# This script uses a backquoted command.

today=`date "+%A, %B %d"`
echo "Hello $USER, today is $today"
```

Figure 9.16 Code listing of a script that stores the output of a backquoted command in a variable.

```
localhost:~ vanilla$ ./script.sh
Hello vanilla, today is Monday, June 17
[localhost:~]
```

Figure 9.17 Output from the script in Figure 9.16.

Doing Arithmetic and Using Expressions

It is frequently useful to have a script add two numbers together, or perform multiplication, division, or other arithmetic. The Bourne shell itself does not provide built-in arithmetic functions. Instead, it uses the standard Unix `expr` command to evaluate *expressions*.

The `expr` command sees expressions as a set of three arguments consisting of two arguments with an *operator* between them, such as

```
3 + 4
```

or

```
$x - $y
```

Table 9.2 lists the operators you are most likely to use with `expr`. Read the `man` page (`man expr`) for the complete list. The math operators supported by `expr` work only on integers and give only integers as results—no decimal places. See the sidebar "Floating-Point Math" for notes about doing this type of calculation.

Table 9.2

Math Operators for Use with expr

All numerical values must be integers. See the `expr` `man` page for other operators.

Expression	Meaning
`$a + $b`	Returns the sum of `$a` and `$b`.
`$a - $b`	Subtracts `$b` from `$a`.
`$a \* $b`	Returns the product of `$a` times `$b`. (You must escape the * with a backslash.)
`$a / $b`	Divides `$a` by `$b`.
`$a % $b`	Returns the remainder after dividing `$a` by `$b`.

Floating-Point Math

Two Unix commands do floating-point arithmetic at the command line or in a shell script: `dc` and `bc`. Both are fairly complex programs. The `dc` command uses "reverse Polish notation" (developed in 1920 by Jan Lukasiewicz; see the RPN page on MoHPC, www.hpmuseum.org/rpn.htm), in which you enter numbers and operators and then ask for a result. For example, to use `dc` to divide 23 by 5 with a precision of four decimal places, you would enter

```
echo "4 k 23 5 / p" | dc
```

This is not pretty. The equivalent command line for `bc` is only slightly better:

```
echo "scale=4; 23 / 5" | bc
```

Read the `man` pages for these commands for the full details.

Try the following task at a shell prompt before you try it in a script.

To evaluate an expression:

- `expr 3 + 4`

  This should give you a result of 7. The spaces before and after the + are required, as `expr` needs to see each item as a separate argument (3, +, and 4).

  Figure 9.18 is a code listing that shows a script using the `expr` command in backquotes to perform integer arithmetic, and **Figure 9.19** shows the output of the script.

To add something to an existing variable:

- Simply use the variable as one of the arguments to `expr`.

  Let's say you want to add 1 to whatever is stored in `$count`. You could use this:

  `` count=`expr $count + 1` ``

  This construct is often used inside loops to count the number of times a loop was executed. See "Using loops," later in this chapter.

```
#!/bin/sh
# This script uses expr to perform integer arithmetic.

total=`expr $1 + $2`
difference=`expr $1 - $2`
product=`expr $1 \* $2`
fraction=`expr $1 / $2`
remainder=`expr $1 % $2`

echo "$total is the sum of $1 and $2"
echo "$difference is the difference between $1 and $2"
echo "$product is the product of $1 and $2"
echo "$fraction is $1 divided by $2"
echo "$remainder is the remainder of dividing $1 by $2"
```

Figure 9.18 Code listing of a script that uses the expr command in backquotes to perform integer arithmetic.

```
localhost:~ vanilla$ ./math.sh 517 23
540 is the sum of 517 and 23
494 is the difference between 517 and 23
11891 is the product of 517 and 23
22 is 517 divided by 23
11 is the remainder of dividing 517 by 23
[localhost:~]
```

Figure 9.19 Output from the script in Figure 9.18.

Using Control Structures

There are times when you want to control which commands in your script actually get executed, in what order, and how many times. In those instances, you use tools called *control structures*. Without control structures, your script is executed line by line, from start to finish. Often this is just fine. The simple Trash script you created earlier in this chapter is an example of this, but the Trash script would be better if it could change its behavior—such as pausing—if it found that it was about to overwrite a file.

In scripting (and in computer programming in general), there are two basic kinds of control structures: *conditionals* and *loops*.

Conditionals are the familiar "If . . . then" construct we use in everyday life—for example, "If you are going to call me after 5 p.m., then use my home number."

We also use loops in everyday language, but less consciously. For example, we say, "Put the dishes on the table" instead of saying, "Put the first dish on the table. Put the second dish on the table. Put the third dish on the table." A loop involves a command or set of commands that are to be repeated.

Using conditionals

In shell scripts, you use conditionals so that your script performs different actions based on questions like "Did the user supply enough arguments to the script?" "Does this file exist?" "Do we have permission to create a file in this directory?" "Is `$a` greater than `$b`?" and so on.

continues on next page

Fundamental to the use of conditionals is the idea of something being *true* or *false*. When using conditionals in shell scripts, you'll test whether the expressions are true or false. We show you some common tests below.

Using the if . . . then conditional

The most basic conditional is the `if` *statement*. When an `if` statement is used, a command or set of commands is executed only if something is true.

While reading through the next task, refer to **Figure 9.20**. It is a code listing of a script that uses an `if` statement, while **Figure 9.21** shows the output from two executions of the script. In the first case, the `if` statement finds a false when comparing **$1** to see if it is equal to `(-eq) $magic_number`, and in the second case the `if` statement finds a true result.

```
#!/bin/sh
# This script uses an if statement

magic_number=17

echo "Checking to see if your guess ($1) is the magic number...."

if [ $1 -eq $magic_number ]
then
    echo "You got it!"
fi

echo "Thanks for playing!"
```

Figure 9.20 Code listing of a script using an `if` statement.

```
localhost:~ vanilla$ ./if.sh 5
Checking to see if your guess (5) is the magic number....
Thanks for playing!
localhost:~ vanilla$ ./if.sh 17
Checking to see if your guess (17) is the magic number....
You got it!
Thanks for playing!
localhost:~ vanilla
```

Figure 9.21 Output from two uses of the script in Figure 9.20 showing the text expression being false and then true.

To use an if . . . then structure:

1. `if [ expression ]`

   An `if` statement begins with the word `if` and is followed by a test expression enclosed in square brackets. There must be a space after the `[` and before the `]`.

   There are two main types of test expressions: *comparisons* and *file tests.*

   Comparison expressions are similar to the expressions used with `expr`, in that they consist of two arguments separated by an operator. Examples of `if` statements using comparison tests are

   ```
   if [ $count -eq 1 ]
   if [ $a -gt $b ]
   if [ $word1 > $word2 ]
   ```

   File-test expressions use one operator and a filename or path. Examples include

   ```
   if [ -f "$filename" ]
   if [ -d "$filename" ]
   ```

   Table 9.3 lists the most common test expressions. See `man test` for the complete list.

continues on next page

Table 9.3

Test Expressions for Use in [ ]

Expression	Meaning
Integer Comparisons	
n1 -eq *n2*	Integer comparison. True if *n1* equals *n2*. Example: `[ $a -eq $b ]`.
n1 -ne *n2*	True if *n1* is not equal to *n2*.
n1 -lt *n2*	True if *n1* is less than *n2*.
n1 -gt *n2*	True if *n1* is greater than *n2*.
n1 -le *n2*	True if *n1* is less than or equal to *n2*.
n1 -ge *n2*	True if *n1* is greater than or equal to *n2*.
String (Text) Comparisons Using ASCII Values of Text	
str1 = *str2*	True if *str1* is identical to *str2*. Example: `[ $guess = $password ]`.
str1 != *str2*	True if *str1* is not identical to *str2*.
str1 < *str2*	True if *str1* is alphabetically lower than *str2*.
str1 > *str2*	True if *str1* is alphabetically higher than *str2*.
-z *string*	True if *string* is not empty. Example: `[ -z $word ]`.
File-Test Expressions	
-e *filename*	True if *filename* exists.
-f *filename*	True if *filename* exists and is a regular file.
-d *filename*	True if *filename* exists and is a directory.
-r *filename*	True if *filename* exists and is readable.
-w *filename*	True if *filename* exists and is writable.
-x *filename*	True if *filename* exists and is executable.
-L *filename*	True if *filename* exists and is a symbolic link.
file1 -nt *file2*	True if *f1* exists and is newer than *f2* (has a more recent modification time).
file1 -ot *file2*	True if *file1* exists and is older than *file2*.
file1 -ef *file2*	True if *file1* exists and refers to the same file as *file2*.

2. `then`

   The next line after you start the `if` statement is simply the word `then`. All the lines between the `then` line and the end of the `if` statement will be executed if the test expression is true.

3. Enter one or more command lines.

   This is where you enter the commands that are executed if the test expression is true.

   For example,

   ```
   echo "If you see this the test
   → returned true"
   ```

   You can have as many lines as you want after the `then` line.

   It is customary (and makes for more readable scripts) to indent every line between the `then` and the end of the `if` statement. In Figure 9.20 you can see how the `echo` statement is indented.

4. The `if` statement is closed off (ended) with a line that says simply

   ```
   fi
   ```

   That's `if` backward. Have a look at Figure 9.20 for a complete example. Figure 9.21 shows output from the script.

✔ Tip

- You can make your scripts a bit easier to read if you put the `then` part of an `if` statement on the same line as the test by using a semicolon after the test:

  ```
  if [ $number -le $guess ] ; then
  echo "$a is less than or equal to $b"
  fi
  ```

You can reverse the meaning of any test expression by adding a `!`, which you can think of as "not."

To reverse the meaning of any test expression:

- Add a `!` to the expression:

  ```
  if [ ! -f "$filename" ]
  ```

  The expression inside the `[ ]` will be true if the file *does* exist and false if the file does not. The spaces around the `!` are required.

The `if` statement is very useful, but what about when you want to do one thing if the test is true and another if it is false? In that case, you add an `else` clause to your `if` statement. Refer to **Figure 9.22** for a code listing of a script that uses an if . . . then . . . else structure, and **Figure 9.23** for sample output from the script.

To create an if . . . then . . . else structure:

1. `if [` *`testexpression`* `]`

   Create the first part of the `if` statement.

   For example, from Figure 9.22:

   ```
   if [ $1 -eq $magic_number ]
   ```

2. `then`

   This line simply begins the block of code that will be executed if the condition is true.

3. Enter the commands for the true part.

   Remember to indent these commands to make the script more readable.

   From 9.22:

   ```
   echo "You got it!"
   ```

   Now, instead of finishing the `if` statement (with `fi`), add a line (not indented) that says simply:

4. else

   The commands that follow the `else` line will be executed if the test is false.

5. Enter the commands for the false part.

   As with the commands for the true part, you may enter as many command lines here as you like.

   Using Figure 9.22 again as an example:

   `echo "Oh no! You didn't get it."`

   Finally, you still end the entire `if` statement with the backward `if`:

continues on next page

```
#!/bin/sh
# This script uses an if...then...else structure

magic_number=17

echo "Checking to see if your guess ($1) is the magic number...."

if [ $1 -eq $magic_number ]
then
        echo "You got it!"
else
        echo "Oh no! You didn't get it."
fi

echo "Thanks for playing!"
```

Figure 9.22 Code listing of a script using an if... then... else structure.

```
localhost:~ vanilla$ ./else.sh 5
Checking to see if your guess (5) is the magic number....
Oh no! You didn't get it.
Thanks for playing!
localhost:~ vanilla$ ./else.sh 17
Checking to see if your guess (17) is the magic number....
You got it!
Thanks for playing!
localhost:~ vanilla
```

Figure 9.23 Output from two tries on the script in Figure 9.22; on the second try, the `if` clause is fulfilled, so the then clause is executed.

6. `fi`

Sometimes `if . . . then . . . else` is not enough. You'd like to try one test, and then if that fails, try another. You could do this by nesting one or more `if` statements inside one another as in **Figure 9.24**, but a better way is to use `elif` clauses, as shown in **Figure 9.25**. **Figure 9.26** shows the output that would result from either script. They both do the same thing in different ways.

`elif` means *else if* and is a way of having multiple tests in the same `if` statement. Only the first true `elif` is used.

```
#!/bin/sh
# This script uses nested if statements.

magic_number=17

echo "Checking to see if your guess ($1) is the magic number...."

if [ $1 -eq $magic_number ]
then
        echo "You got it!"
else
        if [ $1 -gt $magic_number ]
        then
             echo "Your guess ($1) is greater than the magic number."
        fi

        if [ $1 -lt $magic_number ]
        then
             echo "Your guess ($1) is less than the magic number."
        fi
fi

echo "Thanks for playing!"
```

Figure 9.24 Code listing of a script that uses nested `if` statements.

```
#!/bin/sh
# This script uses elif clauses in an if statement.

magic_number=17

echo "Checking to see if your guess ($1) is the magic number...."

if [ $1 -eq $magic_number ]
then
        echo "You got it!"
elif [ $1 -gt $magic_number ]
then
        echo "Your guess ($1) is greater than the magic number."
elif [ $1 -lt $magic_number ]
then
        echo "Your guess ($1) is less than the magic number."
fi

echo "Thanks for playing!"
```

Figure 9.25 Code listing of a script that does the same thing as Figure 9.24 but uses the `elif` clause instead.

```
localhost:~ vanilla$ ./guess.sh 100
Checking to see if your guess (100) is the magic number....
Your guess (100) is greater than the magic number.
Thanks for playing!
localhost:~ vanilla$ ./guess.sh 5
Checking to see if your guess (5) is the magic number....
Your guess (5) is less than the magic number.
Thanks for playing!
localhost:~ vanilla$ ./guess.sh 17
Checking to see if your guess (17) is the magic number....
You got it!
Thanks for playing!
localhost:~ vanilla
```

Figure 9.26 Output from either of the scripts in Figures 9.24 and 9.25.

Using the case conditional

You might be tempted to use a series of elif clauses where you have a variable that is storing one item from a list of possibilities such as start, stop, or restart, and you want to execute a different set of commands based on which one of the words the variable actually has. You could use a series of elif clauses in an if statement to do this, but because this is such a common occurrence, the Bourne shell provides a conditional structure called case exactly for this purpose.

Using a case structure involves setting up a series of *cases*, which are each associated with a pattern that is checked against a single variable. The first case whose pattern matches is executed, while the rest are ignored.

Refer to **Figure 9.27** while reading the following task. Figure 9.27 is a code listing of a script using a case structure. **Figure 9.28** shows the output of the script with four different arguments, each one triggering a different case.

```
#!/bin/sh
# This script uses a case structure.

# We will do different things based on
# the first argument to this script.

time=`date`

case "$1" in
        start)
                echo "Received start command at $time"
        ;;

        stop)
                echo "Received stop command at $time"
        ;;

        restart)
                # To restart we execute this same script twice, supplying
                # arguments of stop and start
                "$0" stop
                "$0" start
        ;;

        *)
                # The * will always match, so this is the default
                # section. Do this if nothing above matched.
                echo "Usage: $0 (start|stop|restart)"
        ;;

esac
```

Figure 9.27 Code listing of a script that uses case structure to perform one of four different cases, depending on the script's first argument.

To use a case structure:

1. `case $variable in`

   The variable can be anything, such as one of the special variables for command-line arguments, like $1 or $USER, or any variable you have assigned earlier in your script.

   Using Figure 9.27 as an example:

   `case "$1" in`

   The contents of the variable will be matched against a series of patterns.

2. `pattern)`

   This is the pattern that the variable must match to activate this case. Note that there is no opening parenthesis. It might look strange but that's the syntax. The pattern can be a literal string of text, as it is in the first three patterns in Figure 9.27, or it can use the same wildcards available on the command line. For example, * will match anything:

   `file*)` matches `file`, `files`, `file system`, and so on.

   The pipe character (|) can be used to specify alternatives:

   `start|go)`

   matches either `start` or `go`.

   Only the first matching case will be executed (or no cases if none of the patterns match).

   In Figure 9.27 the first pattern is

   `start)`

   After you declare a pattern, enter a series of command lines to be executed for that case.

3. Enter one or more command lines.

   This is just like the lines that follow the `then` part of an `if` statement.

4. `;;`

   Each case is terminated with a double semicolon. See Figure 9.27 for four examples. The first one is

   `echo "Received start command at $time"`

   You may have as many cases as you like.

5. Repeat steps 2–4 for each pattern you wish to match.

   Usually the last case uses the pattern

   `*)`

   which matches anything. You use this case to handle the possibility that none of the prior cases matched. You do not need to do this, but it is usually a good idea. Figure 9.27 uses this case to provide a *usage message* stating the allowable arguments for the script.

continues on next page

```
localhost:~ vanilla$ ./case.sh start
Received start command at Mon Jun 17 22:49:15 PDT 2002
localhost:~ vanilla$ ./case.sh stop
Received stop command at Mon Jun 17 22:49:21 PDT 2002
localhost:~ vanilla$ ./case.sh restart
Received stop command at Mon Jun 17 22:49:26 PDT 2002
Received start command at Mon Jun 17 22:49:26 PDT 2002
localhost:~ vanilla$ ./case.sh run
Usage: ./case.sh (start|stop|restart)
localhost:~ vanilla$
```

Figure 9.28 Output from the script in Figure 9.27 showing the effect of using different arguments. Notice how the usage message comes up.

6. Finally, you terminate the entire case structure:

   esac

   That's case spelled backward. The Bourne shell seems to like this backward stuff.

✔ **Tip**

- Notice how the script in Figure 9.27 uses the $0 variable as a command name to execute itself again in the restart case. That's worth remembering.

Using loops

Use a loop when you want a command line or lines to be repeated over and over.

Loops are most commonly used in shell scripts to process each element of a list. These are called *for loops*. An example of using this kind of loop is to iterate over every argument in $@.

Another common use of a loop is to keep performing a series of commands as long as some test keeps returning a true result. These are called *while loops*, and we'll show you how to improve the Trash script using this technique.

We'll start with a for loop. Refer to **Figure 9.29** while reading the following task. Figure 9.29 is a code listing of a simple script that tells you the largest number of all its arguments (it works only with integer arguments). **Figure 9.30** shows a couple of examples of output from the script with different arguments.

```
#!/bin/sh
# This script uses a for loop to find the biggest of its arguments.

# Start by saving the first argument in $biggest
biggest=$1

# Now loop over all the arguments, one at a time
for arg in "$@"
do
        if [ $arg -gt $biggest ] ; then
             biggest=$arg
        fi
done

echo "The biggest number is $biggest"
```

Figure 9.29 Code listing of a script using a for loop to find the largest of its arguments.

```
localhost:~ vanilla$ ./biggest 3 8 9 101 78 344 5 7 8
The biggest number is 344
localhost:~ vanilla$ ./biggest -6 -20 -41 -1 -17
The biggest number is -1
localhost:~ vanilla$
```

Figure 9.30 Output from the script in Figure 9.29.

To use a for loop:

1. `for loop_variable in list`

   The *`loop_variable`* will have a different value each time through the loop. The first time, it will hold the first item from `list`, then the second item, and so on.

   In Figure 9.29 the special variable `$@` is used to create the list. This is the only variable that will be treated as a list of items when enclosed in quotes. In all other cases, enclosing a variable in double quotes causes its contents to be treated as a single item.

   The list can be a series of values like

   ```
   for fate in Clotho Lachesis Atropos
   ```

   `$fate` will hold `Clotho` the first time through the loop, `Lachesis` on the second go-round, and `Atropos` on the third.

   It can come from a variable:

   ```
   winds="Boreas Eurus Notus Zephyrus"
   for wind in $winds
   ```

   Notice that `$winds` is not enclosed in quotes—the shell splits it into separate items based on the spaces, resulting in four winds.

   The list can come from more than one variable:

   ```
   muses="Calliope Clio Erato Euterpe"
   muses2="Melpomene Thalia Polyhymnia"
   muses3="Terpsichore Urania"
   for muse in $muses $muses2 $muses3
   ```

2. `do`

   The next line is simply the word `do` by itself.

   You can put the `do` on the first line if you use a semicolon:

   ```
   for bird in $flight ; do
   ```

3. Enter a series of one or more command lines.

   This marks the top of the loop body. The command lines in the loop body repeat for each item in the list, with the `loop` variable having a different value each time through.

4. `done`

   This terminates the loop body.

The `for` loop is an excellent way to process each element in a list (similar loops in other programming languages are sometimes called *foreach* loops, as in "For each item in the list, do something"). There are times when you don't have a list but still want to repeat a series of commands. Usually the `while` loop will do what you want.

A `while` loop combines a conditional test (like an `if` statement) with a loop body. The test is performed, and if true, the loop body is executed. Then the test is performed again. Lather, rinse, repeat. Unless something happens to alter the outcome of the test, the loop can run forever. Of course, usually you put something in the loop body that alters at least one of the variables in the test. Sometimes the test checks something happening outside the script, perhaps to see if a file still exists.

Refer to **Figure 9.31** while reading the following task. Figure 9.31 is a code listing of a script that uses a `while` loop to count from 0 to 10. Notice how the contents of a variable in the test are altered each time through the loop. **Figure 9.32** shows a run of the script.

To use a while loop:

1. `while [ test_expression ] ; do`

   The test expression is the same thing you used for the `if` statement earlier in this chapter. See Table 9.3 for a list of common test expressions, or `man test` for the complete list.

   The `do` command can go on the next line, but by now we think you want to do it like the pros and use a semicolon to put it on the same line as the test.

2. Enter the commands for the loop body.

   As with the `for` loop, these commands will be executed each time through the loop, as long as the test is true.

   In Figure 9.31 the script adds 1 to the value of `$count` on each pass though the loop. Eventually the test is false (when `$count` is 11, it is no longer "less than or equal to" 10). The script exits the loop and continues with the next line after the loop.

3. `done`

   That's the line that marks the end of the loop, the same as with the `for` loop.

```
#!/bin/sh
# This script uses a while loop to count to 10

count=0
while [ $count -le 10 ] ; do
        echo $count
        count=`expr $count + 1`
done
```

Figure 9.31 Code listing of a script using a `while` loop to count to 10.

```
localhost:~ vanilla$ ./count.sh
0
1
2
3
4
5
6
7
8
9
10
localhost:~ vanilla$
```

Figure 9.32 Output from the counting script. Pretty much what you would expect.

Earlier we promised you an improved version of the Trash script. **Figure 9.33** is a code listing of a script that lets you use the Macintosh Trash from the command line, and checks to see if the file(s) you are trashing might overwrite other files in the Trash. The script mimics the behavior of the Finder by renaming the trashed file if a conflict is found. Notice that the script uses a `while` loop to keep checking to see if a file exists, and if it does, it adds 1 to `$count` and uses the new value in the filename it checks for. Eventually a filename that is not already in the Trash is found, and the trashed file gets moved to the Trash with the new name.

```
#!/bin/sh
# Better trash - script for moving files to the Trash
# from the command line.

# Each user's Trash is a directory called .trash in their
# home directory
trash_directory="$HOME/.Trash"

if [ ! -d "$trash_directory" ] ; then
       echo "Whoa! $trash_directory doesn't exist."
       exit ; # The exit command quits the script immediately
fi

# loop over each command line argument
for file in "$@" ; do
       if [ -e "$file" ] ; then
            count=0
            filename="$file"
            trashname="$trash_directory/$filename"

            # If there is no file with this name in the Trash
            # then the while loop won't execute even once, which is OK.
            #
            while [ -e "$trashname" ] ; do
                     count=`expr $count + 1`
                     trashname="$trash_directory/$filename $count"
            done

            # We now have a $trashname that is not in use
            # Here's where we actually move the file into the Trash
            #
            mv "$file" "$trashname"
            fi
done
```

Figure 9.33 Code listing of a better Trash script. This one uses file tests, a `for` loop, and a `while` loop.

Getting User Input

You've seen one way to get user input into your scripts—by using the command-line arguments and then accessing them with $1, $2, and so on, or $@. But what if you want your script to ask the user for input while it is running? No problem—you use the `read` command.

Refer to **Figure 9.34** while reading the following task. Figure 9.34 is a code listing of a script that asks the user for input and stores the input in a variable. **Figure 9.35** shows the script being used.

```
#!/bin/sh
# This script asks the user for input and stores it in a variable.

echo "Hello $USER, we just want to ask you a few questions."

# Use the -n option to echo to suppress the new line
echo -n "Enter an integer: "
read number

square=`expr $number \* $number`

echo "The  square of $number is $square"
```

Figure 9.34 Code listing of a script using the read command to get user input.

```
localhost:~ vanilla$ ./read.sh
Hello vanilla, we just want to ask you a few questions.
Enter an integer: 7
The  square of 7 is 49
[localhost:~] ./read.sh
Hello vanilla, we just want to ask you a few questions.
Enter an integer: 17
The  square of 17 is 289
localhost:~ vanilla$
```

Figure 9.35 Output from the script in Figure 9.34.

To read user input into a variable:

- `read` *`variable`*

  The `read` command takes one or more arguments that are the names of variables—for example,

  `read var1 var2 var3`

  When executed, `read` waits for user input and reads a line of input from the keyboard (actually from `stdin`—see Chapter 2 for more on standard input).

  `read` splits the input into pieces, based on the spaces between words, and stores each piece in one of the variables.

  If there are more pieces (input) than variables, the extras go in the last variable. This means that if you use `read` with a single variable name, you get an entire line of user input in that one variable. If there are more variables than input, the extra variables are left empty. If the script has

  `read var1 var2 var3`

  and the user types

  `good morning`

  then `var1` will contain `good`, `var2` will contain `morning`, and `var3` will be empty.

Creating and Using Functions

Functions are series of commands that have a name much like miniature scripts that can be stored inside another script. Functions make your code easier to understand and maintain. If you have a series of commands that you use more than once in your script, or that you want to use in more than one script, consider putting it in a function. You give the set of commands a name, and then in your script you use the name instead of repeating all of the command lines that the name refers to. You can pass arguments to functions in a manner similar to passing arguments to commands.

While reading the following task, refer to **Figure 9.36**, which is a code listing of a script that uses a function, and **Figure 9.37**, which shows output from the script.

```
#!/bin/sh
# The script uses a function

magic=77
guess=0

# define a function called "ask"
ask () {
    echo -n "Pick a number between 1 and 100: "
    read guess
}

while [ $guess -ne $magic ] ; do
    ask
    if [ $guess -lt $magic ] ; then
          echo "Try a higher number."
    elif [ $guess -gt $magic ] ; then
          echo "Try a lower number"
    else
          echo "Hey! You got it!"
    fi
done
```

Figure 9.36 Code listing of a script that uses a function.

```
localhost:~ vanilla$ ./function.sh
Pick a number between 1 and 100: 13
Try a higher number.
Pick a number between 1 and 100: 50
Try a higher number.
Pick a number between 1 and 100: 75
Try a higher number.
Pick a number between 1 and 100: 88
Try a lower number
Pick a number between 1 and 100: 80
Try a lower number
Pick a number between 1 and 100: 79
Try a lower number
Pick a number between 1 and 100: 78
Try a lower number
Pick a number between 1 and 100: 77
Hey! You got it!
localhost:~ vanilla$
```

Figure 9.37 Output from the script in Figure 9.36.

To create a function:

1. `name () {`

   The function name can be any combination of letters, numbers, dashes, and underscore characters as long as it isn't the same as a predefined or built-in shell command, such as `if`, `while`, and so forth (see `man builtin`).

2. Enter a series of command lines.

   The body of the function is a series of command lines. Indent the commands in the function to make the script easier to read.

3. `}`

   The } ends the function. Now you can use the function at any point farther on in your script, as if you have added a new command to the Bourne shell language. (You cannot use a function in a script at a point earlier than where the function is defined.)

Functions can take arguments just as a script or command does.

To use arguments in a function:

- Use the special variables for arguments in the function.

  The special variables you have used for script arguments all work inside a function. When used inside a function, they refer to the arguments used with the function, not the script around the function. So the $3 inside a function is the third argument to the function, not the third argument to the script.

Figure 9.38 is a code listing of a script using a function that takes arguments, and **Figure 9.39** is output from that script.

```
#!/bin/sh
# The script uses a function that takes arguments

magic=63
a=0
b=0
sum=0

ask () {
        echo -n "Enter two integers: "
        read a b
}

add () {
        sum=`expr $1 + $2`
}


while [ $magic -ne $sum ] ; do
        ask
        add $a $b
        if [ $sum -lt $magic ] ; then
             echo "Try HIGHER."
        elif [ $sum -gt $magic ] ; then
             echo "Try LOWER."
        else
             echo "VERY GOOD. $a + $b = $magic which is the magic number."
  fi
done
```

Figure 9.38 Code listing of a script using a function that takes arguments.

✔ Tip

- If you have a function or functions that you want to use in more than one script, you should put the function(s) in a separate file and read that file into your script(s) using the `.` command:

  ```
  . file
  ```

  `file` must be a path to the file you want to read. If it is simply a filename, then the file must be in your current directory when you execute the script. The script will read the named file and execute its contents as if they were typed into the script at this point.

```
localhost:~ vanilla$ ./function.sh
Enter two integers: 23 37
Try HIGHER.
Enter two integers: 30 40
Try LOWER.
Enter two integers: 29 40
Try LOWER.
Enter two integers: 27 37
Try LOWER.
Enter two integers: 25 37
Try HIGHER.
Enter two integers: 26 37
VERY GOOD. 26 + 37 = 63 which is the magic
number.
localhost:~ vanilla$
```

Figure 9.39 Output of the script in Figure 9.38.

Where to Learn More

Of course the Bourne shell `man` page, `man sh`, will at least give you a good overview of what else there is to learn, although it may not be the best guide for a beginner to actually work from.

Here are two online tutorials:

- Unix Bourne Shell Scripting (http://unix.about.com/library/course/blshscript-outline.htm)
- Steve Parker's Web site (http://steve-parker.org/sh/sh.shtml)

If you use the `bash` shell, you should read *Learning the bash Shell,* Second Edition, by Cameron Newham and Bill Rosenblatt (O'Reilly; www.oreilly.com/catalog/bash2).

10 Connecting over the Internet

Using Unix means being part of a global system for collaborative computing. The ability to connect with and perform interactive tasks on other Unix machines is built into Mac OS X and every other version of Unix in use today.

Most of the interactions you have with other Unix machines will fall into one of two categories: logging in to another machine to get a command-line interface on the remote machine, or copying files between your machine and a remote machine.

Technically speaking, the programs we describe in this chapter are not limited to interacting with Unix machines; the underlying requirement is simply that they understand the lingua franca of the Internet, TCP/IP. However, Unix is so prevalent that chances are, the system you connect to will be Unix based. The basics of interaction with non-Unix machines, as well as more advanced forms of interaction, such as setting up virtual private networks and automated (unattended) file transfers, are beyond the scope of this book. We will, however, guide you to places where you can learn more about what is possible and how to do it.

About Hostnames

Connecting to another machine over a network requires that you have some way of identifying the remote machine.

All of the tools covered in this chapter use the TCP/IP (Transmission Control Protocol/ Internet Protocol) suite of protocols to communicate across networks, and thus we refer to them generally as *Internet tools.*

When you use the Internet, there are two ways to identify another machine. One is to use an IP (Internet Protocol) address, and the other is to use a *hostname.* Data sent over the Internet always uses IP addresses, but IP addresses are hard for humans to remember. This is where hostnames and domain names come in.

An IP address looks like this: 192.168.23.45. Every computer's numbers are different, but IP addresses always have four parts separated by dots (but see the sidebar "The Next Version of IP Addresses"). Each part is a value between 0 and 255. In fact, each part is actually an 8-bit binary number, from 00000000 (0 in base 10) to 11111111 (255 in base 10). Every machine on the Internet must have at least one unique IP address—it's like its telephone number. You can always use an IP address to connect to another machine over the Internet, but usually you will want to use a more user-friendly text-based domain name.

The familiar format of *www.something.com* is called a *fully qualified domain name* (FQDN). Your computer translates FQDNs into IP addresses through a process of asking other computers on the Internet for the translation, sort of like using directory assistance for telephone numbers. The most common system for doing this translation is the Domain Name System (DNS), but there are others. You can find a bit more about DNS in "Setting Your Machine's Hostname" in Chapter 14, "Installing and Configuring Servers." FQDNs consist of a *top-level domain* (.com, .edu, .int, .us, and so on) on the right-hand end, and then any number of sub-domains on the left, with the leftmost item being the name of one specific computer inside the preceding sub-domain. So in this example,

```
us.rd.yahoo.com
```

.com is the top-level domain, *yahoo* is a sub-domain (a sub-domain of .com), *rd* is also a sub-domain (of yahoo.com), and *us* is a host-name. The whole thing, `us.rd.yahoo.com`, is a fully qualified domain name and can be translated by your computer into an IP address. Because "fully qualified domain name" or even "FQDN" is such a mouthful, it is common practice to say "domain name" or "hostname" when what is really meant is "fully qualified domain name." Technically, domain names and the hostname are just parts of an FQDN, but people are sloppy, what can we say?

The Next Version of IP Addresses

The IP addresses described in this book meet a standard called Internet Protocol version 4, or IPv4. The next version of the standard for IP addresses is Internet Protocol Version 6, or IPv6, which allows for much longer addresses. (IPv4 addresses are 32 bits long. IPv6 addresses are four times that size—128 bits long.) See the IPv6 Information Page (www.ipv6.org) for more information. Mac OS X has built-in support for IPv6.

Authenticity of Hosts and SSH

When you use SSH to connect to another machine, the SSH software on your end (the "client" software) and the `sshd` daemon on the other end (the "server") exchange information about each other.

One of the things the client asks for is the "identity" of the remote host. If you already have the remote machine's encrypted identity stored in your `~/.ssh/known_hosts` or `~/.ssh/known_hosts2` file (depending on which version of the SSH protocol the client and server have agreed to use), the client trusts the server's identity; otherwise, you get the prompt shown in Figure 10.1. If you say "yes" to the prompt, then the client adds the encrypted identity supplied by the server to your `~/.ssh/known_hosts` or `known_hosts2` file.

The most secure way of establishing the identity of the remote host is to obtain the remote host's identity file from that machine and manually add it to your `~/.ssh/known_hosts` or `known_hosts2` file. One way of doing this is to have the remote machine's administrator e-mail the file to you. Because there are variations in how different versions of the SSH software work, you need to get help from the remote machine's administrator to make sure you add the host-identity information in the proper format.

In practice this is rarely done, and people simply answer "yes" to the prompt shown in Figure 10.1 the first time they connect to a machine using SSH.

Logging In to Another Unix Machine

The most basic and common way you interact with other Unix machines from the command line is to log in to them using a command-line interface from your own machine.

Once you log in to another Unix machine using a command-line interface, you can use that machine in the same way as you use your own machine from the command line. Of course, you may not have the same level of permissions that you have on your own machine, and if the remote machine is running a different version of Unix, there will be some differences in availability of commands and variations in how some commands work. Overall, however, you will find yourself in an environment very much like the command-line environment on your own machine.

In this section we describe two ways of getting to a command-line prompt on remote machines. The first (and preferred) method uses SSH to establish an encrypted connection to the remote machine, while the second method uses an older program called Telnet to establish an unencrypted connection. Both SSH and Telnet are useful for more than simply logging in to another machine, but connecting via SSH is not always supported, so sometimes you have to use Telnet.

Secure connections using SSH

SSH stands for *secure shell* and is the name of both a protocol (SSH) and a command (`ssh`).

The SSH protocol sets up an encrypted connection between two machines over a network such as the Internet. The primary tool for using the SSH protocol is the `ssh` command. This means that if you are communicating

continues on next page

with a remote host using SSH and someone is able to tap in to the connection, it is extremely difficult or impossible for that person to read the data flowing between the two machines. For this reason, SSH is the preferred method for logging in to another machine over the Internet.

To log in to other machines over the Internet, you need to have an account on the remote machine. That means having a user name and password. You also need to know the network address of the remote machine—either its IP address or a hostname that your machine can translate into an IP address. As complicated as that sounds, it is actually simple in practice: If you are supposed to be connecting to a remote machine, you will have been given the address to use.

Refer to **Figure 10.1** for the following task. The figure shows the process of logging in to a remote machine using the `ssh` command.

To log in using ssh:

1. `ssh` *`username@hostname`*

   `username` is your user name on the remote system. *`hostname`* is either in the typical domain-name format or an IP address of the remote machine. For example, the following will connect to the machine well.com with the user name puffball:

   ```
   ssh puffball@well.com
   ```

Logging In to Your Own Machine via SSH

Your Mac OS X machine comes with SSH server software installed, but you have to turn it on before you can log in to your machine from another Internet host using SSH. It's pretty easy, though: Open the Sharing pane of System Preferences, go to the Application tab, and check the "Allow remote login" box. That's it.

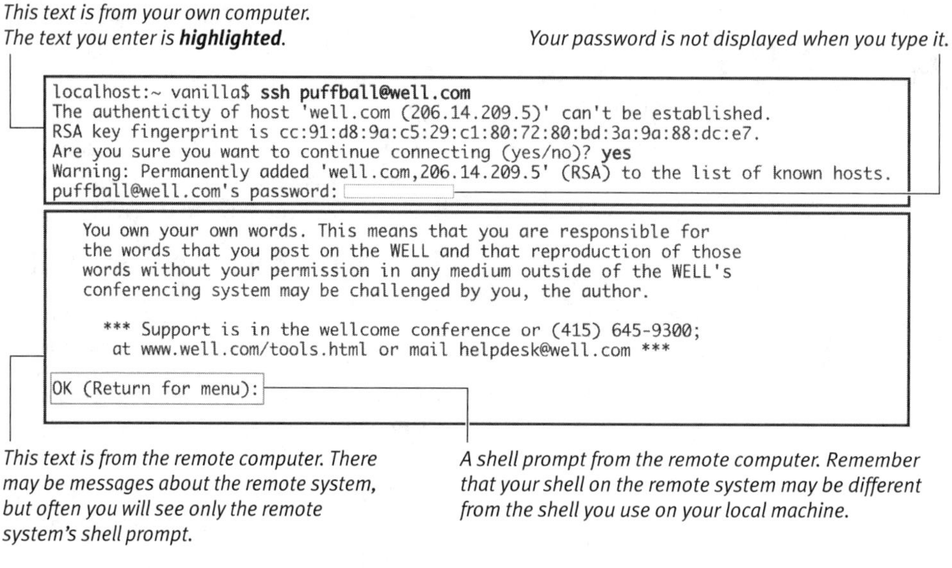

*This text is from your own computer. The text you enter is **highlighted**.*

Your password is not displayed when you type it.

```
localhost:~ vanilla$ ssh puffball@well.com
The authenticity of host 'well.com (206.14.209.5)' can't be established.
RSA key fingerprint is cc:91:d8:9a:c5:29:c1:80:72:80:bd:3a:9a:88:dc:e7.
Are you sure you want to continue connecting (yes/no)? yes
Warning: Permanently added 'well.com,206.14.209.5' (RSA) to the list of known hosts.
puffball@well.com's password:
```

```
    You own your own words. This means that you are responsible for
    the words that you post on the WELL and that reproduction of those
    words without your permission in any medium outside of the WELL's
    conferencing system may be challenged by you, the author.

      *** Support is in the wellcome conference or (415) 645-9300;
       at www.well.com/tools.html or mail helpdesk@well.com ***

OK (Return for menu):
```

This text is from the remote computer. There may be messages about the remote system, but often you will see only the remote system's shell prompt.

A shell prompt from the remote computer. Remember that your shell on the remote system may be different from the shell you use on your local machine.

Figure 10.1 Diagram showing the use of ssh to connect to a remote machine.

If your user name is the same on both the local and remote machines, you may omit the *username@* portion of the command line:

```
ssh well.com
```

Sometimes you get an IP address to use instead of a hostname. You can experiment on your own machine using the special IP address 127.0.0.1, which always means "this machine right here," or use the hostname "localhost," which is a Unix standard name for the local machine. (You might have noticed that we use the hostname `localhost` in the examples of command-line prompts in this book.)

```
ssh username@127.0.0.1
```

or

```
ssh 127.0.0.1
```

or

```
ssh localhost
```

If this is the first time you have used `ssh` to connect to a particular hostname or IP address, you see a prompt as shown in Figure 10.1. Despite the apparent security warning, you should answer "yes" to the question. (You must type the full word `yes`, not just `y`.) See the sidebar "Authenticity of Hosts and SSH."

The next thing you see is the prompt for your password:

```
puffball@well.com's password:
```

2. Enter your password.

Your typing is not displayed, to prevent your password from being visible.

You are then logged in to the remote machine. The remote machine may display an informational message about itself, perhaps telling you the last time you logged in or giving you a telephone number for the system support staff. Often you will get only a prompt from that machine. You can now start entering command lines to the remote machine.

When you want to log out of the remote machine, type

```
logout
```

You return to a shell prompt on your own machine. (`exit` also works, and on some systems Control D will also work.)

✔ Tips

- It is a good idea to open a new Terminal window for each connection to a remote machine (you can have many open at the same time).
- Consider changing the Terminal window title and/or text color for each window in which you are connected to a remote machine. This will help you remember which machine you are "on" in each window. You can make these changes in the Terminal application by pulling down the Terminal menu, choosing Window Settings, and then choosing Shell.
- If you are having trouble on the remote machine while connected via `ssh`, you can terminate the connection (without closing the Terminal window) by using a special sequence of keys:

  Return ~ .

  That's the Return key, followed by the ~ character, followed by a period—press them one at a time, not all together. You can get a list of the available "escape" commands with this sequence of keys:

  Return ~ ?
- Bear in mind that your shell may not be the same on the remote machine as on your local machine. For example, your account on your own machine might be set to use the `bash` shell, while on the remote machine your account might use the `tchsh` shell, so you can expect some slight differences in how the command-line environment behaves. One way to see which shell you are using is

  ```
  echo $SHELL
  ```

Using SSH to run a command on another machine:

One of the nifty things about SSH is that you can use it to run commands on another machine without actually logging in to the remote machine.

For example, the `who` command shows a list of users logged in to a machine. If you want to check who is logged in to a remote machine on which you have an account, you can use the `ssh` command to run the `who` command on the remote machine and see its output on your machine.

To run a single command line on a remote machine:

- `ssh user@host commandline`

  For example,

  `ssh puffball@well.com who`

  runs the `who` command as the user puffball on the remote machine well.com (**Figure 10.2**).

  The command line you run on the remote machine may be a full command line, including options and arguments. For example, to see a list of the files in the remote system's `/etc` directory, you could use

  `ssh puffball@well.com ls -l /etc`

More About SSH

SSH is both the name of a protocol and the name of a widely used Unix command (`ssh`).

As with many facets of Unix, there is more than one variety of the SSH software. Mac OS X comes with OpenSSH, an open-source implementation of the SSH protocol that combines the work of several prior implementations. You can read a brief history at OpenSSH Project History and Credits (www.openssh.org/history.html).

The OpenSSH tool set includes several commands that are installed on your Mac OS X machine, including `ssh`, `sshd`, `scp`, and `sftp`.

```
localhost:~ vanilla$ ssh puffball@well.com who
puffball@well.com's password:
geffrey     pts/1     Jun 25 10:30    (12.112.115.3)
mikkee      pts/7     Jun 25 10:32    (14-226-92-54.clients.attbit.com)
lalla       pts/2     Jun 25 09:21    (werks.kinemia.com)
jmassoun    pts/53    Jun 25 11:10    (huffman.wunterk.com)
rpdoctor    pts/12    Jun 25 06:59    (63.113.8.116)
jperk       pts/26    Jun 25 06:14    (fl-boca-cuda1-c2a-132.pbc.adelphia.net)
fanson      pts/56    Jun 25 10:44    (119-176-36-34-cdsl-rb1:S.0)
```

Figure 10.2 Using ssh to run a command on the remote machine without logging in.

to produce output like that shown in **Figure 10.3**.

Some programs don't simply spit out their output and quit, though—they expect to take over your whole screen and interact with you. For example, the vi editor is a *full-screen* program. It takes over the whole Terminal window and allows you to move around inside that window entering and editing text (review Chapter 6, "Editing and Printing Files," for more on vi). To run these kinds of programs using the ssh command, add the -t option, which makes ssh pretend you are on a terminal on the remote machine. For example:

```
ssh -t puffball@playroom.matisse.net
vi myfile
```

runs the vi editor on the remote machine. When you quit from vi, the SSH connection closes, but the file you edited is still on the remote machine.

```
localhost:~ vanilla$ ssh puffball@playroom.matisse.net ls -l /etc
puffball@playroom.matisse.net's password:
total 1980
drwxr-xr-x    3 root    root    4096 Oct 31     2002 CORBA
-rw-r--r--    1 root    root    2434 Oct 29     2004 DIR_COLORS
-rw-r--r--    1 root    root    2434 Oct 29     2004 DIR_COLORS.xterm
-rw-r--r--    1 root    root    92421 Mar 19    2003 Muttrc
drwxr-xr-x    17 root   root    4096 Feb 19 09:47 X11
-rw-r--r--    1 root    root    2562 Aug  5     2002 a2ps-site.cfg
-rw-r--r--    1 root    root    15228 Aug  5    2002 a2ps.cfg
-rw-r--r--    1 root    root    49 Mar 11 13:03 adjtime
-rw-r--r--    1 root    roo     1122 Mar  6 17:04 aliases
-rw-r--r--    1 smmsp   root    12288 Mar 25 11:31 aliases.db
drwxr-xr-x    2 root    root    4096 Sep 17     2003 alternatives
-rw-r--r--    1 root    roo     317 Aug 28      2002 anacrontab
-rw-------    1 root    root    1 Jul 24        2002 at.deny
-rw-r--r--    1 root    root    212 Aug 26      2002 auto.master
-rw-r--r--    1 root    root    575 Aug 26      2002 auto.misc
-rw-r--r--    1 root    root    1497 Aug 29     2002 bashrc
drwxr-xr-x    2 root    root    4096 Oct 31     2002 bonobo-activation
-rw-r--r--    1 root    root    756 Jun 23      2003 cdrecord.conf
drwxr-xr-x    2 root    root    4096 Jul 19     2005 cron.d
drwxr-xr-x    2 root    root    4096 Mar 25 12:24 cron.daily

(Partial Output)
```

Figure 10.3 You can supply options and arguments to commands run on a remote machine with ssh.

Connecting using Telnet

Before there was the SSH protocol there was the Telnet protocol. The Telnet protocol is at least 25 years old (geeks in the audience: check out RFC 764 if you doubt this) and is the lowest-common-denominator method of logging in to a remote Unix machine. These days it is deprecated in favor of SSH because all of the data in a Telnet connection (including your user name and password) is sent over the network unencrypted. However, a few systems still don't support SSH, and there are things you can do with Telnet besides logging in to another machine.

Just as we have the `ssh` command for using the SSH protocol, we have the `telnet` command for using the Telnet protocol.

When using the `telnet` command, you need the same things as you do for SSH—that is, the remote machine's address (either a hostname or an IP address) and an account on the remote machine (user name and password).

To log in using Telnet:

1. `telnet` *`hostname`*

   As with `ssh`, *`hostname`* can be either a text-based network address, such as well.com, or an IP address, such as 206.14.209.5. If you use a hostname, the `telnet` program asks the operating system to translate the hostname into an IP address. That's why you see an IP address in this line:

   `Trying 206.14.209.5...`

   When you use `telnet`, your machine tells you it is trying to connect to the remote machine. Once it connects, you see text from the remote machine identifying itself, followed by a `login:` prompt from the remote machine (**Figure 10.4**).

2. Enter your user name.

   Once you enter your user name, you should see a password prompt from the remote machine.

This text is from your own computer.

```
localhost:~ vanilla$ telnet well.com
Trying 206.14.209.5...
Connected to well.com.
Escape character is '^]'.
```

```
SunOS 5.6

This is The WELL

Find membership information at http://www.well.com/
Forgot your password?  Go to http://www.well.com/newpass

If you already have a WELL account, type your username.

login:
```

This text is from the remote computer.

Figure 10.4 Using Telnet to log in to a remote machine.

3. Enter your password.

   You are now logged in. Some systems will show you a short message about themselves (called "the message of the day"). In any case, you get a prompt from the remote machine, and you can now type commands to it.

✔ Tip

- If you are having trouble on the remote machine while using `telnet`, you can quit the Telnet program by typing a special keyboard combination that gets you a prompt from the Telnet program itself.

  Notice in Figure 10.4 the line that says

  `Escape character is '^]'.`

  This is part of the text that comes from your own computer before you get the `login:` prompt from the remote machine. The Telnet program is telling you that if you press Control], you'll get a prompt from the Telnet client on your own machine:

  `telnet>`

  and you can then exit the Telnet program (and kill the connection to the remote machine) by typing

  `quit`

Using Telnet to test other systems

Besides using Telnet to log in to a remote machine, you can also use it to test services running on other machines.

You do this by using `telnet` to connect to a remote machine but to a different *port number* than the one normally used for logging in with `telnet`.

When one machine connects to another over the Internet, it always uses a combination of an IP address and a port number. The combination is called a *socket*. The IP address identifies the particular machine, while the port number leads to one of the (possibly many) pieces of software that are "listening" for incoming connections. Each Internet service has a standard port number that it listens on; the server software for `telnet` login, for example, normally listens on port 23. We provide a more extensive discussion of ports in Chapter 12, "Security," and Table 12.1 lists the most commonly used port numbers. You can see the full list your system uses in the file `/etc/services`.

When you use `telnet` to log in, you are using the `telnet` client program to connect to a Telnet server program (called `telnetd`) on the remote machine. Server programs like `telnetd` (and `sshd`, mentioned earlier in this chapter) are said to "listen" on specific port numbers. The `telnet` command normally connects to port 23 on the remote machine.

On the Internet there are standard port numbers for all the common Internet services, so the `telnetd` server listens on port 23, Web servers normally listen on port 80, e-mail servers listen on port 25, the `sshd` server listens on port 22, and so on. This allows all of those services to be running on the same machine and share the same IP address. It is their port numbers that distinguish them; in other words, each service uses a different socket (again, that's the combination of IP address and port number).

You can use the `telnet` command to connect to a remote machine on a port other than the standard Telnet port (23). If the connection itself is successful, you at least know that something is listening on that port on the remote machine. If you are familiar with the protocol that the remote service uses, you may be able to try a test interaction with the remote service.

Refer to **Figure 10.5** while working through the following task.

To connect to a remote Web server to test it:

1. `telnet www.eigenstate.net 80`

   The only new thing about that command line is that you are specifying that `telnet` connect to port 80 on the remote machine instead of the default (port 23).

   If there is anything listening on port 80 on the remote machine, `telnet` should connect to it.

   In Figure 10.5 you see that something is in fact listening—that's why you get the line

   `Connected to www.eigenstate.net.`

   Even though the Web server on the remote machine is waiting for input from you, there will be no prompt.

```
localhost:~ vanilla$ telnet www.eigenstate.net 80
Trying 216.135.166.25...
Connected to www.eigenstate.net.
Escape character is '^]'.
HEAD / HTTP/1.1
Host: www.eigenstate.net
Connection: close

HTTP/1.1 200 OK
Date: Sat, 30 Apr 2005 20:33:47 GMT
Server: Apache
Set-Cookie: eigenstate.net-user=216.135.166.13.1114893229232762; path=/; max-age=31536000;
domain=.eigenstate.net
Last-Modified: Sat, 30 Apr 2005 15:45:44 GMT
ETag: "524171-498-489c5a00"
Accept-Ranges: bytes
Content-Length: 1176
Connection: close
Content-Type: text/html; charset=ISO-8859-1

Connection closed by foreign host.
localhost:~ vanilla$
```

Figure 10.5 Using Telnet to test a remote Web server.

More About HTTP

If you want to learn more about HTTP, you'll find a nice online tutorial and reference in HTTP Made Really Easy (www.jmarshall.com/easy/http), or check out the *HTTP Pocket Reference*, by Clinton Wong (O'Reilly; www.oreilly.com/catalog/httppr).

2. Now you will type a few lines to request some information from the Web server:

   `HEAD / HTTP/1.1`

   Make sure to only press Return once at the end of that line.

   You are asking for the summary information (the "head") about the main page on this Web server (/). Use `GET` instead of `HEAD` to request the full page instead of only the summary information. You are also telling the server that you are using HTTP version 1.1.

3. `Host: www.eigenstate.net`

   This line specifies which domain name you are requesting information about, in case the server software is configured to respond to requests for more than one domain name.

4. `Connection: close`

   Here you are telling the Web server that after it sends you the information, you are requesting that it close the connection.

5. Press Return again.

   Adding a blank line tells the server that you are finished creating your request. If the Web server and network connection are functioning properly, you will immediately see a response like that in Figure 10.5.

   In the response shown in the figure, you see several lines of information, including one that tells you the Web server is running the Apache software and that the Web page we asked about is 1176 bytes long.

Copying Files Across the Internet

There are many reasons to copy files from one machine to another. The most common: downloading software so that you can install it, uploading Web pages you have created to the machine that will serve them, and copying files from one machine to another as a way of backing them up.

If security is a concern (which it should be, most of the time), you should always use one of the secure methods of file transfer, either `scp` (described next) or `sftp` (described in the sidebar "Other Command-Line FTP Clients," below).

The most widely available method for copying files across the Internet is *FTP* (File Transfer Protocol). FTP software (both client and server) is available for virtually every type of operating system, not only Unix. So you might find yourself using FTP from your Unix machine to transfer files to or from a Windows NT machine that is running an FTP server. The big advantage to FTP software is its widespread availability. The biggest downside is that, like Telnet, it transfers everything "in the clear" (that is, unencrypted), including your user name and password.

Preserving ACLs and other Extended Attributes

Most of the command-line file-copy tools described in this chapter have one weakness: They will not transfer certain kinds of file metadata. That includes the "resource forks" created by pre–Mac OS X versions of the Mac OS and the various *extended attributes* introduced in Mac OS X 10.4 for features such as Spotlight. They also don't work with the ACLs described in Chapter 8, "Working with Permissions and Ownership."

You can preserve the resource forks on files created in Mac OS 9 (Classic) by using Aladdin Systems' StuffIt application to compress the file, and then transferring the compressed file. The compressed file is not affected, and when the recipient uncompresses the file, its resource fork and other Mac metadata are preserved.

If both your machine and the remote machine are running Mac OS X 10.4 or later, you can use the `-E` option to the `scp` or `rsync` command (described below). Both Mac OS 9 resource forks and Mac OS X ACL information will be properly copied, as well as the other extended attributes used by Mac OS X features such as Spotlight.

Using scp

The `scp` (*secure copy*) command works very much like the `cp` command (review Chapter 5, "Using Files and Directories"). The basic syntax is

`scp` *`existingfile newfile`*

The key difference between `scp` and `cp` is that any of the files specified can be on another machine, so the proper syntax for `scp` is

`scp` *`user@host:file user@host:file`*

Furthermore, and *this is a really important point*: `scp` automatically uses SSH to make the connection to the remote machine, so the entire transaction is encrypted, including the file(s) being copied across the network.

To send a file from your machine to a remote machine using scp:

- `scp` *`localfile user@host:newfile`*

  where *`localfile`* is a file pathname on the local machine, *`user`* is your user name on the remote machine, *`host`* is the domain name or IP address of the remote machine, and *`newfile`* is a file pathname on the remote machine. If the *`newfile`* path does not begin with a `/`, then it will be interpreted as a path relative to the home directory for *`user`* on the remote machine.

Here are some examples:

`scp Report.doc files.mycompany.com:`

copies the local file Report.doc to your home directory on the remote machine `files.mycompany.com`. The copied file will have the same name on the remote machine because we have only specified the remote hostname, and not the remote filename.

`scp Report.doc puffball@host.com:`
`→ NewReport.doc`

copies the local file Report.doc to puffball's home directory on the remote machine and renames the copy NewReport.doc.

`scp /etc/rc.common puffball@host.com:`
`→ files/`

copies the local file `/etc/rc.common` into a directory called `files` in the home directory of user puffball on the remote machine.

`scp /etc/rc.common host.com:/etc/`
`→ rc.common.save`

copies the local file `/etc/rc.common` to `/etc/rc.common.save` on the remote machine. This assumes your user name is the same on both machines.

To get a file using scp:

1. `scp` *`user@hostname:path path`*

   Examples:

   `scp well.com:myfile.txt .`

   `scp puffball@well.com:myfile.txt`
   `→ myfile_copy.txt`

2. Enter your password.

   See **Figure 10.6**, and notice how `scp` provides a progress indicator. The series of asterisks fills up as the file is copied over the network.

Sometimes you want to copy an entire directory from one machine to another. `scp` handles this with the `-r` option (for *recursive* copy).

To copy an entire directory using scp:

◆ `scp -r` *`original copy`*

where either *`original`* or *`copy`* includes a remote-machine name. Examples:

`scp -r images`
`→ puffball@well.com:new_images`

copies the local directory called `images` to the remote machine, while

`scp -r puffball@well.com:images`
`→ new_images`

copies the remote directory `~puffball/images` to the local current directory and names the copy `new_images`. But be careful—if there is already a local directory named `new_images`, that command line will put the copy inside the existing directory. You can avoid this by adding a trailing `/` to any path that is supposed to be a directory:

`scp -r puffball@well.com:images`
`→ new_images/`

```
localhost:~ vanilla$ scp puffball@well.com:myfile.txt copy.txt
puffball@well.com's password:
myfile.txt  100% |*****************************************|  9939    00:00
localhost:~ vanilla$
```

Figure 10.6 Using scp to copy a file from a remote machine to your local machine.

There are a number of options for scp that you may find useful. You've seen one (the -r option) in the task above. **Table 10.1** lists the most common options for scp, and, as always, you should read the man page for the complete list.

Table 10.1

Options for the scp Command

Option	Meaning/Use
-r	Recursive copy. Used to copy entire directories.
-q	Disables the progress meter (or quiets it).
-p	Preserves permissions and modification times.
-v	Causes lots of debugging information to be displayed (verbose).
-C	Uses compression to speed up copying.
-E	Preserves extended attributes, including ACLs and Mac OS 9 resource forks. Both machines must be running Mac OS X 10.4 or later.
-l *number*	Limits bandwidth used, where *number* is in Kbits/second.

See man scp for the complete list.

Using FTP

FTP is one of the oldest protocols on the Internet and is still widely used for downloading software as well as uploading and downloading files for Web sites and general file-transfer work.

As with virtually all Internet tools, you use FTP by running a client application on your machine that connects to a server application on the remote machine. Mac OS X comes with not one, not two, not three, but (at least!)

Table 10.2

FTP Commands

Command	Meaning/Use
ascii	Sets file-transfer type to plain text.
binary	Sets file-transfer type to binary.
cd	cd directory Changes the current directory on the remote machine.
get	get remotefile [localfile]
hash	Toggles hash-mark printing (progress indicator during file transfer).
lcd	lcd [directory] Changes your current directory on the local machine. With no argument, it changes to your home directory. When you quit FTP, your current directory in the shell will be what it was when you started the FTP program.
ls	ls [directory] Like the regular ls command, lists the names of files and directories; usually uses the "long-form" listing.
mkdir	mkdir directory Creates a new directory on the remote machine.
mput	mput *file1 file2* ... Uploads multiple files.
mget	mget *file1 file2* . . . Downloads multiple files.
put	put *localfile* [*remotefile*]
pwd	Prints your current directory on the remote machine.
quit	Quits the ftp program.

Arguments in square brackets ([ ]) are optional.

four command-line FTP client applications. This chapter focuses on the most common FTP client application, which is called simply `ftp`. The others are `curl`, `sftp`, and `ncftp` (see the sidebar "Other Command-Line FTP Clients").

We are showing you the older and more basic `ftp` program here because we want you to be able to use other Unix machines besides your Mac OS X machine. Still, `ncftp` is a nicer and easier program to use, so as long as you are using Mac OS X, you should read the `man` page for `ncftp` and try using that instead of `ftp`.

The `ftp` client application has its own command prompt, at which you enter commands that are specific to the `ftp` program itself. You can think of it as a miniature shell that has several dozen of its own commands. **Table 10.2** shows the most common FTP commands; see `man ftp` for the complete list.

Using the `ftp` program generally involves the following steps:

- Connecting to the remote machine.
- Logging in with a user name and password.
- Navigating around the directories on the remote machine and/or your local machine.
- Specifying options about how file transfers will be made—for example, specifying that transferred files should be treated as plain text as opposed to binary, or requesting that a progress indicator be displayed during file transfer.
- Giving the actual command to upload or download one or more files.
- Quitting the FTP program to get back to your shell prompt.

Other Command-Line FTP Clients

`curl`

`curl` is a tool for copying files between machines using any one of several different protocols, including FTP, HTTP, and HTTPS. (See `man curl` for the full story.) There are so many options and features in `curl` that we prefer to install and use the `wget` program. It's less powerful but simpler.

`sftp`

`sftp` is actually an FTP-like interface that uses SSH to create a secure connection to the remote machine and then allows you to use commands similar to those of the FTP program to transfer files. If it's available, you should use `sftp` instead of FTP. The commands are mostly the same, but read the `man` page to see a few differences. For example, `sftp` has an `lpwd` command to show your (local) current directory, and a `rename` command that lets you rename remote files.

`ncftp`

`ncftp` is a more user-friendly program than the old `ftp` command. `ncftp` can be used to connect to any FTP server. `ncftp` has a really good `man` page, and you should read that and try using `ncftp` instead of `ftp` when `scp` or `sftp` isn't an option.

The following task assumes that you want to upload a file called poetry.html from the current directory on your local machine to a remote machine called `webhost.somewhere.sf.ca.us`, and that you want the file to end up in the directory `/usr/local/apache/htdocs/written_work` on the remote machine.

A key thing to keep in mind when using the FTP protocol is that you are using two machines simultaneously: your own machine (the "local" machine) and the remote machine.

Refer to **Figure 10.7** throughout the following task.

To upload a file using ftp:

1. `ftp` *`hostname`*

   In Figure 10.7, the hostname is webhost.somewhere.us, so the command line is

   `ftp webhost.somewhere.us`

   Throughout this process, the FTP remote server will send you messages about each action you take. When your client software first connects to the server, you get the message

   `220 FTP Service`

   (The messages you see will vary slightly, depending on the server you connect to.)

   The remote machine's FTP server then prompts you for a user name.

Your shell prompt and the command line that starts the FTP client application.

Your password is not displayed when you type it.

A prompt from the FTP client program.

Everything in this box is from the FTP client application.

```
localhost:~ vanilla$ ftp sbgnews.snapbevgrp.com
Connected to webhost.somewhere.us.
220 FTP Service
Name (webhost.somewhere.us:vanilla): puffball
331 Password required for puffball.
Password:
230 User puffball logged in.
Remote system type is UNIX.
Using binary mode to transfer files.
ftp> cd /usr/local/apache/htdocs/written_work
250 CWD command successful.
ftp> ascii
200 Type set to A.
ftp> put poetry.html
local: poetry.html remote: poetry.html
200 PORT command successful.
150 Opening ASCII mode data connection for poetry.html.
226 Transfer complete.
4691 bytes sent in 0.00882 seconds (531678 bytes/s)
ftp> ls
200 PORT command successful.
150 Opening ASCII mode data connection for file list.
drwxr-xr-x   3 puffball   client        59 Jun 27 11:34 .
drwx--xr-x  10 puffball   client      2048 Jun 27 11:29 ..
-rwxr-xr-x   1 puffball   client      4505 Jun 27 11:34 poetry.html
-rwxr-xr-x   1 puffball   client      4605 Jun 19 21:42 prose.html
226 Transfer complete.
ftp> quit
221 Goodbye.
localhost:~ vanilla$
```

Your shell prompt after you quit the FTP client application.

Figure 10.7 Using FTP to upload a file.

2. Enter a user name.

   You can simply press Return if the user name of your account on the remote machine is the same as your user name on the local machine. In the example, the user name entered is puffball.

   The server gives you a status message:

   `331 Password required for puffball.`

   and prompts you for a password.

3. Enter a password.

   The password is not displayed as you type it. (But the password is sent over the network without encryption, so it may be intercepted and read.)

   You are now logged in to the remote machine.

   The server responds with a series of messages:

   ```
   230 User puffball logged in.
   Remote system type is UNIX.
   Using binary mode to transfer files.
   ```

   The last message tells you the default setting for file transfers and assumes that any file you send (or receive) is a binary file, as opposed to a plain-text file. (A plain-text file is one that contains only ASCII characters, so, for example, a file using Unicode is not a plain-text file.)

   The next thing you see is a prompt from the `ftp` client—this is like a shell prompt in that the client waits for you to enter commands:

   `ftp>`

   While you are logged in using FTP, you have two current directories: one on the local machine and one on the remote machine.

   The FTP server on the remote machine keeps track of your current directory on the remote machine, and the FTP client software keeps track of which directory you are in on your local machine.

   When you first log in using FTP, your current directory on the remote machine is determined by how the remote FTP server is configured, and your local current directory starts off being whatever it was when you typed the `ftp` command to log in.

   In the example here, you are changing directories on the remote machine so that you may upload a file into a specific directory on the remote machine.

4. `cd directory`

   The FTP program has a `cd` command that changes your current directory *on the remote machine.*

   In Figure 10.7 the example is

   ```
   cd /usr/local/apache/htdocs/
   → written_work
   ```

   There is a different command to change your current directory on the local machine:

   `lcd` (local change directory)

   The server responds with a status message:

   `250 CWD command successful.`

5. `ascii`

   In this example, the file being uploaded is a plain-text file (that is, a file containing only ASCII characters), so you must tell the FTP server to change the file-transfer type from binary to ASCII (American Standard Code for Information Interchange, a long way of saying plain text). If you transfer a plain-text file as binary, the file may not have the correct end-of-line characters, and if you transfer a binary file (such as an image or compressed file archive) as plain text, it will almost certainly be damaged and unusable.

   The server responds with

   `200 Type set to A.`

   and you are now ready to upload the file.

continues on next page

6. `put poetry.html`

   This example assumes that the file you are uploading (poetry.html) is in your local directory.

   The server responds with a series of messages as shown in Figure 10.7. In particular, the line

   `local: poetry.html remote: poetry.html`

   tells you that the file will be copied to the remote machine and have the same name on the remote machine. You could upload the file and give the copy a different name:

   `put poetry.html lyrics.html`

7. You can also list the contents of a directory on the remote machine:

   `ls`

   Just like the regular Unix `ls` command, the `ftp ls` command lists file and directory names. Most FTP servers use the long-style listing shown in Figure 10.7.

   You can see by its presence in the listing that the file was copied successfully. If you have more files to transfer, do so.

8. `quit`

   This quits the FTP program, and you get a shell prompt from your local machine.

Compare with Aqua

- There are quite a few graphical interfaces for FTP and a few that handle secure transfers using SSH as well.
- Any Web browser is able to use FTP to download files—when you see a URL that begins with *ftp://*, that instructs the browser to use FTP (instead of the more common HTTP).
- A number of full-fledged FTP client applications provide a GUI for both uploading and downloading. We recommend the Transmit application (www.panic.com/transmit), which also handles the secure SFTP protocol and is available in a 15-day free trial version.
- RBrowser (www.rbrowser.com) handles FTP, SFTP, SSH/`scp`, and other protocols. There are two paid levels of license, and you may download demo versions.
- There used to be several Mac FTP clients that were free of charge, but this no longer seems to be true. The Mac OS X version of the venerable Dartmouth University Fetch program is now $25 from Fetch Softworks (www.fetchsoftworks.com); a 15-day free trial is available. Version 5.0 supports SFTP.

The FTP program has more than five dozen commands, all of which are described in the `man` page, and the more common ones are described in Table 10.2. Still, it is useful to get help while you are actually using the FTP program at the `ftp>` prompt.

To get help inside FTP:

1. ?

   The `ftp` command ? (just a question mark), typed at the `ftp>` prompt, lists all the available FTP commands, as shown in **Figure 10.8**.

   The message "Commands may be abbreviated" means that you only need to type enough of each command name to make it unique. So you can type

   `as`

   instead of

   `ascii`

continues on next page

```
ftp> ?
Commands may be abbreviated.  Commands are:

!             features      mls           prompt        site
$             fget          mlsd          proxy         size
account       form          mlst          put           sndbuf
append        ftp           mode          pwd           status
ascii         gate          modtime       quit          struct
bell          get           more          quote         sunique
binary        glob          mput          rate          system
bye           hash          mreget        rcvbuf        tenex
case          help          msend         recv          throttle
cd            idle          newer         reget         trace
cdup          image         nlist         remopts       type
chmod         lcd           nmap          rename        umask
close         less          ntrans        reset         unset
cr            lpage         open          restart       usage
debug         lpwd          page          rhelp         user
delete        ls            passive       rmdir         verbose
dir           macdef        pdir          rstatus       xferbuf
disconnect    mdelete       pls           runique       ?
edit          mdir          pmlsd         send
epsv4         mget          preserve      sendport
exit          mkdir         progres       set
ftp>
```

Figure 10.8 Using the ? command to get a list of all the available FTP commands.

2. You can also get a one-line description of any individual command:

   `? command`

   For example,

   `? ascii`

   Figure 10.9 shows several examples.

Besides uploading files, you will of course use FTP to download files.

You may be working on a Web site on a remote machine and need to download copies of HTML pages and graphics from that machine. Another common situation would be to use FTP to download the source code for software you want to install (see Chapter 13, "Installing Software from Source Code").

Software is available for download from many publicly accessible FTP servers. Public FTP servers differ from servers on which you have an account (with a user name and password) in that they allow you to log in using the special user name "anonymous" and to use your e-mail address as a password. Generally speaking, you cannot upload files to these "anonymous FTP servers," but you can download files from them.

Often the easiest way to download files from anonymous FTP servers is to use a GUI tool such as a Web browser or the `curl` or `wget` command (covered later in this chapter). But it is also useful to know how to do it the old-school way with a command-line FTP client. You will often be given the location of a file to download as an FTP URL—that is, a URL that starts with *ftp://*. **Figure 10.10** shows how to extract the hostname, directory, and filename from an FTP URL like this:

```
ftp://ftp.gnu.org/gnu/hello/
→ hello-2.1.1.tar.gz
```

Refer to **Figure 10.11** throughout the following task. The steps are *almost* identical to those in the task of uploading a file.

```
ftp> ? ascii
ascii    set ascii transfer type
ftp> ? as
ascii    set ascii transfer type
ftp> ? lcd
lcd      change local working directory
ftp> ? pwd
pwd      print working directory on remote machine
ftp> ? umask
umask    get (set) umask on remote side
ftp>
```

Figure 10.9 Getting one-line descriptions of individual FTP commands.

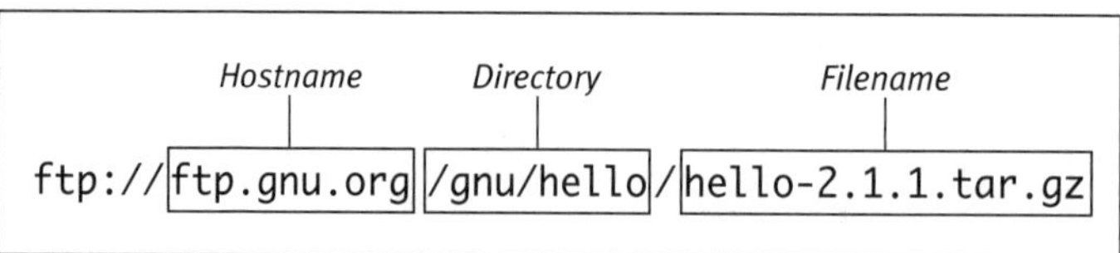

Figure 10.10 Extracting the hostname, directory, and filename from an FTP URL.

```
localhost:~ vanilla$ ftp ftp.gnu.org
Connected to ftp.gnu.org.
220 GNU FTP server ready.
Name (ftp.gnu.org:vanilla): anonymous
230-Due to U.S. Export Regulations, all cryptographic software on this
230-site is subject to the following legal notice:
230-
230-    This site includes publicly available encryption source code
230-    which, together with object code resulting from the compiling of
230-    publicly available source code, may be exported from the United
230-    States under License Exception "TSU" pursuant to 15 C.F.R. Section
230-    740.13(e).
230-
230-This legal notice applies to cryptographic software only. Please see
230-the Bureau of Industry and Security (www.bxa.doc.gov) for more
230-information about current U.S. regulations.
230 Login successful.
Remote system type is UNIX.
Using binary mode to transfer files.
ftp> cd /gnu/hello
250 Directory successfully changed.
ftp> ls
229 Entering Extended Passive Mode (|||47977|)
150 Here comes the directory listing.
-rw-r--r--    1 0      0       16452 Sep 17 1992       hello-1.0-1.1.diff.gz
-rw-r--r--    1 0      0       25676 May 22 1993       hello-1.1-1.2.diff.gz
-rw-r--r--    1 0      0       2919 May 23 1993        hello-1.2-1.3.diff.gz
-rw-r--r--    1 0      0       87942 May 23 1993       hello-1.3.tar.gz
-rw-r--r--    1 0      0       2020 Jun 09 2002        hello-2.1.0-2.1.1.diff.gz
-rw-r--r--    1 0      0       389049 Jun 09 2002      hello-2.1.0.tar.gz
-rw-r--r--    1 0      0       389363 Jun 09 2002      hello-2.1.1.tar.gz
226 Directory send OK.
ftp> hash
Hash mark printing on (1024 bytes/hash mark).
ftp> get hello-2.1.1.tar.gz
local: hello-2.1.1.tar.gz remote: hello-2.1.1.tar.gz
229 Entering Extended Passive Mode (|||9018|)
150 Opening BINARY mode data connection for hello-2.1.1.tar.gz (389363 bytes).
####################################################################################################
####################################################################################################
####################################################################################################
################################################################################
226 File send OK.
389363 bytes received in 00:03 (103.45 KB/s)
ftp> quit
221 Goodbye.
localhost:~ vanilla$
```

Figure 10.11 Downloading a file with FTP.

To download a file using FTP:

1. `ftp hostname`

   This step is exactly the same as in uploading. You are simply connecting to the remote machine.

2. Enter a user name.

   If you have an account on the remote machine, then use it. If your remote user name is the same as your local user name, just press Return; otherwise, type in your remote user name.

   If you are logging in to an anonymous FTP server, use the special user name "anonymous."

   For non-anonymous FTP servers, and for some anonymous FTP servers, you will be prompted for a password.

3. Enter your password, if asked.

   If you are logging in to a machine on which you have an account, enter the password. If you are logging in to an anonymous FTP server, enter your e-mail address.

   Some anonymous FTP servers will not bother asking for a password, as in our example in Figure 10.11.

4. You now change the directory to find the file you want to download:

   `cd directory`

   Using the example from Figures 10.10 and 10.11, the command would be

   `cd /gnu/hello`

   The server gives you a status message and another prompt.

5. `ls`

   Listing the contents of the current directory (on the remote machine) verifies that the file you want is really there.

6. You are now ready to download the file, but first you can tell the server to create a progress indicator during file transfers so that you can see something happening while transferring a large file:

   `hash`

   The `hash` command toggles the file-transfer progress indicator, which means that if it was off (the default), it is turned on, and if it was on, it is turned off.

7. Now you give the command to copy the file to your machine:

   `get filename`

   In the example, the filename is hello-2.1.1.tar.gz, so the command is

   `get hello-2.1.1.tar.gz`

   This copies the file to the current directory on the local machine and gives it the same name. If you want the copy to have a different name, you can type

   `get remotename localnewname`

   The file transfer takes place, and because you turned on the `hash` command earlier, you see a series of hash marks (#), one for each 1024 bytes transferred. When the transfer is complete, the server gives you a status message and the total number of bytes copied. You then get another prompt.

   If you have more files to transfer, you can do that, and when you are done, you quit the `ftp` program.

8. `quit`

   This quits the `ftp` program and takes you back to your shell.

✔ Tips

- Many anonymous FTP servers permit the shorter user name "ftp" instead of "anonymous."
- You usually don't really need to enter an e-mail address—these days the FTP servers rarely check that what you entered even looks like an e-mail address. But it is a courtesy to let the administrators know who is using the resources they are providing free of charge to the world.

Retrieving files using curl

Mac OS X includes the curl command, which allows you to retrieve (and in some cases send) files from servers using several of the common Internet protocols (for example, HTTP and FTP).

To retrieve a Web page using curl:

- `curl url`

  For example:

  ```
  curl http://www.matisse.net/files/
  → glossary.html
  ```

  fetches the page and puts the result on the screen.

✔ Tips

- To save the output of curl to a file, use redirection:

  ```
  curl url > file
  ```

  For example:

  ```
  curl gopher://gopher.well.com/00/WER/
  → forces.adrift > story.txt
  ```

- The curl command has many options. It is designed to be used in scripts without any live human interaction. All of these capabilities make it a bit complex, but powerful. See man curl for the Unix man page.

Retrieving files using wget

Yet another useful command-line tool for retrieving files is the wget command. In our opinion, wget is much easier to use than the curl command described above, especially for retrieving Web pages complete with images and other pages linked into the page.

wget takes a URL as an argument and acts like a Web browser. It fetches the file indicated by the URL and saves it to disk. In addition, if the file is an HTML page with links, wget is smart enough to fetch all the associated pages and images and save them to disk as well, giving you a complete local copy of the Web site.

wget does not come with Mac OS X. It is pretty easy to install, though, using the Fink program described in Chapter 13. **Table 10.3** lists some common options for the wget command.

Table 10.3

Options for the wget Command

There are many more options. These are just a few to whet your appetite.

Option	Meaning
--recursive	Follows links in the URL and downloads the pages and images found. wget normally follows links five levels deep. It creates a directory on your machine that has the same name as the domain name in the URL, and the saved files will all be inside that directory.
--level=depth	Used with --recursive. For example, --level=2 instructs wget to follow links for only two levels (the original page and its links), and links in the following pages).
--convert-links	After downloading, converts links in documents for local viewing. This will mean converting all the links in the pages so that they work properly when you view the pages in a browser from your disk (as opposed to viewing them from the remote site).

To fetch a file using wget:

- `wget url`

  where *url* is any valid URL using the HTTP or FTP protocol. (The `wget-ssl` program supports HTTPS as well.) For example, both of the following are valid command lines:

  ```
  wget http://www.matisse.net/files/
  → glossary.html
  ```

  ```
  wget ftp://ftp.gnu.org/gnu/hello/
  → hello-2.1.1.tar.gz
  ```

  Either of those command lines saves the requested file in the current directory on your machine. The file will have the same name as the remote version (glossary.html or hello-2.1.1.tar.gz in the examples above). **Figure 10.12** shows an example of retrieving an HTML page using `wget`.

✔ Tip

- Be very careful using the `--recursive` option (see Table 10.3), because you can end up downloading hundreds of files.

```
localhost:~ vanilla$ wget http://www.matisse.net/files/glossary.html
-15:47:20-  http://www.matisse.net/files/glossary.html
       => `glossary.html'
Resolving www.matisse.net... done.
Connecting to www.matisse.net[66.47.69.194]:80... connected.
HTTP request sent, awaiting response... 200 OK
Length: 77,217 [text/html]

100%[=================================================>] 77,217        9.20M/s       ETA 00:00

15:47:20 (9.20 MB/s) - `glossary.html' saved [77217/77217]
localhost:~ vanilla$
```

Figure 10.12 Using wget to download an HTML page.

Synchronizing directories using rsync

The rsync command is used to make a directory on one machine identical to a directory on another machine. A very sweet feature of rsync is that it is fast—it sends only the differences between the directories across the network. So if you have already synchronized a directory and a few of the files have changed by the time you run rsync again on that directory, then only the new portions of the changed files get sent across the network. You can read about the algorithm used by rsync at http://rsync.samba.org.

As with scp, if both the local and remote machines are running Mac OS X 10.4 or later, you may use the -E option to rsync to preserve extended attributes such as ACLs.

Furthermore, rsync can use SSH to connect between machines, so the entire process uses an encrypted connection.

When you use rsync to synchronize directories, you give it a source directory and a destination directory. rsync compares the source and destination directories file by file and sends the files required to make sure the destination has all the files that are in the source directory. The following task refers to **Figure 10.13**.

```
localhost:~/Sites vanilla$ rsync -e ssh -avz images puffball@somewhere.us:webdocs
puffball@somewhere.us password:
building file list ... done
images/
images/apache_pb.gif
images/macosxlogo.gif
images/web_share.gif

sent 8406 bytes  received 68 bytes  1540.73 bytes/sec
total size is 8853  speedup is 1.04
localhost:~/Sites vanilla$
```

Figure 10.13 Using rsync with a local directory as the source directory.

To synchronize using a local directory as the source:

1. `rsync -e ssh -avz` *`source_dir user@ host`*`:`*`remote_dir`*

   For example,

   ```
   rsync -e ssh -avz images
   → puffball@somewhere.us:webdocs
   ```

   The `-e ssh` option tells `rsync` to use `ssh` to make an *encrypted* connection as user puffball to `somewhere.us`. The specification for the destination directory uses the same format as `scp` (described earlier in this chapter). (Note: Don't confuse the `-e` option with the `-E` option, which is for synchronizing between two machines both running Mac OS X 10.4 or later. See `man rysnc`.)

   You are prompted for a password just as with `ssh` (because you are in fact using `ssh`).

2. Enter your password.

   Your password is not displayed.

   Table 10.4 explains the `-a`, `-v`, and `-z` options, and a few others.

   The source directory will be the directory called `images`. It is important that you understand the difference between

   `images`

   and

   `images/`

   Adding the / means "the contents of the `images` directory," while `images` *without* the / means "the `images` directory itself." Usually you will *not* put the / at the end of the source directory.

Table 10.4

Some Options for rsync

As always, see the `man` page for the complete list.

Option	Use/Meaning
`-a`	Archive mode. This recursively copies subdirectories and will preserve permissions and file-modification times. Actually a shortcut for all seven of the following options: `rlptgoD`. See `man rysnc` for the meanings of all seven options.
`-v`	Verbose mode. `rsync` gives more information during transfer.
`-z`	Uses compression. Makes transfer of most files faster.
`-e ssh`	Uses SSH to make an encrypted connection.
`-n`	Stands for *not really*. `rsync` shows you what it would do but does not actually transfer anything. Very useful for testing with the `-delete` option (below).
`-delete`	Deletes files on the destination side that do not exist on the source side. Be very careful with this one. Try it with the `-n` option first to see what would be deleted.
`-u`	Updates. Skips files that already exist on the destination side and have a date later than the source side. Only files on the source side that are newer than the destination side are sent.
`-r`	Recursive mode. Copies everything inside the source directory.
`-l`	Copies symbolic links as symbolic links (instead of the files they point to).
`-p`	Preserves permissions.
`-t`	Preserves modification times.
`-E`	Preserves extended attributes, including ACLs and Mac OS 9 resource forks. Both machines must be running Mac OS X 10.4 or later.

See `man rsync` for the complete list.

rsync will use ssh to connect to the host somewhere.us as the user puffball.

The destination directory is the webdocs directory inside puffball's home directory. rsync will copy the source directory into the destination directory.

Figure 10.14 takes the example from Figure 10.13 further. If you were to add a file to the local images directory (for example, adding a file called dancer.jpg) and make a change to one other file (for example, changing web_share.gif), and were to repeat the rsync command, you would get something like Figure 10.14, in which rsync sends only the changed files across the network.

```
[localhost:~/Sites] vanilla% rsync -e ssh -avz images puffball@somewhere.us:webdocs
puffball@somewhere.us password:
building file list ... done
images/
images/dancer.jpg
images/web_share.gif

sent 75475 bytes received 88 bytes  13738.73 bytes/sec
total size is 81380   speedup is 1.08
localhost:~/Sites vanilla$
```

Figure 10.14 Re-synchronizing a directory with rsync. Note that only two files are updated.

The process of synchronizing works both ways—you can use a remote directory as the source.

To synchronize using a remote directory as the source:

1. sync -e ssh -avz *user@host:remote_dir* → *destination*

   You are prompted for a password.

2. Enter your password.

   The positions of the source and destination directories are simply reversed.

   For example,

   ```
   rsync -e ssh -avz puffball@
   → somewhere.us:webdocs/images Sites
   ```

   That source directory is the `webdocs/images` directory inside puffball's home directory on the host somewhere.us, and the destination directory is the `Sites` directory in your current directory.

   Figure 10.15 shows what this looks like at the command line.

   So the result transfers to `Sites/images` the same files as those in the remote `webdocs/images` directory.

✔ Tip

- You can safely experiment with `rsync` by using the `-n` (*not really*) option. `rsync` will show you what it would have done, but will not actually transfer, delete, or overwrite any files.

```
localhost:~ vanilla$ rsync -e ssh -avz puffball@somewhere.us:webdocs/images Sites
puffball@somewhere.us password:
receiving file list ... done
images/
images/flower.gif
wrote 32 bytes         read 3077 bytes       6218.00 bytes/sec
total size is 97294    speedup is 31.29
localhost:~ vanilla$
```

Figure 10.15 Using rsync with a remote directory as the source directory.

Using Lynx—a text-based Web browser

Why use a text-based Web browser, you ask? Well, it is faster than a GUI Web browser (no pictures!), and it provides a convenient way to view and download files from other machines while staying at the command line.

The Lynx Web browser handles HTTP, FTP, gopher, and other protocols. Lynx does not come with Mac OS X but is easily installed using the Fink program as described in Chapter 13.

Lynx is a full-screen command-line program, which means that, like the `vi` editor, it takes over the whole Terminal window.

To start Lynx:

- `lynx` *URL*

  For example:

  `lynx http://www.opendarwin.org/`

  Figure 10.16 is a screen shot showing the Lynx display of www.opendarwin.org.

To navigate in Lynx:

1. Use the down arrow key to select the next link.
2. Use the up arrow key to select the previous link.
3. Press Return to follow the currently selected link.
4. Use the left arrow key to go back to a previous page (as with the back button in a GUI Web browser).

continues on next page

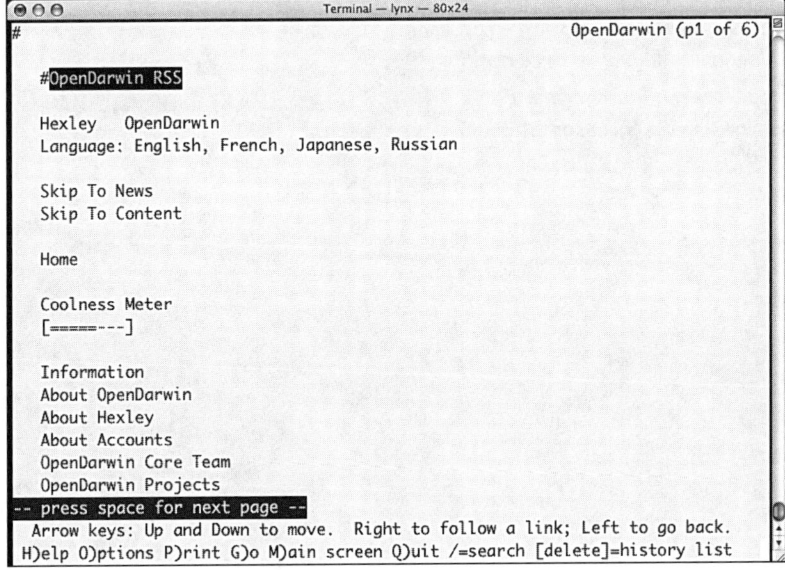

Figure 10.16 Browsing the opendarwin.org Web site with `lynx`.

5. Use the right arrow key to go forward after having used the left arrow key to go back to a previous page (as with the forward button in a GUI Web browser).

6. Press [Spacebar] to scroll down in the current page.

7. Press [-] (the hyphen key) to scroll back in the current page.

8. Press [H] to get the Lynx help screen.
   Remember that you can use the left arrow key to go back to previously viewed pages.

9. Press [Q] to quit Lynx.

To use lynx to fetch a URL and save the result to a file:

- `lynx -dump` *`url`* `>` *`file`*

  For example,

  ```
  lynx -dump http://www.matisse.
  → net/files/glossary.html > glossary
  ```

  fetches the file glossary.html and saves it as glossary. The cool thing about the `-dump` option is that the HTML file is processed by `lynx`, so the resulting file can be read by humans. If you want to preserve the raw HTML codes, add the `-source` option:

  ```
  lynx -dump -source http://www.
  → matisse.net/files/glossary.html >
  → glossary
  ```

  For comparison, you would get the same result from `wget` with

  ```
  wget http://www.matisse.net/files/
  → glossary.html
  ```

  You can also download non-HTML files using `lynx`:

  ```
  lynx -dump ftp://ftp.gnu.org/gnu/
  → hello/hello-2.1.1.tar.gz > hello.
  → tar.gz
  ```

  fetches the file hello-2.1.1.tar.gz and saves it as hello.tar.gz.

  The same result could be obtained with `wget` (if installed):

  ```
  wget ftp://ftp.gnu.org/gnu/hello/
  → hello-2.1.1.tar.gz
  ```

Advanced Interactions

As you probably have guessed, this chapter has covered only the most common ways of interacting with other machines over networks.

As you become more proficient using Unix, you may wish to tackle more-advanced forms of interaction with other machines—for example, creating scripts to perform unattended copying of files, or setting up virtual private networks.

In this section we'll give you some pointers about where you can find information to take you further along the Unix path.

Automated (unattended) file transfers

To perform unattended file transfers, you need to learn about creating scripts (review Chapter 9, "Creating and Using Scripts") and to become familiar with one or more of the file cross-network copying tools, such as `scp` and `rsync`. Because you are likely to do your file transfer using an encrypted connection, you will also want to learn more about SSH.

Here are some resources to use in building up your knowledge and skills:

- Chapter 9.
- For more on scripts, try these two books:
  Learning the bash Shell, Second Edition, by Cameron Newham and Bill Rosenblatt (O'Reilly; www.oreilly.com/catalog/bash2)
  and
  Using csh & tcsh, by Paul DuBois (O'Reilly; www.oreilly.com/catalog/tcsh).
- The `man` pages for `rsync`, `scp`, `sftp`, `ssh`, and `curl` (`curl` is especially designed for use in scripts).
- To learn more about SSH and `ssh`, we recommend OpenSSH (www.openssh.org), which has the addresses of e-mail discussion lists (www.openssh.org/list.html). Start by subscribing to the general list, and read it for a while before asking questions.

Virtual private networks

If you have a private network you wish to connect to another private network (perhaps you have a company with offices in two or more cities), you can lease private lines connecting the offices to create one larger network (or *internetwork*). You can also connect the separate private networks through the public Internet using encrypted connections, creating a virtual private network (VPN).

Here are some resources to use in learning more about VPNs and how to set them up:

- `vpnd`—The Virtual Private Network Daemon (http://sunsite.dk/vpnd).
- Internet Connect (located in the Applications folder) allows you to connect to a VPN.

Sharing disks with other Unix machines

The Network File System (NFS) protocol is the Unix way of doing what the Apple File Protocol (AFP) does in the traditional Macintosh world—it allows machines to mount disks on other machines over networks.

The Webmin system, which we'll describe in Chapter 11, "Introduction to System Administration," may be used to configure NFS. You can find a shareware GUI tool designed to configure NFS on Mac OS X at MBS's NFS Manager page (www.bresink.de/osx/NFSManager.html).

11 Introduction to System Administration

System administration is the job of keeping a system up and running, and providing a suitable environment for whatever work the system is doing—whether it's serving Web pages, being used for software development, or acting as a workgroup file server.

As we've mentioned, Max OS X comes in two versions, the version that we cover in this book (Mac OS X Tiger) and another version called Mac OS X Server Tiger. The two versions are almost identical but do have some differences. For example, Access Control Lists (ACLs) are turned on by default in Mac OS X Server. Mac OS X Server also comes with an iChat server, a Weblog server, and Xgrid (which enables turning a group of Macs into a supercomputer). If you are working on Mac OS X Server, everything in this chapter will work for you, but you'll need to learn about some additional tools.

Most Mac OS X users are working on single-user desktop machines, but some of you are stepping out into the strange new world of running a multiuser system. Perhaps you're giving friends accounts on your machine so that they can `ssh` in and edit Web pages, or running a mail server with accounts for dozens of colleagues. If so, you are starting to be concerned about backing up your users' data (at least you should be concerned about it!), managing users' accounts and permissions on the system, and troubleshooting problems for other people. You have now fallen into what may seem like the rabbit hole of system administration, where everything appears strange. This chapter will help you transcend that complexity and become the author of your own Wonderland, where in our world—the Unix world—you will be known as a *sysadmin*.

In this chapter we will give you a whirlwind tour of the basic elements of system administration. We're sure the information here will provide a good basis for learning even more as your skills and interest grow. Please note that *most of the tasks in this chapter assume that you are logged in as an admin user.* Admin users are specific to Mac OS X and are accounts that have been set to "allow user to administer this computer" when the account was created (see "Adding and deleting users with System Preferences," later in this chapter). Mac OS X admin users have a very powerful capacity—a capacity known in the wider Unix world as "having root." That is, they have the ability to execute any command on the system with the privileges of the all-powerful root account. The first thing a system administrator needs to learn about is the power of root.

✔ Tip

- For an overview of Mac OS X Server Tiger that describes many of the server-only features, see http://images.apple.com/server/pdfs/Mac_OS_X_Server_TO_v10.4.pdf and www.afp548.com/article.php?story=2005041722220621. For Apple's official Server documentation, see www.apple.com/server/documentation. And for more on the command-line administration tools in particular, see http://images.apple.com/server/pdfs/Command_Line_v10.4.pdf.

About root

The traditional Unix approach to system administration makes heavy use of one highly privileged account: root. Every Unix system has exactly one root account.

The root account is not limited by the permissions or ownership settings of any file on the system, so root can edit, delete, rename, move, and otherwise mess with every file on the system. Most basic system processes run as the root user so that they can access any part of the disk and so that other users cannot interfere with them.

Protection of the root password is critical to system security. The root account is all-powerful. There is no way to stop the root account from altering anything on the system.

To maintain the highest level of system security, access to root must be limited to the smallest possible number of people, and the power of root should be used only when strictly necessary.

The root account is often referred to as the *superuser,* and Unix veterans have been known to refer to all non-root accounts as "mere mortals." Determining whether the seemingly all-powerful root is God or the Devil, and how they differ, is left as a theological exercise for the reader.

Because many directories and files that contain system software and configuration settings can be changed only by the root user, most system-administration tasks must be performed by the root account.

On most Unix systems, an administrator uses the root account in one of two ways:

- By logging in as the root user. This method is often disabled, however, in which case the next method is required.

- By logging in as a "regular" user and then switching to the root account with the `su` command. (`su` stands for *substitute user identity* and is described later in this chapter.)

Many systems do not allow the root account to log in directly; those systems require that an administrator use the second method. That way only someone who knows the password to a regular account as well as the root password is able to run commands as root.

The Mac OS X/Darwin approach to root

Mac OS X is designed to reduce to an absolute minimum the situations in which users execute commands as root, while still giving users full control over their machines and allowing them to perform any needed system-administration tasks.

As long as you stick to the Aqua GUI, you never come across "root." Instead, a part of the operating system called the Authentication Manager occasionally prompts you to enter the name and password of an admin user before completing a task that requires root access, such as installing software.

But if you use the command line, the situation is different. Unlike Mac OS X, command-line programs that require root privileges almost never prompt you for a password—they simply fail if they are not executed by root. So at the command line you must know in advance that what you are about to do requires root, and take some action to "become root" before executing certain commands, such as changing a user's password or installing software.

sudo—the Mac OS X way of using root

Mac OS X ships with the root account disabled, and unless you enable it (see "To run any command line as root," below), you can neither log in as root nor use the `su` command to assume the root identity. Instead, Mac OS X uses the `sudo` command (think of "substitute user do...") to provide root access at the command line.

Every time someone uses `sudo`, a record of what that user did is added to the system log file, `/var/log/system.log`.

The `sudo` command itself is not unique to Mac OS X—it is used on many Unix systems. But in Mac OS X, it is normally the *only* way to use root from the command line. In this system, no one has the root password, but instead anyone who is an admin user is a member of the "admin" group, and anyone in group admin is explicitly allowed to use `sudo` to execute any command as root. (Review Chapter 8, "Working with Permissions and Ownership," to learn about groups.)

The `sudo` command allows specific users or groups of users to execute specific commands with the power of root. The `sudo` command has a configuration file (see `man sudoers`) that lists who can perform which commands as root.

The idea behind `sudo` is that a trusted user or group of users can be given the ability to run specific commands, such as restarting a Web server if it crashes.

In Mac OS X, `sudo` is configured so that any user in group admin can execute *any* command with the power of root. The first account you created (perhaps it is the only account you created) on your Mac OS X system is always in group admin. If you are using

continues on next page

a Mac OS X system set up by someone else, then your account may not be in group admin. In order to perform the tasks in this chapter, you need to ask whoever administers your system (that would be the system administrator!) to allow you to be an admin user.

Only admin users are supposed to perform system-administration tasks on Mac OS X.

The most common way you use the `sudo` command is to run a command line as root.

Problems with the Mac OS X Approach to root

The way Mac OS X allows root access is fine if your Mac OS X machine is being used only by you and perhaps a couple of trusted family members and friends, and if it's not on a publicly accessible network.

On the other hand, if your machine is used by many people, especially by people you don't know, or if it's connected to the Internet on a full-time basis, then Apple's approach to root access could be considered problematic.

On most modern Unix systems, in order for users to operate as root, they have to have two passwords: their own (that is, the one they log in with) and the root password (the one they can use only after having logged in as themselves).

The Mac OS X approach requires only that a user be in group "admin" and know his or her own password to gain root privileges. As long as that user is an admin user, his or her account can perform any command as root without the user's having to know any other password.

Compounding the problem (only needing one password instead of two) was the fact that prior to Mac OS X 10.3, the default configuration of Mac OS X left weakly encrypted passwords available to non-root users, and so the `nidump` command could be used by any user to reveal the encrypted passwords of all users. The encryption used was fairly weak, and poor passwords (those based on words or that use simple patterns) can be cracked in a matter of days or hours on modern machines. Starting with Mac OS X 10.3, the default changed so that the encrypted passwords are not available to non-root users, but accounts created before 10.3 and not changed since then will still have the encrypted passwords available to non-root users.

The Mac OS X approach is easier on the user—there's only one password to remember, and for people using their Mac OS X machine as an isolated desktop machine, this is probably fine. However, if the computer is a true multiuser machine in a networked environment—used the way Unix was intended—the wisdom of this approach is debatable.

One measure you should take is to ensure that the password for any admin user is a good one (see the sidebar "Choosing a Safer Password").

Perhaps in future versions of Mac OS X, admin users will be divided into groups with different levels of access to root, but at present (version 10.4), any admin user is essentially equivalent to root.

To run any command line as root:

1. sudo *commandline*

   commandline can be any command line. For example,

   sudo du -sk /Users/*

   runs the du command (for *disk usage*) and shows a summary (-s) of how much disk space is being used (in kilobytes because of the k option) by each directory in the /Users directory, effectively showing every user's disk usage. You could not do this without being root, because many of the files in each user's directory are not readable by other regular users. When the command is run by the root user, it can read the size of every file and produce a complete report (**Figure 11.1**).

   As you can see, the first time you use sudo, unusual messages appear. You receive a little lecture on the use of root, and then sudo prompts you for your password.

2. Enter your password.

   If this is the first time you have used sudo, then sudo creates a directory named after your user name in /var/run/sudo/ (for example, /var/run/sudo/vanilla).

   Each time you use sudo, it checks the modification time on that directory. If the modification time is more than five minutes old, you are prompted for your password again to make sure that you haven't walked away from your keyboard, allowing someone else to try to use sudo.

   Your password is not displayed as you type it. Once sudo accepts your password, it executes the command line you gave it and updates the modification time on your directory in /var/run/sudo.

✔ Tips

- You can force sudo to ask for a password (overriding the 5-minute time period) with

  sudo -k

continues on next page

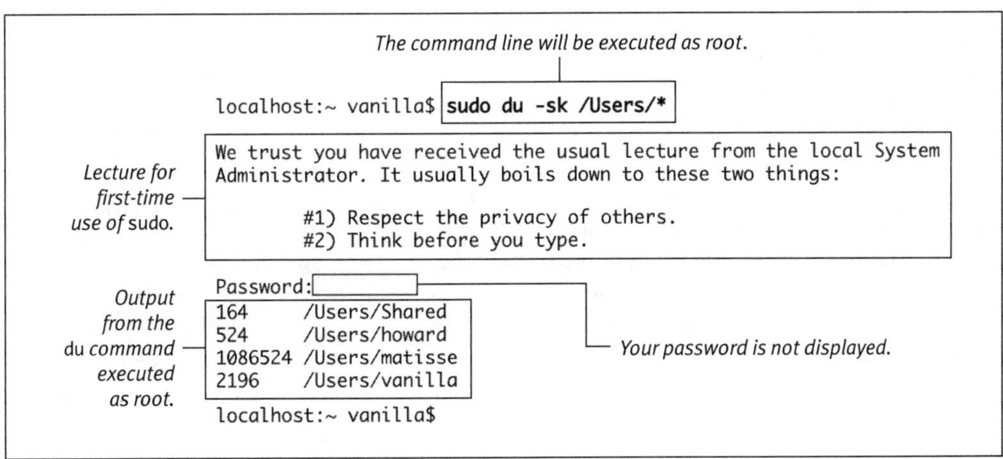

Figure 11.1 Using the sudo command to execute a command line as root.

- The 5-minute grace period can be modified with the visudo command. See **Table 11.1** for a summary of the options for sudo.
- sudo will not work on command lines that use shell built-in commands, such as the cd command. That's because shell built-in commands are not separate programs. See man builtin for a list of shell built-in commands.
- The sudo command has an entire Web site devoted to it: Sudo Main Page (www.sudo.ws). There you can learn the whole story of how it can be used, find security alerts, peruse a troubleshooting FAQ list, and more. For much more on sudo than we can discuss in this book, check out *Mac OS X Server 10.4 Tiger: Visual QuickPro Guide*, by Schoun Regan and Kevin White (Peachpit Press; www.peachpit.com), which also covers configuring sudo.

To start an entire shell as root:

- sudo -s

  After entering your password, you get a different shell prompt (ending with root#) and every command line you run will be executed as root. Exit the root shell with Control D.

Other ways of becoming root

Although using sudo will probably handle all the things you need to do as root from the command line, this wouldn't be Unix if there weren't other ways to do it. Besides, you may come across a situation in which using sudo doesn't achieve what you need. So here are a couple of more ways to become root. We're not including these so much for you to use them as for you to know what is possible.

The default configuration for Mac OS X has the root account disabled—you cannot use the su command to assume the root account's identity, nor can you log in to Aqua as root, nor can you log in to the machine over the Internet as root (using ssh, for example; see Chapter 10, "Connecting over the Internet"). Once you enable the root account, you can do all of these.

Although experienced Unix users will mistakenly think they *must* enable the root account, it is very unlikely that you will need to log in as root using the Aqua interface, nor should you allow people to log in as root over a network. In fact, we don't even recommend it! Still, if you must know, refer to man dsenableroot for more on enabling the root account.

Table 11.1

Common Options for sudo

Remember to see the man page for the complete list.

Option	Meaning/Use
-l	Lists the allowed and forbidden commands for the current user. This is a good way of seeing what you can (and can't) do with sudo.
-k	Kills the 5-minute grace period. sudo requires a password on the next use, no matter how soon it is.
-K	Removes the time-stamp directory entirely. Next time you use sudo, you get the lecture again.
-u *user*	Runs the command line as user instead of as root.
-s	Gives you a root shell. Very dangerous. *Every* command you enter until you exit the new shell is run as root. Uses the shell in the SHELL environment variable if it is set; otherwise, uses the user's default shell.
-H	Sets the HOME environment variable to the home directory of the user whose identity sudo takes on (default is root). Normally sudo does not change the HOME variable.

Compare with Aqua: Becoming root

In its graphical interface, Mac OS X uses an approach very much like the one used with `sudo`. Whenever you use Aqua to attempt a change that requires root access (for example, installing system software using the Software Update command), the GUI prompts you for an administrator name and password.

There is a big difference between the GUI and the command line in this case, however: The GUI "knows" when something must be done by root and prompts you, and it does not provide a way to run arbitrary programs as root. The command line, on the other hand, leaves it all up to you—if you try to perform an action with insufficient privileges, you get an error, and by using `sudo` you can run any command as root. This is very much in the Unix spirit of not trying (or bothering) to protect you from yourself. Unix expects you to avoid doing foolish things because you know you haven't learned how yet, not because it prevents you from trying.

How sudo Makes Command Names Case Insensitive

When you execute a command using `sudo`, the command name is not case sensitive. So,

```
sudo DATE
```

and

```
sudo date
```

do the same thing. This has to do with a combination of how `sudo` looks up command names and the peculiarities of the Mac file system.

As we discussed in Chapter 5, "Using Files and Directories," the standard Mac file system is a "case-preserving, case-insensitive" file system. In some cases in Mac OS X, then, you can ignore case when specifying file and command names. But do not rely upon it. The default shell `bash` (and the Bourne shell on which it is based) does not care about case in the way it looks up commands and filenames, while the `tcsh` shell uses a case-sensitive method. The `sudo` command itself uses a case-insensitive lookup. An example of how this can get tricky is that if you are using `tcsh`, then

```
sudo DATE
```

works, because it is the `sudo` command that is looking up `DATE`, but

```
SUDO date
```

does not, because the `tcsh` shell won't find the `SUDO` command.

Becoming Another User

As we mentioned above, on most Unix systems, a system administrator uses the root account by invoking the su command to *substitute* the root account's identity for his or her own.

If you have enabled the root account on Mac OS X, then users may use the su command to assume the root account's identity.

The su command allows you to temporarily assume the identity of another user on the system. Therefore, users can log in to the system as themselves, "su to root," perform whatever tasks need to be done as root, and then exit from the su session and reassume their own identities.

You can also use the su command to switch to users other than root, which is useful if you want to test a configuration for another user, or run a particular command as another user without bothering to actually log in as that user. Refer to **Figure 11.2** through the following task.

To switch to another user:

1. `su -l` *`user name`*

   The `-l` option (in some versions of su it's abbreviated as simply a hyphen: -) tells su that the new shell should be a *login* shell. The current directory for the new shell is the home directory of the target user.

   User name is the target user; that is, the user you want to switch to. If you omit *`user name`*, then the target user is root.

   For example, to assume the identity of user puffball:

   `su -l puffball`

   To assume the identity of root:

   `su -l`

   You are then prompted for the user's password.

2. Enter the user's password.

   su starts a new shell as the target user. If you used the `-l` option, then the new shell is a login shell that causes the target user's personal configuration files (`.bash_profile`, and so on) to be read. (Review Chapter 7, "Configuring Your Environment with Unix.")

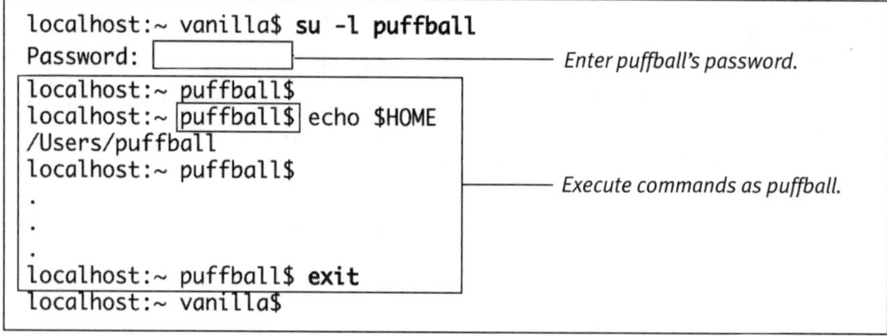

localhost:~ vanilla$ su -l puffball
Password:
Enter puffball's password.
localhost:~ puffball$
localhost:~ puffball$ echo $HOME
/Users/puffball
localhost:~ puffball$
Execute commands as puffball.
localhost:~ puffball$ exit
localhost:~ vanilla$

Figure 11.2 Using su to assume the identity of another user.

If you omitted the `-l` option—for example,

```
su puffball
```

or

```
su
```

—then only the environment variables `USER`, `HOME`, and `SHELL` are set to the values appropriate for the target user, unless the target user is root, in which case the `USER` variable is left unchanged. All other environment variables for the new shell are inherited from your environment.

3. Run commands as the target user.

   Every command you run in the new shell is executed with the permission of the target user.

4. If you used `su` to become root with

   ```
   su -l
   ```

   then when you have finished performing tasks as the target user, exit the shell to go back to being yourself, at your own shell prompt:

   ```
   exit
   ```

✔ Tips

- Once you have a root shell, you can `su` to another user *without* having his or her password.
- You can specify which shell you want `su` to start up for the target user by giving it as an additional argument. For example:

  ```
  su puffball /bin/sh
  ```

- Once again, be aware of the power of root. From the `su man` page: "By default (unless the prompt is reset by a startup file) the super-user prompt is set to '#' to remind one of its awesome power."

Using the System in Single-User Mode

If you want to use the system in this state, you run the command lines

```
/sbin/fsck -fy /
/sbin/mount -uw /
sh /etc/rc
```

These will mount the system disk in read/write mode and run a series of scripts that eventually bring up the familiar Mac OS X graphical interface. However, at the time that this book was being written, this method would not work in Mac OS X 10.4.2. In fact, your machine would hang after the last command line in that sequence. We expect that Apple will soon solve the problem.

Note that Apple intends to phase out the use of the `/etc/rc` script. To learn more about the Mac OS X boot sequence, see the Mac OS X Developer Documentation at http://developer.apple.com/documentation/MacOSX/Conceptual/BPSystemStartup/Articles/BootProcess.html.

Keeping Backups

Keeping a good set of backup files is one of the primary responsibilities of a system administrator. Even if you're the only person on the system, you still want to have backups!

An ideal backup system

- Makes copies that are easy to recover.
- Preserves all file attributes, including ownership, permissions, and creation/modification date.
- Only backs up files that have changed since a particular prior backup. This is called an *incremental* backup.

There are a number of venerable Unix tools for creating backups that are all designed to preserve the ownership, permissions, and modification dates of files when used by root, and are commonly used in scripts that automate the backup process. The most common of these tools are the `tar` (*tape archive*) command and the `dump` and `restore` commands. The `dump` command is designed to make backups and includes the ability to make incremental backups. Another frequently overlooked tool is `pax`—so named because it can handle files created by `tar` and another program, `cpio`, allowing them to peacefully coexist. One valuable feature of `pax`: It allows you to specify files to copy based on their modification date. See `man pax` for details.

Unfortunately, `dump` and `restore` do not work at all on the Mac OS X standard HFS Plus file-system format. And neither `tar` nor `pax` properly handles so-called complex files created by older Mac applications. These files have multiple *data streams* or *forks*. (Review the sidebar "Old Mac Files in the Unix World" in Chapter 5.)

As of this writing (summer 2005), Apple had no plans to create new versions of the standard Unix backup tools that handle HFS Plus file systems or complex files. Starting with version 10.4 of Mac OS X, the `cp` command does properly handle these complex files.

For an excellent technical discussion of the issues, see "The Challenges of Integrating the Unix and Mac OS Environments" (www.wsanchez.net/papers/USENIX_2000/).

So, you cannot use the standard Unix tools to perform standard "full" and "incremental" backups on Mac OS X. You may use the `cp` command with the `-p` option to preserve the files' permissions, modification time, and so forth, but even then the related information in the metadata store and content index do not get backed up.

Doing full and incremental backups from the command line

The bad news is that as of Mac OS X 10.4, the standard Mac OS X installation provides no simple way to perform an incremental backup of your entire system from the command line. The good news is that thanks to the open nature of Darwin and the work of people outside Apple, there are tools you can install that will perform incremental backups. See the sidebar "Darwin Backup Tools for HFS Plus."

Mac OS X does come with a command-line tool called `ditto` that you can use to make almost full backups of your system, and to safely back up any subset of your files—for example, the `/Users` directory. Incremental backups, though, are something `ditto` won't do.

The `ditto` command backs up entire directories, preserving (in most cases) all the file attributes, such as permission, ownership, and dates, and handles complex files.

Using ditto

The `ditto` command comes with Mac OS X and properly handles both standard Unix files and older complex files.

From the `ditto man` page: "Ditto copies one or more source directories to a destination directory. If the destination directory does not exist it will be created before the first source directory is copied."

The `ditto` command preserves the ownership, permissions ("mode"), and modification times of all the files it copies, but will not alter the ownership, mode, or times on any directories that already exist in the destination. Thus, if you change the permissions (or ownership) of a directory you have already copied with `ditto`, and then copy it again to the same destination, the copy will not pick up the new ownership or mode. That is an important limitation—the only way around it would be to use `ditto` only to copy to empty destination directories.

In the following tasks we assume you have an additional disk for backups, perhaps an external FireWire disk. All disks and volumes besides the boot volume are mounted as subdirectories of `/Volumes`, so if you had an external FireWire hard drive named "big disk," for example, it would show up in the file system as `/Volumes/big_disk` (review Figure 5.1 for a schematic diagram of a typical Mac OS X file system).

There are subtle differences in how you use `ditto` when copying directories as opposed to copying individual files. We'll show you directories first.

Darwin Backup Tools for HFS Plus

We are aware of several projects under way to create HFS Plus–compatible command-line tools for performing backups and other file-copying operations.

One such project is `psync`. The `psync` utility is a Perl script created by Dan Kogai that will perform incremental backups and restores on an HFS Plus files ystem. You can obtain `psync` from http://www.dan.co.jp/cases/macosx/psync.html. You may want to refer to Chapter 13, "Installing Software from Source Code." There is also a project called PsyncX that provides a graphical interface (that is, an Aqua interface) to `psync`. PsyncX is available from (http://sourceforge.net/projects/psyncx).

Another project is `hfstar`, a version of the `tar` command that works properly with the HFS Plus file system and with older Mac files. We have tested `hfstar` successfully but not extensively. `hfstar` can be obtained from metaobject (www.metaobject.com/Products.html).

Two other HFS-compatible tools are `hfspax` and `rsyncx`. `hfspax` is intended to replace the `pax` program that comes with Mac OS X. You can get `hfspax` from its creator, Howard Oakley (http://homepage.mac.com/howardoakley). The `rsyncx` utility is available from MacEnterprise.org (www.macosxlabs.org/rsyncx/rsyncx.html).

To back up a directory with ditto:

- `sudo ditto -rsrc` *`source destination`*

  The `-rsrc` option (it is one option, not four) tells `ditto` to preserve the extra data in old-style complex files. This option is the default behavior, but it can be overridden by setting the environment variable `DITTONORSRC`. Using the `-rsrc` option ensures that its behavior will be invoked.

- Enter your password if `sudo` prompts you for it.

  In this task we assume that *`source`* is a directory. You can specify more than one source. The *`destination`* must be a directory, not a file.

  `ditto` will copy the contents of the *`source`* directory (or directories) into the *`destination`* directory.

  For example, to back up all your users' home directories to an external disk mounted on `/Volumes/big_disk`:

  ```
  ditto -rsrc /Users /Volumes/big_disk/
  → backups/Users
  ```

  That command line will copy the contents of `/Users` into `/Volumes/big_disk/backups/Users`.

  It is very important to note that `ditto` will not copy the source directory itself, just its contents. So in the example above, `ditto` does not copy the `/Users` directory, but instead copies everything *inside* `/Users` into

  `/Volumes/big_disk/backups/Users`

✔ Tip

- Use the `-v` option to `ditto` to have it print out the name of every source directory, or use the `-V` option to see the name of every file it copies.

Backups are only good if you can use them to recover files. When you are recovering files from backups (which is, essentially, copying them back), you have one of two common situations: Either you want to recover one or more specific files, or you want to recover entire directories. If you want to recover a directory, you can use `ditto` as described in the task above. If you want to recover specific files, then you need to use `ditto` in a subtly different way.

To use ditto to copy or recover individual files:

- `sudo ditto -rsrc` *`source destination`*

  If that command-line pattern looks the same as the one in the previous task, you are right, it is the same. The difference here is that if the *`source`* is a file (as opposed to a directory), then the *`destination`* may be either a file or a directory. If the *`destination`* is a directory, then the *`source`* file(s) are copied into the directory. If the *`destination`* is a file, then it is overwritten. If the *`destination`* does not exist, then it is created as a file. For example,

  ```
  sudo ditto -rsrc /Volumes/big_disk/
  → backups/Users/vanilla/Documents/
  → Contract.doc/Users/vanilla/
  → Documents/Contract_recovered.doc
  ```

  copies the file Contract.doc from the backup disk to vanilla's Documents folder and calls the copy Contract_recovered.doc.

  As with all uses of `sudo`, you may be prompted for your password if you haven't used `sudo` in the last 5 minutes. If you are prompted, enter your password.

Compare with Aqua: Making Backups

The simplest way to make backups in Aqua is to have a second disk drive—such as an external FireWire drive—and simply copy files using the Finder.

Automated backup software for Mac OS X includes the minimalist PocketBackup, from Pocket Software (www.pocketsw.com), or the industry-standard EMC Dantz Retrospect, from EMC Dantz (www.dantz.com).

PocketBackup (as of version 1.0.1) is most useful for backing up files in your own home directory. In order to use it to properly back up files for multiple users and all system files, you would have to log in to Aqua as root, which is generally a bad idea.

Compare with Aqua: Restoring from Backups

Restoring files from backup copies in Aqua can be as simple as copying them from the backup media using the Finder.

Copying files in the Finder works fine for files that are supposed to be owned by the user doing the copying, but it is not a good idea for system files or sets of files belonging to multiple users, because the ownership and permissions on the files will be wrong (the files will end up being owned by the user who performs the copy, and in some cases you won't even have permission to make another copy). In those cases, you should either use the GUI application that created the backups in the first place (such as EMC Dantz Retrospect) or use the command-line `ditto` program. One good GUI application for making backups in Mac OS X is the shareware Carbon Copy Cloner (CCC), which can make a bootable clone of your boot disk (http://www.bombich.com/software/ccc.html).

Managing User Accounts and Groups

The system administrator's job includes adding new users to the system and managing the ability of various groups to access different parts of the file system (review Chapter 8).

The easiest way to add a user in Mac OS X is with the Accounts pane in System Preferences (see the following task). This not only adds the user, but it also creates his or her home directory and several files that each user needs.

It *is* possible to add a user to your system using the command line, but the process is rather complex and is beyond the scope of this book. (If you really *must* know how, see the sidebar "Adding a User from the Command Line," later in this chapter.)

Adding and deleting users with System Preferences

The Mac OS X System Preferences is a GUI interface for many basic administrative tasks. You access System Preferences from the Apple menu or from the Dock.

To create a new user:

1. Choose System Preferences from the Apple menu or click its icon in the Dock.
   The main System Preferences window opens (**Figure 11.3**).
2. Click the Accounts icon.
   The Accounts pane opens showing the list of users on the left (**Figure 11.4**).
   All the current regular users are shown (not shown are special system accounts, including the root account).

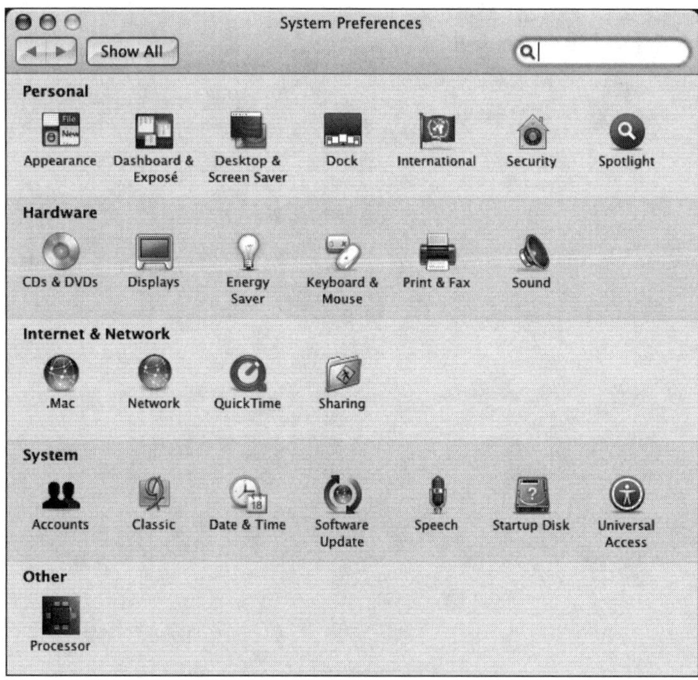

Figure 11.3 The System Preferences window.

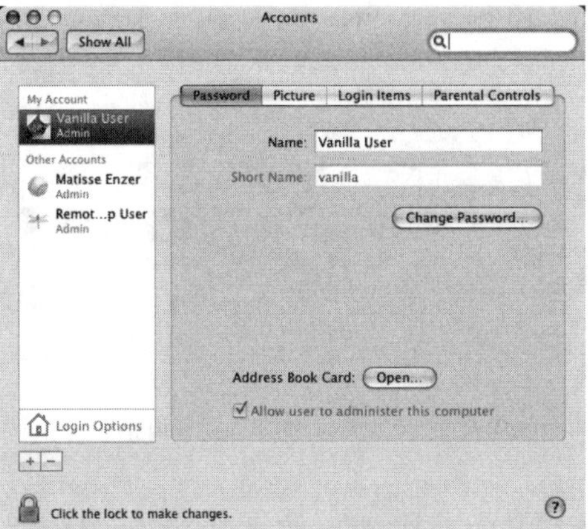

Figure 11.4 The Accounts pane of System Preferences, showing users.

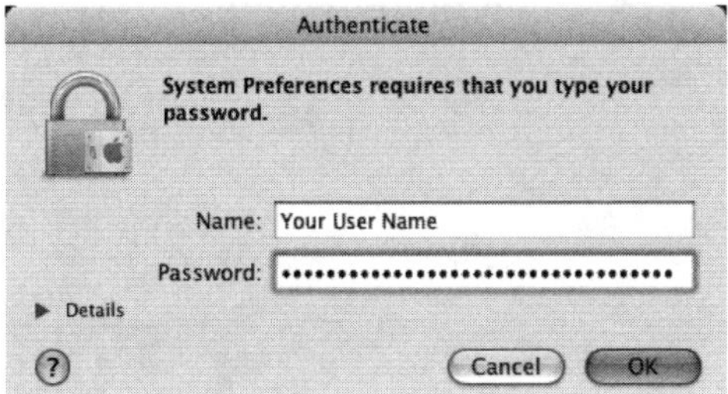

Figure 11.5 The Authenticate dialog, asking for your user name and password.

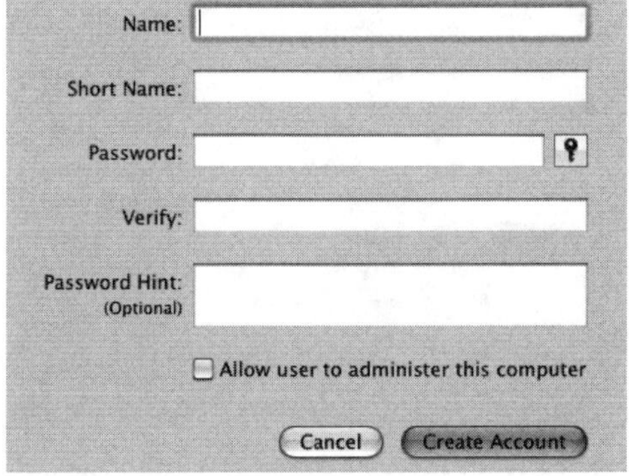

Figure 11.6 The dialog that appears when you click the plus button on the Accounts pane.

3. Click the lock icon.

   You will get a dialog asking for your user name and password (**Figure 11.5**). This is basically the Aqua version of using `sudo`—you are about to assume root privileges for this task. Fill in the dialog and click OK.

4. Back in the Accounts pane, click the plus (+) button, just above the lock icon.

   A dialog slides down with fields for the new user's information (**Figure 11.6**).

5. Fill in the Name and Short Name fields for the new user.

   The Name field is just the everyday name, typically including both first and last name. Mac OS X uses the term *short name* for what all Unix systems call the *user name* or *login name*." On many Unix systems the short name must be eight characters or less and should consist only of lowercase letters and numbers, so you may want to stick with that to be consistent with other Unix systems. But in Mac OS X since 10.2, you can use up to 255 bytes for the short user name. (Note, however, that bytes does not mean characters, because there are multibyte characters, for example, in Japanese.)

6. Fill in the user's new password.

   You type the password twice, and it is displayed as a series of bullets (so someone looking over your shoulder won't see it).

continues on next page

7. If you click the key icon next to the Password field (see Figure 11.6), you get the cool Password Assistant dialog (**Figure 11.7**), which will help you create a good password.

   You may fill in a "password hint" for the user. This will show up in the Aqua Login window if he or she fails three login attempts in a row. (The hint option must also be set in the Login Options pane of the Accounts preferences pane.)

8. If you want the new user to have root access on the machine, check the box next to "Allow user to administer this computer."

   Figure 11.8 shows an example of the new-user dialog filled in and ready to save.

9. Click Create Account.

   At this point the new user has been added to the system, and that person can log in.

   The new-user dialog slides away and the Accounts pane shows the new user's name in the list (**Figure 11.9**).

   The new user's home directory has been created, along with various subdirectories such as his or her Documents folder. Also, a configuration file for the Apache Web server is created for the new user in `/etc/httpd/users/`.

   Add more users if you like.

10. Quit System Preferences.

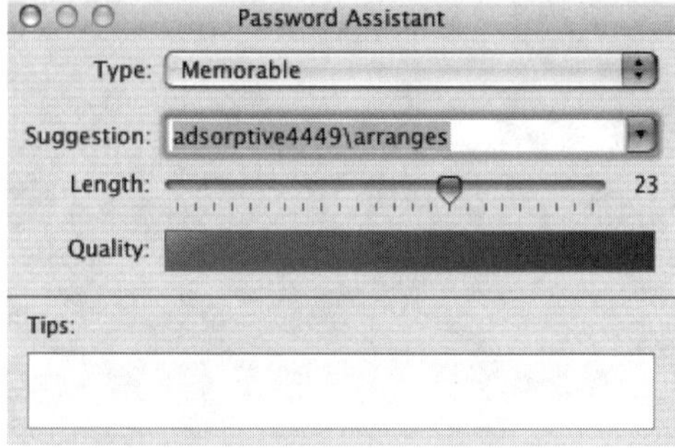

Figure 11.7 The Password Assistant dialog.

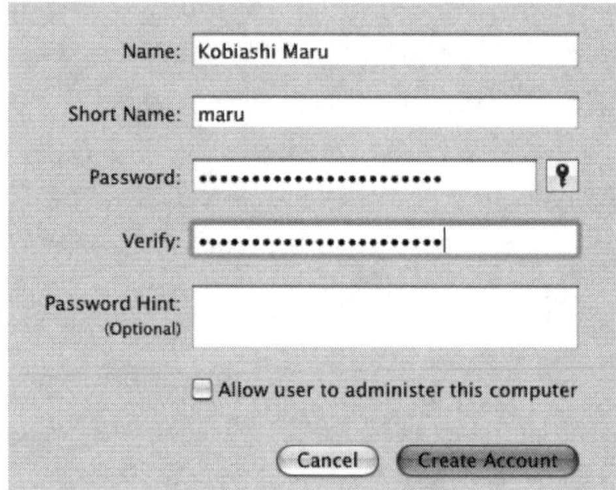

Figure 11.8 The new user dialog all filled in and ready to save.

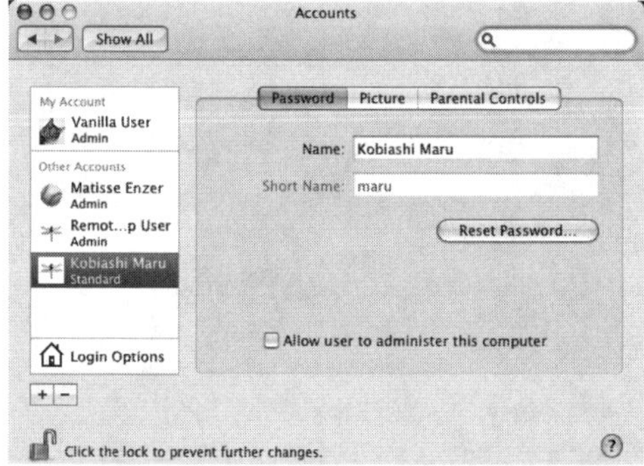

Figure 11.9 The Accounts pane, showing the new user added to the list.

✔ Tip

- Passwords are the backbone of system security. If a malicious person obtained a user's password, he or she could cause serious harm to that person's system: disabling it altogether, obtaining root privileges, or copying any information on the system. Be very careful about giving users the ability to "administer this computer," since that essentially gives them root access and the ability to take complete control of the machine.

Occasionally you'll need to remove a user, and you can use System Preferences to do that as well. It gives you a choice about whether or not to completely delete the user's home directory; the default behavior is to create a disk-image file (a .dmg file) of the user's home directory and place that file in the `/Users/Deleted Users` directory.

To remove a user:

1. Open System Preferences.
2. Click the Accounts icon.
3. Select the user from the list.
4. Click the minus (–) button at the bottom of the list of users (see Figure 11.9).

   You will get a dialog asking if you want to delete the user's home directory immediately or allow a disk image to be placed in `/Users/Deleted Users`.
5. Choose either OK or Delete Immediately.

   If you allow the disk image to be created, you can always remove it later.
6. Quit System Preferences.

continues on next page

Choosing a Safer Password

Good passwords always have a combination of letters, numbers, punctuation marks, and symbols (!@#$%^&*_+-=":;' ><,.?/\|), and never contain a dictionary word. For example, *secret23* would be a terrible password, far too easy for a computerized guessing program to figure out.

One way to make a good password is to use the first letter from each word in a song lyric or poem, and change some of the characters to numbers and punctuation. For example, the lyric "Sporting 50-dollar sneakers and all the money's spent" (from Grandmaster Flash's "All Wrapped Up") might become the password *S50$s&atm.*

In addition to the root password, all user passwords, especially those for admin users, must also be excellent in order for your system to have good security. In Mac OS X, having an admin user's password is equivalent to having the root password. (We'll go into more about choosing good passwords in Chapter 12, "Security.")

✔ Tip

- There may be files outside the user's home directory that were owned by that user. For example, if you are running a Web server, you may have allowed users to put HTML files in /Library/WebServer/Documents. You can create a list of all the files in a directory that are owned by unknown users with the -nouser option to the find command:

```
sudo find /Library/WebServer/Documents
→ -nouser > orphanlist.txt
```

You can then look at the resulting list and decide which files to delete and which to change the ownership of (so that they are owned by a user still on the system).

Adding a User from the Command Line

OK, you want to be a hot-shot Unix sysadmin. At the end of this sidebar we provide a list of things you have to do to add a user from the command line. Each of these steps has several substeps.

Before trying this, download the Apple documentation for Mac OS X Server Command-Line Administration: http://images.apple.com/server/pdfs/Command_Line_v10.4.pdf—and please, experiment on a noncritical machine.

The documentation in the PDF file mentioned above refers to some command-line tools (serversetup, dsimport, createhomedir, and so on). One of them, serversetup, is not installed in the non-Server version of Mac OS X. So unless you are working on the Server version, you will not be able to create new admin users from the command line or perform some of the tests that the documentation describes. The tools are installed in different places on the Server and non-Server versions of Mac OS X. In the non-Server version these commands are installed in /usr/bin and /usr/sbin, so they are already in your PATH. (See Chapter 7 for more about your PATH.)

Here is the basic process:

1. Create a text file containing the required information for the user(s) you are adding. The PDF file mentioned above has examples of this file.
2. Use the dsimport command to import the file. See man dsimport.
3. Use the createhomedir command to create home directories for the user(s). This will also populate the directories with the appropriate files. See man createhomedir.

Note: There is a command-line tool called dsidentity that can be used to create a limited type of user account at the command line. The dsidentity tool is intended for creating accounts that are used only for remote file sharing and similar purposes. See man dsidentity for more.

Managing passwords

Perhaps the most common task for a system administrator is to help users who have forgotten their password. While there is no easy way to find a user's current password, it can be changed easily. You can use System Preferences, but you can also do this easily from the command line. Refer to **Figure 11.10** throughout the following task.

To change a user's password:

1. `sudo passwd user name`

   The *user name* argument is the same as the short name that was entered when the user's account was created. For example,

   `sudo passwd sarafina`

   If you haven't used `sudo` in the last 5 minutes, you are prompted for *your* password, with just

   `Password:`

   After you enter your password, or if you have recently used `sudo`, you will see a prompt from the `passwd` command.

2. Enter the user's new password.
3. Reenter the new password.

   Because the passwords are not displayed, you have to enter them twice to make sure you have it right. If the entries don't match, you'll be prompted to enter them again.

✔ Tips

- Use a secure method to tell the user his or her new password—that is, in person or on a phone line you trust. *Never* send an (unencrypted) password over e-mail or leave it on a voice-mail system.

- The Mac OS X *keychain* knows when you've changed your password and will prompt you to update your keychain the next time you use it.

This command line will be executed as root.

```
localhost:~ vanilla$ sudo passwd sarafina
Password: [          ]
Changing password for sarafina.
New password: [          ]
Retype new password: [          ]
localhost:~ vanilla$
```

Your password is not displayed.

The user's new password is not displayed.

The second entry must match the first.

Figure 11.10 Changing a user's password with the passwd command.

Changing a user's login shell

Although it's not as common an activity as changing passwords, system administrators occasionally are asked (or decide) to change a user's login shell. For example, a user might want to use the tcsh shell as his or her login shell instead of the Mac OS X default (which is bash).

The command-line tool for changing a user's shell in Darwin and Mac OS X is quite different from that used in other versions of Unix (in which you would probably use either usermod or chsh). Darwin and thus Mac OS X use a different system than other flavors of Unix to store and access all the system-configuration information, such as users, groups, and mounted disks. See the sidebar "About lookupd, Open Directory, and Directory Service."

The main command-line tool for dealing with the Directory Services system is dscl (*Directory Service command line*), and that's what you'll use in the following task (**Figure 11.11**)


```
localhost:~ vanilla$ sudo dscl . -change /users/name=puffball UserShell /bin/bash /bin/tcsh
Password:
localhost:~ vanilla$ dscl . -read /users/name=puffball UserShell
UserShell: /bin/tcsh
localhost:~ vanilla$
```

Figure 11.11 Using dscl to change a user's login shell from /bin/bash to /bin/tcsh.

About lookupd, Open Directory, and Directory Service

All Unix systems need a way to store and retrieve system-configuration information about users, groups, networks, and disks. On many other Unix systems, this data is stored (primarily) in text files in the `/etc` directory. For example, `/etc/passwd` usually has all the user accounts, and `/etc/group` has the list of groups.

While Mac OS X/Darwin is able to use the traditional `/etc` files (which it calls BSD Flat Files) to manage system-configuration information, at a more fundamental level it uses a system called Open Directory, which uses the `DirectoryService` and `lookupd` daemons. Apple has rewritten the low-level software libraries (`get_pw` for you C hackers) so that they use `lookupd`. The `lookupd` daemon can use a variety of data sources, including BSD Flat Files, Apple's legacy NetInfo database (see the sidebar "Deeper into NetInfo"), an LDAP server, and more. For more on `lookupd`, see `man lookupd`. For more on Directory Services, see `man DirectoryService` and http://developer.apple.com/darwin/projects/opendirectory/.

To change a user's login shell:

1. `sudo dscl . -change /users/`*`user`*
   `→ UserShell `*`oldshell newshell`*

   For example, to change the shell for user `puffball` from `/bin/bash` to `/bin/tcsh` the command line is

   ```
   sudo dscl . -change /users/puffball
   → UserShell /bin/bash /bin/tcsh
   ```

   If `sudo` prompts you for your password, enter it.

   Now you can check that the change took place:

2. `dscl . -read /users/`*`user`*` UserShell`

   For example:

   ```
   dscl . -read /users/puffball
   ```

✔ Tips

- The `dscl` utility provides `man` tools for reading and changing system-configuration settings. See `man dscl` for the complete story.
- An interesting feature of `dscl` is that it offers an interactive shell-like interface. If you run

  ```
  sudo dscl .
  ```

  you will get a prompt (just a >) from which you can navigate around the data hierarchy using `cd` and `ls`, and issue all of the various `dscl` commands, such as `read`, `change`, `search`, and so on. Again, see `man dscl` for more. Using `dscl` in interactive mode to change a user's shell could look like this:

  ```
  localhost:~ vanilla$ sudo dscl .
  > change /users/puffball
  → UserShell /bin/bash /bin/tcsh
  > read /users/puffball
  → UserShell
  Usershell: /bin/tcsh
  > quit
  localhost:~ vanilla$
  ```

Tracking who uses the system

Every time a user logs in, entries are made in three log files. These files enable you to see who is currently using the system and a history of logins to the system.

Table 11.2 lists these files and the commands used to view them.

Using the commands listed in Table 11.2, you can see a good deal of information about who was and is using your system.

To see a list of users logged in right now:

- `users`

  The `users` command simply lists the user name of anyone who is currently logged in. The output looks like this:

  `vanilla matisse puffball`

To see a list of users and where they logged in from:

- `who`

  The `who` command shows you one line for each login shell each user is running. So if you had three Terminal windows open and another user was logged in over the Internet, `who` would show *five* entries (**Figure 11.12**).

  That's one entry for your Aqua login (the `console` entry), the three Terminal windows (the `ttyp1`, `ttyp3`, and `ttyp4` entries), and an entry for a user logged in over the Internet. The entry for the remote user shows where he or she is logged in from (the host well.com).

  `ttyp` means *teletypewriter, pseudo*. In the old days, people used electromechanical teletypewriters (TTYs) to log in to computers; now those TTYs are emulated in software, hence the *pseudo*.

  Using the `-H` option adds a line of headings to the output.

  The `-u` option adds the idle time for each entry (in hours:minutes).

  Figure 11.13 shows the output with the `-Hu` options.

Table 11.2

Files Used to Track User Logins

File	Purpose and Commands
`var/run/utmp`	Shows who is logged in right now (`tmp` stands for *temporary*). Used by the `users`, `w`, and `who` commands.
`/var/log/wtmp`	Records each login and logout. A binary file, not human-readable. Used by the `last` and `ac` commands. This file is "rolled over" every month by the script `/etc/monthly`. See "Running Regularly Scheduled Commands," later in this chapter.
`/var/log/lastlog`	Records the date and time of each user's last login. The date of the last login is displayed when logging in via a command-line interface (for example, when you open a new Terminal window).

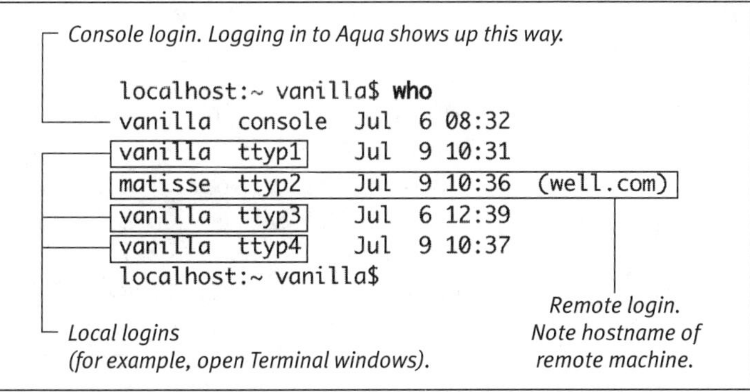

Figure 11.12 Annotated output from the who command.

```
localhost:~ vanilla$ who -Hu
NAME      LINE      TIME          IDLE    FROM
vanilla   console   Jul 9 16:55   22:32
vanilla   ttyp1     Jul 9 12:55   .       (g5-imac.matisse.)
matisse   ttyp2     Jul 9 10:36   .       (well.com)
vanilla   ttyp3     Jul 6 12:39   00:09
vanilla   ttyp4     Jul 9 10:37   00:09
localhost:~ vanilla$
```

Figure 11.13 Output from the who command with -Hu options.

Deeper into NetInfo

The NetInfo system is being phased out of Mac OS X/Darwin but is still in use as of Mac OS X 10.4 and probably will be for a while. NetInfo was originally a hierarchical directory service system like LDAP or Active Directory, but it is now used solely for storing local configuration information. The data stored in NetInfo is mostly data that is stored on other Unix systems in plain-text files: The file `/etc/passwd` has the list of all users, their home directories, and their login shells. In Darwin, `/etc/passwd` is used only when the machine is in single-user mode, but on most Unix systems, `/etc/passwd` is the only database of users.

The official Apple overview of the NetInfo system is available as a PDF document at www.apple.com/server/pdfs/UnderstandingUsingNetInfo.pdf.

To see who is logged in and what they are doing:

- `w`

  The `w` command shows output similar to `who -Hu` but adds a line of information reporting system uptime and load (actually, it is the output from the `uptime` command; see "Monitoring System Usage," later in this chapter). It also tries to show the last command that each user executed. **Figure 11.14** shows output from `w` on a Mac OS X system, and **Figure 11.15** shows partial output from `w` on another Unix system (running Sun's Solaris 2.6 operating system). Notice that that system had 152 users logged in at the time the command was run. Also notice the customized shell prompt (`Love ya babe 34:`) at the top of the code listing.

```
localhost:~ vanilla$ w
11:15AM     up 3 days, 11:53, 5 users, load averages: 0.39, 0.48, 0.60
USER        TTY FROM        LOGIN@           IDLE WHAT
vanilla     co -            Sat08AM 21:38    -
vanilla     p1 -            10:31AM          - bash
matisse     p2 well.com     10:36AM          - find
vanilla     p3 -            Sat12PM          - mail
vanilla     p4 -            10:37AM          - w
localhost:~ vanilla$
```

Figure 11.14 Output of w on Mac OS X.

```
Love ya babe 34: w
11:20am     up 20 day(s), 5:08,     152 users,     load average: 5.98, 6.62, 6.74
User        tty        login@     idle  JCPU  PCPU  what
java        pts/3      5:49am     41    22    16    -bash
swede       pts/8      10:49am    5     5     4     /usr/local/lib/mailwrapper/pine
fluffer     pts/15     11:04am    4     4     more
maxie       pts/35     6:14am     1:32  55    -picospan
flute       pts/58     11:06am    7     2     2     extract -g -f weblog -J -k web /
bottle      pts/44     10:36am                2     ped -t -z /home/b/o/bottle/.muse
risc        pts/19     11:11am    3           more
artgrrl     pts/41     8:35am     1     1     1     ssh -l artgrrl artgrrl.net
omni23      pts/100    11:14am                      lynx villagevoice
starboy     pts/13     11:14am          2           -bash
bunch       pts/60     10:26am    39    8     5     -picospan
bloomsb     pts/162    10:07am          1:08  38    irc NihiAtWrk irc.wagill.com
libre       pts/134    10:48am    2     2     2     /usr/bin/vi /home/l/i/libre/cf.buf
pwolf       pts/90     9:53am     1:28              /usr/bin/ksh
....output abbreviated....
```

Figure 11.15 Abbreviated output from w on a machine running Sun's Solaris 2.6 version of Unix.

To see a history of logins for all users:

- `last`

  The `last` command shows a history of all sessions (login/logout pairs) for the current month (**Figure 11.16**).

  Besides showing user sessions, the `last` log also shows entries for shutdowns, reboots, and crashes.

The information is taken from the `/var/log/wtmp` file, which is emptied out and started again each month by the `/etc/month` script. Last month's file is `/var/log/wtmp.0.gz`, the prior month is `wtmp.1.gz`, and so on up to `wtmp.4.gz`. You can uncompress the older files and supply the filename as an argument with the `-f` option to `last` to look at a previous month's data:

```
cd /var/log
sudo gunzip wtmp.2.gz
last -f wtmp.2
```

```
localhost:~ vanilla$ last
vanillattyp4                          Tue Jul  9 10:37     still logged in
matissettyp2     well.com             Tue Jul  9 10:36 -   11:20       (00:43)
vanillattyp1                          Tue Jul  9 10:31     still logged in
vanillattyp2                          Tue Jul  9 10:31 -   10:36       (00:05)
vanillattyp3                          Sat Jul  6 12:39     still logged in
vanillattyp2                          Sat Jul  6 10:29 -   10:31       (3+00:02)
puffball  ttyp2                       Sat Jul  6 08:43 -   10:29       (01:45)
vanillattyp1                          Sat Jul  6 08:34 -   10:09       (01:35)
matisseconsole   user-112uhed.biz     Sat Jul  6 08:32     still logged in
root     console                      Fri Jul  5 12:30 - 12:32         (00:01)
vanillaconsole   user-112uhed.biz     Fri Jul  5 12:29 - 12:30         (00:00)
puffball  ttyp1  playroom.matisse     Thu Jul  4 11:00 - 12:36         (1+01:35)
vanillattyp2                          Tue Jul  2 16:45 - 14:21         (2+21:36)
vanillattyp1                          Tue Jul  2 16:35 - 11:00         (1+18:24)
vanillaconsole   user-112uhed.biz     Tue Jul  2 16:23 - 12:29         (2+20:05)
reboot ~                              Tue Jul  2 16:20
shutdown  ~                           Tue Jul  2 16:14
root             console  user-112uhed.biz Tue Jul  2 16:14 -   16:14       (00:00)
vanillattyp2                          Tue Jul  2 15:06 -   shutdown    (01:08)
puffball  ttyp1                       Tue Jul  2 15:04 -   shutdown    (01:09)
vanillattyp1                          Tue Jul  2 15:04 -   15:04       (00:00)
vanillattyp3                          Tue Jul  2 11:53 -   shutdown    (04:20)
matissettyp1                          Tue Jul  2 10:10 -   15:04       (04:53)
vanillattyp2                          Mon Jul  1 21:43 -   15:06       (17:22)
vanillattyp1                          Mon Jul  1 21:42 -   10:10       (12:27)

wtmp begins Mon Jul  1 09:18
localhost:~ vanilla$
```

Figure 11.16 Output from the `last` command showing all login sessions, reboots, shutdowns, and crashes for the current month.

To see a history of all logins for one user:

- `last username`

  If you supply a user name as an argument to `last`, it limits the output to the sessions for that user. For example,

  `last puffball`

  gives output like that in **Figure 11.17**.

✔ Tip

- You can use `last` with the pseudo–user names reboot, shutdown, and crash to see all the corresponding entries in the `last` log. For example,

  `last reboot`

  shows all the reboots this month.

To see a summary of login times:

- `ac`

  Short for *connect time accounting*, this shows the total of all sessions since the start of this month (the data comes from `/var/log/wtmp`).

  For example, the output could be

  `total 197.15`

  You can supply a list of one or more user names to get a total for the selected users only. For example,

  `ac puffball`

  shows a total (in hours:minutes) of all of puffball's sessions for the current month, and

  `ac puffball vanilla`

  shows the total for the two users.

  You may use the `-p` option to get a per-user breakdown of the time, or the `-d` option to get a daily subtotal, but not both. **Figure 11.18** shows several different results for the `ac` command with different arguments and options.

```
localhost:~ vanilla$ last puffball
puffball    ttyp2                        Sat Jul  6 08:43 - 10:29        (01:45)
puffball    ttyp1    playroom.matisse    Thu Jul  4 11:00 - 12:36        (1+01:35)
puffball    ttyp1                        Tue Jul  2 15:04 - shutdown     (01:09)

wtmp begins Mon Jul  1 09:18
localhost:~ vanilla$
```

Figure 11.17 Output from `last` showing only one user.

```
localhost:~ vanilla$ ac
        total                197.22
localhost:~ vanilla$ ac -p
        vanilla              196.20
        root                 0.29
        puffball             0.73
        total                197.22
localhost:~ vanilla$ ac -d
Jul     3    total           62.19
Jul     4    total           24.00
Jul     5    total           23.97
Jul     8    total           72.00
Jul     9    total           15.06
localhost:~ vanilla$ ac vanilla
        total                196.20
localhost:~ vanilla$ ac puffball vanilla
        total                196.94
localhost:~ vanilla$ ac -p puffball vanilla
        vanilla              196.21
        puffball             0.73
        total                196.94
localhost:~ vanilla$ ac -d vanilla
Jul     1    total           14.35
Jul     3    total           47.84
Jul     4    total           24.00
Jul     5    total           23.69
Jul     8    total           72.00
Jul     9    total           14.34
localhost:~ vanilla$
```

Figure 11.18 Output from using the ac command with a variety of arguments and options.

✔ Tip

- You can use the `-w` option for `ac` to have it read a different file from the default. For example,

  `cd /var/log`

  `sudo gunzip wtmp.0.gz`

  `ac -w wtmp.0 -p`

  shows a per-day summary for the month whose data is in the file.

Managing groups

In Chapter 8, you learned about how Unix uses groups to grant permission for various file operations (read, write, execute) to groups of users. And earlier in this chapter, you learned that Mac OS X allows any user in the admin group to use `sudo` to execute commands as root.

In this section we're going to show you how to change a user's group assignment, and how to add and remove groups. A common reason to create a new group is if you have several people using your computer and want to allow some of them to have write permission in a directory where the other users do not. You would create a new group and put each of the team members into that group. Users can be members of many groups.

You will be using a Darwin-only tool called `dseditgroup` to manage group information, as well as the Darwin-only `nireport` and `dscl`.

To see all the groups a user belongs to:

- `groups` *`username`*

  For example,

  `groups puffball`

  lists all the groups that puffball is a member of—for example,

  `puffball www`

✔ Tip

- Supposedly, the `groups` command is being made obsolete by the `id` command, which has several options and can show more information about a user. Unfortunately, the `id` command is quite different on different Unix systems. In Mac OS X,

  `id -Gn` *`username`*

  behaves the same as

  `groups` *`username`*

  See `man id` for more.

To see a list of all the groups:

- `dscl . -list /groups PrimaryGroupID`

  This shows a list of all the groups on your system. Each line has the group name and its group ID number as shown in **Figure 11.19**. If you omit `PrimaryGroupID`, then the `gid` numbers are omitted from the output.

To see all the attributes of one group:

- `dscl . -read /groups/`*`groupname`*

  For example:

  `Dscl . -read /groups/admin`

  This produces a list of all the attributes for the admin group, as shown in **Figure 11.20**.

```
localhost:~ vanilla$ localhost:~ vanilla$
→ dscl . -list /groups PrimaryGroupID
accessibility      90
admin              80
amavisd            83
appowner           87
appserveradm       81
appserverusr       79
authedusers        50
bin                7
clamav             82
consoleusers       53
daemon             1
dancers            500
dialer             68
everyone           12
group              11 16
interactusers      51
jabber             84
kmem               2
lp                 26
mail               6
mailman            78
matisse            501
mysql              74
netusers           52
network            69
nobody             -2
nogroup            -1
operator           5
owner              10
postdrop           28
postfix            27
qtss               76
remote             503
securityagent      92
smmsp              25
sshd               75
staff              20
sys                3
tokend             91
tty                4
unknown            99
utmp               45
uucp               66
vanilla            502
wheel              0
windowserver       88
www                70
xgridagent         86
xgridcontroller    85
localhost:~ vanilla$
```

Figure 11.19 Using dscl to see a list of all the groups. Your output will differ.

To see all the users who belong to a group:

- There isn't any easy way to do this. Yes, we know it seems strange, but it's true.

  One partial solution is with

  `dscl . -read /groups/group name` → `GroupMembership`

  That command reads the Directory Service data and shows the users who have been directly added to the group. If there are no users associated with that group, the message "No such key:GroupMembership" will appear. The problem is that there is more than one place where a user can be included in a group. One is in Directory Service data for groups, in which each group has a list of users that belong to it. The command line above will read that for you. But when a user is created, he or she is assigned one group as his or her "primary" group, and that information is stored in the record for the *user*, not for the group.

  In Mac OS X 10.4, new users have a *private* group as their primary group—a group with the same name as the user name. Prior to 10.4, a user's primary group was set to "staff." In either case their user names do *not* appear in the Directory Service database record for the group itself, so the `dscl . -read` command shown above won't find it.

  In order to really find out who all the members of a group are, you would have to examine every user on the system, as well as the group entry in Directory Services. You could write a script to do this, but there's no single command to do it. Sorry.

> **Compare with Aqua: NetInfo Manager**
>
> You can use the GUI application NetInfo Manager to see who is a member of a group, as well as to add and remove groups. Even though NetInfo Manager is a GUI application, it is far less easy to use than most Mac applications. This is one case where the command-line tools are probably easier than the GUI equivalent.


```
localhost:~ vanilla$ dscl . -read /groups/admin
AppleMetaNodeLocation: /NetInfo/DefaultLocalNode
GeneratedUID: FFFFEEEE-DDDD-CCCC-BBBB-AAAA00000050 ABCDEFAB-CDEF-ABCD-EFAB-CDEF00000050
GroupMembership: root matisse vanilla remote
Password: *
PrimaryGroupID: 80
RealName: Administrators
RecordName: admin
RecordType: dsRecTypeNative:groups
SMBSID: S-1-5-32-544
localhost:~ vanilla$
```

Figure 11.20 Using dscl to see all the attributes for one group (the admin group in this example).

To create a new group:

1. First get the list of all groups as described in the task "To see a list of all the groups":

   ```
   dscl . -list /groups PrimaryGroupID
   ```

2. Make up a group name that is not in use.

   Group names should be all lowercase and should contain only letters and numbers.

3. `sudo dseditgroup -o create groupname`

   You must be root to modify the data sources used by Directory Service, hence the use of sudo.

   For example, to create a group called "dancers":

   ```
   sudo dseditgroup -o create dancers
   ```

   Enter your password if sudo prompts you for it.

   If a group already exists with the name you chose, you will be asked if you want to overwrite the existing record.

✔ Tips

- Instead of using sudo, you can use the -p option and you will be prompted for your password:

  ```
  dseditgroup -p -o create groupname
  ```

  Or if you are not logged in as an admin user, you may use the -p and -u options to supply an admin user name:

  ```
  dseditgroup -u user name -p -o
  → create groupname
  ```

  You'll still need the password, of course.

- There are several more options for creating a group with dseditgroup—for example, you can add a comment with the -c option. See man dseditgroup for the complete list.

To add a user to an existing group:

- ```
  sudo dseditgroup -o edit -a username
  → -t user groupname
  ```

  This adds the user *username* to the group *groupname*. For example, to add user "fireboy" to group "dancers":

  ```
  sudo dseditgroup -o edit -a fireboy
  → -t user dancers
  ```

  The change takes effect the next time fireboy logs in.

  Be sure to check your addition with

  ```
  dscl . -read /groups/dancers
  → GroupMembership
  ```

  to ensure that the user fireboy is added, since dseditgroups provides little feedback on failure or success

Starting in Mac OS X 10.4, you can have groups be members of other groups. Any user who is a member of a subgroup is automatically a member of the higher-level group(s). You may only add groups to groups that were created using the new 10.4 tools, such as dseditgroup, described above. (That is, you will get an error if you try to add a group to a "legacy-style" group.)

To display information about a group:

- `dseditgroup group name`

  This will display all the known attributes of the group. **Figure 11.21** shows an annotated example.

To add a group to another group:

- ```
  sudo dseditgroup -o edit -a subgroup
  → -t group parentgroup
  ```

  This adds the group *subgroup* to *parent group*. All users who are in the subgroup are now also members of the parent group. Note that while you can remove subgroups (see below), there is currently no easy way to see a list of subgroups for a particular group.

To remove a user from a group:

- `sudo dseditgroup -o edit -d` *username* `→ -t group` *groupname*

  This removes the user *username* from group *groupname*.

To remove a subgroup from a group:

- `sudo dseditgroup -o edit -d` *subgroup* `→ -t group` *groupname*

  This removes the subgroup *subgroup* from group *groupname*.

To remove a group:

1. `sudo dseditgroup -o delete` *groupname*

   For example, to delete a group called "tango":

   `sudo dseditgroup -o delete tango`

   You will get a prompt telling you the group already exists and asking if you really want to delete it:

   ```
   Delete called on existing record -
   → do you really want to delete,
   → y or n :
   ```

2. `y`

   Typing y confirms the request to delete the group. It's gone as soon as you press Return.

Shows only 15 lines of processes.

```
localhost:~ vanilla$ dseditgroup dancers

Recordname <dancers>
10 attribute(s) found
Attribute[1] is <dsAttrTypeStandard:AppleMetaNodeLocation>
        Value[1] is </NetInfo/DefaultLocalNode>
Attribute[2] is <dsAttrTypeStandard:RecordType>
        Value[1] is <dsRecTypeStandard:Groups>
Attribute[3] is <dsAttrTypeStandard:RecordName>
        Value[1] is <dancers>
Attribute[4] is <dsAttrTypeStandard:PrimaryGroupID>
        Value[1] is <500>
Attribute[5] is <dsAttrTypeStandard:GeneratedUID>
        Value[1] is <ED5CA594-5D8B-4446-94D9-E2092DD0CAA9>
Attribute[6] is <dsAttrTypeStandard:RealName>
        Value[1] is <Group of Dancers>
Attribute[7] is <dsAttrTypeStandard:Comment>
        Value[1] is <A comment>
Attribute[8] is <dsAttrTypeStandard:GroupMembers>
        Value[1] is <7C9F2456-03DE-4D90-A26D-9B961CA250D5>
        Value[2] is <E8AB52F7-7F0C-464C-B5CD-60607814C503>
Attribute[9] is <dsAttrTypeStandard:GroupMembership>
        Value[1] is <matisse>
        Value[2] is <vanilla>
Attribute[10] is <dsAttrTypeStandard:NestedGroups>
        Value[1] is <CA3C67F5-4A4B-4D45-AE44-AF0B70D9664D>
localhost:~ vanilla$
```

The attribute RecordName contains a single value: the group name.

The attribute GeneratedUID contains a universally unique identifier (UUID) for the group (see man uuidgen).

The attribute GroupMembership lists the user names of those who belong to this group. (Does not include users who belong because they are members of subgroups.)

The attribute NestedGroups lists the UUIDs of subgroups.

Figure 11.21 Annotated output from dseditgroup *group name*.

Monitoring System Usage

Staying aware of what's happening on your machine is a big part of system administration. The two most important things to watch on a day-to-day basis are (1) disk space and (2) load on the processor(s). Run out of disk space, and many processes stop working because they have no place to create temporary data. Let a runaway program consume too much processor time, and everything else slows down.

Monitoring disk space

Anticipating the need to add disk space before you run out is an important system-administration function.

You can view both available and used space for the entire system or for any directory in the file system.

To see a summary of disk usage for the entire system:

- `df -lk`

  The `df` command (*display free disk space*) displays information about all the disks mounted on your system. The `-l` option tells `df` to display only locally mounted file systems (omitting network drives and some special entries that are not really disks), while the `-k` option tells `df` to show disk space in kilobytes, instead of the default half-kilobyte (512-byte) units (**Figure 11.22**).

✔ **Tip**

- If you supply a directory as an argument to `df`, it shows a listing for only the file system containing the directory, so

  `df -k .`

  shows a listing only for the file system containing the current directory (which is also a tricky way of finding out which file system the current directory is located in).

  `df -k /Users`

  shows a listing only for the file system containing `/Users`. If the directory is a symlink (see "About Links [the Unix Version of Aliases]" in Chapter 5), then `df` reports on the file system containing the directory that the link points to, not the link itself.

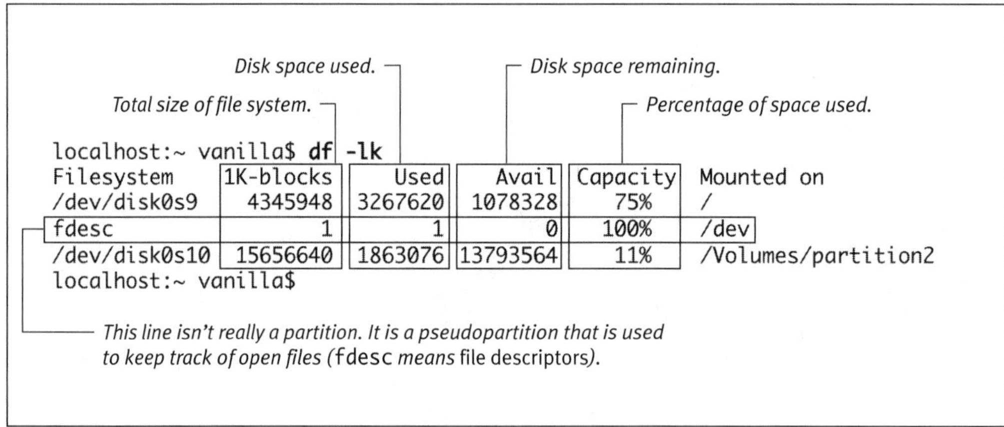

Figure 11.22 Annotated output from `df -lk` displaying free space (in kilobytes) on the system disks.

Table 11.3

Options for the du Command

Option	Meaning/Use
-H	Follows symbolic links in the command-line arguments. (Symbolic links encountered inside directories are not followed.)
-L	Follows all symbolic links.
-P	Does not follow symbolic links.
-a	Displays something for every file counted.
-k	Displays sizes in kilobytes instead of the system default for measuring files (usually 512-byte "blocks").
-c	Displays a grand total at the end.
-s	Displays a subtotal for each directory on the command line.
-x	Does not follow symbolic links that point to directories on other volumes.

To see disk usage for a particular directory:

- `du -sk` *`directory`*

  The `-s` asks for a summary of the target directory, and the `-k` says to show sizes in kilobytes. **Table 11.3** shows all the options for the `du` command.

  To see a summary of the disk space used by puffball's home directory:

  `sudo du -sk /Users/puffball`

  The `sudo` is needed in this case because you might not have read permission on everything in the directory.

Compare with Aqua: Activity Monitor Application

Mac OS X comes with a nice GUI application called Activity Monitor, located in the /Applications/Utilities folder, which lets you monitor active processes, memory, network activity, and so on. Still, you may want to use the command-line tools for several reasons:

- If you are logged in to the machine using `ssh` over the Internet and have access only to the command-line tools.
- If you need information, such as disk usage by directory as supplied by the `du` command, that isn't available in Activity Monitor.
- If you want to redirect activity or resource information to a file, send it in e-mail, or use the information in script.
- If you are already working at the command line, in which case it may be faster to simply type `top` than to launch Activity Monitor.
- If you are on another Unix system. The command-line tools for monitoring the system described in this chapter are available on virtually any Unix system you might use, while Activity Monitor is available only on Mac OS X.

To see disk usage for several directories:

◆ `du -sk dir1 dir2 dir3 . . .`

Simply list as many directories as you like on the command line. The `-s` option generates a subtotal for each one. For example, if you type

`du -sk Documents Pictures Movies`

you get the output shown in **Figure 11.23**.

You can see how much each user is using with

`sudo du -sk /Users/*`

The shell expands the `*` so that `du` gets a list of several directories. You need to `sudo` to get permission to read other users' home directories.

✔ Tip

■ Add the `-c` option to get a grand total of disk space used. For example:

`sudo du -skc /Users/*`

Monitoring processes and load on your machine

If you have read Chapter 2, "Using the Command Line," then you already have seen two of the best tools for monitoring running processes: `ps` and `top`. (See "About Commands, Processes, and Jobs," in Chapter 2.)

Reading the `man` pages for `ps` and `top` yields a great deal of information about the kinds of things you can monitor on your system. Here are some highlights for the `top` command, which shows a wealth of information in real time. You might want to compare what we show here with the various views of system activity in the Activity Monitor application, which we mentioned earlier. For example, in Activity Monitor you may limit the display of active processes to ones associated with windows in the Aqua interface ("Windowed Processes").

More about top

Figure 11.24 is an annotated example of output from `top`, showing the most significant indicators of system use.

Note how the ID of each process is displayed. If a process gets out of control, you can use the `kill` command (described in Chapter 2) to terminate it. You need to use `sudo` to kill processes you didn't start yourself. Be very careful, since you could crash the machine by killing a system process, such as the process `1` (`launchd`).

If you use `top` frequently, you will notice that your system spends a great deal of time doing very little. It is quite common for computers, especially desktop machines used by only a few people, to run at 90 percent idle. Most of the computing power in the world is wasted, just generating heat and performing no useful work. For ways to put those spare CPU cycles to work for a good cause, see Seti@home (http://setiathome.ssl.berkeley.edu), distributed.net (www.distributed.net), and Xgrid (www.apple.com/server/macosx/features/xgrid.html).

Another noteworthy command is `uptime`, which shows the same thing as the first line of output from the `w` command. The `top` command also displays the information from `uptime` in its first few lines, as well as a great deal of other information.

```
localhost:~ vanilla$ du -sk Documents Pictures Movies
82740   Documents
71204   Pictures
320     Movies
localhost:~ vanilla$
```

Figure 11.23 Using du -sk to get disk-use subtotals for several directories.

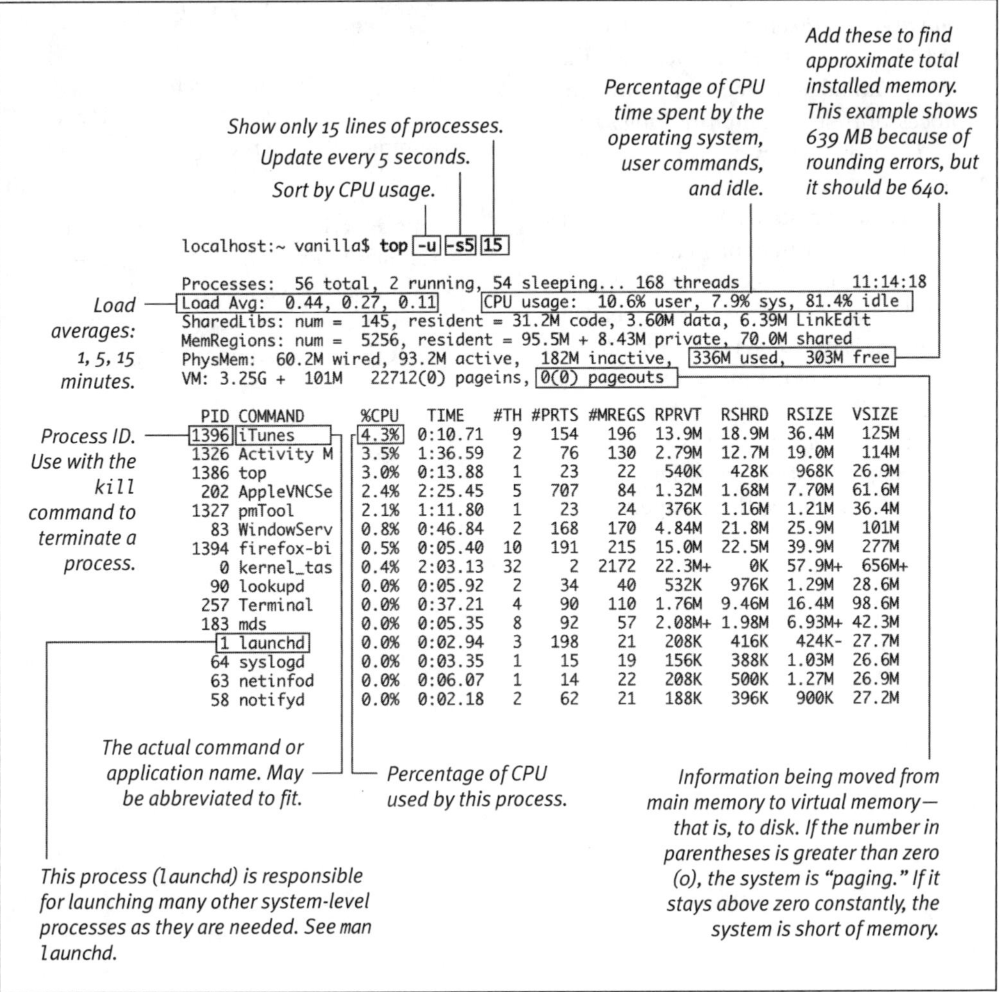

Figure 11.24 Annotated example of output from the top command.

To see system load and uptime:

- `uptime`

  This gives you a single line of output,

  ```
  9:42PM up 3 days, 22:20, 6 users,
  → load averages: 0.42, 0.89, 0.85
  ```

  that shows you the current time, the length of time the system has been up, the number of users logged in, and three *load averages* taken over the past 1, 5, and 15 minutes. The load average is the average number of processes waiting for processor time. In a multitasking system like Unix, only one process is actually running on each CPU at any given instant. The operating system allows each process to run for a tiny fraction of a second and then lets another process run. Because this sharing is enforced by the operating system, it is called *preemptive multitasking* and is one of the major reasons for Unix's stability (as opposed to *cooperative multitasking* in Mac OS 7 through 9, in which applications were supposed to play well together without supervision).

vm_stat—Tool for Monitoring Memory Usage

Another command worth knowing about is `vm_stat` (*virtual memory statistics*), often called `vmstat` on other Unix systems. `vm_stat` reports on several aspects of memory usage, in real time.

`vm_stat` is normally executed as

`vm_stat 5`

which gives a summary since startup and then a new line every 5 seconds. It keeps running until you press Control C.

Interpreting the output of `vm_stat` takes some experience, but the `pageout` column is similar to the data shown by `top`—that column should be zero most of the time. Otherwise, either your system is short of memory or something is using it up.

Running Regularly Scheduled Commands

Regularly scheduled commands are an important part of system administration, and virtually all Unix systems provide a tool called cron that enables this. A typical "cron job" would be a script that rebuilds the locate database every Sunday at 3:15 a.m. (See also the sidebar "Run a Command Once in the Future.")

Starting in Mac OS X 10.4, Apple has introduced an additional tool, called launchd, that provides many of the capabilities of cron and adds other desirable features as well. This chapter will cover both the cron and launchd systems, which allow you to specify a schedule for running any command or script (often called *jobs*). The most common schedules involve running a job at the same time every day, every week, or every month, but both cron and launchd allow you to schedule jobs down to the minute.

About the periodic Command

The periodic command is designed to run all the executable files in a single directory one after the other, in alphabetical order, and is common on Unix systems (such as Darwin) that inherit from FreeBSD. By default the periodic command uses three directories in which scheduled system-administration scripts are kept: /etc/periodic/daily/, /etc/periodic/weekly/, and /etc/periodic/monthly/. For example, the script that updates the database used by the locate command is /etc/periodic/weekly/500.weekly. That same script also runs the makewhatis command that updates the file /usr/share/man/whatis used by man -k (aka the apropos command). You may also specify an arbitrary directory for periodic to look in for scripts to run.

The basic idea is that you have a set of scripts that should all be run at more or less the same time, so you schedule a run of the periodic command for a certain time and tell it which directory to use. Then you can add and remove scripts from the target directory without having to worry about messing with the scheduling function.

In Mac OS X before 10.4, the periodic command was run, um, periodically, via cron. In Mac OS X 10.4, it is run periodically by launchd. See man periodic for more about this command, but note that the man page (as of Mac OS X 10.4.2) still refers to cron.

The periodic command is designed specifically to be run from a crontab file (although in Mac OS X 10.4 it is run via launchd). The argument to the periodic command is the name of a directory inside the /etc/periodic/ directory. For example, the argument daily means that the periodic command will look inside /etc/periodic/daily/ and execute every executable file in that directory in alphabetical order.

The periodic command has a number of configuration options, which are set in the file /etc/defaults/periodic.conf. If you need to override any of the settings, you should do so by editing one of the other files used by periodic (see man periodic). The default settings in /etc/defaults/periodic.conf are set to cause output from the daily scripts to go in the log file /var/log/daily.out, the weekly scripts in /var/log/weekly.out, and the monthly scripts in /var/log/monthly.out.

Scheduling jobs using cron

Let's focus on cron before moving on to launchd. cron is a special kind of program that in Unix we call a *daemon*. The cron daemon executes programs according to a schedule. Daemons are (often small) programs that are launched—sometimes we say "spawned"—to run in the background, waiting to handle various system tasks as they arise. Most server software, such as Web servers, runs as daemons, as do many pieces of the operating system that are constantly running, waiting to do some particular kind of work. In Darwin/Mac OS X, daemons are managed by a master daemon called launchd, which we'll cover later in this chapter.

Every minute, the cron daemon checks the directory /var/cron/tabs for files whose names match user names—for example, root—and reads any new or changed files into memory. The cron daemon also checks the system-administration file /etc/crontab. These files, called *crontabs* (for *chronological tables*), are in a special format (described below) that tells cron what commands to execute and when. Commands in a crontab file are executed as the user who owns the crontab file (except for the special /etc/crontab file; see "About /etc/crontab," below).

When a command from a crontab file is executed, any output from the command is e-mailed to the user owning the crontab file.

Users' crontab files are created and edited with the crontab command, which uses the vi editor (or the editor specified in your VISUAL environment variable) and performs a syntax check on the file before installing it. (This is similar to the working of the visudo command, covered earlier in this chapter.) The system-administration crontab file, /etc/crontab, must be edited directly using an editor such as vi. Unfortunately, the crontab command cannot be used to perform a syntax check on /etc/crontab.

You can view the man page for the crontab command with man crontab, and the man page for what goes inside crontab files with man 5 crontab. (To see why you need to add the 5, review the man command in Chapter 3, "Getting Help and Using the Unix Manual.")

Make certain you are familiar with the text editor you are going to use (vi by default, or whatever is in your VISUAL environment variable) before editing your crontab file.

Run a Command Once in the Future

Mac OS X comes with a standard Unix command called at that is used to run a command once at some future time. The at command depends on another command, atrun, which is disabled by default in Mac OS X, although it may be enabled (see man at).

To run a command every day using cron:

1. `crontab -e`

   The `-e` option says, "I want to *edit* my crontab file."

2. Add the `crontab` command line.

   Let's say you want a summary of your disk-space usage to be added to a file every day at 10:23 p.m.

   The basic command you want to run is

   ```
   /usr/bin/du -skc /Users/vanilla >>
   → /Users/vanilla/disk_use.log
   ```

   You should always use full paths for commands in crontab files because `cron` runs them with a very limited environment (you can find the path to a command with `which` *command*).

   You add a series of five items to the crontab file, specifying when you want the command to run, and then the command line goes after the fifth item. It must be one long line.

   Figure 11.25 is an annotated example of a crontab entry and shows the meaning of each of the time fields and the entry to run the above command every day at 10:23 p.m.

3. Save the file and quit the editor.

   If you are using `vi`, you press Esc and then type `:wq`.

continues on next page

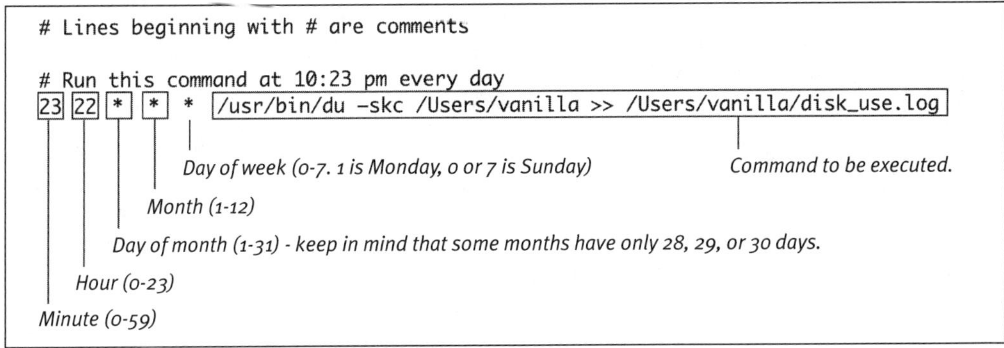

Figure 11.25 Example of a crontab file with an entry to run a command every day at 10:23 p.m. Since it will run every day, you put asterisks in the Day of month, Month, and Day of week fields.

✔ Tip

- When redirecting the output of a command line in your crontab, as in the example above, you can't have multiple commands on the command line. So if you want to run a cron job that consists of a series of commands, then you create a script and run it from your crontab.

  For example, you might have a script like this:

  ```
  #!/bin/sh
  /bin/date
  /usr/bin/du -skc /Users/vanilla
  ```

  You could then run the script with cron and redirect the output of the script (which includes the date) into a log file.

Figure 11.26 shows a series of examples of crontab entries. man 5 crontab gives the full, detailed specification for what is possible in a crontab file. In particular, notice that you can specify ranges of times or dates, so you can run a command every other month, every third hour, or whenever you want. Also, note that lines beginning with # are comments, which can be very helpful, so add some!

```
# This is a comment. I love comments.

# Set the SHELL to use for running cron commands, overrides whatever
# the system default is.
SHELL=/bin/sh

# Mail any output to 'puffball', regardless of whose crontab this is.
MAILTO=puffball



# Use a day name for the day of week
5 4 * * sun echo "run at 5 minutes after 4 every Sunday"

# run five minutes after midnight, every day.
# Also redirects stderr to stdout so errors get emailed.
5 0 * * *   $HOME/bin/daily.job >> $HOME/tmp/out 2>&1

# run at 2:15pm on the first of every month
15 14 1 * * $HOME/bin/monthly


# run at 10 pm on weekdays, annoy Joe
# You can use % to include a <return> in an argument.
0 22 * * 1-5echo "Joe,%%Where are your kids?%" | mail -s "It's 10pm" joe

# You can use ranges, e.g. 1-5 means 1,2,3,4,5
# Run at 9:00am every Monday, Wednesday and Friday
0 9 * * 1,3,5 mail -s "bring me flowers" spouse@work.com

# You can use step values with ranges by putting a / after the range.
#  0-10/3 means 0,3,6,9 (the 10 never gets used) and */2 means "every two"
15 12 * */2 3 echo "run at 12:15 every second month but only on Wednesdays"
17 8-20/2 * * * echo "run at 17 minutes after every 2nd hour from 8am to 7pm everyday"
```

Figure 11.26 Examples of several crontab entries.

Controlling who uses cron

You don't have to allow every user on the system to use cron. If you have a large number of users, there might be some you want to bar from using cron, or you might want to restrict the use of cron to a few users. This is easy to do.

If the file /var/cron/allow exists, then only users who are listed in that file may use cron.

If the file /var/cron/deny exists, then any user listed in that file may *not* use cron.

To restrict cron use to a list of specific users:

1. Edit the file /var/cron/allow.

   This must be done by root, so if you are using the vi editor, the command would be

   ```
   sudo vi /var/cron/allow
   ```

   Enter your password if prompted for it.

   If the file already exists, make a copy of it first, in case you mess it up and need to go back to the original version.

2. Add the user names of those who are allowed to use cron.

   These should appear one per line—for example,

   ```
   vanilla
   puffball
   ```

3. Save the file and quit the editor.

To create a list of users who are not allowed to use cron:

1. Edit the file /var/cron/deny.

   This must be done by root, so if you are using the vi editor, the command would be

   ```
   sudo vi /var/cron/deny
   ```

   Enter your password if prompted for it.

   If the file already exists, make a copy of it first, in case you mess it up and need to go back to the original version.

2. Add user names to the file.

   Enter one user name per line—for example,

   ```
   jackie
   wesley
   ```

3. Save the file and quit the editor.

   Any user listed in the file is unable to use cron.

About /etc/crontab

There is one special crontab file, /etc/crontab, already on your computer for system-administration purposes. Note that starting in Mac OS X 10.4, this file has no entries because the jobs that were handled here in earlier versions of Mac OS X are now handled by launchd. Because it is quite a bit easier to create a new cron job than a new launchd job, you might want to use /etc/crontab for system-administration tasks instead of the more complex launchd (see the next section, "Scheduling jobs using launchd").

Because the /etc/crontab file is run by root, it uses a format a little different than the crontab files for users. The command entries in /etc/crontab use an extra field (the sixth field) that specifies which user the command will run as. This allows root to schedule commands to be run by less privileged users. So instead of the actual command line being everything after the first five fields, the command line to be run from an /etc/crontab entry is everything after the first *six* fields. (The command line is still the last thing in each line.)

continues on next page

Figure 11.27 is an example of an /etc/crontab file that runs a command to show the disk usage of all users. The command is set to run once a week, on Monday at 10:15 a.m. (but it won't run if your computer isn't on!).

Note the MAILTO setting that will cause the output of any cron jobs in the file to go to puffball@someplace.com, and how the job is set to be run as the root user.

Scheduling jobs using launchd

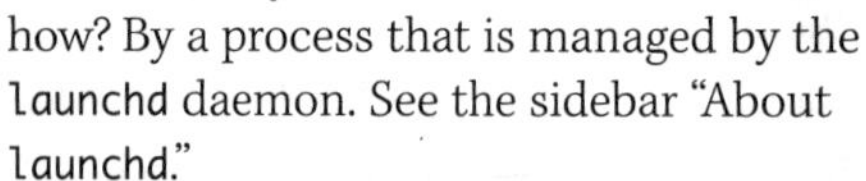

Remember the locate command mentioned in Chapter 4, "Useful Unix Utilities"? We told you that locate uses a database that is rebuilt every week. But how? By a process that is managed by the launchd daemon. See the sidebar "About launchd."

The plist (*Property List*) format is widely used in Mac OS X/Darwin. You configure new scheduled jobs (also called *agents*) for launchd by creating an XML file in the plist format using options specified in the launchd.plist man page (see man launchd.plist), and then passing the file to launchd using a utility called launchctl. Also see man plist and the sidebar "More About the Property List Format."

The launchd framework allows for many configuration options, such as limiting the amount of CPU time or memory used by jobs. The launchctl command controls other aspects of launchd configuration, such as loading and unloading launchd jobs, logging, and monitoring launchd resource usage. (See man launchctl for more.)

The proper location of the XML files you create for launchd agents depends on whether they are per-user or systemwide agents and whether they are installed by regular users or by system administrators. **Table 11.4** shows the standard directories used by launchd. The idea is that some launchd files may be installed or changed only by an administrator, while regular users can install and change their own launchd files, much as they can their own crontab entries.

More About the Property List Format

The plist, or Property List, format is widely used in Mac OS X/Darwin for system-configuration files and by virtually all applications to store user preferences. Have a look in ~/Library/Preferences and you will see many .plist files. The OmniGraffle diagramming application even uses the plist format for its documents (www.omnigroup.com/applications/omnigraffle).

In addition to the man page for the plist format (see man plist), you should also check out the GUI tool for creating and editing plist files at /Developer/Applications/Property List Editor (which is only present if the Developer Tools are installed).

The plist format is an XML (*eXtensible Markup Language*) format. For more on XML, see W3C's "Extensible Markup Language (XML)" page (www.w3.org/XML) and *XML for the World Wide Web: Visual QuickStart Guide*, by Elizabeth Castro (Peachpit Press; www.peachpit.com).

```
# /etc/crontab
SHELL=/bin/sh
PATH=/etc:/bin:/sbin:/usr/bin:/usr/sbin
HOME=/var/log
MAILTO=puffball@someplace.com

#
#minute hourday  month    wday who  command
#
#*/5    *    *    *    *
root/usr/libexec/atrun
#
# Run daily/weekly/monthly jobs.
15 10   *    *    1    root du -skch /Users/*
```

Figure 11.27 Sample of an /etc/crontab file.

The following task describes creating a scheduled job for `launchd` that is installed and runs from your user account. The XML file will be in your home directory, and the process that runs will be owned by your user account. Let's say you want to run a script called `diskusage` that is installed in the `bin` directory of your home directory, so it looks like this:

```
/Users/vanilla/bin/diskusage
```

You can of course name the file whatever you like. We recommend that the name end in .plist because the file is in the `plist` format. See Table 11.4 for other places to put `launchd` configuration files for different purposes.

You can use a text editor such as `vi` to create the file, or you can use the GUI application Property List Editor (located in `/Developer/Applications/`).

continues on next page

Table 11.4

Directories Used by launchd

Directory	Purpose
~/Library/LaunchAgents	Per-user agents provided by the user
/Library/LaunchAgents	Per-user agents provided by the administrator
/Library/LaunchDaemons	Systemwide daemons provided by the administrator
/System/Library/LaunchAgents	Per-user agents installed with the operating system (essentially by Apple)
/System/Library/LaunchDaemons	Systemwide agents and daemons installed with the operating system

About launchd

Introduced in Mac OS X 10.4, `launchd` provides an extensive framework for managing both daemons and non-daemon jobs that `launchd` calls *agents*. That is, in `launchd` documentation, you will see references to agents, which means commands that are managed by `launchd` but do not run as daemons.

In Mac OS X/Darwin, `launchd` is used to launch several processes during system startup (see "The Boot Sequence," later in this chapter). It also provides a capability similar to `cron`—you can use `launchd` to set up scheduled, repeated execution of commands and scripts, although not with quite the same level of fine control that `cron` provides when the jobs execute.

As seen in a typical property list in **Figure 11.28**, the ProgramArguments key is for an array of one or more <string> elements. The first one is the actual command or script that will be executed. Any additional <string> elements are passed as arguments to the command. However, unlike what you do with cron jobs, you are not supplying a command line—you cannot use shell operators like *, >, >>, and |. You are simply supplying an executable and an (optional) series of arguments.

Example of a Systemwide launchd Agent

One example of a systemwide launchd job (or agent) is com.apple.periodic-daily. This job simply executes /usr/bin/periodic with an argument of daily, and runs at 3:15 a.m. every day (assuming the computer is on).

The launchd configuration file for this agent is /System/Library/LaunchDaemons/com.apple.periodic-daily.plist.

See "The Boot Sequence," later in this chapter.


```
<!DOCTYPE plist PUBLIC "-//Apple Computer//DTD PLIST 1.0//EN"
"http://www.apple.com/DTDs/PropertyList-1.0.dtd">
<plist version="1.0">
<dict>
   <key>Label</key>
   <string>diskusage</string>
   <key>ProgramArguments</key>
         <array>
               <string>/Users/vanilla/bin/diskusage</string>
         </array>
   <key>ServiceDescription</key>
   <string>Shows a summary of disk usage in my home directory.</string>
   <key>StartCalendarInterval</key>
   <dict>
               <key>Minute</key>  <integer>45</integer>
               <key>Hour</key>    <integer>3</integer>
               <key>Weekday</key> <integer>1</integer>
         </dict>
</dict>
</plist>
```

Figure 11.28 Example of an XML file for a launchd agent that runs at 3:45 a.m. every Monday. See man launchd.plist for the complete specification of what may go in this type of file.

To run a command every day using launchd:

1. Create the XML file

   `~/Library/LaunchAgents/filename`

   For example (refer to Figure 11.28):

   `~/Library/LaunchAgents/diskuse.plist`

2. If you want to use shell operators, put those in the script that is being executed.

   For example, Figure 11.28 refers to a (made-up) script, `/Users/vanilla/bin/diskusage`, which might look like this:

   ```
   #!/bin/sh
   du -sk /Users/vanilla/* >>
   → /tmp/vanilla.diskusage
   ```

   When `launchd` runs that script, the `*` and `>>` will work as expected because the script is a Bourne shell script (as indicated by the first line). See Chapter 9, "Creating and Using Scripts," for more on Bourne shell scripts.

3. Once you have created the XML file, load it into `launchd` using

   ```
   launchctl load
   → ~/Library/LaunchAgents/filename
   ```

   For example:

   ```
   launchctl load ~/Library/
   → LaunchAgents/diskuse.plist
   ```

   This tells `launchd` to read the file and attempt to load it. You'll get an error message if the file doesn't conform to the specification in `man launchd.plist` or if the command you use in the `ProgramArguments` doesn't exist.

   If you have indicated a `StartInterval` and/or a `StartCalendarInterval`, then you are done—the agent will run at the times specified (assuming the computer is turned on).

✔ Tips

- Read the `man` page for `launchd.plist`. There are quite a number of options available for configuring `launchd` agents. For example, `WatchPaths` can cause an agent to run whenever a listed path is modified, and `EnvironmentVariables` will set environment variables before running a job. See **Table 11.5** for more examples.

continues on page 356

Table 11.5

launchd Configuration Options

Only the `Label` and `ProgramArguments` keys are required; all others are optional. See `man launchd.plist` for the complete list.

Key	Description and Example of Use

`Label`	Required. A unique name for the job.
	`<key>Label</key>`
	`<string>uniquelabel</string>`

`Disabled`	Disables the agent if `true`. See `man launchctl` and the entry for the -w option to the `load` and `unload` commands. Default is `false`.
	`<key>Disabled</key>`
	`<true/>`

`UserName`	If the agent is run by root, this sets the user to run the job as
	`<key>UserName</key>`
	`<string>username</string>`

table continues on next page

Table 11.5 *continued*

launchd Configuration Options

Key	Description and Example of Use
GroupName	If the agent is run by root, this sets the group to run the job as <key>GroupName</key> <string>*groupname*</string>
Program	If present, this specifies the program (command, script, and so on) to be executed. If this key is not present, then the first item in the ProgramArguments array is used instead. (See next entry.) <key>Program</key> <string>program</string>
ProgramArguments	Required. An array of strings that are passed as arguments to the program. If the Program key is not present, then the first item is the program to run. <key>ProgramArguments</key> <array> <string>*argument1*</string> <string>*argument2*</string> </array>
WorkingDirectory	Causes launchd to do a cd into a particular directory just before running the job. <key>WorkingDirectory</key> <string>*fullpath*</string>
EnvironmentVariables	Environment variables to be set just before running the job. The format is a "dictionary of strings," which is the same format as the top-level structure of a launchd plist file itself: <key>EnvironmentVariables</key> <dict> <key>*VARNAME*</key> <string>*value*</string> <key>*VARNAME2*</key> <string>*value*</string> </dict>
Umask	Specifies an argument to pass to the umask command just before running the job. (See "Default Permissions for File Creation," in Chapter 8.) The *value* should be a valid umask such as 077. <key>Umask</key> <integer>*value*</integer>
WatchPaths	The job will be started if any of the paths are modified. <key>WatchPaths</key> <array> <string>*/path1/to/watch*</string> <string>*/path2/to/watch*</string> </array>

table continues on next page

Table 11.5 *continued*

launchd Configuration Options	
Key	**Description and Example of Use**

`QueueDirectories`	Same as `WatchPaths` except the job will be started only if the modified path is a directory and is not empty, so basically only if something is added to or removed from one of the listed directories.
	`<key>QueueDirectories</key>`
	`<array>`
	`<string>`*/path1/to/watch*`</string>`
	`<string>`*/path2/to/watch*`</string>`
	`</array>`

`StartInterval`	Specifies an interval in seconds to run the job, so if you want to run the job every 10 seconds, set it to 10, every 5 minutes, to 300, and so forth.
	`<key>StartInterval</key>`
	`<integer>`*interval*`</integer>`

`StartCalendarInterval`	A dictionary of integers—you may have one key each for `Minute`, `Hour`, `Day`, `Weekday`, and `Month`. You cannot specify multiple values, so (unlike with `cron`) you cannot run a job on Monday–Friday. If a key is missing, then the value for that key is `every one`, so you could run a job every day and then have the script figure out which day it is and decide whether or not to do anything. For the `Day` value use day of month, and watch out for 29–31; not every month has a 31st! For the `Weekday` value, both `0` and 7 are Sunday (1 is Monday).
	`<key>StartCalendarInterval</key>`
	`<dict>`
	`<key>Minute</key>`
	`<integer>`*value 0–59*`</integer>`
	`<key>Hour</key>`
	`<integer>`*value 0–23*`</integer>`
	`<key>Day</key>`
	`<integer>`*value 1–31*`</integer>`
	`<key>Weekday</key>`
	`<integer>`*value 0–7*`</integer>`
	`<key>Month</key>`
	`<integer>`*value 1–12*`</integer>`
	`</dict>`

`StandardOutPath`	Path where all `stdout` from the job goes. Similar to using > to redirect `stdout`. (See "About Standard Input and Output," in Chapter 2.)
	`<key>StandardOutPath</key>`
	`<string>`*/path/somewhere*`</string>`

`StandardErrorPath`	Similar to `StandardOutPath` but redirects `stderr` for the job.
	`<key>StandardErrorPath</key>`
	`<string>`*/path/somewhere*`</string>`

`HardResourceLimits`	Allows you to impose resource limits on the job. See `man launchd.plist` for a list of available settings.

- You can use the plutil command to check a plist file to see if it is a well-formed XML plist file (this won't catch misspelled keys, though):

```
plutil file
```

- Use the StartInterval key to specify an interval in seconds. For example, to run the agent every 5 minutes:

```
<key>StartInterval</key>
<integer>300</integer>
```

- You may load an entire directory of launchd configuration files by passing a directory name to launchctl load instead of a filename:

```
launchctl load directory
```

- You can run an agent immediately at any time with

```
launchctl start Label
```

—for example,

```
launchctl start diskusage
```

The *Label* is taken from the Label entry in the XML file. In Figure 11.28 the *Label* is diskusage.

- The folks at codepoetry have created a shareware GUI tool, Launchd Editor, that simplifies most of the work in creating new launchd agents and daemons (www.codepoetry.net/products/launchdeditor).

To unload a launchd agent:

◆ `launchctl unload path`

The *path* is a path to a launchd configuration file or a directory containing one or more such files.

✔ Tip

- If you add the -w option to the unload subcommand, a Disabled key set to true will be added to the configuration file(s) and the file(s) written back to disk. The -w option must come after the unload subcommand:

```
launchctl unload -w path
```

To list jobs loaded into launchd:

◆ `sudo launchctl list`

This displays a list of the labels of the jobs you have loaded into launchd.

If you do not run the command line as root—that is, if you omit the sudo command—then only your personal launchd agents, the ones you have loaded without using sudo, will be listed. **Figure 11.29** shows typical output, although yours may differ depending on which agents you have loaded.

```
localhost:~ vanilla$ sudo launchctl list
Password:
com.apple.KernelEventAgent
com.apple.mDNSResponder
com.apple.nibindd
com.apple.periodic-daily
com.apple.periodic-monthly
com.apple.periodic-weekly
com.apple.portmap
com.apple.syslogd
com.vix.cron
org.postfix.master
org.xinetd.xinetd
com.openssh.sshd
localhost:~ vanilla$
```

Figure 11.29 Example of typical output from launchctl list showing loaded launchd agents. Your output may differ.

System Log Files

Unix systems keep quite a few log files. Entries in the system logs record a variety of events, such as system startups, e-mail being sent, people logging in, and each use of sudo.

Mac OS X keeps most log files in /var/log, which is the same place as on many versions of Unix. **Figure 11.30** shows a typical listing for that directory. Some entries are text files and some are subdirectories containing multiple log files for a process. You'll notice that most of the filenames end in .gz, indicating that they have been compressed using the gzip program (and can be viewed with zcat; see the man pages).

The log files in /var/log are "rotated" or "rolled over" by the script /etc/periodic/daily/100.clean-logs, which is run by the periodic command. That command is in turn run from a launchd agent called com.apple.periodic-daily in the launchd configuration file /System/Library/LaunchDaemons/com.apple.periodic-daily.plist. (See "Running Regularly Scheduled Commands," earlier in this chapter.)

continues on next page

```
localhost:~ vanilla$ ls /var/log
CDIS.custom         lookupd.log.2.gz    mail.log.4.gz       system.log.3.gz
OSInstall.custom    lookupd.log.3.gz    monthly.out         system.log.4.gz
daily.out           lookupd.log.4.gz    netinfo.log         system.log.5.gz
ftp.log             lpr.log             netinfo.log.0.gz    system.log.6.gz
ftp.log.0.gz        lpr.log.0.gz        netinfo.log.1.gz    system.log.7.gz
ftp.log.1.gz        lpr.log.1.gz        netinfo.log.2.gz    weekly.out
ftp.log.2.gz        lpr.log.2.gz        netinfo.log.3.gz    wtmp
ftp.log.3.gz        lpr.log.3.gz        netinfo.log.4.gz    wtmp.0.gz
ftp.log.4.gz        lpr.log.4.gz        secure.log          wtmp.1.gz
httpd               mail.log            statistics          wtmp.2.gz
lastlog             mail.log.0.gz       system.log          wtmp.3.gz
lookupd.log         mail.log.1.gz       system.log.0.gz     wtmp.4.gz
lookupd.log.0.gz    mail.log.2.gz       system.log.1.gz
lookupd.log.1.gz    mail.log.3.gz       system.log.2.gz
localhost:~ vanilla$
```

Figure 11.30 Listing of the /var/log directory showing the system log files. Your output will differ.

If you have Web sharing turned on (in the Sharing pane of System Preferences, in the Finder), then the Apache Web-server logs are of interest. These are /var/log/httpd/access_log and /var/log/httpd/error_log. Every request handled by the Web server is logged in access_log, and errors are logged (surprise!) in error_log.

If you suspect that something is going wrong with your system, especially if something is happening over and over, looking through the system log files can reveal the cause of the problem.

There isn't any special command needed for most of the logs; they are simply text files, and you can use the tools described in earlier chapters to look at them (see especially Chapter 5). **Table 11.6** lists the most useful tools for looking through log files. While the log format differs for each process, in general all log file entries will include a timestamp, process name, and whatever the programmer decided was important to put in the log.

One particularly common situation involves watching a log file to see what is being added to it. See "To view the end of a file while it is growing," in Chapter 5.

One other important log file is the console log.

The console log is where most error messages go during regular operations. It can be viewed from Aqua using the Console utility: /Applications/Utilities/Console.

Console logs are created each time you log in to Aqua, and each one is owned and readable only by the user whose login created it (of course, root can also read it). In Mac OS X 10.4 the files are kept in directories named after the user ID number for the user (earlier versions of Mac OS X named the directories using the short username.) So, in 10.4 the console logs for the user with user ID 502 are located in /Library/Logs/Console/502/, where you'll find a file called console.log (the current or most recent log), as well as saved log files like console.log.0, console.log.1, and so on. Use ls -l to see the last-modified times. You can translate a use RID to a user name with

```
dscl . -search /users UniqueID userid
```

For example:

```
dscl . -search /users UniqueID 502
```

Table 11.6

Commands for Looking at Files

Command	What It Does
less	Views the file one screen at a time.
grep	Searches for text patterns.
tail	Views the end of a file. The -f (*follow*) option is especially useful for log files.

SYSTEM LOG FILES

The Boot Sequence

As anyone who's turned on a computer knows, a computer has to go through a series of steps before it becomes generally available for use. This process is called *booting*, which is short for *bootstrapping*—itself an abbreviation of "pulling itself up by its own bootstraps." Booting involves a sequence of starting software that in turn launches other software, and so on, until eventually the entire operating system is loaded.

Though you may not have cared about this sequence before, it's useful to know what the steps are when you're administering a machine. We'll give you an overview of the fundamental layers of software involved, and of the various places where something can go awry.

Every type of operating system has a somewhat different boot process, and this includes different flavors of Unix.

The Mac OS X boot sequence is based on `launchd`—a daemon that manages other daemons. We had a lot to say about `launchd` earlier in this chapter in the section "Running Regularly Scheduled Commands."

The official Apple documentation of the Mac OS X boot sequence is at http://developer.apple.com/documentation/MacOSX/Conceptual/BPSystemStartup/Articles/BootProcess.html.

Here's an abbreviated version:

1. When the power comes on, a part of the hardware called the BootROM performs a test of the hardware (Power On Self Test, or POST) and runs a piece of software called Open Firmware. This is the software that selects which operating system to use. In older Macs, Open Firmware can boot into either Mac OS 9 or Mac OS X, but the latest Macs can only boot into Mac OS X.
2. Once BootROM or the user has selected Mac OS X, the next piece of software to take over is the BootX booter, located in `/System/Library/CoreServices`. The system is now using software from the disk. If the cache of device drivers is out of date or corrupted, BootX will search `/System/Library/Extensions` for software drivers needed to communicate with various hardware devices. BootX then runs the kernel of the operating system: `/mach_kernel`.
3. The kernel now runs `launchd`, which is the first process, process ID 1. Prior to Mac OS X 10.4, the kernel would run `mach_init`. But starting with Mac OS X 10.4, `launchd` is used instead.

continues on next page

THE BOOT SEQUENCE

4. The launchd daemon manages many other daemons both during startup and throughout the system's uptime. launchd keeps running until the system is shut down.

   See man launchd and the various launchd configuration files in /System/Library/LaunchDaemons.

   Figures 11.31 and **11.32** show two launchd configuration files from the /System/Library/LaunchDaemons directory. Figure 11.31 shows

   com.apple.periodic-weekly.plist

   which causes launchd to run the command line

   /usr/sbin/periodic weekly

   at 3:15 a.m. every Saturday (day 6). See "Scheduling jobs using launchd," earlier in this chapter, for more on the use of launchd to schedule running commands.

   Figure 11.32 shows the configuration file org.postfix.master.plist

   which starts the Postfix e-mail server daemon /usr/libexec/postfix/master with an option of -e 60 (this causes the daemon to expire after 60 seconds of idle time). The QueueDirectories property tells launchd to watch the directory /var/spool/postfix/maildrop and restart the daemon if anything appears inside that directory.

   See "Creating New LaunchDaemons and StartupItems," later in this chapter, for details on creating a new launchd configuration to start and manage a system daemon.

5. Another step taken by launchd is running the script /etc/rc, which in turn runs the SystemStarter program. Apple intends to phase out the use of /etc/rc at some point in the future.

6. SystemStarter runs a series of scripts found in /System/Library/StartupItems and /Library/StartupItems.

   The scripts in /System/Library/StartupItems are supplied by Apple, and you should *not* change them. The /Library/StartupItems directory is where you may install scripts of your own to launch daemons or other commands at system startup. However, Apple is moving away from SystemStarter, and, as of Mac OS X 10.4, Apple recommends that you use launchd instead. See "Creating New LaunchDaemons and StartupItems," later in this chapter.

7. After launchd has finished starting the system daemons configured in /System/Library/LaunchDaemons and the legacy StartupItems have been run, launchd starts a process called loginwindow, which provides a graphical dialog and handles authenticating users. An administrator can configure Mac OS X to bypass user authentication (using Login Options in the Accounts pane of System Preferences) by having the system automatically log in as a specified user on startup; this is the default on a freshly installed Mac OS X system.

```
<?xml version="1.0" encoding="UTF-8"?>
<!DOCTYPE plist PUBLIC "-//Apple Computer//DTD PLIST 1.0//EN"
"http://www.apple.com/DTDs/PropertyList-1.0.dtd">
<plist version="1.0">
<dict>
  <key>Label</key>
  <string>com.apple.periodic-weekly</string>
  <key>ProgramArguments</key>
  <array>
       <string>/usr/sbin/periodic</string>
       <string>weekly</string>
  </array>
  <key>LowPriorityIO</key>
  <true/>
  <key>Nice</key>
  <integer>1</integer>
  <key>StartCalendarInterval</key>
  <dict>
       <key>Hour</key>
       <integer>3</integer>
       <key>Minute</key>
       <integer>15</integer>
       <key>Weekday</key>
       <integer>6</integer>
  </dict>
</dict>
</plist>
```

Figure 11.31 Contents of the launchd configuration file /System/Library/LaunchDaemons/com.apple.periodic-weekly.plist.

```
<?xml version="1.0" encoding="UTF-8"?>
<!DOCTYPE plist PUBLIC "-//Apple Computer//DTD PLIST 1.0//EN"
"http://www.apple.com/DTDs/PropertyList-1.0.dtd">
<plist version="1.0">
<dict>
  <key>Label</key>
  <string>org.postfix.master</string>
  <key>Program</key>
  <string>/usr/libexec/postfix/master</string>
  <key>ProgramArguments</key>
  <array>
       <string>master</string>
       <string>-e</string>
       <string>60</string>
  </array>
  <key>QueueDirectories</key>
  <array>
       <string>/var/spool/postfix/maildrop</string>
  </array>
</dict>
</plist>
```

Figure 11.32 Contents of the launchd configuration file /System/Library/LaunchDaemons/org.postfix.master.plist.

Creating New LaunchDaemons and StartupItems

In this section we are focusing on the use of `launchd` and `SystemStarter` to manage daemons that are started when the machine boots up and/or are started later as needed. You will use the same procedure you used to create a scheduled job with `launchd`, but with a different configuration in the .plist file. Before starting in on the next task, go back and review "Scheduling jobs using `launchd`," earlier in this chapter.

To create a LaunchDaemon that starts at boot time and runs continuously:

1. Create the configuration file `/Library/LaunchDaemons/`*`filename`*

   For example:

   ```
   sudo vi /Library/LaunchDaemons/
   → calculatord.plist
   ```

   The actual filename can be pretty much anything you like, but we suggest you use the .plist extension since the file will be in the `plist` format. For example, chat-service.plist is better than chat-service.

2. Set the `OnDemand` property to `false`.

   This means including the following in your file:

   ```
   <key>OnDemand</key>
   <false/>
   ```

   Figure 11.33 shows a sample `launchd` configuration file that will cause `launchd` to start up the Calculator application at boot time and keep it running all the time—note that the `OnDemand` property is set to `false`. The default is `true`, so if you leave that property out of the file, then `launchd` will not launch your daemon at boot time; instead it will wait for a "demand." See the next task for more on this.

   If you want the new daemon to run right away (as opposed to waiting for the next reboot), you may load the configuration file using `launchctl`:

   ```
   launchctl load /path/to/file
   ```



```
<?xml version="1.0" encoding="UTF-8"?>
<!DOCTYPE plist PUBLIC -//Apple Computer//DTD PLIST 1.0//EN
http://www.apple.com/DTDs/PropertyList-1.0.dtd >
<plist version="1.0">
<dict>
        <key>Label</key>
        <string>com.apple.calculator</string>
        <key>ProgramArguments</key>
        <array>
              <string>/Applications/Calculator.app/Contents/MacOS/Calculator</string>
        </array>
        <key>OnDemand</key>
        <false/>
</dict>
</plist>
```

Figure 11.33 A sample `launchd` configuration file that keeps the Calculator application running all the time (OnDemand set to `false`).

More on launchd

For more details and examples of using `launchd`, check out the following two articles online: "launchd in Depth" (www.afp548.com/article.php?story=20050620071558293) and "All About launchd Items and How to Make One Yourself" (www.macgeekery.com/tips/all_about_launchd_items_and_how_to_make_one_yourself). Also see the Apple document "Creating Launch-On-Demand Daemons" (http://developer.apple.com/documentation/MacOSX/Conceptual/BPSystemStartup/Articles/LaunchOnDemandDaemons.html) and read the portion of the `launchd.plist` `man` page that describes the `Socket` property.

For example:

```
launchctl load /Library/
→ LaunchDaemons/calculatord.plist
```

If you used the sample code from Figure 11.33, then the Calculator application will launch immediately, and if you quit it, `launchd` will promptly launch it again. To stop the daemon, you use `launchctl` to unload the configuration:

`launchctl unload` *`/path/to/file`*

For example:

```
launchctl unload /Library/
→ LaunchDaemons/calculatord.plist
```

✔ Tips

- If your daemon must run as root, or if you have it switching to a different user (via the `UserName` property in the configuration file), then you must run `launchctl` as root or reboot the machine:

  `sudo launchctl load` *`/path/to/file`*

- Review the `man` page for `launchd.plist` files:

  `man launchd.plist`

  and pay special attention to the `EXPECTATIONS` section at the beginning. There is a list of things that the daemon you are configuring should and should not do. Also, the `man` page has the complete list of the XML properties you can use in the configuration file. (Table 11.5 lists many of them, but the `man` page has the complete list.)

Looking at StartupItems

A StartupItem consists of a directory containing at least two files: the actual system-startup program (usually a script) that has the same name as the directory and should handle arguments of `start` and `stop`, and a file named StartupParameters.plist. **Figure 11.34** is the script `/System/Library/StartupItems/Apache/Apache` which is used by `SystemStarter` to start the Apache Web server at boot time. **Figure 11.35** shows the StartupParameters.plist file for the Apache

```
{
   Description     = "Apache web server";
   Provides        = ("Web Server");
   Uses            = ("Disks", "NFS");
}
```

Figure 11.35 StartupParameters.plist file for the Apache Web server StartupItem: `/System/Library/StartupItems/Apache/StartupParameters.plist`.

```
#!/bin/sh

##
# Apache HTTP Server
##

. /etc/rc.common

StartService ()
{
        if [ "${WEBSERVER:=-NO-}" = "-YES-" ]; then
        echo "Starting Apache web server"
        if [ ! -e /etc/httpd/httpd.conf ] ; then
                cp -p /etc/httpd/httpd.conf.default /etc/httpd/httpd.conf
        fi
        apachectl start
        if [ "${WEBPERFCACHESERVER:=-NO-}" = "-YES-" ]; then
            if [ -x /usr/sbin/webperfcachectl ]; then
                echo "Starting web performance cache server"
                /usr/sbin/webperfcachectl start
        fi
        fi
    fi
}

StopService ()
```

figure continues on next page

Figure 11.34 The `StartupItems` script `/System/Library/StartupItems/Apache/Apache` used by `SystemStarter` to start the Apache Web server at boot time.

Web server (/System/Library/StartupItems/Apache/StartupParameters.plist). The StartupParameters.plist file may be in one of two formats—either the legacy NeXT-style format (shown in Figure 11.34) or in the newer, recommended XML format described in the plist man page (shown in the next task).

StartupItems provided by Apple are in /System/Library/StartupItems, and StartupItems added by users (that's you) should go in /Library/StartupItems. You must be logged in as an admin user or root to create a new StartupItem.

To create a new StartupItem:

1. Create a new directory inside /Library/StartupItems.

   The new directory should have the same name as the service you are installing. For example, if you are installing the MySQL database engine, then you would call the directory MySQL:

   ```
   mkdir -p /Library/StartupItems/MySQL
   ```

   The -p option is necessary because the directory /Library/StartupItems may not already exist, and adding the -p tells mkdir to create the entire path.

continues on next page

Figure 11.34 *(continued)*

```
{
        if [ -x /usr/sbin/webperfcachectl ]; then
            echo "Stopping web performance cache server"
            /usr/sbin/webperfcachectl stop
        fi
        echo "Stopping Apache web server"
        apachectl stop
}

RestartService ()
{
        if [ "${WEBSERVER:=-NO-}" = "-YES-" ]; then
            echo "Restarting Apache web server"
            apachectl restart
            if [ "${WEBPERFCACHESERVER:=-NO-}" = "-YES-" ]; then
            if [ -x /usr/sbin/webperfcachectl ]; then
                echo "Restarting web performance cache server"
                /usr/sbin/webperfcachectl restart
        fi
  fi
  else
  StopService
  fi
}

RunService "$1"
```

2. Create a file named StartupParameters. plist file (for *property list*) in the new directory.

   The filename must be StartupParameters. plist.

   Figure 11.36 shows an annotated version of a StartupParameters.plist file for the MySQL database engine. This example uses the XML format documented in the `plist` man page.

3. Create the startup script itself.

   The best way to learn how to do this is to copy an existing Startup script and modify it. Look at the various scripts in the subdirectories of `/System/Library/StartupItems/`—your script might be able to be a modified copy of one of those. **Figure 11.37** is a code listing of a startup script for the MySQL database engine, but it could be adapted for many purposes. (Review Chapter 9.)

4. Notice the line

   `. /etc/rc.common`

   This appears in all of the Apple-provided StartupItem scripts, and you should probably use it as well. It executes the file `/etc/rc.common`. The file `/etc/rc.common` is another shell script that defines several functions, including the `RunService` function used in Figure 11.37.

   The `/etc/rc.common` script ends by executing `/etc/hostconfig`—yet *another* shell script that simply defines a bunch of variables used by the various Apple-supplied StartupItem scripts. Our example in Figure 11.36 uses a variable called `MYSQL` to determine if the service is supposed to run or not, the StartupItem script for the Apache Web server (`/System/Library/StartupItems/Apache/Apache`; see Figure 11.34) checks `WEBSERVER` variables, and so on.

continues on page 368

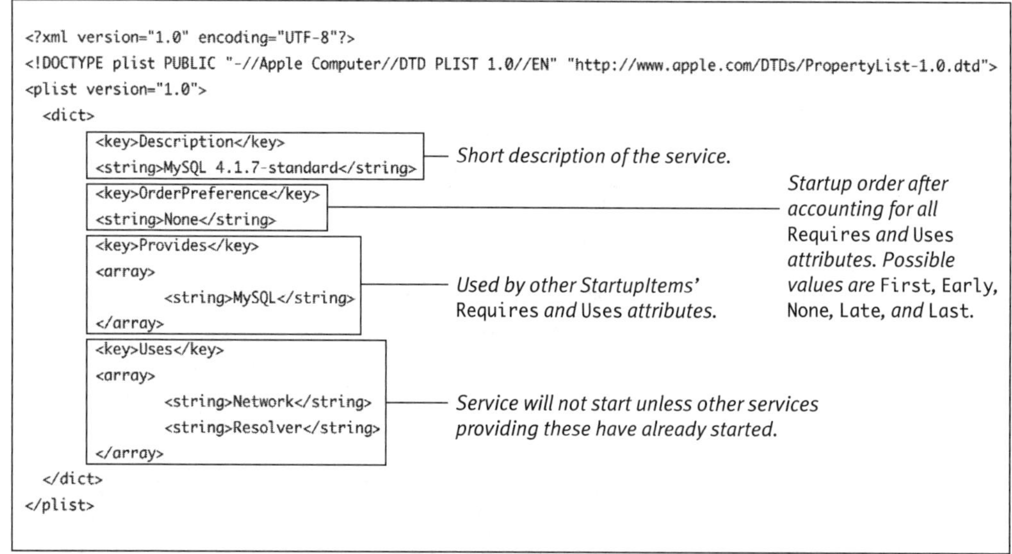

```
<?xml version="1.0" encoding="UTF-8"?>
<!DOCTYPE plist PUBLIC "-//Apple Computer//DTD PLIST 1.0//EN" "http://www.apple.com/DTDs/PropertyList-1.0.dtd">
<plist version="1.0">
  <dict>
      <key>Description</key>
      <string>MySQL 4.1.7-standard</string>
      <key>OrderPreference</key>
      <string>None</string>
      <key>Provides</key>
      <array>
            <string>MySQL</string>
      </array>
      <key>Uses</key>
      <array>
            <string>Network</string>
            <string>Resolver</string>
      </array>
  </dict>
</plist>
```

Short description of the service.
Startup order after accounting for all Requires and Uses attributes. Possible values are First, Early, None, Late, and Last.
Used by other StartupItems' Requires and Uses attributes.
Service will not start unless other services providing these have already started.

Figure 11.36 Example of a StartupParameters. plist file for the MySQL database server.

```
#!/bin/sh
#
# /Library/StartupItems/MySQL/MySQL
#
# A script to automatically start up MySQL on system bootup
# for Mac OS X. This is actually just a wrapper script around
# the standard mysql.server init script, which is included in
# the binary distribution.
#
# (c) 2003 MySQL AB
# Written by Lenz Grimmer <lenz@mysql.com>
#

# Suppress the annoying "$1: unbound variable" error when no option
# was given
if [ -z $1 ] ; then
        echo "Usage: $0 [start|stop|restart] "
        exit 1
fi

# Source the common setup functions for startup scripts
test -r /etc/rc.common || exit 1
. /etc/rc.common

# The path to the mysql.server init script. The official MySQL
# Mac OS X packages are being installed into /usr/local/mysql.
SCRIPT="/usr/local/mysql/support-files/mysql.server"

StartService ()
{
    if [ "${MYSQL:=-NO-}" = "-YES-" ] ; then
        ConsoleMessage "Starting MySQL database server"
        $SCRIPT start > /dev/null 2>&1
    fi
}

StopService ()
{
        ConsoleMessage "Stopping MySQL database server"
        $SCRIPT stop > /dev/null 2>&1
}

RestartService ()
{
        ConsoleMessage "Restarting MySQL database server"
        $SCRIPT restart > /dev/null 2>&1
}

if test -x $SCRIPT ; then
        RunService "$1"
else
        ConsoleMessage "Could not find MySQL startup script!"
fi
```

Figure 11.37 Example of a StartupItem script for the MySQL database server. This would be installed as /System/Library/StartupItems/MySQL/MySQL.

5. Notice how our example in Figure 11.37 defines separate functions called `StartService`, `StopService`, and `RestartService`.

   The `StartService` function is the one that actually runs the service with the line

   ```
   $SCRIPT start > /dev/null 2>&1
   ```

   The `SCRIPT` variable is defined to be the full path to the executable for the service—in this case:

   ```
   SCRIPT="/usr/local/mysql/support-files/
   → mysql.server
   ```

   Inside the `StartService` function is an `if` statement that looks like this:

   ```
   if [ "${MYSQL:=-NO-}" = "-YES-" ]
   ```

   That is a somewhat advanced shell script trick that is checking if `"${MYSQL:=-NO-}"` is the same as `-YES-`.

   The tricky part is `"${MYSQL:=-NO-}"` — that means "Get the value of `$MYSQL`, or if there is no value, then use `-NO-`." The value of `$MYSQL` is going to come from `/etc/hostconfig`—more about that in the next step.

6. Edit `/etc/hostconfig` to add a variable for your new service.

   The `/etc/hostconfig` script just holds a bunch of variables that are normally set by the various tools in System Preferences (referred to as "control panels" in `/etc/hostconfig`). **Figure 11.38** is an example of a typical `/etc/hostconfig` file.

7. Using our example from Figure 11.37, you would want to add the following line to `/etc/hostconfig`:

   ```
   MYSQL=-YES-
   ```

   The idea here is that your new StartupItem script is *always* going to be executed at boot time by `SystemStarter` with an argument of `start`, so you want an easy way to disable it. By having a single place for all StartupItem scripts to check, you can quickly see which ones are enabled and disabled.

8. Test the script from the command line to see that your new service starts up. Depending on the nature of your service, you might need to test it as root (using `sudo`):

   ```
   sudo /Library/StartupItems/
   → MyService/MyService start
   ```

   For example:

   ```
   sudo /Library/StartupItems/
   → MySQL/MySQL start
   ```

9. Reboot the machine for further confirmation.

✔ Tips

- Apple's official documentation for creating new StartupItems is available via a link on http://developer.apple.com/documentation/MacOSX/Conceptual/BPSystemStartup/ (that's one long URL!).

- You'll need to decide what should go in the Requires entry of the StartupParameters.plist. Have a look at the different StartupParameters.plist files in each of the subdirectories of `/System/Library/StartupItems/` and see what is in the Provides entry for each item. You can see all the Provides entries with the following command line:

  ```
  grep Provides /System/Library/
  → StartupItems/*/*.plist
  ```

  or

  ```
  find /System/Library/StartupItems -
  → name "*plist" | xargs grep
  → Provides
  ```

```
##
# /etc/hostconfig
##
# This file is maintained by the system control panels
##
# Network configuration
HOSTNAME=-AUTOMATIC-
ROUTER=-AUTOMATIC-
# Services
AFPSERVER=-YES-
AUTHSERVER=-NO-
AUTOMOUNT=-YES-
CUPS=-YES-
IPFORWARDING=-NO-
IPV6=-YES-
MAILSERVER=-AUTOMATIC-
NETINFOSERVER=-AUTOMATIC-
NFSLOCKS=-AUTOMATIC-
NISDOMAIN=-NO-
RPCSERVER=-AUTOMATIC-
TIMESYNC=-YES-
QTSSERVER=-NO-
WEBSERVER=-NO-
SMBSERVER=-NO-
DNSSERVER=-NO-
COREDUMPS=-NO-
VPNSERVER=-NO-
SNMPSERVER=-NO-
CHATSERVER=-NO-
SPOTLIGHT=-YES-
CRASHREPORTER=-YES-
ARDAGENT=-YES-
ENCRYPTSWAP=-NO-
```

Figure 11.38 A typical /etc/hostconfig file. Yours will look different.

Setting the Hostname

If your machine is being used as a server on the Internet, you usually want it to be identified by a *fully qualified domain name*, or *FQDN*. You've already seen FQDNs, although you might not have known that's what they were called. The URL www.peachpit.com is an FQDN, as is mail.yahoo.com. If your machine has been assigned a FQDN, it may be able to figure out its hostname by itself, but it may not. The hostname command shows what your machine thinks its FQDN or hostname is. See Chapter 14, "Installing and Configuring Servers," for a more detailed discussion of FQDNs, including how to tell your machine which hostname (or FQDN) to use. The really short version of how to do it is that you edit the HOSTNAME entry /etc/hostconfig.

Webmin—a GUI Tool for System Administration

Webmin is a Web-based interface for Unix system administration that allows you to use a Web browser to perform a large variety of tasks, such as managing users and groups, managing servers such as database servers, setting up `cron` jobs, and much more. The basic Webmin package provides one set of features, and others are available as additional modules from Shoutcast administration, MRTG network traffic grapher, and others.

As of this writing, the latest version of Webmin (1.221) will work with Mac OS X 10.4 but does not yet provide support for `launchd`. So you can use it to create `cron` jobs but not `launchd` agents. Webmin is an actively maintained project with many developers contributing to it, so we expect upcoming versions to add more support for new Mac OS X features.

Webmin installs its own tiny Web server that uses the HTTPS protocol if possible. HTTPS is the HTTP protocol plus Secure Socket Layer; it causes all data sent to or from the Web server to be encrypted. This greatly reduces the risk of a packet-sniffing attack (see Chapter 12), which could intercept the Webmin user name and password, giving the attacker the equivalent of root access.

In order for Webmin to use SSL, you must install the Perl module called `Net::SSLeay`. Chapter 13 describes how to do this. If you do not install `Net::SSLeay`, you may still use Webmin, but any use of it when the Web browser is on another machine is vulnerable to packet-sniffing attacks.

Before installing Webmin, be sure to check out http://webmin.com/changes.html. Also read Chapter 13, in particular the section "Manually Installing from Source Code," which goes into more detail about the basic installation procedures you should use.

Troubleshooting Tips

Not that *anything ever* goes wrong with your system, but when something *does* go wrong, there are some things you can try in order to figure out what has happened.

Troubleshooting problems in a Unix system is similar in many ways to troubleshooting on any system: You start by comparing the symptoms of the problem with the patient's medical history. When did the problem start? Oh, right after you installed the system-configuration files you were up all night editing? Hmmm. Maybe that's a clue to the problem . . .

Using the system log files

The system log files (described earlier in this chapter) often have an error message related to the problem you are experiencing. Usually you won't understand the error message, but don't stop there. You can search the Web for information regarding the exact error message you are seeing.

To search the Web for an error message:

1. Copy whatever seems to be the most descriptive part of the error message.
2. Use your favorite Web search engine to search for the error message.

   This usually means enclosing all the words in quotes—for example,

   "DNSAgent: dns_send_query_server - timeout"
3. Consider adding "Mac OS X" or "Darwin" as a separate search string.

   For example, using the Google search engine,

   "DNSAgent: dns_send_query_server - timeout" + "Mac OS X"

   limits the search to pages that contain both of the phrases enclosed in quotes. (We found five pages with that search.)

Permission problems

If you are getting an error that includes the phrase "Permission denied" or something similar, it's a sign that you have a permission problem somewhere—a common problem in Unix. Permission problems crop up because a program might not be able to write to a directory or file it expects to, or because it might not be able to read a file and thus is missing some configuration information.

Tracking down permission problems, like much computer troubleshooting, requires that you think like the machine. Remember that in order to create a file, a process must have write permission for the *directory* containing the file (because the filename is an entry in the directory), while in order to change a file, you must have write permission on the *file* itself.

One quick thing to try is the "Repair Permissions" feature in the GUI application Disk Utility (located in the Utilities folder of the Applications folder). It will restore the permissions on many system files to their Apple-supplied defaults. Review Chapter 8 for details on permissions.

Dealing with "device full" problems

Another problem you are likely to run into sooner or later is when a disk fills up.

If you see an error message that says, "Write Error: No space left on device," you've filled up a disk volume; that is, you've used up all the available storage space. (Note that in Unix documentation the terms *volume* and *partition* are often used interchangeably—for example, in the `man` pages for `df` and `diskutil`.)

continues on next page

Although this doesn't happen every day (hopefully!), the consequences can be pretty harsh: Some programs may simply stop working. For example, a mail server cannot save incoming mail if there is no disk space left.

You can quickly see if you are running out of disk space by using the `df` command (described in "To see a summary of disk usage for the entire system," earlier in this chapter). **Figure 11.39** shows an example of a machine with two disks, one of which has two volumes (also called partitions). In the example, volume s9 on disk0 is almost full.

If you see that any of the regular volumes are over 90 percent capacity, it's time to start worrying. By "regular volumes," we mean the ones where the filesystem column in `df` starts with `/dev/disk`. Remember that `df` displays information about various pseudo-volumes that always show up at 100 percent capacity—for example, the `fdesc` (*file descriptor*) filesystem, which is used to keep track of open files.

This is possible because the operating system keeps a small amount of disk space in reserve to reduce the chance of a volume's filling up. If you see that a disk volume is at 101 percent capacity, then you have a problem *now*.

Basic steps to free up space on a disk volume:

- Delete unneeded files on the critical volume. Remember that using the Trash does not delete files—it moves them. To actually delete the files, use `rm` and/or empty the Trash. See "To clear out users' Trash for them," below.
- Move one or more directories to a different volume and put a symbolic link where the directory used to be. See "To move directories from one disk to another while keeping the original path," below.
- Add more disks, and then move directories to the new disks. In Mac OS X, this is as easy as it has always been on the Mac. With external FireWire and USB hard drives, you don't even need to shut down.

  Note that Mac OS X automatically makes any disks you add show up in `/Volumes`.

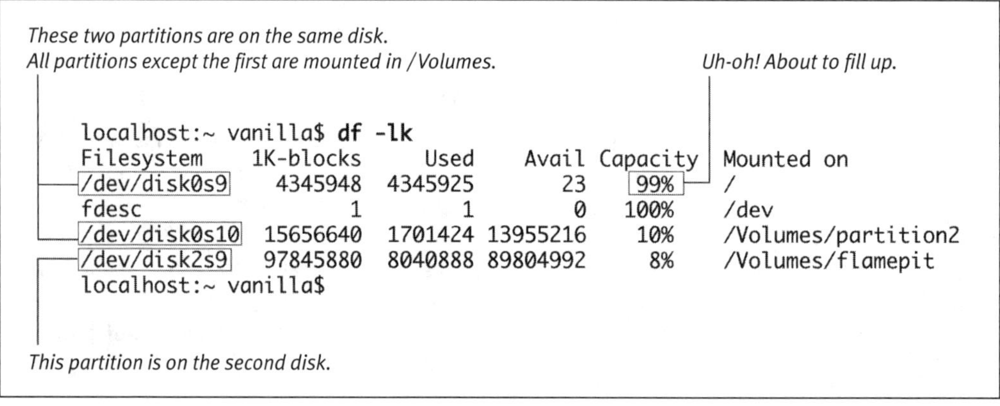

Figure 11.39 Example of output from `df -lk` showing two disks with a total of three volumes (also called *partitions*). Partition s9 on disko is almost full.

On almost all other Unix systems, adding a disk is more complicated, but you can mount new disks on any directory. For example, you could mount a new disk on `/Users` (though you would still have to copy the old contents onto the new disk).

To clear out users' Trash for them:

1. Find each user's Trash directory.

   Each user has a `.Trash` directory in his or her home directory.

   If the volume that's filling up is the one that holds users' home directories, go into each user's home directory and delete his or her `.Trash` directory (it is re-created when the user needs it).

   You'll need to do the next step for each user.

2. `sudo rm -rf ~`*`username`*`/.Trash`

   That removes an entire `.Trash` directory. (In case you are wondering, the `.Trash` directory will be re-created when needed; also, using `rm -rf ~`*`username`*`/.Trash/*` will remove the contents only, but will miss deleting dot-files at the top level of the `.Trash` directory.)

   If you use the Finder to trash a file that is on a different volume than your home directory, then instead of going into `~/.Trash`, that file goes into a different Trash directory.

   There are directories at the root level of the directory on which each volume is mounted. Huh, you say? Here is an example:

   Let's say you have three disk volumes. Perhaps you have two disks, and one of them has two partitions, so you have a total of three disk volumes. Your `df` output might look like that shown in Figure 11.39. (Note the use of the `-lk` options to show only local volumes, and the sizes in kilobytes. Note too that `df` will show only volumes, not the Trash files themselves.)

   In that case, there are three directories, each called `.Trashes`:

   `/.Trashes`

   `/Volumes/partition2/.Trashes`

   `/Volumes/flamepit/.Trashes`

   Each of the directories has subdirectories for each user ID that has trashed files from that volume. So if user puffball has `uid 502`, then there might be

   `/Users/puffball/.Trash`

   `/Volumes/partition2/.Trashes/502`

   `/Volumes/flamepit/.Trashes/502`

   You want to remove the `.Trashes` directory from the critical volume (don't worry, it will be re-created when needed).

3. `sudo rm -rf /`*`volume-in-trouble`*`/.`
   `→ Trashes`

   To remove the `.Trashes` directory for the volume mounted on `/Volumes/partition2`:

   `sudo rm -rf /Volumes/partition2/.`
   `→ Trashes`

If you have one volume that is filling up and another with more space (perhaps you've added a second disk), you can move directories from the full volume to the spacious one and replace the original directory with a symbolic link.

Going Over 100 Percent

On some Unix systems, `df` may show you that a filesystem (as it does with a volume) is *over* 100 percent capacity.

On those systems, the "used" and "available" columns in `df` add up to something less than the column showing the total capacity. On Mac OS X the numbers add up exactly.

To move directories from one disk to another while keeping the original path:

1. Use `ditto` to copy the directory.

   For example, if you want to move the `/Users` directory to the volume mounted on `/Volumes/partition2`, you can use

   ```
   sudo ditto -rsrc /Users
   → /Volumes/partition2/Users
   ```

2. `mv olddir olddir.save`

   For example:

   ```
   mv /Users /Users.save
   ```

   You'll delete it later after making sure that everything is OK.

3. Create a symbolic link where the old directory was, pointing to the new directory.

   For example:

   ```
   ln -s /Volumes/partition2/Users
   → /Users
   ```

   So anything that accesses `/Users` still works.

4. When everything seems OK, delete the old directory.

   For example:

   ```
   rm -rf /Users.save
   ```


Problems booting up

In the unlikely and scary event that your machine won't completely boot up, you may still be able to get things working again—assuming that the machine can at least begin the boot process.

If you are able to boot into single-user mode, then you can attempt to repair file system damage using the `fsck` (*file system check*) command.

To watch all the system-startup messages:

- Hold down both Cmd and V while booting.

  This is called "booting in verbose mode."

  In a normal, healthy boot-up, you see a great deal of text messages scrolling across the screen as the system goes through the boot-up process.

  It is very important to learn what a healthy boot-up looks like so that you'll notice any problems when they occur. Try it a couple of times and watch what a normal start-up looks like. Booting in verbose mode won't directly fix anything, but you may be able to see what's going wrong, or at least copy a message off the screen to give to someone else to assist in troubleshooting.

The last resort

In most cases your disks will be using a *journaling file system*, which makes data corruption extremely unlikely. You can see a list of your volumes with

```
diskutil list
```

and see what kind of file system a volume has with

```
diskutil info volume
```

For example:

```
diskutil list /dev/disk0s2
```

If the output includes `Journaled HFS+`, then the volume has a journaled file system and the following tasks will probably have no effect.

This next task is mainly, useful only if your disk(s) are *not* formatted with a journaling file system, and should be considered a last resort. Do not attempt it unless you are willing to risk losing data (maybe even all the data on your disk) and you have tried all other available approaches.

To check and repair the file system with fsck:

1. Boot into single-user mode.

   You do this by holding down both Cmd and S while the machine starts up.

   If the system isn't too badly messed up, you end up at a prompt like this:

   ```
   localhost#
   ```

   Your next move is to try to check and repair the file system.

2. `/sbin/fsck -fy`

   This is basically the command-line version of the repair feature in Disk Utility.

   See the `man` page for `fsck` to learn more about that command.

   When you get back to a prompt, you can try mounting the root volume and booting the machine.

   When you get back to the prompt, run it again to make sure that the repairs were effective.

continues on next page

Getting More Help

There are plenty of places to get deeper into Unix system administration. Here are a few:

The official Apple documentation for the Darwin layer of Mac OS X can be found at http://developer.apple.com/darwin. Apple offers training and certification for Mac OS X; see http://train.apple.com/.

Another useful set of documentation from Apple is oriented toward developers (programmers) but contains much information of interest to anyone wanting to dig deeper into Mac OS X: http://developer.apple.com/techpubs/macosx/Essentials/SystemOverview.

The Mac OS X Hints Web site (www.macosxhints.com) is a wonderful user-supported site run by Rob Griffiths. It is basically a big bulletin board for Mac OS X information. It's free, but you can make a donation to support it.

Two valuable books in the Unix system-administration world are *Essential System Administration*, Third Edition, by Æleen Frisch (O'Reilly; www.oreilly.com/catalog/esa3); and *Unix System Administration Handbook*, 3rd Edition, by Evi Nemeth, Garth Snyder, Scott Seebass, and Trent R. Hein (Admin.com; www.admin.com).

3. `/sbin/fsck -fy`

   If you get a message saying that your disk "appears to be OK," then `fsck` worked.

   - ▲ If it didn't work, try booting from an external FireWire drive if available, or the installation DVD or CD. You may then be able to run Terminal and possibly view the damaged volumes. You will probably need help from an experienced Unix administrator to mount the damaged volume(s) and fix them. Contacting Apple for assistance isn't a bad idea, either.
   - ▲ If it worked (or even if it didn't), go ahead and reboot the machine.

4. `reboot`

   Hopefully, the machine starts up and all is well.

✔ Tip

- ■ In `/Library/Logs` you may find log files that have some record of things that have gone wrong. Look for files with names such as panic.log and a `CrashReporter` subdirectory. There may also be `CrashReporter` subdirectories in any users' own `Library/Logs` directories—that is, `/Users/`*`user name`*`/Library/Logs/CrashReporter/`.

12

Security

Security, like freedom, is a goal and an ideal, not an absolute condition.

As shipped, Mac OS X is fairly secure. If you use your machine only as a personal computer and do not install any new server software on it, then your only security assignment is to regularly use the Apple Software Update tool (see "Keeping Up-to-Date," later in this chapter).

On the other hand, if you have multiple users or you install new Internet server software on your machine, then you are well advised to pay more attention to security.

Because Unix systems are inherently multiuser, they tend to have many people using them. This means there are likely to be a number of people who have various levels of access to a machine running Unix, and each of these users' accounts is a potential entry point for an attacker. Also, Unix's origin as a system created to foster collaborative work means that security settings default to letting all users on a system have at least read-only access. (In Mac OS X, users' home directories are set up with a higher level of security, but most system files are still readable by all users.)

You achieve security only by preventing unauthorized access to your system. It is also important to monitor your system to see if its security has been breached.

In this chapter we cover the basics of Unix system security, including physical security, choosing and protecting passwords, protecting against attacks over the Internet, and keeping up-to-date with the latest software and security-related announcements.

continues on next page

A note about terminology: Throughout this chapter we use the terms *server* and *service*, and you need to keep in mind their different meanings. *Server* can refer to either a physical machine, as in "That G5 in the corner is our Web-server box," or a piece of software that provides a service—for example, "That G5 in the corner is running the Apache Web server" or "Postfix is the server software that provides e-mail service on this box."

Security Checklist

Here's a checklist to go though when you set up a new system, when you take responsibility for a system, and periodically after that. You'll learn more about each of these steps in the rest of this chapter.

1. Maintain good physical security.
2. Use only strong passwords, and change them regularly.
3. Configure the built-in firewall software to block access to all ports you are not using. (Choose the Sharing pane in System Preferences.)
4. Give as few people admin (root) access as is practical.
5. Change all admin passwords at least once every three months.
6. If the machine provides any services (such as Post Office Protocol [POP], Internet Mail Access Protocol [IMAP], or File Transfer Protocol [FTP]) that use unencrypted passwords, set up special shells for the users of those services so that they cannot log in to a standard shell. This defends against password-sniffing attacks by preventing a sniffed user name and password from being used to log in to a regular shell.
7. Do not allow Telnet access (it uses an unencrypted connection to provide shell access, so everything sent in the connection, including passwords, is susceptible to interception by bad people).
8. Only run servers you actually need. For example, do not run an e-mail server unless you need to.
9. Keep your software (especially servers) up-to-date.
10. Monitor the Computer Emergency Response Team Web site (www.cert.org) or e-mail lists.
11. Periodically search your system for `setuid` root files.
12. Create MD5 checksums of all files in `/etc` and in each of the directories in your `PATH`. Save these on a CD-ROM, and run an `md5sum` check against the list every month.

Physical Security

It might seem obvious, but we think it is worth pointing out that you should keep your computer as physically secure as you want its data to be.

If someone has physical access to your machine, she could boot it into single-user mode and then have the run of the system. (See Chapter 11, "Introduction to System Administration," for more on booting into single-user mode.)

And, of course, if someone has physical access to the machine, he might be able to steal it, install malicious software on it, or even install a hardware keystroke-recording device (see Privacy.org; www.privacy.org/archives/000990.html).

The main idea here is to remember that computers, hard drives, and wires all exist in the physical world, and that the same security precautions you apply to, say, your checkbook should be applied to your computer and your data.

Choosing Good Passwords

Passwords are the foundation of Unix security. All the other security measures are for naught if you have weak passwords (meaning that they're easy to guess or obtain) or if someone is able to obtain a user's password, no matter how good it is.

As we discussed in Chapter 11, a good password is one that is both easy to remember (so it doesn't get written on a note taped to the user's screen) and hard to guess. The latter means that the password should not be susceptible to a *dictionary attack* (described below).

How passwords are vulnerable

Unauthorized people obtain passwords in three ways. Think about whether you're vulnerable to any of these:

- **User error**—This includes writing the password on a note stuck to your screen, or sending a password via e-mail or leaving it in voice mail.
- **Dictionary attacks**—Done by a software program that tries millions of guesses to figure out a password. These attacks start by obtaining the encrypted version of a password and comparing it with every possible encrypted version of a huge list of words and possible passwords (the *dictionary*). If they match, then the attacker knows what the password is.
- **Packet-sniffing attacks**—These occur when a monitoring device is illicitly used to examine all the data flowing on a network. User names and passwords can be "sniffed" out of the data stream with ease, so any unencrypted traffic is completely vulnerable. These attacks are described in more detail below in "Protecting Yourself from Internet Attacks."

The first two vulnerabilities (user error and dictionary attacks) are fairly easy to reduce or eliminate, so we'll tackle those first. The third vulnerability, packet-sniffing attacks, comes from the vulnerability of unencrypted data traveling over a network. Reducing this vulnerability is more complex.

You need to communicate to your users the potential consequences of their passwords' being obtained by an attacker: The system can be rendered unusable, data can be lost or altered, private information can be made public, and the system can be used as a staging area for further attacks.

Passwords are liable to be compromised when users do foolish things like writing them on notes left under their keyboard, letting someone watch them enter their password, or sending a password via e-mail. E-mail messages are like postcards—they can be read at several places along their journey, and there is no way of knowing if the intended recipient is actually the person who reads the e-mail. It is a very bad idea to send unencrypted passwords via e-mail. Ultimately, you prevent the compromise of passwords through user error by educating your users.

Because computers are so fast these days, a dictionary attack using a very large dictionary of possible passwords can be completed in a matter of hours or days. This method includes adding numbers to the beginning and end of every word, so a dictionary attack can guess a password of sunny23 or 7times7.

A dictionary attack can work only if the encryption method used always produces the same encrypted text from the same input (such systems are said to be *deterministic*), and if the attacker's dictionary includes the plain-text password. Sadly, the standard encryption method used to store passwords on Unix systems does indeed produce the same output whenever it is given the same input. (The encryption method used, known as *crypt*, is an advanced version of the World War II–era Enigma encryption system used by the German military and cracked by the Poles and later the British.)

Many modern Unix systems add a layer of defense against dictionary attacks by making the encrypted passwords available only to the root account. On Mac OS X prior to version 10.3, anyone could use the `nidump` command to reveal all of the encrypted passwords. Even in version 10.3, user accounts created in prior versions of Mac OS X were vulnerable to this.

It would be best if computer systems did not use authentication methods that are vulnerable to dictionary and packet-sniffing attacks (see the sidebar "S/Key and Kerberos: Better Authentication Systems" for two examples), but the crypt system of password encryption is so widely used in the Unix world that this will not happen soon (enough).

So, the best available defense against dictionary attacks is to use passwords that are not in anyone's dictionary. This means passwords that contain a combination of letters, numbers, and punctuation, and that do not contain a dictionary word.

S/Key and Kerberos: Better Authentication Systems

There are alternatives to the standard Unix password system, which uses passwords that are vulnerable to dictionary and packet-sniffing attacks.

These alternatives have been around for many years but are still far from being universally adopted:

S/Key—Secure Key is a onetime password (OTP) system—that is, a system that generates and uses passwords that are valid only once. S/Key is a registered trademark of Bell Communications Research (where it was developed), so the acronym OTP is often used instead.

When a user attempts to log in to an OTP-protected system, she gets a "challenge" (some numbers) from the server, which she enters into an OTP response generator on her end, along with her password. The response generator then creates a onetime password, which the user enters into the protected system to obtain access.

An OTP response generator for Mac OS X is SkeyCalc (www.orange-carb.org/SkeyCalc).

Kerberos—Developed at the Massachusetts Institute of Technology, Kerberos (http://web.mit.edu/kerberos/www) is an even more secure system. (Kerberos is the Greek name for the three-headed dog that guarded the entrance to Hades; the dog is also known by its Latin name, Cerberus.) Kerberos exchanges encrypted information between the client and server, and the server issues a temporary "ticket" to the client. Kerberos is designed to be invulnerable to packet sniffing and to situations in which an attacker is able to commandeer a machine between the user and the service he is trying to authenticate into (a "man in the middle" attack). We believe that Apple is considering adding increased support for Kerberos to future versions of Mac OS X.

To choose a good password:

1. Pick a song lyric, poem, or phrase from your favorite story—for example, "Can any human being ever reach that kind of light?" (from "Galileo," by Emily Saliers of the Indigo Girls).
2. Take the first letter of each word in the phrase; so here we have
   Cahbertkol
3. Change some of the letters to numbers.
   The changes should be ones that make sense to you. Perhaps the *C* becomes *100* because *C* is the Roman numeral for 100:
   100ahbertkol
4. Change the result to include some punctuation.
   Perhaps the *k* becomes *%* because it sort of looks like a *%*, and perhaps you add a *?* at the end because the phrase itself is a question. So you have
   100ahbert%ol?
5. Make sure the remaining characters include both upper- and lowercase letters.
   Maybe you make the *h* and *b* uppercase because you like human beings:
   100aHBert%ol?
6. You've got a great password.
   The result is very unlikely to be in anyone's dictionary of passwords and should be easy for you to remember because it is based on something that has personal meaning for you.

✔ Tip

- Many Unix password systems pay attention only to the first eight characters of the password, but there is no harm in using a longer one if it helps you remember. Mac OS X pays attention to the first 32 characters, so you can have a nice long password, like
  M@y your 23000 feet always be SWIFT!

Connecting to the Internet with a Private IP Address

Private TCP/IP network addresses are those that begin with 10., 172.16., or 192.168. (for example, the following are all private addresses: 10.1.1.23, 172.16.20.35, 192.168.1.254).

If your machine has a private address, it can still use the public Internet via a process called *Network Address Translation* (*NAT*).

Private networks often have a NAT server that allows the machines on the local, private network to connect to the Internet.

A NAT server translates the return addresses of all outgoing data so that to the rest of the world, the data is coming from a nonprivate IP address. When responses come back in to the NAT server from the outside world, it again translates and forwards the data to the appropriate machine on the private network.

One effect of using NAT is that machines on the public Internet cannot initiate connections to machines behind the NAT server. The NAT server will pass data to the local, private machines only if it comes in response to a connection started from the local network.

You can read more about private addresses at www.ietf.org/rfc/rfc1918.txt and about NAT at www.ietf.org/rfc/rfc1631.txt and www.ietf.org/rfc/rfc2766.txt.

Protecting Yourself from Internet Attacks

If your computer is connected to a network, then by definition other computers on that network can communicate with your computer. If your network is connected to another network (that is, if it's part of an inter-network), then your exposure is potentially greater. If your computer is connected to the Internet, then it is connected to the world's largest inter-network and your exposure to potentially naughty people is about as big as it gets.

The default configuration for Mac OS X is reasonably secure from Internet attacks. Nonetheless, it is helpful to have a basic understanding of the security risks of connecting to the Internet and of how to protect your machine from attack.

If your machine is connected to the Internet, it may be exposed to unauthorized and malicious people attempting to gain control of it or to harm it in some way. We say "may be" because some ways of connecting your machine to the Internet do not expose it to attack, and there are things you can do to configure your machine to reduce its exposure.

Every machine connected to the Internet has either a public or private IP address.

Some IP addresses are actually not part of the public Internet. These addresses (known as *private addresses*) are used by networks that are, well, private, and not accessible to machines on the public Internet. A machine with a private IP address may still be (indirectly) connected to the Internet. See the sidebar "Connecting to the Internet with a Private IP Address."

continues on next page

On the other hand, if your machine has a publicly reachable IP address, then machines anywhere on the Internet can attempt to initiate connections to it. Basically, they can knock on the door, but they only succeed in making a connection if your machine is "listening" for the type of connection being attempted. For example, if you have activated Web sharing, then other machines can connect to the Web server software running on your machine.

Packet-sniffing attacks

Packet-sniffing attacks are the most insidious type of attack you are likely to deal with. In a packet-sniffing attack, a *sniffer* program running on a computer examines all the data flowing on that machine's local network. This makes all the unencrypted data on that network easily available for examination: user names, passwords, credit card numbers, medical histories, you name it. Any data whatsoever that is traveling unencrypted on a network is open for examination via a packet sniffer.

There are legitimate uses of packet sniffers, primarily having to do with diagnosing networking problems, so the mere existence of a packet-sniffer program doesn't automatically mean that someone is attacking your system or network, but it is certainly something to be concerned about.

To run a packet sniffer, though, one must have full control over the machine on which it is run. On a Unix machine, that means having root access. But a user running a Mac OS 9 or Windows machine can also run packet sniffers. (The packet sniffer needs to be able to alter settings in the network interface card—the Ethernet adapter—to put it into promiscuous mode, in which it reads every packet of data passing by on the wired or wireless network.)

Using easily available tools (see the sidebar "Packet Sniffers and Port Scanners"), it is possible to grab user names and passwords that are being sent over the local network between machines. **Figure 12.1** is a diagram of a typical local area network (LAN) connected to the Internet. The packet sniffer could be on your local network, or on a network where someone is connecting to a server on your network. In either case, the sniffer will be able to obtain unencrypted passwords (and other information) that is

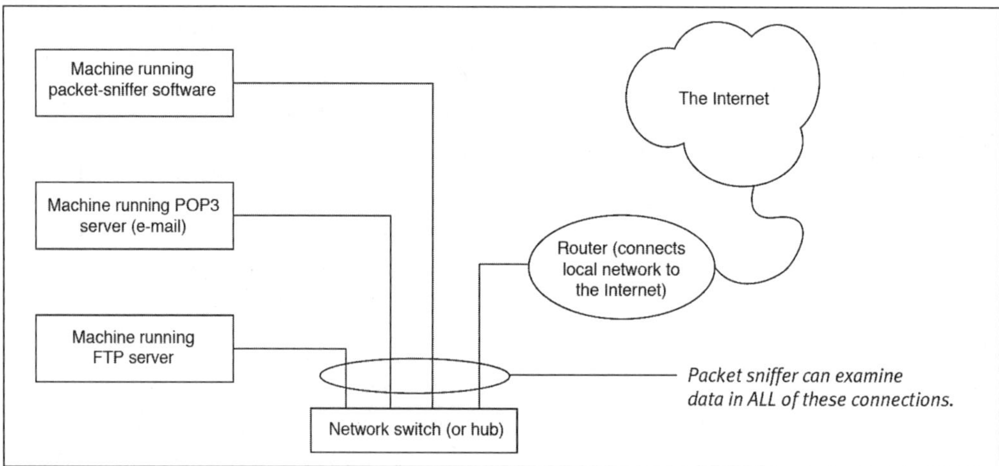

Figure 12.1 Diagram showing a typical LAN connected to the Internet and the reach of a packet sniffer.

What an Attack on IIS Looks Like

If you turn on Web sharing (in the Sharing pane of System Preferences), and if your machine is connected to the Internet with a publicly accessible IP address, you can almost be certain to see entries in the server log file (`/var/log/httpd/access_log`) that reveal attacks directed at Microsoft's IIS server software.

A typical attack will show up in the Web server log as

```
66.169.207.82 - - [13/Jul/2005:07:59:19
→ -0700] "GET /scripts/..%c0%2f../
→ winnt/ system32/cmd.exe?/c+dir
→ HTTP/ 1.0" 404 319
```

That line shows an attack originating from the machine with the IP address 66.169.207.82 on July 13, 2005, at 7:59 GMT. The attack attempted to run a program called `cmd.exe`. The Web server returned a "Page Not Found" code (404), and the attack had no effect besides using up a bit of bandwidth and creating a log entry. On the other hand, had this machine been running Windows NT with an unsecured version of IIS, the attack might have succeeded in gaining control of the machine. Seeing a dozen or more of these attacks every day is quite common.

being sent to your server. So if you are running any services on your machine that use unencrypted passwords for access, it is possible that a user account on your machine could get sniffed, and then the attacker could log in to your machine and cause further mischief.

One defense against packet sniffing is to not run any services that allow login via unencrypted passwords (for example, not running a Telnet or FTP server). In the real world, however, you may need to run some services that use unencrypted passwords. Most e-mail programs use either the POP or IMAP protocol to collect a user's e-mail from the mail server, and the passwords are sent over the network without encryption. If you find yourself running a POP or IMAP server, you should consider setting each user's account so that he or she cannot log in and get a shell prompt from the machine. You might set all the IMAP users to have a login shell of `/usr/bin/false`, which allows them to use IMAP to collect their e-mail but not use the same user name and password to log in and get a shell prompt. That way, even if an IMAP user's password is sniffed, the attacker cannot use it to get a shell prompt and attempt further attacks from the "inside." (Review Chapter 11 for more on how to change a user's login shell.)

Attacks on services

Most attacks against a machine via the Internet occur when an attacker connects to a service running on the target machine and exploits a security hole in that service. For example, there may be a security weakness in Postfix, a program that provides e-mail services. An attacker might connect to the e-mail server on your machine and then attempt to exploit the security vulnerability.

continues on next page

The exact method of each attack is different, depending upon the exact security hole being exploited.

One common type of attack is called a *buffer-overflow* attack. In situations where software has a buffer-overflow vulnerability, that vulnerability can be exploited by an attacker who sends the target software more data than it was designed to handle. If the target software is vulnerable, a portion of memory the target is using gets overwritten by the excess data. The excess data occupies a part of the target's memory where legitimate commands are supposed to be, only now the data may be commands that were supplied by the attacker. Of course, well-designed software doesn't allow this, but sometimes such vulnerabilities exist and are exploited.

Other attacks, known as *denial-of-service* (frequently abbreviated *DoS*) attacks, seek to overload a server with more requests than it can handle, causing the server to either crash or simply be unable to respond to normal requests—much like keeping someone's fax machine constantly busy.

Denial-of-service attacks are very hard to defend against, since they often do not rely upon any weakness in your server software but instead simply keep it too busy to be useful. Thankfully, DoS attacks are not very common, because they require a sustained effort on the part of the attacker, often from multiple machines.

In the most common attacks, software probes a network looking for server software that is known to have a particular weakness, and then attempts to exploit the weakness. Most commonly, this type of attack seeks servers running Microsoft's Internet Information Server (IIS)—its Web-server software—versions of which have been shipped with serious security flaws. Virtually every Web server on the Internet sees multiple daily attacks aimed at IIS software. Of course, since you are running Mac OS X, these attacks mean nothing to you. (See the sidebar "What an Attack on IIS Looks Like.")

An example of a problematic weakness in server software can be found in a "Vulnerability Note" from May 2005 on the US-CERT Web site (www.kb.cert.org/vuls/id/706838) concerning the Virtual Private Network daemon (`vpnd`) installed on Mac OS X. About two weeks after the problem was publicly announced, a security update was available for download from Apple. Notification and installation of the update were automatic for Mac OS X users who had Software Update turned on in System Preferences.

You can see a list of the frequent security updates Apple provides at www.info.apple.com/usen/security/security_updates.html. See "Keeping Up-to-Date," later in this chapter.

Limiting the number of services running on a machine limits both its exposure and the number of things you need to keep up-to-date. For this reason, it is a good idea not to run services you don't need.

To see which services are running:

1. Check the Sharing pane in System Preferences.

   Open System Preferences, click the Sharing icon, and examine the Firewall settings in the Sharing pane. Deactivate any services you are not using.

2. Check which jobs are loaded into `launchd`:

   ```
   sudo launchctl list
   ```

   See also "To list jobs loaded into `launchd`," in Chapter 11.

3. Look for active services in the `/etc/hostconfig` file.

   That would be services marked `-YES-` and possibly `-AUTOMATIC-`.

   Through a somewhat complicated process, scripts that are run by `SystemStarter` (see `man SystemStarter`) use variables set in `/etc/hostconfig` to decide whether or not to actually start a service. Have a look at `/System/Library/StartupItems/Apache/Apache`.

4. Look at the currently open Internet connections.

   `sudo lsof -i`

   The `lsof` command ("list open files"; see `man lsof`) is used to list files and network connections that are in use when the command is run. An example of the output is in **Figure 12.2**.

5. Look in each file in the `/etc/xinetd.d` directory, and in the `/etc/inetd.conf` file (if it exists on your system).

   For more about `xinetd` and `inetd` see the sidebar "The Server of Servers: `inetd`."

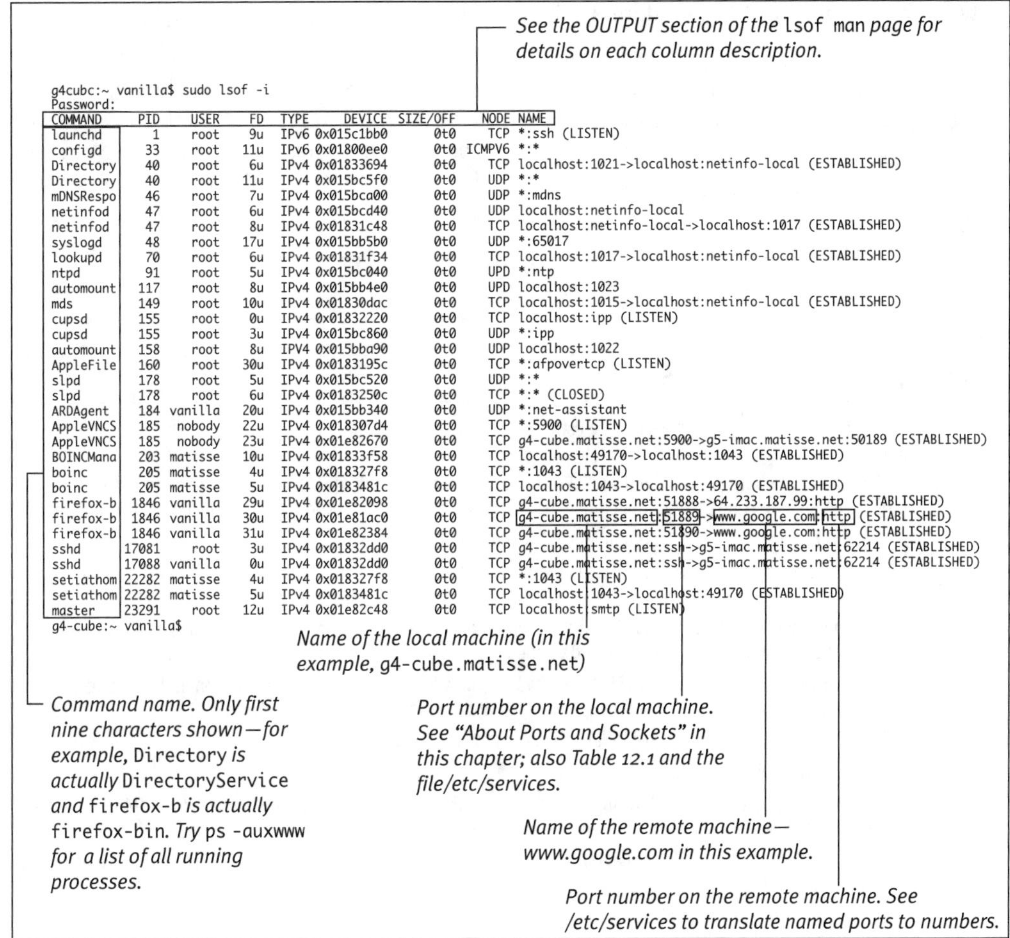

Figure 12.2 Using the `lsof` command with the `-i` option to show active Internet connections.

Besides limiting the server software you run on a machine, you should also limit which ports are accessible.

About ports and sockets

A *socket* is the combination of an IP address and a *port number.*

To understand port numbers, consider that a machine with only a single IP address (which is usually the case) can have many simultaneous Internet connections. Each connection uses a different port number. Here is an analogy: If an IP address is your machine's Internet "street address," then ports are "suite numbers" at that address.

Each Internet service running on a machine "listens" on a specific port number. (Note that "services" are provided by "servers"—documentation such as `man` pages will sometimes use the terms *server* and *service* interchangeably.) For example, the default port for e-mail servers is port 25, for an SSH (Secure Shell) server it is port 22, for Web servers it is port 80, and so on. **Table 12.1** describes the most commonly used ports, and you can see a list of virtually all the ports with commonly used names in the file `/etc/services`.

Port numbers below 1024 (that is, 0–1023) are special—only processes owned by root may listen on these port numbers. See the sidebar "How Do Services Get Assigned to Port Numbers?" for more information.

As we mentioned above, the combination of the IP address and port number is called a *socket.* When you use a Web browser to connect to a Web server, there are two (or more) sockets in use: One involves the server's IP address and port 80, and the other is your local machine's IP address and some other port number (above 1024) to which the server is sending data. So your Web browser sends a request

Table 12.1

Commonly Used Ports

See `/etc/services` for an almost comprehensive list.

Port	Use
20 and 21	FTP servers use both ports 20 and 21. FTP is turned off in the default Mac OS X configuration (it can be turned on in the Sharing pane of System Preferences). FTP passwords are sent over the wire unencrypted ("in the clear").
22	The SSH protocol. Part of the default Mac OS X configuration.
23	Telnet servers listen on port 23. Not used in the default Mac OS X configuration. Telnet passwords are sent in the clear.
25	For e-mail servers—the Simple Mail Transport Protocol (SMTP). Not turned on in the default Mac OS X configuration, but see Chapter 14, "Installing and Configuring Servers."
80	For Hypertext Transfer Protocol (HTTP) used by Web browsers and servers. Not turned on in the default Mac OS X configuration, but see Chapter 14, "Installing and Configuring Servers."
109	POP, version 2. POP servers provide remote access to your e-mail box.
110	The POP protocol, version 3.
	IMAP. A newer, better way of allowing users to pick up their e-mail over networks. In particular, IMAP makes it easy to read your e-mail from more than one computer.
443	HTTPS (HTTP plus Secure Socket Layer). Encrypted version of HTTP. Web sites whose URLs begin with *https* are normally on port 443.
548	AppleShare over TCP/IP. The latest versions of AppleShare encrypt the password before sending it.
4000	ICQ. A popular live chat system.

TCP? UDP?

The descriptions of services shown in `/etc/services` include TCP (Transmission Control Protocol) or UDP (User Datagram Protocol).

TCP and UDP are two different kinds of data packets that are sent over the Internet. Both protocols are part of the TCP/IP suite of protocols (which also includes Internet Control Message Protocol (ICMP) and Internet Protocol (IP).

How Do Services Get Assigned to Port Numbers?

The list of "well-known" and "registered" ports is maintained by IANA—the Internet Assigned Numbers Authority (www.iana.org).

The current official list of port numbers is at www.iana.org/assignments/port-numbers, and the standard Unix file `/etc/services` on your machine is simply a slightly reformatted version of that same information. For many years the IANA was mainly one man: Jon Postel, a true hero of the Internet whose mantra was "Be liberal in what you accept, and conservative in what you send." He gave much good and shaped a world in which the contributions of others flourished. Postel's early death at age 55 was a great blow to the Internet community (see www.postel.org/postel.html). See also Request for Comments 2468 (as in "who do we appreciate...") at ftp://ftp.isi.edu/in-notes/rfc2468.txt.

to port 80 on the server and listens on some other port for the response. (The machine that initiates the connection tells the remote machine which port to send responses to.)

A common security measure involves blocking access to ports on your machine at a point closer to the outside world than where services actually listen for connections. When this is done, a connection cannot be established from a remote machine to that port on your machine. So you are protected even if there is a server (perhaps inadvertently) listening (or trying to listen) on that port.

The primary type of traffic carried on the Internet uses TCP (Transmission Control Protocol). You can test whether a particular port is open or blocked to TCP traffic quite easily by using the `telnet` command, described in Chapter 10, "Connecting over the Internet." Review the section "Connecting using Telnet" in Chapter 10 before proceeding with this task.

To check if a particular port is blocked for TCP traffic:

1. `telnet` *`hostname port`*

   `hostname` can be either a name or an IP address, and *`port`* is the port number you are checking. For example,

   `telnet localhost 25`

   attempts to connect to your own machine on port 25.

   `telnet www.matisse.net 80`

   attempts to connect to port 80 on the machine www.matisse.net.

   Software that blocks ports often blocks access to some hosts (usually any host except itself) and allows access to others (usually just itself, or machines on the local network), so you should try checking from both your own machine and another machine outside your network

continues on next page

(that means you will need a shell account on a Unix machine on another network).

- ▲ If you get a response that says

  `Trying 205.21.36.191...`

  `Connected to localhost.`

  `Escape character is '^]'.`

  (the IP address will be different), that means you have connected to server software on the target machine, and the port is not blocked for access from the machine you are testing from.

  You may get further output from the target machine, depending on what server software you have connected to.

- ▲ If you get a response that says

  `telnet: Unable to connect to remote host: Connection refused`

  the port is not blocked, but there is no server software listening on that port.

- ▲ If you get a response that says

  `Trying 66.47.69.205...`

  (the IP address will be different) and then nothing, the port probably is blocked. Eventually the Telnet program will give up, although this may take a few minutes.

2. Stop the connection.

You do this by pressing Control]. You get a prompt that says

`telnet>`

3. `quit`

This brings you back to your shell prompt.

Any server software can be configured to listen on a nonstandard port, and, generally speaking, servers use "well-known ports" (0–1023) and "registered" ports (1024–49151).

The well-known ports 0–1023 are also called *privileged* ports, and only root can bind a service to a privileged port. On the other hand, any user on the system can run server software that listens on port number 1024 and above.

The following task describes a simple Perl script that reproduces the Port Scan feature of the GUI application Network Utility (located in `/Applications/Utilities`).

One advantage of a script is that you can easily save its output to a file, run it automatically as a `cron` job (see Chapter 11), or pipe it into e-mail. Also, maybe you will come up with a useful modification of the script.

To see which ports are open:

1. Create a Perl script, using the code listing in **Figure 12.3**, in a file named `port_scan.pl` (Review Chapter 9, "Creating and Using Scripts.")

continues on page 392

Packet Sniffers and Port Scanners

Besides simply checking for open ports, any machine on your local network can examine all the data flowing on that network. This means that any machine on a local network is capable of obtaining any user names and passwords that flow across that network, unless they are encrypted before transport.

`Nmap` (www.insecure.org/nmap) is an open-source network mapping tool that has many more features than the simple script in Figure 12.2. `Nmap` doesn't come with Mac OS X but can be easily installed with Fink (see Chapter 13).

Another newer, even more powerful tool is `ettercap`, which can also be installed using Fink (see the sidebar "Tools for Monitoring Your System"). `ettercap` is primarily designed for analyzing machines on the same local network as your machine, and it allows you to do such naughty things as intercepting traffic and collecting passwords.

```
#!/usr/bin/perl
# port_scan.pl
# Simple port-scanning script
# Pointing this script at someone else's machine could be considered
# rude, like trying all the doorknobs on their house.
###########################################################################

use strict;
use IO::Socket::INET;
use Socket;

# The Well Known Ports are 1 through 1023.
# The Registered Ports are 1024 through 49151
# The Dynamic and/or Private Ports are 49152 through 65535
#
my $low_port = 1;  # lowest port number to check
my $high_port = 65535;  # Highest port number to check.

my $host = $ARGV[0];
 _usage() unless ($host);   # Gives usage message if no hostname supplied


my $ip_addr = gethostbyname( $host );
$ip_addr = inet_ntoa( $ip_addr );
print "Scanning $host ($ip_addr), ports $low_port through $high_port\n\n";

for my $port ( $low_port..$high_port ) {
        my $socket = IO::Socket::INET->new(PeerAddr => $host,
                   PeerPort => $port,
                   Proto    => 'tcp',
                   Timeout  => 1,
                   Type     => SOCK_STREAM);
        if ( $socket ) {
                   close $socket;
                   # Is there a standard name for this port?
                   my($protocol,$service) = getservbyport($port,'tcp');
                   my $description;
                   if ( $protocol ) {
                        $description = " ($protocol";
                        if ( $service ) {
                             $description .= ", $service)";
                        } else {
                             $description .= ")";
                        }
                   }
                   print "Connected! Port $port is open. $description\n";
         }
}

sub _usage {
    print STDERR <<"EOF";
Usage: $0 host

'host' may be a hostname or IP address.
Try 'localhost' to test this machine.

EOF
        exit 1;
}
```

Figure 12.3 Code listing of a Perl script that scans a machine and tells which ports are open.

2. Set the file permissions to make the script executable:

   `chmod 755 port_scan.pl`

3. `./port_scan.pl localhost`

   The script will take a long time to run, since it is checking 65535 different ports. **Figure 12.4** shows what the output would look like if you were to activate Secure Login, AppleShare file sharing, Web file sharing, and an e-mail server. (See Chapter 14 for instructions on activating these servers.)

Blocking access to ports

Mac OS X comes with a very powerful tool called `ipfw` for blocking access to ports and doing other "traffic shaping" of Internet connections.

The `ipfw` utility is rather complex, and misconfiguring it can leave your machine in an almost unusable condition, which may force you to boot into single-user mode to fix things. Before you attempt any command-line changes using `ipfw`, be sure to thoroughly read the `man` page and preferably have an experienced person available to help.

```
localhost:~ vanilla$ ./port_scan.pl localhost
Scanning localhost, ports 1 through 65535

Connected! Port 22 is open.  (ssh)
Connected! Port 25 is open.  (smtp)
Connected! Port 80 is open.  (http, www www-http)
Connected! Port 427 is open.  (svrloc)
Connected! Port 548 is open.  (afpovertcp)
Connected! Port 587 is open.  (submission)
localhost:~ vanilla$
```


Figure 12.4 Annotated output of the `scan.pl` script. None of these services are active in the default Mac OS X configuration. See Chapter 14 for instructions on activation.

Fortunately, the Mac OS X System Preferences include a very reasonable GUI configuration tool for `ipfw`, so that's what we'll show you here.

To block ports using the Sharing firewall tool:

1. Open the Sharing pane from System Preferences.
2. Choose the Firewall tab.

   This shows how to start, stop, and configure the built-in firewall (**Figure 12.5** shows the firewall after it has been turned on).
3. Click the Start button.

   The built-in firewall software starts up and blocks access to every port on your machine, except for those explicitly listed and marked as On in the Allow list on this tab.

Warning: There are reports of a bug in Mac OS X 10.4.1 in which access for Apple Remote Desktop will be blocked by the firewall even when Apple Remote Desktop is enabled on the Firewall tab. The workaround is to add a rule allowing TCP traffic on port 5900. See the task below, "To add a firewall rule to allow access on a specific port."

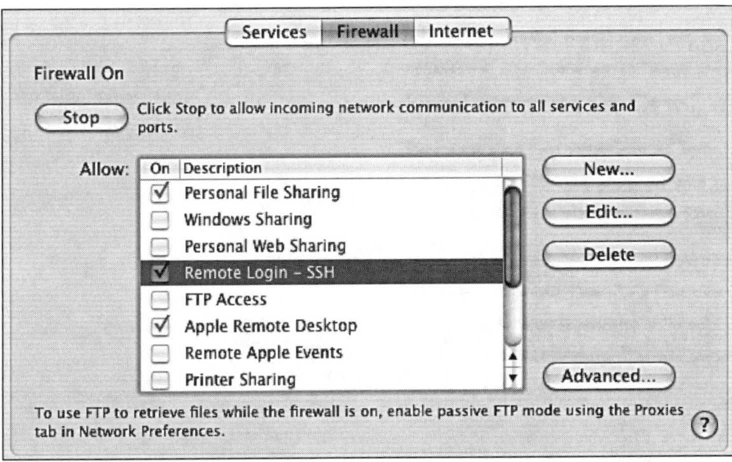

Figure 12.5 Part of the Firewall tab of the Sharing pane from System Preferences.

To see a list of the firewall rules:

- `sudo ipfw show`

  This command line displays all the currently active `ipfw` rules.

  The first column is the rule number (1–65535), the second is how many data packets the rule has processed, the third is bytes, and the rest of the line is the rule itself.

  If the firewall is on, you will see several rules. **Figure 12.6** is an annotated example of output (yours will differ slightly); see `man ipfw` for more details.

  If the firewall is off, there will be only one rule:

  ```
  65535 4946989 3780999653 allow ip
  → from any to any
  ```

✔ Tips

- You may limit the output to a specific rule by supplying the rule number—for example:

  `sudo ipfw show 2190`

- You can see a list of the `ipfw` rules without the packet and byte counts by using `list` instead of `show`:

  `sudo ipfw list`

  or

  `sudo ipfw list 2190`

Firewalk—Another Firewall Tool

Firewalk is a GUI application for configuring `ipfw` on Mac OS X. Firewalk X 2 has more features than the firewall configuration toll built into Mac OS X's System Preferences Sharing tool, including the ability to set a time when rules expire and to have alerts pop up when a rule blocks incoming traffic.

Firewalk X 2 has a $34.99 license fee and is available at www.pliris-soft.com/products/firewalkx.

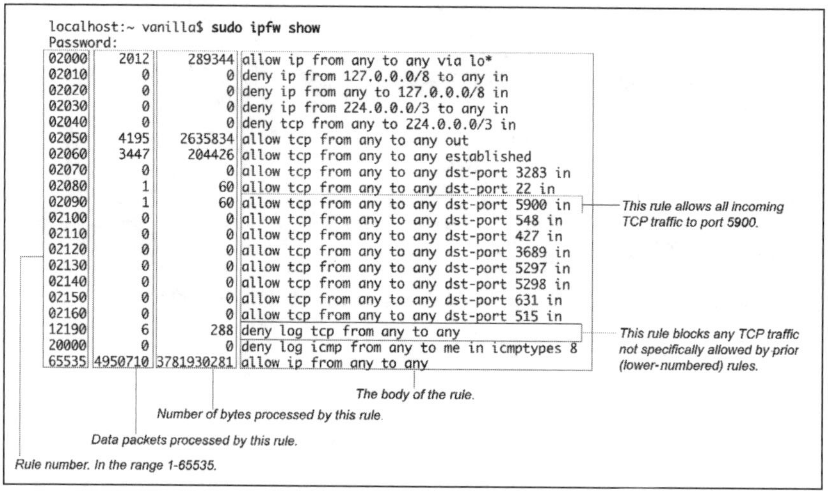

```
localhost:~ vanilla$ sudo ipfw show
Password:
02000    2012      289344 allow ip from any to any via lo*
02010       0           0 deny ip from 127.0.0.0/8 to any in
02020       0           0 deny ip from any to 127.0.0.0/8 in
02030       0           0 deny ip from 224.0.0.0/3 to any in
02040       0           0 deny tcp from any to 224.0.0.0/3 in
02050    4195     2635834 allow tcp from any to any out
02060    3447      204426 allow tcp from any to any established
02070       0           0 allow tcp from any to any dst-port 3283 in
02080       1          60 allow tcp from any to any dst-port 22 in
02090       1          60 allow tcp from any to any dst-port 5900 in
02100       0           0 allow tcp from any to any dst-port 548 in
02110       0           0 allow tcp from any to any dst-port 427 in
02120       0           0 allow tcp from any to any dst-port 3689 in
02130       0           0 allow tcp from any to any dst-port 5297 in
02140       0           0 allow tcp from any to any dst-port 5298 in
02150       0           0 allow tcp from any to any dst-port 631 in
02160       0           0 allow tcp from any to any dst-port 515 in
12190       6         288 deny log tcp from any to any
20000       0           0 deny log icmp from any to me in icmptypes 8
65535 4950710  3781930281 allow ip from any to any
```

This rule allows all incoming TCP traffic to port 5900.

This rule blocks any TCP traffic not specifically allowed by prior (lower-numbered) rules.

The body of the rule.

Number of bytes processed by this rule.

Data packets processed by this rule.

Rule number. In the range 1-65535.

Figure 12.6 Listing the `ipfw` rules (your output will differ somewhat).

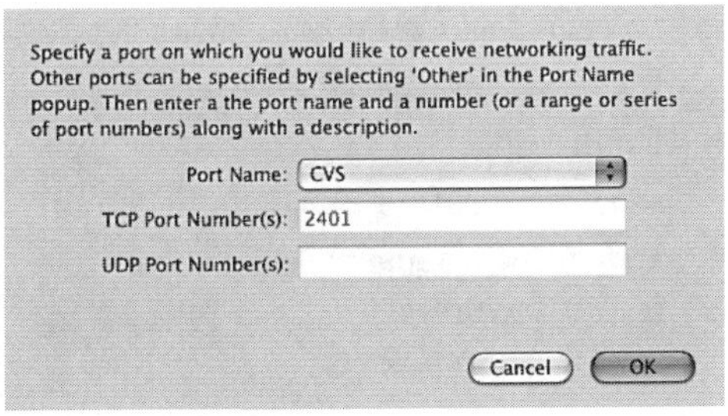

Specify a port on which you would like to receive networking traffic. Other ports can be specified by selecting 'Other' in the Port Name popup. Then enter a the port name and a number (or a range or series of port numbers) along with a description.

Port Name: CVS

TCP Port Number(s): 2401

UDP Port Number(s):

Cancel OK

Figure 12.7 A dialog drops down on the Firewall tab, where you can create a new entry in the built-in firewall tool.

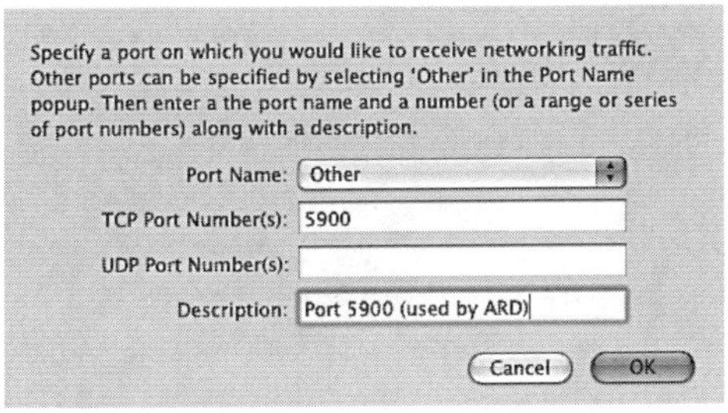

Specify a port on which you would like to receive networking traffic. Other ports can be specified by selecting 'Other' in the Port Name popup. Then enter a the port name and a number (or a range or series of port numbers) along with a description.

Port Name: Other

TCP Port Number(s): 5900

UDP Port Number(s):

Description: Port 5900 (used by ARD)

Cancel OK

Figure 12.8 A new dialog appears with an additional field if you chose Other in the Port Name menu.

The list of allowed ports in the GUI firewall tool can be easily changed.

Deleting an item from the list is a matter of selecting it and pressing Delete. Here's how to add an item to the list (pretty obvious, but we figure we'll walk you through it for fun).

To add a firewall rule to allow access on a specific port:

1. Open the Firewall tab in the Sharing pane of System Preferences.

   If the lock icon is locked, click it and authenticate as an admin user.

2. Click the New button.

   A dialog appears (**Figure 12.7**).

3. Choose an item from the Port Name pop-up menu.

   If you chose Other, then you get a new dialog as shown in **Figure 12.8**.

   In our example, we show how you would allow TCP connections on port 5900. This can be done to correct a bug in the firewall that blocks Apple Remote Desktop (ARD) even when ARD is enabled on the Services tab.

   The two port number fields TCP Port Number(s) and UDP Port Numbers(s) can be either a single port number, such as 5900; a range, such as 6000–6010; or a series, such as 7000, 70023, 7034 (you can separate the items with commas, spaces, or both).

   If you chose a port name from the pop-up menu, the port number will be filled in for you.

4. Click OK.

   The new entry is added to the list of ports and is checked as On (to allow access to that port).

continues on next page

If you wish to block access to the port, uncheck the box for the entry and make sure the firewall is actually "On."

✔ Tips

- Check that the rule was added:
  `sudo ifpw show`
- You can delete an `ipfw` rule with
  `sudo ipfw delete` *`rulenumber`*
  For example:
  `sudo ipfw delete 5900`
  The rule will come back if you stop and restart the firewall.

The Server of Servers: inetd

Mac OS X (like virtually all versions of Unix) comes with a special server program called `inetd` (the *Internet daemon*) as well as the more advanced `xinetd`.

Starting with Mac OS X 10.4, Apple has moved almost all of the services that `xinetd` used to handle to the Apple-created `launchd` system (see "About `launchd`" in Chapter 11) and actually uses `launchd` to launch `xinetd`.

`xinetd` acts as a kind of dispatch office for several networked servers. It is configured using the file `/etc/xinetd.conf`, which typically lists one or more directories containing additional configuration files corresponding to a service handled by `xinetd`. The standard location (used in Mac OS X 10.2) for additional `xinetd` configuration files is the `/etc/xinetd.d` directory, where you'll find more than a dozen small configuration files.

Mac OS X 10.1 and earlier had only the older `inetd` program (no `x`). In Mac OS X 10.2, Apple added `xinetd`, but the `inetd` program may still be running, depending on your system configuration. `inetd` uses a single configuration file, `/etc/inetd.conf`, but we suggest you leave it alone.

The configuration files for `xinetd` tell it which services (such as remote-access services) it is responsible for. `xinetd` can listen on multiple ports, and when it receives a connection, it starts up the appropriate software and hands off the connection to the software it started. Following the general rule of only running servers you actually need, Mac OS X comes with all the entries in `/etc/xinetd.d/` disabled, because none of the services listed are required for normal operation (once again, keep in mind that a *service* is some useful function provided by a *server*). Both `xinetd` and `inetd` do start when your Mac boots up (by the `/System/Library/StartupItems/IPServices/IPservices` script).

Apple recommends that you use the new `launchd` facility instead of `xinetd`, and we suggest you follow that advice (see "Creating New LaunchDaemons and Startup Items" in Chapter 11). If you find that you must run something from `xinetd`, you will need to add in the `/etc/xinetd.d` directory. But until that day comes, you can just be aware that it exists and leave it alone (and of course have a look at the file and the `xinetd man` page).

Searching for Files That Make You root

If root owns a file, and that file has the `setuid` bit set, then when that file is executed it runs with the power of root, regardless of who runs it (review Chapter 8, "Working with Permissions and Ownership"). If a `setuid` root file has its permissions set so that anyone can execute it (known to programmers as *world executable*), then anyone on the system can run the file and perhaps use it to obtain root access.

Some world-executable commands are intentionally "`setuid` root" because they need to access parts of the system normally available only to root. The `lsof` program is one example. These programs are (hopefully) carefully written to prevent anyone from using them to create a new shell or to execute other commands.

You can use the `find` command to search your entire system for `setuid` root files.

As of Mac OS X version 10.4, there are dozens of world-executable `setuid` root programs on the system.

A good security practice would be to create a list of all the `setuid` root programs on your machine, save it somewhere safe (such as on a CD), and periodically compare the saved list with a newly generated version. If you found any new programs on the list, you would want to check with Apple to see if they were really supposed to be there.

This is obviously a time-consuming and annoying process, which is true of most security tasks.

To search for setuid root files:

- `sudo find / -type f -user root -perm -4000`

  The command must be run as root in order to read every file on the system, hence the `sudo` (see Chapter 11 for more on `sudo` and Chapter 4, "Useful Unix Utilities," for more on `find`). The `find` command is being told to search starting at / for files (`-type f`) owned by root (`-user root`) that have the `setuid` bit set (`-perm -4000`).

✔ Tip

- The command will take a while to finish, since it has to look at every file on your system. You might want to pipe the results into e-mail and put it in the background by adding the following to the end of the command line:

  `| mail` *`youremailaddress`* `&`

Keeping Up-to-Date

Mac OS X comes with an application called Software Update that automatically contacts Apple over the Internet to check if there are new versions of any of the Apple-supplied software. These can be as minor as a new version of a program like iTunes, or as major as a new version of Mac OS X itself. One of Software Update's key uses is to maintain the security of your Mac. Apple has been very good about quickly getting new versions of software into its update system when a security problem is discovered.

Because Software Update deals only with Apple-supplied software, you must keep yourself informed of security issues with any other software you install, especially servers. See "Security news and announcements," below.

Software Update

If you are running an Internet-connected Mac, you should be using Software Update.

If your machine has an "always-on" connection to the Internet, you can have Software Update check for updates automatically. If you connect to the Internet intermittently, you can manually request an update check when you are connected.

The GUI Software Update tool is available under the Apple menu. Here's how to run it from the command line:

To run Software Update from the command line:

1. `softwareupdate -list`
   You will see a list of packages available for update (**Figure 12.9**).
2. Pick a package to install:
   `sudo softwareupdate` *`package`*
   Enter your password if prompted for it.
   For example,
   `sudo softwareupdate iCal-2.0.2`
   as shown in **Figure 12.10**.

✔ Tips

- You can turn on automatic checking with the `-schedule` option:
  `sudo softwareupdate -schedule on`
  See `man softwareupdate` for more.
- You can manage the list of ignored updates with the `-ignored` option. See `man softwareupdate` for more.

```
localhost:~ vanilla$ softwareupdate -list
Software Update Tool
Copyright 2002 Apple Computer, Inc.

Software Update found the following new or updated software:

        - SecurityUpd2002-08-02
            Security Update 2002-08-02 (1.0), 5300K - restart required
        - iPod
            iPod Software Updater (1.1), 2140K

To install an update, run this tool with the item name as an argument.
            e.g. 'softwareupdate <item> ...'

localhost:~ vanilla$
```

Figure 12.9 Output from the `softwareupdate -list` command showing a list of available updates.

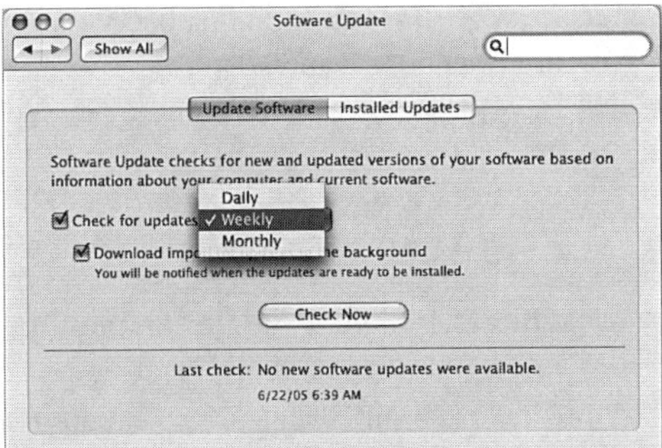

Figure 12.11 You can configure Software Update in the Software Update pane of System Preferences.

To configure automatic Software Update via the GUI:

1. Launch Software Update (found in the Software Update pane of System Preferences).
2. Select the update frequency you desire (**Figure 12.11**).

   It can check automatically on a daily, weekly, or monthly basis. You may also choose to download "important" updates in the background, which means they get downloaded (but not installed) without asking you.

   In either case, you may request an immediate check for aailable updates by clicking Update Now.

continues on next page


```
localhost:~ vanilla$ sudo softwareupdate -install SecurityUpd2002-08-02
Password:
Software Update Tool
Copyright 2002 Apple Computer, Inc.

Downloading "Security Update 2002-08-02"... 10% 20% 30% 40%
50%2002-08-06 22:59:07.143 softwareupdate[2185] File to verify:
/var/root/Library/Caches/a1028.g.akamai.net/5/1028/3093/1/1a1a1a88ff63d249b72392f35785e656c63297c528
97043397067deb57c6278bfe2d82d504346a9bc8f8295a91c03867cb337bf3478cf055960b71c5fd74a51258c53f99/
SecurityUpd2002-08-02.tar
2002-08-06 22:59:09.583 softwareupdate[2185] File verification succeeded
2002-08-06 22:59:09.585 softwareupdate[2185] Verified file now to
install: /tmp/SecurityUpd2002-08-02.pkg.tar
2002-08-06 22:59:09.586 softwareupdate[2185] Returning 1 from VerifyFile

Unarchiving "Security Update 2002-08-02"... 50%
Installing "Security Update 2002-08-02"... 67% 71% 80% 90%
Installing "Security Update 2002-08-02"... 67% 71% 80% 90% 100% done.

You have installed one or more updates that requires that you restart your
computer.  Please restart immediately.
localhost:~ vanilla$
```

Figure 12.10 Output from selecting a package to update using `softwareupdate` at the command line. Your output will differ.

The actual download and installation process will take anywhere from a few minutes to over an hour depending on the size of the update and the speed of your Internet connection.

When Software Update finds that a new version of software is available, it asks if you wish to install it. Sometimes a restart is required when installing new software.

Security news and announcements

Staying up-to-date on security matters involves more than simply running Software Update. It means keeping abreast of the latest news about Mac OS X security issues and the solutions available.

The following online resources are all good places to visit regularly for Mac OS X security news:

- Apple Security Updates page (www.apple.com/support/security/security_updates.html).

  The official Apple source of security news for Mac OS X.

- Mac-specific Security sites:

  SecureMac.com (www.securemac.com).

  MacSecurity.org (www.macsecurity.org).

- An Introduction to Mac OS X Security for Web Developers (http://developer.apple.com/internet/security/securityintro.html).

- US-CERT (United States Computer Emergency Readiness Team, part of the Department of Homeland Security) maintains four e-mail lists for U.S. cyber-security issues (www.us-cert.gov/cas).

  CERT advisories are a major central source of Internet security notifications. If you run a busy Internet site or are simply interested in seeing the latest Internet security issues, you should subscribe to one of the CERT e-mail lists.

  The Australian version of CERT, AusCERT, has created a Unix Security Checklist (www.cert.org/tech_tips/usc20_essentials.html).

- The BugTraq mailing list (http://online.securityfocus.com/archive/1).

  "BugTraq is a full disclosure moderated mailing list for the detailed discussion and announcement of computer security vulnerabilities: what they are, how to exploit them, and how to fix them." (From the BugTraq Web site.)

- The Common Vulnerabilities and Exposures (CVE) list (http://cve.mitre.org/cve).

  Maintained by Mitre (a nonprofit corporation that provides engineering support to the U.S. government), the CVE list is a dictionary of security issues that seeks to present standardized descriptions of security problems.

Books on Unix Security

These two books are intended for experienced Unix users. Both were written by people who have many years of experience in the Unix and Internet security fields. Their authors are well known in the Unix and Internet communities.

Practical UNIX and Internet Security, 2nd Edition, by Simson Garfinkel and Gene Spafford (O'Reilly; www.oreilly.com/catalog/puis).

Building Internet Firewalls, 2nd Edition, by Elizabeth D. Zwicky, Simon Cooper, and D. Brent Chapman (O'Reilly; www.oreilly.com/catalog/fire2).

Monitoring Files for Changes

If an attacker gains root access to your system, one of the first things he is likely to do is alter or replace one or more programs with one of his own making to enable him to gain access again in the future, or to use for launching attacks against other systems.

There are commercial programs available to automate the process of checking files on your system to see if they have been changed, such as Tripwire (see the sidebar "Tools for Monitoring Your System"). You can perform this type of check yourself with the freely available `md5sum` program.

Using md5sum to check for file changes

Mac OS X doesn't come with `md5sum`, but `md5sum` does come with the Fink tool, described in Chapter 13, "Installing Software from Source Code." If you have installed Fink, then you have `md5sum` installed (as `/sw/bin/md5sum`).

The `md5sum` program creates and reads something called a *message digest* or *checksum*. A message digest is a compact summary of a file that is guaranteed to be different for different files. It is sometimes called a *fingerprint* for a file. Although much smaller than the file it represents (only 32 characters long in the case of `md5sum`), an MD5 message digest for a file is different if even a single character in the file is changed.

You use `md5sum` to create MD5 message digests for files before an attack occurs, and then to save the digests on a read-only disc—for example, by putting the list of checksums on a CD.

You can then periodically use `md5sum` to compare the message digests with the actual files to see if any of the files have been changed since the checksums were created.

The following tasks assume that you have `md5sum` installed on your system and that it is in your `PATH`.

To create an MD5 checksum of a single file:

◆ `md5sum` *`file`*

For example,

```
md5sum /bin/ps
```

generates an MD5 checksum of the file `/bin/ps` (which is a `setuid` root program; finding programs that are `setuid` root is covered earlier in this chapter).

The output from `md5sum` is a single line showing the checksum and the file path it was generated from. For example,

```
aa37faf342591346cf6c7bd661bdc42c
→ /bin/ps
```

✔ Tip

■ It is best to use a full path when creating an MD5 checksum if you are going to save the checksum for later use (see the next task). If you use a relative path, you will need to be in the same current directory when you check the file later as you did when you created the checksum.

To save MD5 checksums for every file in a directory:

- `sudo find -L` *path* `-type f -print0 | xargs -0 sudo md5sum > checksums.txt`

  This creates a file (checksums.txt) containing an MD5 checksum for every file inside the *path* directory. For example, if *path* is `/etc`, then the checksums.txt file will contain message digests for every file in `/etc`. **Figure 12.12** shows a portion of that file.

  Here we use the `/etc` directory as an example, but it should be clear that you can use the same technique for any directory on the system. Simply replace `/etc` with another directory name.

  Review the `find` command in Chapter 4. We use the `-L` option to `find` (follow symbolic links) because the `/etc` directory is actually a symbolic link to `/private/etc` (a Mac OS X peculiarity).

✔ Tips

- Remember that you can redirect output and append to (instead of overwrite) an existing file by using the >> operator instead of the > operator. (Review Chapter 2, "Using the Command Line.") With this technique, you can create one big file of checksums from several directories.
- Save the file containing the checksums on a CD-ROM (or other read-only media). Then, once a month (or more often if you suspect mischief), insert the CD-ROM and use `md5sum` to check the files for changes. See the next task for instructions.

```
e55afe6e88abb09f0bee39549f1dfbbd  /etc/afpovertcp.cfg
2853942e1130c71462ceb0e14298005c  /etc/aliases
223e4dc957db876a4ba062d27cd80de2  /etc/aliases.db
6d0bb903a21cb10ae7d4ea7480caf770  /etc/appletalk.cfg
6c7ea61072ab60ee211a3b6b227e1c08  /etc/authorization
03e795153c4d2989a905c564054a367a  /etc/bashrc
670137f7b27cea11f82d494f6a38b869  /etc/crontab
5ac352c94e115a608aaea5e92598793d  /etc/csh.cshrc
4e8f734718af35186084e88c59ac2536  /etc/csh.login
a78abc32d5d5f6967f46106879ff8406  /etc/csh.logout
7b5c15f3d613b148cb883d8795dcef4a  /etc/daily
e5f2ad07e4bc451fb6ccb3107aac248e  /etc/group
5889556f9dd9e9b551d19195dfefc6d6  /etc/hostconfig
e798bde840c94334378c9080e55317c3  /etc/hostconfig.system_default
b4f013ca7bf96a709438817f6440d974  /etc/httpd/httpd.conf
966328a6348ea217d93c7d627dff6330  /etc/httpd/magic
81d6686ca86c74b4afc93fac359f544c  /etc/httpd/mime.types
2ddb6e29cf197be5cee45c4869e5c4a9  /etc/httpd/users/matisse.conf
3ab54679c8551eefb72205bdafa83912  /etc/httpd/users/vanilla.conf
d406d67cc38e0a4ca473d015bfb58e50  /etc/ssh_config
d406d67cc38e0a4ca473d015bfb58e50  /etc/ssh_config.applesaved
d406d67cc38e0a4ca473d015bfb58e50  /etc/ssh_config.applesaved2
d406d67cc38e0a4ca473d015bfb58e50  /etc/ssh_config.applesaved3
```

Figure 12.12 Partial list of MD5 checksums generated with `sudo find -L /etc -type f -print0 | xargs -0 sudo md5sum > checksums.txt`.

- You should consider generating MD5 checksums for all the files in `/etc` and for every directory in your `PATH` (review Chapter 7, "Configuring Your Environment with Unix," for more on your `PATH`) and also for the `/Applications` directory.

Once you have a file containing MD5 checksums, you can have `md5sum` use the file as a reference to see if any of the files in the list have changed.

Note that `md5sum` will tell you only if the file's contents have changed. It will not look for changes in permissions, ownership, or modification date (a file could have been edited and saved with no actual changes, which would have updated its modification time).

To use md5sum to check a list of files for changes:

1. Generate a file containing a list of MD5 checksums as described in the previous task.

   For example, if you followed the instructions for the task above, you will have a file called checksums.txt and will have saved it on a CD-ROM.

   For this task, we assume that the file containing the checksums is on a CD-ROM called "checksums" and that you have inserted the CD-ROM into your machine. The full path to the checksums.txt file is `/Volumes/checksums/checksums.txt`

continues on next page

Tools for Monitoring Your System

There are many tools for monitoring system security. A good place to find a general roundup of available tools is SecureMac.com, a Web site devoted entirely to Mac security issues (www.securemac.com). It has news, security alerts, and software downloads, as well as tutorials and articles on Mac security.

Here are some useful tools:

Snort is an open-source intrusion-detection system. Documentation and source code are available at Snort.org (www.snort.org).

`ettercap` is a packet-sniffer/logging program from Ettercap that can be installed using Fink (http://ettercap.sourceforge.net).

Swatch is a tool for automating the watching of system log files, written in Perl. The official Web site for `swatch` is http://swatch.sourceforge.net/.

Tripwire is a commercial security tool capable of monitoring hundreds (or even thousands) of servers. Although the current version (3.3) doesn't list Mac OS X as a supported platform, it does list FreeBSD 4.4. In any event, Tripwire is widely used in large Unix installations, so you should at least be aware of it (www.tripwire.com).

2. `md5sum -c` *`checksumfile`*

   The `-c` option runs `md5sum` in "check" mode. The *`checksumfile`* argument is the path to the file where you saved the checksum in step 1.

   For example,

   ```
   md5sum -c /Volumes/checksums/
   → checksums.txt
   ```

   `md5sum` reads the *`checksumfile`*, and for each file listed `md5sum` generates a new checksum and compares it with the one you saved. (Figure 12.12 is an example of what the checksums.txt file might contain.)

   If the checksums do not match or if the original file is not found, then `md5sum` issues a warning.

   If the checksums match, then `md5sum` produces no output for that line and moves on to the next line. So even if `md5sum` checks a thousand files, it will produce output only if a checksum doesn't match or if a file is missing. (This is an example of the Unix standard "Silence means success.")

   Figure 12.13 shows an example in which `md5sum` finds that two files in the list have changed and one file from the list is missing.

✔ Tip

- To be really useful for detecting security problems, MD5 checksums need to be saved somewhere they cannot be altered by an attacker. This means copying the file containing the checksum to a read-only media, such as a CD-ROM.

```
localhost:~ vanilla$ md5sum -c /Volumes/checksums/checksums.txt
md5sum: MD5 check failed for '/etc/afpovertcp.cfg'
md5sum: MD5 check failed for '/etc/httpd/users/vanilla.conf'
md5sum: can't open /etc/ssh_config.applesaved3
localhost:~ vanilla$
```

Figure 12.13 Using `md5sum` to examine a list of files. Three changes are found: Two files have changed, and one is missing.

13 Installing Software from Source Code

Thousands of software applications run on Mac OS X. These applications come in two forms: *precompiled* and *source code*. With precompiled software, all you have to do is install it and it is ready to run. Shrink-wrapped applications like Adobe Photoshop and Microsoft Excel are sold in precompiled form and are not available as source code (they are *closed-source* software, not *open-source* software). Unix software applications are sometimes available in both precompiled and source-code forms, but many applications are available only in the latter form.

Programmers create source code as text files that can be read by users. Except in the case of scripts (review Chapter 9, "Creating and Using Scripts"), source code must be converted into software the computer can understand; this is done with a process called *compiling*. The source code is fed through another piece of software (called a *compiler*), which produces a machine-readable file (*object code*); this is the actual software you run on your machine. The Mac OS X Developer Tools include the compilers you need to convert software from source code into machine-readable code (if you have not already installed the Developer Tools, see the sidebar "The Mac OS X Developer Tools: Xcode Tools").

Object code works only with specific combinations of hardware architecture and operating system. For example, software compiled to run on a PowerPC chip on the Mac OS X operating system will not run on a Pentium running Windows. Note, however, that by late 2006 Apple expects to ship computers running Mac OS X on Intel chips, and it will be possible for developers to create "universal binaries" that will run on Mac OS X on either the legacy PPC machines or the new Intel-based Macs, similar to when Apple switched from the Motorola 68000-series chips to the PPC chips.

In order to take advantage of the full range of software available for Mac OS X, you need to learn how to install software from source code. It is actually fairly easy, and once you're done, you'll have access to an amazing variety of software.

In this chapter we will first explain the general process for installing from source code, and then we'll show you how to install Fink, which automates the process for many software packages. We will also show you in detail how to install software manually without the aid of Fink.

You will need to have your computer connected to the Internet in order to download software.

Installing from Source Code—the Basics

Installing software from source code always involves the same basic steps: Download the compressed source code, *unpack* it (the term most frequently used in the Unix world for expanding compressed code), move to the new directory using `cd`, compile, and install. The mantra that Unix veterans use is

```
./configure
make
make test or make check
make install
```

Here's a more detailed look at the general steps involved.

To install software from source code:

1. Obtain the source code. Usually you do this by downloading a compressed `tar` file from a Web site. (Review Chapter 4, "Useful Unix Utilities.")
2. Uncompress the file containing the source code (this automatically creates a directory). The most common way to do this at the command line is to use the `tar` command with `xfvz` options.
3. `cd` into the newly created directory.
4. Read the README and INSTALL files (the filenames are in all caps so that they stand out clearly—you should always read these files).

   They will tell you how to configure and install the software.
5. All the following steps need to be executed as root, so give yourself a root shell with

   `sudo -s`

   (review Chapter 7, "Configuring Your Environment with Unix," for more on shells; see Chapter 11, "Introduction to System Administration," for more on root and `sudo`).

6. Following the instructions in the INSTALL file, configure the source code so that it's ready for the compiler.

   The most common configuration method is to run a script called `configure` that comes with the source code. Type

   ```
   ./configure
   ```

   The configuration process sometimes asks you questions about your system, which directory you want to install the software in, and what options you want to include. In most cases you can simply accept the default answers, because the configuration process automatically determines the information it needs (such as asking, "Do you have multiple processors?") and creates one or more files (called *makefiles*) it uses to run the compiler process in the next step. The INSTALL file is your main reference for specific issues that arise, such as the meanings of available options and when to use them.

7. Compile the software.

   This will almost certainly be a matter of simply running the `make` command, which reads the makefiles and runs the commands they contain. *Makefiles* are scripts for building software. You will see quite a bit of output on your screen while `make` runs the compiler. We show examples of this later in this chapter.

8. Run any tests included with the source code.

   Some packages include preinstallation tests that can be run with `make test` or `make check`. Refer to the INSTALL file for specifics.

9. Perform the actual installation process.

   Again, follow the instructions from the INSTALL file—usually a matter of running `make install`.

   If errors are reported, start by rereading the README and INSTALL files and searching on the Web for the exact text of the error message(s).

10. You're done.

The Mac OS X Developer Tools: Xcode Tools

The Developer Tools, which contain the `gcc` compiler you need to install software from source code, come on the Mac OS X installation DVD (or on one of the CDs if your copy of Mac OS X came on CDs). The DVD or CD may be labeled "includes Xcode Tools." Xcode is a marketing name for the Mac OS X Developer Tools, and you will sometimes see the terms used interchangeably.

The Xcode Tools are also available from Apple's developer Web site (http://developer.apple.com).

Using Fink to Install Software

Fink is an open-source system that automates the process of downloading, configuring, compiling, and installing hundreds of Darwin packages (remember, Darwin is the version of Unix at the core of Mac OS X). By "package," we simply mean a piece of software along with its associated documentation and configuration files. Rather than your having to follow all the steps outlined in the previous section, Fink downloads, compiles, and installs a package with a single command (the Fink Web site at http://fink.sourceforge.net/ offers a variety of packages, from games to graphics, available for download, as does the Webmin Web site [www.webmin.com]).

See the sidebar "More About Fink," for late-breaking news about the program.

To install Fink, start by downloading the software. Fink comes precompiled, so you don't have to compile it to use it.

To install Fink:

1. From your Web browser, open the Fink download page:
   http://fink.sourceforge.net/download
2. Click the link to download the latest version of the *installer disk image* (a file that, when mounted as a disk, contains the installation program for a particular piece of software).

   Figure 13.1 (showing how the Web page for downloading Fink appeared during production of this book) highlights the link to click. The Web page you get may be a bit different, but note that there is a list of different versions of Fink for different versions of Mac OS X.

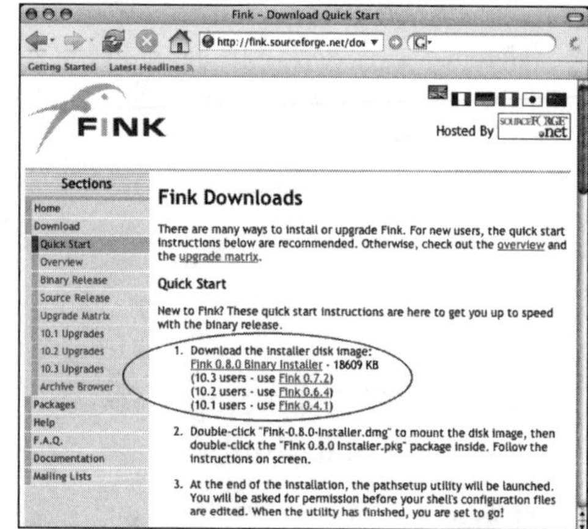

Figure 13.1 The Fink download page. The file you want to download is the "installer disk image." Note that there are different versions of Fink for different versions of Mac OS X.

Fink and X Windows

Many of the packages available for installation with Fink rely on the X Windows system. X Windows is a large collection of software that provides a platform-independent graphical user interface (GUI) environment. Most Unix software that provides a GUI relies upon X Windows to handle the creation of windows, dialogs, and buttons. Apple's version of X Windows is on your Mac OS X installation DVD (or CDs) and is also available for no charge at the X11 page (www.apple.com/macosx/features/x11).

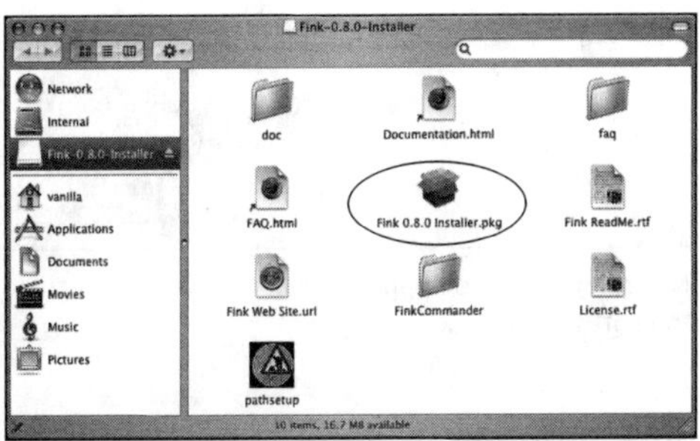

Figure 13.2 A Finder window showing the Fink Installer disk image, mounted as if it were a disk. You see the Fink installer package and associated files.

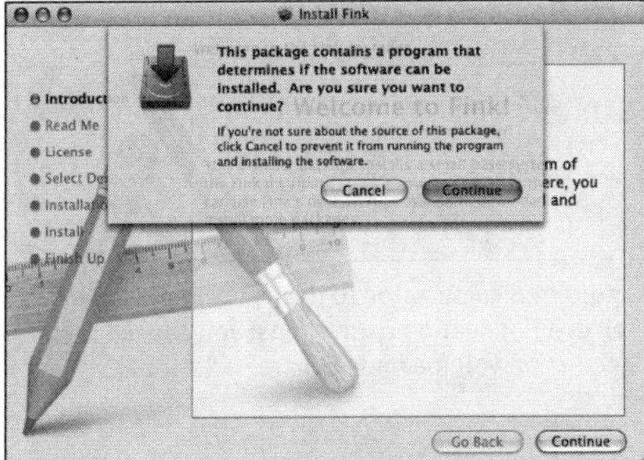

Figure 13.3 Double-clicking the Fink Installer.pkg icon launches the installer program.

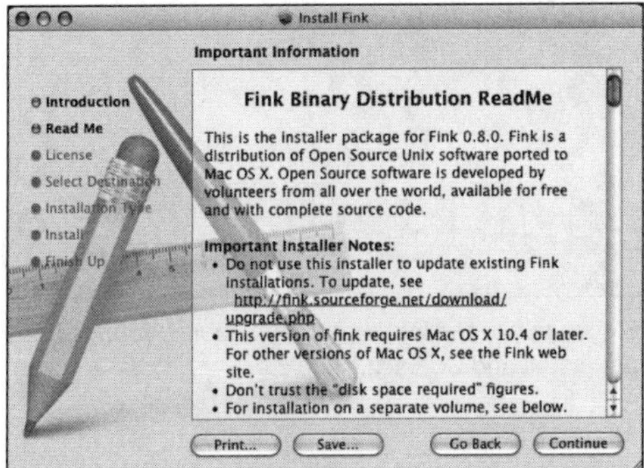

Figure 13.4 The Read Me pane of the Fink installer.

Follow the download instructions and save the file on your system's hard disk.

Depending on your browser configuration, the disk image may be automatically mounted. If not, double-click the disk-image file in the Finder to mount it. You should end up with a Finder window that looks similar to **Figure 13.2**.

3. Double-click the Fink Installer.pkg file to launch the Fink installation program. In Figure 13.2, it's the icon labeled Fink 0.8.0 Installer.pkg. You get a standard Mac OS X software installer window (**Figure 13.3**).

   The dialog that drops down asks you about running a program to determine if the installation will work.

4. Click the Continue button in the dialog.

   The dialog goes away.

5. Click the Continue button in the lower right-hand corner of the window.

   You see the Read Me information for Fink (**Figure 13.4**). Read it. It may have important information about the latest version.

6. Click the Continue button.

   You see the Software License Agreement. Read it. Note that Fink is licensed under the GNU General Public License (GPL), which we mentioned in Chapter 1, "What Is Unix, and Why Is It Good?" The GPL says that you may use Fink without any cost or obligation. However, if you redistribute Fink, you are obligated to make the source code available to all those to whom you distribute it.

continues on next page

7. Click the Continue button.

   You get a dialog asking if you agree with the software license agreement (**Figure 13.5**).

8. Click Agree to accept the license terms.

   The installer switches to the Select a Destination pane, which asks you to select a disk on which to install Fink (**Figure 13.6**).

   If you have more than one volume showing, click the one you want to use. We recommend installing Fink on the boot volume.

   If you do not agree to the license terms, you may not use the software. Click Disagree and quit the installer.

9. Click the Continue button.

   You see the Installation Type pane (**Figure 13.7**). This is here just to give you a chance to confirm before the installation proceeds.

10. Click the Install button.

    The Authenticate window opens, asking you to enter your password because the installer is going to run as root (**Figure 13.8**).

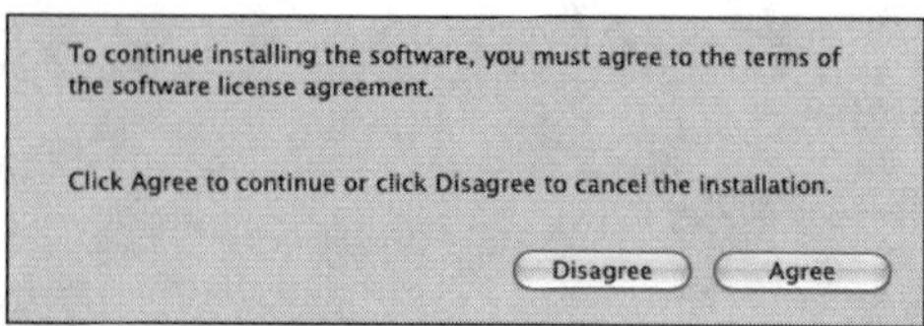

Figure 13.5 A dialog appears, asking if you agree to the software license.

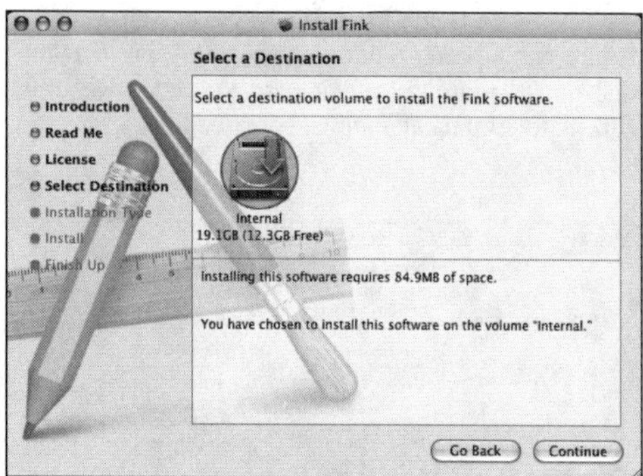

Figure 13.6 If you agree to the license terms, the Select a Destination pane opens; you choose the installation volume for Fink here.

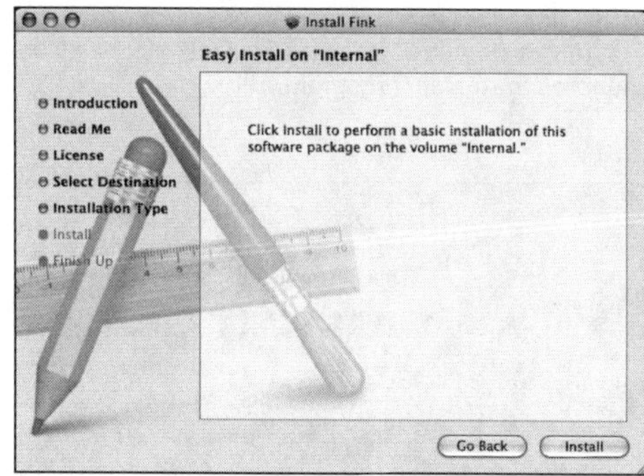

Figure 13.7 In the Installation Type pane, your choices are Install and Go Back.

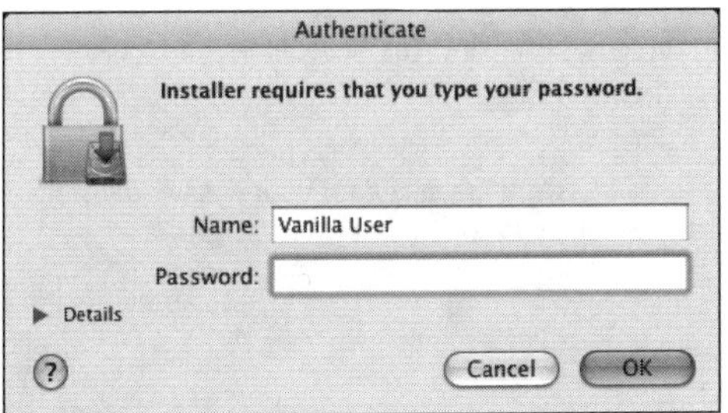

Figure 13.8 The Authenticate window, where your name is already filled in.

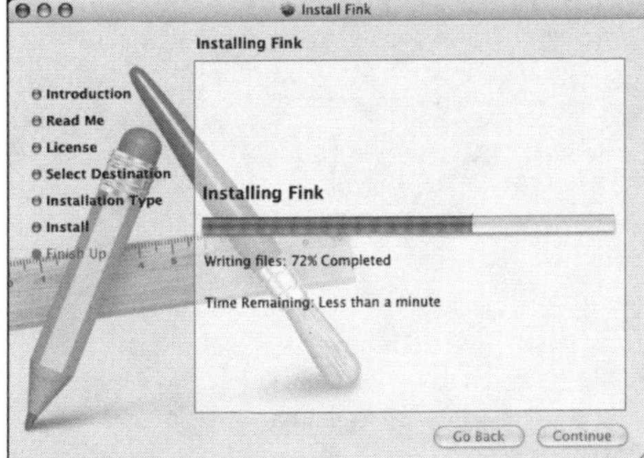

Figure 13.9 The Fink installation in progress.

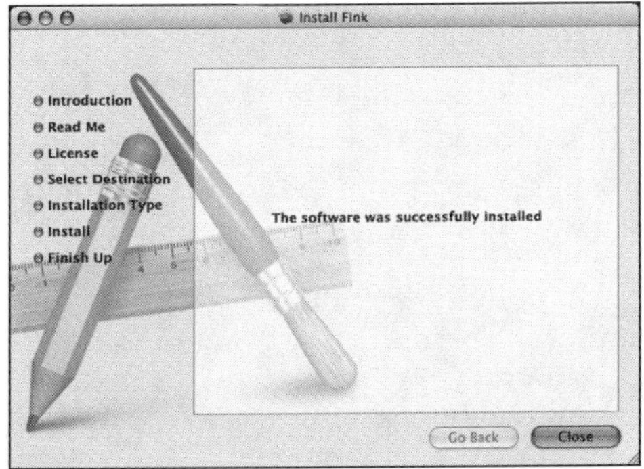

Figure 13.10 When the installation is done, the progress bar is filled; click Close to finish.

11. Enter your password and click the OK button.

    Throughout this book we assume you are logged in as an admin user, if not, then you must use the name and password of an admin account, not your own.

    Click the Continue button in the lower right-hand corner of the Install pane; the installation begins (**Figure 13.9**).

    When the installer has finished, the progress bar is complete and the Close button is highlighted (**Figure 13.10**).

12. Click Close to finish the installation.

    The installer creates a new directory called `sw` on the volume you selected. If you selected the boot volume, Fink is installed in `/sw` (which is what we recommend). If you installed Fink on any volume other than your system-startup volume, you must make a symlink called `/sw` that points to the installed location. For example, if you installed Fink on a partition called Extra Disk, you will create the symlink at the command line with

    ```
    sudo ln -s "/Volumes/Extra
    → Disk/sw" /sw
    ```

    (Review Chapter 5, "Using Files and Directories," for details on symlinks.)

    Fink is now installed.

    If you have the Terminal application open, we suggest quitting and restarting it to make sure your shells pick up the new Fink configuration (see the tip, next page).

continues on next page

✔ Tip

- The installer will have modified your shell configuration. If you are using the `bash` shell (the Mac OS X default), the `.bash_profile` in your home directory will have a new line:

  ```
  test -r /sw/bin/init.sh &&
  → . /sw/bin/init.sh
  ```

  That line checks if `/sw/bin/init.sh` is readable and then runs it. The `init.sh` script modifies a number of environment variables by adding the Fink directories to them; in particular it modifies your `PATH` and `MANPATH` environment variables to include the directories used by Fink. Go ahead and read the script—it won't bite. There is a similar script, `/sw/bin/init.csh`, for the `tcsh` and `csh` shells.

  The Fink program itself is located in `/sw/bin/fink`, and software you install using Fink will also be installed in `/sw/bin`. The `man` pages for Fink and the software it installs are located in `/sw/share/man`.

The next step is to configure Fink as root from the command line. In order to automate the process of downloading, compiling, and installing software, Fink needs to know some things about how your computer is connected to the Internet.

To configure Fink:

1. `sudo fink configure`

   Fink must be configured as root, so you use the `sudo` command to run `fink configure` (see Chapter 11). You are asked for your password (**Figure 13.11**).

```
localhost:~ vanilla$ sudo fink configure
Password:
```

Figure 13.11 You are asked for your password to enable the sudo command.

2. Enter your password, and press [Return].

   Fink asks a series of questions. The default answers will appear inside square brackets ([ ]), and in many cases the default will be nothing—that is, there will be nothing inside the square brackets. That's OK. Unless you know that the answer should be different from the default, press [Return] to accept.

   Figure 13.12 shows the questions asked by version 0.8.0 of Fink. In the example we have accepted all the defaults.

continues on next page


```
localhost:~ vanilla$ sudo fink configure
Password:

OK, I'll ask you some questions and update the configuration file in
'/sw/etc/fink.conf'.

In what additional directory should Fink look for downloaded tarballs? []
Which directory should Fink use to build packages? (If you don't know what this
means, it is safe to leave it at its default.) []
Should Fink try to download pre-compiled packages from the binary distribution
if available? [Y/n]

(1)    Quiet (do not show download statistics)
(2)    Low (do not show tarballs being expanded)
(3)    Medium (will show almost everything)
(4)    High (will show everything)

How verbose should Fink be? [2]

Proxy/Firewall settings
Enter the URL of the HTTP proxy to use, or 'none' for no proxy. The URL should
start with http:// and may contain username, password or port specifications.
E.g: http://username:password@hostname:port  [none]
Enter the URL of the proxy to use for FTP, or 'none' for no proxy. The URL
should start with http:// and may contain username, password or port
specifications. E.g: ftp://username:password@hostname:port  [none]
Use passive mode FTP transfers (to get through a firewall)? [Y/n]

Mirror selection
All mirrors are set. Do you want to change them? [y/N]

Writing updated configuration to '/sw/etc/fink.conf'...
localhost:~ vanilla$
```

Figure 13.12 Fink asks you a series of questions. In this example we are accepting the default for every question—so we pressed [Return] for each one.

✔ Tips

- Notice how the configuration process ends with writing to the file `/sw/etc/fink.conf`. **Figure 13.13** shows the contents. You can manually edit this file in the future if you wish, or rerun
  `sudo fink configuration`
- Of course, there is a `man` page: `man fink` will show it to you, and `fink --help` will give you a summary of available commands and options (**Figure 13.14**).
- If you have problems during the Fink installation, see the sidebar "More About Fink" for links to the Fink homepage and mailing lists.

More About Fink

The Fink Web site is at http://fink.sourceforge.net.

Fink has an HTML user's guide, which is included in the installation disk image. You can open the file with a Web browser. The user's guide is also available online at http://fink.sourceforge.net/doc.

You can find links to mailing lists about Fink at http://fink.sourceforge.net/lists.

```
# Fink configuration, initially created by bootstrap.pl
Basepath: /sw
RootMethod: sudo
Trees: local/main stable/main stable/crypto
Distribution: 10.4-transitional
Mirror-apt: http://bindist.finkmirrors.net/bindist
Mirror-cpan: ftp://ftp.funet.fi/pub/languages/perl/CPAN/
Mirror-ctan: ftp://tug.ctan.org/tex-archive/
Mirror-debian: ftp.debian.org
Mirror-gimp: ftp://ftp.gimp.org/pub/gimp/
Mirror-gnome: ftp://ftp.gnome.org/pub/GNOME/
Mirror-gnu: ftp://ftp.gnu.org/gnu
Mirror-kde: ftp://ftp.kde.org/pub/kde/
Mirror-master: http://distfiles.master.finkmirrors.net/
Mirror-rsync: rsync://master.us.finkmirrors.net/finkinfo/
Mirror-sourceforge: http://west.dl.sourceforge.net/sourceforge/
MirrorContinent: nam
MirrorCountry: nam-us
MirrorOrder: MasterFirst
ProxyPassiveFTP: true
UseBinaryDist: true
Verbose: 1
```

Figure 13.13 The Fink configuration file, `/sw/etc/fink.conf`.

Now that you have Fink installed and configured, let's start using it.

Fink can show you all of the software packages available for installation. New software packages are added to the list frequently.

```
localhost:~ vanilla$ fink --help
Fink 0.23.10

Usage: fink [options] command [package...]
  fink install pkg1 [pkg2 ...]

Common commands:
  install        - install/update the named packages
  remove         - remove the named packages
  purge          - same as remove but also removes all configuration files
  update         - update the named packages
  selfupdat      - upgrade fink to the lastest release
  update-all     - update all installed packages
  configur       - rerun the configuration process
  list           - list available packages, optionally filtering by name,
                 see 'fink list -help' for more options
  apropos        - list packages matching a search keyword
  describe       - display a detailed description of the named packages
  index          - force rebuild of package cache
  validate       - performs various checks on .info and .deb files
  scanpackages   - rescans the list of binary packages on the system
  cleanup        - removes obsolete package files if newer versions are available
  dumpinfo       - show how fink parses parts of a package's .info file
  show-deps      - list run-time and compile-time package dependencies

Options:
  -h,       --help                - display this help text
  -q,       --quiet               - causes fink to be less verbose, opposite of -verbose
  -V,       --version             - display version information
  -v,       --verbose             - causes fink to be more verbose, opposite of -quiet
  -y,       --yes                 - assume default answer for all interactive questions
  -b,       --use-binary-dist     - download pre-compiled packages from the binary
                                  distribution if available
  --no-use-binary-dist            - don't use pre-compiled packages from the binary
                                  distribution (opposite of -b)

See the fink(8) manual page for more commands and options.
Visit http://fink.sourceforge.net/ for further information.
```

Figure 13.14 Using `fink --help` to get a summary of available commands and options.

To list available packages:

- `sudo fink list`

  brings up a list of all the available packages (**Figure 13.15**). Packages that are already installed are marked with an `i`, such as the `apt` package.

```
localhost:~ vanilla$ sudo fink list
Reading package info...

Information about 1766 packages read in 16 seconds.
     abs            0.908-12      Opensource spreadsheet
 i   apt            0.5.4-51      Advanced front-end for dpkg
     barcode        0.98-12       Barcode generation library and CLI front-end
     bluefish       1.0-20        Web-oriented text editor
 i   bzip2          1.0.2-12      Block-sorting file compressor
     contacts       1.1-1         Little command line OS X address book viewer
     cssed          1:0.2.1-13    CSS editor
     darkstat       2.5-3         Smaller network traffic analyzer
 i   darwin         8.1.0-1       [virtual package representing the kernel]
     dialog         0.9b-200208   Displays dialog boxes from shell scripts
     ethereal       0.10.9-11     Powerful network protocol analyzer
 i   fink           0.23.10-21    The Fink package manager
 i   fink-mirrors   0.24.4.1-1    Mirror infrastructure
     freehelix      98-11         Nucleic acid helix analysis program
     gimp           1.2.5-3       The GNU Image Manipulation Program
     gnupg          1.2.4-2       Gnu privacy guard - A Free PGP replacement
 i   gzip           1.2.4a-6      The gzip file compressor
     ht2html        2.0-1         Python-based web page template processor
     keychain       2.0.3-1       User-friendly front-end to ssh-agent(1)
     launch         1.0.0-2       Replacement for OS X "open" command
     libjpeg        6b-16         JPEG image format handling library
 i   macosx         10.4.1-1      [virtual package representing the system]
     mysql          4.1.10-1      Open Source SQL database
     openldap-ssl   2.1.22-25     LDAP directory services implementation
     pine           4.58-21       Text based tool for managing emails
     pstree         2.17-1        Shows the ps listing as a tree
     ruby18         1.8.1-1       Interpreted, object-oriented script language
     sitecopy       0.14.2-1      Web site uploader
     svn            1.1.4-11      Subversion - svnserve, tools
 i   tar            1.14-1        GNU tar - tape archiver
     web2png        2.4.6-2       Batch-converts entire web-pages with gif2png
     wget           1.8.2-2       Automatic web site retreiver
     xcircuit       3.3.12-1      Circuit drawing app with schematic capture
     yorick         1.6.02-2      Interpreted language and scientific graphics
     zoinks         0.2.7-11      Programmer's editor and IDE
     ztools         981107-1      Set of Z-Machine tools
localhost:~ vanilla$
```

Figure 13.15 Using the `fink list` command to show all available packages. Installed packages are marked with an `i`. The listing has been abbreviated. This figure is an abridged version of typical output, which will normally be over 1500 lines long.

✔ Tips

- The use of sudo in this case is not really required. You can run the `fink list` command without root privileges, but if `fink` detects that its cache of packages is out of date, it will be able to update the cache only if run as root.
- The list of available packages is very long—well over 1500 packages. To be able to scroll back in the Terminal application and read it all, make sure the Terminal screen buffer is large enough: Check in the Terminal menu, under Window Settings in the Buffer controls. You also may want to redirect the output of `fink list` to a file for viewing with `less` or `vi`:

  `fink list > /tmp/finklist.txt`

One of Fink's most useful features is that it keeps track of all the software it has installed, so upgrading and removing software is easy.

To list only installed packages:

◆ `fink list -i`

  gets you a list of only the installed packages (**Figure 13.16**).

Now the fun part: actually installing a package using Fink. We'll install the `wget` program as an example. `wget` is a command-line tool for retrieving files from Web sites and FTP sites. Mac OS X comes with a similar command, `curl`, but in our opinion `wget` is much easier to use.


```
localhost:~ vanilla$ fink list -i
Information about 1766 packages read in 6 seconds.
 i   apt                                 0.5.4-51      Advanced front-end for dpkg
 i   apt-shlibs        0.5.4-51            Advanced front-end for dpkg
 i   base-files        1.9.5-1             Directory infrastructure
 i   bzip2             1.0.2-12            Block-sorting file compressor
 i   bzip2-dev         1.0.2-12            Developer files for bzip2 package
 i   bzip2-shlibs      1.0.2-12            Shared libraries for bzip2 package
 i   cctools           576-1               [virtual package representing the develop...
 i   cctools-extra     1:525-1             Extra software from cctools
 i   cctools-sing...   1.0-1               [virtual package, your dev tools support ...
 i   darwin            8.1.0-1             [virtual package representing the kernel]
 i   debianutils       1.23-11             Misc. utilities specific to Debian (and F...
 i   dpkg              1.10.21-204         The Debian package manager
 i   fink              0.23.10-21          The Fink package manager
 i   fink-mirrors      0.24.4.1-1          Mirror infrastructure
 i   fink-prebinding   0.7.1-2             Tools for enabling prebinding in Fink
 i   gcc3.3            3.3-1               [virtual package representing the gcc 3.3...
 i   gcc4.0            4.0.0-1             [virtual package representing the gcc 4.0...
 i   gettext           0.10.40-19          Message localization support
 i   gettext-bin       0.10.40-19          Executables for gettext package
 i   gettext-dev       0.10.40-19          Developer files for gettext package
 i   gettext-tools     0.10.40-19          Developer executables for gettext package
```

continues on next page

Figure 13.16 Using `fink list -i` to list installed packages. Your output may differ.

To install a package using Fink:

1. `fink install wget`

   You must be root to install software with Fink, so it will automatically invoke `sudo` behind the scenes and you will be prompted for your password.

   Fink automatically downloads, compiles, and installs the software.

   Figure 13.17 shows typical output for the entire process of Fink downloading and installing `wget`.

   The amount of time involved will depend on the speed of your Internet connection and of your computer.

   You will get a shell prompt when Fink is done. The software is now installed.

2. Try using the newly installed software:

   `wget http://www.matisse.net/files/`
   `➝ glossary.html`

   This retrieves my Glossary of Internet terms and saves it in your current directory as glossary.html (**Figure 13.18**). See `man wget` for details on `wget`.

✔ Tips

- To cause the output from `wget` to go to `stdout` instead of a file on disk, use the `-O -` option (`-O` sets the output file, `-` is a special filename for `stdout`):

  `wget -O -` *`url`*

- Fink installs some informational files for each package in `/sw/share/doc`. In particular, there should be a README file for each package in a subdirectory named after the package; for example:

  `/sw/share/doc/wget/README`

continues on page 420

Figure 13.16 *continued*

```
 i   gimp-print7-...   4.2.6-1        [virtual package representing Apple's ins...
 i   gzip              1.2.4a-6       The gzip file compressor
 i   libiconv          1.9.1-11       Character set conversion library
 i   libiconv-bin      1.9.1-11       Executables for libiconv package
 i   libiconv-dev      1.9.1-11       Developer files for libiconv package
 i   libncurses5-...   5.4-2004102    Shared libraries for libncurses5 package
 i   macosx            10.4.1-1       [virtual package representing the system]
 i   ncurses           5.4-2004102    Executable files for ncurses
 i   ncurses-dev       5.3-2003101    Development files for ncurses package
 i   ncurses-shlibs    5.3-2003101    Shared libraries for ncurses package
 i   system-java       1.4.2-1        [virtual package representing Java 1.4.2]
 i   system-java-dev   1.4.2-1        [virtual package representing Java SDK 1....
 i   system-java13     1.3.1-1        [virtual package representing Java 1.3.1]
 i   system-java1...   1.3.1-1        [virtual package representing Java 1.3.1 ...
 i   system-java14     1.4.2-1        [virtual package representing Java 1.4.2]
 i   system-java1...   1.4.2-1        [virtual package representing Java 1.4.2 ...
 i   system-java3d     0-1            [virtual package representing Java3D]
 i   system-javaai     0-1            [virtual package representing Java Advanc...
 i   system-perl       5.8.6-1        [virtual package representing perl]
 i   system-xfree86    2:4.4-2        [placeholder for user installed x11]
 i   system-xfree...   2:4.4-2        [placeholder for user installed x11 devel...
 i   system-xfree...   2:4.4-2        [placeholder for user installed x11 share...
 i   tar               1.14-1         GNU tar - tape archiver
 i   unzip             5.52-11        Decompression compatible with pkunzip
localhost:~ vanilla$
```

```
localhost:~ vanilla$ fink install wget
Password:
Information about 1766 packages read in 2 seconds.
The following package will be installed or updated:
 wget
/sw/bin/apt-get -q --ignore-breakage --download-only install wget=1.8.2-2
Reading Package Lists...
Building Dependency Tree...
The following NEW packages will be installed:
  wget
0 packages upgraded, 1 newly installed, 0 to remove and 0  not upgraded.
Need to get 346kB of archives. After unpacking 1249kB will be used.
Get:1 http://bindist.finkmirrors.net 10.4-transitional/release/main wget 1.8.2-2 [346kB]
Fetched 346kB in 3s (105kB/s)
Download complete and in download only mode
dpkg -i /sw/var/cache/apt/archives/wget_1.8.2-2_darwin-powerpc.deb
Selecting previously deselected package wget.
(Reading database ... 4090 files and directories currently installed.)
Unpacking wget (from .../wget_1.8.2-2_darwin-powerpc.deb) ...
Setting up wget (1.8.2-2) ...
* Wget: (wget). The non-interactive network downloader.
install-info(/sw/share/info/wget.info): creating new section `Net Utilities'

localhost:~ vanilla$
```

Figure 13.17 Using Fink to download and install the wget program.

```
localhost:~ vanilla$ wget http://www.matisse.net/files/glossary.html
--08:34:02--  http://www.matisse.net/files/glossary.html
   => `glossary.html'
Resolving www.matisse.net... done.
Connecting to www.matisse.net[216.135.166.2]:80... connected.
HTTP request sent, awaiting response... 200 OK
Length: 115,145 [text/html]

100%[====================================>] 115,145        1.23M/s    ETA 00:00

08:34:02 (1.23 MB/s) - `glossary.html' saved [115145/115145]

localhost:~ vanilla$
```

Figure 13.18 Using the newly installed wget command to retrieve and save a document.

- If you are using the `tcsh` shell, run the `rehash` command after installing new software to update the shell's list of available commands.

The database that Fink uses for package information contains short descriptions of the available packages. You can see a package description with the `fink describe` command.

To show details about a package:

- `fink describe` *package*

  For example, to see the package description for the `launch` program,

  `fink describe launch`

  produces the output shown in **Figure 13.19**. Not all packages have a description, but most do.

To search for packages by keyword:

- `fink apropos` *package*

  To search for packages whose name or one-line description contains *audio*, use

  `fink apropos audio`

  which produces output like that shown in **Figure 13.20**.


```
localhost:~ vanilla$ fink describe launch
Information about 1766 packages read in 3 seconds.

launch-1.0.0-2: Replacement for OS X "open" command
 launch is a replacement for "open" which:
 * Opens URLs, directly or in your preferred helper application.
 * Lets you specify applications by their four-char creator (e.g. 'ToyS') or
   Java-style bundle ID (e.g. com.apple.scripteditor), both of which allow
   you to move or rename an app.
 * Asks applications to print documents, something the OS X Finder is missing.
 * Launches applications in the background, or launches Carbon applications in
   Classic.
 * Shows info about any item on disk, including its file type, creator, data
   and resource fork sizes, dates and bundle ID.
 .
 Web site: http://web.sabi.net/nriley/software/
 .
 Maintainer: Ben Hines <bhines@alumni.ucsd.edu>

localhost:~ vanilla$
```

Figure 13.19 Using `fink describe` *package* to provide a brief description of a package, even one not yet installed.

Table 13.1

Updating and Removing Packages with Fink

ACTION	COMMAND
Update a specific package	`fink update package`
Update all installed packages	`fink update-all`
Update Fink itself	`fink selfupdate`
Remove a package	`fink remove package`

Updating and removing packages with Fink

One of the most excellent (dude!) features of Fink is the ease with which you can use it to update installed packages.

Updating a package in Fink is simply a matter of using the `fink update` command. You can update a single package by specifying a package name on the command line, but even cooler is the fact that you can update *all* installed packages with the `fink update-all` command.

Fink also makes it easy to have it update itself and to remove any package installed with it. **Table 13.1** summarizes the commands for updating and removing packages installed with Fink.

```
localhost:~ vanilla$ fink apropos audio
Information about 1766 packages read in 3 seconds.
  audiofile          0.2.6-10      Audio File Library *Developement Files*
  audiofile-bin      0.2.6-10      Audio File Library *Binaries*
  audiofile-sh...    0.2.6-10      Audio File Library *Shared Libraries*
  flac               1.1.1-11      Free lossless audio codec
  flac-bin           1.1.1-11      Free lossless audio codec - encoder/decoder
  flac-nox           1.1.1-11      Free lossless audio codec - No X11
  flac-nox-bin       1.1.1-11      Free lossless audio codec - encoder/decoder
  flac-nox-shlibs    1.1.1-11      Free lossless audio codec - shared libs
  flac-shlibs        1.1.1-11      Free lossless audio codec - shared libs
  flac-xmms          1.1.1-11      Free lossless audio codec - xmms plugin
  gnome-audio        1.4.0-3       Audio files for Gnome
  ladspa             1.12-12       Linux Audio Developer's Simple Plugin API
  libao2             0.8.4-10      Audio output library
  libao2-shlibs      0.8.4-10      Audio output library
  libmad             0.15.1b-1     MPEG audio decoder library
  libmad-shlibs      0.15.1b-1     MPEG audio decoder library
  libvorbis0         1.0.1-1       Vorbis audio codec development headers an...
  libvorbis0-s...    1.0.1-1       Vorbis audio codec shared libraries
  madplay            0.15.2b-3     MPEG audio decoder and player
  mpg123             pre0.59s-8    Real time MPEG Audio Player for Layer 1,2...
  mpgtx              1.1-13        Command line MPEG audio/video toolbox
  normalize          0.7.4-3       Audio file volume normalizer
  sdl-mixer          1.2.5-12      SDL multi-channel audio mixer library
  sdl-mixer-sh...    1.2.5-12      SDL multi-channel audio mixer library
localhost:~ vanilla$
```

Figure 13.20 Using `fink apropos` *keyword* to search for available packages by keyword.

Manually Installing from Source Code

Most of the Unix software you are likely to want to use is available via Fink, but as you get into more advanced uses of Unix, you will find that some software isn't available through Fink. You need to know how to compile and install software manually. The process for installing virtually all open-source Unix software is described here (except for using the CPAN system to install Perl modules, which we describe later in this chapter).

For the following task, we will use a sample program that is designed to demonstrate the process of manually downloading, compiling, and installing a Unix application from the command line. The program is the classic sample program `hello world`.

You use the `wget` program to download the source code from the command line. If you haven't already installed `wget` using Fink, do that now (described in the previous section).

To manually install a package from source code:

1. `sudo -s`

   The installation process must be performed as root, because you will be adding files to directories owned and writable only by root.

   To avoid typing `sudo` before every command, you are simply spawning a new shell as root. Notice that your shell prompt changes (**Figure 13.21**). Remember to exit from the new shell (with the `exit` command) after the installation is done. We'll remind you.

2. Enter your password, and press Return.

   The next step is to create the directory where you are saving the source code.

   The conventional place for all user-installed software is in subdirectories of `/usr/local`.

   The source code goes in a subdirectory of `/usr/local/src`, and the actual program (the compiled executable file itself) goes in `/usr/local/bin`.

3. `mkdir -p /usr/local/src/hello`

   That command creates the directory `/usr/local/src/hello` and any intermediate directories that may not exist (such as the `src` directory).

```
localhost:~ vanilla$ sudo -s
Password:
localhost:~ root#
```

Figure 13.21 Your shell prompt changes when you start a new shell as root.

4. `cd /usr/local/src/hello`

   This changes your current directory to `/usr/local/src/hello`.

   (Here's a mini-tip: You can also do

   `cd !$`

   because `!$` translates to the last argument of the previous command, in this case `/usr/local/src/hello`.)

5. `wget http://ftp.gnu.org/gnu/hello/` → `hello-2.1.1.tar.gz`

   The `wget` command retrieves the compressed `tar` file (also known as a *tarball*) and saves it in the current directory (**Figure 13.22**).

   Next you will unpack the compressed `tar` file.

continues on next page

```
localhost:/usr/local/src/hello root# wget http://ftp.gnu.org/gnu/hello/hello-2.1.1.tar.gz
-06:56:06-  http://ftp.gnu.org/gnu/hello/hello-2.1.1.tar.gz
  => `hello-2.1.1.tar.gz'
Resolving ftp.gnu.org... done.
Connecting to ftp.gnu.org[199.232.41.7]:80... connected.
HTTP request sent, awaiting response... 200 OK
Length: 389,363 [application/x-tar]

100%[===================================>] 389,363      103.52K/s    ETA 00:00

06:56:10 (103.52 KB/s) - `hello-2.1.1.tar.gz' saved [389363/389363]

localhost:/usr/local/src/hello root#
```

Figure 13.22 Using `wget` to retrieve a compressed `tar` file (a *tarball*) of source code.

Learning More About Compiling Software

Almost all the Unix software you will download and install is written in the C programming language and uses a couple of common tools to manage the process of configuring the source code and compiling it.

The classic text on C is *The C Programming Language,* by Brian W. Kernighan and Dennis M. Ritchie (Prentice Hall; http://cm.bell-labs.com/cm/cs/cbook). Also check out *C Programming: Visual QuickStart Guide* by Larry Ullman and Marc Liyanage (Peachpit Press; www.peachpit.com/title/0321287630).

The `make` program is widely used for managing software development, especially software written in C. The standard text on `make` is *Managing Projects with make,* Second Edition, by Andy Oram and Steve Talbott (O'Reilly; www.oreilly.com/catalog/make2).

6. `tar xfvz hello-2.1.1.tar.gz`

   This creates a new directory called `hello-2.1.1`.

   The options to `tar` are the following: `x` for "extract," `f` for "from a file," `v` for "verbose," and `z` for "the file is compressed with `gzip`." The verbose option causes the display of the name of each file and directory extracted from the archive; in all, you will see more than 200 files listed (**Figure 13.23**).


```
localhost:/usr/local/src/hello root# tar xfvz hello-2.1.1.tar.gz
hello-2.1.1/
hello-2.1.1/intl/
hello-2.1.1/intl/ChangeLog
hello-2.1.1/intl/Makefile.in
… omitting display of many files from the intl/ subdirectory
hello-2.1.1/intl/VERSION
hello-2.1.1/po/
hello-2.1.1/po/Makefile.in.in
… omitting display of files in the po/ subdirectory
hello-2.1.1/README
hello-2.1.1/ABOUT-NLS
hello-2.1.1/AUTHORS
hello-2.1.1/COPYING
hello-2.1.1/ChangeLog
hello-2.1.1/INSTALL
hello-2.1.1/Makefile.am
hello-2.1.1/Makefile.in
hello-2.1.1/NEWS
hello-2.1.1/THANKS
hello-2.1.1/TODO
hello-2.1.1/aclocal.m4
hello-2.1.1/config.guess
hello-2.1.1/config.h.in
hello-2.1.1/config.rpath
hello-2.1.1/config.sub
hello-2.1.1/configure
hello-2.1.1/configure.ac
 .
 .
 .
```

Figure 13.23 Using `tar` to extract files from the compressed archive. (Abridged output; total output will be more than 200 lines.)

7. `cd hello-2.1.1`

   Now your current directory is the directory containing the actual source code. Check the files, looking especially for README and INSTALL files.

8. `ls`

   You will see that there are indeed both README and INSTALL files (**Figure 13.24**); read them both.

9. `less README`

   The README file usually tells you what the program is for, who wrote it, where to find more information, and how to report bugs.

10. `q`

    This quits from the `less` program.

11. `less INSTALL`

    The INSTALL file should tell you, in detail, how to install the software. Install files can be quite complex because they try to address many different versions of Unix and the many options that someone might use. In general, as we noted at the beginning of this chapter, the basic instructions tell you to run the following:

    `./configure`

    `make`

    `make test` or `make check`

    `make install`

    It is a good idea to read through the INSTALL files carefully the first dozen or so times you install software manually. After that, always read enough to confirm that nothing unusual is required for the installation.

    One common option described in INSTALL files controls where you install the software. The convention is to use a prefix of `/usr/local`, so executables go in `/usr/local/bin`, `man` pages in `/usr/local/man`, software libraries in `/usr/local/lib`, and so on. Do not use something else unless you have a very good reason. Installing software in the default location keeps your system consistent with the rest of the world and makes for easier maintenance.

12. `q`

    to quit from `less`.

    In the case of this sample program, you will use the default configuration, so the next steps are very simple.

continues on next page


```
localhost:/usr/local/src/hello/hello-2.1.1 root# ls
ABOUT-NLS       Makefile.am     config.guess    depcomp         mkinstalldirs
AUTHORS         Makefile.in     config.h.in     doc             po
BUGS            NEWS            config.rpath    install-sh      src
COPYING         README          config.sub      intl            tests
ChangeLog       THANKS          configure       m4
ChangeLog.0     TODO            configure.ac    man
INSTALL         aclocal.m4      contrib         missing
localhost:/usr/local/src/hello/hello-2.1.1 root#
```

Figure 13.24 Using `ls` to see the files in the unpacked directory.

13. `./configure`

This runs a script that probes your system and creates another script using the information found (**Figure 13.25**). The `configure` script creates a file called Makefile, which is used by the next command.

```
localhost:/usr/local/src/hello/hello-2.1.1 root# ./configure
checking for a BSD-compatible install... /usr/bin/install -c
checking whether build environment is sane... yes
checking for gawk... no
checking for mawk... no
checking for nawk... no
checking for awk... awk
checking whether make sets ${MAKE}... yes
checking for gcc... gcc
checking for C compiler default output... a.out
checking whether the C compiler works... yes
checking whether we are cross compiling... no
checking for suffix of executables...
checking for suffix of object files... o
checking whether we are using the GNU C compiler... yes
checking whether gcc accepts -g... yes
checking for style of include used by make... GNU
... omitting many lines to save space...
configure: creating ./config.status
config.status: creating Makefile
config.status: creating contrib/Makefile
config.status: creating doc/Makefile
config.status: creating intl/Makefile
config.status: creating man/Makefile
config.status: creating po/Makefile.in
config.status: creating m4/Makefile
config.status: creating src/Makefile
config.status: creating tests/Makefile
config.status: creating config.h
config.status: executing depfiles commands
config.status: executing default-1 commands
config.status: creating po/POTFILES
config.status: creating po/Makefile
config.status: executing default commands
localhost:/usr/local/src/hello/hello-2.1.1 root#
```

Figure 13.25 The `configure` script probes your system and configures the source code for compilation. (Output here is abridged.)

14. make

The make command reads Makefile, created by configure, and runs a series of commands to compile the software. (Both configure and Makefile are plain-text files—you can look inside them if you are curious.) **Figure 13.26** shows abridged output from make. Depending on how large and complex the software is, and how fast your computer is, the compilation process can take many minutes or even longer.

continues on next page

```
localhost:/usr/local/src/hello/hello-2.1.1 root# make
make  all-recursive
Making all in contrib
make[2]: Nothing to be done for `all'.
Making all in doc
make[2]: Nothing to be done for `all'.
Making all in intl
gcc -c -DLOCALEDIR=\"/usr/local/share/locale\" -DLOCALE_ALIAS_PATH=\"/usr/local
… several lines omitted …
rm -f libintl.a
ar cru libintl.a intl-compat.o bindtextdom.o dcgettext.o dgettext.o gettext.o f
ranlib libintl.a
cp ./libgnuintl.h libintl.h
/bin/sh ./config.charset 'powerpc-apple-darwin8.1.0' > t-charset.alias
mv t-charset.alias charset.alias
sed -e '/^#/d' -e 's/@''PACKAGE''@/hello/g' ref-add.sin > t-ref-add.sed
mv t-ref-add.sed ref-add.sed
sed -e '/^#/d' -e 's/@''PACKAGE''@/hello/g' ref-del.sin > t-ref-del.sed
mv t-ref-del.sed ref-del.sed
Making all in po
make[2]: Nothing to be done for `all'.
Making all in src
source='hello.c' object='hello.o' libtool=no \
depfile='.deps/hello.Po' tmpdepfile='.deps/hello.TPo' \
depmode=gcc3 /bin/sh ../depcomp \
… several lines omitted …
Making all in man
perl help2man --name="Friendly Greeting Program" ../src/hello >hello.1
Making all in m4
make[2]: Nothing to be done for `all'.
Making all in tests
make[2]: Nothing to be done for `all'.
make[2]: Nothing to be done for `all-am'.
localhost:/usr/local/src/hello/hello-2.1.1 root#
```

Figure 13.26 The make command runs the compilation process. (Output here is abridged.)

15. `make check`

Some software packages come with a set of preinstallation tests to run after compiling the software but before installing it. In this case, the INSTALL file says that we can run the tests with `make check` (**Figure 13.27**). Many packages use `make test` for the same purpose. (By the way, the argument to the `make` command is called a *target*.)

Up to now you have not changed anything on your disk outside the directory containing the source code. The next step is to install the software in the location where it will be available to all users on the system.


```
localhost:/usr/local/src/hello/hello-2.1.1 root# make check
Making check in contrib
make[1]: Nothing to be done for `check'.
Making check in doc
make[1]: Nothing to be done for `check'.
Making check in intl
make[1]: Nothing to be done for `check'.
Making check in po
make[1]: Nothing to be done for `check'.
Making check in src
make[1]: Nothing to be done for `check'.
Making check in man
make[1]: Nothing to be done for `check'.
Making check in m4
make[1]: Nothing to be done for `check'.
Making check in tests
make  check-TESTS
PASS: hello-1
PASS: world-1
PASS: nothing-1
==================
All 3 tests passed
==================
make[1]: Nothing to be done for `check-am'.
localhost:/usr/local/src/hello/hello-2.1.1 root#
```

Figure 13.27 Running the preinstallation tests. In this case there were three tests; all passed.

16. `make install`

The make program shows you what it does to install the software. In this case it uses the `install` program (`/usr/bin/install`) (**Figure 13.28**), which has a man page you can read if you are curious. The software is now installed.

continues on next page

```
localhost:/usr/local/src/hello/hello-2.1.1 root# make install
Making install in contrib
make[2]: Nothing to be done for `install-exec-am'.
make[2]: Nothing to be done for `install-data-am'.
Making install in doc
make[2]: Nothing to be done for `install-exec-am'.
/bin/sh ../mkinstalldirs /usr/local/info
mkdir --p – /usr/local/info
 /usr/bin/install -c -m 644 ./hello.info /usr/local/info/hello.info
 install-info --info-dir=/usr/local/info /usr/local/info/hello.info
* Hello, world!: (hello). GNU `Hello, world'.
install-info(/usr/local/info/hello.info): no file /usr/local/info/dir, retrieving backup file
/var/backups/infodir.bak.
install-info(/usr/local/info/hello.info): creating new section `Greeting Printing Program'
...dozens of lines omitted...
Making install in po
...dozens of lines omitted...
Making install in src
/bin/sh ../mkinstalldirs /usr/local/bin
mkdir -p -- /usr/local/bin
  /usr/bin/install -c hello /usr/local/bin/hello
make[2]: Nothing to be done for `install-data-am'.
Making install in man
make[2]: Nothing to be done for `install-exec-am'.
/bin/sh ../mkinstalldirs /usr/local/man/man1
mkdir -p -- /usr/local/man/man1
 /usr/bin/install -c -m 644 ./hello.1 /usr/local/man/man1/hello.1
Making install in m4
make[2]: Nothing to be done for `install-exec-am'.
make[2]: Nothing to be done for `install-data-am'.
Making install in tests
make[2]: Nothing to be done for `install-exec-am'.
make[2]: Nothing to be done for `install-data-am'.
make[2]: Nothing to be done for `install-exec-am'.
make[2]: Nothing to be done for `install-data-am'.
localhost:/usr/local/src/hello/hello-2.1.1 root#
```

Figure 13.28 The make `install` program performs the actual installation of the software. (Output here is abridged.)

17. `exit`

    This exits from the root shell you started in step 1. Your prompt changes back to your normal prompt. Note that your current directory reverts to whatever it was when you started the root shell (**Figure 13.29**).

    If you are using the `tcsh` shell as your shell, type `rehash` so that `tcsh` will rebuild its list of available commands.

    Now you can try running the newly installed software. The new program has been installed as `/usr/local/bin/hello`, so you want to make sure that `/usr/local/bin` is in your `PATH`. Also, the `man` page is installed as `/usr/local/man/man1/hello.1`, so make sure that `/usr/local/man` is in your `MANPATH`—see Chapter 7 to learn how to alter your `PATH` and `MANPATH`.

18. `hello`

    The program produces output as shown in **Figure 13.30**. If you get an error that says

    `-bash: hello: command not found`

    see step 17 above—you probably need to adjust your `PATH` to include `/usr/local/bin`. Or use the full path `/usr/local/bin/hello`.

19. You're done.

    Congratulations—you've installed software from source code.

✔ Tips

- Read the `man` page: `man hello`

  The `hello` source-code package (like many GNU packages) also installs documentation in a format called Info. Read `man info` to learn about the Info format and the `info` command so that you can run `info hello`.

- You can save a record of the compilation process to a file by redirecting the output of `make` to a file:

  `make > compilation.log`

  or

  `make install > install.log`

- You can remove all the files created in the source directory by the compilation process with

  `make clean`

  (If you want to remove files that have been installed with `make install`, you must remove them manually from their installed locations. In some rare cases there might be an "uninstall" target in the makefile, in which case you could do `make uninstall`.)

- The `configure` script saves the configuration it builds in another shell script, called `config.status`, which you can run to re-create the configuration, including any options you selected.

- If you are using the `tcsh` shell as your shell, run `rehash` so that `tcsh` will rebuild its list of available commands.

```
localhost:/usr/local/src/hello/hello-2.1.1
→ root# exit
localhost:~ vanilla$
```

Figure 13.29 Exiting from the root shell brings you back to the directory you were in when you started it.

```
localhost:~ vanilla$ hello
Hello, world!
localhost:~ vanilla$
```

Figure 13.30 Running the newly installed software to see what it does.

Installing Perl Modules

If you've started using Unix a lot, there is a good chance you will also use Perl a lot. Perl is a powerful and easy-to-learn language that's well suited for both large and small programming tasks. A beginner can learn how to write a simple Perl script in a day, and an experienced programmer can use Perl to solve complex problems efficiently.

One of the things that make Perl so powerful is CPAN (Comprehensive Perl Archive Network). CPAN is a truly amazing collection of freely available Perl modules (we'll tell you where to find out more about CPAN later in the chapter).

A *Perl module* is a piece of software that adds features to Perl, such as the ability to do date and time arithmetic, to connect to databases, or to use strong encryption. Perl modules can be written in Perl, C, and other languages; most are written in C and/or Perl. The version of Perl installed with Mac OS X comes with more than 250 modules (the "standard modules") already installed. The CPAN system provides more than a thousand more.

You can download and build Perl modules using a series of steps very similar to the steps described above. The main difference is that instead of running a shell script (`./configure`) to build the makefile and configure the software for compilation, you run a Perl script by using the command line `perl Makefile.PL`. Also, Perl modules almost always come with tests that run when you do `make test`. But wait—there's more.

One of the standard modules included with Perl on Mac OS X is the CPAN module—essentially the Perl version of Fink (in fact, the CPAN module predates Fink by several years). As with Fink, your computer must be connected to the Internet to use the CPAN module.

Using the Perl CPAN module, you can easily install Perl modules in a couple of steps.

The first time you use the CPAN module, you must configure it.

Also, in order to use CPAN from Mac OS X, you need to set your `FTP_PASSIVE` environment variable to a true (that is, nonzero) value. This will tell the FTP software used by the CPAN module (the Perl `libnet` module) to use

continues on next page

When Things Go Wrong

Sometimes running `./configure` doesn't work smoothly. Usually, if something goes wrong with `configure`, it is because the script could not find something on your system that it needs.

Sometimes `configure` works, but compilation fails when you run `make`.

As you gain experience with compiling software, you may be able to fix the problem yourself, perhaps by installing a piece of software required by the one that didn't compile.

The first place to look for help is in the README and INSTALL files. Make sure you have read anything pertaining to Mac OS X or Darwin mentioned in those files. Look for references to other help resources, such as a Web site or mailing list. If you send a message to someone asking for help, be very respectful of his or her time. Make sure to include an exact copy of any error messages you received and any options you used when running `configure`.

passive mode, which will enable FTP connections to work even with the Mac OS X firewall software on (see Chapter 12, "Security"). Chapter 7 covers more on setting environment variables, but here's a quick task.

To set your FTP_PASSIVE environment variable to "true":

- export FTP_PASSIVE=1

  That works for the bash shell; if you are using the tcsh shell, the command line is

  setenv FTP_PASSIVE 1

  You really should make the setting part of your shell configuration (again, see Chapter 7) by adding the command line to the .bash_profile in your home directory (or .tcshrc, for tcsh users).

To configure CPAN:

1. sudo cpan

   Here you are running the cpan command as root. The cpan command is a small script that basically is a shortcut for running the following command line:

   perl -MCPAN -e shell

   The CPAN module provides its own little shell interface—its prompt is cpan>, and it takes commands to search for and install Perl modules.

   You use sudo because the CPAN module will be making changes in system directories (it will save its configuration in /System/Library/Perl/5.8.6/CPAN/Config.pm and will install new modules in various subdirectories of /Library/Perl). Note that the "5.8.6" in that path refers to a specific version of Perl (the one installed in Mac OS X 10.4) and will change in the future.

   If this is the first time you have used the CPAN module, it will ask you to configure it (**Figure 13.31**).

   (Make sure you have set your FTP_PASSIVE environment variable to 1; see the previous task.)

```
localhost:~ vanilla$ sudo cpan
Password:

/System/Library/Perl/5.8.6/CPAN/Config.pm initialized.


CPAN is the world-wide archive of perl resources. It consists of about
100 sites that all replicate the same contents all around the globe.
Many countries have at least one CPAN site already. The resources
found on CPAN are easily accessible with the CPAN.pm module. If you
want to use CPAN.pm, you have to configure it properly.

If you do not want to enter a dialog now, you can answer 'no' to this
question and I'll try to autoconfigure. (Note: you can revisit this
dialog anytime later by typing 'o conf init' at the cpan prompt.)

Are you ready for manual configuration? [yes]
```

Figure 13.31 Running the cpan command for the first time starts a configuration process.

2. Enter your password if asked.

   The CPAN module asks if you are ready to do a manual configuration.

3. Accept the default (yes) by pressing Return.

   The CPAN module asks you for the name of a directory where it will store files during installation (**Figure 13.32**).

4. /usr/local/CPAN

   This is one of the few places where you will enter something different from the default. The CPAN module will create the directory if it doesn't exist.

   If you make a mistake while typing, you can erase the whole line you have entered by pressing Control U.

   The module now asks about the size of the cache it will keep of files used during installations. The default of 10 MB is a good choice (**Figure 13.33**).

5. Accept the default (10) by pressing Return.

   The module now asks if it should check the size of the cache when it starts up. The default (atstart) is what you want (**Figure 13.34**).

continues on next page

```
The following questions are intended to help you with the
configuration. The CPAN module needs a directory of its own to cache
important index files and maybe keep a temporary mirror of CPAN files.
This may be a site-wide directory or a personal directory.


First of all, I'd like to create this directory. Where?

CPAN build and cache directory? [/Users/vanilla/.cpan] /usr/local/CPAN
```

Figure 13.32 Setting the directory that CPAN will use to download and build Perl modules, overriding the default by entering /usr/local/CPAN.

```
How big should the disk cache be for keeping the build directories
with all the intermediate files?

Cache size for build directory (in MB)? [10]
```

Figure 13.33 Selecting the size of the CPAN cache.

```
By default, each time the CPAN module is started, cache scanning
is performed to keep the cache size in sync. To prevent this,
disable the cache scanning with 'never'.

Perform cache scanning (atstart or never)? [atstart]
```

Figure 13.34 The CPAN module asks when to scan the cache to limit its size.

6. Accept the default by pressing Return.

   The module asks if it should try to keep an index of information about modules (using another module called `Storable`). Again, accept the default (yes) (**Figure 13.35**).

7. Press Return to accept the default.

   The module asks you about the character set supported by your terminal. Unless you are sure you know what you are doing, you should accept the default (yes indicates ISO-8859-1, the standard English character set) (**Figure 13.36**).

8. Press Return to accept the default.

   The module explains that it can create a file that provides command history in the CPAN shell interface, and then asks you for the filename and the number of lines to store (**Figure 13.37**). We suggest accepting the default values.

```
To considerably speed up the initial CPAN shell startup, it is
possible to use Storable to create a cache of metadata. If Storable
is not available, the normal index mechanism will be used.

Cache metadata (yes/no)? [yes]
```

Figure 13.35 The CPAN module asks if it should try to keep an index of information to speed startup.

```
The next option deals with the charset your terminal supports. In
general CPAN is English speaking territory, thus the charset does not
matter much, but some of the aliens out there who upload their
software to CPAN bear names that are outside the ASCII range. If your
terminal supports UTF-8, you say no to the next question, if it
supports ISO-8859-1 (also known as LATIN1) then you say yes, and if it
supports neither nor, your answer does not matter, you will not be
able to read the names of some authors anyway. If you answer no, nmes
will be output in UTF-8.

Your terminal expects ISO-8859-1 (yes/no)? [yes]
```

Figure 13.36 The CPAN module asks about the character set supported by your terminal.

```
If you have one of the readline packages (Term::ReadLine::Perl,
Term::ReadLine::Gnu, possibly others) installed, the interactive CPAN
shell will have history support. The next two questions deal with the
filename of the history file and with its size. If you do not want to
set this variable, please hit SPACE RETURN to the following question.

File to save your history? [/usr/local/CPAN/histfile]
Number of lines to save? [100]
```

Figure 13.37 The module asks two questions (filename and number of lines) about a file to store a command history for the CPAN shell interface.

9. Press [Return] twice to accept the default for both questions.

   The next question deals with the fact that some modules depend on others' having already been installed.

   You can instruct the module to ask you before installing prerequisite modules (ask), to ignore prerequisites (not recommended), or to "follow" the requirements and install prerequisites when discovered.

   The default is to ask before installing, but we suggest you change that to `follow` (**Figure 13.38**).

   The module then asks about a series of programs that it uses. You should accept the default for each of them by pressing [Return].

10. Press [Return] for each program shown in **Figure 13.39**.

    (Notice the `wget` program—you installed that using `wget` earlier in this chapter. You can also install `lynx` using Fink, if you like.)

    (Don't worry if the `lynx` and `ncftpget` programs are not found—the module will work without them.)

continues on next page

```
The CPAN module can detect when a module that which you are trying to
build depends on prerequisites. If this happens, it can build the
prerequisites for you automatically ('follow'), ask you for
confirmation ('ask'), or just ignore them ('ignore'). Please set your
policy to one of the three values.

Policy on building prerequisites (follow, ask or ignore)? [ask] follow
```

Figure 13.38 The CPAN module asks for your policy on building prerequisite modules. You tell it to "follow."

```
The CPAN module will need a few external programs to work properly.
Please correct me, if I guess the wrong path for a program. Don't
panic if you do not have some of them, just press ENTER for those. To
disable the use of a download program, you can type a space followed
by ENTER.

Where is your gzip program? [/sw/bin/gzip]
Where is your tar program? [/sw/bin/tar]
Where is your unzip program? [/usr/bin/unzip]
Where is your make program? [/usr/bin/make]
Warning: lynx not found in PATH
Where is your lynx program? []
Where is your wget program? [/sw/bin/wget]
Warning: ncftpget not found in PATH
Where is your ncftpget program? []
Where is your ncftp program? [/usr/bin/ncftp]
Where is your ftp program? [/usr/bin/ftp]
What is your favorite pager program? [/usr/bin/less]
What is your favorite shell? [/bin/tcsh]
```

Figure 13.39 The CPAN module asks about a series of programs it wants to use. You accept the default for each question. (Your list might differ a bit.)

The module now asks about parameters for the `perl Makefile.PL` command (**Figure 13.40**).

11. Don't supply any extra parameters; just accept the default by pressing Return.

    The module asks for parameters for the `make` command (**Figure 13.41**).

    If you have a dual-processor machine, enter

    `-j3`

    Otherwise, don't enter anything.

12. Press Return

    You are asked about options for the `make install` command. The CPAN module offers an option to try to uninstall potentially conflicting packages, which is a good idea (**Figure 13.42**).

```
Every Makefile.PL is run by perl in a separate process. Likewise we
run 'make' and 'make install' in processes. If you have any
parameters (e.g. PREFIX, LIB, UNINST or the like) you want to pass
to the calls, please specify them here.

If you don't understand this question, just press ENTER.

Parameters for the 'perl Makefile.PL' command?
Typical frequently used settings:

  POLLUTE=1 increasing backwards compatibility
  LIB=~/perl     non-root users (please see manual for more hints)

Your choice:  []
```

Figure 13.40 The CPAN module asks about options for the `perl Makefile.PL` command. You just press Return.

```
Parameters for the 'make' command?
Typical frequently used setting:

  -j3  dual processor system

Your choice:  []
```

Figure 13.41 Options for the `make` command. Enter `-j3` if you have a dual-processor machine; otherwise, don't enter anything.

```
Parameters for the 'make install' command?
Typical frequently used setting:

  UNINST=1  to always uninstall potentially conflicting files

Your choice:  [] UNINST=1
```

Figure 13.42 Options for the `make install` command. Enter UNINST=1.

13. `UNINST=1`

The installation process for many modules involves asking you questions. You can tell the CPAN module how long to wait for an answer (in seconds) before stopping an installation process. The CPAN module recommends a setting of 0, which means "wait forever," so if you walk away from your computer during an installation, the module will wait until you come back (**Figure 13.43**).

14. Press Return to accept the default (0).

The module now asks you about proxy servers. If your computer is set up behind a firewall, there may be one or more proxy servers you must use to access Web sites or FTP sites on the Internet.

Ask your network administrator if you are not sure. If you don't have a network administrator, then you almost certainly don't have proxy servers, so just accept the default (nothing) for each of the next three questions (**Figure 13.44**).

If you have a proxy server, enter it in the form of a URL:

`http://proxy.paranoid.sf.ca.us/`

continues on next page

```
Sometimes you may wish to leave the processes run by CPAN alone
without caring about them. As sometimes the Makefile.PL contains
question you're expected to answer, you can set a timer that will
kill a 'perl Makefile.PL' process after the specified time in seconds.

If you set this value to 0, these processes will wait forever. This is
the default and recommended setting.

Timeout for inactivity during Makefile.PL? [0]
```

Figure 13.43 Setting the time-out period. The default (0 for "wait forever") is a good choice.

```
If you're accessing the net via proxies, you can specify them in the
CPAN configuration or via environment variables. The variable in
the $CPAN::Config takes precedence.

Your ftp_proxy?
Your http_proxy?
Your no_proxy?
```

Figure 13.44 Press Return to accept the default (which is nothing—an empty value) for the proxy-server questions.

15. Press Return three times to accept the default for each of the proxy-server questions.

For the next step, the module needs to download a list of servers.

The download process can sometimes take a long time to begin. If you see that the CPAN module is "stuck" retrying the download process over and over, you can get it to try a different method of connecting to the remote system and/or try a different server by pressing Control C (**Figure 13.45**). If you press Control C twice quickly, it will abort the entire process.

continues on page 440

```
You have no /usr/local/CPAN/sources/MIRRORED.BY
  I'm trying to fetch one
LWP not available
CPAN: Net::FTP loaded ok
Fetching with Net::FTP:
  ftp://ftp.perl.org/pub/CPAN/MIRRORED.BY
Couldn't fetch MIRRORED.BY from ftp.perl.org
Fetching with Net::FTP
  ftp://ftp.perl.org/pub/CPAN/MIRRORED.BY.gz
Couldn't fetch MIRRORED.BY.gz from ftp.perl.org

Trying with "/sw/bin/wget -O -" to get
   ftp://ftp.perl.org/pub/CPAN/MIRRORED.BY
-08:04:16-  ftp://ftp.perl.org/pub/CPAN/MIRRORED.BY
    => `-'
Resolving ftp.perl.org... done.
Connecting to ftp.perl.org[204.152.191.7]:21... connected.
Logging in as anonymous ... Logged in!
==> SYST ... done.    ==> PWD ... done.
==> TYPE I ... done.  ==> CWD /pub/CPAN ... done.
==> PORT ... done.    ==> RETR MIRRORED.BY ...
Error in server response, closing control connection.
Retrying.
```

. . . nine retries omitted . . .

```
-08:14:05-  ftp://ftp.perl.org/pub/CPAN/MIRRORED.BY
   (try:10) => `-'
Connecting to ftp.perl.org[204.152.191.7]:21... connected.
```

continues on next page

Figure 13.45 The CPAN module had problems downloading a file and kept retrying. Pressing Control C causes the module to attempt a different method, which worked in this case.

Figure 13.45 *continued*

```
Logging in as anonymous ... Logged in!
==> SYST ... done.    ==> PWD ... done.
==> TYPE I ... done.  ==> CWD /pub/CPAN ... done.
==> PORT ... done.    ==> RETR MIRRORED.BY ... ← User pressed Control C
Trying with "/sw/bin/wget -O -" to get
  ftp://ftp.perl.org/pub/CPAN/MIRRORED.BY.gz
-08:14:06-  ftp://ftp.perl.org/pub/CPAN/MIRRORED.BY.gz
           => `-'
Resolving ftp.perl.org... done.
Connecting to ftp.perl.org[207.45.221.24]:21... connected.
Logging in as anonymous ... Logged in!
==> SYST ... done.    ==> PWD ... done.
==> TYPE I ... done.  ==> CWD /pub/CPAN ... done.
==> PORT ... done.    ==> RETR MIRRORED.BY.gz ...
No such file `MIRRORED.BY.gz'.

Issuing "/usr/bin/ftp -n"
Trying 207.45.221.24...
Connected to ftp.cpan.ddns.develooper.com.
220 mirror.teleglobe.net server ready
331 Anonymous login ok, send your complete email address as your password.
230-*********************************************************************
230- mirror.teleglobe.net hosted in Newark, NJ
230-
230- You are connection 18. Total connections allowed is 1000.
```

. . . omitting several lines of comments . . .

```
230 Guest access granted for anonymous.
Remote system type is UNIX.
Using binary mode to transfer files.
Local directory now /usr/local/CPAN/sources
250 CWD command successful.
250 CWD command successful.
250-The Comprehensive Perl Archive Network (http://www.cpan.org/)
250-master site has been from the very beginning (1995) hosted at FUNET,
250-the Finnish University NETwork.
250-
250-
250 CWD command successful.
200 Type set to I.
local: MIRRORED.BY remote: MIRRORED.BY
500 EPSV not understood.
227 Entering Passive Mode (207,45,221,24,216,67).
150 Opening BINARY mode data connection for MIRRORED.BY (147970 bytes)
100% |*************************************|   144 KB   78.05 KB/s    00:01
226 Transfer complete.
147970 bytes received in 00:01 (74.42 KB/s)
221-Goodbye from mirror.teleglobe.net hosted in Newark, NJ
221
GOT /usr/local/CPAN/sources/MIRRORED.BY
```

Once the module has the list of servers (see the MIRRORED.BY file mentioned in Figure 13.45), it asks you about the sites from which it will download source code for Perl modules (**Figure 13.46**).

16. Enter a number corresponding to the area of the world you are in so that you will download from servers closest to you.

Figure 13.46 shows 5 entered for North America.

The module gives you a list of countries to choose from (**Figure 13.47**).

```
Now we need to know where your favorite CPAN sites are located. Push
a few sites onto the array (just in case the first on the array won't
work). If you are mirroring CPAN to your local workstation, specify a
file: URL.

First, pick a nearby continent and country (you can pick several of
each, separated by spaces, or none if you just want to keep your
existing selections). Then, you will be presented with a list of URLs
of CPAN mirrors in the countries you selected, along with previously
selected URLs. Select some of those URLs, or just keep the old list.
Finally, you will be prompted for any extra URLs - file:, ftp:, or
http: - that host a CPAN mirror.

(1) Africa
(2) Asia
(3) Central America
(4) Europe
(5) North America
(6) Oceania
(7) South America
Select your continent (or several nearby continents) [] 5
```

Figure 13.46 Telling the CPAN module what part of the world you are in.

```
(1) Canada
(2) Mexico
(3) Puerto Rico
(4) United States
Select your country (or several nearby countries) [] 2 4
```

Figure 13.47 The CPAN module asks you to choose from a list of countries.

17. Enter one or more numbers separated by spaces.

    In Figure 13.47, we entered 2 and 4 for Mexico and the United States.

    You see a list of CPAN sites from your chosen countries, from which you are asked to select as many sites as you like (**Figure 13.48**). If the list is longer than what fits in your Terminal window, you can use the scroll bar to see the sites that scrolled off the top.

18. Enter three numbers separated by spaces. In Figure 13.48, we entered `5 2 14`.

    Do not enter commas; just separate the numbers with spaces. You might try opening a different Terminal window and using `ping` and `traceroute` (see Chapter 4) to the hostnames of some sites to see which are most easily reachable from your network.

    You can enter as few as one and as many as you like. Three is a good number. The CPAN module tries the first site first, and if it gets no answer, it tries the second, and so on.

    The module then asks if you want to enter more sites (**Figure 13.49**).

continues on next page

```
(1) ftp://cpan.upn.mx/pub/CPAN (Mexico)
(2) ftp://ftp.msg.com.mx/pub/CPAN/ (Mexico)
(3) ftp://archive.progeny.com/CPAN/ (United States)
(4) ftp://carroll.cac.psu.edu/pub/CPAN/ (United States)
(5) ftp://cpan-du.viaverio.com/pub/CPAN/ (United States)
(6) ftp://cpan.calvin.edu/pub/CPAN (United States)
(7) ftp://cpan.cs.utah.edu/pub/CPAN/ (United States)
(8) ftp://cpan.erlbaum.net/ (United States)
(9) ftp://cpan.llarian.net/pub/CPAN/ (United States)
(10) ftp://cpan.mirrors.redwire.net/pub/CPAN/ (United States)
(11) ftp://cpan.mirrors.tds.net/pub/CPAN (United States)
(12) ftp://cpan.netnitco.net/pub/mirrors/CPAN/ (United States)
(13) ftp://cpan.teleglobe.net/pub/CPAN (United States)
(14) ftp://cpan.thepirtgroup.com/ (United States)
(15) ftp://csociety-ftp.ecn.purdue.edu/pub/CPAN (United States)
(16) ftp://ftp-mirror.internap.com/pub/CPAN/ (United States)
44 more items, hit SPACE RETURN to show them
Select as many URLs as you like,
put them on one line, separated by blanks [] 5 2 14
```

Figure 13.48 You are asked to choose sites from which to download modules.

```
Enter another URL or RETURN to quit: []
```

Figure 13.49 You are given a chance to enter more sites if you want to.

19. Press Return to move on.

The CPAN module is now configured (**Figure 13.50**).

The module writes the configuration to

/System/Library/Perl/5.8.6/CPAN/
→ Config.pm

(which is a text file—you can examine it if you are curious).

20. quit

This quits the CPAN shell and returns you to your Unix shell (**Figure 13.51**).

You have been using the CPAN module's shell interface—the cpan> at the end of Figure 13.50 is the CPAN module shell prompt, not to be confused with the shell prompt from your Unix shell.

✔ Tip

- You can rerun the configuration process in the future by starting the CPAN shell and then, at the cpan> prompt, giving the command

  o conf init

  The old configuration file will be saved as Config.pm~, so if you look in /System/Library/Perl/5.8.6/CPAN/ you will see both Config.pm and Config.pm~.

```
New set of picks:
  ftp://cpan-du.viaverio.com/pub/CPAN/
  ftp://ftp.msg.com.mx/pub/CPAN/
  ftp://cpan.thepirtgroup.com/

commit: wrote /System/Library/Perl/5.8.6/CPAN/Config.pm

cpan shell - CPAN exploration and modules installation (v1.7601)
ReadLine support available (try 'install Bundle::CPAN')
cpan>
```

Figure 13.50 The CPAN module shows the sites you picked and where it saved your configuration: /System/Library/Perl/5.8.6/CPAN/Config.pm.

```
cpan> quit
Lockfile removed.
localhost:~ vanilla$
```

Figure 13.51 Quitting the CPAN module and returning to your Unix shell prompt.

Now that you have configured the CPAN module, you can use it to install Perl modules.

To start the CPAN module:

1. `sudo cpan`
2. Enter your password if asked.

   You get the CPAN shell prompt:

   `cpan>`

✔ Tip

- You can quit by typing `quit` at the `cpan>` prompt.

The following tasks assume that you have started the CPAN module and are at a `cpan>` prompt.

To search for a Perl module:

1. `m /^Date::/`

   The `m` is a `cpan` shell command meaning "search for Module names." Other search commands are `a` (authors), `b` (bundles—groups of related modules), `d` (distributions, like bundles), and `i` (anything: author, bundle, distribution, module—but the `i` command usually finds too much stuff).

   This searches module names that begin with `Date::`. (The search is *not* case sensitive.)

   CPAN modules are named in a hierarchical fashion, using the double colon (`::`) as the separator. So there is `Date::Calc`, `Date::Calc::Iterator`, and so on. Often, installing a module will also install one or more modules "below" it in the hierarchy.

   You may recognize the search pattern as a *regular expression*. The ^ means "search for this at the beginning of the string." Review Chapter 4 for more details. So to search for (the several dozen) modules that have the string `google` in their names:

   `m /google/`

continues on next page

Upgrading the CPAN Module

When you start up the CPAN module, you may see a notice recommending that you upgrade the module to a newer version. Do this by typing

`install Bundle::CPAN`

at a `cpan>` prompt.

In some cases, this process may take a very long time, so don't do this unless you are prepared to let the process run for an hour or possibly more (depending on the speed of your Mac and your Internet connection). Usually it takes only a few minutes on a fast Internet connection.

Furthermore, you may be asked to go through the CPAN configuration process again after an upgrade if new features have been added. The CPAN module generally remembers your previous configuration choices and presents them as defaults.

In the case of the /^Date::/ example, you get a rather long list (**Figure 13.52**).

Let's assume that you know you want something to do date calculations, so the module Date::Calc seems appropriate.

You can get more information about the module with the next step.

```
cpan> m /^Date::/
Module       Date::Baha::i                  (G/GE/GENE/Date-Baha-i-0.16.tar.gz)
Module       Date::Business                 (D/DE/DESIMINER/Date-Business-1.2.tar.gz)
Module       Date::Calc                     (S/ST/STBEY/Date-Calc-5.4.tar.gz)
Module       Date::Calc::Iterator           (B/BR/BRONTO/Date-Calc-Iterator-1.00.tar.gz)
Module       Date::Calc::Object             (S/ST/STBEY/Date-Calc-5.4.tar.gz)
Module       Date::Calendar                 (S/ST/STBEY/Date-Calc-5.4.tar.gz)
Module       Date::Calendar::Profiles       (S/ST/STBEY/Date-Calc-5.4.tar.gz)
Module       Date::Calendar::Year           (S/ST/STBEY/Date-Calc-5.4.tar.gz)
Module       Date::Chinese                  (R/RB/RBOW/Date-Chinese-1.03.tar.gz)
Module       Date::Christmas                (H/HF/HFB/Date-Christmas-1.02.tar.gz)
Module       Date::Convert                  (M/MO/MORTY/DateConvert-0.16.tar.gz)
```

. . . omitted many entries . . .

```
Module       Date::Tie                      (F/FG/FGLOCK/Date-Tie-0.17.tar.gz)
Module       Date::Time                     (Contact Author Tobias Brox <tobix@irctos.org>)
Module       Date::Tolkien::Shire           (T/TB/TBRAUN/Date-Tolkien-Shire-1.12.tar.gz)
Module       Date::Transform                (C/CT/CTBROWN/Date-Transform-0.11.tar.gz)
Module       Date::Transform::Closures      (C/CT/CTBROWN/Date-Transform-0.11.tar.gz)
Module       Date::Transform::Constants     (C/CT/CTBROWN/Date-Transform-0.11.tar.gz)
Module       Date::Transform::Extensions    (C/CT/CTBROWN/Date-Transform-0.11.tar.gz)
Module       Date::Transform::Functions     (C/CT/CTBROWN/Date-Transform-0.11.tar.gz)
Module       Date::WeekOfYear               (G/GN/GNG/Date-WeekOfYear-1.01.tar.gz)
137 items found

cpan>
```

Figure 13.52 Searching for all the Date:: modules (abridged output).

2. `m Date::Calc`

   From the description of the module (**Figure 13.53**), it looks as if we might want this one.

   (Note: The `cpan shell` command

   `m Date::Calc`

   is different from

   `m /Date::Calc/`

   The first gets information about one specific module; the second searches using a regular expression.)

   You can look at the README file for any module available through CPAN (even modules you have not installed), with the `readme` command.

continues on next page


```
cpan> m Date::Calc
Module id = Date::Calc
  DESCRIPTION      Gregorian calendar date calculations
  CPAN_USERID      STBEY (Steffen Beyer <sb@engelschall.com>)
  CPAN_VERSION 5.4
  CPAN_FILE        S/ST/STBEY/Date-Calc-.4.tar.gz
  DSLI_STATUS      Mdch (mature,developer,C,hybrid)
  INST_FILE        (not installed)

cpan> m Date::Tolkien::Shire
Module id = Date::Tolkien::Shire
  DESCRIPTION      J.R.R. Tolkien's hobbit calendar
  CPAN_USERID      TBRAUN (Tom Braun <tbraun@pobox.com>)
  CPAN_VERSION 1.12
  CPAN_FILE        T/TB/TBRAUN/Date-Tolkien-Shire-1.12.tar.gz
  DSLI_STATUS      RdpO (released,developer,perl,object-oriented)
  INST_FILE        (not installed)

cpan>
```

Figure 13.53 Getting information about specific modules by name.

3. `readme Date::Calc`

This retrieves the README file and displays it (using the `less pager` command described in Chapter 5) (**Figure 13.54**).

The next step is to install the module. Again, to perform the following task, have your `FTP_PASSIVE` environment variable set to 1.

```
cpan> readme Date::Calc
Running readme for module Date::Calc
LWP not available
CPAN: Net::FTP loaded ok
Fetching with Net::FTP:
  ftp://cpan-sj.viaverio.com/pub/CPAN/authors/id/S/ST/STBEY/Date-Calc-5.4.readme

Displaying file
  /usr/local/CPAN/sources/authors/id/S/ST/STBEY/Date-Calc-5.4.readme
with pager "/usr/bin/less"

        ====================================
        Package "Date::Calc" Version 5.4
        ====================================


This package is available for download either from my web site at

        http://www.engelschall.com/u/sb/download/

or from any CPAN (= "Comprehensive Perl Archive Network") mirror server:

        http://www.perl.com/CPAN/authors/id/S/ST/STBEY/


Abstract:
-----

This package consists of a C library (intended to make life easier for C
developers) and a Perl module to access this library from Perl.
```

. . . output abridged . . .

Figure 13.54 Seeing a module's README file.

Installing Perl Modules

To install a Perl module from the cpan shell prompt:

◆ `install ModuleName`

For example:

`install Date::Calc`

That's all there is to it.

You can do the same thing from your Unix shell prompt with

`sudo cpan -i Date::Calc`

You will see a great deal of output as the install process proceeds (an abridged example is shown in **Figure 13.55**).

✔ Tips

- See the sidebar "Using the `Date::Calc` Module" for an example of using this module.
- Perl modules have documentation built into their source code (which is different from how Unix `man` pages work). To read the documentation for an installed Perl module, use the `perldoc` command from a shell prompt (not from the `cpan>` prompt):

  `perldoc Date::Calc`

  In fact, on some Unix systems, including Mac OS X, you can also use the `man` command to read the documentation for Perl modules:

  `man Date::Calc`

```
cpan> install Date::Calc
CPAN: Storable loaded ok
Going to read /usr/local/CPAN/Metadata
  Database was generated on Sat, 02 Jul 2005 11:58:14 GMT
Running install for module Date::Calc
Running make for S/ST/STBEY/Date-Calc-5.4.tar.gz
```

. . . output abridged . . .

```
Fetching with Net::FTP:
  ftp://cpan-sj.viaverio.com/pub/CPAN/authors/id/S/ST/STBEY/CHECKSUMS
CPAN: Compress::Zlib loaded ok
Checksum for /usr/local/CPAN/sources/authors/id/S/ST/STBEY/Date-Calc-5.4.tar.gz ok
Scanning cache /usr/local/CPAN/build for sizes
Date-Calc-5.4/
Date-Calc-5.4/t/
```

. . . output abridged . . .

```
-- Unsatisfied dependencies detected during [S/ST/STBEY/Date-Calc-5.4.tar.gz] ---
  Bit::Vector
  Carp::Clan
```

. . . output abridged . . .

```
  CPAN.pm: Going to build S/ST/STBEY/Bit-Vector-6.4.tar.gz
```

. . . output abridged . . .

continues on next page

Figure 13.55 Installing a module (abridged output). Notice how additional required modules were installed because we configured CPAN to "follow" dependencies (see Figure 13.38).

Figure 13.55 *continued*

```
   CPAN.pm: Going to build S/ST/STBEY/Carp-Clan-5.3.tar.gz
```

. . . output abridged . . .

```
Running make for S/ST/STBEY/Date-Calc-5.4.tar.gz
   Is already unwrapped into directory /usr/local/CPAN/build/Date-Calc-5.4

   CPAN.pm: Going to build S/ST/STBEY/Date-Calc-5.4.tar.gz
```

. . . output abridged . . .

```
Running make test
PERL_DL_NONLAZY=1 /usr/bin/perl "-MExtUtils::Command::MM" "-e" "test_harness(0, 'blib/lib',
'blib/arch')" t/*.t
t/f000 ok
t/f001 ok
t/f002 ok
```

. . . output abridged . . .

```
All tests successful, 4 tests skipped.
Files=48, Tests=2436, 12 wallclock secs ( 6.43 cusr +  1.48 csys =  7.91 CPU)
   /usr/bin/make test - OK
Running make install
```

. . . output abridged . . .

```
  /usr/bin/make install UNINST=1 - OK
cpan>
```

Learning More About CPAN

If you are going to do any Perl programming beyond the most basic level, you should know how to find out more about CPAN.

Like all Perl modules, CPAN has built-in documentation; read it with `perldoc CPAN`.

The main CPAN Web site is at www.cpan.org. The CPAN Frequently Asked Questions document (www.cpan.org/misc/cpan-faq.html) answers many questions, including "What is Perl?" and "What is CPAN?"

Using the Date::Calc Module

Since you've gone to the trouble of installing it, here's a little script that uses the `Date::Calc` module.

The code listing shown in **Figure 13.56** will prompt you for a date in U.S. format (for example, July 15, 2004) and a number of days to add, and will display the new date. To try the script, create a file, enter the text from Figure 13.56, make the file executable, and run the script. (You'll need the skills you learned in Chapter 5 and Chapter 8, "Working with Permissions and Ownership," to create the file and make it executable.)

```
#!/usr/bin/perl
#
# Add days to a date. Get a date back.
#############################################

use Date::Calc qw( Decode_Date_US Add_Delta_Days Date_to_Text_Long );

print "Enter a date in any US format (month, day, year): ";
$date = <STDIN>; # get input from user
chop $date; # remove the newline character

( $y, $m, $d ) = Decode_Date_US( $date );

print "How many days to add? ";
$add_days = <STDIN>;
chop $add_days;

( $y, $m, $d ) = Add_Delta_Days( $y,$m,$d,$add_days );

$new_date = Date_to_Text_Long($y,$m,$d);

print "New date is $new_date\n";
```

Figure 13.56 Code listing of a Perl script that uses the `Date::Calc` module.

To see a list of installed modules with new versions available:

- `autobundle`

  (That command must be entered at the `cpan` shell prompt.)

  The CPAN module examines all the Perl modules installed on your system, compares the installed version number with the latest available version number, and displays a list of modules where your installed version is older than the latest available version.

  Figure 13.57 shows an abridged version of the output. You can install the new version of a module with

  `install` *`module`*

  For example:

  `install Compress::Zlib`

✔ Tips

- You can install *all* the available new versions with one command, from your Unix shell prompt:

  `sudo cpan -r`

  This could take a while, so be patient. Also, you may be prompted by the install script to answer questions for some modules, so you can't just let this run and go to lunch. You need to stick around to answer the questions if they arise.

- It bears repeating that you can read the documentation for any installed Perl module with

  `perldoc` *`ModuleName`*

  (Remember that the module name usually includes one or more pairs of colons—for example, `Test::Harness`.)


```
cpan> r

Package namespace   installed   latest   in CPAN file
Archive::Tar        1.22        1.24     K/KA/KANE/Archive-Tar-1.24.tar.gz
Archive::Zip        1.14        1.15     S/SM/SMPETERS/Archive-Zip-1.15.tar.gz
B                   1.07        1.09     N/NW/NWCLARK/perl-5.8.7.tar.gz
CGI                 3.05        3.10     L/LD/LDS/CGI.pm-3.10.tar.gz
Class::ISA          0.32        0.33     S/SB/SBURKE/Class-ISA-0.33.tar.gz
Compress::Zlib      1.33        1.34     P/PM/PMQS/Compress-Zlib-1.34.tar.gz
Convert::UUlib      1.03        1.051    M/ML/MLEHMANN/Convert-UUlib-1.051.tar.gz
Cwd                 3.01        3.09     K/KW/KWILLIAMS/PathTools-3.09.tar.gz
DB_File             1.810       1.811    P/PM/PMQS/DB_File-1.811.tar.gz
Devel::PPPort       3.03        3.06     M/MH/MHX/Devel-PPPort-3.06.tar.gz
Digest              1.08        1.10     G/GA/GAAS/Digest-1.10.tar.gz
Encode              2.08        2.10     D/DA/DANKOGAI/Encode-2.10.tar.gz
```

. . . output abridged . . .

```
115 installed modules have no parseable version number

cpan>
```

Figure 13.57 Listing modules that have newer versions available.

14 Installing and Configuring Servers

As you've probably gathered, managing servers is one of the most valuable—and most complex—aspects of running a Unix machine. It's something Unix does very well because of its reliability.

In this chapter we'll show you how to install and configure the basic server applications. We'll set up your machine's Internet domain name, activate file sharing using both AppleShare and FTP, and explain secure login. From there, you'll configure your Mac to be an e-mail server, activate the Apache Web server, and add a simple *CGI* (*Common Gateway Interface*) script to the server.

After that, we'll show you how to install and configure the MySQL database engine. We even show you a simple Perl script that connects to and uses the database.

Some of these server applications are already installed in Mac OS X and can be activated with a mouse click. But of course we will show you how to do it all from the command line.

With this chapter in particular we are assuming that you have read the earlier chapters and are quite comfortable working at the command line and editing files.

You will need to be logged in as an administrative user for most of the tasks in this chapter, as almost all of them require that you perform tasks as root, using the `sudo` command.

Setting Your Machine's Hostname

When dealing with networks, you will often encounter the term *hostname*. This term can cause some confusion because of the difference between its technical meaning and its common usage. The term hostname is frequently used where the correct term would be *fully qualified domain name* (*FQDN*).

Hostname technically refers to a name given to a specific machine (or host) without any mention of a domain name. So a machine's hostname could be "mailserver1," "frodo," or "amelia." The hostname is typically (but not always) a single word rather than multiple words separated by dots. On the other hand, an FQDN always includes a domain name, and thus always has one or more dots in it. For example, www.peachpit.com is an FQDN.

In Chapter 11, "Introduction to System Administration," we explained that people tend to refer to Internet hosts by their FQDNs, (such as www.peachpit.com), while machines on the Internet identify each other using IP addresses. FQDNs ultimately point to IP addresses, not to hostnames.

What can be very confusing is that the actual hostnames of machines on the Internet are often not used in their FQDNs. For example, the machine that is reachable with the FQDN www.peachpit.com might have a hostname of server23. And here's the *really* confusing part: The term *hostname* is widely used to refer to what are actually FQDNs, so it is very common to read something that says, "Enter a hostname, such as www.peachpit.com," and, for better or worse, we stick to the popular usage in this book.

Throughout this chapter we talk about setting up server software on your computer so that other machines can connect to it using various network protocols (for example, to send e-mail to your computer or to use a Web browser or FTP client to connect to your computer). If you want people to be able to connect to your server using an FQDN instead of an IP address, then you need to arrange for an FQDN to "point" to your machine's IP address. This is done using something called the *domain name system* (DNS.)

FQDNs refer to specific machines and are created by whoever controls the domain involved. For example, the FQDN

www.matisse.sf.ca.us

refers to the machine that has the IP address 216.135.166.2. That FQDN is created by whoever controls the

.matisse.sf.ca.us

domain (that would be me, the author).

The controller of a domain may create as many sub-domains and FQDNs as he or she wishes within the domain. Basically, you can add as many different elements as you like to the left side of domain names you control.

If you are running your Mac in a large office environment, you should probably contact your office's network administrator to find out what the FQDN is for your machine, or have the administrator create one for you.

If you are a home- or small-office user, then your Internet service provider (ISP) has probably established FQDNs for the IP address(es) that it assigned to you. Unfortunately, the FQDN for your machine's IP address is probably something like "user135-walla-walla.high-speed.ispname.com."

You may also have reserved a new domain name through one of the many domain-name registries. You will need to contact that registry and ask it to set up the FQDN for you, giving it the FQDN you want and the IP address for your machine. It will often take several days or even weeks to get through the bureaucratic process.

So in order for your machine to have the FQDN that you want, you must arrange for the following:

- Your machine must have a static IP address. This is one that does not change each time you reboot the machine. Look in the Network pane of System Preferences, on the TCP/IP tab. Select the port you want to use, such as Built-in Ethernet, from the Show pop-up menu. The Configure method should be set to Manually (**Figure 14.1**). For an exception to this rule, see the sidebar "Dynamic DNS."
- The owner of an Internet domain name must create a configuration entry that associates your IP address with a domain name (making it an FQDN).

Mac OS X tries to figure out the FQDN for your machine when it boots up, but if you want the operating system to set its hostname to an FQDN other than the one it finds automatically, you need to change a system-configuration file.

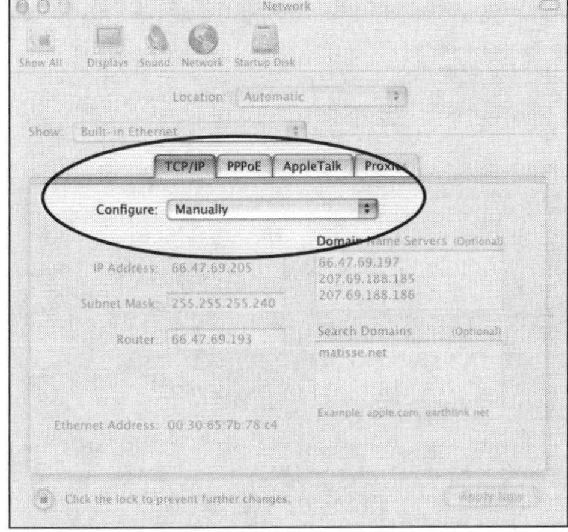

Figure 14.1 The TCP/IP tab of the Network pane of System Preferences, where you set the Configure method to Manually for a static IP address.

To see the hostname your Mac is using:

- `hostname`

  This will show the FQDN that your Mac is currently using.

  Technically, the hostname is only the left-most part of the FQDN, and you can see that part alone by adding the `-s` option:

  `hostname -s`

✔ Tip

- Sometimes in a script you want to get the hostname part of the FQDN so that you can use it in the name of a log file or something similar. In a Bourne shell script you would use

  ```
  hostpart=`hostname -s`
  ```

  and in a `tcsh` (`csh`) script you would use

  ```
  set hostpart=`hostname -s`
  ```

  That sets `$hostpart` to contain only the host part of the FQDN.

The system of translating domain names to IP addresses (and vice versa) is handled by the *DNS* worldwide database of domain names and IP addresses. This distributed database is made up of tens of thousands of servers, called *domain name servers*, each of which is responsible for a small portion of the overall database. Each domain name is controlled by one server (the primary DNS server for that domain), with one or more backup servers (secondary DNS servers) that copy information from the primary one.

Only the operator of a primary DNS server can create a new FQDN. Even if you set the hostname of your Mac, the rest of the world will not be able to use that hostname to reach your Mac unless a DNS record associates that hostname with your Mac's IP address.

To see the DNS records for a hostname:

- `dig` *name*

  The `dig` command will show you information about the *name*—which you usually enter as an FQDN—for example,

  `dig www.eigenstate.net`

  Figure 14.2 shows an annotated example of a `dig` query and response.

  The `ANSWER SECTION` is where the IP address will be shown. In some cases an FQDN may map to multiple IP addresses; for example, try

  `dig www.yahoo.com`

  See `man dig` for more details on the `dig` command.

✔ Tips

- A very important item in Figure 14.2 is the `ANSWER SECTION`, which shows us that an `A` record exists associating the IP address 216.135.166.25 with the FQDN www.eigenstate.net.
- E-mail servers use their FQDN to identify themselves when they send e-mail to another machine. In most cases, the receiving server will reject the connection unless the DNS "A record" for the sending machine's IP address matches the FQDN with which the sending e-mail server identifies itself. In other words, the machine you are sending *to* wants to be able to look at the IP address of your machine.

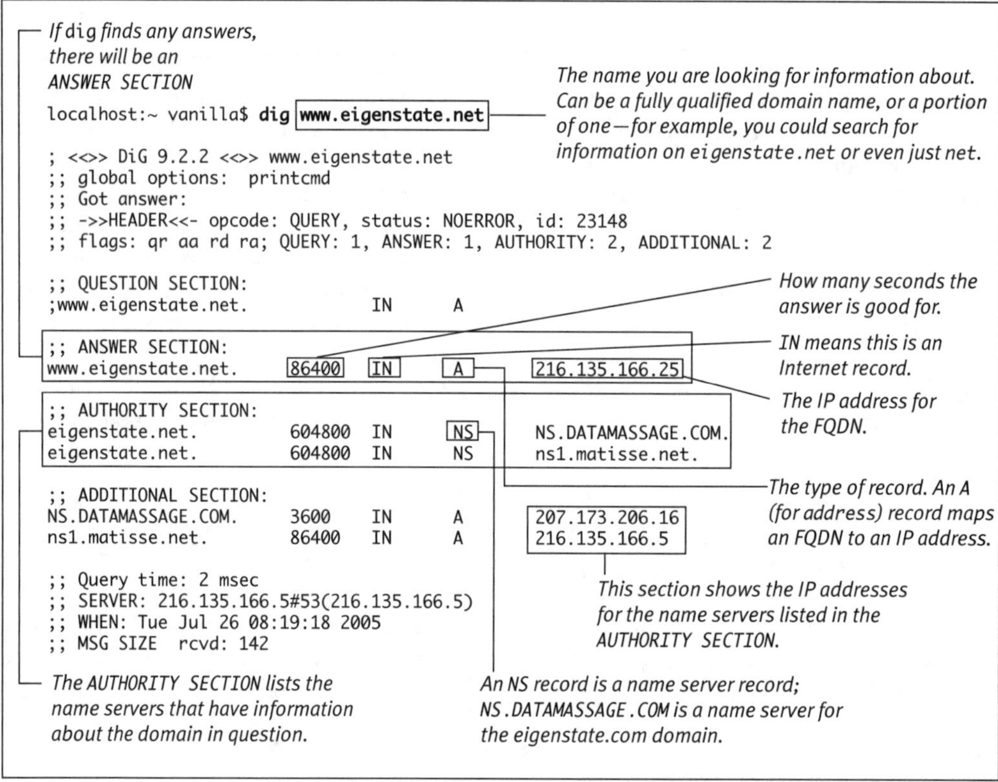

Figure 14.2 Annotated example of output from the `dig` command.

The receiving server automatically gets the IP address when your machine connects to it. Then the receiving server wants to translate that IP address into an FQDN that matches your e-mail server. This is largely an anti-spam measure.

- Another way to see the IP address(es) for an FQDN is the `host` command—for example:

  `host www.eigenstate.net`

  or

  `host www.yahoo.com`

To see the fully qualified domain name for an IP address:

- `dig -x` *`ipaddress`*

  For example:

  `dig -x 216.135.166.25`

  If there is an FQDN for the IP address, it will be shown in the `ANSWER SECTION` of the output from `dig`.

If the FQDN you intend to use for your machine is different from the one returned by the hostname command, then you must change a system-configuration file to tell your Mac to use the FQDN you want. The exact method of doing this varies among different versions of Unix, but here's the Darwin approach.

Note: For several tasks in this chapter, you'll have to become root, make a backup of your `/etc/hostconfig` file, and then edit it. We've listed the three steps of the task here, but later in the chapter we combine them, with a reference back here.

To change the /etc/hostconfig system-configuration file:

1. Become root:

   `sudo -s`

2. Make a backup copy of `/etc/hostconfig`:

   ```
   cp /etc/hostconfig/etc/
   → hostconfig.YYYYMMDD
   ```

   Use today's date for *`YYYYMMDD`*. The `/etc/hostconfig` file can be changed only by root.

   `YYYYMMDD` is the current year, month, and day from today's date. If you were doing this on July 23, 2003, the command line would read

   ```
   cp /etc/hostconfig /etc/
   → hostconfig.20030723
   ```

3. Edit the file `/etc/hostconfig` using your favorite command-line editor—for example, `vi`:

   `vi /etc/hostconfig`

   Review Chapter 6, "Editing and Printing Files," for more on editing files.

4. Make whatever changes are need to the `hostconfig` file.

   You will use the steps from this task in several tasks in this chapter.

Whenever you change a system-configuration file, you should always make a copy of it first. That way, you can easily revert to whatever state the file was in before you messed it up . . . um, before you changed it.

Dynamic DNS

Most home users of the Internet do not have static IP addresses. Instead, their Internet service providers assign a different address (from a pool of addresses) each time a customer connects.

There is a way that you can have an FQDN that points to a machine whose IP address changes each time it boots up. You arrange with a service that provides *dynamic DNS*. With this service, your computer contacts the dynamic DNS provider each time it gets a new IP address, and the dynamic DNS provider updates its database so that your FQDN points to your current IP address.

See Dynamic DNS Providers List (www.technopagan.org/dynamic).

To set the machine's hostname temporarily:

- `sudo hostname newhostname`

  This will set the machine's hostname to *newhostname*—for example:

  `sudo hostname test.example.com`

  The change will last only until the next reboot. See the next task for how to set the hostname on each startup.

This next task requires a reboot, so only proceed with it when you are ready to reboot the machine.

To set the machine's hostname on every startup:

1. Per the task above, become root, back up `/etc/hostconfig`, and edit the file using `vi`.
2. Change the line that says

   `HOSTNAME=-AUTOMATIC-`

   to have your FQDN, instead of `-AUTOMATIC-`. So if your FQDN is sailing.seas.uk, you would use

   `HOSTNAME=sailing.seas.uk`
3. Save your changes and quit the editor. (In `vi`, you press Esc and then type `:wq`.)
4. Restart the machine.

   In Mac OS X 10.2 (only), you can restart just the networking functions with

   `SystemStarter restart Network`

   In other versions of Mac OS X, you must restart the machine for the change to take effect. However, see the previous task for how to set the hostname temporarily, without a reboot.
5. Test it:

   `hostname`

   should show the FQDN you entered.

Running Your Own DNS Server

Mac OS X comes with the software necessary to run your own DNS server. To effectively run your own DNS server for a particular domain, such as fuzzybears-are-cute.com, your Mac needs to be on all the time and have a static IP address. Also, you must notify the domain's registrar that you want your Mac to be the primary DNS server for the domain.

Controlling the AppleShare Server

AppleShare is the Macintosh system for sharing files and disks across networks. Of course, you can activate AppleShare file sharing from the Sharing pane of System Preferences (on the Services tab) by selecting Personal File Sharing. But where's the fun in that?

The AppleShare file server listens on port 548. If you are using firewall software, make sure that access to port 548 is not blocked.

To activate AppleShare from the command line:

1. Per the task "To change the `/etc/hostconfig` system-configuration file" above, become root, back up `/etc/hostconfig`, and edit the file using `vi`.
2. Change the line that says
   `AFPSERVER=-NO-`
   to
   `AFPSERVER=-YES-`
3. Save your changes and quit the editor.
4. Start AppleShare:
   `SystemStarter start AppleShare`
   AppleShare is now active.
5. Stop being root:
   `exit`
   You should be back at your regular shell prompt.

✔ Tip

- If you want to keep AppleShare from starting at boot time, reverse the change you made in step 2 above—that is, change `AFPSERVER=-YES-` back to `AFPSERVER=-NO-`.

You can turn AppleShare off from the GUI using the Services tab of the Sharing pane in System Preferences, which also allows you to activate it, and you can also shut it down from the command line.

Once Apple updates the AppleShare StartupItems script (`/System/Library/StartupItems/AppleShare/AppleShare`) to handle an argument of `stop`, you will be able to use that script to stop AppleShare. Until then, you can still do it with a few more steps. (As of Mac OS X 10.4.2, the AppleShare script still cannot stop or restart the AppleShare server.)

As with everything in Unix, there are many reasons for wanting to do something from the command line instead of through a graphical interface. For example, you might want to create a shell script to perform a task, or you might want to perform the task manually while logged in to your Mac at the command line from another machine on the Internet.

To shut down AppleShare from the command line:

1. `sudo killall AppleFileServer`

   That's it. The AppleFileServer stops.

   The `killall` command will attempt to stop all processes whose name matches its argument, and whose UID matches the UID of the user running the command. So, unless you run the command as root, `killall` will only kill processes that you own. When run by root (as we did here using `sudo`), `killall` will send a `TERM` signal to all processes whose name matches the argument. See "About Commands, Processes, and Jobs" in Chapter 2, "Using the Command Line," for more on processes and who owns them.

   Next, you should verify that the process is really gone.

2. `ps -auxwww | grep AppleFileServer`

   This should return only one line—the line for the `grep` process itself—because that line contains the string `AppleFileServer`.

Activating the SSH Server

Mac OS X comes with the sshd server, which provides secure login capability using the SSH (Secure Shell) protocol. We covered SSH in some detail in Chapters 10 ("Connecting over the Internet") and 12 ("Security"). In an SSH connection, all traffic between client and server is encrypted. Activating the SSH server enables other machines to connect to yours over the Internet using the SSH protocol. Review Chapter 10 for more on using ssh, scp, sftp, and other SSH-based tools.

You can activate and deactivate the SSH server by going to the Sharing pane of System Preferences, clicking the Services tab, and selecting or deselecting the Remote Login box, but here's the Unix way (actually, this is the Darwin way—most other Unix systems would use a different series of steps).

The SSH server listens on port 22. If you are using firewall software, make sure that access to port 22 is not blocked.

To activate the SSH server:

◆ `sudo launchctl load -w`
`→ /System/Library/LaunchDaemons/ssh.`
`→ plist`

That's it. The SSH daemon (sshd) will now listen for incoming connections on port 22.

Review Chapter 11 for more on the launchctl utility. And, of course, read the man page for launchctl.

✔ Tips

- In Mac OS X 10.3 the SSH daemon was run using the xinetd daemon. The configuration file was /etc/xinetd.d/ssh, and you could change the

  `disable = yes`

  line to

  `disable = no`

  and then do

  `sudo kill -HUP `cat/var/run/xinetd.`
  `→ pid``

  (note that those are backquotes [`], not apostrophes [']).

- In Mac OS X 10.2 and earlier, sshd was controlled by a StartupItem similar to the AppleShare StartupItem covered in tasks above, and so in 10.2 and 10.1 you can use the same approach for sshd that we showed you for the AppleFileServer.
- Incoming SSH connections are logged to /var/log/secure.log.

To shut down the SSH server from the command line:

◆ `sudo launchctl unload -w /System/`
`→ Library/LaunchDaemons/ssh.plist`

That should stop sshd and prevent it from starting up on reboot.

✔ Tips

- Be careful about doing this when logged in using SSH! Your current connection will continue to work, but you will not be able to start a new one.
- In Mac OS X 10.3 you can stop sshd by editing /etc/xinetd.d/ssh and setting the disable property to yes, and then doing

  `sudo kill -HUP `cat /var/run/xinetd.`
  `→ pid``

- In Mac OS X10.2 you can use an approach similar to the one described earlier in this chapter for AppleShare. The SSH StartupItem in 10.2 is /System/Library/StartupItems/SSH/SSH, and the entry in /etc/hostconfig is SSHSERVER.

Configuring an Internet E-mail Server

If your machine is connected to the Internet, you can use it to send e-mail from the command line. If your machine is connected all the time ("24/7," as they say), then you can use it as a server to receive incoming e-mail and store messages in mailboxes for each user on your system.

Mac OS X comes with a common open-source e-mail server called Postfix. (Mac OS X 10.2 used another, even more common server called Sendmail.) In this section we will show how to configure the Postfix mail server to receive incoming e-mail and save messages to the appropriate mailbox for each user.

Postfix actually provides two kinds of e-mail services: It is a *Mail Transport Agent* (*MTA*) and a *Mail Delivery Agent* (*MDA*). MTAs handle the exchange of e-mail between MTAs across the Internet. That is, MTAs talk to other MTAs across networks. MDAs handle incoming messages and store them in the appropriate mailbox for each user. (In more complex configurations, a mail server may also forward incoming mail to other machines for further processing.)

Before proceeding with the following task, make sure your machine has an FQDN that has a DNS entry associating the FQDN of your machine's IP address. See "Setting Your Machine's Hostname," at the beginning of this chapter, for more details. The Postfix configuration will automatically read what the `hostname` command returns and use that as the FQDN for which it expects to be receiving e-mail (although you can override that behavior).

To configure Postfix to receive e-mail addressed to your FQDN:

1. `hostname`

   You will need to know the FQDN that you machine thinks it has. Running the `hostname` command shows this to you. Make a note of the result.

2. Become root, entering your password if prompted:

   `sudo -s`

   You are going to perform several commands as root in this task, so we have you start a root shell rather than run `sudo` for each command line. Your shell prompt will change. Now you are going to back up the `launchd` configuration file that controls Postfix.

3. `cd /etc/postfix`

   This changes your working directory to where the Postfix configuration files are kept.

4. `cp main.cf main.cf.`*`YYYYMMDD`*

   You are making a backup of the file. Replace *`YYYYMMDD`* with the year, month, and day of the current date—for example:

   `cp main.cf main.cf.20050921`

5. Edit `main.cf`.

   Here's where you make some changes:

   - If the return value from the `hostname` command is *not* the FQDN you want to use, then find the `INTERNET HOST AND DOMAIN NAMES` section and add the line

     `myhostname =` *`fqdn`*

     where *`fqdn`* is the one you want to use. For example:

     `myhostname = susie.example.com`

The FQDN you use must be one that maps to your machine's IP address. Otherwise, people will not be able to use it to send e-mail to your machine.

- ▲ If the return value from `hostname` is the FQDN you want to use, Postfix will figure it out and automatically use it, so you do not need to change the `myhostname` setting.

6. Change the line near the end of `main.cf` in the section beginning with the comment `THE FOLLOWING DEFAULTS ARE SET BY APPLE` from

   `inet_interfaces = localhost`

   to

   `inet_interfaces = localhost,`
   `→ $myhostname`

   This tells Postfix to listen on the IP address associated with the hostname. You should also add a comment (lines starting with #) explaining what you did.

7. `launchctl stop org.postfix.master`

   This stops the Postfix master daemon, if it happens to be running.

8. `cd /System/Library/LaunchDaemons`

   Change your working directory so that the pathnames you type next won't be so long.

9. `launchctl unload -w org.postfix.`
   `→ master.plist`

   This sets the Disabled key in the `launchd` configuration file and writes it back to disk. (See Chapter 11 for more on `launchctl` and `launchd`.)

10. `cp org.postfix.master.plist org.`
    `→ postfix.master.`*`YYYYMMDD`*

    Here you are making a backup copy of the plist file. Change *`YYYYMMDD`* to be the current year, month, and day.

11. Edit the file `org.postfix.master.plist`.

    Using `vi` or another text editor, edit the file and make the following changes:

    - ▲ Add a new key, `OnDemand`, set to `false`.
    - ▲ Remove the second and third strings from the `ProgramArguments` array (the `-e` and `60` strings).
    - ▲ Remove the entire `QueueDirectories` section. **Figure 14.3** shows before-and-after examples. Make sure to save the file before exiting your editor.

continues on next page

The file before editing (text to be removed shown in ~~strikethough~~):

```
<?xml version="1.0" encoding="UTF-8"?>
<!DOCTYPE plist PUBLIC "-//Apple Computer//DTD PLIST 1.0//EN"
"http://www.apple.com/DTDs/PropertyList-1.0.dtd">
<plist version="1.0">
<dict>
        <key>Disabled</key>
        <true/>
        <key>Label</key>
        <string>org.postfix.master</string>
        <key>Program</key>
```

continues on next page

Figure 14.3 Before-and-after examples of the file.

12. `launchctl load -w org.postfix.`
 `→ master.plist`

 This loads the new plist file into `launchd`. The `-w` flag changes the Disabled key to `false` and writes the file back to disk.

13. `launchctl start org.postfix.master`

 This tells `launchd` to start the Postfix daemon.

14. Stop being root:

 `exit`

 You should be back at your regular shell prompt.

15. Check firewall settings.

 Look in the Sharing pane of System Preferences and click the Firewall tab. If you have the firewall on, open up port 25. See Chapter 12, and in particular the section "About ports and sockets," for more on the firewall.

Figure 14.3 *(continued)*

```
        <string>/usr/libexec/postfix/master</string>
        <key>ProgramArguments</key>
        <array>
             <string>master</string>
             <string>-e</string>
             <string>60</string>
        </array>
        <key>QueueDirectories</key>
        <array>
             <string>/var/spool/postfix/maildrop</string>
        </array>
</dict>
</plist>
```

The file after editing (new text shown in *italics*):

```
<?xml version="1.0" encoding="UTF-8"?>
<!DOCTYPE plist PUBLIC "-//Apple Computer//DTD PLIST 1.0//EN"
"http://www.apple.com/DTDs/PropertyList-1.0.dtd">
<plist version="1.0">
<dict>
        <key>Disabled</key>
        <true/>
        <key>OnDemand</key>
        <false>
        <key>Label</key>
        <string>org.postfix.master</string>
        <key>Program</key>
        <string>/usr/libexec/postfix/master</string>
        <key>ProgramArguments</key>
        <array>
             <string>master</string>
        </array>
</dict>
</plist>
```

16. Test the setup.

    Send yourself e-mail from another system (or ask a friend to do it), using the FQDN for your Mac OS X machine.

✔ Tips

- Watch the mail-server log file while testing. Type

  `sudo tail -f /var/log/mail.log`

  to see the mail server accept each incoming message.

- The central source for information about Postfix is Postfix.org (http://postfix.org/). There you can find documentation, howtos and FAQs, mailing lists, and more.

Sending Mail Addressed to an IP Address

It is perfectly valid to send e-mail that is addressed to an IP address rather than a domain name. To do so, you must enclose the IP address in square brackets:

puffball@[198.137.241.43]

If you are doing this from the command line, make sure to escape the brackets:

`puffball@\[198.137.241.43\]`

because they would otherwise be interpreted by the shell as the `test` command. See `man test`: Looking carefully at the NAME line in the manual, see the `[` character? It's another name for the `test` command.

Forwarding e-mail to different addresses

Sometimes you want e-mail that arrives for one address to be automatically forwarded to another address. There are a couple of ways to do this. What we describe here works when you want to forward e-mail to an account that already exists on your system. It is also possible to set up virtual users—e-mail addresses on your system that do not correspond to actual user accounts but rather to things like roles or departments (for example, sales@bigthree.com). Setting up virtual users in Postfix is beyond the scope of this book, but you can find instructions for doing it at the Postfix Virtual Domain Hosting Howto (www.postfix.org/VIRTUAL_README.html).

To forward e-mail for an existing user account:

1. Create a file called `.forward` in the home directory of the user whose e-mail is to be forwarded.

   The file should contain a single line: the e-mail address you want to forward to. For example,

   ```
   sudo echo "user@newaddress.net" >
   ➝ ~user/.forward
   ```

   where *user* is the user name of the user on your system and the address is whatever address you want to forward the mail to.

   Enter your password if prompted for it.

   If you want a copy of the forwarded e-mail to stay on your system, use this format:

   ```
   \user, user@newaddress.net
   ```

2. Set the ownership on the file:

   ```
   sudo chown user .forward
   ```

Spam Sucks

Spam e-mail is unsolicited material, usually asking for money or selling products, sent to multiple e-mail addresses (the name comes from the Monty Python sketch involving the seemingly endless repetition of the word *spam*).

Spam wastes bandwidth, and, more important, it wastes the one thing none of us can ever get more of: time.

If you are running a mail server that is being hit with spam, you should look into anti-spam features. (The Mac OS X GUI e-mail client, Mail, has anti-spam features you can use to help with your personal e-mail account.)

Probably the premier anti-spam software for mail servers is SpamAssassin (http://spamassassin.org).

There is a Mac OS X how-to for SpamAssassin at www.stupidfool.org/docs/sa.html.

Providing Remote Access to Users' E-mail: IMAP and POP

Another kind of mail server allows users to connect and download or read their e-mail from other machines. These servers provide remote access to users' mailboxes (kept in `/var/mail` on Mac OS X) and utilize either the complex and powerful *IMAP* (*Internet Mail Access Protocol*) or the simpler but less capable *POP* (*Post Office Protocol*).

For information on IMAP, go to the IMAP Connection (www.imap.org). It has a searchable database of IMAP software, such as clients and servers (www.imap.org/products/database.php).

If you are considering setting up your Mac OS X machine to provide remote access to users' e-mail, we suggest that you use an IMAP server. This will allow your users to read their mail from multiple remote machines (such as from home or the office), as well as provide better security, since IMAP servers can be configured to use encryption.

Two no-cost open-source IMAP servers:

- The University of Washington's IMAPd (IMAP daemon), available at the IMAP Information Center (www.washington.edu/imap).
- The Cyrus IMAP server, which is designed for use on "e-mail-only" servers where regular users are not permitted to log in (http://asg.web.cmu.edu/cyrus/imapd).

Here are three commercial IMAP servers (which also handle POP):

- CommuniGate Pro (www.stalker.com/CommuniGatePro). A free version is available, but it adds a line of advertising to each message.
- The Kerio Mailserver. Offers support for Microsoft's Entourage e-mail client (www.kerio.com/kms_home.html).
- Post.Office, from Tenon Intersystems (www.tenon.com/products/post_office).

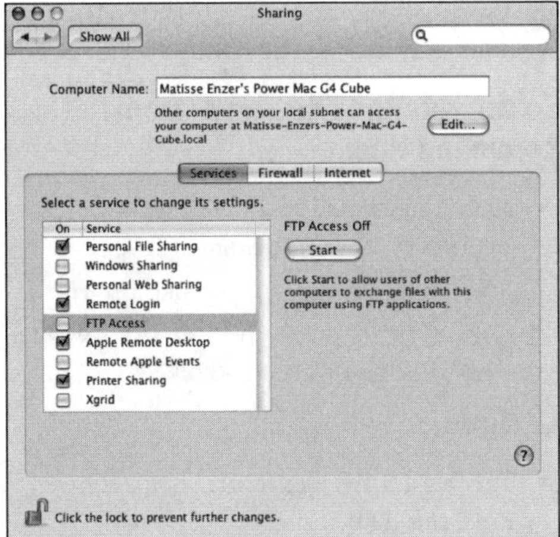

Figure 14.4 System Preferences with the Sharing pane and the Services tab selected.

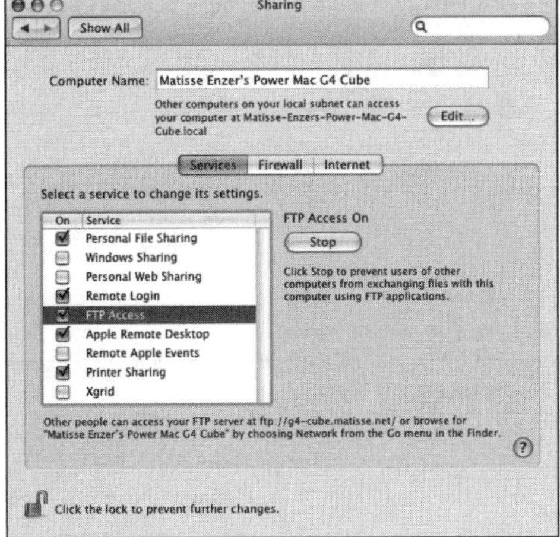

Figure 14.5 The FTP server is now running—the Start button has changed to Stop.

Activating the FTP Server

FTP (File Transfer Protocol) is the oldest such protocol on the Internet and is still widely used. Virtually all Web browsers are capable of acting as clients with FTP servers, and there are several GUI and command-line clients for FTP (see Chapter 10).

FTP connections are not encrypted, so all data, including user names and passwords, sent over an FTP connection is vulnerable to being intercepted and read. You should never use or allow FTP to be used to transfer unencrypted confidential information, or use user name/password combinations that give access to confidential information elsewhere.

Mac OS X comes with an FTP server that can be activated from the Sharing pane of System Preferences.

To activate the FTP server using the GUI:

1. Open the Sharing pane of System Preferences and choose the Services tab (**Figure 14.4**).

   If the lock icon in the lower left is locked, click it and authenticate as an admin user.

2. Click the FTP Access item.

3. Either click the Start button or check the box next to FTP Access.

   The pane shows the FTP server as running, and the Start button changes to Stop (**Figure 14.5**). (If your button already said Stop, your FTP server was already running.)

   In the Unix layer of Mac OS X, the operating system simply does the following (as root):

   ```
   launchctl load -w System/Library/
   → LaunchDaemons/ftp.plist
   ```

continues on next page

which tells `launchd` to load a daemon labeled `com.apple.ftpd`. You can see that it is loaded with

```
sudo launchctl list
```

(See the `launchd` section in Chapter 11.)

4. Close System Preferences.
5. Test the server. Do this by logging in via FTP, preferably from another machine, or you can also do it from your own machine.

✔ Tips

- If you have the firewall running, FTP access to your machine will not work for many users, because the firewall will block "passive FTP" access. See the task "To allow Passive FTP access through the firewall," below.
- The FTP daemon that Apple uses in Mac OS X 10.4 is `tnftpd`. See `man tnftpd` and `man ftpd.conf` for details on its capabilities.
- To inactivate the FTP server, just repeat steps 1 and 2 above and click Stop.

Of course, you can also activate the FTP server without ever leaving the command line.

To activate the FTP server from the command line:

- ◆ `sudo launchctl load -w /System/`
  `→ Library/LaunchDaemons/ftp.plist`

  If you have the firewall turned on, you must allow access on port 21. See Chapter 12 for more on the firewall tool.

✔ Tips

- **Table 14.1** lists various files used by `ftpd`, the FTP server.
- You can deactivate the FTP server from the command line with

  ```
  sudo launchctl unload -w /System/
  → Library/LaunchDaemons/ftp.plist
  ```
- See Chapter 11 for more on `launchctl` and `launchd`.

Table 14.1

Files Used by ftpd

File	Use
/usr/libexec/ftpd	The FTP server itself. See man ftpd.
/etc/ftpusers	List of users who may not connect to the FTP server.
/etc/ftpchroot	List of users whose use of FTP is restricted to their home directory. See man chroot.
/etc/ftpwelcome	Contents of this file are displayed when a user logs in via FTP.
/etc/nologin	If this file exists, it is displayed to users attempting to log in, and access is refused.
/var/log/ftp.log	Log of FTP connections and file transfers.
/var/log/ftpd	Log of file FTP connections.

About Passive vs. Active FTP

The FTP protocol has two modes: Active and Passive.

Many client machines will be unable to use Active mode connections to FTP servers because the firewall on the client machine or local network will block the data connection from the server back to the client. Active mode may also be blocked if the client is using *Network Address Translation* (*NAT*) to obtain access to the network, and has a non-routable IP address. FTP uses two connections (also called *channels*) between the client and server—a *command* connection and a *data* connection. In both Active and Passive modes the client initiates the command connection to port 21 on the FTP server. (Review "About ports and sockets," in Chapter 12, for more on port numbers.)

In Active mode the server (not the client) initiates the data connection back to the client from port 20 on the server machine. In Passive mode the client, not the server, initiates the data connection to a random port number between 1024 and 65535 on the server. (The server may tell the client to select from a smaller range.)

In Active mode the client machine must be able to accept the data connections that are initiated by the FTP server, and this will often be blocked by firewall software on the client side. In Passive mode the client initiates both connections, so the firewall on the client side will typically allow it.

In Active mode the FTP server must have port 21 open in its firewall configuration (if it is using a firewall). In Passive mode the server must have port 21 *and* all or some of the ports above 1023 open. That is what we are going to show you how to do in the following task.

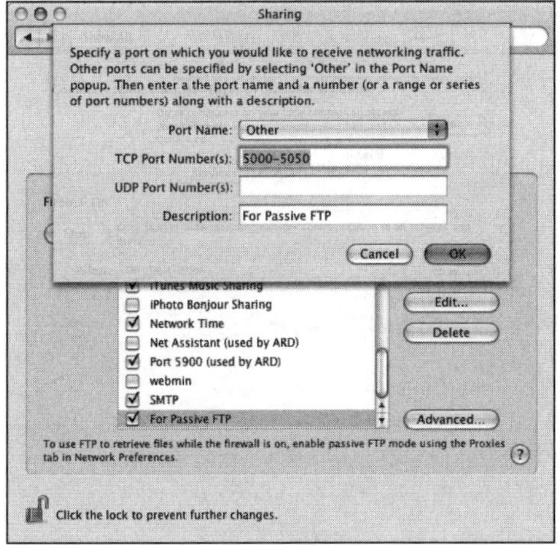

Figure 14.6 Opening ports 5000–5050 on the Firewall tab of the Sharing pane in System Preferences.

To allow Passive FTP access through the firewall:

1. Open a range of ports in the firewall.

   Figure 14.6 shows an example of opening ports 5000 through 5050.

2. Add the `portrange` directive to `/etc/ftpd.conf`.

   If that file doesn't exist, create it.

   You need to add the following line to the file:

   `portrange    min    max`

   where *`min`* is the lower port number you used in step 1, and *`max`* is the higher number—for example:

   `portrange    5000    5050`

3. Restart the FTP server.

   You can do this on the Services tab of the Sharing pane in System Preferences, or from the command line with

   ```
   sudo launchctl unload -w /System/
   → Library/LaunchDaemons/ftp.plist
   sudo launchctl load -w /System/
   → Library/LaunchDaemons/ftp.plist
   ```

Allowing anonymous FTP access

Before there were Web sites, there were anonymous FTP sites.

An anonymous FTP server allows users who do not have an account on your system to download files. You can see how HTTP and Web servers have become the dominant tools for this role. Still, FTP is widely used to allow public downloading (and, less frequently, uploading) of files.

Anonymous FTP involves the user's logging in with a special account called "anonymous" (the user name "ftp" can also be used as a shorter alternative).

Anonymous FTP logins do not need a password. It is traditional to use one's e-mail address as a password.

The FTP server is designed to take special security precautions for anonymous logins to make sure that anonymous users cannot access anything outside the directory established for anonymous FTP use.

To allow anonymous FTP access (no password):

1. `sudo -s`

   You will need to perform all the following steps as root, so here you are starting a root shell.

   ▲ If the FTP server is running, stop it:

   `launchctl unload -w /System/`
   `→ Library/LaunchDaemons/ftp.plist`

2. `dsidentity -a ftp -c "Anonymous FTP User"`

   This creates a new "identity" account on your system, which will have a real user name ("ftp" in this case) but a home directory and login shell of `/dev/null`, which is perfect for our purposes here.

   See `man dsidentity` and the sidebar "Adding a User from the Command Line," in Chapter 11, for some discussion of the intricacies of adding a "normal" user account from the command line.

3. `mkdir -m 555 /Users/ftp`

   Since the `dsidentity` command doesn't create a home directory for the new ftp user, you create one here. The directory can be anywhere on your file system. The `-m 555` option sets the permissions (mode) on the directory to `-r-xr-xr-x`, so no one has write permission on the directory (but root can still write to it). We use `/Users/ftp` as an example here, but you could just as well create `/var/ftp` or `/usr/local/ftp`, for example. If you choose a different location than `/Users/ftp`, make sure to adjust your actions in steps 3, 4, and 5 to use the proper directory.

Security Concerns About FTP

The FTP server in Mac OS X is not activated by default, and you should be careful about activating it, since FTP uses unencrypted passwords.

Review Chapter 12 for the dangers of sending unencrypted passwords over a network. See also "Reducing the security risks from an FTP server," later in this section.

At a minimum, you should add `deny` and `denyquick` directives for all admin users to the file `/etc/ftpusers` to prevent any admin-user passwords from being exposed to packet-sniffing attacks.

4. `mkdir -m 555 /Users/ftp/pub`

   This is the top-level directory where you will put files for people to download. When users log in to your FTP server, they will be in this directory.

   Optionally create a `.message` file in this and/or any subdirectories. The FTP server will display the contents of a `.message` file that it finds in any directory the user enters. A typical use would be to explain the contents of a particular directory.

5. Put some files in `/Users/ftp/pub`.

   These are the files you are making publicly available. You can put as many as you like. You can (and should) have subdirectories for different groups of files. As noted in step 4 above, if you put a `.message` file in a directory, it will be displayed when an FTP user enters that directory.

6. Create or edit `/etc/ftpd.conf`.

   You want to end up with a file that looks like that in **Figure 14.7**.

continues on next page

```
# /etc/ftpd.conf
# This is a comment. I love comments.
# Based on the  examples/ftpd.conf in the source code.
# Full source code available from http://freshmeat.net/projects/tnftpd
# See  man tnftpd    and  man ftpd.conf

# Set maximum    transfer rate to 16384 bytes/second (128 Kbits/sec)
rateget all      16384

# Check PORT command for validity; prevents denial of service attempt.
checkportcmd     all

# For anonymous connections, when a directory is entered show the contents
# of `.message' if it exists, and notify about any files that start
# with `README'.
display          guest          .message
notify           guest          README*

# Prevent uploads & modification commands for anonymous connections
upload           guest          off

# Limit the number of simultaneous `guest' class connections to 5,
# and display /etc/ftptoomany when this limit is reached.
limit            guest          5         ftptoomany

# Disconnect if an invalid username is entered, do not even ask for password
denyquick        guest
chroot           guest          /Users/ftp
homedir          guest          /pub

# Specify a range of port numbers to use for passive connections.
# If a firewall is in use these ports must be opened up.
portrange        all            5000          5050
```

Figure 14.7 Example of `/etc/ftpd.conf` set up for anonymous FTP access.

Mac OS X 10.4 doesn't come with an /etc/ftpd.conf file, relying entirely on the FTP server's default configuration, but a later version of Mac OS might have installed one. If the file already exists, make a backup copy before editing. Note that the chroot directive in /etc/ftpd.conf must point to the directory you created in step 4 above.

▲ If you have not already done so, follow the steps in the task "To allow Passive FTP access through the firewall," earlier in this chapter. Mainly this means opening up a range of ports in your firewall.

7. Edit /etc/ftpusers.

   Make a backup copy before editing the file. You want to end up with a file like that in **Figure 14.8**. You are allowing access to your FTP server *only* via anonymous FTP.

   ▲ If you want to allow some users to access the server via non-anonymous FTP, you can add more lines in the format

   `user name allow`

   But recall that FTP is an unencrypted protocol, so passwords and files are susceptible to interception.

8. Create the file /etc/ftptoomany.

   This file will be displayed to users trying to connect if the limit specified by the limit directive in /etc/ftpd.conf is reached. The file might contain "We are too busy—limit of 50 users reached. Please try again later."

9. Start the FTP server.

   From the command line:

   ```
   launchctl load -w /System/Library/
   → LaunchDaemons/ftp.plist
   ```

   or use the Sharing pane in System Preferences.

   The FTP server logs activity to /var/log/ftp.log, so you can watch it (perhaps in a separate Terminal window) with

   `tail -f /var/log/ftp.log`

```
#       This is a comment. I love comments.
#       /etc/ftpusers - access control for tnftpd
#       Based on the  examples/ftpusers  file in the source code.
#       Full source code available from http://freshmeat.net/projects/tnftpd
#       See  man ftpusers   and  man tnftpd

# This configuration is for an anonymous-only FTP server
# Permit anonymous ftp connections (both entries are required,
# because the username `anonymous' is often used.)
#
ftp             allow
anonymous       allow

# Deny access to all other usernames
*           deny
```

Figure 14.8 Example of /etc/ftpusers set up to allow only anonymous FTP access.

10. `exit`

    This terminates the root shell you started in step 1 and gets you back to your regular shell prompt.

11. Log in and try anonymous FTP access.

    You can use any FTP client you like. The `/pub` directory is where the file will be. The hostname to connect is the FQDN for your machine (see "Setting Your Machine's Hostname," at the beginning of this chapter) or your machine's IP address. Or, if you are connecting from the same machine, you can use the hostname "localhost." Examples include

    ```
    ftp your.hostname.example.com
    ftp nnn.nnn.nn.nnn
    ftp localhost
    ```

    When you connect, enter a username of either anonymous or ftp. When asked for a password, you can supply anything—or nothing (just press Return).

    If you are using an FTP client such as a Web browser, then the URL is

    ftp://*hostname*/

    Accesses will be logged to the file `/var/log/ftp.log`.

Sometimes you want to allow anonymous FTP users to upload files as well as download them.

The proper way to do this involves creating a special directory (typically called `incoming`) where FTP users can use the `put` command to upload files. When properly set up, the incoming directory does not allow users to see the files it contains (although if they can guess a filename, they can download it), and if they upload a file with the same name as an existing file, the new file is renamed by adding a *.1* to the filename (or *.2*, or *.3*, and so on).

The following task assumes that you have already set up anonymous FTP access.

To allow anonymous FTP users to upload files to your server:

1. `sudo -s`

   You'll need to be root for this task, so start a root shell. Enter your password if asked.

2. Create a new directory called `incoming` in the FTP `pub` directory.

   So if your FTP `pub` directory is `/Users/ftp/pub`, then the command line is

   ```
   mkdir -m 333 /Users/ftp/pub/incoming
   ```

   The permission mode `333` means that all users may write and execute the directory but may not read it (of course root can read it). This allows anonymous FTP users to `cd` into the directory and upload files but not to list the directory's contents.

   - ▲ If you like, create a `.message` file inside the new incoming directory. The file will be displayed when FTP users enter the directory.

3. Make changes to `/etc/ftpd.conf`.

   Make a backup copy and then edit `/etc/ftpd.conf`, removing or commenting-out this line:

   ```
   upload          guest    off
   ```

   and adding these lines:

   ```
   # Set max size in bytes for uploads.
   maxfilesize     guest      10485760
   ```

   (10485760 bytes is 10 megabytes—you may change that to anything you like, or `-1` for no limit).

4. `exit`

   This terminates the root shell you started in step 1 and returns you to your regular shell prompt.

continues on next page

5. You're done.

   Anonymous FTP users can now upload files into the `incoming` directory.

✔ Tip

- You may want to create a script that's run from `cron` to send e-mail to someone whenever files are added to the `incoming` directory. See the section "Running Regularly Scheduled Commands," in Chapter 11, for instructions on setting up a `cron` job or a LaunchDaemon. **Figure 14.9** is a sample script you could set to run every 15 minutes (or whatever frequency seems convenient).

  If it's run as a `cron` job, the output from the script is e-mailed (by `cron`). On the other hand, a LaunchDaemon can be configured to watch a directory and run a script whenever the directory is not empty.

  The script produces output the first time it finds files in the `/Users/ftp/pub/incoming` directory, and it creates a marker file (just a file whose presence is an indication of something) to avoid sending e-mail every time it runs (you remove the marker file to re-enable the script).

```
#!/bin/sh
# Script for checking if files have been uploaded via Anonymous FTP
# This script could be run as a cron job, perhaps every 15 minutes.
# It will produce output the first time it finds files in the
# /Users/ftp/pub/incoming directory.
# After cleaning out the incoming directory you need to also remove
# the marker file so this script will send email again.

# Name of file that we use as a marker
NOTICE_FILE="incoming_has_files"

# cd to the ftp pub directory
cd /Users/ftp/pub


# Get the contents of the incoming/ directory
contents=`/bin/ls incoming/`

if [ "$contents" != "" ] ; then
   if [ ! -e "$NOTICE_FILE" ] ; then
                echo "Anonymous FTP incoming files:"
                echo "$contents"
                # Create the notice file so we don't get email again
                # until someone clears it out.
                /bin/date > "$NOTICE_FILE"

                echo "Remember to remove ~ftp/$NOTICE_FILE"

        fi
fi

# Otherwise, remain silent
```

Figure 14.9 Code listing of a sample script to be used as a cron job, to send notification when files are added to the anonymous FTP upload directory.

Reducing the security risks from an FTP server

Because of the security risk from password sniffing, you must assume that any user name and password used to access your FTP server can be obtained by an unauthorized person.

If you are running an FTP server to provide only anonymous access, then this is not an issue, since the account used for anonymous FTP is not one that people can use to log in to your machine.

You can reduce the risks that come from running an FTP server by treating all FTP logins in a manner similar to anonymous logins:

- Set up separate FTP-only accounts that cannot be used to log in on the command line.
- Configure the FTP server to place access restrictions on the FTP-only accounts so that they cannot access anything outside their home directories.
- Forbid any user except anonymous-access and the special FTP-only accounts from logging in via FTP.

See Chapter 12 for more Unix security information.

To increase the security restrictions when a user logs in via FTP:

- Add the user name to `/etc/ftpchroot`.

  This prevents the user from accessing any files outside his or her home directory when logging in via FTP (`chroot` means "change the root directory the user sees"; see `man chroot`).

  If the file `/etc/ftpchroot` doesn't exist, you must create it. You must be root (use `sudo`) to create or edit that file. It simply contains one user name per line. **Figure 14.10** shows an example.

```
# Users who get a chroot'd environment
# (See  man chroot )
puffball
mary
johnftp
xaos
jackftp
```

Figure 14.10 Example of a `/etc/ftpchroot` file.

One of the best things you can do to reduce the risks created by running an FTP server is to allow only specially restricted FTP-only accounts to access your system via FTP.

Secure Alternatives to FTP

The primary secure alternatives to FTP are file transfers that use the SSH protocol. Chapter 10 covers the client side of these methods using the `ssh` and `sftp` commands.

To create FTP-only user accounts:

1. Create a new user account.

   See "To create a new user," in Chapter 11.

   This account will be configured so that it has access only via FTP. The password for this account should *not* be the same as the password for another account.

2. Change the user's shell to `/usr/bin/false`.

   See "Changing a user's login shell," in Chapter 11.

   Having `/usr/bin/false` as the login shell for an account means that as soon as someone logs in, he or she is instantly logged out.

   We want to prevent someone who obtains this account's password from logging in at the command line, where that user's opportunity for mischief is much greater than through FTP. Logging in via FTP and logging in to a command-line shell are two different things.

   When a user logs in at the command line, the operating system executes his or her login shell—that is, the program that accepts command-line input (review Chapter 2). The program `/usr/bin/false` is a tiny program that quits as soon as it is started and gives a *return code* meaning "false" to whatever program ran it.

   The FTP server will allow logins only from accounts whose login shell is listed in the file `/etc/shells`, so if this is the first FTP-only account you have created, you must add `/usr/bin/false` to the list of valid shells in the file `/etc/shells`. **Figure 14.11** shows `/etc/shells` with the added entry.

3. Add the new user name to `/etc/ftpchroot`.

   If a user name is listed in the file `/etc/ftpchroot`, then the FTP server applies additional access restrictions to the account, preventing access to any file outside the account's home directory.

To prevent a particular user from connecting to the FTP server:

◆ Add a `deny` entry for the user to `/etc/ftpusers`.

For example, to deny FTP access to user "quagmire," add the following line to `/etc/ftpusers`:

```
quagmire      deny
```

```
# List of acceptable shells for chpass(1).
# Ftpd will not allow users to connect who are not using
# one of these shells.

/bin/bash
/bin/csh
/bin/ksh
/bin/sh
/bin/tcsh
/bin/zsh
/usr/bin/false
```

Figure 14.11 The file `/etc/shells`, with `/usr/bin/false` added.

Apache: A Web Server

Apache is the most popular Web server on the Internet. It's easy to obtain and install, stable and secure, and reasonably easy to configure and modify; it handles both small and large Web sites; and it has a huge number of available options. Several common versions of Unix come with Apache already installed—including, of course, Mac OS X.

Apache gets its name from its history. Back at the dawn of the Web (circa 1993), the folks at the National Center for Supercomputing Applications (NCSA), at the University of Illinois at Urbana-Champaign, created the NCSA Web-server application, called HTTPD (*Hypertext Transfer Protocol daemon*). It was (and is) an open-source application, and many people contributed code for it, known as *patches*. So many patches were contributed that it became known as "a patchy server." "A patchy" morphed into "Apache."

Activating Apache

As with AppleShare and the SSH server, you can activate and deactivate the Apache Web server from the Sharing pane of System Preferences, on the Services tab, by clicking the Start/Stop button or checking the box for Personal Web Sharing.

Web servers listen on port 80 by default. If you are using firewall software, make sure that access to port 80 is not blocked. (Activating Apache via System Preferences does this automatically.)

Here's the command-line version. Astute readers will note that these tasks are almost identical to the ones for the SSH server.

Apache Documentation

Mac OS X comes with the complete Apache documentation in HTML format.

If you turn on Personal Web Sharing in the Sharing pane of System preferences, you can browse the documentation with the URL

http://127.0.0.1/manual/

Or, if Web sharing is not on, then with this URL:

file:///Library/WebServer/Documents/manual/index.html.html

(Yes, *html* appears twice in that filename.)

More documentation, as well as specific how-to documents, is available through the Apache HTTP Server Project (http://httpd.apache.org/docs-project). The site contains a document on performance tuning, for example (http://httpd.apache.org/docs/misc/perf-tuning.html).

To activate Apache from the command line:

1. Per the task "To change the `/etc/hostconfig` system-configuration file," become root, back up `/etc/hostconfig`, and edit the file using a text editor such as `vi`.

   Note that this leaves you in a root shell.

2. Change the line that says

   `WEBSERVER=-NO-`

   to

   `WEBSERVER=-YES-`

3. Save your changes, and quit the editor.

4. Start the Apache server:

   `apachectl start`

   The Apache Web server is now active.

   The `apachectl` script (`/usr/sbin/apachectl`) is used by the Mac OS X StartupItem for Apache, so you can also do

   `SystemStarter start Apache`

   But the `apachectl` script offers more options. See `man apachectl`.

5. Stop being root:

   `exit`

   You should be back at your regular shell prompt.

✔ Tips

- To keep the Apache server from starting at boot time, reverse the change from step 2 above. That is, change `WEBSERVER=-YES-` back to `WEBSERVER=-NO-`.
- Apache logs all connections to `/var/log/httpd/access_log`, and error-message and startup/shutdown events to `/var/log/httpd/error_log`.
- If you have the firewall running, you must open access on port 80 for people to reach your Web server.

More About the Apache Startup Script

The Apple-supplied StartupItem script, /System/Library/StartupItems/Apache/Apache, actually executes the standard Apache startup script, apachectl.

On Mac OS X, apachectl is installed as /usr/sbin/apachectl. It is a Bourne shell script—you can look at it with any text editor to see how it works.

On most Unix systems where Apache is installed, the apachectl script itself is used to start (and stop) Apache, because that script handles arguments of start, stop, restart, and others. There is a man page for apachectl showing all of its options.

You can use apachectl directly (ignoring /etc/hostconfig), if you want.

On Mac OS X, it will be perfectly effective for you to start Apache with

```
sudo apachectl start
```

and to stop it with

```
sudo apachectl stop
```

To browse your Web server:

- Enter the URL for your Web server into your favorite Web browser.
- If you are browsing from the same machine the server is on, you can simply use
  http://localhost/
  Note: That URL will not work in the Microsoft Internet Explorer browser; instead use http://127.0.0.1/
- If you want to browse your machine from another machine, you need to know your machine's FQDN or IP address: www.mozilla.org or http://207.200.81.215/.

✔ Tips

- The main HTML directory for your Web server is /Library/WebServer/Documents, which is defined in the Apache-configuration file (/etc/httpd/httpd.conf) by the DocumentRoot directive.
- Mac OS X automatically creates a separate Apache-configuration file for each user you create, through the Accounts pane in System Preferences. The user-configuration files are in /etc/httpd/users and are named after each user—for example:
  /etc/httpd/users/puffball.conf
  The last line of the main Apache-configuration file reads all the files in the /etc/httpd/users directory when Apache starts up. The default is for each user to have his or her own directory of HTML pages, which is the Sites directory in each user's home directory. The URL for a user's personal Web page is
  http://*domainname*/~*username*/
  For user "puffball," it would be
  http://localhost/~puffball/
  or
  http://*domainname*/~puffball/

You can also shut down the Apache server from the command line.

To shut down the Apache server from the command line:

- `sudo apachectl stop`

  Enter your password if prompted.

  When the Apache server starts up, it writes its *process ID* (*pid*) number into the file `/var/run/httpd.pid`. The `apachectl` script uses that file to find the pid number and stop the server. See the sidebar "More About the Apache Startup Script."

Adding a CGI script

One of the most important—and exciting—things you can do with Apache is to build your first Common Gateway Interface (CGI) script. CGI is the standard for how Web servers communicate with other software. A CGI program can be written in any language, as long as it adheres to the CGI standard.

Basically, CGI works this way: The Web server is configured to treat certain requests as CGI requests. When the Web server gets a CGI request, it executes a program instead of simply sending back an HTML page. The CGI program then does . . . something. It might contact a database or send some e-mail. (A CGI program can be written to do anything any other program can do.) It then sends a response back to the Web server, which in turn passes that response back to the Web browser. Often that response is an HTML document generated on the fly, perhaps based on a database connection.

Typically, CGI requests begin with `/cgi-bin`, but they can begin with anything the person doing the configuration decides. In Mac OS X, the Apache server is configured so that any request starting with `/cgi-bin` is a CGI request, and Apache looks for the CGI program to execute in the directory `/Library/WebServer/CGI-Executables`.

So if Apache gets a request for `/cgi-bin/shopping.pl`, it will execute the file

```
/Library/WebServer/CGI-Executables/
→ shopping.pl
```

The process of installing your first CGI program involves creating the program (we will use a simple script in this case), and telling the Web server where the CGI programs are and which requests to treat as CGI requests. We'll use a simple script as an example. This Perl script produces an HTML page that shows all the environment variables present at the time the script is run. Apache sets a large number of environment variables when it executes a CGI script. These environment variables contain a great deal of information about the Web server and the request, so a script like this is very useful for troubleshooting and debugging.

To create a CGI script:

1. `cd /Library/WebServer/CGI-Executables`

   This is where you will create the new script.
2. Copy the script from **Figure 14.12** into a new file called test.pl.

   The URL for this script will be

   http://localhost/cgi-bin/test.pl

   You do not need to be root for this step, but you must be in group admin. (Throughout this book we assume you are an admin user.)
3. Make the script executable:

   `chmod 755 test.pl`

continues on page 480

```
#!/usr/bin/perl
# Simple CGI test script
# Displays environment variables in HTML format
# Save as /Library/WebServer/CGI-Executables/test.pl
######################################################################

# Anything printed out gets sent back to the Web server
# and then to the Web browser.

# Print everything up until the line that starts with BUNNY
print <<"BUNNY";
Content-type: text/html

<html>
<head>
<title>CGI Test Output</title>
</head>

<body bgcolor="#ffffff">
<h1>CGI Test Output</h1>

<table>
<tr>
        <th>Variable<th>
        <th>Value</th>
</tr>
BUNNY

# Iterate over all the environment variable names.
foreach $variable ( sort keys %ENV ) {
        print <<"BUNNY";
        <tr>
        <td><font color="blue">$variable</font></td>
        <td><font color="red">$ENV{$variable}</font></td>
        </tr>
BUNNY
}

print <<"BUNNY";

</table>
</html>
BUNNY
```

Figure 14.12 Code listing of a simple CGI script that displays its environment variables.

4. Test the script from the command line:

   ./test.pl

   You should get output similar to that in **Figure 14.13**.

5. Test the script from a Web browser.

   To test from the same machine, you can use the URL

   http://localhost/cgi-bin/test.pl

   You can also use your IP address or host-name instead of "localhost." Of course, if your machine has an FQDN, you can use that too, and it should work from anywhere on the Internet.

continues on next page

```
[g4-cube:/Library/WebServer/CGI-Executables] vanilla% ./test.pl
Content-type: text/html

<html>
<head>
<title>CGI Test Output</title>
</head>

<body bgcolor="#ffffff">
<h1>CGI Test Output</h1>

<table>
<tr>
        <th>Variable<th>
        <th>Value</th>
</tr>
            <tr>
            <td><font color="blue"> ENV_SET</font></td>
            <td><font color="red"> </font></td>
            </tr>
            <tr>
            <td><font color="blue"> GROUP</font></td>
            <td><font color="red"> staff</font></td>
            </tr>
            <tr>
            <td><font color="blue"> HOME</font></td>
            <td><font color="red"> /Users/matisse</font></td>
.
.
. Output continues...
```

Figure 14.13 Abbreviated output from the CGI test script at the command line.

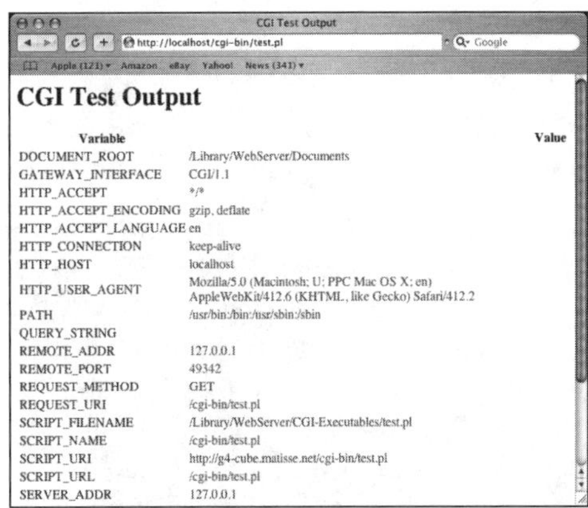

CGI Test Output

Variable	Value
DOCUMENT_ROOT	/Library/WebServer/Documents
GATEWAY_INTERFACE	CGI/1.1
HTTP_ACCEPT	*/*
HTTP_ACCEPT_ENCODING	gzip, deflate
HTTP_ACCEPT_LANGUAGE	en
HTTP_CONNECTION	keep-alive
HTTP_HOST	localhost
HTTP_USER_AGENT	Mozilla/5.0 (Macintosh; U; PPC Mac OS X; en) AppleWebKit/412.6 (KHTML, like Gecko) Safari/412.2
PATH	/usr/bin:/bin:/usr/sbin:/sbin
QUERY_STRING	
REMOTE_ADDR	127.0.0.1
REMOTE_PORT	49342
REQUEST_METHOD	GET
REQUEST_URI	/cgi-bin/test.pl
SCRIPT_FILENAME	/Library/WebServer/CGI-Executables/test.pl
SCRIPT_NAME	/cgi-bin/test.pl
SCRIPT_URI	http://g4-cube.matisse.net/cgi-bin/test.pl
SCRIPT_URL	/cgi-bin/test.pl
SERVER_ADDR	127.0.0.1

Figure 14.14 A Web-browser window showing output from the CGI test script.

```
<Directory "/Users/vanilla/Sites/">
        Options Indexes MultiViews
        AllowOverride None
        Order allow,deny
        Allow from all
</Directory>

ScriptAlias "/~vanilla/cgi-bin/" "/Users/
vanilla/Sites/cgi-bin/"
```

Figure 14.15 Code listing of user vanilla's Apache-configuration file (`/etc/httpd/users/vanilla.conf`) after adding a line to enable a `cgi-bin` directory.

Learning More About CGI

The CGI standard has been very stable, but it is still evolving.

You can read about the effort to formalize the CGI 1.1 specification at the Common Gateway Interface—RFC Project Page (http://ken.coar.org/cgi/).

An introductory book for creating CGI programs with Perl is *Perl and CGI for the World Wide Web: Visual QuickStart Guide*, Second Edition, by Elizabeth Castro (Peachpit Press; www.peachpit.com).

Figure 14.14 shows the output from the script in a browser window, so we know it works.

6. Congratulations—you've created a CGI script and are hosting dynamically generated HTML pages.

If you want to install a CGI script somewhere besides the default location, you will need to make a change to the Apache-configuration file.

To install a CGI program in your personal Sites directory:

1. Create a `cgi-bin` directory inside your `Sites` directory:

   `mkdir ~/Sites/cgi-bin`

2. Copy the script from Figure 14.12 into the new `cgi-bin` directory.

   ▲ If you already created a script in the previous task, you can just copy that file.

   ▲ If you are creating the script as a new file, be sure to make its mode executable by all when you are done:
   `chmod +x` *`filename`*

3. Become root, entering your password if prompted:

   `sudo -s`

4. Edit the Apache-configuration file.

   You will be editing the Apache configuration for just your one user. For example, for the user vanilla:

   `vi /etc/httpd/users/vanilla.conf`

   Add the following line to the file:

   ```
   ScriptAlias "/~vanilla/cgi-bin/"
   ⇢ "/Users/vanilla/Sites/cgi-bin/"
   ```

   Figure 14.15 shows the resulting file.

   Be sure to save the changes to the file before you quit the editor.

continues on next page

5. Test the Apache-configuration file:

   `apachectl configtest`

   The `apachectl` command checks all of the Apache-configuration files for errors (the main configuration file and those for each user); the output looks like that in **Figure 14.16**.

6. Restart the Apache server:

   `apachectl graceful`

   The `apachectl` command has two ways of restarting the server. The argument `graceful` allows any current connections to finish before the server restarts, while the argument `restart` kills all current connections before the server restarts.

7. Stop being root:

   `exit`

   You should be back at your normal shell prompt.

8. Test the CGI through a Web browser.

   Assuming you logged in as the user vanilla's account, the URL is http://localhost/~vanilla/cgi-bin/test.pl.

   You should get almost exactly the same result as in the previous task and Figure 14.14, only the values of some of the environment variables will be different (have a look at `REQUEST_URL`, `SCRIPT_FILENAME`, and `SCRIPT_NAME` in particular).

Apache Version 1.3.x vs. 2.x

Mac OS X 10.4 comes with version 1.3.26 of Apache. In May 2002, though, Apache version 2.0 was released.

The 2.x family of Apache is a major rewrite of Apache, offering significantly improved speed on some systems (for the geeks in the audience, Apache 2.x supports POSIX threads). The new features in Apache 2 are listed at httpd.apache.org/docs-2.0/new_features_2_0.html.

Apache 2 has been slow to catch on, mostly because Apache 1.3.x is so good, and some of the more popular add-on modules for Apache 1.3 have not yet been rewritten for Apache 2. Still, Apache 2 is the future, and if you are thinking of being heavily involved in managing a Web site, you should look into Apache 2.


```
[g4-cube:/Users/vanilla/Sites/cgi-bin] root# apachectl configtest
Processing config directory: /private/etc/httpd/users/*.conf
 Processing config file: /private/etc/httpd/users/matisse.conf
 Processing config file: /private/etc/httpd/users/puffball.conf
 Processing config file: /private/etc/httpd/users/scott.conf
 Processing config file: /private/etc/httpd/users/vanilla.conf
Syntax OK
[g4-cube:/Users/vanilla/Sites/cgi-bin] root#
```

Figure 14.16 Using the `apachectl` command to check the Apache-configuration files for syntax errors.

The MySQL Database Server

Databases are everywhere these days. It's all part of the increasing role of information in society. There is more information, and more need to organize it. Even your cell phone has a database.

MySQL is a *relational database management system* (*RDBMS*) that understands *Structured Query Language* (*SQL*) (pronounced either by saying the letters individually or the word "sequel"). The ideas of tracking relationships within a database and of being able to query it for information have been around for 20 years and are fundamental precepts to the way almost all corporate databases run today.

MySQL is a powerful, stable, open-source RDBMS that you can use without cost, but you can also purchase commercial support for it from the developers at MySQL (www.mysql.com).

If a database engine (that's another name for an RDBMS) understands SQL, then other applications can talk to it in a standardized fashion. Software written to communicate with one SQL database can usually communicate with any other with only minimal changes.

An RDBMS can contain many databases, such as one for "purchases" and one for "sales." Each database in turn may have many tables, identifying "customers," "invoices," and "invoice line items." A *table* is a collection of data entries that all have exactly the same list of headings, called *columns* or *fields*. Each table can have many columns, such as "ID number," "name," "address," and "phone."

A database is essentially a tool for organizing information. Relational databases are databases that can contain several tables of information, which can be linked to each other. A database of purchase histories might contain one table that lists customers (the "customer table"), another that lists invoices (the "invoice table"), and a third that lists invoice line items (the "invoice line-items table"). An entry in the invoice table might have only the invoice number, customer number, and invoice date. Thus, an entry in the invoice table is not actually a complete invoice; rather, it holds only the information that is unique to one invoice. This avoids the necessity of keeping a copy of the customer address for every invoice. The customer's ID number is in the invoice table and is used to look up the customer address for each invoice in the customer table. This connection between the tables is called a *relationship*.

continues on next page

To produce a complete invoice, the system would need to pull a record from the invoice table and then pull information from the two related tables (the customer table and the invoice line-items table). This is possible because each record in the invoice table has a customer ID number (which is used to find a customer) and an invoice ID. Each record in the invoice line-items table has an invoice ID, so by finding all the records in the invoice line-items table with a particular invoice ID, the database can find all the line items for one invoice. **Figure 14.17** is a diagram showing the relationships between the tables in a sample database.

Learning how to use a database, totally apart from setting one up, is quite a project. But you have to have a database in order to start learning, and installing an industrial-strength database on Mac OS X is actually very easy.

Installing MySQL

You can install MySQL from source code using Fink or the other methods described in Chapter 13, "Installing Software from Source Code." With Fink, you can easily remove the entire installation. However, an even easier way to install MySQL is to download the MySQL installer package from the MySQL Web site.

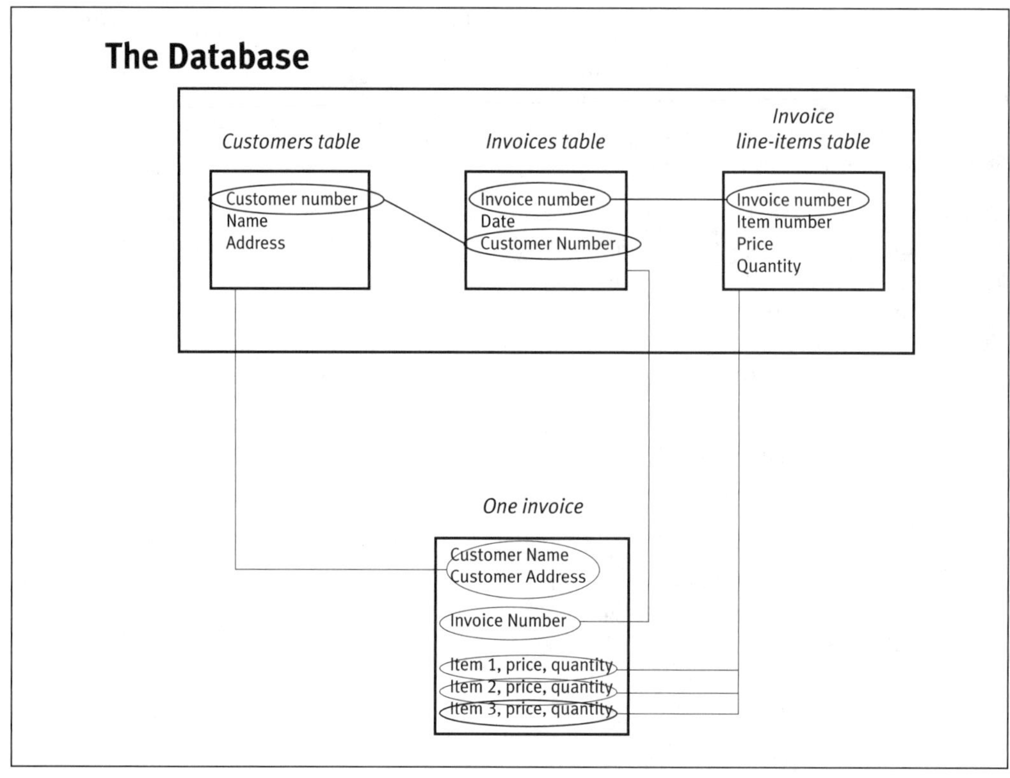

Figure 14.17 Diagram showing the relationships between tables in a relational database.

To install MySQL using precompiled binaries:

1. Download the installer-package disk image from MySQL.

   The disk image is available from http://dev.mysql.com/downloads/mysql/.

   Look for the "Mac OS X downloads" and pick the appropriate version. **Figure 14.18** shows a partial screen shot of the MySQL download page.

continues on next page

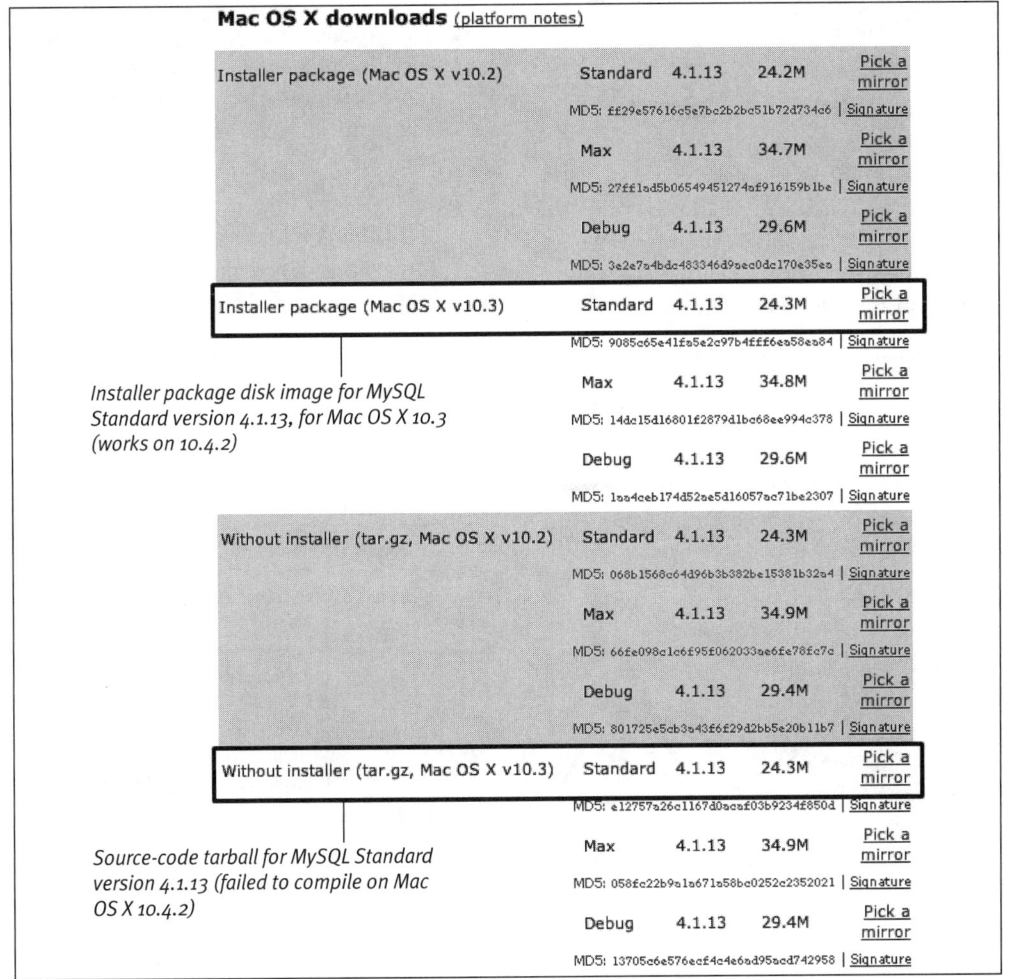

Figure 14.18 Partial screen shot of the MySQL download page showing various alternatives for Mac OS X.

2. Double-click the installer package and follow the instructions to install the MySQL database server and many utility programs.

   The main installation location is

   `/usr/local/mysql-VERSION`

   For example:

   `/usr/local/ mysql-standard-4.1.13-`
   `→ apple-darwin6.8-powerpc`

   A symbolic link, `/usr/local/mysql`, is created pointing to the new location.

   All of the installed files will be in `/usr/local/mysql`. Initially there are two databases: `mysql` and `test`. The `mysql` database is where MySQL stores information about itself—users, passwords, and so on.

3. Double-click the MySQLStartupItem installer package and follow the instructions.

   This installs a StartupItem (`/Library/StartupItems/MySQLCOM`) that provides the MySQL service. An entry is also created in `/etc/hostconfig`.

4. Check the firewall.

   MySQL listens on port 3306. If you are running firewall software, be sure to configure it to allow access to this port if you want other machines to be able to connect to your MySQL server.

5. Set the MySQL root password.

   The MySQL database gets installed with no password protection. You should set a password right away. Immediately proceed to the next task, "To set the MySQL root password."

✔ Tips

- Besides `man` pages for all the MySQL utility programs, the MySQL user's manual includes a tutorial, performance-tuning tips, and detailed reference material on all aspects of MySQL. The manual is available online at http://dev.mysql.com/doc/ and may be browsed and searched online, as well as downloaded and stored on your local disk in HTML and PDF formats. For books about MySQL, see http://dev.mysql.com/books/.
- The installer puts over 50 programs in `/usr/local/mysql/bin/` and the commonly used ones have built-in help available if run with the `-help` option—for example:

  `mysqldump -help`

  See **Table 14.2** for a list of the commonly used MySQL commands.

Table 14.2

Commonly Used MySQL Commands

(All installed in `/usr/local/mysql/bin`.)

Command	Description
`mysql`	Command-line client program for issuing SQL commands and seeing the results.
`mysqladmin`	For changing the root password, shutting down the database server, reloading access controls, and so on.
`mysqldump`	Dumping the contents of an entire database or one or more tables as an SQL text file. Very useful for making backups. Output can be piped to the `mysql` utility to create a copy of a database.
`mysqlimport`	Reads delimited text files into a database.

GUI Tools for MySQL Administration

There are a number of graphical tools for administering MySQL. Webmin (www.webmin.com) has a MySQL module that works nicely. Another Web-based tool, phpMyAdmin, is available in 50 languages (www.phpmyadmin.net).

The folks at MySQL AB (the makers of MySQL) have released Mac OS X versions of their MySQL Administrator (http://dev.mysql.com/downloads/administrator) and MySQL Query Browser (http://dev.mysql.com/downloads/query-browser). These are proper Mac applications that allow you to administer MySQL. They are very fast and offer nice built-in tools for creating and saving SQL queries, comparing results from two queries, and so on. As of this writing, these tools are available for Mac OS X 10.3, but not yet for 10.4.

Configuring and starting MySQL

Configuring MySQL involves several steps: creating a root password for MySQL, starting the `mysqld` program itself, learning how to use the `mysql` command-line tool, creating one or more MySQL users, creating a MySQL database, setting the access controls for the new database, and creating tables in the new database. Once all this is done, you can insert and retrieve data from the tables in the new database. Though this is more detail than we've gone into for most tasks in this book, we feel that it's appropriate because database mastery is a key asset for knowledgeable Unix users. See also the sidebar "GUI Tools for MySQL Administration."

MySQL has its own list of users, which are totally separate from the user accounts on your system. When you install MySQL, it has one user already installed—root. This can be a bit confusing—the MySQL root account is totally different from the Unix root account. It can—and should—have a different password and is used only for managing MySQL.

The MySQL root account starts off with no password, so the first thing you should do is set a password for the MySQL root account.

For the following tasks, we are assuming you have added the directory `/usr/local/mysql/bin` to your `PATH`. If you haven't done that, do it now (see Chapter 7, "Configuring Your Environment with Unix," for instructions).

To set the MySQL root password:

1. Become root:

   ```
   sudo -s
   ```

   Enter your Unix password if prompted. You need to be the Unix root user to start MySQL.

2. Start the MySQL database server.

   If you installed the StartupItem package in the previous task, then you can start the server with

   ```
   SystemStarter start MySQL
   ```

   See **Figure 14.19**.

   That command runs the StartupItem script `/Library/StartupItems/MySQLCOM`, which in turn actually runs another script, which you can run directly if you need to:

   ```
   /usr/local/mysql/support-files/mysql.
   → server start
   ```

   That script runs the database server daemon: `mysqld`.

   The `mysqld` daemon must be running in order to set a password for the MySQL root account.

3. `mysqladmin -u root password 'mypassword'`

   That sets the MySQL root password to *mypassword*. Note that the new password is enclosed in single quotes.

   For example, to set the MySQL root password to Gr56%kQ, the command is

   ```
   mysqladmin -u root password
   → 'Gr56%kQ'
   ```

   From now on, when you use the `mysqladmin` command, you need to add the `-p` option, which will tell `mysqladmin` to ask you for a password, and then enter the password you just created. For example,

   ```
   mysqladmin -u root -p status
   ```

   will prompt for a password, and when you enter it, you will get status information about the MySQL database engine.

4. Clear the password out of your shell's command history.

   Because your command history (see Chapter 2) is written to disk, when your shell exits, you want to ensure that the password you just typed doesn't get written where someone might be able to see it.

   - If you are using the default shell (`bash`):

     ```
     unset HISTFILE
     ```

   - If you are using the `tcsh` shell:

     ```
     history -c
     ```

5. `exit`

   This exits the root shell you started in step 1, and you should be back to your regular shell prompt.

To start MySQL from the command line:

- `sudo SystemStarter start MySQL`

  or, if you have not installed the StartupItem, then

  ```
  sudo /usr/local/mysql/support-files/
  → mysql.server start
  ```

```
g4-cube:~ root# SystemStarter start MySQL
Starting MySQL database server
g4-cube:~ root#
```

Figure 14.19 Starting the `mysqld` daemon using the StartupItem script.

To shut down MySQL from the command line:

- `sudo SystemStarter stop MySQL`

  or, if you have not installed the StartupItem, then

  ```
  sudo /usr/local/mysql/support-files/
  → mysql.server stop
  ```

  You can also use

  ```
  mysqladmin -u root -p shutdown
  ```

  and then enter the MySQL root password when prompted. Notice that this method uses the MySQL root password, not your password.

MySQL has dozens of available options. You put options into the MySQL options file, `/etc/my.cnf`. (The options file is also called the *configuration file.*) If that file does not exist, then reasonable default values are used.

Four sample configuration files are provided in `/usr/local/mysql/support-files/`, each corresponding to how heavily used your MySQL server will be: `my-huge.cnf`, `my-large.cnf`, `my-medium.cnf`, and `my-small.cnf`.

The files contain some documentation about the various options, and the MySQL manual discusses options files in section 4.3.2 (see http://dev.mysql.com/doc/mysql).

To install a MySQL options/configuration file:

1. Choose one of the sample options files from `/usr/local/mysql/share/mysql`.
2. Make a backup copy of `/etc/my.cnf`.

   For example:

   ```
   cp /etc/my.cnf /etc/my.cnf.20051221
   ```
3. Copy the file to `/etc/my.cnf`.

   For example:

   ```
   sudo cp /usr/local/mysql/share/mysql/
   → my-medium.cnf /etc/my.cnf
   ```
4. Edit the file to adjust the options to your liking. You need to be root in order to edit the file.
5. Start or restart MySQL. (See tasks above.)

Connecting to MySQL

The main way to manage MySQL is to connect to the `mysqld` daemon using the `mysql` command-line utility. (See also the sidebar "GUI Tools for MySQL Administration.") Most of the commands you use inside the `mysql` utility are SQL commands, called *statements*. The MySQL manual has extensive coverage of SQL in section 13, "SQL Statement Syntax," as well as a complete tutorial in section 3, "MySQL Tutorial," which we strongly recommend that you read and perform.

In the following tasks, we use two databases that are created when you install MySQL. One is called "mysql"—it's the "master database" containing information about MySQL itself, as well as all the databases, users, and access-control information. The other is called "test"; it's an empty database used for—you guessed it—testing.

When you connect to MySQL, you must do so as a MySQL user. Until you create more MySQL users, the only one that exists is the MySQL root user, so we use that user in this task. You do *not* need to be root to perform the following task. You are logging in to the MySQL server as the "MySQL" root user, which is not the same as the Unix root user (it just has the same name in order to confuse you).

To use the mysql utility to connect to the mysqld daemon:

1. `mysql -u root -p`
2. Enter the MySQL root password.

   You are now connected to `mysqld`. **Figure 14.20** shows the command line for connecting, and then the output and prompt from the `mysql` utility.

   The `mysql` utility is an interactive program, like the `ftp` command. `mysql` provides its own prompt, where you type commands to it. You can think of it as a shell program just for MySQL.
3. `show databases;`

   This shows a list of all the databases that `mysqld` is managing (**Figure 14.21**).

You can enter commands in the `mysql` utility (called *SQL statements*) on multiple lines. That is, you can press Return in the middle of an SQL statement because the SQL statement doesn't actually end (and get executed) until you enter one of the following and press Return:

`;`

`\g`

`\G`

The first two have the same meaning. The third one, `\G`, does a nice job of formatting output that would be too wide for your screen when using either of the first two forms.

```
localhost:~ vanilla% mysql -u root -p
Enter password:
Welcome to the MySQL monitor.  Commands end with ; or \g.
Your MySQL connection id is 1 to server version: 4.1.13-standard

Type 'help;' or '\h' for help. Type '\c' to clear the buffer.

mysql>
```

Figure 14.20 Connecting to `mysqld` using the `mysql` command-line utility.

```
mysql> show databases;
+------+
| Database |
+------+
| mysql    |
| test     |
+------+
2 rows in set (0.01 sec)

mysql>
```

Figure 14.21 Using the `show databases` command in the `mysql` utility to display a list of all MySQL databases.

4. `use mysql;`

   This tells the `mysql` utility that you want to communicate with the MySQL database (**Figure 14.22**).

5. `show tables;`

   This command lists all the tables in the currently selected database—in this case, the MySQL database (**Figure 14.23**).

continues on next page

```
mysql> use mysql;
Reading table information for completion of table and column names
You can turn off this feature to get a quicker startup with -A

Database changed
mysql>
```

Figure 14.22 Telling the `mysql` utility which database you want to communicate with.

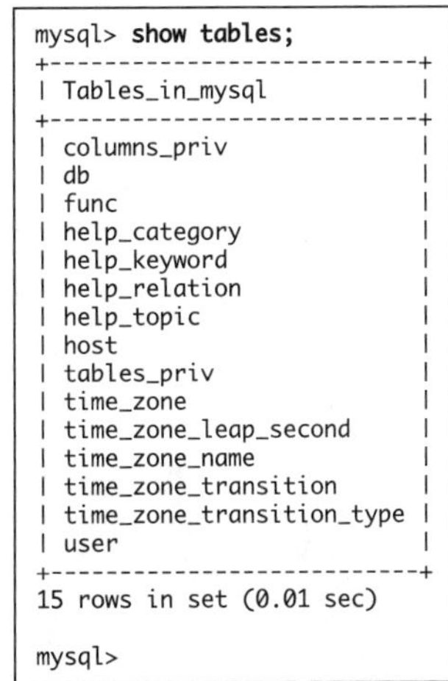

```
mysql> show tables;
+---------------------------+
| Tables_in_mysql           |
+---------------------------+
| columns_priv              |
| db                        |
| func                      |
| help_category             |
| help_keyword              |
| help_relation             |
| help_topic                |
| host                      |
| tables_priv               |
| time_zone                 |
| time_zone_leap_second     |
| time_zone_name            |
| time_zone_transition      |
| time_zone_transition_type |
| user                      |
+---------------------------+
15 rows in set (0.01 sec)

mysql>
```

Figure 14.23 Using the show `tables` command to see all the tables in the currently selected database.

6. `DESCRIBE user;`

   This command (which need not be capitalized) describes all the fields (or columns) in the user table. **Figure 14.24** shows the output. The output shows the column (Field) name, the data type for the column, whether the column can contain NULL (empty) values, whether the column is indexed (in which case the Key column has a value in it), and finally the column's default value. In this example 21 fields have a default value of `N`, 7 have no default, and 3 have a default value of `0`.

7. `quit`

   This exits the `mysql` utility, taking you back to your shell prompt. Notice that you did not need a semicolon at the end of that command.

✔ Tips

- Commands, table names, and field (column) names are not case sensitive, so `describe` and `DESCRIBE` mean the same thing. We show SQL commands in uppercase for clarity only.

```
mysql> DESCRIBE user;
+-----------------------+-----------------------------------+------+-----+---------+-------+
| Field                 | Type                              | Null | Key | Default | Extra |
+-----------------------+-----------------------------------+------+-----+---------+-------+
| Host                  | varchar(60)                       |      | PRI |         |       |
| User                  | varchar(16)                       |      | PRI |         |       |
| Password              | varchar(41)                       |      |     |         |       |
| Select_priv           | enum('N','Y')                     |      |     | N       |       |
| Insert_priv           | enum('N','Y')                     |      |     | N       |       |
| Update_priv           | enum('N','Y')                     |      |     | N       |       |
| Delete_priv           | enum('N','Y')                     |      |     | N       |       |
| Create_priv           | enum('N','Y')                     |      |     | N       |       |
| Drop_priv             | enum('N','Y')                     |      |     | N       |       |
| Reload_priv           | enum('N','Y')                     |      |     | N       |       |
| Shutdown_priv         | enum('N','Y')                     |      |     | N       |       |
| Process_priv          | enum('N','Y')                     |      |     | N       |       |
| File_priv             | enum('N','Y')                     |      |     | N       |       |
| Grant_priv            | enum('N','Y')                     |      |     | N       |       |
| References_priv       | enum('N','Y')                     |      |     | N       |       |
| Index_priv            | enum('N','Y')                     |      |     | N       |       |
| Alter_priv            | enum('N','Y')                     |      |     | N       |       |
| Show_db_priv          | enum('N','Y')                     |      |     | N       |       |
| Super_priv            | enum('N','Y')                     |      |     | N       |       |
| Create_tmp_table_priv | enum('N','Y')                     |      |     | N       |       |
| Lock_tables_priv      | enum('N','Y')                     |      |     | N       |       |
| Execute_priv          | enum('N','Y')                     |      |     | N       |       |
| Repl_slave_priv       | enum('N','Y')                     |      |     | N       |       |
| Repl_client_priv      | enum('N','Y')                     |      |     | N       |       |
| ssl_type              | enum('','ANY','X509','SPECIFIED') |      |     |         |       |
| ssl_cipher            | blob                              |      |     |         |       |
| x509_issuer           | blob                              |      |     |         |       |
| x509_subject          | blob                              |      |     |         |       |
| max_questions         | int(11) unsigned                  |      |     | 0       |       |
| max_updates           | int(11) unsigned                  |      |     | 0       |       |
| max_connections       | int(11) unsigned                  |      |     | 0       |       |
+-----------------------+-----------------------------------+------+-----+---------+-------+
31 rows in set (0.03 sec)

mysql>
```

Figure 14.24 Using the DESCRIBE command to see the descriptions of all the fields in the user table.

- You can specify which database to connect to on the command line when you run the `mysql` utility—for example,

  ```
  mysql -u root -p test
  ```

  starts the `mysql` program and connects to the test database right away.

- The `mysql` tool has a command history much like your Unix shell's. You can use the up arrow and down arrow keys to scroll through command lines you have entered.

Creating a new database

When you create a new database in MySQL, it has no access controls whatsoever, unless you have put them in place before creating the database. So the process we show you for creating a new database in MySQL involves first setting up the access controls and then creating the empty database. Please note that section 5 of the MySQL user's manual goes into great detail about MySQL access controls. Section 5.6 in particular covers the MySQL access-control system.

To set up the access controls, connect to the MySQL master database, mysql. That is the database where MySQL keeps information about itself and any databases you create. Once again, we are assuming you have added `/usr/local/mysql/bin` to your `PATH`.

At the end of this chapter, we show you a simple Perl script that connects to MySQL. The script assumes you have created the sample database and user described below.

To create a new database in MySQL:

1. `mysqladmin -u root -p create` *`dbname`*

   where ***dbname*** is the name of the new database. For example, to create a database called "sample":

   ```
   mysqladmin -u root -p create sample
   ```

2. Enter the MySQL root password.

   The database now exists but has no tables or access control. See the next two tasks to set up access control and create tables in the database.

✔ Tip

- You may also create a new database from within the `mysql` shell program, if you connect as the MySQL root user. Use the following SQL statement:

  ```
  create database dbname;
  ```

Access control in MySQL can be quite complex. The simple version we show you here creates a single MySQL user with its own password. The user is allowed to connect to one database and will have a great deal of access to the database, but not total access. The user is able to retrieve information from the database ("SELECT" data) and to add, delete, and change records in the database. He or she is able to connect to the database only from the same machine that MySQL is running on (localhost) and can create and remove—but not alter—the structure of tables in the database.

The graphical interfaces for MySQL provided by the Webmin, phpMySQL, and MySQL Administrator applications simplifies much of MySQL administration. See the sidebar "GUI Tools for MySQL Administration," earlier in this chapter.

Properly setting up a new database in MySQL involves first creating its access controls. This ensures that a new database never exists even for a moment without access control.

To configure access control for a database:

1. If `mysqld` is not already running, then start it.
2. `mysql -u root -p mysql`

   You are connecting to the "master" database, mysql, as user root.
3. Enter the MySQL root password.
4. Create a new MySQL user.

   Commands in the `mysql` tool can be many lines long.

   The following command inserts a new row into the user table, creating a MySQL user named "daffy":

   `INSERT INTO user SET`

   `Host='localhost', User='daffy'`

   To execute the command, enter a semicolon, or `\g` or `\G`, and press Return, as shown in **Figure 14.25**:

   `;`

   The above command is an SQL statement. In this case, you are inserting data into a table called "user" in the mysql database.

   The new user is added, and is set to be allowed to connect only from this machine (that's the `localhost` setting) and to have no permissions to do anything yet (the default).
5. Look at the record ("row") for the new user:

   `SELECT * FROM user`

   `WHERE User='daffy'`

   `\G`

   The * means that we are asking for all the fields in the record.

   We use the `\G` end-of-command code here because otherwise the output would not fit nicely on the screen (**Figure 14.26**).

   Notice how all of the fields except the Password field have something in them. When you created this record in step 4,

```
mysql> INSERT INTO user SET
       -> Host='localhost', User='daffy'
       -> ;
Query OK, 1 row affected (0.03 sec)

mysql>
```

Figure 14.25 Creating a new MySQL user named "daffy."

```
mysql> SELECT * FROM user WHERE
    -> User='daffy'
    -> \G
*************************** 1. row ***********
Host: localhost
                 User: daffy
             Password:
          Select_priv: N
          Insert_priv: N
          Update_priv: N
          Delete_priv: N
          Create_priv: N
            Drop_priv: N
          Reload_priv: N
        Shutdown_priv: N
         Process_priv: N
            File_priv: N
           Grant_priv: N
      References_priv: N
           Index_priv: N
           Alter_priv: N
         Show_db_priv: N
           Super_priv: N
Create_tmp_table_priv: N
     Lock_tables_priv: N
         Execute_priv: N
      Repl_slave_priv: N
     Repl_client_priv: N
             ssl_type:
           ssl_cipher:
          x509_issuer:
         x509_subject:
        max_questions: 0
          max_updates: 0
      max_connections: 0
1 row in set (0.06 sec)
mysql>
```

Figure 14.26 Using an SQL SELECT statement to view a record from the database.

you set the values for the User and Host fields, and the default values shown in Figure 14.26 were filled in for all the fields you did not set. One field, the Password field, has no default, so it is empty.

6. Set the user's password.

   The following SQL statement updates the user table, setting the contents of the field Password to an encrypted version of "qu@cker"—you should use a different password, of course, but just remember what you use!

   ```
   UPDATE user SET
   → Password=password('qu@cker') WHERE
   → User='daffy';
   ```

   The value put into the Password field is the result of using the MySQL `password()` function to encrypt the supplied password (**Figure 14.27**).

7. Check that the update worked:

   ```
   SELECT User,Password FROM user
   WHERE User='daffy';
   ```

   In this case, you are asking for only two fields from the record: the User field and the Password field (**Figure 14.28**).

continues on next page

```
mysql> UPDATE user SET Password=password('qu@cker')
    ->  WHERE User='daffy';
Query OK, 1 row affected (0.03 sec)
Rows matched: 1  Changed: 1  Warnings: 0
mysql>
```

Figure 14.27 Using an SQL UPDATE statement to set the user's password.

```
mysql> SELECT User,Password FROM user
    -> WHERE User='daffy';
+-------+-------------------------------------------+
| User  | Password                                  |
+-------+-------------------------------------------+
| daffy | *59E155CA427C9377E9B924967BD8AD16798FC0F5 |
+-------+-------------------------------------------+
1 row in set (0.00 sec)

mysql>
```

Figure 14.28 Using a SELECT statement to retrieve only two fields from a record.

8. `DESCRIBE db;`

   This shows all the column (field) descriptions in the db table (**Figure 14.29**).

9. Create an entry for the new database.

   Here's how to create an entry for a new database called "sample." The database doesn't exist yet—you are simply preparing access controls for it first.

   ```
   INSERT INTO db
   VALUES ('localhost','sample','daffy',
   'Y','Y','Y','Y','Y','Y','N','N','N','
   N','N','N');
   ```

   See **Figure 14.30**.

   Here you have given the user daffy permission to connect to the sample database from the local machine (not over the Internet) and have granted the user select, insert, update, and delete privileges. The six "Y" values correspond to the fourth, fifth, sixth, seventh, eight, and ninth fields listed in Figure 14.29.

   Using this form of the `INSERT` statement, you must supply exactly the right number of values, one for each column. Otherwise, you will get an error message like this:

   ```
   ERROR 1136: Column count doesn't
   match value count at row 1
   ```

```
mysql> DESCRIBE db;
+-----------------------+-----------------+------+-----+---------+-------+
| Field                 | Type            | Null | Key | Default | Extra |
+-----------------------+-----------------+------+-----+---------+-------+
| Host                  | char(60)        |      | PRI |         |       |
| Db                    | char(64)        |      | PRI |         |       |
| User                  | char(16)        |      | PRI |         |       |
| Select_priv           | enum('N','Y')   |      |     | N       |       |
| Insert_priv           | enum('N','Y')   |      |     | N       |       |
| Update_priv           | enum('N','Y')   |      |     | N       |       |
| Delete_priv           | enum('N','Y')   |      |     | N       |       |
| Create_priv           | enum('N','Y')   |      |     | N       |       |
| Drop_priv             | enum('N','Y')   |      |     | N       |       |
| Grant_priv            | enum('N','Y')   |      |     | N       |       |
| References_priv       | enum('N','Y')   |      |     | N       |       |
| Index_priv            | enum('N','Y')   |      |     | N       |       |
| Alter_priv            | enum('N','Y')   |      |     | N       |       |
| Create_tmp_table_priv | enum('N','Y')   |      |     | N       |       |
| Lock_tables_priv      | enum('N','Y')   |      |     | N       |       |
+-----------------------+-----------------+------+-----+---------+-------+
15 rows in set (0.00 sec)

mysql>
```

Figure 14.29 Output from DESCRIBE db showing the column descriptions for the db table.

```
mysql> INSERT INTO db VALUES ('localhost','sample','daffy',
'Y','Y','Y','Y','Y','Y','N','N','N','N','N','N');
Query OK, 1 row affected (0.01 sec)

mysql>
```

Figure 14.30 Inserting a new record into the db table.

10. Check that the new record looks OK:

    `SELECT * FROM db`

    `WHERE User='daffy'\G`

    as shown in **Figure 14.31**.

11. `flush privileges;`

    This tells MySQL to reload its access controls. MySQL now knows about the access controls you just created.

    You could also do this from a Unix shell prompt with

    `mysqladmin -u root -p reload`

12. `create database sample;`

    This creates a new, empty database. You can also do this from a Unix shell prompt with

    `mysqladmin -u root -p create sample`

13. Quit the `mysql` tool:

    `quit` (or `exit`)

    You're back at your Unix shell prompt.

14. Connect to the new database as user daffy:

    `mysql -u daffy -p sample`

15. Enter daffy's password.

    You are now connected to the sample database as the MySQL user daffy (**Figure 14.32**).

16. Quit the `mysql` utility:

    `quit`

```
mysql> SELECT * FROM db WHERE User='daffy'\G
*************************** 1. row ***************************
                 Host: localhost
                   Db: sample
                 User: daffy
          Select_priv: Y
          Insert_priv: Y
          Update_priv: Y
          Delete_priv: Y
          Create_priv: Y
            Drop_priv: Y
           Grant_priv: N
      References_priv: N
           Index_priv: N
           Alter_priv: N
Create_tmp_table_priv: N
     Lock_tables_priv: N
1 row in set (0.00 sec)

mysql>
```

Figure 14.31 Selecting a record from the db table.

```
localhost:~ vanilla$ mysql -u daffy -p sample
Enter password:
Welcome to the MySQL monitor.  Commands end with ; or \g.
Your MySQL connection id is 5 to server version: 4.1.13-standard

Type 'help;' or '\h' for help. Type '\c' to clear the buffer.

mysql>
```

Figure 14.32 Connecting to the sample database as the MySQL user daffy.

To add a table to a database:

1. Connect to the database.

   To connect to the sample database as the user daffy:

   `mysql -u daffy -p sample`

2. Enter the MySQL user's password (Figure 14.32).

3. Create the table.

   The following SQL statement creates a table called "table_one" with three fields. The "name" field will hold up to 20 characters, the "address" field up to 30, and the "phone" field up to 20; and the "id" field will hold an integer (a number) that will be automatically filled in each time a record is added. The `PRIMARY KEY` instruction tells MySQL to use the id field as a sort of master index for the table. Searching the table based on that field will go faster than a search based on other fields.

   ```
   CREATE TABLE table_one (
   name char(20),
   address char(30),
   phone char(20),
   id int NOT NULL auto_increment,
   PRIMARY KEY(id)
   );
   ```

   Figure 14.33 shows the result, and also the result of the next step. Section 13.1.5 of the MySQL user's manual covers the `CREATE TABLE` syntax in detail (see http://dev.mysql.com/doc/mysql/en/sql-syntax.html).

4. `show tables;`

   This shows that the new table has been created.

   If you want to see how `mysql` describes your table, use

   `DESCRIBE table_one;`

5. Quit the `mysql` utility:

   `quit`

✔ Tip

- You can see the SQL statement used to create any table with the special SQL statement

  `show create table tablename\G`

  This can be a useful way to learn how tables are constructed.

For the following tasks, we assume that you are connected to the sample database as the user daffy, as described above.

```
mysql> CREATE TABLE table_one (
    -> name char(20),
    -> address char(30),
    -> phone char(20),
    -> id int NOT NULL auto_increment,
    -> PRIMARY KEY (id)
    -> );
Query OK, 0 rows affected (0.01 sec)

mysql> show tables;
+----------------+
| Tables_in_sample |
+----------------+
| table_one      |
+----------------+
1 row in set (0.00 sec)

mysql>
```

Figure 14.33 Creating a new table with a CREATE statement.

About the SQL WHERE clause

Many of the SQL statements we show you here use the SQL WHERE clause to limit which records are affected by the SQL statement. The options for using a WHERE clause are varied, but usually you specify a column and the value it must contain for the SQL statement to "catch" a record. Section 13.2.7 of the MySQL user's manual has some good examples of using a WHERE clause in an SQL statement.

To add a new record (row) to a table:

- Use an INSERT statement.

  There are three forms of the INSERT statement. Section 13.2.4 of the MySQL user's manual covers INSERT syntax in detail. Here is one way to insert a new row into a table:

  ```
  INSERT INTO table_one
  SET name = 'Margaret',
  address='Constantinople';
  ```

  In this case, even though you did not specify a value for the id column, it will be filled in automatically, because it is an auto_increment field. The phone field remains empty.

```
mysql> SELECT name,address,id FROM table_one;
+----------+----------------+----+
| name     | address        | id |
+----------+----------------+----+
| Margaret | Constantinople |  1 |
| Larry    | Ohio           |  2 |
| Margaret | Pompeii        |  3 |
+----------+----------------+----+
3 rows in set (0.00 sec)

mysql>
```

Figure 14.34 Using a SELECT statement to select only the name, address, and id columns.

To select data from a table:

- Use a SELECT statement.

  The SELECT statement is covered in section 13.2.7 of the MySQL user's manual.

  We are covering this after the INSERT statement so that you will have some data to select! But SELECT statements are actually the most common in using databases.

  The following SQL statement selects the name, address, and id fields for all records from table_one:

  ```
  SELECT name,address,id
  FROM table_one;
  ```

  Figure 14.34 shows the result (we cheated and added two more records when you weren't looking). We can see that there are two Margarets—one in Constantinople with id 1, and one in Pompeii, with id 3.

  If you do not include a WHERE clause in the SELECT statement, it fetches every record in the table.

  To do the same SELECT statement, but to find only records where the name is Margaret, you would use

  ```
  SELECT name,address,id
  FROM table_one
  WHERE name='Margaret';
  ```

To change the values in an existing record:

◆ Use an UPDATE statement.

Section 13.2.10 of the MySQL user's manual covers UPDATE in detail. Here is an example of changing Margaret's address to "Istanbul":

```
UPDATE table_one
SET address='Istanbul'
WHERE name='Margaret';
```

That is OK, unless there is more than one Margaret in the table, in which case they would *all* get moved to Istanbul—maybe not what they wanted.

In our sample table, the id field was designated as a PRIMARY KEY, which means that no two rows will ever have the same value in that column. So if you know that the record you want to update has an id of 1, you would use

```
UPDATE table_one
SET address='Istanbul'
WHERE id=1;
```

Because the id field is an integer field, you do not enclose its value in single quotes.

How would you know that the record had an id of 1? You would have had to SELECT that data from the table first. See the next task.

To delete a row from a table:

◆ Use a DELETE statement.

Unless you want to delete every row in a table, always include a WHERE clause in your DELETE statements. DELETE is covered in section 13.2.1 of the MySQL user's manual.

To delete the Margaret who lives in Pompeii:

```
DELETE FROM table_one
WHERE id=3;
```

as shown in **Figure 14.35**.

```
mysql> DELETE FROM table_one
    -> WHERE id=3;
Query OK, 1 row affected (0.00 sec)

mysql>
```

Figure 14.35 Using a DELETE statement to delete a record.

Creating a script that uses SQL

Now that you have that lovely new database running, we are going to show you a very simple Perl script that uses MySQL.

The script uses the popular *Perl DBI* (*DataBase Independent*) module, which allows Perl scripts to be written to work with a variety of SQL databases. You add a second Perl module for the particular database engine you are using. So our script will also use the `DBD::mysql` module.

If this sort of thing interests you (and who would not be fascinated by such an enthralling subject?), then we suggest you have a look at the book *Programming the Perl DBI*, coauthored by Alligator Descartes and the creator of the Perl DBI module, Tim Bunce (O'Reilly; www.oreilly.com). Installing Perl modules is covered in Chapter 13.

To install the Perl DBI and DBD::mysql modules:

1. Install the MySQL database server.
2. Make sure the MySQL server is running.
   Now you can use the instructions in Chapter 13 to install the `DBI` and `DBD::mysql` modules.
   The short version for the `DBI` module is
   ```
   sudo cpan -i DBI
   ```
   (You may need to do
   ```
   export FTP_PASSIVE=1
   ```
   first.)

   For the `DBD::mysql` module, you need to use the `CPAN` shell and add a little extra command so that the install script will know to use the MySQL user "test" when testing the installation. The short version would be
   ```
   sudo cpan
   ```
   Then, at the `cpan>` prompt:
   ```
   o conf makepl_arg -testuser=test
   install DBD::mysql
   ```
   The `DBD::mysql` install process performs several hundred tests. Sometimes a few of the tests will fail but the module is still usable. You can force `CPAN` to install the module in spite of the test failures by using this command at the `cpan>` prompt:
   ```
   force install DBD::mysql
   ```
   (We had to do this for `DBD::mysql` back in version 2.1020, which failed two tests on Mac OS X 10.2. `DBD::mysql 3.0002` installed cleanly on Mac OS X 10.4.2.)

Once you have installed the Perl modules, you can create a simple script that will talk to the MySQL database engine. The script in the following task assumes you have created the "sample" database described earlier.

To create a Perl script that uses MySQL:

1. Copy the code from **Figure 14.36** (on the facing page) into a file called database.pl.

   Change the line

   `$password = 'd**kb0y';`

   to have the password for user `daffy`.

2. Make the file executable, but not readable by others:

   `chmod 700 database.pl`

   The file contains a MySQL user name and password, so you make it executable for yourself but not readable by others; that way, they can't find the password. If the MySQL user whose password is in the script has only `SELECT` privileges on the database, then it would be safe to let others see the password (assuming that there is no private information in the database).

3. Test the script:

   `./database.pl`

   You are prompted for a name. Type one that you know is in the database, and press Return. **Figure 14.37** shows an example of what happens when the script doesn't find anyone, and when it does.

4. Congratulations!

   You are now a Unix database-application programmer.

```
localhost:~/bin vanilla$ ./database.pl
Enter a name: Johnny
Didn't find anyone with the name Johnny

localhost:~/bin vanilla$ ./database.pl
Enter a name: Margaret
ID: 1
Name: Margaret
Address: Constantinople
Phone:

ID: 4
Name: Margaret
Address: Ithaca
Phone: 000-333-1111

hostname:~/bin vanilla$
```

Figure 14.37 Using the Perl script to search the database.

Learning More About SQL

Obviously, there is a great deal more to SQL than we show you here. Section 13 of the MySQL user's manual is a good reference. An online tutorial for beginners is available at A Gentle Introduction to SQL (www.sqlzoo.net). Two books about SQL are *SQL: Visual QuickStart Guide*, Second Edition, by Chris Fehily (Peachpit Press; www.peachpit.com), and *SQL in a Nutshell*, Second Edition, by Kevin Kline (O'Reilly; www.oreilly.com).

Another very popular open-source SQL database is PostgreSQL (pronounced post-gres-KYOO-well) (www.postgresql.org).

```
#!/usr/bin/perl
# Simple script that uses MySQL
#
##############################################################################

# Tell Perl we want to use the DBI module
use DBI;

# Ask the user for a name to search the database for.
print "Enter a name: ";
$name = <STDIN>;
chop $name;  # strip the newline character

# Items needed to connect to MySQL
$database = 'sample';
$user     = 'daffy';
$password = 'd**kb0y';
$hostname = 'localhost';

# dsn is the "Distiguished Service name". It includes the name of the
# DBD module we are using (mysql)
$dsn = "DBI:mysql:database=$database;host=$hostname";

# dbh is the "Database handle"
$dbh = DBI->connect($dsn, $user, $password);

# Here's SQL statement we'll use
$sql = "SELECT id,name,address,phone FROM table_one WHERE name=?";

# These lines check the SQl statement for errors
$sth = $dbh->prepare($sql);
$sth->execute($name);

# Here we actually fetch the data
$found_rows = $sth->fetchall_arrayref( {} );

$sth->finish;  # tell the database we are done with this request

# If we didn't find anything, give a message and quit
unless ( @{$found_rows} ) {
  print "Didn't find anyone with the name $name\n";
  exit;
}

# If we get this far we found at least one row.
# Print our all the found rows.
foreach $row ( @{$found_rows} ) {
        print "ID: $row->{id}\n";
        print "Name: $row->{name}\n";
        print "Address: $row->{address}\n";
        print "Phone: $row->{phone}\n";
        print "\n";  # extra blank line
}
```

Figure 14.36 Code listing of a Perl script that searches a database for a name supplied by the user.

Even More Servers

Even if the subject of running servers on your Mac OS X machine is not of great interest to you, we suggest that you study Chapters 11, 12, and 13 thoroughly, and follow up on the additional resources mentioned in each of those chapters. It will be especially helpful for you to connect with other Unix users, as they will be the most valuable sources of assistance in all your Unix endeavors.

Darwin-only Unix Commands

A

This appendix lists command-line programs that are found only or almost only in Darwin, the open-source version of Unix used in Mac OS X.

For more information on Darwin, including access to the source code, see http://developer.apple.com/darwin. To read the Unix manual entry for a command, type `man command` at a shell prompt. For example, use `man authopen` to read the `authopen` documentation.

In the following table, the first column shows the command name followed by the Unix manual section in parentheses. See Chapter 3, "Getting Help and Using the Unix Manual," for an explanation of the different sections of the Unix manual. Entries in Section 5 of the manual (for example, `plist`) are documentation for configuration files and file formats, not commands.

Unix Commands Unique to Mac OS X/Darwin

Command(man sec.)	Description	Installed Location
agvtool(8)	Apple-generic versioning tool for Xcode.	/Developer/Tools
asr(8)	Apple Software Restore; copy volumes (such as from disk images).	/usr/sbin
authopen(1)	Open file with Mac OS X authorization.	/usr/libexec
bless(8)	Set volume bootability and startup-disk options.	/usr/sbin
blued(8)	The Mac OS X Bluetooth daemon.	/usr/sbin
bootpd(8)	DHCP/BOOTP/NetBoot server.	/usr/libexec
BuildStrings(1)	Programmer tool to generate .h and .r files.	/Developer/Tools
cd9660.util(8)	ISO 9660 file-system utility.	/System/Library/Filesystems/cd9660.fs
chkpasswd(8)	Verify user password against various systems.	/usr/libexec
ConsoleMessage(8)	Send a message to SystemStarter.	/usr/libexec
configd(8)	System Configuration Daemon.	/usr/sbin
coreaudiod(1)	Daemon for CoreAudio-related purposes.	/usr/sbin
CpMac(1)	Copy files, preserving metadata and forks.	/Developer/Tools
crashdump(8)	Crash-reporting tool.	/usr/libexec
crashreporterd(8)	Crash-detection and panic-logging daemon.	/usr/libexec
create_nidb(8)	Create a NetInfo database from flat files.	/usr/libexec
defaults(1)	Read and set Mac OS X user defaults.	/usr/bin
DeRez(1)	Decompile resources (programmer tool).	/Developer/Tools
DirectoryService(8)	Directory Service daemon. See also dscl(1).	/usr/sbin
diskarbitrationd(8)	Disk-arbitration daemon.	/usr/sbin
disklabel(8)	Manipulate and query Apple Label disk label.	/sbin
diskutil(8)	Modify, verify, and repair local disks.	/usr/sbin
ditto(1)	Copy files and directories; provides Mac-specific options not available in cp.	/usr/bin
dnsextd(8)	BIND Extension daemon.	/usr/sbin
dscl(1)	Directory Service command-line utility.	/usr/bin
dsconfigad(8)	Configure the Active Directory Plug-in.	/usr/sbin
dsconfigldap(1)	Add/remove LDAP server configurations.	/usr/sbin
dseditgroup(1)	Manipulate groups in Directory Service.	/usr/sbin
dsenableroot(8)	Enable or disable the root account.	/usr/sbin
dsidentity(1)	Add/remove "identity" (non-login) user accounts.	/usr/sbin
fibreconfig(8)	Configure settings for Fibre Channel disks.	/sbin
fsaclctl (no man page)	Enable/disable Access Control Lists (ACLs).	/usr/sbin
GetFileInfo(1)	Get Mac-only attributes of files and directories.	/Developer/Tools

Unix Commands Unique to Mac OS X/Darwin *continued*

COMMAND(man SEC.)	DESCRIPTION	INSTALLED LOCATION
hdid(8)	Disk-image loading and decompression.	/usr/bin
hdiutil(1)	Manipulate disk images (preferred over hdid).	/usr/bin
hfs.util(8)	HFS/HFS Plus file-system utility.	/System/Library/ Filesystems/hfs.fs
ifcstart(8)	Rebuild file caches used by international components.	/usr/libexec
installer(8)	System-software and package-installer tool.	/usr/sbin
kerberosautoconfig(8)	Configure Kerberos for Open Directory.	/sbin
kextcache(8)	Create or update kernel-extension caches.	/usr/sbin
kextd(8)	Load kernel extensions on demand.	/usr/libexec/kextd
kextload(8)	Load, validate, and generate symbols for a kernel extension.	/sbin
kextstat(8)	Display status of dynamically loaded kexts.	/usr/sbin
kextunload(8)	Terminate and unload kernel extensions.	/sbin
kuncd(8)	The Kernel User Notification Center daemon.	/usr/libexec
launchctl(1)	Command-line interface to launchd.	/bin
launchd(8)	Systemwide and per-user daemon/agent manager.	/sbin
launchd.conf(5)	Commands for launchctl to run when launchd starts.	man page, not a command.
launchd_debugd(8)	Simple HTTP server to display launchd job data.	See man page.
launchd.plist(5)	Documentation for launchd configuration files.	man page, not a command.
launchproxy(8)	Provide inetd emulation for launchd.	/usr/libexec
lookupd(8)	Directory information and cache daemon.	/usr/sbin
mdcheckschema(1)	Schema-validation tool for mdimport files.	/usr/bin
mdfind(1)	Command-line version of Spotlight search.	/usr/bin
mdimport(1)	Import file hierarchies into the Spotlight data store.	/usr/bin
mdls(1)	List the metadata attributes for the specified file.	/usr/bin
mdutil(1)	Manage the metadata stores used by Spotlight.	/usr/bin
memberd(8)	Group-membership resolution daemon.	/usr/sbin
memberd.plist	File located at /usr/share/man/man8/ memberd.plist.	Not a command.
MergePef(1)	Programmer tool. Merges "PowerPC Executable Format" (PEF) files.	/Developer/Tools
mkextunpack(8)	Programmer tool for multikext (mkext) archives.	/usr/sbin
mount_cddafs(8)	Mount an audio CD.	/sbin

Unix Commands Unique to Mac OS X/Darwin *continued*

Command(man sec.)	Description	Installed Location
MvMac(1)	Move files, preserving metadata and forks.	/Developer/Tools
newfs_hfs(8)	Construct a new HFS Plus file system.	/sbin
nibtool(1)	Programmer tool to print, verify, and update nib files (nib files contain user-interface objects).	/usr/bin
niutil(1)	NetInfo utility—read and write NetInfo data.	/usr/bin
ntfs.util(8)	NTFS file-system utility.	/System/Library/Filesystems/ntfs.fs
open(1)	Open files and directories (double-click from command line).	/usr/bin
opendiff(1)	Graphically compare or merge files or directories.	/usr/bin
osacompile(1)	Compile AppleScripts and other OSA language scripts.	/usr/bin
osalang(1)	Show information about installed OSA languages.	/usr/bin
osascript(1)	Execute AppleScripts and other OSA language scripts.	/usr/bin
pbcopy(1)	Copy from STDIN to the pasteboard (clipboard).	/usr/bin
pbpaste(1)	Paste from the pasteboard (clipboard) to STDOUT.	/usr/bin
pbhelpindexer(1)	Index the HTML documentation for Developer Tools.	/Developer/Tools
pbprojectdump	Take an Xcode project file and output a more nested version of the project structure.	No man page.
pl(1)	Convert between ASCII and binary plist formats.	/usr/bin
plist(5)	Property-list format documentation.	Not a command.
plutil(1)	Check property-list syntax and/or convert format.	/usr/bin
pmset(1)	Modify power-management settings.	/usr/bin
PPCExplain(1)	Programmer help for PPC assembly code.	/Developer/Tools
ResMerger(1)	Programmer tool for merging resource data.	/Developer/Tools
Rez(1)	Programmer tool to compile resources.	/Developer/Tools
RezWack(1)	Programmer tool to flatten file.	/Developer/Tools
say(1)	Convert text to audible speech.	/usr/bin
screencapture(1)	Capture screen shots to file or clipboard.	/usr/sbin
screenreaderd(8)	VoiceOver daemon; gives audible feedback on user activity and responds to user requests for VoiceOver feedback.	/usr/sbin
scsid(8)	SCSI subsystem daemon.	/usr/libexec
scutil(8)	Manage system configuration (configd) parameters.	/usr/sbin
securityd(1)	Security context daemon for authorization and cryptographic operations.	/usr/libexec

Unix Commands Unique to Mac OS X/Darwin *continued*

COMMAND(man SEC.)	DESCRIPTION	INSTALLED LOCATION
SetFile(1)	Set Mac attributes of files and directories.	/Developer/Tools
softwareupdate(8)	Mac OS X System Software Update tool.	/usr/sbin
SplitForks(1)	Divide two-fork HFS file into AppleDouble resource and data files.	/Developer/Tools
StartupItemContext(8)	Execute a program in StartupItem context.	/usr/libexec
sw_vers(1)	Show operating-system version information.	/usr/bin
system_profiler(8)	Show system hardware and software configuration.	/usr/sbin
SystemStarter(8)	Start, stop, and restart system services.	/sbin
textutil(1)	Convert between various file formats.	/usr/bin
ufs.util(8)	UFS file-system utility.	/System/Library/Filesystems/ufs.fs
uninstall-devtools.pl(8)	Remove Xcode Tools or Developer installation.	/Developer/Tools
UnRezWack(1)	Split a RezWack file into separate files.	/Developer/Tools
uuidgen(1)	Utility to generate a new Universally Unique ID (UUID).	/usr/bin
vpnd(8)	Mac OS X VPN service daemon.	/usr/sbin
wait4path(1)	Wait for given path to show up in the file system.	/bin
WaitingForLoginWindow(8)	Draw to the screen until LoginWindow is ready.	/usr/libexec
xcodebuild(1)	Build an Xcode project.	/usr/bin
xgridctl(8)	Xgrid daemon's control interface.	/usr/sbin

INDEX

Symbols
! (bang), 245
" " (double quotes)
  escaping with \, 195, 247
  protecting spaces with, 46
(sharp), 245
#! (shebang), 245
$@ variable, 252–253
$USER environment variable, 36
& (ampersand), 33
' ' (single quotes)
  escaping with \, 195, 247
  protecting spaces with, 46
* (asterisk)
  cautions using, 102
  function of, 39, 98
  matching characters with, 47, 48
. command, 176, 276
. directories, 126
.. directories, 126
/ (forward slash)
  escaping with \, 176
  searching forward in text strings, 165–166
  searching relative or absolute paths, 29
  using in pathnames, 12, 13
  using with relative and full paths, 124
: (colon), 12
< character, 33
> character
  redirecting output, 33
  setting environment variables with, 195
>> character
  appending to existing file, 33, 39
  redirecting output, 33, 38
  setting environment variables with, 195
? (question mark)
  entering as command, 295–296
  searching backward in text strings, 166
[ ] (square brackets)
  creating character class with, 48
  function of, 98
  text expressions for conditional structures, 261
^ (caret), 48
\ (backslash)
  escape sequences for `bash`, 202
  escaping / character with, 176
  escaping quotes with, 195, 247
  protecting spaces with, 46
` (backquote), 33, 60, 255
{ } (curly brackets), 98
| (pipe), 33
~ (tilde)
  changing case of character under cursor, 172
  representing home directory with, 127

A

absolute modes
  about, 225
  changing permissions with, 228–230
  common permission settings for, 229
  setting permissions with, 229
  values of digits in, 228
absolute paths, 29
Accounts pane (System Preferences), 323, 324
ACL (Access Control List)
  adding entry, 236, 238
  `chmod` options for, 237
  enabling, 236
  examples of, 239
  permissions, 236–239
  preserving extended attributes and, 288
  removing or altering, 238
ACL indicator, 219
Activity Monitor, 341, 342
admin users
  logging in as substitute user, 311
  using root account, 310

AFP (Apple File Protocol), 307
agents, 351
algebraic equations, 246, 247
aliases. *See also* shell aliases
  about, 151
  shell, 198–201
  symlinks vs., 152
alphabetical sorting, 84
ampersand (&) character, 33
anonymous FTP access, 468–471
ANSWER SECTION of `dig` command output, 454
Apache Web server, 475–482
  about, 7, 20, 475
  activating from command line, 476
  browsing with, 477
  creating CGI script, 478–482
  documentation for, 475
  `StartupItem` script for, 477
  versions of, 482
appending output to file, 50
Apple File Protocol (AFP), 307
AppleScript
  learning, 77
  running from command line, 57, 77
AppleShare servers, 457–458
AppleTalk printers, 184–186
applications
  defined, 11
  reading system preferences for, 209
`apropos` command, 68
Aqua interface
  about, 6
  Activity Monitor, 341, 342
  becoming root in, 315
  `cat` command vs., 39
  configuring applications from command line, 188
  `cp` command vs., 37–39
  directories in Unix and, 123
  displaying permissions in, 220
  files and directories in Unix and, 120
  graphical interfaces for FTP, 294
  making and restoring backups, 321
  `mv` command vs., 39
  `pwd` command vs., 35–36
  returning to login window, 25
  searching in `grep` vs., 98
  showing hidden Finder files, 122
  using NetInfo Manager, 337
  using Trash from command line, 253–254
archives, unpacking `tar`, 82
arguments
  accessing with `shift` command, 253
  command-line, 28
  commands used with, 32
  full and relative path used as, 124–125
  functions with, 275
  passing to scripts, 251–254
  referring to list of, 253–254
  replacing command-line, 110
  scripts using command-line, 252–254
  using from within `tcsh` shell alias, 199
arithmetic operators in scripts, 257–258
asterisk (*)
  cautions using, 102
  function of, 39, 98
  matching characters with, 47, 48
`at` command, 346
atoms
  creating, 101–102
  finding one-character variations, 101
  finding repeated, 102, 103
  rules and tools for building, 103
attributes
  metadata, 104, 105, 145–146, 150
  preserving extended, 288
  viewing group, 336, 337
Authenticate dialog, 323
`autobundle` command, 450
automated file transfers, 307
`-aux` options, 42
`awk` command
  origin of name, 15, 89
  printing one field from file, 89
  processing whitespace with `cut` and, 90

B

background
  running command in, 53–56
  stopping job in, 54
backquote character (`), 33, 60, 255
backslash (\), 46
backups
  `ditto` command for, 318–319
  making full and incremental, 318
  restoring files in Aqua, 321
bang (!) character, 245
`bash` (Bourne again shell)
  about, 16, 26, 189
  adding directory to `PATH`, 197
  changing environment variables in, 194
  creating permanent aliases, 199
  creating temporary aliases, 198–199
  customizing shell prompt, 202–204
  default shell for Mac OS X, 190
  escape sequences for prompt, 202
  modifications after installing Fink, 412
  shell functions in, 200–201
BBEdit, 168
Berkeley Software Distribution (BSD) Unix, 5, 6, 8

/bin directory
  about, 40
  creating personal, 58
blocking access to ports, 392–396
blogs, 22
boot sequence
  booting in verbose mode, 374
  booting into single-user mode, 25
  bootstrapping, 359
  checking and repairing file system, 375–376
  steps in, 359–361
  troubleshooting, 374–376
boot volume, 121
BootROM, 359
Bourne again shell. *See* bash
browsing
  with Apache Web server, 477
  Lynx Web browser, 118, 305–306
BSD4.4-Lite, 8
BSD (Berkeley Software Distribution) Unix, 5, 6, 8
buffer-overflow attacks, 386

C

C programming language, 7, 20
cache size for Perl modules, 433
Calculator application, 362–363
caret (^), 48
case conditionals, 266–268
case sensitivity
  case insensitive searches with grep, 95
  changing case in vi, 172
  sudo command and, 315
  Unix and Mac OS Extended file systems, 129
cat command
  about, 36, 112
  Aqua interface vs., 39
  seeing entire file without pausing, 135
  viewing text with, 134
cd command
  about, 11, 39
  changing directories with, 35, 128–129
CGI (Common Gateway Interface)
  creating script for Apache Web server, 478–482
  further resources on, 481
  installing program in personal Sites directory, 481–482
characters
  escaping with backslash, 46
  matching, 47, 48
  negating class of, 48
cheat sheets for vi, 164
checklist for system security, 378
chgrp command, 231–232
child processes, 11
chmod command
  ACL options with, 237
  origin of name, 15
  permission options for, 229, 230
chown command, 231, 232–233
chroot command, 473
Classic Mac metadata, 149–150
clipboard, 78
closed-source software, 405
colon (:), 12
columns, 483
command line, 23–61. *See also* configuring Unix environments
  about standard input and output, 49
  adding user from, 326
  Apache Web server activated from, 476
  AppleShare servers configured from, 457–458
  arguments in, 32
  background commands run from, 53–56
  blocking ports with ipfw utility, 392
  common commands from, 35
  copying/pasting between clipboard and, 78
  creating shell script from, 58–61
  editing files from, 15
  Finder configured from, 209–210
  Fink configured from, 412–414
  FTP server activated from, 466
  getting to via Terminal, 24–25
  listing basic Unix commands, 40–41
  logging into interface, 25
  Mac defaults system configured from, 187, 208–210
  making full and incremental backups from, 318
  monitoring system activity from, 341
  MySQL controlled from, 488, 489
  opening files from, 57
  operators and special characters in, 32–33
  parts of, 28
  piping output from any command to mail, 113–114
  printing from, 179, 181–182
  protecting spaces in, 45–46
  relative and absolute paths, 29
  running as root, 313–314
  running command from, 27
  searching for files with mdfind, 106
  seeing updated list of processes, 44
  sending e-mail from, 113
  SSH servers controlled from, 459
  stopping commands, 33
  System Preferences configured from, 208
  text editing from, 57
  Trash used from, 253–254
  Unix environments configured from, 187
  updating software from, 398

INDEX

using, 14, 23
using command-line arguments in script, 252–254
wildcards in, 39, 47–48
command mode
changing text in, 170
deleting text in `vi`, 169
`vi` editor, 158, 161
commands. *See also specific commands*
applying to each file found, 110–111
arguments with, 32
background, 53–56
backquoted, 255–256
common, 35
creating pipelines of, 51–52
CUPS, 180
defined, 11
getting help for, 34
listing basic, 40–41
for looking through logs, 358
Mac applications vs. Unix, 29
MySQL, 486
names of Unix, 15
options with, 30–31
piping output to e-mail, 52
regularly scheduled, 345–356
running daily, 347–348
running from command line, 27
running shell scripts like, 244–245
stopping, 33
switching to `vi` edit mode, 163
types of Unix, 28
using within commands for scripts, 255–256
using within variable, 248–249
viewing built-in help for, 71–72
`vi` editor, 176
Common Gateway Interface. *See* CGI
Common Unix Printing System (CUPS), 180
compiling software
defined, 405
learning more about, 423
Comprehensive Perl Archive Network. *See* CPAN
compressing files with `gzip`, 79–80
computers. *See also* remote computers
hostname for, 278, 369, 452–456
monitoring processes and system load, 342–344
physical security of, 379
sharing disks with other Unix, 307
showing system status with shell script, 59–61
using in single-user mode, 317
concatenate. *See* `cat` command
conditionals, 259–268
about, 259–260
`case`, 266–268
`if...then`, 260–262
`if...then...else` structure, 262–265
`./configure` shell scripts, 426, 431
configuring
CPAN, 432–443
defaults system, 187, 208–210
Finder to display hidden files, 210
Fink, 412–414
`launchd` daemon, 353–355
MySQL database server, 487–488
Postfix, 460–463
shells, 190–191
Terminal vs. shells, 188
`vi` editor, 207
configuring Unix environments, 187–210. *See also* environment variables
about, 187–188
changing mask, 205–206
changing `PATH`, 196–197
configuring shell, 190–191
configuring Terminal vs. shell, 188
customizing shell prompt, 202–205
finding shell configuration files, 189
Mac defaults system, 187, 208–210
prompt macros for `tcsh` shell, 204
settings for `vi`, 207
shell aliases, 198–201
working with environment variables, 192–195
content index, 104
Control C, 33
control structures, 259–271. *See also* conditionals; loops
conditionals, 259–268
defined, 259
loops, 268–271
cooperative multitasking, 344
copying
across Internet, 288
from command line and pasting to clipboard, 78
`ditto` for file, 320
files, 37, 139
`vi`, 173–174
correcting permission problems, 235
counting lines, words, and bytes, 83
`cp` command
about, 11
backing up with, 318
copying files and directories, 139–140
options for, 140
selecting files to be copied, 37
CPAN (Comprehensive Perl Archive Network)
about, 431
building on prerequisite modules, 435
choosing servers to download from, 440–441
configuring, 432–443
configuring terminal and shell interface, 434
further resources, 448

INDEX

installing Perl module from cpan shell prompt, 447–448
proxy-server options in, 437–438
retrying download process in, 438–439
searching for Perl modules, 443–446
selecting cache size for, 433
setting FTP_PASSIVE environment variable to true, 431–432
starting, 443
upgrading, 443
viewing Perl modules and available versions, 450

cron daemon
restricting use of, 349
scheduling jobs with, 346

crontab files
about, 346
/etc/crontab files, 349–350
running daily commands with, 347–348

csh (Bourne shell)
about, 26, 189
changing environment variables in, 195

CUPS (Common Unix Printing System), 180

curl client, about, 291

curly bracket ({ }) characters, 98

cursor
adding text before, after, or above, 162–163
changing character under, 172
changing text in relationship to, 170–171
moving in vi, 164–165

cut command
printing single field from file, 86–88
processing whitespace with awk and, 90

cw command, 170

D

daemons. *See* cron daemon; launchd daemon

Darwin
adding user from command line, 326
backup tools for HFS Plus, 319
booting into Darwin layer, 25
changing login shells, 328–329
creating users and groups, 216
Darwin-only Unix commands, 505–509
grep version with, 95
location of system-startup scripts, 242
logo marking commands for, 76
lookupd, Open Directory, and Directory Services, 329
mdfind command, 75, 104, 106
NetInfo system, 331
nidump command, 213–215
origins of, 5, 6
release date for, 8
root accounts in, 311
utilities for Mac OS X, 76–78
Web sites for, 8

Darwin layer, 25

Darwin Streaming Server, 20

data forks, 140, 318

databases. *See also* MySQL database server
about, 483–484
adding table to, 498
configuring access control for MySQL, 494
creating, 493–497

Date::Calc module, 449

date command, 38

dd command, 169

defaults command, 209–210

defaults system
configuring, 187, 208–210
defined, 187

DELETE statement, 500

deleting
files and directories, 142
permissions for file, 222
row from tables, 500
text in vi, 169

DESCRIBE command, 492, 496

"device full" problems, 371–374

device names, 12

df command
checking disk space with, 372–373
viewing system disk usage, 340

dictionary attacks, 380

dig command, 454

. (direct) command, 176, 276

directories. *See also* full paths; home directory; relative paths; root directory
. and .., 126
about, 130
absolute mode values for permissions, 230
adding to PATH, 197
archiving with tar, 81–82
backing up with ditto, 320
changing working, 128–129
copying with cp command, 139–140
copying with scp, 289–290
creating, 138
defined, 9, 11
deleting, 142
disk usage for, 341, 342
displaying working, 123
folders as, 12
getting information about, 143
hidden files, 131
installing CGI program in personal Sites, 481–482
listing, 27, 35–36, 130–131
moving to another disk keeping original path, 374

permissions for, 220, 222
personal bin, 58
renaming or moving, 141
returning to home, 129
showing recursive listings, 133
sorting, 132
synchronizing with rsync, 301–304
testfile for permissions, 218
Unix and Aqua concepts of, 123
discarding command output, 50
disk space
checking and freeing up, 372
"device full" problems, 371–374
monitoring, 340–342
displaying input backward, 93–94
ditto command
about, 318–319
backing up directory with, 320
copying or recovering files with, 320
DNS (domain name system)
about, 452
dynamic, 455
seeing records for hostnames, 454–455
DNS server, 453, 456
domain name system. *See* DNS
domain names, 278
DoS (Denial of Service) attacks, 386
. directories, 126
.. directories, 126
dot files. *See also* hidden files
shell configuration files as, 189
downloading
choosing servers for CPAN, 440–441
files with FTP, 297–298
Perl modules, 431–432
X Windows, 408
dscl (Directory Service command line) utility
changing user's login shell, 328–329
creating groups, 338
listing all groups with, 336
viewing attributes of group, 336, 337
dseditgroup command, 338–339
dsidentity tool, 326
du command, 341, 342, 343
dump command, 318
dynamic DNS, 455

E

echo command, 35, 36
edit mode (vi editor), 157–158, 161–163
editing, 155–178. *See also* emacs editor; vi editor
adding text (vi), 162–163
changing text (vi), 170–173
cheat sheets (vi), 164
command mode (vi), 158, 161
commands for editing files, 112
commands for text editing (vi), 176
copy-and-paste function (vi), 173–174
cursor movement (vi), 164–165
deleting text (vi), 169
edit mode (vi), 157–158, 161–163
emacs for, 112, 155, 177, 178
files from command line, 15
navigation (vi), 164–167
repeating last command (vi), 176
saving (vi), 167
search-and-replace (vi), 174–176
text from command line, 57
undoing changes (vi), 173
vim and vi, 156
word wrap (vi), 163
egrep command
about, 95
creating atom with, 101–102
finding lines where one character varies, 101
options for, 97
regular expressions with, 98
rules and tools for building atoms, 103
testing regular expressions, 100–101
using wildcard character with, 102, 103
elif (else if) statements, 264–265
emacs editor
about, 112, 155
starting, 177
using, 178
e-mail
configuring firewall settings for, 462
forwarding for existing user accounts, 463
Pine program, 114
piping output to, 52
sending from command line, 113
spam, 464
e-mail servers, 460–464
configuring Postfix, 460–463
forwarding e-mail for existing user accounts, 463
providing remote access to IMAP and POP servers, 464
sending mail to IP addresses, 463
enabling
ACLs, 236
SSH server software, 280
encryption
encrypted passwords in Mac OS X, 312
encrypted transactions with scp, 288
password, 381
env command, 193
environment variables, 192–195. *See also* PATH environment variable
$USER, 36

common, 193
making durable changes in, 195
setting, 194–195
setting FTP_PASSIVE to true, 431–432
using in shell scripts, 250
viewing, 193
error messages
interpreting, 371
watching system-startup, 374
Esc key, 176
escaping characters
escape sequences for bash, 202
using backslash for, 46, 176, 195, 202, 247
/etc/crontab files, 349–350
/etc/ftpchroot/ command, 473
/etc/hostconfig system-configuration file, 455
ettercap, 390, 403
ex editor, 156
execute permissions
about, 221
cautions with, 224
for files and directories, 222
expr command, 257–258
expressions
shell script test, 261–262
test, 261
using in scripts, 257–258
extended attributes, 288
eXtensible Markup Language. *See* XML
extracting output from data, 86–88

F

fg command, 54, 55
fields, delimiting with spaces, 86
file command, 148
file systems. *See also* HFS Plus file system
case sensitivity of Unix and Mac OS Extended, 129
checking and repairing, 375–376
corruption and journaling, 375
definitions of, 13
NFS, 307
filename completion, 46, 125, 127
filename extensions in OS X, 13
filenames
about Unix, 124–127
case sensitivity and, 129
distinguishing file type information after, 148
starting vi with or without, 160
file-path designations, 12
files. *See also* backups; editing; permissions; printing
adding or removing read permissions, 226
applying command to found, 110–111
automated transfer of, 307
changing /etc/hostconfig system-configuration, 455
checksum for, 401–404
commands for viewing and editing, 112
compressing with gzip, 79–80
converting format with textutil, 91–92
copying, 37, 139–140, 320
correcting permission problems, 235
counting lines, words, and bytes in, 83
creating, 138
creating with vi, 157–159
crontab, 347–348
curl command for retrieving, 299
deleting, 142, 222
downloading with FTP, 297–298
editing from command line, 15
/etc/crontab, 349–350
finding modified, 109
finding out type of, 147–148
finding strings in, 95
Fink configuration, 414
getting information about, 143
links to, 151–154
listing, 27
listing beginning or end of, 136
listing by matching patterns, 133
listing metadata attributes of, 145–146
listing permissions for, 220
locked, 149, 150
metadata for, 150
monitoring additions to system log, 137
monitoring for security, 401–404
moving and renaming, 39
names identify location of, 38
names of Unix, 124–127
navigating with emacs, 178
ownership of, 211, 219
permission testfile, 218
permissions for, 211, 219, 221, 222, 234
printing from command line, 182
README, 425
removing unknown user's, 326
renaming or moving, 141
retrieving with wget command, 299–300
reversing contents of input, 93–94
saving (vi), 167
saving output to, 50
searching for, 106, 108–111
seeing entire file without pausing, 135
sending and receiving remote, 288–289
setting permissions in absolute mode, 229
showing hidden, 122, 123, 131, 210
spaces in names of, 45
taking mail message body from, 114
taking output from, 50
type and size of, 144
Unix and Aqua hierarchy of, 120, 121

Unix changes to Mac OS filesystem and, 12
uploading to FTP servers, 292–294, 471–472
used by `ftpd`, 466
used for tracking user logins, 330
viewing text, 134–137

`find` command
applying to each file found, 110
finding modified files, 109
searching for files with, 108–111

Finder
copying files with Unix vs., 37
moving files to Trash, 142
`pwd` command vs., 35–36
showing hidden files, 122, 123, 210
showing settings with `defaults` command, 209
view of Trash folder in, 254

Fink, 408–421
about, 408, 414–415
configuring, 412–414
further resources, 414
help for, 415
installing, 408–412
listing available packages with, 416–417
package installation with, 418–420
updating and removing packages, 421

Firewalk, 394

firewalls. *See also* ports
allowing access to specific ports, 395–396
blocking ports, 393
configuring e-mail settings for, 462
enabling FTP connections with, 431–432
using Apache Web server with, 476
viewing list of rules for, 394–395

flags. *See* options

floating-point math, 257

`FocusFollowsMouse` command, 210

folders. *See also* directories
directories as, 12
Unix and Aqua hierarchy of, 120, 121

fonts for command-line, 24

`for` loops, 268, 269

foreground, 54

forks, data and resource, 140, 318

forward slash (/)
escaping with \, 176
searching forward in text strings, 165–166
used in Unix pathnames, 12, 13

FQDN (fully qualified domain names)
defined, 278
identifying mail servers with, 454–455
IP address requirements for, 453
receiving e-mail addressed to, 460–463
using as server hostname, 369, 452–453
viewing for IP address, 455

FreeBSD programs, 22

`fsck` command, 375–376

FTP (File Transfer Protocol), 290–298
about, 288, 290
Active and Passive modes, 467
Aqua graphical interfaces for, 294
command-line clients for, 291
commands for, 290
downloading files with, 297–298
file retrieval with `wget` command, 299–300
getting help for, 295–296
retrieving files using `curl` command, 299
synchronizing directories with `rsync`, 301–304
uploading file using, 292–294

FTP servers
activating from GUI, 465–466
allowing anonymous users to upload files, 471–472
allowing Passive FTP access through firewall, 467
anonymous FTP user access, 468–471
denying access to, 474
files used by `ftpd`, 466
reducing security risks of, 473–474
using from command line, 466

`ftp` tool, 118

FTP-only user accounts, 474

full backups, 318

full paths
. directories and, 126
relative paths vs., 124
using with symbolic links, 151, 152

fully qualified domain names. *See* FQDN

functions
adding to more than one script, 275
using in shell scripts, 274–276

further resources
Apache Web server, 475
AppleScript, 77
`awk` and `sed` commands, 89
CGI, 481
compiling software, 423
CPAN, 448
Fink, 414
hidden files, 137
HTTP, 287
`launchd` daemon, 363
MySQL database server, 486
Perl, 93
regular expressions, 100
shell scripts, 276
SQL, 502
system administration, 375
Unix security, 400

G

GCC (Gnu Compiler Collection), 7
GetFileInfo command, 149, 150
gid (group ID), 212
GIMP (GNU Image Manipulation Program), 21
Gimp-Print printer drivers, 183
glob-patterns. *See* wildcards
Gnu Compiler Collection (GCC), 7
GNU General Public License (GPL), 6, 179
GNU (Gnu's Not Unix), 80
GNU Image Manipulation Program (GIMP), 21
GNU/Linux operating system, 3
Google, 73
Greer, Ken, 189
grep command, 95–104
  Aqua searches vs., 98
  finding lines starting or ending with strings, 99
  finding lines that don't match, 97
  finding lines where atom is repeated, 102, 103
  options for, 97
  origin of name, 15, 96
  recursive searches in directory, 97
  regular expressions with, 98
  searching for strings in multiple files, 96
  searching output of another command, 97
  using, 95
groff command, 70
group ID (gid), 212
groups. *See also* managing user accounts and groups
  about, 212
  adding to another group, 338
  adding users to existing, 338
  attributes of, 336, 337
  creating, 216, 338
  displaying information about, 338
  finding all user belongs to, 215
  listing all, 336
  managing, 335–339
  removing subgroups, users, and, 339
  seeing all users in, 337
  setgid properties for ownership, 232
  user private, 212, 337
  viewing all, 214, 215
  viewing file ownership information for, 219
groups command, 336
gunzip command, 80
gzip command, 79–80

H

hard disks. *See also* volumes
  "device full" problems, 371–374
  device names for, 12
  freeing space on, 372–373
  hierarchy of files and folders on, 121
  monitoring disk space, 340–342
  moving directories to another disk with original path, 374
  sharing with other Unix systems, 307
hard links
  about, 151, 153
  creating, 154
head command
  about, 112
  showing file beginning with, 136, 137
help. *See also* Unix manual
  finding on Web, 73
  Fink, 415
  FTP, 295
  getting from other people, 74
  reading command, 34
  viewing command, 71–72
  ways of getting, 63
-help option, 72
--help option, 71
HFS Plus file system
  about, 129
  backup utilities incompatible with, 318
  Darwin backup tools for, 319
hidden files
  further resources for, 137
  showing Finder, 122, 123, 210
  viewing, 131
home directory
  defined, 9, 10
  representing with tilde, 127
  returning to, 129
hostnames, 452–456
  defined, 278, 452
  seeing DNS records for, 454–455
  setting computer's, 369, 452–453, 456
  viewing computer's, 453
HTML (Hypertext Markup Language)
  about, 7
  converting manual pages to, 70
HTTP (HyperText Transport Protocol), 287

I

ICMP (Internet Control Message Protocol) packets, 116
id command, 336
if...then conditionals, 260–262
if...then...else conditionals, 262–265
IIS (Internet Information Server) attacks, 385, 386
IMAP servers, 464
incremental backups, 318
inetd, 396
init, 11

input. *See also* stdin
  about, 49
  creating script to reverse, 93–94
  reading user input into variables, 273
insert mode in vi editor, 157–158, 161–163
INSERT statements, 499
installing, 405–446. *See also* Fink
  basic steps for source code, 406–407
  CGI program in personal Sites directory, 481–482
  DBI and DBD::mysql modules, 501
  Fink for source-code installation, 408–421
  MySQL options/configuration file, 489
  MySQL server, 484–486
  Perl modules, 431–450
  saving source code compilation logs, 430
  source code manually, 422–430
  Webmin, 370
  wget command, 418–420
Internet, 277–307. *See also* Telnet
  automated file transfers, 307
  checking for active hosts, 115–116
  copying files across, 288
  hostnames, 278
  identifying IIS attacks, 385
  logging into another Unix machine, 279
  logging into remote machine with Telnet, 284–285
  Lynx Web browser, 305–306
  ports for services, 285, 286
  preserving ACLs and extended attributes, 288
  preventing packet-sniffing attacks, 380, 384–385, 390
  protecting against attacks, 383–396
  sharing disks with other Unix machines, 307
  SSH protocol and ssh command, 279–283
  tracing route to host on, 116–117
  Unix tools for, 118
  verifying host authenticity with SSH, 279
  viewing active connections to, 387
  virtual private networks, 307
Internet Control Message Protocol (ICMP) packets, 116
Internet Information Server (IIS) attacks, 385, 386
Internet Protocol addresses. *See* IP addresses
interpolating variables, 246–247, 248
interpreters, 245
IP (Internet Protocol) addresses
  domain names, 278
  FQDN and, 452–453
  private, 383
  sending e-mail to, 463
  support for IPv6, 278
  viewing FQDN for, 455
ipfw utility
  blocking ports from command line, 392
  listing firewall rules, 394
iTunes, 77

J

Java, 19
jobs
  running in background, 53–56
  suspending, 54, 55, 56
Jobs, Steve, 5
jobs command, 54–56
Jolitz, Bill, 8
journaling file system, 375
Joy, Bill, 5, 189

K

Kerberos, 381
kernel, 8
Kernighan, Brian, 7
kill command
  about, 54
  using, 33
-k option, 31
Kron, David, 189
ksh shell, 26, 189

L

last command, 333
launchd daemon
  about, 351
  configuration options for, 353–355
  directories used by, 351
  example of systemwide launchd agent, 352
  further resources on, 363
  listing jobs loaded into, 356
  replacing function of xinetd, 396
  role in boot sequence, 359–361
  running daily commands with, 353
  scheduling jobs with, 350–352
  starting applications at boot time with, 362–363
  unloading launchd agent, 356
launching. *See* starting
less command
  about, 112
  options and resources for, 137
  paging text with, 134
lines
  changing text to specific numbered, 172
  copying current, 173
  counting, 83
  finding specific, 99
  finding where one character varies, 101
  that don't match, 97
  with variation in characters, 101
  where atom is repeated, 102, 103
links
  hard, 151, 153, 154

symbolic, 151, 152
types of, 141
Linux, 3, 6, 8
listing. *See* `ls` command
`ln` command, 152
`locate` command, 107
locked files, 149, 150
login shell, changing, 328–329
logins
to another Unix machine, 279
to command line interface, 25
monitoring activities of logged-in users, 332
to remote machine with Telnet, 284–285
`ssh` command for, 280–281
summary of times for, 334–335
tracking user, 330
viewing history of, 333–334
logo for Darwin commands, 76
`lookupd` daemon, 329
loops, 268–271
about, 259, 268
`for`, 268, 269
`while`, 268, 269, 270–271
`lp` printing, 181
`lpr` printing, 181
`lpstat` command, 182
`ls` command
checking new directories, 138
listing file information, 143–144
listing files and directories, 27
recursively listing directory contents, 133
seeing Unix file-type information, 148
showing directory contents, 130–131
sorting directories by time or reverse order, 132
viewing permissions and ownership, 219
viewing root directory contents, 120–121
Lynx Web browser
about, 118
fetching URL and saving result to file, 306
starting and navigating in, 305–306

M

Mac OS 9
Mac OS X vs., 9
paths illustrated in OS X and, 12
running servers in, 20
Mac OS X. *See also* Darwin
Activity Monitor, 341, 342
`at` command in, 346
Classic Mac metadata, 149–150
compressing files, 80
creating users and groups, 216
Darwin and, 5, 6
Darwin-only Unix commands, 505–509
Darwin-specific utilities for, 76–78
default shell, 26, 190
defaults system, 187, 208–210
enabling ACLs, 236
enabling SSH server software, 280
filename case sensitivity, 129
filename completion, 46, 125, 127
filename extensions, 13
location of system-startup scripts, 242
Mac OS 9 vs., 9
`man` pages for, 63
NetInfo system, 331
open-source technology and, 7
paths illustrated in OS 9 and, 12
reliably running servers in, 20
root accounts in, 311, 312
running DNS server with, 456
sections of Unix manual, 64
short names, 212, 323
`ssh` connections, 20
`sudo` command vs. root accounts, 217, 311–312
support for IPv6 addresses, 278
system log file location, 357–358
text files in Unix and, 155
Unix programming and scripting tools, 15–16
Unix's relationship with, 2, 5
updating keychain passwords, 327
using Terminal in, 24
Mac OS X Developer Tools, 407
Mac OS X Server Tiger
about, 309, 310
command line administration on, 326
Mac OS Extended file system, 129
macros, prompt, 204
`mail` command, 113, 114
Mail Delivery Agent (MDA), 460
Mail Transport Agent (MTA), 460
Mailman, 22
Majordomo, 22
`make` command, 423, 427–429
`man` command, 34
`man` pages. *See also* Unix manual
about, 63
converting to HTML, 70
converting to PDFs, 69
illustrated, 67
printing, 69–70
searching for, 68
syntax for displaying, 66
managing user accounts and groups, 322–339
changing login shell, 328–329
managing groups, 335–339
passwords, 327
System Preferences for adding and deleting users, 322–326

manual. *See* Unix manual
manually installing source code, 422–430
math operators, 257
md5sum program
  about, 401
  checking files for changes, 403–404
  creating checksum for files, 401–403
MDA (Mail Delivery Agent), 460
mdfind command
  about, 75
  queries using, 106
  Spotlight and, 104
mdls command, 104, 145–146
metadata. *See also* metadata attributes
  Mac OS X updating of, 104
  working with Classic Mac, 149–150
metadata attributes
  about, 104, 105
  listing with mdls command, 145–146
  setting, 150
mkdir command, 37, 138
monitoring
  disk space, 340–342
  files for security, 401–404
  processes and load, 342–344
  system load and uptime, 344
  tools for system security, 403
  virtual memory statistics, 344
monospace fonts, 24
more command, 134
moving files, 141
MTA (Mail Transport Agent), 460
Multics, 4, 6
multiuser environments, 10
mv command
  Aqua interface vs., 39
  function of, 38
  options for, 141
  preserving resource forks with, 140
MySQL database server. *See also* tables
  about, 483–484
  adding table to database, 498
  changing values in existing record, 500
  common commands for, 486
  configuring and starting, 487–488
  connecting to, 489–493
  connecting to mysqld daemon, 490–493
  creating database, 493–497
  installing, 484–486
  installing and running Perl script with, 501–503
  installing options/configuration file, 489
  RDBMS illustrated, 484
  SQL WHERE clause and statements, 499–500
  tools for administering, 487
mysqld daemon, 490–493

N

nano editor
  about, 112
  limitations of, 155
  pico vs., 57
  saving changes, 60–61
  starting, 59
NAT (Network Address Translation), 383
navigating
  with emacs, 178
  with Lynx Web browser, 305–306
  with vi, 164–167
ncftp client, 291
negating character class, 48
nested directories, 138
NetInfo Manager, 331, 337
Network Address Translation (NAT), 383
Network File System (NFS) protocol, 307
Network Utility, 115–117
  features of, 117
  launching, 115
  Traceroute with, 116–117
  using Ping, 115–116
NeXT, 5, 8
NFS (Network File System) protocol, 307
nidump command, 213–215, 312
Nmap, 390
numerical sorting, 84

O

object code, 405
open command, 57, 76
Open Directory, 329
opening
  ports for Passive FTP protocol, 467
  Terminal, 24
open-source software
  about, 2–3
  defined, 405
  Mac OS X use of, 7
OpenSSH tool set, 282
operators
  listing of, 33
  math, 257
  using in command lines, 32–33
options
  mv command, 141
  combining, 31
  command, 30–31
  cp command, 140
  cut command, 88
  du command, 341
  link, 151

multiple arguments combined with, 32
as part of command line, 28
ps command, 43
rsync command, 302
scp command, 290
sudo command, 314
used for man page display, 66–67
osascript command, 57, 76–77
output. *See also* stdout
about standard, 49
appending to file, 50
discarding command, 50
echo command, 35
extracting from data, 86–88
piping from any command to mail, 113–114
printing command, 182
saving to files, 50
taking from files, 50
top command, 343
ownership
about, 211, 212
changing group and user, 231–233
setuid and setgid properties, 232
understanding permissions and, 218
viewing current directory file, 219

P

packages
listing with Fink, 416–417
searching for by keyword, 420, 421
showing details of downloaded, 420
updating and removing with Fink, 421
packet sniffers, 384, 390
packet-sniffing attacks, 380, 384–385, 390
pager programs, 134
parent directories, 126
parent processes, 11
partitions. *See* hard disks; volumes
passwd command, 327
Password Assistant dialog, 324
passwords
allowing FTP access without, 468–471
choosing safe, 325, 380–382
managing, 327
safer Mac, 312, 325
setting MySQL root, 488
using with sudo command, 313
pasting
with vi editor, 173–174
to clipboard from command line, 78
deleted text, 174
PATH environment variable
about, 192
adding bin directory to, 58–59
changing, 196–197
relative and absolute paths, 29
paths
full and relative paths as arguments, 124–125
illustrated, 12
searching absolute, 29
pax command, 318
pbcopy command, 78
pbpaste command, 78
PDFs, converting manual pages to, 69
periodic command, 345
Perl, 431–450. *See also* CPAN
about, 19, 92–93
building on prerequisite modules, 435
configuring CPAN, 432–443
configuring module's terminal and shell interface, 434
creating script to reverse input, 93–94
defined, 7, 431
displaying input backward, 94
downloading and building Perl modules, 431–432
installing DBI and DBD::mysql modules, 501
installing module from cpan shell prompt, 447–448
listing installed modules and updates, 450
resources for learning, 93
script using Date::Calc module, 449
searching for modules, 443–446
setting cache size for modules, 433
using CPAN, 431–432
viewing open ports with, 390–392
permanent shell aliases, 200
permissions. *See also* absolute modes; ACL; groups; symbolic modes; user accounts
about, 211
absolute modes, 225, 228–230
ACLs for, 236–239
correcting problems with, 235
defaults for new files, 234
deleting files and, 222
examples of, 223–224
options for chmod command, 229, 230
overriding warnings about, 167
setting and changing, 225–230
troubleshooting, 371
types of, 221
umask definitions of, 212
understanding ownership and, 218
viewing for current directory files, 219
physical security of computers, 379
pico editor, 57
PID (process ID), 41
pine command, 114
Ping, 115–116
pipe character (|), 33

pipeline, 49
piping command output
  to another command, 51
  to e-mail, 52, 114
Plan 9, 7
`plist` (Property List) format, about, 350
PocketBackup, 321
POP servers, 464
port numbers
  about, 388–389
  assigned to services, 285, 286, 388–389
port scanners, 390
ports
  allowing access to specific, 395–396
  blocking access to, 392–396
  checking if blocked for TCP traffic, 389–390
  numbers assigned to services, 285, 286, 388–389
  opening for Apache Web server, 476
  opening for Passive FTP protocol, 467
  viewing open, 390–392
POST (Power On Self Test), 359
Postfix
  about, 7
  configuring, 460–463
PostScript
  printing manual pages with, 69
  printing with, 180, 181
preemptive multitasking, 2, 11, 344
primary groups, 212, 214
printer drivers, 183
printers
  printer driver support, 183
  printing from non-default, 183
  printing to AppleTalk, 184–186
  setting default, 183
  viewing information about, 182
printing, 179–186
  about, 179
  AppleTalk printers for, 184–186
  from command line, 179, 181–182
  `lp` vs. `lpr`, 181
  Mac CUPS system for, 180
  `man` pages, 69–70
  non-default printers for, 183
  PostScript, 69, 180, 181
  single field from file, 86–88, 89
private IP addresses, 383
process ID (PID), 41
processes
  defined, 10, 41
  monitoring, 342
  seeing updated list of, 44
  viewing own, 41
  viewing system, 42–43
programming in Unix, 15–16
prompt macros for `tcsh` shell, 204
protected memory, 2
`ps` command
  options for, 43
  viewing processes with, 41–43
`psync` utility, 319
puns in Unix, 4
`pwd` command, 35–36

Q

question mark (?)
  entering as command, 295–296
  searching backward in text strings, 166
quitting
  Apache Web server, 478
  `emacs`, 178
  MySQL from command line, 489
  `vi`, 168

R

RDBMS (relational database management system), 483
`read` command, 272–273
read permissions
  about, 221
  adding or removing file, 226
  file and directory, 222
  group, 227
README files
  purpose of, 425
  viewing Perl module, 445–446
records
  adding to tables, 499
  changing values in existing, 500
recovering files with `ditto`, 320
redirecting `stderr`, `stdin`, and `stdout`, 50
regex atoms. *See* atoms
regular expressions
  about, 96, 98
  creating atom from range of numbers or letters, 102
  creating atom matching any character not in list, 101–102
  finding lines where one character varies, 101
  finding lines with specific strings, 99
  further resources on, 100
  searching for Perl module using, 443–446
  testing, 100–101
relational database management system (RDBMS)
  about, 483
  illustrated, 484
relative paths
  absolute and, 29
  full paths vs., 124

searching, 29
symbolic links with, 151, 152
using more complex, 125
remote computers
copying files with scp command, 288
logging into with Telnet, 284–285
remote access to IMAP and POP servers, 464
running command line with ssh utility, 282–283
sending and receiving remote files, 288–289
synchronizing directories, 301–304
testing with Telnet, 285–287
using directory as synchronization source, 304
verifying host authenticity of, 279
removing
members of groups, groups, and subgroups, 339
packages, 421
user accounts, 325–326
renaming files, 141
replacing all occurrences of text, 91
resource forks, 140, 318
restoring files
from backups in Aqua, 321
restore command for, 318
retrying CPAN download process, 438–439
reverse command in Perl, 93–94
reverse sorting
directories with, 132
numerically, 85
reversing input, 93–94
reversing meaning of test expressions, 262
reverting to last saved version of text, 173
Ritchie, Dennis M., 5, 7, 8
rm command, 37, 142
rmdir command, 142
root account
about, 217. *See also* sudo command
administration and, 310–311
other ways of becoming root, 314
problems with Mac OS X approach to, 312
running command line as, 313–314
searching for setuid root programs, 397
sudo command and, 217, 311–312
root directory
defined, 120
viewing contents of, 120–121
viewing file information for, 144
rsync command, 301–304
about, 301
options for, 302
remote directory as source for synchronizing, 304
synchronizing with local directory as source, 302–303
Ruby on Rails, 21

S

S/Key password system, 381
Samba, 21
Sanchez, Wilfredo, 189
saving
changes in emacs, 178
file in vi, 167
and quitting in vi editor, 168
source code installation compilation logs, 430
saving output to file, 50
scheduling jobs, 345–356
about /etc/crontab files, 349–350
cron for, 346–348
launchd daemon for, 350–352
restricting who uses cron, 349
scp (secure copy) command
about, 118
copying directory with, 289–290
options, 290
sending and receiving remote files with, 288–289
using, 288
scripts. *See also* shell scripts
about, 241
./configure, 426, 431
Perl script using MySQL, 502
scripting in Unix, 15–16
shebang line of, 245
shell configuration files as, 189
using Date::Calc module, 449
for viewing open ports, 390–392
viewing system-startup, 16–18
searching, 95–103. *See also* grep command; regular expressions; Spotlight
absolute paths, 29
by file name and type, 108
creating atom matching any character not in list, 101–102
find command for, 108–111
forward and backward in vi text string, 165–166
Google for Unix help, 73
grep for, 95
lines that don't match, 97
lines where atom is repeated, 102, 103
lines with strings, 99
lines with variation in characters, 101
locate command for, 107
man page, 68
modified files, 109
output of another command, 97
packages by keyword, 420, 421
queries using mdfind, 106
setuid root programs, 397
using patterns in search, 98

INDEX

security, 377–404
about, 377–378
attacks on services, 385–388
checklist for system, 378
choosing safe passwords, 325, 380–382
concerns about FTP, 468
denying FTP server access, 474
further resources, 400
maintaining with Software Update, 398–400
monitoring files for changes, 401–404
news and announcements about, 400
physical, 379
preventing packet-sniffing attacks, 380, 384–385, 390
private IP addresses, 383
reducing risks of FTP servers, 473–474
S/Key and Kerberos authentication, 381
searching for `setuid` root programs, 397
tools for monitoring, 403
Unix influence on file, 12
using Webmin with SSL, 370
`sed` utility, 89, 91
`SELECT` statements, 499
selecting data from tables, 499
Sendmail, 7
servers, 451–503. *See also* Apache Web server; MySQL database server
Apache Web, 475–482
AppleShare, 457–458
changing `/etc/hostconfig` system-configuration file, 455
checking for active Internet hosts, 115–116
choosing CPAN, 440–441
configuring e-mail, 460–464
controlling SSH, 459
definition of, 278
DNS, 456
FTP, 465–474
function of `xinetd` for, 396
MySQL, 483–484
remote access to IMAP and POP, 464
running from Mac OS X, 20
setting machine's hostname, 452–456
sharing disks with other Unix machines, 307
services
attacks on, 385–388
defined, 378
port numbers assigned to, 389
viewing active, 386–388
`setenv` command, 193
`setuid` and `setgid` properties for ownership, 232
`setuid` root programs, 397
`sftp` client, 291
`sftp` utility, 118
`sh` (Bourne shell)
about, 189
automating tasks with scripts, 242
changing environment variables in, 194
Sharing pane (System Preferences), 393, 465
sharp (#) character, 245
shebang (#!) character, 245
shell aliases, 198–201
`bash` shell functions, 200–201
defined, 198
permanent, 200
temporary, 198–199
shell prompts
changing when start new shell as root, 422
customizing, 202–205
defined, 24, 26
illustrated, 24
shell scripts, 241–276. *See also* control structures
`./configure`, 426, 431
about, 16
arithmetic operators and expressions in, 257–258
`case` conditionals, 266–268
command-line arguments in, 252–254
creating, 58–61, 243–244
environment variables in, 250
functions within, 274–276
getting user input with `read` command, 272–273
loops, 268–271
passing arguments to, 251–254
Perl, 19
running without using path, 244–245
shebang line of, 245
showing system status with, 59–61
test expressions in, 261
Trash, 271
uses for, 242
using commands within commands, 255–256
variables in, 246–250
viewing system-startup script, 16–18
shells
about most common, 189
changing login, 328–329
changing `umask`, 205–206
configuring, 190–191
customizing prompt for, 202–205
default OS X, 26
defined, 26
determining shell in use, 190
finding configuration files for, 189
job number and process ID displayed in, 53
starting as root, 314
Terminal vs., 188
types of, 26, 189
`shift` command, 253
short names
defined, 212, 323
logging in with, 25
Show Info window (Aqua), 220

shutting down
  AppleShare servers, 458
  SSH servers, 459
Snort, 403
sockets, 388
soft links. *See* symbolic links
Software Update
  configuring via GUI, 399–400
  running from command line, 398, 399
  Vulnerability Note (May 2005), 386
Software Update pane (System Preferences), 399
Solaris, 3, 8
`sort` command, 84–85
sorting
  alphabetical, 84
  directories, 132
  numerical, 84
  text, 84–85
source code, 405–446
  basic steps for installation, 406–407
  installing software from, 406–407
  manually installing, 422–430
  open-source software, 2–3, 7, 405
  saving installation compilation logs, 430
spaces
  delimiting fields with, 86
  in file names, 45
  protecting in command line, 45–46
  searching for string in multiple files including, 96
spam, 464
special characters
  listing of, 33
  using in command lines, 32–33
Spotlight
  `grep` searches vs., 98
  `mdfind` command and, 104
  searching data viewed with `textutil`, 92
SQL (Structured Query Language). *See also* MySQL database server
  about, 483
  further resources on, 502
SQL database engines, 21
SQL statements
  about, 489, 490
  `DELETE`, 501
  `INSERT`, 499
  `SELECT`, 499
  `UPDATE`, 500
square bracket ([ ])
  function of, 98
  text expressions for conditional structures, 261
`-s` option, 30, 31
SSH (Secure Shell)
  defined, 7
  enabling in Mac OS X, 280
  encrypted transactions with `scp`, 288
  logging into another Unix machine, 279
  running command on remote computer, 282–283
  SSH protocol and `ssh` command, 279–283
  SSH servers, 459
  using, 20
  verifying host authenticity with, 279
`ssh` utility
  about, 118
  running command line on remote machine with, 282–283
  SSH protocol and, 279–283
SSLs (Secure Socket Layers), 370
Stallman, Richard M., 177, 179
starting
  CPAN, 443
  `emacs`, 177
  Lynx Web browser, 305
  MySQL, 488
  `nano` editor, 59
  Network Utility, 115
  shell as root, 314
  system with startup script, 16–18
  `vi` editor, 160
`StartupItems`
  about, 364–365
  creating, 365–369
  script for Apache Web server, 477
statements. *See* SQL statements
stationery files, 147
`stderr`
  about, 49
  redirecting, 50
`stdin`
  about, 49
  redirecting, 50
`stdout`
  about, 49
  extracting data from fields, 87–88, 89
  piping command output to another command, 51
  piping command output to e-mail, 52, 114
  redirecting, 33, 50
  searching output of another command, 97
sticky bits, 222
stopping commands, 33
strings
  finding specific lines with, 99
  searching for in files, 95
  searching for in multiple files, 96
  searching forward and backward in `vi` text, 165–166
Structured Query Language (SQL), 483
`su` command, 311, 316–317
subdirectories, 12
`sudo` command
  command names not case sensitive with, 315
  command options for, 314

Mac OS X use of, 311–312
monitoring use of, 311
root account vs., 217, 311–312
running root from command line with, 313–314
suspending jobs
about, 54
continuing suspended job in background, 56
suspending top command, 55
Swatch, 403
switches. *See* options
symbolic links
about, 151
creating, 152
symbolic modes
about, 225
adding or removing file permissions, 226
adding or removing group permissions, 227
changing permissions with, 225
listing of changes for, 225
symlinks. *See* symbolic links
synchronizing directories, 301–304
syntax
adding options to commands, 30–31
command line, 28
displaying `man` page, 66
system administration, 309–376. *See also* managing user accounts and groups
about, 309
adding and deleting users with System Preferences, 322–326
admin users, 310–311
boot sequence, 359–361
changing user's login shell, 328–329
creating `LaunchDaemon` at boot time, 362–363
emptying Trash for users, 373
further resources, 375
keeping backups, 318–321
managing groups, 335–339
managing passwords, 327
monitoring disk space, 340–342
root accounts, 310–315
scheduling commands, 345–356
StartupItems, 364–369
switching to another user account, 316–317
system log files, 357–358
tracking system users, 330–334
troubleshooting tips, 371–376
using system in single-user mode, 317
using Webmin, 370
viewing history of logins, 333–334
system load, 342–344
system logs
checking additions to, 137
identifying IIS attacks, 385
interpreting error messages, 371
location of, 357–358
monitoring use of `sudo`, 311
System Preferences
activating FTP Server from Sharing pane, 465–466
allowing access to specific ports, 395–396
blocking ports from Sharing pane, 393
configuring from command line, 208
controlling AppleShare servers from, 457
illustrated, 322
opening ports for Passive and Active FTP protocol, 467
reading for applications, 209
Software Update pane, 399
TCP/IP tab of Network pane, 453

T

tables
adding records to, 499
adding to database, 498
defined, 483
deleting row from, 500
relationships between, 483
selecting data from, 499
`tail` command
about, 112
checking additions to system logs, 137
seeing file end with, 136
`tar` (tape archive) command, 81–82, 318
`tar` files
retrieving with `wget`, 423
unpacking compressed, 423–424
TCP (Transmission Control Protocol), 389
TCP/IP tab (System Preferences Network pane), 453
TCP/IP (Transmission Control Protocol/Internet Protocol), 5, 6, 278
`tcsh` shell
about, 26, 189
adding directory to `PATH`, 197
changing environment variables in, 195
customizing prompt for, 205
permanent aliases, 200
prompt macros for, 204
`setenv` command, 193
temporary aliases, 199
Telnet, 284–287
about, 118, 284
logging in using, 284–285
logging into another Unix machine with, 279
testing remote systems with, 285–287
temporary shell aliases, 198–199
Terminal
changing shell used by, 190
configuring shell vs., 188
`FocusFollowsMouse` command, 210

getting to command line via, 24–25
restarting after configuring Fink, 411
vi display in, 156
testing
CGI script for Apache Web server, 480–481
creating testfile for permissions, 218
regular expressions, 100–101
remote systems with Telnet, 285–287
test expressions in shell scripts, 261–262
text
adding in vi edit mode, 162–163
changing in vi, 170–173
counting lines, words, and bytes, 83
deleting in vi, 169
displaying unique lines of, 85
paging, 134
replacing all occurrences of, 91
searching and replacing with vi, 174–176
searching for inside files, 95–103
seeing entire file without pausing, 135
sorting, 84–85
Unix vs. Mac files, 155
viewing beginning or ending of file, 136
text editors. *See* emacs editor; vi editor
text files
shell scripts as, 243
viewing, 134–137
textutil command, 91–92
Thompson, Ken, 7, 8
tilde (~) character
changing case of character under cursor, 172
representing home directory with, 127
time, displaying, 38
top command, 342–344
Torvalds, Linus, 6, 8
touch command, 138
Traceroute, 116–117
Transmission Control Protocol/Internet Protocol (TCP/IP), 5, 6, 278
Trash
emptying for users, 373
moving files to, 142
script for, 271
using from command line, 253–254
view of folder in Finder, 254
.Trash directory, 142
Tripwire, 403
troubleshooting, 371–376
boot up, 374–376
"device full" problems, 371–374
interpreting error messages, 371
moving directories to another disk keeping original path, 374
permission problems, 371
system in single-user mode, 317

U

u command, 173
UDP (User Datagram Protocol), 389
UFS partitions, 129
uid (user ID), 212
umask command
changing shell's, 205–206
effect on new file permissions, 234
file permissions assigned by, 212
undoing changes in vi, 173
uniq command, 85
Unix. *See also* configuring Unix environments
about, 2
about multiuser environments, 10
capabilities of Mac OS X, 10
changes to Mac OS filesystem and files, 12
command names in, 15
commands as separate programs in, 28
Darwin-only Unix commands, 505–509
directories in Aqua and, 123
editing files from command line, 15
editing text from command line, 57
file permissions and ownership, 211
filename case sensitivity in, 129
files and directories in Aqua and, 120
hierarchy of files and folders in, 120, 121
history of, 5–8
key development dates, 8
listing basic commands, 40–41
Mac applications vs. commands in, 29
moving files to Trash, 142
parent and children processes, 11
preemptive multitasking, 2, 11, 344
preserving resource fork with files, 140, 318
programming and scripting in, 15–16
puns and word games in, 4
putting command in background, 55
root accounts, 217
ssh connections within, 20
stability on Mac OS X, 2
text files in Mac and, 155
user name and ID, 212
users and groups in, 212
using command line, 14
versions of, 1, 3
viewing file-type information, 147–148
Unix manual, 63–74
about, 63
displaying page of, 64–67
getting help for Darwin-only Unix commands, 505
help for commands, 34, 71–72
illustrated, 67
printing pages, 69–70
searching for man page, 68

sections of Mac OS X/BSD, 64
shell, 26
using, 64
unlocking files, 149, 150
unpacking compressed tar files, 423–424
UPDATE statement, 500
updating
finding security updates online, 400
packages, 421
passwords for keychain, 327
Perl modules, 450
upgrading CPAN, 443
uploading files to FTP servers, 292–294, 471–472
uptime command, 342, 344
URLs, fetching and saving, 306
$USER environment variable, 36
user accounts. *See also* managing user accounts and groups
about, 212
adding to existing groups, 338
admin user accounts, 310–311
changing login shell, 328–329
configuring access control for MySQL database, 494
creating, 216, 322–324
file ownership information for, 219
forwarding e-mail for existing, 463
FTP-only, 474
monitoring login history, 333–334
name and number of, 212
removing, 325–326
restricting use of cron, 349
root accounts, 217
seeing all groups user belongs to, 336
seeing list of users logged in, 330–331
setuid properties for ownership, 232
switching to other, 316–317
system, 10
viewing all, 212–214
user ID, 212
user private group, 212, 337
users. *See* user accounts
users command, 330
utilities, 75–118. *See also specific utilities*
awk program, 89–90
compressing files with gzip, 79–80
cut command, 86–88, 90
defined, 75
find command, 108–111
ftp, 118
grep, 95–104
locate command, 107
Lynx, 118
mail command, 113–114
mdfind command, 75, 104, 106
Network Utility, 115–117
open command, 76
osascript command, 76–77
packet sniffers and port scanners, 390
pbcopy command, 78
pbpaste command, 78
Perl, 92–94
pine command, 114
scp, 118
scripting new, 242
sed, 91
sort command, 84–85
ssh, 118
tar command, 81
telnet, 118
textutil command, 91–92
uncompressing files with gunzip, 80
uniq command, 85
unpacking tar archive, 82
viewing and editing files, 112
wc command, 83

V

variable interpolation, 246–247, 248
variables
adding to expr command, 258
assigning and interpolating, 246–247, 248
commands used within, 248–249
defined, 192
reading user input into, 273
saving command output in, 256
shell script, 246–250
using environment variables in script, 250
using within other, 248
working with environment, 192–195
verbose mode, 374
versions
Apache Web server, 482
grep, 95
IPv6 addresses, 278
Unix, 1, 3
viewing Perl modules and available, 450
vi editor, 156–177
about, 112, 155
adding text, 162–163
changing text, 170–173
cheat sheets, 164
command mode, 158, 161
commands for, 176
configuration file for, 189
configuring, 207
copy-and-paste function, 173–174
creating file with, 157–159
cursor movement, 164–165

INDEX

deleting text in, 169
edit mode, 157–158, 161–163
navigation in, 164–167
practice directory for, 156
quitting, 168
repeating last editing command, 176
saving files, 167
search-and-replace function, 174–176
starting, 160
undoing changes, 173
using vim and, 156
word wrap, 163
viewing
active Internet services and connections, 387
all groups, 214, 215
commands for viewing files, 112
computer's hostname, 453
current aliases, 199
entire file without pausing, 135
environment variables, 193
file size, 144
firewall rules, 394–395
FQDN for IP address, 455
group information, 338
help for commands, 34, 71–72
hidden files, 122, 123, 131, 210
history of logins, 333–334
open ports, 390–392
Perl README files, 445–446
processes, 41–44
system load and uptime, 344
system processes, 42–43
system-startup script, 16–18
text, 134–137
working directory, 123
vim editor, 156
vimtutor, 156
virtual private networks (VPNs), 307
vm_stat command, 344
volumes. *See also* hard disks
Aqua's hierarchical display of, 120
boot, 121
freeing space on, 372–373
Unix, 121
vpnd vulnerabilities, 386
VPNs (virtual private networks), 307

W

:w command, 167
w command, 332
wc command, 83
Web servers. *See also* Apache Web server
Apache, 475–482
testing remote, 286–287
Web sharing, 385
Web sites
finding Mac OS X applications, 22
history of Unix, 8
resources for help, 74
Webmin, 370
wget command
about, 417
installing, 418–420
retrieving files with, 299–300
retrieving tar file with, 423
WHERE clause, 499–500
which command, 111
while loops, 268, 269, 270–271
who command, 330, 331
wildcards. *See also* asterisk
using in command line, 39, 47–48
using with egrep, 102, 103
WindowServer, 11
word wrap in vi, 163
working directories
changing, 128–129
displaying, 123
write permissions
about, 221
adding or removing group, 227
for files and directories, 222

X

x command, 169
X Windows
about, 21–22
where to download, 408
xargs command, 110
Xcode Tools, 407
xinetd, 396
XML (eXtensible Markup Language)
file for launchd agent, 352
plist format in, 350

Z

zsh shell, 26, 189